D1758749

30150   019072609

The origins and spread of agriculture and pastoralism in Eurasia

Drummond Lib.

The origins and spread of agriculture and pastoralism in Eurasia

Edited by

David R. Harris

Institute of Archaeology, University College London

UCL
PRESS

EDINBURGH UNIVERSITY LIBRARY

WITHDRAWN

© David R. Harris and contributors, 1996

This book is copyright under the Berne Convention.
No reproduction without permission.
All rights reserved.

First published in 1996 by UCL Press
Reprinted 1999

UCL Press Limited
1 Gunpowder Square
London EC4A 3DF

The name of University College London (UCL) is a registered trade mark used by
UCL Press with the consent of the owner.

British Library Cataloguing in Publication Data
A catalogue record for this book is available from the British Library.

ISBN: 1-85728-537-9   HB
            1-85728-538-7   PB

Typeset in Times New Roman.
Printed and bound by
Bookcraft (Bath) Ltd, England.

Contents

Preface   ix
David R. Harris

List of contributors   xiii

1   Introduction: themes and concepts in the
study of early agriculture   1
David R. Harris

Part One: Thematic perspectives

2   Growing plants and raising animals: an anthropological
perspective on domestication   12
Tim Ingold

3   Ecology, evolutionary theory and agricultural origins   25
Mark. A. Blumler

4   The spread of agriculture and nomadic pastoralism:
insights from genetics, linguistics and archaeology   51
L. Luca Cavalli-Sforza

5   Language families and the spread of farming   70
Colin Renfrew

6   Tracking early crops and early farmers: the potential
of biomolecular archaeology   93
Martin Jones, Terry Brown, Robin Allaby

7   The impact of diseases upon the emergence of agriculture   101
Les Groube

8   Plate tectonics and imaginary prehistories: structure and
contingency in agricultural origins   130
Andrew Sherratt

Part Two: Southwest Asia

9   The mode of domestication of the founder crops of
        Southwest Asian agriculture   142
        Daniel Zohary

10   Late Pleistocene changes in wild plant-foods available
        to hunter–gatherers of the northern Fertile Crescent:
        possible preludes to cereal cultivation   159
        Gordon Hillman

11   The emergence of crop cultivation and caprine herding
        in the "Marginal Zone" of the southern Levant   204
        Andrew Garrard, Susan Colledge, Louise Martin

12   Animal domestication – accident or intention?   227
        Hans-Peter Uerpmann

13   The beginning of caprine domestication in Southwest Asia   238
        Tony Legge

14   The context of caprine domestication in the Zagros region   263
        Frank Hole

15   The one-humped camel in Asia: origin, utilization
        and mechanisms of dispersal   282
        Ilse Köhler-Rollefson

Part Three: Europe

16   The development of agriculture and pastoralism in Greece:
        when, how, who and what?   296
        Paul Halstead

17   The cultural context of the first use of domesticates
        in continental Central and Northwest Europe   310
        Julian Thomas

18   The agricultural frontier and the transition to farming
        in the circum-Baltic region   323
        Marek Zvelebil

19   The first farmers of southern Scandinavia   346
        T. Douglas Price

20   Aboriculture in Southwest Europe: *dehesas* as managed
        woodlands   363
        Richard J. Harrison

Part Four: Central Asia to the Pacific

21   The beginnings of agriculture in western Central Asia   370
      David R. Harris & Chris Gosden

22   The origins and spread of agriculture and pastoralism
      in northwestern South Asia   390
      Richard H. Meadow

23   New evidence for early rice cultivation in South,
      Southeast and East Asia   413
      Ian C. Glover & Charles F. W. Higham

24   Jomon and Yayoi: the transition to agriculture in
      Japanese prehistory   442
      Keiji Imamura

25   The origins and spread of agriculture in the Indo–Pacific
      region: gradualism and diffusion or revolution
      and colonization?   465
      Peter Bellwood

26   People–plant interactions in the New Guinea highlands:
      agricultural hearthland or horticultural backwater?   499
      Tim Bayliss-Smith

27   Early agriculture and what went before in Island Melanesia:
      continuity or intrusion?   524
      Matthew Spriggs

28   The origins of tropical vegeculture: Zingiberaceae, Araceae
      and Dioscoreaceae in Southeast Asia   538
      Jon G. Hather

Part Five: Conclusion

29   The origins and spread of agriculture and pastoralism
      in Eurasia: an overview   552
      David R. Harris

      Index   575

To our prehistoric predecessors who started it all,
and in memory of two intellectual pioneers of our subject:
V. Gordon Childe and Carl O. Sauer

Preface

The most fateful change in the human career can be said to have occurred some 10,000 years ago when the transition from foraging to farming began. During the preceding 150,000 years anatomically modern humans had successfully colonized almost all habitable and accessible areas of the earth and in so doing had learned to subsist, as "hunter–gatherers", on a great diversity of plant and animal foods. But human population densities remained low throughout these many millennia, and even by the beginning of the Holocene about 10,000 years ago the total world population probably numbered at most only a few million (cf. Groube's contribution to this volume).

The most fundamental and far-reaching consequence of the "agricultural revolution" in the early Holocene was that it enabled more food to be obtained, and more people supported, per unit area of exploited land. It thus facilitated long-term sedentary settlement and the maintenance of larger and more complex social groups, which in turn enabled urban society to develop. But this is not to suggest that the transition to agriculture was an unmixed blessing. By reducing the range of wild foods exploited, and increasing dependence on a much smaller repertoire of "domesticated" plants and animals, it ushered in a decline in nutrition, which, coupled with greater disease transmission in more crowded permanent settlements, probably caused, in the short term at least, an overall deterioration in human health.

If the consequences of the agricultural revolution have been so far-reaching, it is not surprising that it continues to stimulate multi-disciplinary scientific enquiry – as the contents of this book clearly demonstrate. My own involvement in the subject began when I was a graduate student at the University of California, Berkeley, under the inspiring tutelage of Carl Sauer; and later when it fell to me, as President of the Prehistoric Society, to propose a topic for the Society's 1993 international conference, I suggested that we should examine afresh, in a broad inter-disciplinary context, the familiar theme of the transition to agriculture. I did so because, despite the recent appearance of several publications on the subject (referred to below in the Introduction), I believed that we could gain new understanding of the processes involved by focusing on the circumstances in which agriculture and pastoralism arose and spread within one large landmass, i.e. Eurasia. A further reason for suggesting this topic was the fact that much relevant new evidence had been obtained in recent years from archaeological and other investigations in several parts of Europe and Asia. The time therefore seemed ripe for a re-examination of the subject within this broad but geographically delimited comparative framework.

If the conference was to fulfil these hopes it seemed essential to have among the participants a broadly representative group drawn from leading contributors to the subject in different fields. In the event, the speakers shared expertise in anthropology, archaeology, botany, biochemistry, demography, ecology, epidemiology, genetics, geography, linguistics and zoology; and many were (and still are) actively involved in relevant field and laboratory work.

During the three days of the conference, which took place at the Institute of Archaeology in London over the week-end of 24–26 September 1993 and was attended by 130 people, papers were given by 23 invited speakers, all of which are included in revised form in this book. Marek Zvelebil was unfortunately prevented from giving his paper and in his place Nanna Noe-Nygaard kindly spoke at short notice on palaeoenvironmental changes at the mesolithic/neolithic transition in Denmark. Generous time – over 40 per cent of the total – was deliberately allowed for discussion, which took place following groups of related papers and in a long concluding session. This added greatly to the interest and enjoyment of the conference, and many points made in discussion are reflected in the published versions of the papers. Colleagues who kindly agreed to chair individual sessions contributed much to the success of the discussions, and I would like to thank them all. They were: Martin Bell, Barbara Bender, Juliet Clutton-Brock, Peter Fowler, Clive Gamble, Peter Jewell, Susan Limbrey, Roger Mercer and Andrew Moore.

The whole conference depended critically for its success on Judith Harris, who was then the Administrative Assistant to the Prehistoric Society and who handled the preconference organization superbly, with the valued assistance of Mary Moloney and of Katherine Wright as the conference treasurer. I also wish to thank the students who helped with slide projection, tape recording, the serving of tea and coffee and in many other ways, and to acknowledge gratefully the financial support provided by the British Academy, the Prehistoric Society and the Institute of Archaeology.

We left the conference with a new sense of collective commitment to the subject and with much new knowledge gained personally. Then began the inevitably long drawn-out process of revising papers, and of editing the entire volume. Although it was never my intention to attempt comprehensive geographical coverage of the whole of Eurasia – and there are major "gaps" in the book in that sense – I decided to approach two colleagues after the conference who I knew could make very pertinent contributions to the book: Tim Bayliss-Smith and Julian Thomas. I want particularly to thank them for producing, at relatively short notice, very valuable papers on, respectively, New Guinea and Northwest and Central Europe. I also thank the following colleagues who were not speakers at the conference but who agreed to co-author papers with some of those who were: Robin Allaby, Terry Brown, Susan Colledge, Chris Gosden, Charles Higham and Louise Martin. I greatly appreciate, too, the energy and enthusiasm with which the Institute's Librarian, Belinda Barratt, helped me track down many obscure and incomplete references, the meticulous care with which Roger Jones and Kate Williams at UCL Press handled the production process, and the skill with which Tim Aspden of the UCL Geography Department prepared many of the figures.

Above all I owe a debt of gratitude to my assistant, Mary Moloney, who has uncomplainingly – and indeed with great good humour – produced the many revisions of all 30 contributions to this book, as well as pursuing errant authors by letter, fax and phone! Had I not had her help, the interval between conference and publication would have been much longer.

The scenes on the book's cover, showing cultivation of Eurasia's two great grain crops, wheat and rice, with men and women labouring in the fieds and domestic cattle yoked to the plough, aptly portray one of the essential differences between foraging and farming: the greater energy and effort invested in the soil by farmers – "in the sweat of thy face shalt thou eat bread". I hope that the effort required to read this book will be less taxing, and that it will bring us closer to understanding the complexities of how agriculture began.

DAVID R HARRIS
Institute of Archaeology
University College London
University of London
25 July 1995

Conventions used

Radiocarbon dates

In this book bc and bp refer to uncalibrated radiocarbon dates. BC, BP and AD are used to indicate calibrated radiocarbon dates and calendric dates.

Southwest Asia

This term is generally used in this book in preference to "the Near East" to denote the geographical region between the eastern Mediterranean and the Indus Valley and between the Black and Caspian Seas and southern Arabia.

List of contributors

Robin G. Allaby, Department of Biochemistry and Molecular Biology, University of Manchester Institute of Science and Technology, UK

Tim Bayliss-Smith, Department of Geography, University of Cambridge, UK

Peter Bellwood, Department of Archaeology and Anthropology, Australian National University, Canberra, Australia

Mark Blumler, Department of Geography, State University of New York, Binghamton, New York, USA

Terry A. Brown, Department of Biochemistry and Molecular Biology, University of Manchester Institute of Science and Technology, UK

L. Luca Cavalli-Sforza, Department of Genetics, Stanford University School of Medicine, Stanford, California, USA

Susan M. Colledge, McDonald Institute of Archaeological Research, University of Cambridge, UK

Andrew N. Garrard, Institute of Archaeology, University College London, University of London, UK

Ian C. Glover, Institute of Archaeology, University College London, University of London, UK

Chris Gosden, Pitt Rivers Museum, University of Oxford, UK

Les Groube, l'Ancien Presbytère, Mellionnec, France (formerly Department of Anthropology, University of Papua New Guinea)

Paul Halstead, Department of Archaeology and Prehistory, University of Sheffield, UK

David R. Harris, Institute of Archaeology, University College London, University of London, UK

Richard J. Harrison, Department of Archaeology, University of Bristol, UK

Jonathan G. Hather, Institute of Archaeology, University College London, University of London, UK

Charles F. W. Higham, Department of Anthropology, University of Otago, Dunedin, New Zealand

Gordon C. Hillman, Institute of Archaeology, University College London, University of London, UK

Frank Hole, Department of Anthropology, Yale University, New Haven, Connecticut, USA

Keiji Imamura, Department of Archaeology, University of Tokyo, Japan

Tim Ingold, Department of Social Anthropology, University of Manchester, UK

Martin K. Jones, Department of Archaeology, University of Cambridge, UK

Ilse Köhler-Rollefson, Department of Biology, TH Darmstadt, Germany

Anthony J. Legge, Department of Archaeology, Centre for Extra-Mural Studies, Birkbeck College, University of London, UK

Louise A. Martin, Institute of Archaeology, University College London, University of London, UK

Richard H. Meadow, Zooarchaeology Laboratory, Peabody Museum of Archaeology and Ethnology, Harvard University, Cambridge, Massachusetts, USA

T. Douglas Price, Department of Anthropology, University of Wisconsin-Madison, Madison, Wisconsin, USA

Colin Renfrew, Department of Archaeology, University of Cambridge, UK

Andrew Sherratt, Department of Antiquities, Ashmolean Museum, University of Oxford, UK

Matthew Spriggs, Division of Archaeology and Natural History, Research School of Pacific and Asian Studies, Australian National University, Canberra, Australia

Julian Thomas, Department of Archaeology, University of Southampton, UK

Hans-Peter Uerpmann, Institut für Ur- und Frühgeschichte, Eberhard-Karls-Universität, Tübingen, Germany

Daniel Zohary, Professor of Genetics, Department of Evolution, Systematics and Ecology, The Hebrew University, Jerusalem, Israel

Marek Zvelebil, Department of Archaeology and Prehistory, University of Sheffield, UK

CHAPTER ONE

Introduction: themes and concepts in the study of early agriculture

David R. Harris

The questions of how, when, where and why people first domesticated plants and animals, and abandoned the foraging life for that of farming, are central to an understanding of the history of humanity. The transition to agriculture not only had revolutionary ecological and economic consequences; it was also associated with the development of settled life and it led ultimately (in some parts of the world) to the emergence of urban civilization. Progress in understanding the transition depends on multidisciplinary investigations – to which archaeologists, anthropologists, biologists, geographers and other scientists have all contributed. As a field of scholarly enquiry it has a pedigree that reaches back at least to the second half of the nineteenth century, in such pioneering works as those of Darwin (1868), Hehn (1870), de Candolle (1882) and Hahn (1896). It was given fresh impetus in the early twentieth century by two seminal statements, one by a botanist (Vavilov 1926) and one by an archaeologist (Childe 1928), which, respectively, introduced the concept of "centres of origin" of cultivated plants (and, by extension, of agriculture) and formulated the concept of the Neolithic (or Agricultural) Revolution. Both these contributions profoundly influenced subsequent thinking about, and investigations of, the origins of agriculture (Harris 1990, 1994), and that they continue to do so, directly or indirectly, is evident in many of the chapters in this book.

After the Second World War, archaeologists started specifically to investigate the beginnings of agriculture in the field, and to involve botanists and zoologists in their endeavours. Such multidisciplinary projects were pioneered by Robert Braidwood in Iraq (Braidwood & Braidwood 1950) and by Richard MacNeish in Mexico (MacNeish 1950), and these were followed in the 1950s by other excavations of early neolithic/agricultural sites, principally in the Near East (Southwest Asia), for example those carried out by Kathleen Kenyon at Jericho (Kenyon 1960) and by James Mellaart at Haçilar and Çatal Hüyük (Mellaart 1958, 1962). By the 1960s the search for "agricultural origins" had become a prime preoccupation of many archaeologists, and it took centre stage in the "processual" revolution of that decade, particularly in the theoretical contributions of Lewis Binford (1968) and Kent Flannery (1968). The transformation of thinking about the beginnings of agriculture that took place then was encapsulated by Binford (ibid.: 327) when he asserted that "the question to be asked is not why agricultural and food-storage techniques were not developed everywhere, but why they were developed at all"; and it introduced into the debate not only systems theory but more general ecological concepts, which were employed at that time by British students of the subject (e.g. Harris 1969, Higgs & Jarman 1969) as well as by the "New Archaeologists" on the other side of the Atlantic.

Although the pursuit of "agricultural origins" has lost much of its intellectual glamour since the heady days of the late 1960s and early 1970s, it has remained a major focus of archaeological research and has continued to generate many international conferences and symposia (e.g. Harlan et al. 1976, Hutchinson et al. 1977, Megaw 1977, Reed 1977, Clark & Brandt 1984, Farrington 1985, Ford 1985, Clutton-Brock 1989, Harris & Hillman 1989, Milles et al. 1989, Anderson 1992, Cowan & Watson 1992, Gebauer & Price 1992) as well as several comprehensive individual studies (e.g. Cohen 1977, Rindos 1984, MacNeish 1992, Zohary & Hopf 1993). This procession of publications contains an impressive volume of new data on early agriculture and plant and animal domestication, but, more significantly, it also reflects a shift away from the search for ever earlier evidence, in the form of the oldest dated cereal grain or domestic caprine bone, to an attempt to trace transitions from "hunting and gathering" to "agriculture" in all their ecological and cultural complexity in particular regions of the world. This research agenda is also increasingly being aided by the application of a wide range of new scientific techniques to the retrieval, identification, dating and analysis of plant, animal and human remains and the archaeological contexts in which they are found.

Given the plethora of recent conferences and resulting publications on agricultural "origins" and "transitions", it may seem otiose to have produced yet another. But this book differs from most of its predecessors by focusing on the single landmass of Eurasia. To understand better the processes by which agriculture originated and spread, we need to examine the evidence in broad, explicitly comparative frameworks, particularly because there is a tendency for the results of individual excavations to be interpreted in terms of local cultural sequences, with insufficient comparison made with evidence from other areas. Ideally, and eventually, such comparison should be carried out at a global scale, but at present there is insufficient evidence worldwide to justify attempting such an ambitious enterprise. We are, I suggest, likely to gain greater understanding of these complex processes by examining, in depth but not in complete isolation, the evidence currently available for each of the major continental landmasses: Eurasia, Africa and the Americas. At present, less is securely known about the origins and spread of agriculture in Africa and the Americas than in Europe and Asia, where investigation has concentrated particularly on Southwest Asia and on the postulated spread of agriculture from there to and through Europe. We know relatively less about the beginnings of agriculture elsewhere in Asia, but in recent years investigations in Central, South, Southeast and East Asia, as far east as Japan and New Guinea, have produced sufficient new data to justify an attempt to compare, and partially at least even to synthesize, the evidence for Eurasia as a whole. To attempt this was one of the main reasons for organizing the conference from which this book derives.

The conference had, however, an additional, more theoretical aim. This was to bring to bear on the discussion distinctive thematic perspectives – social, ecological, genetic, linguistic, biomolecular, epidemiological and geographical – all of which are highly relevant to, and some of which are largely ignored in, debates on the origins and spread of agriculture. These seven thematic perspectives constitute, in effect, an extended introduction to the regionally specific parts of the book, which depend to a greater extent on the more conventional archaeological and biological categories of evidence. The distinction between the more theoretical introductory chapters and the more substantive regional ones is not of course absolute; indeed, the introductory ones contain much evidence that relates to specific areas, periods and processes, and the later ones contain many explicit and implicit theoretical statements. But the first part does provide a multidisciplinary, thematic prelude that informs, and sometimes calls into question, assumptions and conclusions in the regional chapters that comprise the second, third and fourth parts of the book.

The emphasis, in the book as a whole, is on the types of specific archaeological and biological data that can provide the chronological and geographical frameworks on which interpretations should rest and against which hypotheses should be tested. It is less concerned with the social contexts in which transitions to agriculture occurred. This is not to deny the importance of the social dimension – indeed several contributors do examine it in some depth – but rather to accept that the continental-scale, comparative approach adopted depends heavily on the temporally and spatially specific types of evidence that archaeology and biology are best able to provide. There is also relatively little attention given in the book to the nature and early development of different *systems* of agriculture and pastoralism, although, again, certain contributors (particularly, for example, Harrison, Ingold and Köhler-Rollefson) do explore this aspect of the subject. The evolution of distinctive systems of agro–pastoralism is a huge topic in itself, which deserves separate treatment and it is only tangentially touched upon in this volume.

Further introductory comment on the structure and content of the book is unnecessary, but it is worth highlighting three topics that recur frequently and which are central to interpretations of the evidence for early agriculture. The first of these concerns the terminology we use to define agriculture and pastoralism; the second concerns the concept of centres of origin of cultivated plants; and the third concerns the role of diffusion in the adoption and establishment of agriculture.

Terminology

The published literature on "agricultural origins" is characterized by a confusing multiplicity of terms for the conceptual categories that define our discourse. There is little agreement about what precisely is meant by such terms as agriculture, horticulture, cultivation, domestication and husbandry. This semantic confusion militates against clear thinking about the phenomena we investigate, leads to misunderstanding, and can provoke unnecessary disputes over interpretation of the evidence. I have previously suggested that, rather than regard such terms as denoting autonomous categories of human activity, they can be defined in relation to one another, along evolutionary continua of interaction between people and the plants and animals they depend on for food and other products. Since proposing such a model for people–plant interaction (Harris 1989), I have modified the original categories and also suggested a parallel classificatory continuum of people–animal interaction (Harris 1996). The main systems of plant and animal exploitation defined in each model are given below in Table 1.1 in the hope that they will help to clarify the terminology we use and provide a useful prelude to the rest of this book.

Table 1.1   An evolutionary classification of systems of (above) plant and (below) animal exploitation (simplified from Harris 1996: Figs 1 and 2).

Wild plant-food procurement	Plant-food production		Crop-production dominant
	Wild plant-food production dominant		
Gathering and collecting	*Cultivation* with small-scale clearance of vegetation and minimal tillage	*Cultivation* with larger-scale land clearance and systematic tillage	*Agriculture* based largely or exclusively on the cultivation of domesticated plants

Decreasing dependence on wild plants ⟶

Increasing dependence on domesticated plants ⟶

Time ⟶

Predation	Protection	Domestication
Generalized hunting (and scavenging) Specialized hunting (and scavenging) Fishing	Taming Protective herding Free-range management	Livestock raising by settled agriculturalists Transhumance Nomadic pastoralism

Decreasing dependence on wild animals ⟶

Increasing dependence on domesticated animals ⟶

Time ⟶

Table 1.1 greatly oversimplifies the diverse ways in which humans have exploited plants and animals, and it is not intended to imply any inevitable evolutionary progression from one system of exploitation to another. Nor does it imply that all domesticates have followed an essentially similar pathway to domestication. For example, some animals, such as the reindeer, are likely to have entered into a domesticatory relationship with people via protective herding *and* taming (Ingold 1980: 95–133), whereas others may have done so exclusively as tamed infant animals, as Uerpmann suggests (in this volume) for both sheep and goats.

Centres of origin

The second topic that calls for comment – the concept of centres of origin of cultivated plants – has permeated discussions of early agriculture since the time of de Candolle. However, it was Vavilov's delineation – initially of five and later of up to twelve – world centres of origin of cultivated plants that exerted a particularly strong and persistent influence on Western scholars, from 1945 onwards (Harris 1990: 11–15). As early as 1926 he argued that the centres of varietal diversity, and origin, of cultivated plants were to be found in mountainous regions, which were also "the home of primeval agriculture" (Vavilov 1926: 219). He rejected the notion that the concentration of crop varieties that he observed in such regions was the result only of the diversity of environmental conditions in the mountains, arguing that it was also the result of "historical facts", and he even suggested that "in locating the centres where cultivated plants have originated we come near to establishing the principal homesteads of human culture" (ibid.: 218–20). From Vavilov's "centres" one can trace an intellectual thread forwards to Portères' (1950, 1962) "cradles of ancient agriculture", Sauer's (1952) "hearths" of (agri-) cultural innovation, and Harlan's (1971) and Hawkes's (1983) "nuclear centres" of agriculture and civilization. So pervasive has been the concept of centres that there can be few students of early agriculture who have not been influenced by it, although it has increasingly been criticized, particularly on genetic grounds, for example by Zohary (1970).

The main weakness of Vavilov's concept has always been his equation of centres of crop diversity with centres of earliest agriculture. The recognition that areas of varietal diversity of crops were much more extensive than his original centres led his successors to distinguish between primary and secondary centres, the need for which he had himself anticipated (op. cit. 1926: 243). Thus, Zhukovsky, who, like Vavilov before him, was Director of the Institute of Plant Industry in Leningrad, introduced the concept of "primary gene microcentres", which contained the wild relatives of the cultivated species and which he contrasted with "secondary gene megacentres". The latter were in effect Vavilov's centres expanded to include most of the world, and they consisted of the vast areas to which cultivars have been dispersed and in which much varietal diversity has since arisen (Zhukovsky 1970). The value of Zhukovsky's revision of Vavilov's scheme was to distinguish clearly between centres of *origin* of cultivars (his microcentres) and regions of crop diversity (his megacentres), but his work had little impact on Western scholars. This contrasts with the wide influence of a paper by another re-interpreter of Vavilov's scheme, Harlan, who published his version of it in 1971. He argued that only three of Vavilov's centres merited recognition as such, on the grounds that agriculture had originated independently in each of them. He further proposed that most of the remaining Vavilovian centres should be subsumed in three tropical non-centres that were conceived as large areas of diffuse crop origins, each linked by processes of diffusion to its nearest subtropical or temperate centre to the north; thus, Africa was paired with Southwest Asia (the Near East), Southeast Asia with North China, and South America with Mexico (Harlan 1971). Harlan's revision of Vavilov's scheme was based on the assumption that agriculture arose independently in three "nuclear" centres of ancient civilization from which it subsequently spread to the three non-centres – an assumption that cannot be substantiated unequivocally from present archaeological and botanical evidence (as this book demonstrates for Eurasia). In 1983 a similar but more complex revision of Vavilov's centres was proposed by Hawkes, who postulated four "nuclear centers of agricultural origins" (the Near East, northern China, southern Mexico, and central to southern Peru), associated with ten "regions of diversity" to which "domesticated plants spread from the nuclear centers" and eight outlying "minor centers, probably of more recent origin . . . where only a few crops . . . seem to have originated" (Hawkes 1983: 71–2).

Although Vavilov's successors have elaborated and refined his original concept, and have tried to distinguish more clearly than he did between centres of crop diversity and areas of origin of agriculture, conceptual confusion between these two phenomena persists. Nor does the evidence everywhere support the assumption that plants were domesticated and agriculture developed earlier in all the so-called nuclear centres than elsewhere. Rather than continue to try to define, for the world as a whole, a series of "primary" and "secondary" centres of plant domestication and early agriculture, we need to focus research more on the evolutionary history of individual crops and regional crop associations – as Zohary does most effectively in this volume for the "founder crops" of Southwest Asian agriculture. The same reasoning applies to research on the origins of domestic animals, as is demonstrated by the chapters on caprine domestication in this volume by Hole, Legge and Uerpmann, but, in this field of study – unlike the emphasis on crop diversity in the study of plant domestication – research has focused more on the areas of distribution of the known or presumed wild ancestors than on the areas of diversity of domestic breeds (cf. Zeuner 1963, Clutton-Brock 1981). Perhaps students of animal domestication have benefited by not having a "Vavilov" to define "centres" for them!

Discussion of the validity and value of the concept of centres of origin of domesticates in investigating the origins and spread of agriculture raises another, more difficult, problem. This is the question of the relative importance, or frequency, of single or multiple domestications of the same, or closely related, taxa. If it can be determined whether a particular plant or animal was domesticated once only, or several times in different areas, we can gain important insights into the early history of agriculture and pastoralism. We need to be able to answer that question for each crop and domestic animal, but to do so we must know the identity of the wild progenitors and be sufficiently confident about their distribution at the postulated time or times of domestication to draw well founded conclusions about where the process occurred.

The question of single versus multiple origins of domesticates cannot be answered at a general level: detailed biological and archaeological investigation of individual taxa is required, region by region. This must continue to be a major part of the research agenda for the study of "agricultural origins", and it is well represented in this volume. It is explicitly examined, for example, by Zohary who argues persuasively for single or only very few "domestication events" in the development of grain agriculture in Southwest Asia, by Blumler who suggests that this holds true for most "primary" crops, and by Uerpmann who suggests that a unique constellation of circumstances in the "proto-neolithic villages" of the Levant led to the domestication of sheep and goats.

As has already been stressed, such hypotheses depend on assumptions about the areas of distribution of the wild progenitors at the time of initial domestication, and here we encounter another major difficulty: the question of whether environmental changes have so altered those areas of distribution since the time of domestication as to invalidate inferences based on the modern distributions of the wild progenitors. This problem raises particular difficulties in regions that experienced major environmental changes at and after the Pleistocene/Holocene transition, such as Southwest Asia, and it is addressed in this volume by Hillman in his detailed examination of the palynological evidence for changes in the vegetation of the "northern Fertile Crescent".

Diffusion

From the difficulties encountered in trying to determine areas of origin, we now turn to the third topic, which invites introductory comment: the role of diffusion in the adoption and establishment of agriculture. No one can doubt that diffusion processes have played a large part in the rise to world dominance of agricultural economies – indeed the concepts of "origins" and "spread" are inseparably linked, as the title of this volume implies – but opinion varies greatly as to the relative importance in cultural evolution of "diffusion" and "independent invention". In the 1960s and 1970s there was a strong tendency to reject earlier "crude" diffusionist explanations of cultural change and to posit multiple independent innovations – in agriculture and domestication as in other aspects of past human behaviour. This tendency was evident, for example, in re-evaluations of prevailing assumptions about the spread of agriculture from Southwest Asia to Europe (e.g. Dennell 1983, Barker 1985).

More recently a greater readiness to emphasize again the role of diffusion has become apparent, and it is clearly evident in this volume. However, this shift is not just a swing in the pendulum of academic fashion. It stems from a more subtle appreciation – by anthropologists, archaeologists, geographers and other social scientists – of the complexity of the processes by which cultural innovations spread and are adopted. In the study of early agriculture this tendency has shown itself particularly in the continuing debate between those who see the beginnings of agriculture in Europe as a result of the "demic diffusion" of migrant neolithic farmers and pastoralists from Southwest Asia (e.g. Ammerman & Cavalli-Sforza 1984) and those who prefer to emphasize the importance of the selective adoption of introduced domesticates and other cultural items by the indigenous mesolithic hunter–gatherer populations (e.g. Zvelebil & Rowley-Conwy 1986). This difference can be characterized as one between primary ("demic") and secondary (sometimes called "cultural") diffusion, and the varying emphases given to these processes in interpretations of the European Neolithic is exemplified in this volume in the chapters by Halstead, Price, Thomas and Zvelebil (see also the concluding "overview"). The role of demic diffusion in spreading agriculture and pastoralism is given greater emphasis, on a grander scale, by Cavalli-Sforza and by Renfrew in their contributions, which link the distributions of particular human genes and of languages to the spread of agriculture in, and even beyond, Eurasia. Bellwood, too, gives great weight in his chapter to demic diffusion and also links the spread of languages in the Indo–Pacific region and elsewhere to that of agriculture.

The relative importance of independent origins and subsequent diffusion remains, of course, a cardinal question in the study of early agriculture. In attempting to answer it, we need carefully to evaluate all the evidence available in particular regional and continental contexts, and in so doing to identify significant gaps in our knowledge that need to be filled by future research. It is my hope that this book will help to achieve that goal for the great landmass of Eurasia, where so many of the decisive developments took place that set humankind on the path to civilization.

References

Ammerman, A. J. & L. L. Cavalli-Sforza 1984. *The neolithic transition and the genetics of populations in Europe*. Princeton, New Jersey: Princeton University Press.

Anderson, P. C. (ed.) 1992. *Préhistoire de l'agriculture: nouvelles approches expérimentales et ethnographiques* [Monographie 6, Centre de Recherches Archéologiques]. Paris: Editions du CNRS.

Barker, G. 1985. *Prehistoric farming in Europe*. Cambridge: Cambridge University Press.

Binford, L. R. 1968. Post-Pleistocene adaptations. In *New perspectives in archeology*, S. R. Binford & L. R. Binford (eds), 313–41. Chicago: Aldine.

Braidwood, R. J. & L. Braidwood 1950. Jarmo: a village of early farmers in Iraq. *Antiquity* 24, 189–95.

Childe, V. G. 1928. *The most ancient East: the oriental prelude to European prehistory*. London: Kegan Paul, Trench, Trubner.

Clark, J. D. & S. A. Brandt (eds) 1984. *From hunters to farmers: the causes and consequences of food production in Africa*. Berkeley: University of California Press.

Clutton-Brock, J. 1981. *Domesticated animals from early times*. London: Heinemann and the British Museum (Natural History).

— (ed.) 1989. *The walking larder: patterns of domestication, pastoralism, and predation*. London: Unwin Hyman.

Cohen, M. N. 1977. *The food crisis in prehistory: overpopulation and the origins of agriculture*. New Haven, Connecticut: Yale University Press.

Cowan, C. W. & P. J. Watson (eds) 1992. *The origins of agriculture: an international perspective*. Washington DC: Smithsonian Institution Press.

Darwin, C. 1868. *The variation of animals and plants under domestication*, vol 1. London: John Murray.

de Candolle, A. 1882. *Origine des plantes cultivées*. Paris: Germer Baillière.

Dennell, R. W. 1983. *European economic prehistory: a new approach*. London: Academic Press.

Farrington, I. S. (ed.) 1985. *Prehistoric intensive agriculture in the tropics*. Oxford: British Archaeological Reports, International Series 232 i & ii.

Flannery, K. V. 1968. Archeological systems theory and early Mesoamerica. In *Anthropological archeology in the Americas*, B. J. Meggers (ed.), 67–87. Washington DC: Anthropological Society of Washington.

Ford, R. I. 1985. The processes of plant food production in prehistoric North America. In *Prehistoric food production in North America*, R. I. Ford (ed.), 1–18. Anthropological Paper 75, Museum of Anthropology, University of Michigan.

Gebauer, A. B. & T. Douglas Price (eds) 1992. *Transitions to agriculture in prehistory* [Monographs in World Archaeology 4]. Madison, Wisconsin: Prehistory Press.

Hahn, E. 1896. Die Haustiere und ihre Beziehungen zur Wirtschaft des Menschen. Leipzig: Duncker & Humblot.

Harlan, J. R. 1971. Agricultural origins: centers and noncenters. *Science* 174, 468–74.

Harlan, J. R., J. M. J. de Wet, A. B. L. Stemler (eds) 1976. *Origins of African plant domestication*. The Hague: Mouton.

Harris, D. R. 1969. Agricultural systems, ecosystems and the origins of agriculture. In *The domestication and exploitation of plants and animals*, P. J. Ucko & G. W. Dimbleby (eds), 3–15. London: Duckworth.

— 1989. An evolutionary continuum of people–plant interaction. In *Foraging and farming: the evolution of plant exploitation*, D. R. Harris & G. C. Hillman (eds), 11–26. London: Unwin Hyman.

— 1990. Vavilov's concept of centres of origin of cultivated plants: its genesis and its influence on the study of agricultural origins. *Biological Journal of the Linnean Society* **39**, 7–16.

— (ed.) 1994. *The archaeology of V. Gordon Childe: contemporary perspectives*. London: UCL Press.

— 1996. Domesticatory relationships of people, plants and animals. In *Redefining nature: ecology, culture and domestication*, R. Ellen & K. Fukui (eds), 437–63. Oxford: Berg.

Harris, D. R. & G. C. Hillman (eds) 1989. *Foraging and farming: the evolution of plant exploitation*. London: Unwin Hyman.

Hawkes, J. G. 1983. *The diversity of crop plants*. Cambridge, Massachusetts: Harvard University Press.

Hehn, V. 1870 (1885). *Kulturpflanzen und Haustiere in ihrem übergang aus Asien nach Griechenland und Italien sowie in das übrige Europa*. Berlin: Gebrüder Brontraeger. (An English translation by J. S. Stallybrass was published in 1885 as *The wanderings of plants and animals from their first home*. London: Swan Sonnenschein.)

Higgs, E. S. & M. R. Jarman 1969. The origins of agriculture: a reconsideration. *Antiquity* **43**, 31–41.

Hutchinson, J., J. G. D. Clark, E. M. Jope, R. Riley (eds) 1977. *The early history of agriculture*. Oxford: Oxford University Press.

Ingold, T. 1980. *Hunters, pastoralists and ranchers: reindeer economies and their transformations*. Cambridge: Cambridge University Press.

Kenyon, K. M. 1960. Jericho and the origins of agriculture. *The Advancement of Science* **66**, 118–20.

MacNeish, R. S. 1950. A synopsis of the archaeological sequence in the Sierra de Tamaulipas. *Revista México de Instituto Antropología* **11**, 79–96.

— 1992. *The origins of agriculture and settled life*. Norman: University of Oklahoma Press.

Megaw, J. V. S. (ed.) 1977. *Hunters, gatherers and first farmers beyond Europe: an archaeological survey*. Leicester: Leicester University Press.

Mellaart, J. 1958. Excavations at Haçilar: first preliminary report. *Anatolian Studies* **8**, 127–56.

— 1962. Excavations at Çatal Hüyük. *Anatolian Studies* **12**, 41–65.

Milles, A., D. Williams, N. Gardner 1989. *The beginnings of agriculture*. Oxford: British Archaeological Reports, International Series 496.

Portères, R. 1950. Vieilles agricultures africaines avant le xvième siècle: berceaux d'agriculture et centres de variation. *L'Agronomie Tropicale* **5**, 489–507.

— 1962. Berceaux agricoles primaires sur le continent africain. *Journal of African History* **3**, 195–210.

Reed, C. A. (ed.) 1977. *Origins of agriculture*. The Hague: Mouton.

Rindos, D. 1984. *The origins of agriculture: an evolutionary perspective*. Orlando, Florida: Academic Press.

Sauer, C. O. 1952. *Agricultural origins and dispersals*. New York: American Geographical Society.

Vavilov, N. I. 1926. *Studies on the origin of cultivated plants*. Leningrad: Institut Botanique Appliqué et d'Amélioration des Plantes.

Zeuner, F. E. 1963. *A history of domesticated animals*. London: Hutchinson.

Zhukovsky, P. M. 1970 (1975). *World gene pool of plants for breeding. Mega-genecenters and endemic micro-genecenters* [in Russian]. Leningrad: Publishing House "Nauka", Leningrad Division. (English translation, 1975. Leningrad: N. I. Vavilov Institute of Plant Industry).

Zohary, D. 1970. Centers of diversity and centers of origin. In *Genetic resources in plants – their exploration and conservation*, D. H. Frankel & E. Bennett (eds), 33–42. Oxford: Blackwell Scientific.

Zohary, D. & M. Hopf 1993. *Domestication of plants in the Old World: the origin and spread of cultivated plants in West Asia, Europe, and the Nile Valley*, 2nd edn. Oxford: Oxford University Press.

Zvelebil, M. & P. Rowley-Conwy 1986. Foragers and farmers in Atlantic Europe. In *Hunters in transition*, M. Zvelebil (ed.), 67–93. Cambridge: Cambridge University Press.

PART ONE
Thematic perspectives

CHAPTER TWO

Growing plants and raising animals: an anthropological perspective on domestication

Tim Ingold

According to the received categories of archaeological and anthropological thought, there are basically just two ways of procuring a livelihood from the natural environment, conventionally denoted by the terms *collection* and *production*. My aim in this chapter is to review this distinction, and ultimately to dissolve it. I proceed in three steps. First, I trace something of its history, showing how it is embedded in a grand narrative of the human transcendence of nature, in which the domestication of plants and animals figures as the counterpart of the self-domestication of humanity in the process of civilization. The second step is to consider how people who actually live by gardening, tilling the soil or keeping livestock understand the nature of their activity, drawing on examples from South America, Melanesia and West Africa. Indigenous knowledge, almost by definition, differs from Western thought and science in that it is grounded in an immediate and thoroughly practical engagement with the constituents of the environment, rather than in the assumption of human detachment from – and superiority over – the world of nature. The third step is to reconsider what it means to grow plants and to raise animals, taking this condition of engagement as a starting point. I argue that the work of the farmer or herdsman does not "make" crops or livestock, but rather serves to set up certain conditions of development within which plants and animals take on their particular forms and behavioural dispositions. My conclusion is that neither production nor collection offers an adequate conceptualization of what people are doing in their activities of livelihood. Rather, we are dealing with processes of *growth*, in which human beings, animals and plants come into being, each in relation to the others, within a continuous field of relationships.

The human transformation of nature

The distinction between production and collection was first coined by Friedrich Engels. In a note penned in 1875, he pointed to production as the most fundamental criterion of what he saw as a kind of "mastery" of the environment that was distinctively human: "The most that the animal can achieve is to *collect*; man produces, he prepares the means of life. . . which without him nature would not have produced. This makes impossible any unqualified transference of the laws of life in animal society" to human society" (Engels 1934: 308). The essence of production, for Engels, lay in the deliberate planning of activity, by intentional and self-conscious agents, "towards definite, preconceived ends" (ibid.: 178, 237). Animals, through their activities, might exert lasting and quite radical effects on their environments, but these effects are by and large unintended: the non-human animal, Engels thought, did not labour in its surroundings *in order* to change them; it had no conception of its task.

Curiously, however, whenever Engels turned to consider concrete examples of human mastery in production, he drew them exclusively from the activities of agriculture and pastoralism, wherein plants, animals and the landscape itself had been demonstrably transformed through human design (ibid.: 34, 178–9). Opposing the foraging behaviour of non-human species to the human husbandry of plants and animals, Engels left a gap that could only be filled by calling into being a special category of humans known to him and his contemporaries as "savages" – although now, more politely, as hunter–gatherers. The savage had, as it were, come down from the trees but had not yet left the woods: suspended in limbo between evolution and history, he was a human being who had so far failed to realize the potential afforded by his unique constitution. Ever since, the humanity of hunter–gatherers has been somehow in question. They may be members of the species, *Homo sapiens*, but their form of life is such as to put them on a par with other animal kinds, which also derive their subsistence by collecting whatever is "to hand" in the environment. As the archaeologist Robert Braidwood wrote in 1957, "a man who spends his whole life following animals just to kill them to eat, or moving from one berry patch to another, is really living just like an animal himself" (Braidwood 1957: 22).

It was this latent ambiguity that subsequently allowed the archaeologist, V. Gordon Childe, to take up the distinction between collection and production – in terms virtually identical to those proposed by Engels – to draw a line not between humans and animals, but between "neolithic" people and their successors on the one hand, and "palaeolithic" hunters and gatherers on the other. In crossing this line, the ancestors of present-day farmers, herdsmen and urban dwellers were alleged to have set in motion a revolution in the arts of subsistence without parallel in the history of life. Ushered in by the invention of the science of selective breeding, it was a revolution that turned people, according to Childe, into "active partners with nature instead of parasites on nature" (Childe 1942: 55). Although contemporary authors might phrase the distinction somewhat differently, the notion of food production as the singular achievement of human agriculturalists and pastoralists has become part of the stock-in-trade of modern prehistory. And understanding the origins of food production has become as central a preoccupation for prehistorians as has understanding the origins of humankind for palaeo-anthropologists: where the latter seek the evolutionary origins of human beings *within* nature, the former seek the decisive moment at which humanity *transcended* nature, and was set on the path of history.

Underlying the collection/production distinction, then, is a master narrative about how human beings, through their mental and bodily labour, have progressively raised themselves above the purely natural level of existence to which all other animals are confined, and in so doing have built themselves a history of civilization. Through their transformations of nature, according to this narrative, humans have also transformed themselves. It is a fact about human beings, states Maurice Godelier, that alone among animals, they "*produce society in order to live*" – and in so doing, "create history" (Godelier 1986: 1, original emphasis). By this he means that the designs and purposes of human action upon the natural environment – action that yields a return in the form of the wherewithal for subsistence – have their source in the domain of social relations, a domain of mental realities ("representations, judgements, principles of thought"), which stands over and above the sheer materiality of nature (ibid.: 10–11).

Godelier goes on to distinguish five "kinds of materiality", depending upon the manner and extent to which human beings are implicated in their formation. First is that part of nature which is wholly untouched by human activity; secondly, there is the part that has been changed on account of the presence of humans, but indirectly and unintentionally; the third is the part that has been intentionally transformed by human beings and depends upon their attention and energy for its reproduction; the fourth part comprises materials that have been fashioned into instruments such as tools and weapons; and the fifth may be identified with what we would conventionally call the "built environment": houses, shelters, monuments, and the like (ibid.: 4–5). In this classification the critical division falls between the second and third kinds, for it is also taken to mark the distinction between the wild and the domestic. The third part of nature is taken to consist, primarily, of domesticated plants and animals, whereas the biotic components of the first and second parts are either wild or, at most, in a condition of pre-domestication. Moreover, Godelier points to the domestication of plants and animals as a paradigmatic instance of the transforming action of humanity upon nature. This leaves us, however, with two unresolved problems.

The first concerns the status of hunters and gatherers who have sought not to transform their environments but rather to conserve them in a form that remains, as far as possible, unscarred by human activity. If, as Godelier asserts, "human beings have a history because they transform nature" (ibid.: 1), are we to conclude that humans who do not transform nature lack history? For his own part, Godelier resists this conclusion: "I cannot see any theoretical reason to consider the forms of life and thought characteristic of hunters, gatherers and fishers as more natural than those of the agriculturalists and stockbreeders who succeeded them" (ibid.: 12). The activities of hunter–gatherers, like those of all human beings at all times, and unlike those of all non-human animals, are prompted by mental representations that have their source in the intersubjective domain of society. Yet apart from the construction of tools and of shelters (which correspond respectively to the fourth and fifth kinds of materiality), these representations are not inscribed in the substrate of nature. Hunter–gatherers have a history, but theirs is a history that is written neither in the pages of documents nor upon the surface of the land. Overturning the classical conception of hunter–gatherers as arch-representatives of humanity in the state of nature, Godelier reaches the rather paradoxical conclusion that it is in their societies that the boundary between culture and nature, the mental and the material, is most clear cut. The more the material world is subordinated to the ends of art, the more it is "humanized", and the more the nature/culture boundary is dissolved (ibid.: 4).

The second problem is one to which Godelier alludes in a footnote, but fails to take further. It is that for most non-Western people, "the idea of a transformation of nature by human beings has no meaning" (ibid.: 2, *n.* 1). Thus, the peoples of the past who were initially responsible for domesticating plants and animals must have had quite different ideas about what they were doing. In the next section I present a range of comparable ideas drawn from the ethnography of contemporary non-Western societies. The point to stress at this juncture is that the idea of history as consisting of the human transformation of nature, like the ideas of nature itself and of society as an entity counterposed to nature, has a history of its own during a particular period in a particular part of the world. By tracing this history back to its roots, we may find that it has grown out of a set of understandings very different from those familiar to us today, yet much closer to the apparently exotic cosmologies of non-Western "others".

It is beyond the scope of this chapter to document the history of Western thinking about humanity and nature: Glacken's (1967) massive treatise on the subject remains unsurpassed. Suffice it to say that the essence of the kind of thought we call "Western" is that it is founded in a claim to the supremacy of human reason. Entailed in this claim is a notion of making things as an imprinting of prior conceptual design upon a raw material substrate. Human reason is supposed to provide the form, nature the substance in which it is realized. This idea was the fulcrum of Marx's theory of value, according to which it was the work of shaping up the material from its raw to its final state that bestowed value on what was already "given" in nature. It made no difference, in principle, whether that work was represented by the labour of the artisan, in the manufacture of equipment, or by that of the farmer or stockbreeder, in the husbandry of plants and animals. Both were conceived as instances of productive making – the human transformation of nature.

Yet in arriving at his theory of value, Marx turned on its head an older idea, most fully developed in the writings of the French physiocrats, Quesnay and Turgot, in the eighteenth century. For these writers too, the role of the artisan was to imprint a rational design upon material supplied by nature. But in doing so, he created no new value. On the contrary, his work was understood to involve nothing more than a rearrangement of what nature had already brought into existence. The real source of wealth, according to physiocracy, was the land, and it lay in its inherent fertility. And for this reason, the activities of those who worked the land, in growing crops and raising animals, were understood to be fundamentally different in character from the activities of those whose tasks lay in the field of manufacture.

In an elegant analysis, Gudeman (1986: 80–84) has shown how the economic doctrines of physiocracy were closely modelled on the theory of perception and cognition proposed some 70 years previously by John Locke. In Locke's economy of knowledge, the natural world is a source of raw sensations impinging upon the receptor organs of the passive human observer. The mind then operates on these received sensory data, separating and combining them to form complex ideas. In just the same way, according to the physiocrats, the land furnishes its inhabitants with basic raw materials, to which human reason adds form and meaning. As Gudeman puts it, "in this 'intellectual' economics, agriculture is to artisanship as sensation was to mental operation" (ibid.: 83). The role of the farmer is to receive the substantive yield of the land, that of the artisan is to deliver the formal designs of humanity. Where the farmer's work is productive, in that it results in an influx of wealth to the human community, it is nevertheless passive because the creative agency in bringing forth this wealth was attributed to the land itself and, behind that, to divine intervention. Conversely the artisan's work is non-productive, because it adds nothing to human wealth, but is nevertheless active because it is impelled by human reason (ibid.: 87).

In this view of things, although it would still be fair to describe the act of making things as a human transformation of nature, such making is not the equivalent but the very *opposite* of production, just as artisanship is the opposite of agriculture. Production is a process of growing, not making. The farmer, and for that matter the raiser of livestock, submits to a productive dynamic that is immanent in the natural world itself, rather than converting nature into an instrument to his own purpose. Far from "impressing the stamp of their will upon the earth", to adopt Engels' imperialistic phrase (1934: 179), those who toil on the land – in clearing fields, turning the soil, sowing, weeding, reaping, pasturing their flocks and herds, or feeding animals in their stalls – are assisting in the reproduction of nature, and derivatively of their own kind.

In classical Greece, too, agriculture and artisanship were clearly opposed, belonging – as Vernant remarks (1983: 253) – "to two different fields of experience which are to a large extent mutually exclusive". The contrast between growing things and making things was delightfully phrased by the Sophist author Antiphon, writing in the fifth century BC, who invites us to imagine an old wooden bed, buried in the ground, taking root and sprouting green shoots. What comes up, however, is not a new bed, but fresh wood! Beds are made, but wood grows (ibid.: 260). As a grower of crops rather than a maker of artefacts, the farmer was not seen to act upon nature, let alone to transform it to human ends. Work on the land was more a matter of falling into line with an overarching order, at once natural and divinely ordained, within which the finalities of human existence were themselves encompassed. Even were it technically possible to transform nature, the very idea would have been regarded as an impiety (ibid.: 254).

If there is a certain parallel here with the doctrines of physiocracy, despite the immense lapse of time, it is doubtless because both classical Greek and eighteenth-century physiocratic authors were able to draw on a fund of practical experience in working on the land. When it came to farming, they knew what they were talking about. But with regard to artisanship, their respective notions could not have been more different. For according to classical Greek writers, the forms the artisan realized in his material issued not from the human mind, as constructs of a rational intelligence, but were themselves inscribed in the order of nature. Thus, the idea of making as an imposition of rational design upon raw material would have been entirely alien to Greek thought. "The artisan is not in command of nature; he submits to the requirements of the form. His function and his excellence is. . . to obey" (ibid.: 294). This, of course, is the precise inverse of Godelier's assertion that in the husbandry of plants and animals, in making tools and constructing buildings – i.e. in the production of the third, fourth and fifth kinds of materiality – it is nature that submits to the requirements of human form. The idea that production consists in action *upon* nature, issuing from a superior source in society, is an essentially modern one.

Indigenous knowledge: four ethnographic examples

Our next step is to consider some of the ways in which contemporary non-Western people understand their relations with cultivated plants and domestic animals. In what follows I present four ethnographic examples. The first is taken from Phillipe Descola's (1994) study of the Achuar Indians of the Upper Amazon, the second draws on Marilyn Strathern's (1980) work on the people of the Mount Hagen region of the Papua New Guinea Highlands, and the third is based on a recent study by Walter van Beek & Pieteke Banga (1992) of the Dogon of Mali, in West Africa. For my fourth and final example I return to South America, and to the study by Stephen Gudeman & Alberto Rivera (1990) of the peasant farmers of Boyacá, in Colombia.

The Achuar of the Upper Amazon

The Achuar cultivate a great variety of plant species, of which the most ubiquitous is manioc, in gardens that have been cleared through a "slash-and-burn" technique from primary forest. The focus of domestic life is the house, which stands at the centre of its garden, surrounded in turn by a vast expanse of forest. Although a man is expected to prepare a garden plot for each of his wives, the cultivation, maintenance and harvesting of plots is exclusively women's work. All members of the household regularly participate in gathering activities, which are concentrated in familiar areas of the forest within close reach of the garden. Beyond that is the zone of hunting, a risky space in which men dominate, and into which women venture only when accompanied by their husbands.

Gathering, for the Achuar, is a relaxed affair – an occasion for a pleasant day out. But hunting is a quite different matter. Men's relations with the animals they hunt are modelled on the human relation of affinity: like human in-laws, the creatures of the forest are inclined to be touchy, and their feelings have continually to be assuaged with liberal doses of seductive charm. Above all, it is necessary to keep on the right side of the "game mothers", the guardian spirits of the animals, who exercise the same kind of control over their charges as do human mothers over their own children and domestic animals (Descola 1994: 257). Moreover, motherhood also extends to a woman's relations with the plants she grows in her garden. She has, as it were, two sets of offspring, the plants in her garden and the children in her home, and because the two are in competition for the nurture she can provide, relations between them are far from harmonious. Manioc, for example, is attributed with the power to suck the blood of human infants. Thus, despite its peaceful appearance, the garden is as full of menace as is the surrounding forest (ibid.: 206).

Applying orthodox concepts of anthropological analysis, we might be inclined to oppose the forest and the garden along the lines of a distinction between the wild and the domesticated, as though the edge of the woods also marked the outer limits of the human socialization of nature, and the point of transition at which production gives way to collection. But this, as Descola shows, would be profoundly at odds with Achuar understandings. For in the construction and maintenance of their gardens, the Achuar do not see themselves as engaged in a project of domesticating the pristine world of the forest; indeed the colonial image of the conquest of nature is entirely foreign to their way of thinking. For them, the forest is itself a huge garden, albeit an untidy one, and the relations between its constituents are governed by the same principles of domesticity that structure the human household, but on a superhuman scale. The tension between garden plants and children mirrors, on a reduced scale, the tension between forest creatures and human hunters; likewise a woman's care for her crops and domestic animals is writ large in the care of the "game mothers" for the species in their charge. In short, the Achuar garden figures as a microcosm of the forest: "it is not so much the cultural transformation of a portion of wild space as the cultural homology in the human order of a cultural reality of the same standing in the super-human order"; human society is a scaled-down version of the society of nature, the garden plot "temporarily realizes the virtualities of a homely wilderness" (ibid.: 220).

The people of Mount Hagen

The people of the Mount Hagen region of Papua New Guinea (henceforth "Hageners") grow crops – especially taro, yams and sweet potato – in forest clearings; they also raise pigs. They have a word, *mbo*, for the activity of planting, which is also used for things that are planted such as cuttings pushed into the ground. By extension it can refer to any other point of growth within the general field of human relations: thus, a breeding pig can be *mbo* in respect of the herd it will engender, and people can be *mbo* in respect of their placement in clan territory. The antithesis of *mbo* is *rømi*. This latter term is used for things or powers that lie beyond the reach of human nurture. The principal cultivated tubers have their wild counterparts, and these are *rømi*, as are wild pigs and other forest creatures. There are also *rømi* spirits who tend these wild plants and animals, just as people tend their gardens and pigs (Strathern 1980: 192). Indeed, at first glance, the terms *mbo* and *rømi* seem to have their more or less exact equivalents in our conventional notions of "wild" and "domestic" respectively.

Completely absent from the Hagen conception, however, is the notion of a domestic environment "carved out" from wild nature. *Mbo* does not refer to an enclosed space of settlement, as opposed to the surrounding bush or forest. Hageners do not seek to subjugate or colonize the wilderness; although the spirit masters of forest creatures have their spheres of influence as humans have theirs, the aim is "not to subdue but to come to terms with them" (ibid.: 194). *Rømi* is simply that which lies outside the limits of human care and sociability. Significantly, although the opposed term *mbo* takes its primary meaning from the act of planting, it is not used for any other stage of the horticultural process, nor for garden land itself (ibid.: 200). In planting, one does not transform nature, in the sense of imposing a rational order upon a given materiality. Rather, one places a seed or cutting in the ground so that it may take root and grow. As its roots extend into the soil, so the plant draws nourishment from its environment, gradually assuming its mature form.

Like the Achuar, Hageners draw a parallel between growing plants and growing children. The child, placed at birth within a field of nurture – as the plant is placed in the soil – steadily grows into maturity as a responsible, self-aware being, drawing sustenance from its relationships with others even as the latter, like the plant's roots, extend ever further outwards into the social environment (Strathern 1980: 196). There is no sense, however, in which the child starts life as a thing of nature, to which a moral dimension of rules and values is added on through a process of socialization. The child does not begin as *rømi*, and become *mbo*. It is *mbo* from the outset, by virtue of its planting within the field of human relationships. So too, in their cultivation of tubers and raising of pigs, Hageners do not impose a social order upon an environment consisting of "nature in the raw". They rather constitute, as inherently social, the very environment within which their plants and animals come into being, take root and grow to maturity.

The Dogon of Mali

The Dogon, like many other African peoples (Morris 1995: 306), make a sharp contrast between the categories of *ana* (village) and *oru* (bush) (van Beek & Banga 1992: 67). In and around the village, people cultivate the staple crop of millet, and keep gardens of onions and tobacco. But they also depend on the bush in may ways. It is a source of firewood for cooking, brewing and firing pottery. Timber is needed, too, for building houses and granaries, and for fencing gardens. The bush also yields meat, relishes and tree fruits, leaves for use as cattle fodder, and various medicinal herbs. However, the dependence of the village on the bush goes much deeper than this list of products would indicate. For in the Dogon view, the bush is nothing less than the source of life itself, and with it of all knowledge, wisdom, power and healing. But by the same token, it is greatly to be feared. It is a zone of movement and flux, in which all the fixedness and certainties of village life are dissolved. Everything shifts and changes – even trees and rocks can walk from place to place. The many spirits that roam the bush can exchange body parts with living people, human hunters venturing there become like the animals they hunt, and as they do so their existence in the present is swallowed up in a temporal horizon that merges past and future, life and death (van Beek & Banga 1992: 67–8).

Dogon cosmology envisages a kind of entropic system in which the maintenance of the village depends upon a continual inflow of vital force from the bush, which is worn down and used up in the process. If the village is a place of stability, where things stay put and proper distinctions are maintained, it is also a place of stagnation. In an almost exact inversion of the modern Western notion of food production as the manifestation of human knowledge and power over nature, here it is nature – in the form of the bush – that holds ultimate power over human life, whereas the cultivated fields and gardens are sites of consumption rather than production, where vital force is *used up*. "Knowledge dissipates. . . and power evaporates unless reinvigorated from the bush" (ibid.: 69).

Peasant farmers of Boyacá

The rural folk of Colombia say that it is the earth that gives them their food; the role of human beings is to assist it in bringing forth its crops. As one farmer is reported to have put it: "Man helps the land; the earth produces the fruit" (Gudeman & Rivera 1990: 25). Likewise, hens give eggs, sheep give lambs and cows calves. Here, too, the farmer is called upon to assist in the animals' labour, much as a midwife assists at a birth. But the ultimate source of the "strength" or "force" (*la fuerza*) that enables people to work, animals to reproduce and crops to grow lies in the land itself. The earth is conceived as a repository of strength created and sustained by God (ibid.: 18). Thus, crops draw strength from the land, humans in turn gain strength by consuming their crops (or the produce of animals whose strength was drawn from their consumption of fodder), and expend that strength in work on the land that enables it to yield up yet more of its strength to the cycle.

Gudeman & Rivera detect in this folk model distinct echoes of eighteenth-century physiocracy. Indeed, they go so far as to suggest that it offers a window on much earlier notions current among farming peoples of the Old World, which still resonate through the practices of Colombian rural folk as well as through the texts of European political economists. The physiocratic view that only the land yields value, which the farmer harnesses on behalf of society, has its counterpart in the Colombian farmers' notion that human life is powered by the strength of the earth. Both views, moreover, invert the modern Western conception that sees in the land not an active agent but an inert source of raw materials to be shaped up to a human design. Marx (1930: 173) wrote of the earth as foremost among the instruments of labour, and ever since we have tended to think of production as a process wherein land is placed in the service of humanity. But Colombian rural folk place themselves in the service of the land. And they regard their capacity to work not as some inner aspect of their being, as in the Marxian concept of "labour-power", but as God's gift of strength, bestowed through the land and its produce, and expended in their activity (Gudeman & Rivera 1990: 103–4).

Making things, finding things and growing things

Let me now return to the pair of opposed concepts with which I began, namely collection and production. There is no doubt that the primary meaning of production in the age of manufacture is that of *making things*, the construction of artificial objects by rearranging, assembling and transforming raw materials supplied by nature. Defined in opposition to production, collection comes to mean *finding things*: picking up one's supplies, as it were "ready-made", from the environment. But how can you "make" a pig, a yam, or a crop of millet? And how, for that matter, can such things be made in advance?

I believe this modern emphasis on production as making accounts for the special significance that tends to be attached to the so-called "artificial selection" of plants and animals as the key criterion for distinguishing food production from food collection, and hence for determining the point of transition from hunting and gathering to agriculture and pastoralism. Contemporary biotechnology and genetic engineering excepted, it is not literally possible to "make" an animal or plant, in the sense of constructing it to a blueprint of human design. What one can do, however, is to isolate a breeding population within which individuals are selected for reproduction according to the degree to which they conform to an ideal type. Indeed, it is only by reference to such an ideal, suspended within the collective representations of the human community, that we can logically distinguish between artificial and natural selection (Ingold 1994: 5–6). This is probably why the notion of domestication has come to be so closely tied up with that of breeding: it is the closest thing to moulding the forms of plants and animals to a preconceived design. And this, in turn, is why prehistorians investigating the origins of food production are inclined to look for evidence of the morphological divergence of the plant or animal species in question from its original "wild" form, as proof that production was going on.

This procedure, however, generates its own anomalies. For in many parts of the world, both in the past and still today, people are apparently engaged in the husbandry of plants and animals that do not differ appreciably from their wild counterparts. Kept as pets in the houses of the Achuar are a range of "domestic wild animals" – various primates, birds and peccaries (Descola 1994: 90). The forests of Highland New Guinea are full of wild domestic pigs, as well as a variety of plants that also appear in cultivated swiddens. And the fields of the neolithic villagers of Beidha, in Jordan, according to Hans Helbaek, were sown with "cultivated wild barley" (Helbaek 1966: 62, cf. Jarman 1972: 16).

The source of these anomalies lies in the very dichotomy between collection and production. In terms of this dichotomy, human beings must *either* find their food ready-made in nature *or* make it themselves. Yet ask any farmer and he or she will say, with good cause, that the produce of the farm is no more made than it is found ready-made. It is *grown*. So our question must be as follows. Granted that by making things we mean the transformation of pre-existing raw materials, *what do we mean by growing things*? On the answer to this question must hinge the distinctions between gathering and cultivation, and between hunting and animal husbandry.

Two common themes to emerge from the ethnographic cases presented in the previous section point towards a solution. First, the work that people do, in such activities as field clearance, fencing, planting, weeding and so on, or in tending their livestock, does not literally make plants and animals, but rather establishes the environmental conditions for their growth and development. They are "mothered", nurtured, assisted – generally cosseted and helped along. Secondly, growing plants and raising animals are not so different, in principle, from bringing up children. Of course it is true that modern Western discourse, too, extends the notions of cultivation and breeding across human, animal and plant domains, referring in the human case to a refinement of taste and manners (Bouquet 1993: 189–90). Such refinement, however, is represented as a socially approved form of mastery over supposedly innate human impulses, and is the counterpart to the kind of mastery over the environment that is implied by the notion of domestication as the social appropriation of nature. When Achuar women compare their children to the plants in their gardens, or when Hageners use the language of planting for both children and pigs, they do not have this model of socialization in mind. As Strathern puts it (1980: 196): "the child grows into social maturity rather than being trained into it". What each generation provides, whether in growing plants, raising animals or bringing up children, are precisely the developmental conditions under which "growth to maturity" can occur.

Where does this leave the distinctions between gathering and cultivation, and between hunting and animal husbandry? The difference surely lies in no more than this: the *relative scope of human involvement in establishing the conditions for growth*. This is not only a matter of degree rather than kind, it can also vary over time. Weeds can become cultigens, erstwhile domestic animals can turn feral. Moreover, a crucial variable, I suggest, lies in the temporal interlocking of the life-cycles of humans, animals and plants, and their relative durations. The lives of domestic animals tend to be somewhat shorter than those of human beings, but not so short as to be of a different order of magnitude. There is thus a sense in which people and their domestic animals grow older together, and in which their respective life-histories are intertwined as mutually constitutive strands of a single process. The lives of plants, by contrast, can range from the very short to the very long indeed, from a few months to many centuries.

Now as Laura Rival has pointed out, the planned intervention in and control over nature that we conventionally associate with the idea of domestication can only be envisaged in respect of plants "whose growth is much faster relative to human growth and maturation processes" (Rival 1993: 648). It is as though humans could stand watch over the development of their crops without growing significantly older themselves. But the more slow-growing and long-lived the plant, the more artificial this assumption appears to be. In the case of the most enduring plants of all – such as certain large long-lived trees – the assumption becomes wholly untenable. Indeed, for the most part, trees do not fit at all comfortably within the terms of the orthodox distinction between the wild and the domesticated, which may account for the curious fact that despite their manifest importance to people (as our Dogon example shows), they are all but absent from archaeological and anthropological discussions of the nature and origins of food production. Of an ancient tree that has presided over successive human generations it would seem more appropriate to say that it has played its part in the domestication *of* humans rather than having been domesticated *by* them. In short, what is represented in the literature, under the rubric of domestication, as a transcendence and transformation of nature may be more a reflection of an increasing reliance on plants and animals that, by comparison with humans, are relatively fast-growing and short-lived.

I have suggested that regimes of plant and animal husbandry may best be distinguished in terms of the ways in which human beings involve themselves in establishing the conditions for growth. For example, in the cultivation of gardens, more is done to assist the growth of plants than when they are gathered from the bush. To grasp this idea, all that is required is a simple switch of perspective: instead of thinking about plants as part of the natural environment for human beings, we have to think of humans and their activities as part of the environment for plants. But behind this switch there lies a point of much more fundamental significance. If human beings on the one hand, and plants and animals on the other, can be regarded alternately as components of each others' environments, then we can no longer think of the former as inhabiting a social world of their own, over and above the world of nature in which the lives of all other living things are contained. Rather, both humans and the animals and plants on which they depend for a livelihood must be regarded as fellow participants in the *same* world, a world that is at once social and natural. And the forms that all these creatures take are neither given in advance nor imposed from above, but emerge within the relational context of this mutual involvement.

With this conclusion in mind, let me return to Godelier's five kinds of materiality, which were also distinguished according to the manner and extent of human involvement in their existence. In what way does Godelier's formulation differ from our own? The answer is that for Godelier, the formative role of humans lies in their capacity as beings who, to various degrees, act *upon*, intervene *in*, or do things *to*, a domain of nature that is external to their socially constituted selves. According to the argument I have presented, by contrast, human beings do not so much transform the material world as play their part, along with other creatures, in the world's transformation of itself (Ingold 1993: 164). In this view, nature is not a surface of materiality upon which human history is inscribed; rather history is the process wherein both people and their environments are continually coming into being, each in relation to the other. This is one way of interpreting Marx's celebrated yet enigmatic remark that "history itself is a *real* part of *natural history* – of nature developing into man" (Marx 1964: 143, original emphases). By the same token, it is also man developing into nature. Or in other words, human actions in the environment are better seen as incorporative than inscriptive, in the sense that they are built or enfolded into the forms of the landscape and its living inhabitants by way of their own processes of growth.

I should like to conclude with a few words on the question of magic. It is frequently observed in the ethnography of non-Western societies that subsistence practices, above all those of hunting animals and growing plants, are accompanied by magical songs, incantations or rites in which the animal or vegetable objects of peoples' attentions are addressed as if they were capable of being influenced, moved or persuaded by the same devices that appeal to human beings. This has been a source of considerable puzzlement. I believe, however, that the puzzle is largely an artefact of our own categories. For the division between the two worlds of society and nature, which also underwrites the dichotomy between production and collection, forces us to categorize human action, too, into two kinds. There is *communicative* action, that people direct towards one another in society, and *technical* action, directed by people onto the object-world of nature. *Magical* action, then, is defined as acts that – although ostensibly communicative – are supposed by practitioners themselves to have technical efficacy. To us, native people appear confused, mixing up what we insist are separate categories of action (Leach 1976: 30).

Yet the problem is ours, not theirs. As Descola points out for the Achuar, once one accepts – as they do as a matter of course – that cultivated plants are beings rather than mere things, it makes perfectly good sense to attempt to maintain a harmonious relationship with them, by means of magical songs that would be used to the same end in the field of human relations (Descola 1994: 214). Our mistake is to suppose that magic is intended to produce actual, physical effects in the world. In point of fact, none of the peoples who employ magic thinks of it as in any sense a substitute for hard work. What magic does is to dispose people in a particular *relationship* to the constituent beings of their environment, to orient and focus their attention so as to achieve a kind of resonance or sensory attunement.

In short, the native practitioner recognizes intuitively what the Western analyst finds so hard to grasp, namely that people act on their surroundings from *within*. From the outset, they are embedded in ties to the earth and to the manifold beings that spring from it: they are already "with" their environment prior to doing anything "to" it. And magic is for "being with" rather than "doing to": indeed one might call it a form of poetic involvement. In this connection it is worth recalling an observation that Bronislaw Malinowski made concerning the gardens of the Trobriand Islanders, in his classic monograph *Coral gardens and their magic*. "The gardens", he wrote, "are, in a way, a work of art" (1935, I: 80). As such, they are foci of great aesthetic appreciation. There is far more to gardening than the mere production of food, just as there is more to a song than the production of notes. If food were the only object of people's activities, there would perhaps be no need for magic. But for practitioners, growing crops and raising animals are not just ways of producing food; they are forms of life.

References

Bouquet, M. 1993. *Reclaiming English kinship*. Manchester: Manchester University Press.
Braidwood, R. J. 1957. *Prehistoric men*, 3rd edn. Chicago: Natural History Museum.
Childe, V. G. 1942. *What happened in history*. Harmondsworth: Penguin.
Descola, P. 1994. *In the society of nature: a native ecology in Amazonia* [translated by N. Scott]. Cambridge: Cambridge University Press.
Engels, F. 1934. *Dialectics of nature*. Moscow: Progress Publishers.
Glacken, C. J. 1967. *Traces on the Rhodian shore: nature and culture in Western thought from ancient times to the end of the eighteenth century*. Berkeley: University of California Press.
Godelier, M. 1986. *The mental and the material* [translated by M. Thom]. London: Verso.
Gudeman, S. 1986. *Economics as culture: models and metaphors of livelihood*. London: Routledge & Kegan Paul.
Gudeman, S. & A. Rivera 1990. *Conversations in Colombia: the domestic economy in life and text*. Cambridge: Cambridge University Press.
Helbaek, H. 1966. Pre-pottery neolithic farming at Beidha. *Palestine Exploration Quarterly* **98**, 61–6.
Ingold, T. 1993. The temporality of the landscape. *World Archaeology* **25**, 152–74.
— 1994. From trust to domination: an alternative history of human–animal relations. In *Animals and human society: changing perspectives*, A. Manning & J. Serpell (eds), 1–22. London: Routledge.
Jarman, H. N. 1972. The origins of wheat and barley cultivation. In *Papers in economic prehistory*, E. S. Higgs (ed.), 15–26. Cambridge: Cambridge University Press.
Leach, E. R. 1976. *Culture and communication*. Cambridge: Cambridge University Press.
Malinowski, B. 1935. *Coral gardens and their magic*. London: Allen & Unwin.
Marx, K. 1930 (1890). *Capital*, vol. I [translated by E. & C. Paul from the 4th German edn of *Das Kapital*. London: Dent.
— 1964. *The economic and political manuscripts of 1884* [translated by M. Milligan; D. J. Struik (ed.)]. New York: International Publishers.
Morris, B. 1995. Woodland and village: reflections on the "animal estate" in rural Malawi. *Journal of the Royal Anthropological Institute* (NS) **1**, 301–15.
Rival, L. 1993. The growth of family trees: understanding Huaorani perceptions of the forest. *Man* **28**, 635–52.
Strathern, M. 1980. No nature, no culture: the Hagen case. In *Nature, culture and gender*, C. MacCormack & M. Strathern (eds), 174–222. Cambridge: Cambridge University Press.
van Beek, W. E. A. & P. M. Banga 1992. The Dogon and their trees. In *Bush base: forest farm: culture, environment and development*, E. Croll & D. Parkin (eds), 57–75. London: Routledge.
Vernant, J. P. 1983. *Myth and thought among the Greeks*. London: Routledge & Kegan Paul.

CHAPTER THREE

Ecology, evolutionary theory and agricultural origins

Mark A. Blumler

> . . . human beings are not the only actors who make history. Other crea-
> tures do too, as do large natural processes, and any history that ignores
> their effects is likely to be woefully incomplete.   (Cronon 1993: 13)

The study of prehistory is an interdisciplinary endeavour. Given the information
explosion and ever-increasing specialization, however, the mastery of even a small
subdiscipline is well-nigh impossible today. Consequently, one of the more intractable
problems in interdisciplinary research is transdisciplinary communication (Blumler
1993a). It becomes increasingly difficult to stay abreast of developments outside one's
own (sub) field and, almost unavoidably, complexities are neglected while theory
remains out of date. Moreover, minority perspectives are often unwittingly mistaken
for the majority viewpoint because only a few individuals, with little critical review,
serve as explicators of the outside discipline's body of knowledge. All this is true of
anthropological understanding of ecology and evolutionary theory (Orlove 1980), and
it is exacerbated because a remarkable paradigm shift, towards a non-equilibrium view
of nature, is now in full swing within ecology (Worster 1990, Sinton 1993, Zimmerer
1994). Sufficient momentum has built up in recent years that it now seems clear that
this shift is not simply a fad that will soon be abandoned; it is in part a logical extension
of previous paradigm shifts in the physical sciences (e.g. quantum mechanics, chaos
theory), but more importantly it reflects the accumulation of a huge mass of empirical
ecological data that cannot be reconciled with the old paradigm. On the other hand,
because the paradigm shift is still incomplete, it is uncertain how far the pendulum
will swing and what the final form of the new perspective will be. This non-equilibrium
view of nature is only beginning to filter into related fields such as environmental
science, environmental history (Worster 1990, Cronon 1993, Sinton 1993), geography
(Blumler 1984, 1992a, 1993b, Veblen 1985, Baker 1989, Parker 1993, Zimmerer 1994)
and anthropology. Excellent recent critiques of ecological anthropology incorporate
some aspects of the new perspective (e.g. Orlove 1980, Joyce 1988), but they are incomplete, and in this fast-changing intellectual environment they do not go far enough.

Within archaeology and anthropology, historical factors such as the reactions
against environmental determinism and diffusionism have also distorted ecological

understanding. Understandably, most archaeologists have a less sophisticated understanding of nature than of culture and they consequently develop hypotheses about agricultural origins that tend to the cultural determinist. I am more inclined to the Sauerian viewpoint, which although strongly opposed to environmental determinism, nonetheless recognizes that nature and culture were equal players, interacting with each other in non-linear fashion (e.g. Sauer 1952, Byrne 1987, Moore & Hillman 1992, Wright 1993, Diamond 1994a, Sherratt in this volume; and on Sauer, see Blumler 1992b, 1993a, Price & Lewis 1993). In this sense, the Sauerian approach is consonant with the new ecological paradigm.

The main purpose of this chapter is to discuss the major misconceptions about nature that one encounters in the archaeological literature, and the implications for agricultural origins. One important implication is that the environmental component of the neolithic transition was extremely complex, probably crucial, and that we need increased levels of ecological research to achieve a better understanding of it. I argue here that in Southwest Asia, at least, environment, climatic change, and wild cereal ecology each facilitated the beginnings of agriculture.

The social context

It is a truism that social values constrain scientific interpretation (Worster 1977, Gould 1981, Trigger 1989). It is perhaps less often recognized that this is even more characteristic of those fields in the social sciences and humanities, for example, that are on the periphery of science and frequently attempt to draw upon it. Within science, hypothesis testing and accumulation of contrary empirical data force reinterpretation, albeit often only with great reluctance; indeed, "feedback correction" from "encounters with reality" (Barnes 1977: 10) is difficult to avoid in science. For example, applications of traditional ecological theory to the management of parks, reserves and resources have often failed spectacularly, forcing examination of underlying assumptions (Botkin 1990).

Because scholars in neighbouring disciplines are seldom entirely abreast of scientific data and issues, they are more likely to adhere to discarded theories that conform to their (partly socially determined) preferences. For example, although most geneticists (e.g. Beadle 1977, Iltis 1983) dismiss Mangelsdorf's (Mangelsdorf et al. 1964) hypothesis on the origin of maize, some archaeologists continue to prefer it (Mac-Neish 1992), in part, perhaps, out of personal friendship, but also because his model is consonant with the way that most archaeologists *would like to believe* that agriculture developed. Mangelsdorf's model posits a gradual evolution of the domesticate, and a significant human impact upon nature (i.e. the extinction of wild maize); it also argues for that holy grail of research on agricultural origins, an archaeological sequence (in this case at Tehuacán) from wild progenitor to domesticate. Contrast this with Iltis's (1983) hypothesis, in which domestication is almost instantaneous and does not require prolonged interactions between progenitor and humans (Blumler & Byrne 1991), and Tehuacán is seen to display "domesticates but not domestication" (Pickersgill & Heiser 1977: 829).

Ecology and evolutionary biology have developed primarily in a Western intellectual context and they reflect that background (Glacken 1967, Worster 1977, McIntosh 1985, Botkin 1990). Many traditional concepts in both disciplines are Judeo-Christian in origin; others reflect Cartesian dualism, linear thinking, and the rise of the Enlightenment ideal of progress. Nineteenth-century Romanticism also was a major influence, especially on ecology. Ecological anthropology tends both to romanticize and to demean nature, and to interpret ecological theory accordingly. Ecologists themselves frequently suffer from the same tendencies, although the accumulation of contrary empirical data is enabling them to shake off those pre-scientific beliefs that persist more stubbornly, especially among environmentalists but also among anthropologists and others on the periphery of ecology (Blumler 1993c). In fact, the paradigms that are currently being replaced in ecology and evolutionary biology (the paradigm shift is less dramatic but of longer standing in the latter) derive especially from Herbert Spencer, whose ideas held remarkable sway over American academe at the turn of the century (Glick 1974, McIntosh 1985). Ironically, archaeologists, anthropologists and environmentalists, who would be repulsed by Spencer's social Darwinism, unwittingly subscribe to ecological and evolutionary theory that is markedly Spencerian.

Biology's contribution to the debate on agricultural origins has come primarily from crop geneticists and European palynologists. Aside from the latter, ecologists have had minimal input. For the most part, these scholars have communicated relatively little theory to archaeologists, Harlan's excellent discussions of crop genetics constitute a notable exception (1975, Harlan et al. 1973, cf. Blumler & Byrne 1991). Consequently, archaeologists have depended upon second-hand renderings of ecology and evolutionary theory, as in the writings of "neo-evolutionary" and "neofunctionalist" anthropologists (Orlove 1980), and rare discussions in the agricultural origins literature that range from the more (e.g. Flannery 1968, Harris 1969) to the less intelligent (e.g. Rindos 1984, see Blumler & Byrne 1991). Even Flannery's astute, systems theory approach was highly selective. Neofunctionalists such as Flannery gravitated towards Odum's (1953, 1969, Margalef 1968) views on ecosystems, apparently not realizing that his was a minority perspective in ecology (see Orlove 1980, McIntosh 1985, Glenn-Lewin et al. 1992).

Misconceptions about nature: ecology

Table 3.1 lists some widespread misconceptions about nature current among anthropologists and archaeologists. Even ecologically minded archaeologists such as Flannery generally see nature as a static, passive backdrop to cultural change – as a series of systems used and altered by humans. This is a reworking of the Christian theme of a nature created for man's (sic) use and domination. It is related to several other widely accepted misconceptions: the Western (ultimately, Cartesian) dichotomy of human disturbed / nature undisturbed, the idea that human impacts are typically unilinear and degradational, and the balance-of-nature concept (itself a Christian carryover derived from the belief that each species was separately created to fill its own niche and exist in Edenic harmony with all others). These ideas were incorporated into

Table 3.1 Some misconceptions about nature that are
widespread among archaeologists and anthropologists.

Ecology
Nature undisturbed/human disturbed
Nature as a passive, static backdrop to cultural change
Balance-of-nature
Plant community concept
"Climax"
Succession as ubiquitous and linear
Annuals = disturbance
Human impacts on nature are linear, degradational
Evolution
Coevolution leads to obligate mutualisms
Evolution is gradualistic, progressive
Natural selection is overwhelmingly predominant

Clements' (1916) succession theory, which was later combined with systems theory in Odum's (1969) variant of the ecosystem concept. Odum's ideas have proved far more popular with anthropologists (and environmentalists) than with ecologists, in part because his equilibrium view of nature allows one to treat nature as perfect but passive (a view that also derives from systems theory's assumption of homeostasis (e.g. Ashby 1960), which is consonant with the idea of the balance-of-nature). Flannery's (1968) "deviation-amplifying cycles" (i.e. positive feedback loops) were placed on to a nature that without humans was essentially governed by negative feedback.

Climatic change is threatening to this homeostatic view, which may explain Flannery's (1969, 1986a) abhorrence of it. The current concern over global warming has fostered increased recognition that climatic change occurs at all timescales, can be very rapid, and was particularly dramatic across the Pleistocene/Holocene boundary, that is, at about the time that agriculture began in Southwest Asia and perhaps in several other centres (Byrne 1987, Wright 1993). Consequently, some archaeologists are reconsidering the possibility that environmental change was a key factor in the agricultural transition (Henry 1989, Bar-Yosef 1991, McCorriston & Hole 1991, Bar-Yosef & Belfer-Cohen 1992, Moore & Hillman 1992, Hole 1993, and in this volume Hillman, Hole and Sherratt). In contrast, Flannery has gone to some length to dismiss climatic change, in effect disagreeing with the palynologists on the Guilá Naquitz team (Flannery & Wheeler 1986, Schoenwetter & Smith 1986), and attempting, through a flawed computer simulation, to prove that climate change would have militated against agriculture (Reynolds 1986). The major problem with the computer simulation is that it models a shift to a drier climate as if variability would decrease at the same time. This is the reverse of reality, because increasing aridity is highly correlated with increasing variability (Lydolph 1985). In the Guilá Naquitz simulation, it is the decrease in variability, not in the mean that produces the model result (Blumler unpublished). If the computer model were applied to a shift to a drier climate with an *increase* in variability, which would be more realistic, it would predict a faster transition to agriculture than in the absence of climatic change.

Within ecology, the equilibrium concept is rapidly giving way to another set of

THE FAR SIDE   By GARY LARSON

The woods were dark and foreboding, and Alice sensed that sinister eyes were watching her every step. Worst of all, she knew that Nature abhorred a vacuum.

Figure 3.1 Undisturbed conditions constitute a sort of ecological vacuum, which nature, in a sense, "abhors". (*The Far Side,* © 1992 Farworks, Inc. Distributed by Universal Press Syndicate. Reprinted with permission. All rights reserved.)

beliefs, characterized as a non-equilibrium view of nature (Connell 1978, de Angelis & Waterhouse 1987). Rather than in balance, nature is now seen as chaotic (Schaffer 1985, Worster 1990), although scholars in ancillary disciplines remain reluctant to adopt the new paradigm: "The popular perception of balance in nature is a damnable heresy that persists in most fields of applied ecology and resource management to the detriment of establishing realistic goals and guides" (Johnson 1985, cited in Brown 1993).

Ecologists now recognize that disturbance is pervasive even in the absence of humans (Grubb 1977, Connell 1978, Sousa 1984, Veblen 1985, Botkin 1990, Sprugel 1991). I have coined the phrase, "Nature abhors a lack of disturbance", meaning that a lack of disturbance constitutes a sort of ecological vacuum (Fig. 3.1), which nature will fill by such events as pest outbreaks and fires. (Blumler 1992c, 1993b). In the old dualistic view of humans as separate from nature (see Glacken 1967, Worster 1977, Toulmin 1990), we were thought either to civilize and improve nature (the progressionist view) or, more recently, to have degradational impacts on nature(the environmentalist view). The latter perspective, which assumes that natural disturbance is rare, persists but is slowly receding before the increasing evidence that the reality is complex (Walker et al. 1981, Coughenor et al. 1985, Botkin 1990, Rackham 1990, Roberts 1990, Helldén 1991, Mace 1991, Blumler 1992a, 1993b, 1995a, 1995c, Thomas 1993). A metaphor for nature more in line with current ecological theory would be a kaleidoscope, within which humans are enmeshed and have diffuse and often conflicting impacts (Blumler 1994, 1995c)

Accordingly, the plant community concept is also under attack. The notion that species tend to associate in characteristic groupings that are repeated across the landscape is basic to Clementsian theory and to the European school of ecology known as phytosociology (literally, the study of how plant taxa associate in groups (Braun-Blanquet 1932)). English-speaking plant ecologists generally reject the concept except as an unavoidable if misleading necessity in vegetation description, classification and mapping (Gleason 1926, Curtis 1959, Whittaker 1975, Brown 1993). They do so in part because they reject the Lamarckian/Spencerian basis of the community concept (McIntosh 1985), and also because of an overwhelming accumulation of contrary empirical data. In particular, pollen and other palaeoecological evidence demonstrates that species which associated with each other in the past do not do so today, and *vice versa* (Davis 1981, de Angelis & Waterhouse 1987, Joyce 1988, Roberts 1989, van Devender 1990, Anderson & van Devender 1991, Spear et al. 1994). On shorter timescales, too, species composition fluctuates and cannot be taken as being in equilibrium with the prevailing climate (Walker et al. 1981, Baker 1989, Walker 1989, Botkin 1990, Parker 1993). As Colinvaux (1987, cited in Nicholas 1988) put it, "The world is Gleasonian, not Clementsian" and, as Lewis (1992) pointed out, the community concept is analogous to the discredited geographical notion of the region.

The major implication for the study of agricultural origins is that present-day plant communities almost certainly were not identical 10,000 years ago, and that whole communities did not shift north and south, or up and down slope, as climate changed. Rather, each individual species shifted location according to its own requirements and adaptations, forming new species groupings. In this sense, the present is only a partial key to the past. This has some bearing on van Zeist's (1969) puzzlement over the pollen record from the Zagros, which suggests that oaks were rare at the time that agriculture began. As he correctly pointed out, the scarcity of trees would normally be taken to imply a very dry climate, but the wild cereals themselves generally occur in the oak-park zone today (cf. Hillman's detailed discussion of the palynological evidence in Ch. 10 in this volume). From a modern ecological perspective, three plausible explanations suggest themselves:

- the climate was suitable for oaks, but their migration rate from their Pleistocene refuge areas was so slow that they had not yet reached the Zagros (the small amounts of oak pollen present in the Zagros cores could be from long-distance transport)

- the climate was suitable for the maintenance of already existing stands of oaks, but not for their initial establishment, which may require special conditions (Blumler 1995a, cf. Grubb 1977, Mensing 1992, Parker 1993)
- the climate was suitable for wild cereals but not for oaks, despite the fact that they generally occur together today; this might be possible if the summer drought, which has no effect on winter annuals such as the wild cereals, was then even more severe than it is today.

Although eventually van Zeist and others opted for the first explanation (e.g. van Zeist & Bottema 1977, Roberts 1989, Bottema 1991, Moore & Hillman 1992), van Zeist (1969) initially chose the third, suggesting that there was either a shorter rainy season or a hotter summer during the early Holocene. It is unlikely that the rainy season was shorter, however, because wild wheat requires a fairly long growing season (Blumler unpublished). Modelling of changes in incoming solar radiation attributable to Milankovich cycles (COHMAP 1988) supports the supposition that summer temperatures were hotter in the Zagros 10,000 years ago than today (cf. Byrne 1987). Summer solar radiation would have been considerably greater then than at present. This is not to say that the migration hypothesis is false: all three of the above explanations may be valid, in different parts of the Zagros.

A related implication is that phytosociological classifications of vegetation, models of successional relationships and conclusions about human impacts must be taken with a large dose of salt. Unfortunately, phytosociologists seldom test hypotheses; consequently, the field remains intellectually stuck in the nineteenth century in some respects (Whittaker 1962, Blumler 1984, 1992a, 1993b). Because many of the scholars who carry out research on palaeoenvironments in neolithic hearth areas such as Southwest Asia are European, phytosociology's overly Lamarckian view of vegetation and overly dualistic understanding of human–nature interactions sometimes influence palaeo-vegetation reconstructions (Blumler 1993b, 1995a).

Another concept experiencing rapid revision and generally regarded as the most important in plant ecology is that of succession-to-climax (Connell & Slatyer 1977, Glenn-Lewin et al. 1992). Figure 3.2 is a simplified succession diagram that illustrates the salient features of the original, Clementsian model (Clements 1916, Blumler 1993b). After disturbance clears off the vegetation, a sequence or succession of species occupies the site, progressively trending from small short-lived herbaceous to longer-lived taller woody plants, until the largest species that the regional climate can support become dominant – the so-called "climax" state. The model is linear, developmental and progressive (i.e. profoundly Western). It is one of a series of evolutionary models developed in different disciplines at the turn of the century that were based explicitly on Herbert Spencer's ideas (Drury & Nisbet 1971, McIntosh 1985). Some feminists argue that linear hierarchical dualistic models are a male thing (Gray 1979, Kheel 1985) (the underlying dualisms in this case are bare ground/dense forest, disturbed/undisturbed, humans/nature). I have my doubts, given the highly dualistic nature of feminist writings, but it does seem possible that Clements' succession model represents a case of unconscious male psychosexual wish fulfilment: vegetation proceeds from small and flaccid to hard woody and upthrusting, becoming ever bigger and better until the ideal climax is reached. And here's the bio-Utopian kicker: it is a

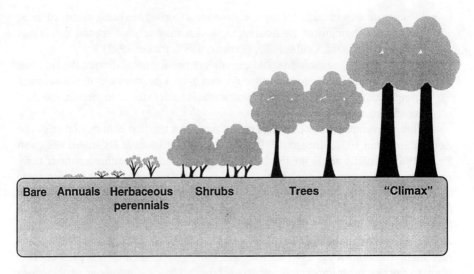

| Bare | Annuals | Herbaceous perennials | Shrubs | Trees | "Climax" |

Figure 3.2   A simplified but otherwise typical succession diagram. A rough, schematic sketch like this one reveals the underlying assumptions, but also trivializes the model. On the other hand, the more carefully drawn, often beautiful, depictions in ecology textbooks idealize the model, thus encouraging its acceptance by the reader.

perpetual climax, because Clements believed that disturbance is rare in the absence of humans, so that most of the Earth's surface was covered by climax vegetation most of the time, until we started mucking things up.

Of course, climax also has positive *non*-sexual connotations, so Clements' choice of term encouraged its idealization. Consequently, twentieth-century management of parks and reserves emphasized the presumed climax, with well known untoward effects: for example, the fire exclusion (Smokey the Bear) policy in American national parks and national forests caused a build-up of excess fuel and, eventually, catastrophic fires (Pyne 1982, Minnich 1983). The climax concept derived in part from the Romantic notion of the forest primeval, which in turn was a reworking of the Edenic myth; that is, Clements effectively combined the Edenic myth with the Enlightenment ideal of progress, and situated them in nature. No wonder environmentalists and others who romanticize nature continue to embrace his ideas so wholeheartedly (Worster 1977, 1990), even as ecologists abandon the paradigm as contrary data accumulate. And no wonder ecologists have not yet modified their views as much as the empirical evidence suggests they should (Blumler 1992a, 1993a,b).

Ecologists now recognize that the notion of a final stable condition is dubious, and consequently usually enclose "climax" within quotation marks. Just as anthropologists no longer believe in "stages" of cultural development yet still find it difficult to conceptualize about the long sweep of human prehistory and history without incorporating the notion, so too ecologists know that the climax concept is of limited validity yet cannot help thinking about vegetation as if climax were a real phenomenon. Elsewhere, I have invoked the Sapir–Whorf hypothesis as a possible explanation for this difficulty (Blumler 1993b). Our language may incorporate linearity. Ecologists do recognize that succession is not always linear or progressive, and that disturbance may be necessary to allow so-called "late successional" species to replace earlier ones (the "inhibition" model of Connell & Slatyer 1977). I have argued (Blumler 1993b) that cases of inhibition should probably not be regarded as succession at all, because they violate the rule that disturbance sets the sequence back to square one. In general, the succession model works reasonably well in humid regions, where there is an advantage to being tall because one can shade out one's neighbours. But it breaks down in dry regions, especially where there is seasonal drought, because then competition for water in the soil may be more important than competition for light (Blumler 1992a, 1993b). Under these circumstances, many growth forms can compete with each other on more or less equal terms, and even annual plants sometimes outcompete all others (Blumler 1984, 1992a, 1993b). However, the bio-Utopian and linear nature of the traditional succession model continues to exert such a powerful hold that even "non-equilibrium" ecologists continue to apply it at times in inappropriate situations.

The notion of stable climax also dominates the literature on agricultural origins, especially in its emphasis on weedy or early successional plants (e.g. Anderson 1952, Flannery 1969, 1986a, Hawkes 1969, Bohrer 1972, Lewis 1972, Harlan 1975, Smith 1978, Rindos 1984, Köhler-Rollefson 1988, Bottema 1990; cf. Blumler 1994). Because traditional succession theory treated disturbance as rare, external to the system and mainly associated with humans, nature could be regarded as an "exotic other" with respect to human societies, and weeds and annuals, associated with humans, exotic others with respect to nature. This placement of weeds outside nature, in effect making them (and, to a lesser extent, annuals) the "outcasts" of plant ecology, has given rise to many misconceptions, because weed ecologists have as yet been relatively uninfluenced by the new ecological thinking (see Blumler 1984, 1992a, 1994, 1995c) For instance, it is now generally accepted that most plant species are adapted to and even require some form of disturbance (Grubb 1977, Connell 1978), but thus far ecologists have not recognized the obvious implication concerning the traditional dualism of weeds as disturbance species, and wild (non-weedy) species as not. And in California, conservation biologists use fire, grazing, mowing and herbicides to favour wild native perennials over introduced annuals that otherwise take over, yet they refer to the latter as weeds (Blumler 1992c).

In the agricultural origins literature, Daniel Zohary's work on wild wheat and other cereal grasses stands out as a singular exception to the Clementsian view (Harlan & Zohary 1966, Zohary 1969, 1983, 1989, Zohary & Hopf 1988; also, Harlan 1967). Contrary also to the entire body of phytosociological literature on Southwest Asian vegetation (including the voluminous and in most respects remarkable publications of Zohary's father (e.g. M. Zohary 1962, 1973)), D. Zohary noted that these vigorous annual plants require little (I would add, if any (Blumler 1984, 1992b, 1993c, 1995c)) disturbance. Hillman also recognizes that "weeds" can be abundant in natural vegetation (Hillman et al. 1989).

An important implication is that those agricultural origins hypotheses that depend upon the climax concept (e.g. Bohrer 1972, Lewis 1972) and/or the equating of progenitors with weeds (e.g. Anderson 1952) need to be re-evaluated. This is not to say that such models should be rejected out of hand. For instance, Lewis's fire/domestication hypothesis is probably invalid for wild wheat and barley because those species are not usually favoured by fire or other disturbances; but the hypothesis may well apply in modified form to the progenitors of Southwest Asian legume domesticates, because fire often favours annual legumes (Blumler 1991). Similarly, dump-heap hypotheses (e.g. Anderson 1952) are unlikely to apply to all early domesticates, but may well apply to some. Some of the progenitors of the first agricultural plants *are* weedy, though many are not (Blumler & Byrne 1991, Blumler 1994).

Misconceptions about nature: evolution

Cultural ecology (Steward 1955, Service 1962) is based to a considerable degree upon so-called evolutionary (more properly, developmental) models of increasing human societal complexity over the course of time. Like Clementsian succession, these models are progressionist, linear and gradualistic. Orlove (1980: 239; see also Nicholas 1988, Trigger 1989) noted that they resemble "the long discarded view in biology that evolution is progressive and leads toward new and better forms in succeeding periods." Or, to quote Stephen Jay Gould:

Traditional concepts of evolution, at least in their translation to popular culture, favor a slow and stately process, ruled by sensible adaptation along its pathways and expanding out towards both greater complexity of the highest forms and more bountiful diversity throughout. (Gould 1994: 23)

These models seem more resonant with Spencer, and perhaps Marx, than Darwin. Even Darwin was more progressionist than some of his admirers are willing to admit (Richards 1992), but he was far less so than Spencer. In any case, modern evolutionary biologists are considerably less sanguine about progressive tendencies in evolution (Ruse 1993). In particular, they doubt the linear simplicity of the nineteenth-century paradigm, recognizing episodes of mass extinction as well as considerable evolutionary backing and filling. Gradualism also is no longer considered the rule. Probably only a minority of evolutionary biologists subscribe to Eldredge & Gould's (1972) "punctuated equilibrium" model, but most accept that great fluctuations in evolutionary rates can and do occur (Blumler & Byrne 1991, Bowring et al. 1993). Steward, Service, and later neo-evolutionists assumed that gradualistic developmental evolutionary models were consonant with evolutionary theory, but this is no longer true. In a sense, biological evolution no longer corresponds entirely to the dictionary (non-biological) definition of the word, with its emphasis on development.

Also, it is now almost universally accepted that random forces play a major role in evolution, although scientists vary in the degree of importance accorded to selection and random processes (Wilson 1975, Wright 1982, Kimura 1983, Eckert & Barrett 1992, Blumler 1995c). Pan-selectionism is out (Gould & Lewontin 1979, Hinde 1991). An area of some debate and reflection at the present time concerns whether even the apparently obvious tendency towards greater complexity and diversity over the course of the palaeontological record necessarily reflects an evolutionary rule or is mere happenstance (Bonner 1988, Nitecki 1988, 1990, McShea 1991, 1993, Boya-jian & Lutz 1992, Lewin 1992, Ruse 1993). Gould (1989) has forcefully and, as always, eloquently argued that evolution is historically contingent rather than directed along predictable lines (such as towards progressive complexity). According to Gould, if there were (are?) a million Earths supporting life, on only one would sentient creatures appear. On others, organisms might remain single-celled indefinitely. I should point out that, despite his eminence as an evolutionary biologist, Gould often, as in this case, takes extreme positions (my own views on evolutionary theory are con-siderably more orthodox than his). At the same time, however, there is now a general consensus among evolutionary biologists that evolutionary "laws" or tendencies are often diffuse or weak.

> . . . each lineage is a unique entity with its own idiosyncrasies: and each evolu-tionary trajectory through a temporal series of environments encounters so many random effects of great magnitude that I expect historical individuality to [be] overwhelm[ing] . . . I regard each species as a contingent item of history with an unpredictable future. I anticipate that a species will arise in a single place and then move along an unexpected pathway.   (Gould 1994: 3)

Gould's contrast between the importance of contingency in history and the search for predictability in evolution (which is an historical process) is very relevant to archaeology. Archaeologists also study an historical process, but often strive for pre-dictability. I believe this is because archaeology is more scientific than most social sciences, and certainly more so than history; therefore, neo-evolutionary models that predict the development of cultural complexity from hunter–gatherer simplicity to the present are more popular among archaeologists than among historians, for whom the emphasis is on contingency (this is not to argue that no historian has ever attempted to derive predictable laws of history). There is a clear analogy with the evolutionary record, in that human societies have become generally more complex as population has increased, but there also have been exceptions and de-intensifications, and there is no reason to assume that the trend necessarily represents some universal law. Archaeologists are returning to a more historical view (Trigger 1989), but this does not seem to have influenced thinking about agricultural origins as yet.

Instead, developmental models that assume a long, progressive sequence of increas-ingly complex manipulations of wild or semi-wild plants, culminating in agriculture and domestication, remain popular (e.g. Harlan 1975, Cohen 1977, Rindos 1984, Ford 1985). Harris (1989) proposed a similar model that is explicitly *not* progressive, but does appear to be gradualist and developmental. It is unfortunate that, just as archae-ologists were ready to move away from developmental models, Rindos (1984) came along and misrepresented evolutionary theory as determinist, selectionist, develop-mental and gradualist. He also misrepresented coevolution as the evolution of obligate, 1:1 mutualisms, whereas it is much more characteristic for coevolutionary interactions to be diffuse, complex, involve many species, and incorporate both positive (mutual-istic) and negative (parasitic or amensal) components (Blumler & Byrne 1991). For example, fruits often contain laxative substances, presumably so that passage through the gut will be rapid, thus increasing the chance that seeds swallowed with the fruit will survive unharmed. This is fine for the seed, but not so nice for the birds and mammals that participate in the, on balance "mutualistic", coevolutionary relationship!

Proponents of developmental models of agricultural origins support their hypotheses with citations of documented examples of hunter–gatherers who engage in pseudo-agricultural practices. A spatial analysis suggests an alternative interpretation, however. Most if not all of the pseudo-agricultural examples come from hunter–gatherers who live in proximity to, and are or were in contact with, farmers. Related groups that are geographically more distant from agriculturalists are less likely to engage in pseudo-agricultural activities, although environment may be closely similar. This is true, for instance, in Australia and California. Consequently, diffusion is a more parsimonious explanation for the pseudo-agricultural practices than is their independent invention by the hunter–gatherers (Heizer & Elsasser 1980, Blumler & Byrne 1991; cf. Yen 1989). Today, there is increasing awareness that extrapolating the ethnographic present to the past entails the highly problematic assumptions of hunter–gatherer stasis and cultural isolation (Wolf 1982, Trigger 1989).

Until recently, however, the neo-evolutionary and neofunctionalist schools, and indeed all of anthropology, have treated cultures as separate but equal, that is, developing independently. Within the agricultural origins literature, at least, this seems to reflect a quasi-scientific orientation, giving rise to the reductionist (and essentialist) separation of cultures into different units for purposes of study. Adoption of the ecosystem concept also focused attention on *in situ* development and away from spatial interactions, because of the emphasis on human adaptation to a particular (local) ecosystem. Probably most important was the highly polarized debate over Sauer's (1952) book, which entrenched the anti-diffusionist, or independent-inventionist, position. The neo-evolutionary paradigm both reinforced and was reinforced by independent inventionism (cf. Trigger 1989: 331).

But this view of culture is highly dubious. For instance, Diamond (1993, 1994a,b) has pointed out that southern regions – Australia and especially Tasmania, Tierra del Fuego and Khoisan southern African before the Bantu invasions – were almost certainly backward technologically because of their geographical isolation, not because of environment, nor, obviously, because of race. Actually, Diamond weakens his argument in relation to southern Africa by suggesting that agriculture did not develop independently there because there were no domesticable plants or animals. In this, he is incorrect: the wild progenitors of several African crops, although domesticated in the north, are also native to southern Africa (Blumler 1992b). It is not that there were no domesticable plants (and, presumably, animals) there, but rather that no one bothered to domesticate them. An obvious implication that many cultural geographers would understand (e.g. Vidal de la Blache 1911, 1926; see Archer 1993) is that cultural development, especially the evolution of complexity, is primarily interactive. As Eric Wolf (1982: ix) put it, neo-evolutionist anthropologists ". . . seem to have forgotten that human populations construct their cultures in interaction with one another and not in isolation".

Many archaeologists – especially those concerned with the imperialist era, of course, but also students of earlier periods – have accepted Wolf's argument (Trigger

1989). A geographer can only respond with a sigh of relief and a heartfelt: "It's about time!" It remains for this perspective to penetrate the agricultural origins literature, however. This is not surprising, given the strength of the anti-diffusionist views of most archaeologists concerned with agricultural origins, and the dominant influence that those views have had on theorizing about prehistory (e.g. Harlan 1975, Renfrew & Cherry 1986). Even Renfrew's (1987) book on the Indo–European question had an (unrecognized, for the most part) *anti*-diffusionist motivation, in that it condensed two diffusions (of agriculture and of Indo–Europeans) into one (A. C. Renfrew: pers. comm.).

I suggest that the reaction against diffusionism has caused many anthropologists and archaeologists to adopt a theoretically weak position that *is not in accord with their own empirical conclusions* (Blumler 1992b, 1993a, 1995b; similar comments apply to the reaction against environmental determinism). For instance, Mangelsdorf (1953) argued, in support of his view that independent invention and diffusion are approximately equal in importance, that writing was invented four times. Now he may have underestimated the number of inventions of writing; but I do not believe anyone has claimed that it was invented more than about eight times. Compared to the number of written languages in existence today, this number is minuscule, proving that diffusion of writing has been far more important than its independent invention. Similarly, no one would argue that 50 per cent of all Bronze Age ethnic groups invented bronze independently. Yet archaeological theory presumes that diffusion and independent invention are equally likely, or even that diffusion is less likely than invention (Mangelsdorf 1953, Harlan 1975, Riley et al. 1990). This is absurd, as consideration of any random set of innovations quickly demonstrates (Blumler 1992b). Sauer's (1952) preference for only one or possibly two origins of agriculture was extreme, but not as extreme as the position staked out by most anthropologists and archaeologists studying agricultural origins that independent invention is at least as important as diffusion. The empirical genetic evidence now being brought to bear on the question clearly shows that independent inventionism is untenable (Zohary 1989 and Ch. 9 in this volume, Blumler 1992b, Uerpmann Ch. 12 in this volume). Table 3.2 illustrates the point (see Blumler 1992b for the analysis upon which the table is based).

The traditional belief that evolution is gradual and developmental has its analogy in the oft repeated assertion that the origin of agriculture was "a process not an event." As there is not a single archaeological sequence showing a clear transition from wild progenitor to primary domesticate, I would argue that there is no substantive evidence for this claim. In contrast, Eldredge & Gould's (1972) punctuated-equilibrium model views evolution as occurring primarily in short explosive bursts, between which there are prolonged periods of stasis. This corresponds remarkably well to the old notion of a Neolithic or Agricultural Revolution, famously enunciated by the archaeologist Gordon Childe (1928, and see Harris 1990). Ironically, Gould, of all biologists, is the most sympathetic to the humanist and social science perspective; yet his view of biological evolution does not correspond to the archaeological consensus about cultural evolution, and in particular, that regarding agricultural origins. In contrast, traditional evolutionary perspectives, which in so many ways correspond to archaeological thinking about the past, are today exemplified especially by E. O. Wilson, of socio-

Table 3.2 Most probable number of domestication events for some putative primary crops (Blumler 1992b and unpublished), illustrating that most apparently were domesticated only once in any given hearth region. Note that even in those cases where domestication took place more than once, the domestication events may not have been truly independent.

| Region | Crop | Most probable number of domestications | | |
		One	Two	Several
Southwest	Emmer wheat	✓		
Asia	Einkorn wheat	✓		
	Barley		✓	
	Pea	✓		
	Lentil	✓	✓	
	Chickpea	✓		
	Broad bean	✓		
	Bitter vetch		✓	
	Flax	✓		
Mexico	Maize	✓		
	Common bean	✓		
	Tepary bean	✓		
	Runner bean		✓	
	Capsicum peppers	✓		
	Amaranths	✓		
	Squash (*C. pepo*) *		✓	
Andes	Common bean			✓
	Potato	✓		
Africa	Finger millet	✓		
	Pearl millet	✓		
	Yam bean		✓	
Other	Sunflower	✓		
	Rice		✓	
	Sweet potato	✓		

* Includes a possible eastern North American domestication

biology fame (or infamy) – "The most overt, living Darwinian enthusiast for absolute progress" (Ruse 1993: 58). As I have suggested above, the consensus view in evolutionary biology lies somewhere between these two extremes. Perhaps it is time that archaeologists also consider that the origin(s) of agriculture may have been an event(s) as much as a process (cf. Bar-Yosef & Belfer-Cohen 1992: 39–40) – a view evidently supported by Moore & Hillman (1992: 491) with regard to Southwest Asia, where the "economic and cultural transformations that marked the transition from Epipaleolithic to Neolithic . . . appear to have been rapid".

Biologists' understanding of nature is admittedly a cultural construction, but the anthropological/archaeological view is a cultural construction of biology's cultural construction. Consequently, this review has been somewhat negative, in pointing out respects in which archaeological thinking does not reflect current biological thought. Let me now try to outline some positive implications of the new paradigms by sketching, in the next section, an argument that environment, climatic change, and wild-progenitor ecology were all important in the neolithic transition.

But first, I should stress that although my manner of presentation has suggested that the new paradigms are good and traditional views bad, this is overly dualistic. Gradual evolution, for instance, occurs at times and may be very important. Succession does sometimes approximate the linear Clementsian model rather well. Human impacts unquestionably are enormous, although in the new perspective it might be better to say that these impacts occur within nature rather than upon it (cf. Gould 1992). "Weed" is not an invalid concept, but a confused and overly dualistic one; and so on. Consequently, I do not wish to suggest that traditional hypotheses concerning agricultural origins are entirely invalid. Anderson's (1952: 136–50) dump-heap hypothesis, for instance, has limited validity. Wild progenitors can be arranged in a continuum according to their basic biology and ecology, from those species particularly likely to flourish on dump-heaps and enter into a relationship with humans, to those that are unlikely to have been domesticated in the manner that Anderson suggested. Cannabis, for instance, is a natural for dump-heap domestication (as Anderson pointed out), and cucurbits may be too. On the other hand, legumes seem poorly suited because they are disfavoured by the normally high nitrogen status of dump-heap soils. Wild cereals also seem poor candidates, because grasses generally are relatively late colonizers of disturbed areas compared to some broad-leaved herbs such as the wind-blown composites, and because the small amount of grain that could be produced on a refuse-heap would not be of great interest to hunter–gatherers. For this reason, dump plants that produce edible vegetables, potential containers (e.g. gourds), spices or drugs – supplements and luxuries rather than staples – are most likely to attract the attention of hunter–gatherers.

Environmental context of agricultural origins

Table 3.3 illustrates the relationship between agricultural origins and seasonal drought, the annual habit, and large seed size in crop progenitors.

It appears that agriculture began in both the Old and the New World, in several

Table 3.3 Relationship between agricultural origins, seasonal drought, annual habit, and large seed size in crop progenitors (from Blumler 1992a).

Neolithic hearth	Seasonal drought	Annuals in flora	Progenitors with large seeds	Chronology (years bp)
Southwest Asia	Summer (extreme)	Many	All except flax	10,000
North China	Winter (cold)	Few (foxtail millet)	No	9,000
Central China	Winter	Few? (rice)	Yes	9,000
Southeast Asia	Winter (variable)	Variable	Rice, Job's tears	9,000
Mexico	Winter	Many	Teosinte, legumes, cucurbits	8,000
Bolivia/Peru	Winter	Many	Legumes, cucurbits	8,000
Sahel/Sudan	Winter	Many	Sorghum, rice	5,000
Eastern North America	None	Few	Pumpkin, sunflower	4,000
Chile	Summer	Many	*Bromus mango*	?

centres, at approximately the same time. Cohen (1977), Flannery (1986b) and Byrne (1987) noted that this coincidence needs explanation, but Cohen's population-pressure hypothesis and Flannery's argument – that people had finally settled in to all available habitats and consequently had nowhere to which they could migrate in response to stress – seem inadequate. Neither explains how population pressure or "settling in" could have occurred as early in the New as in low to mid-latitudes of the Old World. This leaves Byrne's climatic change model as the only plausible expla-nation, unless the Neolithic in Mesoamerica and Peru turn out to be more recent than believed. This is possible, given the revised AMS radiocarbon dates for New World domesticates (Fritz 1994). On the other hand, the three centres that arose most recently may be derivative of developments in earlier hearths.

Secondly, as Byrne (1987) pointed out, all centres experience a pronounced dry season, except eastern North America. North China's drought also is relatively insig-nificant, because it occurs during the cold season (the other summer-rain regions have warm winters). Seasonal drought is likely to favour agriculture both because the corresponding seasonality of resource availability induces stress and requires food storage, and because cultivation is comparatively easy in such environments. Thirdly, annual plants come into their own where there is seasonal drought (Blumler 1984, Byrne 1987), so it is not surprising that they tend to be abundant in the floras of the hearth regions, and are frequently abundant in the vegetation. Finally, the earliest plant domesticates in most of the neolithic centres included annual grasses, legumes or cucurbits, which manufacture unusually large seeds. Large seed size is rare in annual plants and is closely associated with seasonal drought (Blumler 1992a). If one excludes the aquatic wild rice (*Zizania*), which might have been difficult to domesti-cate, the only region with large-seeded annual grasses that was *not* a centre of agri-cultural origin is Morocco/southern Spain (Blumler 1992a, 1994). Most annuals, even in seasonally dry regions, produce small seeds, so those that were domesticated are highly unusual – evolutionary monstrosities in a sense (Blumler 1994) – as are their domesticated derivatives. However, large seeds seem to be only slightly more attrac-tive to gatherers than smaller ones (Blumler 1992a, Wright 1994); the great advantage may come in the transition to primitive agriculture, because large-seeded annuals are relatively easy to cultivate (Blumler 1992a, 1994).

The correlation between agricultural origins and seasonal drought, annual habit and large seeds is not perfect. Given that the archaeological record is so incomplete, it is not known for certain that large-seeded annuals were domesticated before smaller-seeded ones (such as the New World chenopod-amaranths), except in South-west Asia. But the correlation is close enough to be suggestive. Moreover, as Byrne (1987) pointed out, in the early Holocene seasonal drought would have been more extreme in all the centres (with the possible exception of the central Andes) than it is today or than it was during the previous glacial phase. This means that annuals, espe-cially large-seeded ones, should have been more important in the vegetation than they are today or than they were previously.

Finally, the exceptions may be more apparent than real. For instance, recent archaeological discoveries have drastically narrowed the temporal and spatial gaps between northern China and the rice-growing centre to the south (cf. Bellwood and

Glover & Higham, in this volume), so that it has become increasingly possible that millet growing was derived from rice cultivation, in areas where the latter was not feasible. In any case, northern China is geomorphologically remarkable: the huge, highly erodible loess plateau would have supported dense stands of foxtail millet naturally, and it contributes such a heavy sediment load to the Huanghe (Yellow) River that millet would also probably have covered large areas of new substrate laid down each year in the enormous floodplain. In all probability, wild rice also was present in the early Holocene, when temperatures were warmer than today. Thus, annuals are likely to have been abundant, despite the relatively weak seasonal drought.

California, which is very similar environmentally to Southwest Asia, is an interesting case. Most of the cultural features suggested to be important in Southwest Asian agricultural beginnings (sedentism, storage facilities, broad-spectrum resource use, etc.) were also characteristic of prehispanic California – another reason why I suspect that purely cultural explanations for the adoption of agriculture are incomplete. This leaves three salient differences:
- California's summer drought is not quite as extreme as Southwest Asia's today (Naveh 1967, Blumler 1984, Byrne 1987)
- past climates of the two regions may have differed considerably (Byrne 1987, Blumler 1992a)
- the "Fertile Crescent" has many large-seeded, annual grasses and legumes, from which all the early domesticates except flax were derived, whereas California has no, or almost no, large-seeded annuals (Blumler 1992a, 1994, see Baker 1972) – a striking example of evolutionary non-convergence.

Yet another difference is that California was probably less affected by the period of the Younger Dryas, which is increasingly regarded as the trigger of the Southwest Asian Neolithic (Bar-Yosef & Belfer-Cohen 1992, Moore & Hillman 1992, Hole 1993). The Younger Dryas may have brought extremely dry conditions to Southwest Asia (Yechieli et al. 1993), and it was apparently followed immediately by agriculture. Thus, the "oasis theory" (Childe 1928) is back. The evidence has been well reviewed by the authors cited above, and I will add only two comments. First, Near Eastern archaeologists may assume that the Younger Dryas was cold and dry and, indeed, winters probably were colder than today. But climate models predict that summers were considerably hotter than they are at present (Rind et al. 1986, COHMAP 1988). This is especially likely to have been true in the northern part of the Fertile Crescent (cf. Hillman in Ch. 10 in this volume). Secondly, although it is sometimes argued that agriculture began in the southern Levant (McCorriston & Hole 1991, Bar-Yosef & Belfer-Cohen 1992, Hole in Ch. 14 in this volume), wild einkorn does not grow south of the Bekaa Valley today, because the rainy season is too short. Therefore, either domestication took place somewhere to the north, or the rainy season was longer when agriculture began. Moore & Hillman (1992) quite plausibly suggested that there were fluctuations in the seasonal distribution of rainfall as well as in aridity during the period in question.

Wild cereal ecology

The preceding discussion leads on to the question of what was going on with the wild cereal grasses during the millennia leading up to agriculture. In a non-equilibrium perspective, it is unlikely that they always grew where they do today, or that they remained ever-abundant (except for unusual climatic episodes such as the Younger Dryas). Influenced by Odum's (1953) bio-Utopian belief that species diversity is maximized in climax or near-climax forests and is low in dry regions, Flannery (1969) mistakenly asserted that the oak-park zone of Southwest Asia has few plant species. Therefore, he argued, it is not surprising that pure stands of wild cereals are widespread. In fact, regions of mediterranean climate regions are species-rich, and the oak-park zone has perhaps the highest herbaceous species diversity on Earth – frequently over 100 species per 1000m² (Naveh & Whittaker 1979, Blumler 1993b). Therefore, dense stands of wild cereal are a paradox and a puzzle. For high species diversity to be maintained, the stands must collapse rather often, allowing other species to flourish at least temporarily. This happens today and probably also happened during the Epipalaeolithic. Other annual grasses (notably wild oats) often mix in with wild emmer and barley stands so thoroughly today that efficient harvest is impossible (Ladizinsky 1975). How pure were the stands in the past? The scarcity of wild oats in the archaeobotanical record suggests that it may not have been abundant. Is this plausible? Considerable basic research into wild-progenitor ecology is needed before such questions can be answered authoritatively. We understand wild-cereal genetics far better than wild-cereal ecology, and we do not understand the genetics well enough. Important questions concerning stand density under varying natural conditions, edaphic tolerances, fire tolerance (Blumler 1991), and response to harvesting are discussed in the literature primarily by informed (sometimes uninformed) arm-waving. With these caveats, I offer here some arm-waving of my own.

Ecologically, the wild cereals are differentiated primarily according to the length of their growing seasons, from germination to maturity (Fig. 3.3). This relates mainly to the length of the rainy season, although there also seem to be some differences in temperature tolerances and edaphic preferences. A similar gradient of differentiation occurs in the domesticated cereals. Judging by present distributions, all species tolerate some degree of aridity: wild oats will grow to maturity down to about 250mm annual rainfall, wild barley to 300mm, and wild emmer to perhaps 350mm (wild oats and barley also range into still drier regions along wadis, where soil moisture is much higher than the rainfall figures would suggest); wild einkorn and wild rye, although less well studied, are probably similar. Thus, changes in species composition in the archaeobotanical record are most likely to reflect changes in the amount of rain and the length of the rainy season, although temperature can interact with rainfall to determine growing-season length.

I suspect also that temperature and moisture conditions during seed maturation determine to a large extent the relative success of wild oats versus wild emmer and barley. The latter have extremely long awns; although cereal breeders have puzzled over this feature for decades (Grundbacher 1963), it appears that the awns are most advantageous when the weather is very hot and dry at the end of the growing season.

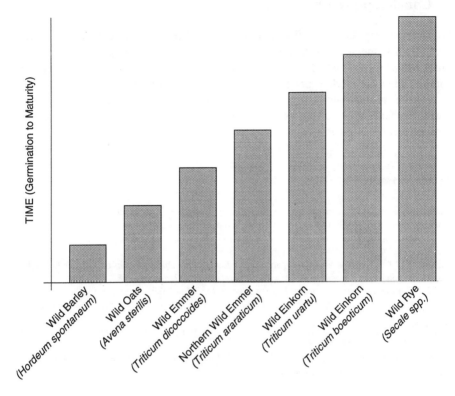

Figure 3.3   Southwest Asian wild cereal grasses arranged by length of the growing season, from the shortest (wild barley) to the longest (wild rye).

On the other hand, wild oats, with its shorter awns and more indeterminate growth, is probably better equipped to deal with gently rising temperatures and late-spring rains. Again, comparison of domesticated oats with emmer and barley supports this supposition (Leonard & Martin 1963). If this is so, then the relative proportion of wild emmer and barley as opposed to wild oats is likely to have varied over the millennia depending on timing of rainfall, late-spring temperatures, and the contrast between winter and late-spring temperatures. Because winter insolation was approaching a minimum and summer insolation a maximum at 10,000 bp (COHMAP 1988), the spring warm-up was probably extremely rapid, which would have favoured wild emmer and barley. Late-spring insolation would have peaked on a slightly different time schedule, but also should have been higher than today during the period immediately preceding the Neolithic. If so, the stands may have been more pure during the Natufian. But I have piled speculation upon speculation in reaching this conclusion; much more work is needed to clarify these matters.

Concluding comment

I have attempted to show that climate, climate change, and the evolution of domesticable plant species each facilitated the Agricultural Revolution. Many archaeologists may wish that the old paradigm about nature were valid, because it was so much simpler than the modern perspective. A nature that is as complex as culture only makes the prehistorian's task that much more difficult. Conversely, many sociobiologists probably wish culture were simpler, so that they could concentrate on biological explanations for behaviour. Unfortunately, that ain't the way it is.

References

Anderson, E. 1952. *Plants, man, and life*. Berkeley: University of California Press.

Anderson, R. S. & T. R. van Devender 1991. Comparison of pollen and macrofossils in packrat (*Neotoma*) middens: a chronological sequence from the Waterman Mountains, southern Arizona. *Review of Paleobotany and Palynology* **69**, 1–28.

Archer, K. 1993. Regions as social organisms: the Lamarckian characteristics of Vidal de la Blache's regional geography. *Annals of the Association of American Geographers* **83**, 498–514.

Ashby, E. 1960. *Design for a brain*, 2nd edn. New York: John Wiley.

Baker, H. G. 1972. Seed weight in relation to environmental conditions in California. *Ecology* **53**, 997–1010.

Baker, W. L. 1989. Landscape ecology and nature reserve design in the Boundary Waters Canoe Area, Minnesota. *Ecology* **70**, 23–35.

Barnes, B. 1977. *Interests and the growth of knowledge*. London: Routledge & Kegan Paul.

Bar-Yosef, O. 1991. The early Neolithic of the Levant: recent advances. *The Review of Archaeology* **12**, 1–18.

Bar-Yosef, O. & A. Belfer-Cohen 1992. From foraging to farming in the Mediterranean Levant. In *Transitions to agriculture in prehistory* [Monographs in World Archaeology 4], A. B. Gebauer & T. D. Price (eds), 21–48 . Madison: Prehistory Press.

Beadle, G. W. 1977. The origin of *Zea mays*. In *Origins of agriculture*, C. A. Reed (ed.), 615–35. The Hague: Mouton.

Blumler, M. A. 1984. Climate and the annual habit. MA thesis, Department of Geography, University of California, Berkeley.

— 1991. Fire and agricultural origins: preliminary investigations. In *Fire and environment: ecological and cultural perspectives, proceedings of an international symposium*: S. C. Nodvin & T. A. Waldrop (eds), 351–8. General Technical Report SE–69, United States Department of Agriculture, Southeastern Forest Experiment Station, Asheville, North Carolina.

— 1992a. Seed weight and environment in mediterranean-type grasslands in California and Israel. PhD dissertation, Department of Geography, University of California, Berkeley.

— 1992b. Independent inventionism and recent genetic evidence on plant domestication. *Economic Botany* **46**, 98–111.

— 1992c. Some myths about California grasslands and grazers. *Fremontia* **20**, 22–7.

— 1993a. On the tension between cultural geography and anthropology: commentary on Christine Rodrigue's "Early animal domestication". *The Professional Geographer* **45**, 359–63.

— 1993b. Successional pattern and landscape sensitivity in the Mediterranean and Near East. In *Landscape sensitivity*, D. S. G. Thomas & R. J. Allison (eds), 287–305. Chichester: John Wiley.

— 1993c. California landscape ideals and ecological theory as deterrents to conservation. Paper presented at the Association of Pacific Coast Geographers Annual Meeting, Berkeley, September 17, 1993.

— 1994. Evolutionary trends in the wheat group in relation to environment, Quaternary climate change and human impacts. In *Environmental change in drylands*, A. C. Millington & K. Pye (eds), 253–69. Chichester: John Wiley.

— 1995a. Palynology, ecological theory, and forest history in the Mediterranean and Near East. Paper presented at the Institute of British Geographers Annual Conference, Newcastle, January 4, 1995.

— 1995b. Theories of cultural development and the diffusion/independent invention debate. Paper presented 1995.

— 1995c. Invasion and transformation of California's valley grassland, a Mediterranean analogue ecosystem. In *Human impact and adaptation: ecological relations in historical times*, R. Butlin & N. Roberts (eds), 308–32. Oxford: Blackwell.

Blumler, M. A. & R. Byrne 1991. The ecological genetics of domestication and the origins of agriculture. *Current Anthropology* **32**, 23–54.

Bohrer, V. L. 1972. On the relation of harvest methods to early agriculture in the Near East. *Economic Botany* **26**, 145–55.

Bonner, J. T. 1988. *The evolution of complexity by means of natural selection*. Princeton, New Jersey: Princeton University Press.

Botkin, D. 1990. *Discordant harmonies: a new ecology for the twenty-first century*. New York: Oxford University Press.

Bottema, S. 1990. Holocene environment of the southern Argolid: a pollen core from Kiladha Bay. In *Excavations at Franchthi Cave, Greece, fascicle 6: Franchthi Paralia: the sediments, stratigraphy, and offshore investigations*, T. J. Wilkinson & S. T. Duhon (eds), 117–38. Bloomington: Indiana University Press.

— 1991. Développement de la végétation et du climat dans le bassin Méditerranéen Oriental à la fin du Pléistocène et pendant l'Holocène. *L'Anthropologie* **95**, 695–728.

Bowring, S. A., J. P. Grotzinger, C. E. Isachsen, A. H. Knoll, S. M. Pelechaty, P. Kolosov 1993. Calibrating rates of Early Cambrian evolution. *Science* **261**, 1293–8.

Boyajian, G. & T. Lutz 1992. Evolution of biological complexity and its relation to taxonomic longevity in the Ammonoidea. *Geology* **20**, 983–6.

Braun-Blanquet, J. 1932. *Plant sociology*. New York: McGraw-Hill.

Brown, D. A. 1993. Early nineteenth-century grasslands of the midcontinent plains. *Annals of the Association of American Geographers* **83**, 589–612.

Byrne, R. 1987. Climatic change and the origins of agriculture. In *Studies in the Neolithic and Urban Revolutions: the V. Gordon Childe Colloquium*, L. Manzanilla (ed.), 21–34. Oxford: British Archaeological Reports, International Series 349.

Childe, V. G. 1928. *The most ancient East: the Oriental prelude to European prehistory*. London: Kegan Paul.

Clements, F. E. 1916. Plant succession: an analysis of the development of vegetation. *Carnegie Institute of Washington Publications* **242**, 1–512.

Cohen, M. N. 1977. *The food crisis in prehistory*. New Haven, Connecticut: Yale University Press.

COHMAP 1988. Climatic changes of the last 18,000 years: observations and model simulations. *Science* **241**, 1043–51.

Connell, J. H. 1978. Diversity in tropical rain forests and coral reefs. *Science* **199**, 1302–10.

Connell, J. H. & R. O. Slatyer 1977. Mechanisms of succession in natural communities and their role in community stability and organization. *The American Naturalist* **111**, 1119–44.

Coughenor, M. B., J. E. Ellis, D. M. Swift, D. L. Coppock, K. Galvin, J. T. McCabe, T. C. Hart 1985. Energy extraction and use in a nomadic pastoral ecosystem. *Science* **230**, 619–25.

Cronon, W. 1993. The uses of environmental history. *Environmental History Review* **17**, 1–22.

Curtis, J. T. 1959. *The vegetation of Wisconsin*. Madison: University of Wisconsin Press.

Davis, M. B. 1981. Quaternary history and the stability of forest communities. In *Forest succession*, D. C. West, H. H. Shugart, D. B. Botkin (eds), 132–53. New York: Springer.

de Angelis, D. L. & J. C. Waterhouse 1987. Equilibrium and non-equilibrium concepts in ecological models. *Ecological Monographs* **57**, 1–21.

Diamond, J. 1993. Ten thousand years of solitude. *Discover* **14**, 48–57.

— 1994a. Spacious skies and tilted axes. *Natural History* **103**, 16–23.
— 1994b. How Africa became black. *Discover* **15**, 72–81.
Drury, W. H. & I. C. T. Nisbet 1971. Inter-relations between developmental models in geomorphology, plant ecology, and animal ecology. *General Systems* **16**, 57–68.
Eckert, C. G. & S. C. H. Barrett 1992. Stochastic loss of style morphs from populatons of tristylous *Lythrum salicaria* and *Decodon verticillatus* (Lythraceae). *Evolution* **46**, 1014–29.
Eldredge, N. & S. J. Gould 1972. Punctuated equilibria: an alternative to phyletic gradualism. In *Models in paleobiology*, T. J. M. Schopf (ed.), 82–115. San Francisco: Freeman, Cooper.
Flannery, K. V. 1968. Archeological systems theory and early Mesoamerica. In *Anthropological archeology in the Americas*, B. J. Meggers (ed.), 67–87. Washington: Anthropological Society of Washington.
— 1969. Origins and ecological effects of early domestication in Iran and the Near East. In *The domestication and exploitation of plants and animals*, P. J. Ucko & G. W. Dimbleby (eds), 73–100. London: Duckworth.
— (ed.) 1986a. *Guilá Naquitz: Archaic foraging and early agriculture in Oaxaca, Mexico*. Orlando, Florida: Academic Press.
— 1986b. The research problem. In *Guilá Naquitz: Archaic foraging and early agriculture in Oaxaca, Mexico*, K. V. Flannery (ed.), 3–18. Orlando, Florida: Academic Press.
Flannery, K. V. & J. C. Wheeler 1986. Comparing the Preceramic and modern microfauna. In *Guilá Naquitz: archaic foraging and early agriculture in Oaxaca, Mexico*, K. V. Flannery (ed.), 239–46. Orlando, Florida: Academic Press.
Ford, R. I. 1985. The processes of plant food production in prehistoric North America. In *Prehistoric food production in North America*, R. I. Ford (ed.), 1–18. Anthropological Paper 75, Museum of Anthropology, University of Michigan.
Fritz, G. J. 1994. Are the first farmers getting younger? *Current Anthropology* **35**, 305–9.
Glacken, C. J. 1967. *Traces on the Rhodian shore: nature and culture in Western thought from ancient times to the end of the eighteenth century*. Berkeley: University of California Press.
Gleason, H. A. 1926. The individualistic concept of the plant association. *Bulletin of the Torrey Botanical Club* **53**, 1–20.
Glenn-Lewin, D. C., R. K. Peet, T. T. Veblen 1992. Prologue. In *Plant succession*, D. C. Glenn-Lewin, R. K. Peet, T. T. Veblen (eds), 1–10. London: Chapman & Hall.
Glick, T. F. (ed.) 1974. *The comparative reception of Darwinism*. Austin: University of Texas Press.
Gould, S. J. 1981. *The mismeasure of man*. New York: Norton.
— 1989. *Wonderful life: the Burgess Shale and the nature of history*. New York: Norton.
— 1992. Form and scale in nature and culture: modern landscape as necessary integration. In *Between home and heaven: contemporary American landscape photography*, (no eds), 74–83. Washington DC: Smithsonian Institution & University of New Mexico Press.
— 1994. In the mind of the beholder. *Natural History* **103**, 14–23.
Gould, S. J. & R. Lewontin 1979. The spandrels of San Marco and the Panglossian paradigm: a critique of the adaptationist programme. *Proceedings of the Royal Society of London, Series B* **205**, 581–98.
Gray, E. D. 1979. *Green paradise lost*. Wellesley, Massachusetts: Roundtable Press.
Grundbacher, F. J. 1963. The physiological function of the cereal awn. *The Botanical Review* **29**, 366–81.
Grubb, P. J. 1977. The maintenance of species richness in plant communities: the importance of the regeneration niche. *Biological Reviews* **52**, 107–45.
Harlan, J. R. 1967. A wild wheat harvest in Turkey. *Archaeology* **20**, 197–201.
— 1975. *Crops and man*. Madison: American Society of Agronomy.
Harlan, J. R. & D. Zohary 1966. Distribution of wild wheats and barley. *Science* **153**, 1074–80.
Harlan, J. R., J. M. J. de Wet, E. G. Price 1973. Comparative evolution of cereals. *Evolution* **27**, 311–25.
Harris, D. R. 1969. Agricultural systems, ecosystems and the origins of agriculture. In *The domestication and exploitation of plants and animals*, P. J. Ucko & G. W. Dimbleby (eds), 3–15. London: Duckworth.
— 1989. An evolutionary continuum of people–plant interaction. In *Foraging and farming: the*

evolution of plant exploitation, D. R. Harris & G. C. Hillman (eds), 11–26. London: Unwin Hyman.

— 1990. *Settling down and breaking ground: rethinking the Neolithic Revolution*. Amsterdam: Stichting Nederlands Museum voor Anthropologie en Praehistorie, Twaalfde Kroon-Voordracht.

Hawkes, J. G. 1969. The ecological background of plant domestication. In *The domestication and exploitation of plants and animals*, P. J. Ucko & G. W. Dimbleby (eds), 17–29. London: Duckworth.

Heizer, R. F. & A. B. Elsasser 1980. *The natural world of the California Indians*. Berkeley: University of California Press.

Helldén, U. 1991. Desertification – time for an assessment? *Ambio* **20**, 372–83.

Henry, D. O. 1989. *From foraging to agriculture*. Philadelphia: University of Pennsylvania Press.

Hillman, G. C., S. M. Colledge, D. R. Harris 1989. Plant-food economy during the Epipalaeolithic period at Tell Abu Hureyra, Syria: dietary diversity, seasonality, and modes of exploitation. In *Foraging and farming: the evolution of plant exploitation*, D. R. Harris & G. C. Hillman (eds), 240–66. London: Unwin Hyman.

Hinde, R. A. 1991. A biologist looks at anthropology. *Man* **26**, 583–608.

Hole, F. 1993. Critical parameters of domestication: temporal, climatic, environmental. Paper presented at the Prehistoric Society Conference on the Origins and Spread of Agriculture and Pastoralism in Eurasia, London, 25 September, 1993.

Iltis, H. H. 1983. From teosinte to maize: the catastrophic sexual transmutation. *Science* **222**, 886–94.

Johnson, H. B. 1985. Consequences of species introductions and removals on ecosystem function – implications for applied ecology. In *Proceedings of the VIth International Symposium on Biological Control of Weeds*, E. S. Delfosse (ed.), 27–56. Vancouver: Agriculture Canada.

Joyce, A. A. 1988. Early/Middle Holocene environments in the Middle Atlantic region: a revised reconstruction. In *Holocene human ecology in northeastern North America*, G. P. Nicholas (ed.), 185–214. New York: Plenum Press.

Kheel, M. 1985. The liberation of nature: a circular affair. *Environmental Ethics* **7**, 135–49.

Kimura, M. 1983. *The neutral theory of molecular evolution*. Cambridge: Cambridge University Press.

Köhler-Rollefson, I. 1988. The aftermath of the Levantine Neolithic Revolution in the light of ecological and ethnographic evidence. *Paléorient* **14**, 87–96.

Ladizinsky, G. 1975. Collection of wild cereals in the Upper Jordan Valley. *Economic Botany* **29**, 264–7.

Leonard, W. H. & J. H. Martin 1963. *Cereal crops*. New York: Macmillan.

Lewin, R. 1992. *Complexity: life at the edge of chaos*. New York: Macmillan.

Lewis, H. T. 1972. The role of fire in the domestication of plants and animals in southwest Asia: a hypothesis. *Man* **7**, 195–222.

Lewis, M. W. 1992. *Green delusions*. Durham, North Carolina: Duke University Press.

Lydolph, P. E. 1985. *The climate of the Earth*. Lanham, Maryland: Rowman & Allanheld.

Mace, R. 1991. Overgrazing overstated. *Nature* **349**, 280–1.

MacNeish, R. S. 1992. *The origins of agriculture and settled life*. Norman: University of Oklahoma Press.

Mangelsdorf, P. C. 1953. Review of "Agricultural origins and dispersals", by Carl O. Sauer. *American Antiquity* **19**, 87–90.

Mangelsdorf, P. C., R. S. MacNeish, W. C. Galinat 1964. Domestication of corn. *Science* **143**, 538–45.

Margalef, R. 1968. *Perspectives in ecological theory*. Chicago: University of Chicago Press.

McCorriston, J. & F. Hole 1991. The ecology of seasonal stress and the origins of agriculture in the Near East. *American Anthropologist* **93**, 46–69.

McIntosh, R. P. 1985. *The background of ecology*. Cambridge: Cambridge University Press.

McShea, D. W. 1991. Complexity and evolution: what everybody knows. *Biology and Philosophy* **6**, 303–24.

— 1993. Evolutionary change in the morphological complexity of the mammalian vertebral column. *Evolution* **47**, 730–40.

Mensing, S. A. 1992. The impact of European settlement on blue oak (*Quercus douglasii*) regeneration and recruitment in the Tehachapi Mountains, California. *Madroño* **39**, 36–46.

Minnich, R. A. 1983. Fire mosaics in southern California and north Baja California. *Science* **219**, 1287–94.

Moore, A. M. T. & G. C. Hillman 1992. The Pleistocene to Holocene transition and human economy in Southwest Asia: the impact of the Younger Dryas. *American Antiquity* **57**, 482–94.

Naveh, Z. 1967. Mediterranean ecosystems and vegetation types in California and Israel. *Ecology* **48**, 445–59.

Naveh, Z. & R. H. Whittaker 1979. Structural and floristic diversity of shrublands and woodlands in northern Israel and other mediterranean countries. *Vegetatio* **41**, 171–190.

Nicholas, G. P. 1988. Ecological leveling: the archaeology and environmental dynamics of early Post-glacial land use. In *Holocene human ecology in northeastern North America*, G. P. Nicholas (ed.), 257–96. New York: Plenum.

Nitecki, M. (ed.) 1988. *Evolutionary progress*. Chicago: University of Chicago Press.

— 1990. *Evolutionary innovations*. Chicago: University of Chicago Press.

Odum, E. P. 1953. *Fundamentals of ecology*. Philadelphia: Saunders.

— 1969. The strategy of ecosystem development. *Science* **164**, 262–70.

Orlove, B. S. 1980. Ecological anthropology. *Annual Review of Anthropology* **9**, 235–73.

Parker, K. C. 1993. Climatic effects on regeneration trends for two columnar cacti in the northern Sonoran Desert. *Annals of the Association of American Geographers* **83**, 452–74.

Pickersgill, B. & C. B. Heiser 1977. Origins and distribution of plants domesticated in the New World tropics. In *Origins of agriculture*, C. A. Reed (ed.), 803–35. The Hague: Mouton.

Price, M. & M. Lewis 1993. The reinvention of cultural geography. *Annals of the Association of American Geographers* **83**, 1–17.

Pyne, S. J. 1982. *Fire in America*. Princeton, New Jersey: Princeton University Press.

Rackham, O. 1990. The greening of Myrtos. In *Man's role in the shaping of the eastern Mediterranean landscape*, S. Bottema, G. Entjes-Nieborg, W. van Zeist (eds), 341–8. Rotterdam: Balkema.

Renfrew, A. C. 1987. *Archaeology and language*. Cambridge: Cambridge University Press.

Renfrew, A. C. & J. F. Cherry (eds) 1986. *Peer polity interaction and socio-political change*. Cambridge: Cambridge University Press.

Reynolds, R. G. 1986. An adaptive computer model for the evolution of plant collecting and early agriculture in the eastern Valley of Oaxaca. In Flannery (1986a: 439–500).

Richards, R. J. 1992. *The meaning of evolution: the morphological construction and ideological reconstruction of Darwin's theory*. Chicago: University of Chicago Press.

Riley, T. J., R. Edging, J. Rossen 1990. Cultigens in prehistoric eastern North America: changing paradigms. *Current Anthropology* **31**, 525–41.

Rind, D., D. Peteet, W. S. Broecker, A. Mcintyre, W. F. Ruddiman 1986. Impact of cold North Atlantic sea surface temperatures on climate: implications for the Younger Dryas cooling (11–10K). *Climate Dynamics* **1**, 3–33.

Rindos, D. 1984. *The origins of agriculture: an evolutionary perspective*. Orlando, Florida: Academic Press.

Roberts, N. 1989. *The Holocene*. Oxford: Basil Blackwell.

— 1990. Human-induced landscape change in South and Southwest Turkey during the later Holocene. In *Man's role in the shaping of the eastern Mediterranean landscape*, S. Bottema, G. Entjes-Nieborg, W. van Zeist (eds), 53–67. Rotterdam: Balkema.

Ruse, M. 1993. Evolution and progress. *Trends in Ecology and Evolution* **8**, 55–9.

Sauer, C. O. 1952. *Agricultural origins and dispersals*. New York: American Geographical Society.

Schaffer, W. M. 1985. Order and chaos in ecological systems. *Ecology* **66**, 93–106.

Schoenwetter, J. & L. D. Smith 1986. Pollen analysis of the Oaxaca Archaic. In Flannery (1986a: 179–237).

Service, E. R. 1962. *Primitive social organization: an evolutionary perspective*. New York: Random House.

Sinton, J. 1993. When Moscow looks like Chicago: an essay on uniformity and diversity in landscapes and communities. *Environmental History Review* **17**, 23–41.

Smith Jr, C. E. 1978. The vegetational history of the Oaxaca Valley. In *Prehistory and human ecology of the valley of Oaxaca* (vol. 5: pt 1), K. V. Flannery & R. E. Blanton (eds), 1–30. Memoirs 10, Museum of Anthropology, University of Michigan.

Sousa, W. P. 1984. The role of disturbance in natural communities. *Annual Review of Ecology and Systematics* **15**, 353–91.

Spear, R. W., M. B. Davis, L. C. K. Shane 1994. Late Quaternary history of low- and mid-elevation vegetation in the White Mountains of New Hampshire. *Ecological Monographs* **64**, 85–109.

Sprugel, D. G. 1991. Disturbance, equilibrium, and environmental variability – what is natural vegetation in a changing environment? *Biological Conservation* **58**, 1–18.

Steward, J. 1955. *Theory of culture change*. Urbana: University of Illinois Press.

Thomas, D. S. G. 1993. Sandstorm in a teacup? Understanding desertification. *Geographical Journal* **159**, 318–31.

Toulmin, S. 1990. *Cosmopolis: the hidden agenda of modernity*. Chicago: University of Chicago Press.

Trigger, B. G. 1989. *A history of archaeological thought*. Cambridge: Cambridge University Press.

van Devender, T. R. 1990. Late Quaternary vegetation and climate of the Sonoran Desert, United States and Mexico. In *Fossil packrat middens: the last 40,000 years of biotic change in the arid West*, J. L. Betancourt, T. R. van Devender, P. S. Martin (eds), 134–65. Tucson: University of Arizona Press.

van Zeist, W. 1969. Reflections on prehistoric environments in the Near East. In *The domestication and exploitation of plants and animals*, P. J. Ucko & G. W. Dimbleby (eds), 35–46. London: Duckworth.

van Zeist, W. & S. Bottema 1977. Palynological investigations in western Iran. *Palaeohistoria* **19**, 19–95.

Veblen, T. T. 1985. Stand dynamics in Chilean *Nothofagus* forests. In *The ecology of natural disturbance and patch dynamics*, S. T. A. Pickett & P. S. White (eds), 31–51. Orlando, Florida: Academic Press.

Vidal de la Blache, P. 1911. Les genres de vie dans la géographie humaine. *Annales de Géographie* **20**, 289–304.

— 1926. *Principles of human geography*. New York: Henry Holt.

Walker, B. H. 1989. Diversity and stability in ecosystem conservation. In *Conservation for the twenty-first century*, D. Western & M. C. Pearl (eds), 121–30. Oxford: Oxford University Press.

Walker, B. H., D. Ludwig, C. S. Holling & R. M. Peterman 1981. Stability of semi-arid savanna grazing systems. *Journal of Ecology* **69**, 473–98.

Whittaker, R. H. 1962. Classification of natural communities. *Botanical Review* **28**, 1–239.

— 1975. *Communities and ecosystems*, 2nd edn. New York: Macmillan.

Wilson, E. O. 1975. *Sociobiology*. Cambridge, Massachusetts: Harvard University Press.

Wolf, E. R. 1982. *Europe and the people without history*. Berkeley: University of California Press.

Worster, D. 1977. *Nature's economy: the roots of ecology*. San Francisco: Sierra Club.

— 1990. The ecology of order and chaos. *Environmental History Review* **14**, 1–18.

Wright Jr, H. E. 1993. Environmental determinism in Near Eastern prehistory. *Current Anthropology* **34**, 459–69.

Wright, K. I. 1994. Ground-stone tools and hunter–gatherer subsistence in southwest Asia: implications for the transition to farming. *American Antiquity* **59**, 238–63.

Wright, S. 1982. The shifting balance theory and macroevolution. *Annual Review of Genetics* **16**, 1–19.

Yechieli, Y., M. Magaritz, Y. Levy, U. Weber, U. Kafri, W. Woelfli, G. Bonani 1993. Late Quaternary geological history of the Dead Sea area, Israel. *Quaternary Research* **39**, 59–67.

Yen, D. E. 1989. The domestication of environment. In *Foraging and farming: the evolution of plant exploitation*, D. R. Harris & G. C. Hillman (eds), 55–75. London: Unwin Hyman.

Zimmerer, K. S. 1994. Human ecology and the "new ecology": the prospect and promise of integration. *Annals of the Association of American Geographers* **84**, 108–25.

Zohary, D. 1969. The progenitors of wheat and barley in relation to domestication and agricultural dispersal in the Old World. In *The domestication and exploitation of plants and animals*, P. J. Ucko & G. W. Dimbleby (eds), 47–66. London: Duckworth.

— 1983. Wild genetic resources of crops in Israel. *Israel Journal of Botany* **32**, 97–127.

— 1989. Domestication of the Southwest Asian Neolithic crop assemblage of cereals, pulses, and flax: the evidence from the living plants. In *Foraging and farming: the evolution of plant exploitation*,

D. R. Harris & G. C. Hillman (eds), 358–73. London: Unwin Hyman.
Zohary, D. & M. Hopf 1988. *Domestication of plants in the Old World: the origin and spread of cultivated plants in West Asia, Europe, and the Nile Valley*. Oxford: Oxford University Press.
Zohary, M. 1962. *Plant life of Palestine*. New York: Ronald Press.
— 1973. *Geobotanical foundations of the Middle East* [2 vols]. Stuttgart: Gustav Fischer.

CHAPTER FOUR

EDINBURG UNIVERSITY LIBRARY
WITHDRAWN

The spread of agriculture and nomadic pastoralism: insights from genetics, linguistics and archaeology

L. Luca Cavalli-Sforza

The mode of spread of agriculture

The population of modern humans has increased progressively since the initial expansion of *Homo sapiens* from Africa opened new territory for settlement. The human population probably increased at least fivefold in the period from about 60,000 or 70,000 to 10,000 years ago. This estimate is based on the consideration that Africa forms about 20 per cent of the land surface of the world. It assumes that there was no increase in efficiency of use of the land over that time period, which is unlikely, and it is therefore probably an underestimate. Whatever the total human population was at the beginning of the Holocene around 10,000 years ago (cf. Groube in Ch. 7 in this volume), just before the beginnings of agriculture and animal breeding, it is likely to have been near saturation for the prevailing hunter–gatherer technology, so that population pressure was probably at the time an important stimulus to innovations in food production (Cohen 1977), leading to the development of plant and animal domestication in several different regions of the world. It is possible, or indeed likely, that contemporaneous climatic changes, which in turn caused floral and faunal changes, contributed significantly to generating the need for new technological developments, which led gradually to the replacement of food collection by food production.

There may have been many more or less independent attempts at plant or animal domestication, but it is clear that a few regions of origin of agriculture had a disproportionate importance in spreading certain key plants and animals. Thus, Southwest Asia was certainly the major centre of diffusion of wheat, barley, sheep, goats, and probably cattle and pigs, to Europe, Egypt and South Asia. Similarly important was the domestication of millets and pigs in North China; of rice, pigs and buffaloes in South China and perhaps in South or Southeast Asia; of maize, squash, beans and many other plants in Central America and northeastern South America. All these developments were almost simultaneous, underlining the likelihood that global cli-

51

matic changes had an important impact on the sequence of events. Other important agricultural developments took place in various parts of Africa. The Sahara may have been an independent early centre of cattle domestication. Millet, sorghum and other plants were domesticated in the modern Sahel, and Ethiopia contributed several other domesticates. (See Ammerman & Cavalli-Sforza (1984: 9–33) for a summary of world centres of agricultural origin.)

The ways in which farming diffused from the nuclear areas of agricultural origin have only very rarely and briefly been discussed explicitly by archaeologists. The two simplest hypotheses that can explain it are the diffusion of farming technology, and the diffusion of farmers themselves. It is not easy to choose between them on the basis of archaeological data alone; moreover, the two hypotheses are not mutually exclusive. A study of bones from neolithic cemeteries could help, but unfortunately most bone characteristics can be substantially altered by diet, and discrimination between the two hypotheses may be difficult or even impossible. An attempt at such analysis by Sokal et al. (1991, 1992) showed that there was insufficient early neolithic bone data available in Europe to allow such discrimination. An earlier unpublished attempt by the present author reached the same conclusion. Other sources of information have been applied to the problem more successfully; they have been discussed and summarized by Ammerman & Cavalli-Sforza (1984), and they include the following findings.

- The rate of advance of farmers from Southwest Asia to Europe can be measured from archaeological data; it is 1 km per year, on average, and somewhat higher along the coasts of the Mediterranean than in the interior of Europe. The expansion to Scandinavia was delayed by the climate prevalent there at the time of first arrival.

- The above rate is compatible with that predicted on the basis of Fisher's (1937) theory on the rate of advance. This theory, originally based on the spread of an advantageous gene, can be extended to that of an expanding population, an epidemic or a cultural innovation, and so on. The main prediction is that the rate of advance is constant in time and depends on two factors: the rates of population growth and individual migration. The former is expressed as the initial growth rate in a logistic growth curve, and the latter as a diffusion constant, akin to molecular movement, as in Brownian motion. Observations of human mobility show that this is an imperfect but useful description of human movement (Cavalli-Sforza 1963). The rate of advance predicted by Fisher's theory is equal to the geometric mean (the square root of the product) of the rates of population growth and migration.

Unfortunately, archaeological data can hardly supply estimates of the geographical mobility and population growth curves of early farmers, but ethnography can help. The rate of advance of agriculture inferred for Europe is compatible with the hypothesis that farmers, not farming, spread (i.e. by *demic diffusion* as opposed to *cultural diffusion*), assuming rates of fertility and mobility of early farmers comparable to those observed in ethnographically similar situations. Further evidence can come from ethnographic observations of recent expansions of farmers, for example the Bantu expansion in central and southern Africa.

- The comparison of observed rates of advance of farming with those expected under the hypothesis of demic diffusion is only an indirect indication that it is farmers and not farming that spread from the area of origin. In the absence of adequate skeletal and other archaeological data, a more direct indication can be derived from modern genetic data, because the spread of agricultural settlers from an area of origin into regions inhabited sparsely by hunter–gatherers, who initially had a different genetic background, is very likely to generate a genetic gradient observable even today.

- The existence of the genetic gradients expected on the hypothesis of demic diffusion has been demonstrated by an analysis of principal components (PCs) of gene frequencies. This is a statistical method that can dissect different, independent demic expansions and pinpoint their areas of origin by the analysis of maps of many genes. A first study of the maps of 39 genes (Menozzi et al. 1978) showed that the postulated spread of farmers from Southwest Asia into Europe was in excellent agreement with the map of the first PC of European gene frequencies. The map of the first PC can also be described as the most important pattern latent in the complex gene geography of Europe. The resemblance between this map and that of the times of first arrival of agriculture, as indicated by radiocarbon dates for the earliest neolithic sites in Europe, was found to be extraordinarily high. This was confirmed by a later analysis using a greater number of genes (95) (Cavalli-Sforza et al. 1993, 1994). Simulations confirmed the potential of PCs to separate different migrations and pinpoint their origins when these were sufficiently distinct geographically (Rendine et al. 1986). Other statistical methods using correlations of the archaeological and the genetic data (Sokal et al. 1991, 1992) confirmed these conclusions.

- Ethnographic studies of modern hunter–gatherers (e.g. African Pygmies) confirm that marriage between them and farmers does take place, although only rarely and mostly in one direction (farmers taking hunter–gatherer wives, who are absorbed with their children into the dominant farming culture). The consequent gene flow from hunter–gatherers into the society of advancing farmers is enough to generate the observed genetic gradient. And whenever drastic deforestation occurs as a result of the advance of agriculturalists, the only hope of survival for the hunter–gatherers is to adopt agriculture, thus increasing the number of farmers and the gene flow of hunter–gatherers into the farming society.

All the above points show that *both* the hypotheses, of the spread of farmers and of farming, are correct; if they were not, the observed genetic gradient would not form.

The response of some archaeologists to this hypothesis was initially critical, especially on the basis of observations at the extreme European periphery of the neolithic expansion. Here, mesolithic cultures could be shown to have survived longer in close proximity to the incoming neolithic cultures (cf. Price, Thomas and Zvelebil in this volume). On this basis Zvelebil (1986) tried to criticize the demic hypothesis of the spread of farming. But his observations are not incompatible with farmers' demic diffusion. In fact, in another paper he accepts demic diffusion for most of Europe (Zvelebil 1989), disputing its validity only for peripheral areas such as Spain, where farming arrived much later and where hunter–gatherer cultures were more advanced.

Genetic analysis of the Iberian peninsula demonstrates clearly, however, that Zvelebil's objection is invalid (Bertranpetit & Cavalli-Sforza 1991). Here, the genetic data suggest that the spread of neolithic people was definitely more limited. In part this may be attributable to the greater development of Iberian mesolithic cultures, which came into contact with agriculture several millennia after the beginning of the spread of agriculture into Europe. Also, at the geographical periphery of the expansion, genetic data are less powerful in showing the demic spread, because the original genetic background of the farmers is greatly diluted. In fact, in the Iberian peninsula the PC most likely to correspond to the neolithic spread of agriculture is the second, and not the first as in the rest of Europe (in Iberia the first represents the retreating mesolithic population, i.e. the Basque people, versus the rest of the Iberians, and the second represents the neolithic population) (Figs 4.1a,b).

Wider archaeological acceptance of the demic hypothesis of agricultural diffusion followed publication of Colin Renfrew's ideas on the link between the spread of agriculture and of languages (Renfrew 1987, 1989). However, he did not make use of the genetic data that we had provided. Instead he noted that population expansions in a vacuum, as in an uninhabited region, or a near vacuum, as in a region that is not densely inhabited but can be rapidly populated by the new settlers, is likely to be accompanied by the establishment of the language of the settlers. He therefore advanced the hypothesis that farmers who spread from Southwest Asia to Europe and India brought Indo–European languages with them. He suggested that the original area where proto-Indo–European was spoken was Anatolia. Some linguists had already advanced a similar hypothesis on other grounds (see Mallory 1989). But other possible areas of origin of Indo–European languages were favoured among linguists, in particular one suggested by another archaeologist, Marija Gimbutas (see below).

The mode of spread of nomadic pastoralism

A common view of the origin of nomadic pastoralism is that it was a secondary development among farmers who occupied marginal ecological areas where agricultural production could not adequately sustain increasing populations, but where certain animal domesticates could prosper. After a long period of adaptation, some of these developments proved capable of generating new, powerful economies that had previously undiscovered advantages, and were remarkably well adapted to extreme marginal, especially arid, environments.

The most successful domesticates, used for food and in part for traction, were cattle, which became in many cultures synonymous with wealth, and were used as money. But the horse and the camel were best suited to transportation, in addition to being excellent sources of food, and they were used for the development of exceedingly efficient armies that made possible rapid, extensive conquests of large areas. In northern Africa progressive desiccation in the Sahara resulted in cattle first, then horses, and finally camels becoming major sources of food and other support for nomadic populations.

The horse was native to the Eurasian steppes, and its domestication gave the opportunity for their inhabitants, and those of the oases of Central Asia, to originate a great number of expansions, starting around 5,000 years ago or perhaps earlier. The area that saw the first expansions of pastoral nomads, the Volga–Don region, was at or near the centre of many other successive expansions, perhaps driven by descendants of the first local pastoral nomads. Gimbutas focused scholarly attention on this "Kurgan" region, so-called from the Russian name of the many prehistoric mounds found in this and neighbouring areas, which were the tombs of nomadic chiefs. She suggested that the Kurgan Culture expanded repeatedly (she proposed three periods of expansion in the direction of Europe from 6,000 to 3,000 years ago) and was responsible for carrying Indo–European languages to Europe (Gimbutas 1970, 1973, 1977, 1979, 1980). The western part of the steppes remained in continuous demographic eruption. In historical times, Scythians, Sarmatians, Alans, Avars, Goths and other peoples moved from the steppe or from nearby regions towards various parts of Europe. The last major successful movement was that of the (non-Indo–European speaking) Magyars who crossed the Carpathians to occupy Hungary at the end of the ninth century AD. The dates suggested by Gimbutas may have to be modified in the light of more recent information, but her major hypotheses seem to be confirmed by later work by Anthony and others (Anthony 1994, Anthony & Vinogradov in press).

On the other hand, cultures closely related to the Kurgan Culture and situated in mid-Central Asia, just east of the Volga–Don region, are believed to have originated expansions to the south and southeast. It has been widely accepted for some time that these transmitted the Indo–Iranian branch of Indo–European languages through Turkestan to Iran, Afghanistan, Pakistan and India.

Meanwhile, however, starting in the third century BC, the eastern part of the Eurasian steppe witnessed a development similar to the earlier one in the western steppe. Huns, Mongols and Turkic people formed armies, against which the Great Wall of China was built but proved powerless. They occupied large parts of Asia, including China in the thirteenth century AD, India, Iran and Turkey. The Eastern Roman Empire fell finally to the Turks in the fifteenth century. They advanced through southeastern Europe to the gates of Vienna, and conquered all of the Middle East and North Africa, thus creating an empire that fell only with First World War.

All these conquests were largely attributable to the military use of the horse, which underwent many successive improvements [but cf. Renfrew's comments, in Ch. 5 in this volume, on the lack of evidence for horses having been ridden for military purposes before about 1500 BC: ed.]. Many nomadic pastoralists seem to have developed a very successful specialization as warriors. Their long seasonal migrations (transhumance) from winter to summer camps gave them opportunities to develop skills in logistics and warfare, and they also achieved high levels of cultural sophistication in crafts, languages and literature, Sanskrit for instance, which has the oldest written grammar of the Western world dated to $c.600$ BC.

The horse may have been the *deus ex machina* of most of these expansions. Another domestic animal, the camel, was responsible for another group of expansions, in the deserts as opposed to the steppes. There are two domesticated species, the dromedary of Arabia (*Camelus dromedarius*) and the Bactrian camel of Central Asia (*C. bactrianus*). The dromedary was dispersed widely from its Arabian homeland, west and south into Africa and north and east to India (see Köhler-Rollefson: this volume). It was well adapted to the desert as a riding, pack and military animal, and it played a vital part in the conquest of North Africa and Spain by the Arabs in the seventh and early eighth centuries AD. They owed their success largely to the mobility of their army, which could act swiftly in the difficult Saharan environment thanks to their camels. From the mid-eleventh to the thirteenth century Arab Bedouins carried out a series of raids and invasions of North Africa (the Hilalian invasions), which again depended heavily on camels. Other nomads of the Sahara – Berbers, Tuaregs, Tubus and Beja – still depend largely on camels for trading (as they used also to do for raiding).

The process of expansion of pastoral nomads shows major differences from that of farmers. Because pastoral nomads are adapted to marginal desert environments and their way of life is based mainly on a small range of domestic animals, they cannot reach high population densities. Their agricultural activities can only be minimal, especially because they have to sustain this livestock by extensive seasonal movements between grazing grounds. They therefore rely on settled farmers for agricultural supplies, and the most efficient way to guarantee such supplies is to dominate the farmers politically. There is however great variation in the social relations of pastoral nomads and farmers (Khazanov 1984). The most successful example of symbiosis between them is perhaps that generated in the Indian subcontinent, the origin of which can be traced back at least to the second millennium BC in what is today Pakistan.

It has already been pointed out that pastoral nomads, who probably originated in the region of the Kurgan Culture in Central Asia, expanded across Iran and Afghanistan and reached Pakistan and India. Here they encountered the agricultural Harappan civilization in the Indus valley. By about 1500 BC, when the Harappan civilization was already in decline, there are archaeological signs of another, more modest, culture of people who lived outside the cities of the Harappan civilization. This is probably the archaeological signature of pastoral nomads, who later spread eastwards to India. The fusion of the former agricultural civilization and the culture of the later pastoral-nomadic arrivals was a long process and gave rise to a unique social system, that of Indian castes. This is essentially a strictly hierarchical society where genetic exchange between castes is non-existent or minimal; the hierarchy of castes is fixed by religion, and the caste of priests/philosophers/teachers/entrepreneurs, the Brahmins, is everywhere dominant. Most castes are characterized by profession and territory, which are inherited. Traditional Indian epic poems such as the Mahabharata, have been interpreted by modern ecologists (Gadgil & Thapar 1990) as the history of wars between the incoming nomads and the established farmers, and, later, between the nomads and their now allied farmers against hunter–gatherers, whose forests were burnt in order to appropriate their territory for pasture and for cultivation. This process was initiated by Brahmins who pioneered the infiltration of the forest.

In research that I have carried out in collaboration with Gadgil (not yet published), it has been shown that there is a close correlation between the first PC of genes in the Indian subcontinent and the map of the dates of first archaeological appearance of the horse, an animal that did not exist in India before the arrival of pastoral nomads. To some extent, this correlation extends to languages. It is likely that languages spoken in South Asia when agriculture began there were largely of the Dravidian family. In prehistoric Southwest Asia, in the Euphrates–Tigris area, most languages belonged to the Afro–Asiatic family, spoken at that time also in Arabia and North Africa. Some however, such as Sumerian, belonged, according to some linguists, to an old linguistic family once widespread in most of Eurasia, of which Basque, some Caucasian languages, and the Sino–Tibetan and the Na–Dene families survive today (Ruhlen 1991). In Iran and probably in Pakistan, languages spoken at the time of early farming were Dravidian. They were perhaps spread to Pakistan and India by farmers from the eastern part of the Euphrates–Tigris region (Renfrew 1987 & this volume, Cavalli-Sforza 1988), and today Dravidian languages are spoken by some tribes in southern Pakistan, in parts of northern India, and in the southeastern part of the Indian peninsula. The strongest evidence for this hypothesis is supplied by the Elamite language, once spoken in Elam (in southwestern Iran). Elamite is known because in the mid-third millennium BC it was written in cuneiform characters and has been translated. Because it is now thought that there is a close affinity between Elamite and Dravidian (McAlpin 1981), it has been suggested that the Dravidian family of languages should be called Elamo–Dravidian (Ruhlen 1991). When Indo–European languages were brought to the Indian subcontinent by nomadic pastoralists from the Central Asian steppes during the second millennium BC, they replaced Dravidian languages almost everywhere except in southeastern India.

The detection of agricultural and pastoral expansions by genetic geography

Population expansions bring about the spread of genes and culture (essentially language, customs and artefacts) of the new settlers. They should be distinguished from migrations. For example, it is likely that when the Magyars migrated to Hungary at the end of the ninth century AD, they left nobody, or only few people, behind in the areas they previously occupied. One would call this a migration and not an expansion. For an expansion to occur, there must be population growth in addition to migration: there is not only a shift of location of the migrants, but also an extension of territory occupied by the population as a whole, part of which remains in the territory of origin and part of which occupies new areas. Expansions may cause very extensive colonization, as happened when Europeans colonized the Americas, Australia and South Africa after the beginning of transoceanic navigation in the sixteenth century AD. Similarly, in the first millennium BC, the Greek and Phoenician expansions resulted in extensive colonization in both the eastern and the western Mediterranean.

The condition required for an expansion to take place is population growth causing local overcrowding, and *partial* migration of the saturated population. In general there tends to be some new factor behind population growth, which, in the human case, is usually the occurrence of technological innovations that increase the local availability of food, favour geographical expansion (e.g. new methods of transportation) or confer some military or political advantage.

Under certain conditions, the study of genetic geography can give precise information on both migrations and expansions. Simulations have shown that it is easier to detect expansions from genetic data the greater the initial differences in gene frequencies between old residents and new settlers (which depends on the remoteness of their genetic relationship), and the greater the demographic importance of the expansion. These factors are determined by the magnitude of the ratio of the number of new settlers to that of old residents in the area of the expansion, by the subsequent demographic development of the two populations after the expansion, namely their relative growth, and by the genetic exchanges between them. Further complications can be generated by later movements to the area of other populations, but principal component analysis can help to dissect them.

As has already been pointed out earlier in this chapter, the genetic approach has been very rewarding in the study of the expansion of agriculture into Europe. The considerable increase of population density made possible by agriculture strongly favours the detection of farmers' expansions into territories previously occupied by hunter–gatherers. The potential increase of population density, even under primitive agriculture, is very high compared with that characteristic of the foraging (hunter–gatherer) food economy: an increase by at least a factor of ten. Most successful agricultural settlements have taken place in forested areas, which were slowly cleared by the advancing farmers. This reduced, or at least slowed down, encroachment on to the hunter–gatherers' territories. Furthermore, at least in Europe, different types of terrain often favoured farming and hunting–gathering activities respectively. Under these conditions there is a higher chance of survival, or at least a slower rate of disappearance, of the hunter–gatherers' culture. Ethnographic data indicate that hunter–gatherers have in general shown little interest in adopting farming; for instance, in tropical Africa the Pygmies have maintained their former customs at least in part despite the presence for 2,000 years or more of Bantu farmers in the same areas (Cavalli-Sforza 1986).

In the case of pastoral–nomadic expansions, one might *a priori* expect that when they occur in areas already occupied by farmers, living at relatively high population densities, they would be less likely to cause major genetic gradients. It seems that the settlement of pastoral nomads in such areas can prosper, especially if it does not disturb the welfare of the previous settlers excessively, and that it is at least partially synergistic with respect to them. The chance of detecting such expansions genetically then depends mostly on the initial difference in gene frequencies between the new and the old settlers. But the parallel development of two populations with different customs has unexpected complications. Most pastoral nomads who originated in the Eurasian steppes and expanded from them seem to have shared a tendency to caste formation, as observed historically in Greek, Roman and Indian societies. This may have been a trend already present among the steppe pastoral nomads, or it may simply be a likely development whenever there is confrontation between pastoral–nomadic invaders and previous agricultural settlers. Under such conditions, systems of social stratification are the probable outcome. In extreme cases the fate of the previous settlers has been annihilation or enslavement; but less extreme forms of serfdom or other modes of political control are more common. The generation of genetically closed segments of society ordered hierarchically, as bona fide castes are, is one form of societal evolution of which the strict Indian model represents a unique example.

The only simulations of admixture between incoming colonists and previous residents that we have published (Sgaramella-Zonta & Cavalli-Sforza 1973, Rendine et al. 1986) are geared towards representing the spread of farmers among hunter–gatherers. They therefore include a very simple treatment of the two major processes of interaction: acculturation (acquisition of the agricultural technology by foragers) and genetic exchange between the two populations, by pooling them into a single phenomenon: the "migration" of hunter–gatherers to the local farming societies, which takes place in the published model at a constant rate. This simplification is justified by the fact that both processes lead eventually to the same consequence, which can be called gene flow from the hunter–gatherers to the farming society, and it is the only one that strictly matters from the point of view of population genetics. For greater precision the two phenomena might be kept distinct in simulations, but the end result is likely to be very similar, whether they are kept together or separated. This gene flow was modelled as a function of the numbers of farmers and of hunter–gatherers in each region, and of a constant rate of social migration, i.e. the net migration of individuals from the hunter–gatherers' to the farmers' society per generation. This could also be called the "acculturation rate", but it is in fact a measure of "social" migration (i.e. among social classes) plus acculturation. The process of population increase per unit of time in each region is represented by the following system of equations:

$$dA/dt = k_a (1-A/A') + gAH$$
$$dH/dt = k_h (1-H/H') - gAH$$

where A and H are the numbers of farmers and hunter–gatherers at time t in each subregion of the whole region considered; k_a and k_h are their relative growth rates in a logistic growth system; and A' and H' are the maximum numbers of individuals supported in the region at saturation by the two food economies. The difference between the growth rates k_a and k_h have little influence and they could be taken as equal without too much effect on the results of the simulation, although they will usually be biased in favour of farmers. g is the "social migration–acculturation" constant.

There is thus, in this model, no direct interference between the processes of population growth in the two segments of societies. The value of g is the single most important factor determining the slope of the genetic gradient to be found in the general area at the end of the process of expansion. It can perhaps be easily understood, at least qualitatively, that with a high value of g, implying a rapid rate of hunter–gatherers acculturating to agriculture (either because they enter the farmers' society, e.g. by marriage, or because they adopt farming customs), the genetic gradient will fall very rapidly just outside the area of origin of agriculture, and, in essence, the initial difference in genetic geography among farmers and hunter–gatherers will remain unchanged for a long time. By contrast, a low value of g will cause the gene frequencies of farmers to extend to the whole area in which they settle, with very little influence of the hunter–gatherers' genes. The slope of the genetic gradient will be very small and the final genetic result will be that farmers' genes will largely replace those of hunter–gatherers. These expected behaviours are explained in some detail in Ammermann & Cavalli-Sforza (1984).

Simulation has also shown that the genetic gradient is rather resistant to later disappearance such as might arise from local migratory exchanges among neighbours, which are always present in any society. General genetic homogeneity (or, at least, greater homogeneity) is the final state, in the absence of other causes of evolution, especially with the present trend to greater and greater human admixture. But as long as local, individual migration, not caused by expansions, is (or was) at the level prevalent in agricultural societies prior to modern industrial development, one can only observe a slow smoothing of existing genetic differences and gradients. By contrast, major expansions tend to cause major genetic gradients because of local population growth under the factors responsible for expansion, and especially the increase in saturation densities attributable to technological innovations.

As already noted, in the simulation model developed by Sgaramella-Zonta & Cavalli-Sforza (1973), which is at the basis of that used by Rendine et al. (1986), there is no direct interference of the processes of population growth going on in the two societies, hunter–gatherers and farmers. But it is likely that when pastoral nomads in substantial numbers successfully invade an area previously settled only by farmers, heavy interference in the population growth of the latter will result. Areas previously under cultivation will be used for pasture, if necessary acquired by the use of force. A reduction in the number of farmers at saturation and an increase in that of pastoralists will follow. Further disruptions of the farmers' political and social system will ensue.

An example of this process can be seen in the decay of civilian life after the fall of the Roman Empire, under the rule of barbarians. It has been guestimated that in the first five centuries after the fall of Rome the population in the former western Roman Empire fell to half its original numbers (Cipolla pers. comm.). There are other causes of increment of the relative Darwinian fitness of pastoralists at the expense of that of farmers, due to the social privileges the former take for themselves, and the tributes levied by them. One would want to repeat simulations with a new set of equations to take all these factors into account. An attempt was made, with the addition of a new term to the above equations (iAH^2), where H are now the incoming nomads, A the previously resident farmers and i is a constant expressing the intensity of interference of H on A. This term will have a negative sign in the dA/dt equation and a positive one in the dH/dt equation. The g term will reverse its sign with respect to the system of equations given earlier, because the general tendency is for some women of the socially inferior group to enter by marriage into the socially dominant group, whereas the reverse movement of women is usually barred by custom. Farmers are now the socially inferior group.

The expectations of this model involving interference in population growth by the incomers have been explored by simulation only in a limited way, in an unpublished collaboration with M. Feldman and his students. Observations from real data do indicate genetic gradients that are likely to be attributable to expansions of pastoral nomads. For instance, one finds a clear genetic gradient from the areas of the Kurgan Culture towards Europe. Whereas the first PC of Europe is essentially determined by the immigration of farmers from Southwest Asia (Fig. 4.1a) and the second by differences between northeastern Europe and the centre-south (probably because of expansion of western Siberian people of the Uralic language family in the extreme north of Europe, and perhaps also because of their adaptation to northern climatic conditions; Fig. 4.1b), the third PC shows an expansion with a clearcut area of origin north of the Caucasus (Fig. 4.1c). This coincides with the Kurgan area, which Gimbutas

(1970, 1973, 1977, 1979, 1980) has suggested is the area of origin of the expansion of Bronze Age pastoral nomads. The relative importance of the three European PCs is quite different: the first, attributable to farmers, is responsible for 28.1 per cent of the total variance, the second for 22.2 per cent, and the third for only 10.6 per cent

Figure 4.1   Synthetic maps of Europe and western Asia, using the first five principal components from 95 gene frequencies calculated by Cavalli-Sforza et al. (1994). Principal components (PCs) are a useful mathematical method of summarizing graphically patterns in large data collections that easily escape direct inspection. They allow a "stratigraphic approach" to genetic data. Each PC is a weighted mean of all the gene frequencies investigated in all populations; weights are calculated so as to maximize the variation among populations, generating the first PC. A second PC is generated by new weights selected so as to maximize the residual variation and generate a PC uncorrelated with the first; the process is repeated for the third, which is uncorrelated with the first and second, and so on. The scale of variation of each PC is represented by eight classes; the central values correspond to the mean of each PC and the two extremes or "poles" correspond to positive and negative values, which are chosen arbitrarily. The two poles represent the opposite extreme tendencies of the pattern represented by the PC. When expansions have occurred, as in these cases, one of the two poles usually corresponds to the area of origin of the expansion and the other to the areas where populations show the greatest genetic difference from that at the origin of the expansion. The poles that correspond to the areas of origin for the first four PCs are shown in black and seem to correspond, in order, to the neolithic expansion from Southwest Asia, the expansion of Uralic language speakers from western Siberia, the expansion of pastoral nomads from the Kurgan area, and Greek colonization in the Mediterranean region. The black area on the fifth map represents the "contraction" of the Basques. Maps (a), (b), (c) and (e) are reproduced, with permission, from Cavalli-Sforza et al. 1994: 292–4; map (d) is a redrawn version of Fig. 5.11.4 in the same reference.

(a)

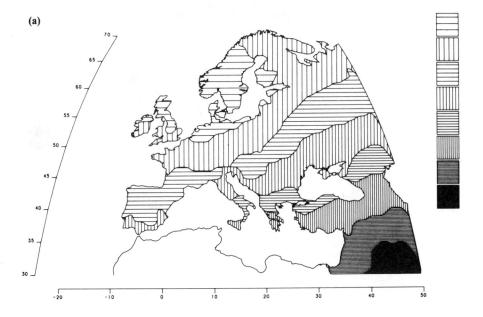

(b)

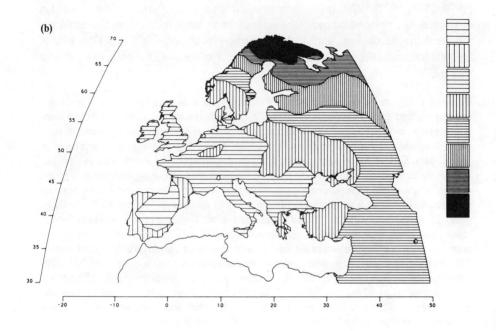

(c)

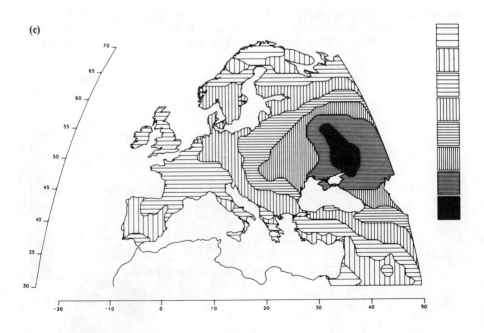

(d)

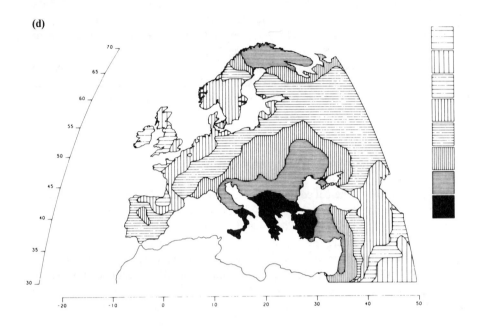

(e)

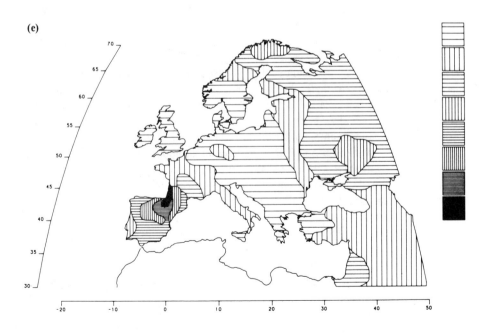

(Cavalli-Sforza et al. 1994). A preliminary analysis of the stability of the PCs has shown that the first five are well reproducible (Piazza et al. 1995). The fourth and fifth are responsible for 7.0 per cent and 5.3 per cent of the variance and are most likely to represent, respectively, Greek colonization in the first millennium BC (and earlier) (Fig. 4.1d), and the genetic "resistance" of early (palaeolithic and mesolithic) western Europeans to exogamy with later arrivals, in the Neolithic and successive periods (Fig. 4.1e). The genetic area pinpointed by the fifth PC corresponds rather precisely with the Basque-speaking area (Fig. 4.1e).

Genetic geography and chronology

What do maps of principal components tell us about dates? One cannot expect any precise contribution to chronology, only a relative one, similar to that offered by archaeological stratigraphy. It is likely that the first four European PCs are in approximate chronological order. The first is dated by archaeology and the relevant expansion, that of neolithic farmers from Southwest Asia (or more specifically Anatolia), took place between $c.9,500$ and $c.5,500$ years ago. The third appears to correspond to the Kurgan, which Gimbutas dates to the Bronze Age expansion, between $c.6,000$ and $c.3,000$ years ago. However, it is unlikely that the only expansion from this area was that which started in the early Bronze Age. It is likely that there were later expansions from the same or a similar area. There is, for instance, a reasonable basis, considering the similarity of their pastoral–nomadic cultures, for thinking that some later inhabitants of the Kurgan area in historical times, such as the Scythians (contemporary with Herodotus, $c.500$ BC), were descendants from the Bronze Age inhabitants of the same region. The Scythians were responsible for an expansion of their own towards Europe. Later descendants of the Kurgan people who also settled in Europe were the "barbarians" who were responsible for the collapse of the Roman Empire in the fifth century AD. Thus, the expansion started by the Kurgan people some 6,000 years ago may have continued until $c.1,500$ years ago and may have contributed to the considerable success of pastoral nomads emanating from the Kurgan region in partially imposing their genes on a large part of Europe. The third PC explains about one third of the variance explained by the first PC, and perhaps this ratio may give an idea of the relative magnitude of the population displacements involved. However, it is not clear, theoretically, that there should be a direct proportionality between the fraction of the population attributable to an expansion and the fraction of variance explained.

I have already mentioned that the Uralic expansion from western Siberia is likely to be responsible for the second PC. Its dates are not known, but they may well be between those of the first and third PCs. They are unlikely to violate the hypothesis that the order of PCs follows the chronological order of expansions. By contrast, the dates of the expansion associated with the fourth PC, that of the Greek colonization, are better known and cluster around 2,500 years ago, at least for the Greek colonization towards the west (to southern Italy). However, there was further migration from Greece to southern Italy in the Byzantine period, shortly after the fall of the western Roman Empire. Taking the average of the beginning and end of the expansion periods, the dates of the four expansions corresponding to the first four PCs are approximately 7,500, ?, 4,000 and 2,000 years ago. The question mark refers to the dates of the Uralic expansion, which should be intermediate between 7,500 and 4,000 if we accept the rule that the sequence of PCs respects that of time. Little is known about the movement of Uralic-language speakers from western Siberia to northeastern Europe, but the time window indicated above may well be correct.

Why should the order of PCs, which is constructed on the basis of the importance of the fractions of total variance of gene frequencies that they explain, correspond to the chronological sequence of the corresponding expansions? The simplest explanation is that, the older in time an expansion, the greater the difference in gene frequencies expected between different geographical regions and hence, as mentioned earlier, the greater the genetic impact of the expansion. This is because the major evolutionary factor responsible for such differences, random genetic drift, is greater on average the lower the population densities in the area. Evolution of modern humans has probably caused an almost regular increase over time of population size and density; hence, the older the time of an expansion, the lower the expected population density, the greater the geographical variation of gene frequencies (i.e. the greater the genetic differences among populations at the time) and the greater the variance explained by the corresponding PC. However, caution is appropriate in applying this reasoning, because results inevitably change with the area being considered in the analysis, and interpretation must take them into account. For example: the fifth PC in Europe shows a very local anomaly, in the Basque region (Fig. 4.1e). It might be expected that this should be evident in the first PC, considering that Basque settlement pre-dates any other expansion. But the Basque anomaly is not itself an expansion, at least not relative to the whole area involved in the analysis of PCs; it is rather a contraction. However, it does acquire the importance it deserves if the analysis is confined to the relevant region, i.e. the Iberian peninsula (Bertranpetit & Cavalli-Sforza 1991) where the first PC is found to refer to the contrast between the Basque and the non-Basque regions. The same remains true if we extend the analysis to France and Spain, and even if one includes Germany (Calafell & Bertranpetit 1994); in fact, the Basque "anomaly" has equal, perhaps even greater, importance in southwestern France, which shares archaeologically, culturally, linguistically and genetically the characteristics of the adjacent area of northern Spain. This Franco–Iberian region is the part of pre-neolithic Europe that most effectively shielded its culture and its genes from external influences, with partial success.

Population expansions and the spread of languages

Basque is an example showing that the persistence of languages over long periods may offer further important clues. Although languages do change, sometimes beyond recognition in a relatively short time, as we know from examples of language replacements in historical times, in major population expansions they are likely to accompany migrating peoples closely. Renfrew suggested, on this basis, that neolithic farmers leaving Anatolia spread Indo–European languages to Europe and South Asia, and he has since hypothesized that all agricultural expansions spread languages or language families that were spoken initially in the areas of origin (Renfrew 1987, 1994 and this volume). The idea that Anatolia was the area of origin of all Indo–European languages had previously been suggested by some linguists (e.g. Dolgopolsky, Gamkrelidze and Ivanov) but was heavily criticized by others (e.g. Mallory 1989). Gimbutas independently hypothesized that pastoral nomads from the Kurgan area spread Indo–European languages to Europe, and not only to Iran and the Indian subcontinent – an hypothesis that was widely accepted. Our genetic research is in agreement with her ideas, in so far as it has produced genetic evidence for an expansion from the Kurgan area. Renfrew (1987) disagreed with Gimbutas, thinking that the scanty archaeological data from the Kurgan area did not support her hypothesis of an early spread from there. However, support for her conclusions has come recently from archaeological observations and radiocarbon dates (Anthony & Brown 1991, Anthony 1994, Anthony & Vinogradov 1995).

Renfrew (1987) considered two alternatives for the origin of the Indo–Iranian branch of Indo–European languages: one first suggested by him, that it originated among farmers in Southwest Asia, and the traditional view that it originated in the Kurgan area. He seems later to have withdrawn the first hypothesis, agreeing with others that Indo–Iranian languages spread from the Asian steppes, and replaced Dravidian languages in Iran and most of India (Renfrew 1994). He did not, however, withdraw his original suggestion that Indo–European languages were spread by neolithic farmers from Anatolia to Europe. It should be noted that this hypothesis is not incompatible with Gimbutas' hypothesis. It is perfectly possible that neolithic farmers brought early Indo–European languages not only to Europe but also to southern Russia, together with agriculture, and that their descendants who developed nomadic pastoralism in the Kurgan steppes carried their languages, which were still of Indo–European origin but transformed from the original in the three or four millennia that had meanwhile elapsed. If this fusion of hypotheses from Renfrew and Gimbutas is correct, the proto-Indo–European language reconstructed by linguists on the basis of modern Indo–European languages must be much closer to that which was spoken in the Kurgan area some five or six millennia ago, than to the pre-proto-Indo–European spoken by Anatolian farmers.

There are other examples of language families or subfamilies spread by farmers, one of the most important of which is that of the Bantu languages, which originated in an area between Nigeria and Cameroon in the past 3,000 years or earlier (see references in Cavalli-Sforza et al. 1994). Another example is that of the Sino–Tibetan languages that eventually spread to all of China as a result of political pressures generated during the unification of the country in the final centuries of the first millennium BC (Mountain et al. 1992). There may have been three major centres of origin of agriculture in China (but cf. Bellwood and Glover & Higham in this volume): one in the north, one in the east-centre and one in the southwest, and they show powerful genetic and cultural effects. The northern centre was probably responsible for the spread of Sino–Tibetan languages in China, but only after it gained political power. Tibetans show greater genetic similarity with northern than with southern Chinese, and they are known historically to have originated in northern China. The genetic and linguistic co-evolution of northern Chinese and Tibetans may go back to early neo-lithic times when agriculture originated in the northern centre.

I will not try to do justice here to the expansions of pastoral nomads of the eastern Eurasian steppe, who were typically speakers of languages of the Altaic family (which includes the subfamilies Turkic, Mongolian and (usually) Tungus) and who were active mainly in central and eastern Asia, but they obviously deserve full discussion. And finally, although strictly speaking it takes us beyond the geographical scope of this volume, the pastoral–nomadic expansions that took place in Africa in the past 3,000 years invite brief comment. The Sahara was an early theatre of agricultural and pastoral developments, which were probably secondary to Southwest Asian origins. There is some archaeological indication of a very early, independent origin of cattle domestication in Libya over 8,000 years ago (Mori 1974), but biological data (Loftus et al. 1994) suggest different origins for European and Indian cattle, with most North African cattle clustering with the European group. The progressive desiccation of the Sahara, which began over 4,000 years ago, forced cultivators, and around 3,000 years ago also pastoralists, to look for less arid conditions elsewhere, essentially farther south, and African pastoralists of Saharan origin subsequently spread to most of Africa. However, there is little if any correlation between language families and the spread of pastoral nomadism south of the Sahara. African pastoralists (who are physically distinct, being tall, lean and long-limbed) belong to all three of the major African language families: Nilo–Saharan, Niger–Kordofanian and Afro–Asiatic. However, Nilo–Saharan languages are most prevalent among African pastoralists and Nilo–Saharan may be the original source of their languages.

Acknowledgements

Research by the author and colleagues referred to here was mostly done with finan-cial help from National Institutes of Health grants GM20467 and 28428. The figures are reproduced from *The history and geography of human genes* by L. Cavalli-Sforza et al. (Princeton, New Jersey: Princeton University Press, 1994); permission to repro-duce them is gratefully acknowledged. I am most grateful to Professor David Harris for invaluable editorial help.

References

Ammerman, A. J. & L. L. Cavalli-Sforza 1984. *The neolithic transition and the genetics of populations in Europe*. Princeton, New Jersey: Princeton University Press.

Anthony, D. W. 1994. The earliest horseback riders and Indo–European origins: new evidence from the steppes. In *Die Indogermanen und das Pferd*. B. Hänsel & S. Zimmer (eds), 185–95. Budapest: Archaeolingua.

Anthony, D. W. & D. R. Brown 1991. The origins of horseback riding. *Antiquity* **65**, 22–38.

Anthony, D. W. & N. B. Vinogradov 1995. Birth of the chariot. *Archaeology* **48**(2), 36–41.

Bertranpetit, J. & L. L. Cavalli-Sforza 1991. A genetic reconstruction of the history of the population of the Iberian peninsula. *Annals of Human Genetics* **55**, 51–67.

Calafell, F. & J. Bertranpetit 1994. Principal component analysis of gene frequencies and the origin of Basques. *American Journal of Physical Anthropology* **93**, 201–15.

Cavalli-Sforza, L. L. 1963. The distribution of migration distances, models and applications to genetics. In *Human displacements: measurement, methodological aspects*. J. Sutter (ed.), 139–58. Monaco: Editions Sciences Humaines, Entretiens de Monaco en Sciences Humaines.

— 1986. *African pygmies*. Orlando, Florida: Academic Press.

— 1988. The Basque population and ancient migrations in Europe. *Munibe* **6**, 129–37.

Cavalli-Sforza, L. L., P. Menozzi, A. Piazza 1993. Demic expansions and human evolution. *Science* **259**, 639–46.

— 1994. *The history and geography of human genes*. Princeton, New Jersey: Princeton University Press.

Cohen, M. N. 1977. *The food crisis in prehistory: overpopulation and the origins of agriculture*. New Haven, Connecticut: Yale University Press.

Fisher, R. A. 1937. The wave of advance of advantageous genes. *Annals of the Eugenic Society of London* **7**, 355–69.

Gadgil, M. & R. Thapar 1990. Human ecology in India: some historical perspectives. *Interdisciplinary Science Reviews* **15**, 209–23.

Gimbutas, M. 1970. Proto-Indo–European culture: the Kurgan culture during the fifth, fourth, and third millennia BC. In *Indo–European and Indo–Europeans*, G. Cardona, H. M. Hoenigswald, A. Senn (eds), 155–95. Philadelphia: University of Pennsylvania Press.

— 1973. The beginning of the Bronze Age in Europe and the Indo–Europeans 3500–2500 BC. *Journal of Indo–European Studies* **1**, 163–214.

— 1977. The first wave of Eurasian steppe pastoralists into Copper Age Europe. *Journal of Indo–European Studies* **5**, 277–338.

— 1979. The three waves of the Kurgan people into Old Europe. *Archives Suisses d'Anthropologie Générale* **43**, 113–17.

— 1980. The Kurgan wave migration (*c*.3400–3200 BC) into Europe and the following transformation of culture. *Journal of Near Eastern Studies* **8**, 273–315.

Khazanov, A. M. 1984. *Nomads and the outside world*. Cambridge: Cambridge University Press.

Loftus, R. T., E. M. David, D. G. Bradley, P. M. Sharp, P. Cunningham 1994. Evidence for two independent domestications of cattle. *Proceedings of the National Academy of Sciences of the USA* **91**, 2757–61.

Mallory, J. P. 1989. *In search of the Indo–Europeans: language, archaeology and myth*. London: Thames & Hudson.

McAlpin, D. W. 1981. Proto-Elamo–Dravidian: the evidence and its implications. *Transactions of the American Philosophical Society* **71**, 3.

Menozzi, P., A. Piazza, L. Cavalli-Sforza 1978. Synthetic maps of human gene frequencies in Europeans. *Science* **201**(4358), 786–92.

Mori, F. 1974. The earliest Saharan rock engravings. *Antiquity* **48**, 87–92.

Mountain, J. L., W. S-Y. Wang, R. Du, Y. Yida, L. L. Cavalli-Sforza 1992. Congruence of genetic and linguistic evolution in China. *Journal of Chinese Linguistics* **20**, 315–31.

Piazza, A., S. Rendine, R. Minch, P. Menozzi, J. Mountain, L. L. Cavalli-Sforza 1995. Genetics and the origin of European languages. *Proceedings of the National Academy of Sciences of the USA* **92**, 5836–40.

Rendine, S., A. Piazza, L. L. Cavalli-Sforza 1986. Simulation and separation by principal components of multiple demic expansions in Europe. *The American Naturalist* **128**, 681–706.

Renfrew, C. 1987. *Archaeology and language: the puzzle of Indo–European origins*. London: Jonathan Cape.

— 1989. The origins of Indo–European languages. *Scientific American* **261**(4), 82–90.

— 1994. World linguistic diversity. *Scientific American* **270**(1), 104–10.

Ruhlen, M. 1991. *A guide to the world's languages*, vol. 1: *classification (with postscript)*. Palo Alto, California: Stanford University Press.

Sgaramella-Zonta, L. & L. L. Cavalli-Sforza 1973. A method for the detection of a demic cline. In

Genetic structure of populations, N. E. Morton (ed.), 128–35. Honolulu: University of Hawaii Press.

Sokal, R. R., C. Wilson, N. L. Oden 1991. Genetic evidence for the spread of agriculture in Europe by demic diffusion. *Nature* **351**, 143–5.

Sokal, R. R., N. L. Oden, C. Wilson 1992. Patterns of population spread. *Nature* **355**, 214.

Zvelebil, M. 1986. Mesolithic societies and the transition to farming: problems of time, scale and organisation. In *Hunters in transition*, M. Zvelebil (ed.), 167–87. Cambridge: Cambridge University Press.

— 1989. On the transition to farming in Europe or what was spreading with the Neolithic: a reply to Ammerman. *Antiquity* **63**, 379–83.

CHAPTER FIVE

Language families and the spread of farming

Colin Renfrew

My aim in this chapter is to suggest that there is so major a correlation between the distribution of the world's language families (a concept from the field of historical linguistics) on the one hand, and that of farming dispersals (seen from the perspective of prehistoric and historic archaeology) on the other, that major reappraisals may be necessary in both of these disciplinary fields, at a global level. And if that claim is insufficiently bold, let it be added that an adequate understanding of world genetic diversity and its origins will scarcely be possible without an insight into this fundamental relationship.

It will be suggested here that farming dispersals, generally through the expansion of populations of farmers by a process of colonization or demic diffusion, are responsible for the distribution and areal extent of many of the world's language families. Other language-family distributions may be assigned to other processes: to initial colonization, to episodes of élite dominance or to late, climate-related colonization. And certainly the mechanisms of farming dispersal may vary in individual cases: processes of acculturation are involved as well as colonization. The nature of the farming economy naturally varies from place to place – in some areas, for instance, the underlying process is the spread of nomadic pastoralism with the emphasis on domesticated animals rather than plants. As the conference that gave rise to this volume very clearly showed, farming itself is not readily encapsulated within a single short definition. Moreover, there are discussions and disagreements among linguists about the appropriate classification and definition of various language families. There is thus always the risk, perhaps even the certainty, of over-simplification when formulating a broad generalization of very wide applicability. But the aim must be first to formulate the generalization in a clear manner in order to demonstrate as lucidly as possible its potential explanatory power. At the same time it must be admitted that any specific case is, in the nature of things, very much more complex in its individual circumstances. The complexity of each particular instance cannot be encapsulated within a simple, general formulation, and must be addressed with an appropriately detailed competence of local knowledge: linguistic, ecological and archaeological. Obviously a single scholar cannot possess that detailed level of knowledge in more than a very few cases, and I certainly do not claim to. But the generality is indeed worth stating, for all the over-simplification and naïveté that such a statement must entail.

In undertaking such a task it is appropriate to note that much the same insight is shared by several scholars who have already contributed in this field. Notable among them, both for the generality of his vision, and for his detailed treatment of the Austronesian case, is Peter Bellwood (1991a, 1991b, and Ch. 25 in this volume). Shnirelman (1988, 1989) and de Laubenfels (1981) have already made some of the points presented here, as has Grover Krantz (1988) for the European area, and recently Charles Higham (in press, Glover & Higham: Ch. 23 in this volume) for Southeast Asia and the Austric languages. It is appropriate also to note that some comments on an earlier formulation of this view as applied to Europe (Renfrew 1987) have developed the discussion in a positive and useful way. Sherratt & Sherratt (1988) have helped to show graphically how what might hold for Europe could apply equally to other areas of western Asia and adjacent lands. Zvelebil & Zvelebil (1988, 1990) have usefully stressed the role of the pre-existing hunter–gatherer populations in processes of farming dispersal, which are much more complex in practice than the simple application of the "wave of advance" model, first advocated by Ammerman & Cavalli-Sforza (1973), might suggest. And Christopher Ehret (1988) has made the important further point that language change or language switch can take place in hunter–gatherer communities in contact with farming communities, even though the hunter–gatherers may not themselves adopt the new and intrusive farming economy. John Robb (1991, 1993) has recently and with justice stressed the role of lineage and language extinctions in the formation of spatial patterns of surviving languages. In the field of historical linguistics Robert Austerlitz (1980) and Johanna Nichols (1992) have opened up new paths, in what one may term linguistic geography or geolinguistics, by the explicit consideration of the scale and density of language families (for instance through the calculation of genetic-unit density ratios). David Harris (1989 and Ch. 1 in this volume) and Matthew Spriggs (Ch. 27 in this volume) are among those who have shown, in the tradition of Eric Higgs among others, that the notion of farming is itself not an unproblematic one, and that horticulture and in some cases domestication can precede by many millennia the development of full-scale agro-ecosystems, with their dependence on agriculture.

When we turn to the possibilities offered by molecular genetics (Renfrew 1992a) in relation to languages and language families, it is pertinent to note the work of Cavalli-Sforza and his colleagues (Cavalli-Sforza et al. 1988, 1994), and of Langaney and his colleagues in Geneva (Excoffier et al. 1987), Torroni and his colleagues for the Americas (Torroni et al. 1992, 1993, 1994), as well as various groups who have considered the genetic as well as the linguistic and cultural diversity of the Pacific (e.g. Kirch & Green 1987, Flint et al. 1986, Hagelberg & Clegg 1993). Although much of this work has been focused upon genetic diversity in modern populations and its origins, it is anticipated that the opportunities offered by ancient DNA will increasingly come into play (Paabo 1993). The contribution to the discussion made by sophisticated statistical handling of the genetic evidence should also be acknowledged (e.g. Sokal et al. 1991, Barbujani & Pilastro 1993).

In the field of linguistic taxonomy, the non-specialist is very much at the mercy of the linguists, and here one sometimes feels the truth of the adage "*quot homines, tot sententiae*". I should certainly wish to acknowledge how much, as a neophyte in linguistic matters, I have benefited from the magisterial survey of the world's languages by Merritt Ruhlen (1987, 1991). This is greatly influenced by the studies of Joseph Greenberg, but although his classification of the African languages (Greenberg 1963) has been widely followed, that for the Americas (Greenberg 1987) created a storm of linguistic controversy (e.g. Campbell 1988). However, it should be noted that the hypothesis on language families and farming dispersals advanced here in no way rests upon the specific approach to linguistic classification advocated by Greenberg and Ruhlen. It applies with even greater force to the sometimes smaller linguistic units discussed by Voegelin & Voegelin (1977, see Austerlitz 1980). So although I am personally sympathetic to the "lumping" approach of Greenberg and Ruhlen, as well as to the Russian Nostratic school (Dolgopolsky 1923, 1987, 1993, Kaiser & Shevoroshkin 1988), I would like to stress that its assumptions do not form a basis for the present chapter. Many of the elements of the "emerging synthesis" between historical linguistics, genetics and prehistoric archaeology (Renfrew 1991: 22) are becoming clear even without these somewhat controversial innovations in linguistic taxonomy.

Language families: distribution and explanation

There are, it is generally estimated, some 5,000 different languages in the world today. Their systematic study is, of course, the subject matter of the fields of comparative and historical linguistics. For more than two centuries it has been recognized that many of the languages of the world can be grouped into language families, of which the Indo–European family was one of the first to be recognized. The Uralic family was identified even earlier. Other families of Europe or Asia and beyond, which are now widely recognized, are the Dravidian, the Afro–Asiatic (formerly "Hamito–Semitic"), the Eskimo–Aleut, the South Caucasian (Kartvelian), the North Caucasian (often divided into the Northwest Caucasian and Northeast Caucasian families) and so forth.

Inevitably, as with any classificatory enterprise, there are discussions and disagreements about where to draw appropriate borders. Thus, the Altaic family (comprising the Turkic, Mongolian and Tungus groups or families) is not universally accepted as a valid taxonomic entity (Miller 1991), whereas other linguists have, on the other hand, proposed widening it to include Japanese, Korean and Ainu. The languages of Southeast Asia have likewise proved difficult to classify (Egerod 1991). Many scholars today would recognize the Austronesian family (which includes the Polynesian languages and others) as a valid entity. And many again would link the Sinitic and Tibeto–Burman languages into a broader, more widely inclusive, Sino–Tibetan family. There is less agreement about the relationships within the family or group of families sometimes classified under the term "Austric", including the Austro–Tai and Austro–Asiatic families. This is a point further touched on below.

Along with such families of evidently related languages, there are individual languages or isolates that have proved much more difficult to classify. Basque, in Europe, is one of these, as are Burushaski and Nahali in India, Ket in central Asia, and Giulyak in Northeast Asia (see Voegelin & Voegelin 1977, Ruhlen 1987).

The languages of Africa have been classified into four major groupings by Greenberg (1963): Khoisan, Niger–Kordofanian, Nilo–Saharan and Afro–Asiatic. The Australian languages include a major language family (Pama–Nyungan) in central and southern Australia, along with a whole disparate series of families in northern Australia. They are all generally regarded as distantly related.

On the other hand, when it comes to the languages of New Guinea, it is accepted that there is an extraordinary range of linguistic diversity. The language families in question are sometimes lumped together under the name "Indo–Pacific", but whereas Greenberg, Ruhlen and the linguistic "lumpers" regard this as a valid genetic classification (i.e. would see these languages as related), other scholars regard their similarities as the result rather of convergence processes, and would accept the term "Indo–Pacific" simply as a convenient geographical designation for a language area rather than for a genetically rated taxonomic unit. Much the same is true for the Americas. Most scholars accept the validity of the Eskimo–Aleut and Na–Dene families. But whereas Greenberg (1987) would class the others into a single, very large macrofamily, "Amerind", many linguists would see the native languages of the Americas as belonging to a whole series of unrelated families (Campbell 1988). The term "Amerind" would not be accepted by them other than as a designation for a language area meaning "native language of the Americas not within the Eskimo–Aleut or Na–Dene families".

The issue of language-family density in North America and Eurasia was considered some years ago by Austerlitz (1980), who noted that language families and language isolates (which together he termed "genetic units") were more tightly packed together – in North America (and indeed in South America) than in Europe and Asia. He formulated a "genetic unit density ratio" (GUDR), which has a value of 2.95 genetic units per million square kilometres in North America as against only 0.68 for Eurasia. He saw this degree of difference as a problem requiring explanation, and offered four lines of approach:

(a) the expansion of political units (in Eurasia) involving the absorption of entire populations and hence languages and even language families
(b) the view that isolation breeds diversity: "that one GU entered the New World and, due to long and hermetic isolation, developed into two GUs in the course of time", and so on repeatedly
(c) that epidemics of gigantic proportions have wiped out vast populations (and hence languages and GUs) of the Old World
(d) that several proto-families in the Old World migrated to the New World, without leaving significant stragglers, and hence depleted the Old World of some already existing proto-families that were thus transported in toto into the New World.

In the event, Austerlitz preferred the fourth of these potential explanations, which to the present writer is the least plausible. But his formulation of the problem itself was perhaps the more important contribution and it has been taken up by Johanna Nichols in her recent volume (1992) *Linguistic diversity in space and time*. Here she proposes the useful contrasting concepts of linguistic "spread zones" and "residual zones". The Caucasus, with its well known concentration of linguistic diversity is an example of the residual zone. She notes, among other factors, the linguistic diversity and greater antiquity of the indigenous language stocks there, and the concept of the Caucasus as a linguistic refugium (Nichols 1992: 13–14).

In contrast she puts forward, as an example of a spread zone, the Eurasian steppe, dominated by a single language family, of relative shallow time-depth and with other characteristics. As she summarizes the position (Nichols 1992: 17), a spread zone may be "defined as the combination of language spread, language succession, and low genetic density over some sizable area (at least a quarter of a million square miles)." These important observations by Austerlitz and Nichols set the scene for some speculation, which leads in a direction rather different from their own.

Farming dispersal and the age-density hypothesis

Looking at the explanations offered by Austerlitz for the high GUDR in the Americas as contrasted with Eurasia, it may be suggested that with his first two explanations, (a) and (b), he came close to offering an adequate account. Indeed, his discussion lacks only one basic ingredient: a consideration of farming dispersal. His first explanation (a), is a concise statement of the process of language displacement, that one might term élite dominance (Renfrew 1989). But the expansion of political units by this process in general implies some hierarchical social structure within the societies in question of the kind present only in cultures of the later prehistoric and historic periods and not in earlier, more egalitarian communities. As I suggest below, the phenomenon of farming dispersal has been of greater general significance on most continents. I suggest that, among the cases of spread zones named by Nichols, the territories occupied by the Indo–European, the Polynesian, the Bantu and the Semitic (Afro–Asiatic) language families offer instances of farming dispersal. I have suggested elsewhere that the late Altaic language distribution and that of the Indo–Aryan branch of the Indo–European family may both be regarded as instances of élite dominance. But in general the lower GUDR for Eurasia may be explained, in large part, by the various cases of farming dispersal.

On the other hand it is interesting that the second explanation (b), offered by Austerlitz for the high density in the Americas, comes very close to that later put forward by Greenberg (1987) to account for his proposed "Amerind" macro-family: namely a very early episode of initial colonization with subsequent divergence.

Here it is possible, I think, to formulate the general hypothesis that areas with a high GUDR, and possessing the higher degree of linguistic diversity and the more limited territorial extent of language families characteristic of the "residual zones" of Nichols, are to be explained by:

(a) the very considerable lapse of time since the initial colonization of the area by the early ancestral proto-language or languages – at a date generally preceding the end of the Pleistocene period some 10,000 years ago – with the consequent opportunities for linguistic divergence; and

(b) the absence of later episodes of farming dispersal or élite dominance that would have led to the replacement of the original languages by others of more recent origin in a manner characteristic of Nichols' spread zones.

Here the north Caucasian languages, for instance, would be regarded as descendants of proto-languages spoken in that area from a very early date, before the end of the Pleistocene, and never subsequently succeeded through processes of language replacement. Much the same point can be made of the languages of New Guinea, listed in Table 5.1 as "Indo–Pacific". The inverted commas are intended to indicate that the designation here is to be seen as a geographical one, a language area, rather than as an assertion of genetic unity. The same point can be made for the native languages of Central and South America. In the present context it does not matter whether one regards these as independent language families arriving in the Americas long ago by a succession of colonizations, or as the product of divergence processes operating upon a single ancestral family over a very long period of time. The term "Amerind", expressed thus in inverted commas, may be regarded as specifically a geographical designation, designating a language area.

The languages seen below in Table 5.1 fall into these two broad classes, which can be labelled A and B. In Class A lie most of those families and groups of families that would score a high GUDR according to Austerlitz. In many cases they occupy what Nichols would term a residual zone. In Class B lie the families whose distribution is the product of more recent dispersals. These will in general score a low GUDR, and in many cases they occupy what Nichols would designate a spread zone.

The correspondence is of course not perfect. In particular the Americas contain several language families whose present distributions may well be the result of more recent dispersal processes (of Class B rather than Class A). Part of the distribution of the Uto–Aztecan languages, for instance, may be attributable to episodes of élite dominance. The distribution of the Otomanguean family, to take another example, may be the product of farming dispersal associated with the domestication of maize. And the distribution of the Algonquin languages may be the product of comparable dispersal processes. Nonetheless, the initial observation of Austerlitz seems to be a valid one, and the high GUDR for the Americas may be seen to correlate with the adherence of many of the language families of the Americas to Class A of Table 5.1. The current language distribution in the Americas is evidently the consequence of very early initial colonization processes, even if the pattern has been complicated in some areas by subsequent dispersal episodes.

The four principal processes at work (I to IV of Table 5.1) are seen illustrated by four maps in two recent articles (Renfrew 1992b, 1994). However, these do considerably over-simplify the position, as indeed does Table 5.1. But they serve to emphasize an important central point: that the explanation for the present pattern of world linguistic diversity is at once processual *and* historical. That is to say, it may be seen to be the product of general processes, intelligible to us today. But at the same time, any specific case can only be understood adequately through reference also to specific local conditions and contingencies. I suggest, therefore, that the important linguistic insights offered by Austerlitz and Nichols are well founded, but that the underlying explanation for the patterns they indicate is at once simpler and more concrete than their own. It is necessary to set the processes at work into specific historical contexts,

Table 5.1   Explaining world linguistic diversity.

The present distribution of each language family or language area is accounted for by one of the following five processes:

CLASS A: Pleistocene

I. *Initial colonization prior to 12,000 bp*
"Khoisan", "Nilo–Saharan" (plus later "aquatic" expansion), North Caucasian, South Caucasian, "Indo–Pacific" (plus later farming changes), North Australian, "Amerind", localized ancestral groups of II and II (below)

CLASS B: Post-Pleistocene

II *Farming dispersal after 10,000 bp*
Niger–Kordofanian (specifically the Bantu languages), Afro–Asiatic, Indo–European, Elamo–Dravidian, Early Altaic, Sino–Tibetan, Austronesian, Austro–Asiatic

III *Northern, climate-sensitive adjustments after 10,000 bp*
Uralic–Yukaghir, Chukchi–Kamchatkan, Na–Dene, Eskimo–Aleut

IV *Elite dominance*
Indo–Iranian, Later Altaic, Southern Sino–Tibetan (Han)

V *Long-distance maritime colonization since AD 1400*
Mainly Indo–European (English, Spanish, Portuguese, French)

for linguistic phenomena do not operate in isolation from cultural or demographic ones. It must be that linguistic changes, cultural changes and, where appropriate, genetic changes (in the molecular sense) are all aspects and consequences of concrete historical events that it should be possible to situate unequivocally in time and space. It is here that prehistoric archaeology should have significant contributions to offer. The outlines of the historical picture are only now beginning to emerge, and there are many points requiring development and perhaps correction. They depend, it is suggested here, upon relatively few demographic and social processes. The most significant of these processes, following initial colonization, is farming dispersal.

Farming dispersals

The following concise and over-simplified statement (Table 5.2) summarizing the process of farming dispersal is taken from two recent articles (Renfrew 1991, 1992a). This simple statement naturally covers very different realities in different parts of the world. One very important variable, for instance, is the relative importance of domestic animals in relation to domestic plants. In Southeast Asia it is the plants that seem of preponderant importance. But in North Africa and in parts of western Europe, domestic animals (notably sheep and goats) seem to have been part of an early dispersal, followed only later in some areas by the adoption of cereal agriculture. Likewise, in Central Asia and beyond, the development of a pastoral nomadic economy, although at all times partially reliant upon cereal cultivation, laid particular emphasis upon domesticated sheep and goats as well as horses (although the use of horses mainly for riding, and then for military purposes, may have been a much later development).

The simple formulation of Table 5.2 should be read against the discussion of the various meanings of the term "farming" and the various kinds of horticultural and agri-

Table 5.2 Farming dispersal.

A nuclear area is defined supporting initially a specific range of wild plants (and sometimes animals) that later proved amenable to domestication. The farming "package" of plants (and, where appropriate, animals), along with the appropriate exploitative techniques, becomes an expansive one dependent upon three factors:

I *Suitability for* transplantation into *new ecological niches* of the plants (and animals), when sustained with the appropriate exploitative technology by the accompanying human population, with propagation (i.e. seeding/planting or controlled breeding), protected growth (by weeding and manuring, or controlled feeding, e.g. by transhumance) and organized harvesting (or culling).

II *Increased birth rate* and reduced rate of human infant mortality, and sometimes increased postinfantile life-expectancy, associated with aspects of the new subsistence regime. These accompany the *sedentary* life that farming facilitated.

III *Greater intensity of production* as measured in terms of food (calories) per unit area, permitted by the new economy. Agricultural economies, even of a simple and non-intensive nature, are characteristically 50 times more productive in this sense than mobile hunter–gatherer economies, or have the capacity to be so.

In favourable cases the language or languages of the nuclear area are transmitted along with the plant and animal domesticates, either through demic diffusion of the farming population (the "wave of advance model"), or through adoption by local hunter–gatherer groups of the new language along with the new agricultural economy (acculturation: the "availability model"). The genetic effects of the two mechanisms are significantly different.

---

cultural systems discussed in this volume, notably by David Harris and Matthew Spriggs. It should be noted moreover that in some areas (nuclear areas in the sense of Table 5.1) the domestication of plants does not necessarily lead to an expansive agricultural system such as gives rise to a farming dispersal. Spriggs (in Ch 27 in this volume) has discussed the various stages in the transition in New Guinea from early horticulture to full-scale agro-ecosystems. This lack of expansive tendency may be in part attributable to the specific properties of the domesticated plants in question, and in part also to the characteristics of the social systems in which they were exploited.

There is, of course, no need for the emphasis here upon farming dispersals to lead to the resurgence of a new form of environmental or ecological determinism. Recent discussions of the origins of agriculture have moved away from such determinist positions, and stressed the innovative role of the societies in which farming was first developed (e.g. Cauvin 1989). Probably there are parts of Table 5.2 that could with profit be reworded to take note of that point.

It may be, also, that the important issue raised in the final paragraph of Table 5.2 requires greater emphasis. The nature of the farming dispersal depends not only upon the societies and the ecology within the original nuclear zone of farming origin in each case; it depends crucially also upon the nature of the societies and the local ecology of those areas to which farming ultimately spread (Zvelebil & Zvelebil 1988, and cf. Thomas, Zvelebil and Price in Chapters 17, 18 and 19 in this volume). These are all matters that require more careful analysis if the dispersal phenomenon is to be understood adequately in each case. And of course there is usually a long aftermath to consider, following the initial dispersal process. The linguistic pattern of today is inevitably a palimpsest, recording in various ways the sequence of processes and changes that have taken place since the crucial episode of farming dispersal. Here it may be appropriate, for heuristic reasons, to stress the decisive role of such episodes in the formation of language families. But even if that emphasis is warranted, there is very much more to be said in each specific case. Quite apart from the operation of processes of linguistic divergence and convergence, there are likely, over a long period of time, to have been local episodes of élite dominance. These may not have altered the broad structure in terms of language families. But they will have been crucial in the history of the emergence and development of individual languages.

Turning now to some specific cases, the Austronesian dispersal, one of the best documented, has been so coherently discussed by Bellwood (1985, 1987, 1989, 1991a) and by other scholars (e.g. Kirch 1986, Terrell 1988), that it does not require re-statement here. They have given good reason for thinking that the nuclear area in question was in the first instance in Southeast Asia, near Taiwan, whence the principal early maritime radiations may have taken place, with a subsequent focus in eastern Melanesia for the colonization of Polynesia. It should be noted that in Polynesia at least this was not only a farming dispersal but an initial colonization also, because the Polynesian islands are believed to have been uninhabited before the farming dispersal.

The social, economic and demographic processes underlying the dispersal of the Bantu languages have also been very thoroughly discussed, notably by Phillipson (1977, 1985a, 1985b). There seems now to be considerable agreement between the archaeological perspective and the linguistic view propounded by Greenberg in 1963.

For Southeast Asia the position is only now becoming clearer. Bellwood (1991a,b) has indicated the relationship between the Austronesian and the Austro–Tai or Daic families (basing his opinion upon linguistic work by Paul Benedict and others). In his view, comparable processes of farming dispersal would underlie the distributions of both language families. The "Austric" language phylum, in addition to the Miao–Yao languages, is sometimes defined to include the Austro–Tai and Austro–Asiatic families (Ruhlen 1991: 154; see Egerod 1991). Higham (in press) has drawn attention to the significance of recent linguistic work by Blust (1993) in which he argues for a common origin for the Austro–Asiatic and Austro–Tai families (and hence for the genetic reality of the Austric macro-family). The linguistic arguments for a single origin and expansion lead Higham and Blust to propose an origin for the Austro–Asiatic language family and for rice cultivation in the nuclear Yunnan–Burma border area, with a farming dispersal (of rice farmers) down the Brahmaputra River into eastern India (for the Munda languages within the Austro–Asiatic family), down the Mekong (for the Mon–Khmer languages of the Austro–Asiatic family), and down the Red River Valley (for the Viet languages within the Kon–Khmer group). The Austro–Tai family would, similarly, find its origin among the early rice cultivators of southern China, where the early site of Hemudu in the lower Yangzi Valley is well known to prehistorians (cf. Glover & Higham in Ch. 23 in this volume).

Higham & Thosarat (1994: ch.8; Higham in press) have described the major rivers of Southeast Asia metaphorically as being like the spokes of a wheel, with the hub in the eastern foothills of the Himalayas. Here we may make reference to the diagram devised by Sherratt & Sherratt (1988) to model what may in some ways be the analogous process of farming dispersal in western Asia.

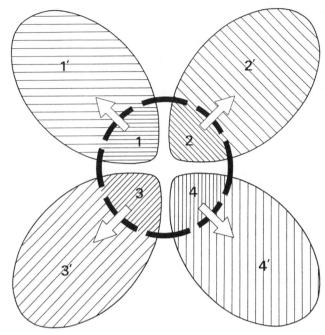

Figure 5.1
Generalized model of farming dispersal. Within the circle lies the nuclear area for farming origins, with linguistic diversity represented by the four languages, 1–4. In many cases, farming dispersal leads to rapid propagation of these languages outwards to the larger areas indicated. (From Sherratt & Sherratt 1988: 589; reproduced by permission of the authors and Antiquity Publications Ltd.)

Higham, following Blust, sees an eastward dispersal for the Yangzi farmers responsible for the dispersal of proto-Austro–Tai, and a westward dispersal for the ancestors of the Munda (of the Austro–Asiatic family). The Austric hypothesis leads Higham to think in terms of a single focus or nuclear area of rice cultivation for those speaking the proto-languages ancestral to both the Austro–Asiatic and Austro–Tai families. The new evidence for the linguistic unity of the Austric micro-family thus leads to a reformulation by Higham of the farming-dispersal hypothesis for Southeast Asia in a form that should certainly be testable through further fieldwork in that area.

The diagram, originally proposed by Sherratt & Sherratt for Southwest Asia (Fig. 5.1) has been expressed in more concrete form (Renfrew 1991: 13, fig. 5) in a map reproduced here as Figure 5.2.

As in the Southeast Asian case, a nuclear area is recognized, and here four possible episodes of farming dispersal are indicated. Dispersal 1 on the map is proposed for the origin of the Afro–Asiatic language family. There is general consensus among linguists about the validity of the family as such, but most have sought an origin for it somewhere in North Africa or in Ethiopia, although no very coherent process of dispersal has been put forward. Within the present context of discussion, a farming dispersal from western Southwest Asia is clearly a strong possibility. For there is general agreement that it is in this region that the goat and possibly the sheep exploited in North Africa, as well as wheat and barley, were domesticated (Zohary & Hopf 1988, and in this volume Garrard et al., Hole, Legge, Uerpmann, Zohary). However, it must be admitted that the real situation must be a great deal more complex than that. Cultivation of wheat and barley came later, it seems, to Saharan Africa than the exploitation of sheep and goat, and other indigenous African species also played a significant role. Indeed, it is perfectly possible, as several scholars have argued, to see indigenous African origins for farming. But that does not account for the Southwest Asian origin of sheep and goats, and then of wheat and barley.

The human genetic evidence (Excoffier et al. 1987) lends some support to the view that the population of northern Africa is to be distinguished from that of sub-Saharan Africa, and is more closely related to that of Southwest Asia. But that is not entirely the case for the people speaking languages of the Cushitic and Omotic families (within Afro–Asiatic) of the Sudan and Ethiopia. Here at any rate it would be more appropriate to think of acculturation and gene flow, involving the adoption of farming and the incoming proto-language by the pre-existing population, rather than in terms of a simple colonization process. These are proposals that have yet to be worked out in detail, using the developing archaeological record for the area in question. It is already clear that a simple "wave of advance" model is not entirely satisfactory in this case. Individual language families within the Afro–Asiatic macro-family have their own local histories, which have to be established in each instance. But at the general level, the

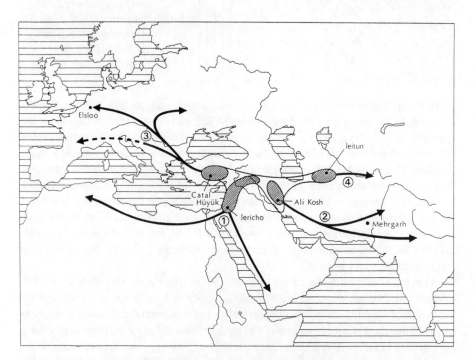

Figure 5.2   Linguistic origins and farming dispersals: a concrete example.
The hypothetical nuclear area contains the homelands of four proto-languages (shaded). It is hypothesized that farming dispersal processes led to the later distribution of the following language families: (1) Afro–Asiatic, (2) Elamo–Dravidian, (3) Indo–European, (4) Altaic. It should be noted that the hypothetical Nostratic macro-family contains all four language families and that the homeland indicated may be the homeland of proto-Nostratic around 10000 bc. (From Renfrew 1991: 13; reproduced by permission of the author and Cambridge University Press.)

very broad and continuous distribution of the Afro–Asiatic languages does require explanation. North Africa, in Nichols' terms, represents a spread zone (with a low value for the GUDR proposed by Austerlitz). A farming dispersal from Southwest Asia is a likely explanation.

The southeastern lobe of the "Near Eastern nuclear area" encompasses the ancient province of Elam. A genetic affinity between ancient Elamite and the Dravidian languages has been proposed by McAlpin (1974, 1981). It is evident, therefore, that there is a case for the dispersal of proto-Dravidian by this process, across to the Indian subcontinent. There the Dravidian languages are now found in the south (with the notable exception of Brahui in Pakistan), but most scholars see the present pattern as a consequence of the subsequent dispersal of the Indo–Iranian branch of Indo–European entering the subcontinent from the north during a later prehistoric period.

In this context the important early farming site of Mehrgarh in northwestern Pakistan is of crucial significance, offering as it does the earliest evidence for cereal cultivation on the subcontinent (Jarrige 1980). Glover & Higham (in Ch. 23 in this volume) have discussed the later inception of rice cultivation, which as Higham (in press) has indicated may be related to the arrival in the subcontinent of the first speakers of Munda or proto-Munda languages in a subsequent farming dispersal from the nuclear areas of rice cultivation in Southeast Asia. It is significant, therefore, that, while stressing various indigenous aspects of development in the subcontinent, Richard Meadow agreed, in discussion at the conference that gave rise to this book, that the earliest cereal cultivation at Mehrgarh represents the importation of domesticates from Southwest Asia, a point confirmed in discussion by Zohary (see Meadow in Ch. 22 in this volume; and Zohary & Hopf 1988). The earliest domesticated goats there are also introduced from outside. As Zohary emphasized, the presence of local varieties of cereal crops need not be taken as evidence for the local domestication of these species in the first place, because every region has its own local varieties. That the earliest domesticates at Mehrgarh were imported from western Asia does not, of course, entail that the early population there spoke a proto-Elamo–Dravidian language dispersed from the same nuclear area. But the possibility is there, and the hypothesis would certainly offer an explanation for the affinities between Elamite and the Dravidian languages noted by McAlpin.

One aspect of the Dravidian situation does, however, give pause for thought. There are now several communities in southern India composed not of farmers but of hunter–gatherers, and there were certainly more in earlier times. The farming-dispersal hypothesis clearly loses ground somewhat if farming practices were not in fact consistently dispersed. But as noted earlier, Ehret (1988) has made the important point that hunter–gatherers sometimes adopt an incoming language without switching to the incoming subsistence strategy. There is also the possibility that in some cases farmers and cultivators may have reverted later to a hunter–gatherer economy. It is not clear at present whether either explanation is satisfactory for southern India and Sri Lanka, and the Elamo–Dravidian farming-dispersal hypothesis cannot yet be considered to be well established.

There are uncertainties also about the early origins of the Altaic speakers of Central Asia (Miller 1991), hypothetically represented as dispersal 4 on Figure 5.2. The languages in question are within the Turkic and also the Mongolian families of Altaic: it is less clear how the Tungus families in eastern Asia (often also grouped in the Altaic macro-family) would be relevant. The Turkic and Mongolian peoples are strongly associated with nomadic pastoralism. And it seems perfectly reasonable to suggest that one focus for the development of a nomadic pastoral economy would be within what is now Turkmenistan and Khazakstan (Masson & Sarianidi 1972). The very early existence of farming sites such as Jeitun is well known (see Harris & Gosden in Ch. 21 in this volume). That there should have been a subsequent and independent origin of nomadic pastoralism in that region, firmly rooted in that early farming background, seems entirely reasonable. It would have taken place at perhaps the same time as the comparable process in the Ukraine, itself rooted in the early farming Tripolye culture and its offshoots. The case for the Turkmenian origins of proto-Altaic remains to be made in detail, but the suggestion seems plausible.

The case for a farming dispersal for proto-Indo–European (Renfrew 1987) has already been quite widely discussed, and widely accepted at least among archaeologists for southeastern Europe, the Balkans and the Danube (Dolukhanov 1994). As Zvelebil & Zvelebil have pointed out (1988, 1990), the matter becomes more complicated in northern and western Europe. Here it seems pertinent to refer to the recent paper by Zilhão (1993) on the spread of agro–pastoral economies in Mediterranean · Europe. His figure 10 is reproduced here as Figure 5.3.

Zilhão shows clearly how the "wave of advance" model for the spread of farming is not applicable to Iberia (cf. Cavalli-Sforza in Ch. 4 in this volume). But this does not lead him to adopt instead the "availability" acculturation model propounded by Zvelebil & Rowley-Conwy (1986). For him the early farmers on the west coast of Iberia are still colonists, and it is fair to assume that they will have brought their own language with them. The pattern he proposes is thus of a primary area located in Greece, the Balkans and southern Italy, from which a first pulse took settler groups along the Danube (open circles) and to the west Mediterranean shores (Cardial sites: black circles) and as far as the west Iberian coast. "A second pulse, after 6000–5500 BP, took agro-pastoral economies to northern Iberia, western France, the Low Countries, the British Isles and Scandinavia, probably through adoption of the new system by the local hunter–gatherer groups" – the region in question being indicated outside the broken line (Zilhão 1993: 51). This is a good example of the sort of second-order elaboration to be expected when any simple model (such as the "wave of advance" model for farming and language dispersal) is applied to the specific circumstances of a local region.

The alternative and still quite widely argued view is the "Kurgan" hypothesis of Gimbutas (see Mallory 1989, and Cavalli-Sforza in Ch. 4 in this volume), which rests for its processual impetus upon the early domestication of the horse in the Ukraine (which is well attested) and its use by invading mounted nomadic pastoralists (which is not well attested at all). During the conference that gave rise to this book, I found it helpful to discuss the issue of horse domestication with Hans-Peter Uerpmann. He has shown clearly (Uerpmann 1990) that there were wild populations of the horse in western Europe from the end of the Pleistocene. Moreover, he has argued for a local domestication of the horse not only in Iberia but more widely in western Europe, so that the domesticated horses at such Beaker sites as Roucadour Level A1 and New-

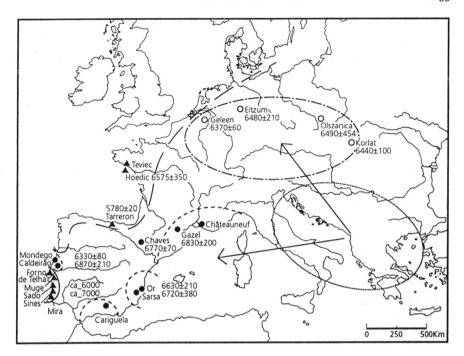

Figure 5.3 The Neolithization of central and western Europe, as outlined by Zilhão (1993: 51). This may be seen as an instance of farming dispersal, responsible for the introduction of proto-Indo–European into the areas indicated. (Reproduced by permission of the author and Sheffield Academic Press.)

grange would be of west European, not Ukrainian, origin. This, perhaps unsurprisingly, seems to undermine the basic motivating force of the "Kurgan" theory as it applies to central and western Europe.

But there is in any case absolutely no evidence that the horse was actually ridden for military purposes *anywhere* before about 1500 BC. Even the early domesticated horses of the Ukraine may have been too small to have been of military significance. Certainly we see depictions of horses quite widely in the second millennium BC, but nearly always pulling chariots. It seems clear that, throughout Europe and Southwest Asia, war chariots preceded mounted horsemen as a military resource. This is also very clear for North India and Pakistan in the Hymns of the Rig Veda, where the "steeds" in question are nearly always pulling chariots. Barnes indicates (1993: 157) that the earliest evidence for horse-riding in China comes from the early Zhou period (around 1000 BC), and that the first evidence there for horse riding in warfare, superseding chariot use among the eastern nomads, is not documented until 484 BC.

This is not the place for an extended discussion of the Indo–European question. But it seems likely that the development of a nomadic pastoralist economy did indeed begin early in the Ukraine, as Anthony (1986) and others have suggested. However, initially it was not based to any significant extent upon horse riding. In the initial phase the horse was a food resource, like other domestic animals (Levine 1990). This does not exclude the possibility that horses were used as beasts of burden, or even ridden as pack animals as other small equids (notably donkeys) are in various areas today. It was in this phase that the Indo–European colonization of the Iranian plateau will have begun. North India may also have been colonized at this early time, well before the development of the "heroic" society (with horse-drawn chariots) described in the Rig Veda. Mounted warfare was a phenomenon that made its appearance in the first millennium BC, and it is relevant only to the development of "heroic" Iron Age societies in Europe, not to earlier phases.

This aside on the domestication of the horse and its uses, although it does not take us beyond the scope of the book as a whole, does go beyond that of the present chapter. The main point to be made here is that farming dispersal remains the primary candidate for the original introduction of proto-Indo–European into Europe, although several millennia of subsequent processes and historical episodes will have brought a considerable degree of complexity to elaborate the primary processes, which, as Zilhão indicates, were themselves sufficiently complex.

Two further points need to be made about farming dispersals. As we have seen from the New Guinea case, farming economies were not necessarily highly expansive. The language families of the Americas remain to be considered from this point of view. Evidently the initial colonization of the Americas took place during the Pleistocene period. Taken together, the native languages of the Americas (excluding the Na–Dene and Eskimo–Aleut languages) belong to Class A of Table 5.1. But to say this (whether one regards "Amerind" as representing merely a language area, or as a genetic unity as Greenberg has argued) does not deny that individual language families (and the Uto–Aztecan, Otomangnean and Algonquin were mentioned earlier) may owe their current distributions to subsequent dispersal processes. I am not in a position to make that case at present, but there is no doubt that it remains to be made. A comparable observation may be offered for the Nilo–Saharan language family. Although I have placed it here within Class A, arguments have been put forward (not reviewed here) to see the current distribution of the Nilo–Saharan languages as a further case of farming dispersal (Bellwood 1991b).

The second point relates to the puzzling uniformity of the Pama–Nyungan language family of the hunter–gatherers of central and southern Australia (Dixon 1980). Linguists are agreed that these languages are closely related. Indeed, central and southern Australia look linguistically more like one of Nichols' spread zones of Class B than a residual zone (a term more appropriately applicable to northern Australia). Whether the uniformity observed is best explained by a dispersal process, or perhaps by one of convergence as R. W. Dixon (pers. comm.) has suggested, will be a matter for future consideration. But it reminds us that such areas of uniformity can arise among hunter–gatherers. They are not a property reserved exclusively to farmers and their successors.

These significant complexities should not, however, be allowed to obscure the basic coherence and, at a first-order level, simplicity of the hypothesis linking farming dispersals and language families. The very considerable scale of the geographical area occupied by some of these language families deserves to be stressed. And, although it may well be possible to offer explanations for the particularities of individual families and their distributions in terms of local episodes of élite dominance or other historical contingencies, for whole language families, as Bellwood has stressed (this volume), such special explanations are hardly adequate. Processes of real ecological, demographic and social significance must underlie the formation and distribution of the world's major language families. In many cases, the profound changes brought about by the dispersal of farming systems from the areas of their inception are the only ones of sufficient scope to explain the consequences.

The genetic dimension

Modern molecular genetics offers a series of increasingly powerful and precise techniques for investigating questions of descent and of migrations of human populations. In many cases they should therefore be able to offer valid insights into the hypotheses offered by archaeologists and by historical linguists about early processes and events. But the converse is also true. If it is indeed the case that farming dispersals have played a major role in determining the distributions of language families, and if these distributions were to a significant extent established by processes of human colonization, migration or demic diffusion, then it is clear that a population history that ignores these processes is bound to be an inadequate one. This, to my mind, is a defect of several recent attempts to show good correlation between linguistic groups and molecular genetics on a world scale. The claim has sometimes been made (e.g. Cavalli-Sforza et al. 1988, Cavalli-Sforza 1991) that such comparisons show the basic comparability of the processes of linguistic and genetic evolution. But the correlations in patterning arising from a series of dispersals in relatively recent times (broadly those indicated in Class B of Table 5.1 here) are not at all the same as those that genuinely result from long-term co-evolution in relative geographical isolation (i.e. those indicated in Class A of Table 5.1).

Not surprisingly, the main thrust of much molecular genetic work has been directed towards understanding the origins of our own species, *Homo sapiens*. Here the widely held "out of Africa" view (which maintains that all modern humans derive from African ancestors of the species *Homo erectus*) may be contrasted with the "multi-regional evolution" position that sees *Homo erectus* ancestors in different parts of the world making a contribution (notably Southeast Asia as well as Africa). It is not the purpose here to discuss this issue, other than to note the initial support offered to African genesis by work on mitochondrial DNA (Cann et al. 1987). Although the computational methods by which they constructed their phylogenetic trees have been criticized, the overall conclusion – the exclusively African origins of *Homo sapiens* – is shared by the majority of workers using data also from nuclear DNA and from classical genetic markers. But it is pertinent to note that even here there are interpretational differences. Nei & Roychoudhury (1993), although agreeing the African origin (and thus the first split in the tree between African populations and others), see the second split as separating "Caucasian" (i.e. European, Southwest Asian and North African) populations from all other non-African populations. This differs from the descent tree constructed by Cavalli-Sforza and his colleagues (1988), where after the first African/non-African split, the second major split of populations separates the North Eurasian supercluster (Caucasians, Northeast Asians, Amerindians) from the Southeast Asian supercluster (Southeast Asians, Australians, Papua New Guineans and Pacific Islanders). But it is pertinent to note that Langaney and his colleagues in Geneva take a different view (Langaney et al. 1992, Excoffier & Langaney 1989), arguing that caucasoid populations could be the closest to an ancestral population from which all other continental groups would have diverged. Sanchez-Mazas & Langaney (1988) use classical blood-group systems to reach similar conclusions. The molecular genetic evidence does not yet speak with one voice on this fundamental issue.

But even in this debate there is the risk, I suspect, that modern populations, whose location is in fact the product of relatively recent dispersals, are being taken to represent the product of very early initial colonizations. For example, Sanchez-Mazas & Langaney (1988: 161) note: "Of particular interest are the genetic profiles observed in East Africa which are closer to Europeans". If farming dispersals are ignored, this observation could indeed be taken as evidence for affinity between African and European populations, and hence as militating against the "first split" in a phylogenetic tree between African and non-African populations. But if, as suggested here, the current distribution of the Afro–Asiatic languages is the result of a later farming dispersal from Southwest Asia, any Southwest Asian or European genetic affinities for those groups in East Africa that speak Afro–Asiatic languages could be seen in a very different light. Great care must be taken to avoid argumental circularities. The choice of populations undertaken to reflect the initial colonization of the globe must not ignore the evidence for much later farming dispersals.

At first sight, the evidence from molecular genetics bearing upon farming dispersals and the distribution of language families is very encouraging. Cavalli-Sforza (1988, 1991) has drawn attention to the high frequency of the rhesus-negative zone in the Basque country in just that area where the Basque language survives at the centre of a wider distribution of Basque toponyms (Cavalli-Sforza, L. & F. 1993: 340). This lends general support to the Indo–European / farming-dispersal hypothesis argued again here, because the high rhesus-negative gene frequency and the (non-Indo–European) Basque language would both be seen as relics of the early, pre-Indo–European population of Europe that was effectively swamped, genetically and linguistically, in the farming dispersal process. But although this argument has an appealing plausibility, it lacks certain connecting links. It is not made clear why the rhesus-negative blood group should show so marked an effect, where so many other genetic markers do not (Cavalli-Sforza et al. 1994). If we knew from other sources that the native, pre-Indo–Europeans had a high rhesus-negative gene frequency, and the incoming proto-Indo–European farmers a low one, this would indeed be impressive. But we do not have that independent evidence.

The most intensive discussion of the farming-dispersal hypothesis has centred upon the analysis of gene-frequency distribution maps for Europe as a whole, which have been analyzed statistically by a variety of techniques. The map illustrated here (Fig. 5.4) represents the first principal component (reflecting 28.1% of the total genetic variation) from the study undertaken by Cavalli-Sforza et al. (1993; see also Cavalli-Sforza in Ch. 4 in this volume). Analysis by Sokal et al. (1991) gives strong

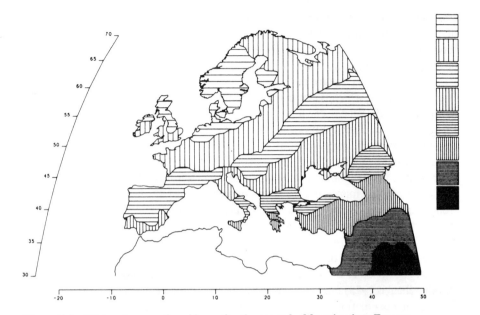

Figure 5.4 Molecular genetic evidence for the spread of farming into Europe.
The map illustrates the first principal component (PC) of molecular genetic variation in Europe,
suggesting demic diffusion from Anatolia, probably associated with the spread of farming. The
range between the maximum and minimum values of the PC has been divided into eight equal
classes, which are indicated by different intensities of shading. The direction of increase of PC
values is arbitrary. (From Cavalli-Sforza et al. 1994: 292; reproduced by permission of the
authors and Princeton University Press.)

confirmation that the gene-frequency cline is indeed the product of the farming dispersal at the beginning of the neolithic period. But they have pointed out that this does
not, in itself, demonstrate that this was the time when the proto-Indo–European language first came to Europe. It is logically possible that this was the result of a different
and later migratory process, as Gimbutas would argue (Mallory 1989). In a more comprehensive series of analyses Sokal et al. (1992) were unable to find clear evidence
to support the association of the Indo–European languages either with a hypothetical
Kurgan invasion or with the early neolithic farming dispersal.

At the same time, however, the very strong molecular-genetic support given to the
farming-dispersal hypothesis itself is significant. It suggests that the criticisms of
Zvelebil & Zvelebil (1988, see also Zvelebil & Rowley-Conwy 1986), although
rightly (in my view) stressing the role of the local populations, especially in northern
and western Europe (see Fig. 5.3 above), do not call into question the reality of this
process in southeastern and central Europe and along the Danube, as well as in the
central Mediterranean region. And although it is certainly possible in theory that these
first farmers spoke some entirely different (presumably Anatolian) language, there is
no trace – or at least none has been indicated – of such a language today. Already the
picture is sufficiently complex, with a pre-Indo–European stratum (represented by
Basque and perhaps Etruscan) followed by early Indo–European with the first farm-

ers, and then quite possibly by proto-Slavic languages in eastern Europe at the time of the supposed Kurgan incursions. The molecular-genetic evidence thus gives comfort and support to the farming-dispersal view propounded here, but it does not unequivocally demonstrate it.

Much the same is true for the statistical testing, using classical genetic data, of the larger hypothesis, which is summarized graphically in Figures 5.1 and 5.2. Barbujani & Pilastro (1993) have considered the hypothesis that the populations speaking Elamo–Dravidian, Indo–European, Altaic and Afro–Asiatic languages originated from a unified founding population in the nuclear area, as the farming-dispersal hypothesis would predict. They found support for the hypothesis in the first three regions, but insufficient data were available from North Africa to give a conclusive result there for the fourth. In this, as in some other cases, the lack of enough samples from living populations places a serious restriction upon the work. It is hoped that, through the initiative of the Human Genome Diversity Project, more adequate samples will in due course become available, so that such analyses can be carried out using a more comprehensive dataset.

It is to be hoped also that one day the extraction of ancient DNA from early human remains (Paabo 1993) may give a direct insight into the genetic particularities of the first farming populations in this area and in others, and hence will contribute directly to the discussion. It is encouraging to note that early human material in the Pacific is already being used to illuminate early population questions there (Hagelberg & Clegg 1993), although here too the interpretation is not immediately easy.

It is perhaps in the Americas that molecular genetic evidence has been giving the clearest answers to longstanding archaeological problems. Recent work on mitochondrial DNA from native American populations has indicated that all the native Americans sampled clustered into one of four distinct lineages. Only one of these was found in Na–Dene speaking populations, but all four in the Amerind ones (Torroni et al. 1992, 1993, 1994). On the face of it, this of course, lends very strong support to the Greenberg three-wave hypothesis mentioned earlier (Greenberg 1987). Moreover, much of the variation was "tribal specific", leading to the conclusion that the process of tribal formation began early in the history of the Amerind populations, with relatively little intertribal genetic exchange occurring subsequently. Indeed, the patterning in the data actually permits a clear distinction to be made among the different tribes studied in southern Mexico, and although conforming in general to the linguistic family relationships proposed by Greenberg, went on in some cases to question particular aspects of his classification. These results at present offer the most elegant application of the techniques of molecular genetics to the problems of historical linguistics.

It should be noted, however, that the time depth involved is frequently greater than for farming dispersals, where the time depth is restricted to about 10,000 years. This is one reason why these techniques may prove difficult to apply effectively to the processes discussed here. Another is that farming dispersals inevitably produce mixing and a significant degree of gene flow. The sort of clear-cut results and patterns now coming from studies of mitochondrial DNA in the Americas are facilitated by isolation and by a very restricted gene flow between groups and communities.

Despite this cautionary note, there is no doubt that genetic and linguistic data can, in favourable circumstances, be brought to bear effectively upon each other, and upon questions of prehistoric dispersal and demography. There is the very real hope that some of the issues raised in the present chapter, and some of the hypotheses outlined, will be clarified over the next decade or so by the progress of molecular genetics. Moreover, through the use of the polymerase chain reaction, these techniques may soon be applied to ancient human material and hence be brought to bear more directly upon a variety of problems in prehistory.

References

Ammerman, A. J. & L. Cavalli-Sforza 1973. A population model for the diffusion of early farming in Europe. In *The explanation of culture change: models in prehistory*, C. Renfrew (ed.), 335–58. London: Duckworth.

Anthony, D. W. 1986. The "Kurgan culture", a reconsideration. *Current Anthropology* 27, 291–313.

Austerlitz, R. 1980. Language-family density in North America and Eurasia. *Ural-Altaische Jahrbücher* 52, 1–10.

Barbujani, G. & A. Pilastro 1993. Genetic evidence on origin and dispersal of human populations speaking languages of the Nostratic macrofamily. *Proceedings of the National Academy of Sciences of the USA* 90, 4670–3.

Barnes, G. L. 1993. *China, Korea and Japan: the rise of civilisation in East Asia*. London: Thames & Hudson.

Bellwood, P. 1985. *Prehistory of the Indo–Malaysian archipelago*. New York: Academic Press.

— 1987. *The Polynesians*, 2nd edn. London: Thames & Hudson.

— 1989. The colonization of the Pacific, some current hypotheses. In *The colonisation of the Pacific, a genetic trail*, A. V. S. Hill & S. W. Serjeantson (eds), 1–58. Oxford: Oxford University Press.

— 1991a. The Austronesian dispersal and the origins of languages. *Scientific American* 265, 88–93.

— 1991b. Prehistoric cultural explanations for widespread language families. Paper presented to the conference "Archaeology and linguistics: understanding ancient Australia", Darwin, 8–12 July.

Blust, R. 1993. Beyond the Austronesian homeland: the Austric hypothesis and its implications for archaeology. Paper read at a meeting on Austronesian languages at the University Museum, University of Pennsylvania, Philadelphia, November 1993.

Campbell, L. 1988. Review of J. H. Greenberg, *Language in the Americas* (Stanford: Stanford University Press, 1987). *Language* 64, 591–615.

Cann, R. L., M. Stoneking, A. C. Wilson 1987. Mitochondrial DNA and human evolution. *Nature* 325, 31–6.

Cauvin, J. 1989. La néolithisation au Levant et sa première diffusion. In *Néolithisations, Proche et Moyen Orient, Méditerranée orientale, Nord de l'Afrique, Europe méridionale, Chine, Amerique du Sud*, O. Aurenche & J. Cauvin (eds), 1–36. Oxford: British Archaeological Reports, International Series 516.

Cavalli-Sforza, L. L. 1988. The Basque population and ancient migrations in Europe. *Munibe (Antropologia y Arquelogia) Supplemento* 6 (San Sebastian), 129–37.

— 1991. Genes, populations and languages. *Scientific American* 265, 72–8.

Cavalli-Sforza, L. & F. Cavalli-Sforza 1993. *Chi siamo, la storia della diversità umana*. Milano: Mondadori.

Cavalli-Sforza. L. L., A. Piazza, P. Menozzi, J. Mountain 1988. Reconstruction of human evolution: bringing together genetic, archaeological and linguistic data. *Proceedings of the National Academy of Sciences of the USA* 85, 6002–6.

Cavalli-Sforza, L. L., P. Menozzi, A. Piazza 1993. Demic expansions and human evolution. *Science*

259, 639–46.

Cavalli-Sforza, L. L., A. Piazza, P. Menozzi 1994. *The history and geography of human genes*. Princeton, New Jersey: Princeton University Press.

de Laubenfels, D. J. 1981. Ethnic geography of the neolithic. *Mankind Quarterly* 1981, **22**, 119–43.

Dixon, R. M. W. 1980. *The languages of Australia*. Cambridge: Cambridge University Press.

Dolgopolsky, A. B. 1973. Boreisch – Ursprache Eurasiens? *Ideen des Exacten Wissens, Wissenschaft und Technik in der Sowietunion* **73**, 19–30.

— 1987. The Indo–European homeland and lexical contacts of proto-Indo–European with other languages. *Mediterranean Language Review* **3**, 7–31.

— 1993. More about the Indo–European homeland problem. *Mediterranean Language Review* **6**, 230–48.

Dolukhanov, P. 1994. *Environment and ethnicity in the ancient Middle East*. Aldershot, England: Avebury.

Egerod, S. 1991. Far Eastern languages. In *Sprung from some common source: investigations into the prehistory of languages*, S. M. Lamb & E. D. Mitchell (eds), 205–31. Stanford, California: Stanford University Press.

Ehret, C. 1988. Language change and the material correlates of language and ethnic shift. *Antiquity* **62**, 564–73.

Excoffier, L. & A. Langaney 1989. Origin and differentiation of human mitochondrial DNA. *American Journal of Human Genetics* **44**, 73–85.

Excoffier, L., B. Pellegrini, A. Sanchez-Mazas, C. Simon, L. Langaney 1987. Genetics and the history of sub-Saharan Africa. *Yearbook of Physical Anthropology* **30**, 151–94.

Flint, J., A. V. S. Hill, D. K. Bowden, S. J. Oppenheimer, P. R. Sill, S. W. Serjeantson, J. Bana-Koiri, M. P. Bhatia Alpers, A. J. Boyce, D. J. Weatherall, J. B. Clegg 1986. High frequencies of α-thalassaemia are the result of natural selection by malaria. *Nature* **321**, 744–9.

Greenberg, J. H. 1963. *The languages of Africa*. Bloomington: Indiana University Press.

— 1987. *Languages in the Americas*. Stanford: Stanford University Press.

Hagelberg, E. & J. B. Clegg 1993. Genetic polymorphism in prehistoric Pacific islanders determined by analysis of ancient bone DNA. *Proceedings of the Royal Society of London B* **252**, 163–70.

Harris, D. R. 1989. An evolutionary continuum of people–plant interaction. In *Foraging and farming: the evolution of plant exploitation*, D. R. Harris & G. C. Hillman (eds), 11–26. London: Unwin Hyman.

Higham, C. F. W. in press. Archaeology and linguistics in Southeast Asia; implications of the Austric hypothesis. Paper delivered to the Indo–Pacific Prehistory Conference, Chiang Mai, Thailand, January 1994.

Higham, C. F. W. & R. Thosarat 1994. *Khok Phanom Di, a cemetery of early rice cultivators in Thailand*. Fort Worth, Texas: Harcourt, Brace, Jovanovich.

Jarrige, J-F. 1980. The antecedents of civilisation in the Indus Valley. *Scientific American* **243**, 122–33.

Kaiser, M. & V. Shevoroshkin 1988. Nostratic. *Annual Review of Anthropology* **17**, 309–29.

Kirch, P. V. 1986. Rethinking East Polynesian prehistory. *Journal of the Polynesian Society* **95**, 9–40.

Kirch, P. V. & R. C. Green 1987. History, phylogeny and evolution in Polynesia. *Current Anthropology* **28**, 431–6.

Krantz, G. S. 1988. *Geographical development of European languages*. Bern: Peter Lang.

Langaney, A., D. Roessli, N. Hubert van Blyenburgh, P. Dard 1992. Do most human populations descend from phylogenetic trees? *Human Evolution* **7**, 47–61.

Levine, M. A. 1990. Dereivka and the problem of horse domestication. *Antiquity* **64**, 727–40.

McAlpin, D. W. 1974. Towards Proto-Elamo–Dravidian. *Language* **50**, 89–101.

— 1981. Proto-Elamo–Dravidian: the evidence and its implications. Philadelphia, *Transactions of the American Philosophical Society* **71**(3), 3–155.

Mallory, J. P. 1989. *In search of the Indo–Europeans: language, archaeology and myth*. London: Thames & Hudson.

Masson, V. M. & V. I. Sarianidi 1972. *Central Asia: Turkmenia before the Achaemenids*. London: Thames & Hudson.

Miller, R. A. 1991. Connections among the Altaic languages. In *Sprung from some common source*, *investigations into the prehistory of languages*, S. M. Lamb & E. D. Mitchell (eds), 293–327. Stanford: Stanford University Press.

Nei, M. & A. K. Roychoudhury 1993. Evolutionary relationships of human populations on a global scale. *Molecular Biology and Evolution* **10**, 927–43.

Nichols, J. 1992. *Language diversity in space and time*. Chicago: University of Chicago Press.

Paabo, S. 1993. Ancient DNA. *Scientific American* **269**, 60–6.

Phillipson, D. W. 1977. The spread of the Bantu languages. *Scientific American* **236**, 106–14.

— 1985a. *African Archaeology*. Cambridge: Cambridge University Press.

— 1985b. An archaeological reconsideration of Bantu expansion. *MUNTU* **2**, 69–84.

Renfrew, C. 1987. *Archaeology and language, the puzzle of Indo–European origins*. London: Jonathan Cape.

— 1989. Models of change in language and archaeology. *Transactions of the Philological Society* **87**, 103–55.

— 1991. Before Babel: speculations on the origins of linguistic diversity. *Cambridge Archaeological Journal* **1**, 3–23.

— 1992a. Archaeology, genetics and linguistic diversity. *Man* **27**, 445–78.

— 1992b. World languages and human dispersals: a minimalist view. In *Transition to modernity, essays on power, wealth and belief*. J. A. Hall & I. C. Jarvie (eds), 11–68. Cambridge: Cambridge University Press.

— 1994. World linguistic diversity. *Scientific American* **270**(1), 104–10.

Robb, J. 1991. Random causes with directed results: the Indo–European spread and the stochastic loss of lineages. *Antiquity* **65**, 287–91.

— 1993. A social prehistory of European languages. *Antiquity* **67**, 747–60.

Ruhlen, M. 1987. *A guide to the world's languages*, vol. I. Stanford: Stanford University Press.

— 1991. *A guide to the world's languages*, vol I: *Classification (with Postscript)*. Stanford: Stanford University Press.

Sanchez-Mazas, A. & A. Langaney 1988. Common genetic pools between human populations. *Human Genetics* **78**, 161–6.

Sherratt, A. & S. Sherratt 1988. The archaeology of Indo–European: an alternative view. *Antiquity* **62**, 584–95.

Shnirelman, V. A. 1988. Historical linguistics through the eyes of the non-linguist. Paper presented to the Conference "Language and Prehistory", University of Michigan, November 1988.

— 1989. *Vozniknovenie proizvodjasoego xozjaistva [The emergence of a food-producing economy]*. Moskow: Nauka.

Sokal, R. R., N. L. Oden, C. Wilson 1991. New genetic evidence supports the origin of agriculture in Europe by demic diffusion. *Nature* **351**, 143–4.

Sokal, R. R., N. L. Oden, B. Thomson 1992. Origins of the Indo–Europeans: genetic evidence. *Proceedings of the National Academy of Sciences of the USA* **89**, 7669–73.

Terrell, J. 1988. *Prehistory in the Pacific Islands*. Cambridge: Cambridge University Press.

Torroni, A., T. G. Schurr, C-C. Yang, E. J. E. S'athmary, R. C. Williams, M. S. Schanfield, G. A. Troup, W. C. Knowler, D. N. Lawrence, K. M. Weiss, D. C. Wallace 1992. Native American mitochondrial DNA analysis indicates that the Amerind and the Na–Dene populations were founded by two independent migrations. *Genetics* **130**, 153–62.

Torroni, A., T. G. Schurr, M. F. Cabell, M. D. Brown, J. V. Neel, M. Larsen, D. G. Smith, C. M. Vullo, D. C. Wallace 1993. Asian affinities and continental radiation of the four founding native American mtDNAs. *American Journal of Human Genetics* **53**, 563–90.

Torroni, A., Y-S. Chen, O. Semino, A. S. Santachiara-Beneceretti, C. R. Scott, M. T. Lott, M. Winter, D. C. Wallace 1994. Mitochondrial DNA and Y-chromosome polymorphisms in four native American populations from southern Mexico. *American Journal of Human Genetics* **54**, 303–18.

Uerpmann, H-P. 1980. Die Domestikation des Pferdes im Chalkolitikum West- und Mitteleuropas. *Madider Mitteilungen* **31**, 109–42.

Voegelin, C. F. & F. M. Voegelin 1977. *Classification and index of the world's languages*. New York: Elsevier.

Zilhão, J. 1993. The spread of agro–pastoral economies across Mediterranean Europe: a view from the far west. *Journal of Mediterranean Archaeology* **6**, 5–63.

Zohary, D. & M. Hopf 1988. *Domestication of plants in the Old World: the origin and spread of cultivated plants in West Asia, Europe, and the Nile Valley*. Oxford: Oxford University Press.

Zvelebil, M. & P. Rowley-Conwy 1986. Foragers and farmers in Atlantic Europe. In *Hunters in transition*, M. Zevelebil (ed.), 67–93. Cambridge: Cambridge University Press,

Zvelebil, M. & K. V. Zvelebil 1988. Agricultural transition and Indo–European dispersals. *Antiquity* **62**, 574–83.

— 1990. Agricultural transition, "Indo–European origins", and the spread of farming. In *When worlds collide: the Bellagio papers*, T. L. Markey & J. A. C. Greppin (eds), 237–66. Ann Arbor: Karoma.

CHAPTER SIX

Tracking early crops and early farmers: the potential of biomolecular archaeology

Martin Jones, Terry Brown, Robin Allaby

The ecology of agricultural spread

The two notable aspects of agriculture that have continuously engaged archaeological attention are the lateness of its appearance and the rapidity of its spread. We have often hoped within archaeology that the key to agriculture's remarkable history could be revealed in that first appearance, where its potentiality for rapid spread could be found in embryonic form. There has been a shift in the emphasis of recent research – which was reflected in the balance of papers given at the conference that gave rise to this book – from the nature of agriculture's origins to the actual form and structure of its spread. The reasons for this have been various. In the first place, the two premises of the simple demographic motor that has been assumed to power the spread of agriculture, and the universal tendency of human populations to maximize rather than optimize their numbers, have both been strongly questioned in the light of ethnographic evidence (cf. Ellen 1982, Harris & Hillman 1989). In the second place, the genetic transformations to which we have attached the term "domestication" are looking increasingly less like the unique and remarkable evolutionary thresholds implicit in the subsequent burst of activity. However much the first generation of such genetic transformations may display a series of distinctive traits (Zohary in Ch. 9 in this volume), in the wider context of evolutionary biology we might regard them as relatively trivial episodes involving quite minor genetic transitions (cf. Hillman & Davis 1990).

The latter point has been developed in detail by Rindos (1984). He argues that it no longer seems reasonable to regard the genetic transformation of a few annual plants and herbivores as unusual. Co-evolutionary transformations in which species' functional interdependence increases through time are widespread. Moreover, such transformations are habitually accompanied by some loss of reproductive autonomy in the symbionts, commonly cited as the characteristic feature of agricultural domestication.

If we take Rindos's arguments against the background of recent developments in our understanding of Quaternary environmental change, we can extend this demystification of domestication to include its chronology. Various of the environmental fluctuations of the late Pleistocene and early Holocene have at one stage or another been drawn into explanations of agricultural origins. These have included rapid changes in aridity (Childe 1936), sea level (Binford 1968) and temperature (Wright 1993). Such explanations have tended to emphasize particular events, rather than the overall variability of the "protocratic" Quaternary episode of which they are all part. It is during these protocratic episodes, which correspond to the thawing out of each interglacial, that the biosphere is probably at its furthest from an equilibrium state with global temperature (Delcourt & Delcourt 1991). It is during these periods of dis-equilibrium that extinctions and speciations are more probable, a point well attested by many examples from the most recent protocratic episode (approximately 15000–9000 bp), which involved the disappearance and appearance both of individual species (Graham & Lundelius 1984) and of the particular combinations we delineate as biological "communities" (Huntley 1990). We might therefore argue that there is nothing intrinsically unusual, from the point of view of evolutionary biology, about the scattered instances of speciation, accompanied by enhanced reproductive dependency on humans, which have been shown to have occurred in various parts of the planet during the last temperature transition. Experimental simulation of such processes of domestication (in wheat and barley) has further demonstrated how small the evolutionary distance is between wild and domestic forms (Hillman & Davis 1990).

Following Rindos in shifting the problematic from the origin of genetic "domestication" to the subsequent success of that co-evolutionary coupling in the context of agricultural spread, and the well known accompanying changes in material culture and the spatial organization of society, we may further question how soon that spread generated formations that were remarkable in ecological terms. The notion of a Neolithic Revolution as a fundamental ecological threshold is conceptually linked with the notion of a wave of advance that is truly "tidal", washing away the inferior ecosystems in its path, a wave that can be tracked by radiocarbon dates and by the flickering of "indicator species" in contemporary pollen curves.

In the Eurasian landmass, the pollen evidence can be examined in some detail in conjunction with a radiocarbon timescale, and synthesized in the manner of the valuable pollen atlas assembled by Huntley & Birks (1983). Although their atlas has been available for more than a decade, there has been little archaeological response to their inference that the first four or five millennia of agricultural spread are essentially invisible in the composite pictures that they produce. "Indicator species" and localized woodland clearances can be used to demonstrate the ecological presence of humans as one among many taxa within the biosphere, but it is also true that the ecological presence of several other taxa, for example the earthworm and the oak tree, could be demonstrated with rather greater force. The absence for several millennia of an appreciable biological impact of agriculture becomes even clearer in the pollen diagrams of the eastern Mediterranean region, whose insensitivity to the unprecedented neolithic transformation of the biosphere supposedly happening around them has been ascribed to recurrent misfortune in the location of pollen-bearing deposits (Bottema & Woldring 1990). We would only observe that that misfortune apparently recurs across the entire European continent. This apparent paradox has been developed further by Willis & Bennett (1994) in the context of the locations of Balkan pollen diagrams and archaeological sites. Even where the two are quite closely located, agricultural impact is still not visible.

Although paucity of settlement evidence is easier to explain, by arguing for poor preservation and lack of fieldwork, the pollen evidence resonates with Dennell's argument about the opacity of the westward spread of agriculture across Europe from its Southwest Asian heartlands (Dennell 1983). The Anatolian landmass does not display the litter of deserted neolithic farmsteads that might be expected in the wake of a tidal advance. Zvelebil (1986) has further elaborated the erratic nature of the spread of agriculture across northern Europe, a spread that would surprise a demographic biologist by its sluggishness rather than its speed. Between the two regions, Hodder (1990: 116–7) has inferred from environmental evidence that Linearbandkeramic farms were lost in an untamed woodland, capturing an image of early European farmers not as victors in a conquest of nature but as simply another part of the general ecological diversification of the mid-Holocene landscape, a diversification visible in a range of biological communities. In summary, from a biological standpoint, it is not only the origins but also the early spread of agriculture across Eurasia that seems in biological terms unremarkable.

It is not until well into agriculture's history, four millennia after it began to spread across Europe and two millennia after it had reached the northwest of the continent, that permanent transformations of the ecosystem, associated with agricultural communities, are for the first time evident from the pollen record on a continental scale (as opposed to locally anywhere along the path of spread). Various transformations are evident. Between the eastern Mediterranean and the Hungarian Plain, the extent of steppe increases significantly, at the expense of woodland (Bottema & Woldring 1990, Huntley & Birks 1983). The sclerophyll woodland of the Aegean spreads westwards across the Mediterranean region (Huntley & Birks 1983, Lewthwaite 1982). Podzolization and peat formation accelerate in northwestern Europe (Bell & Walker 1992), and in northeastern Europe spruce woodland extends around the Baltic and in Scandinavia (Huntley & Birks 1983). Each of these regional transformations is associated with a substantial transformation in the contemporary archaeological evidence for agriculture, and it may be that each of them has its roots in an agricultural spread that is finally having an impact within the biosphere that is out of the ordinary, after millennia of more discrete presence. In order to understand how agriculture came to dominate, rather than simply to enhance, the European ecosystem, we clearly need to investigate its expansion and movement at all these stages and in all these regions.

Questions concerning the structure and chronology of agricultural spread across Europe have been further brought into focus within the debate engendered by Renfrew's essay on its association with language dispersal (Renfrew 1987 and cf. Ch. 5 in this volume), and in particular the responses of Sherratt & Sherratt (1988), and Zvelebil & Zvelebil (1988, 1990) drawing on their own regional syntheses of agricultural transition (Zvelebil 1986). Renfrew's initial formulation draws primarily upon the demic-diffusion model of Ammerman & Cavalli-Sforza (1973), which implicitly treats agricultural transition as a threshold to unfettered exponential growth, in a manner that, as discussed above, may sit unhappily with some of the regional data for that spread. Zvelebil & Zvelebil (op. cit.) place the demic-diffusion model alongside the contrasting model of indigenous adaptation (Dennell 1983, Barker 1985), and Zve-lebil's own combination of the two (Zvelebil 1986). The value of this debate has been to reopen questions of the relationship between language, material culture and farm-ing, and to develop scenarios of the complexity of that interrelationship, some of which are presented in Sherratt & Sherratt (1988) and in Zvelebil & Zvelebil (1988), as well as in Chapters 17, 18 and 19 in this volume by Thomas, Zvelebil and Price.

The potential of biomolecular archaeology

We wish to argue that a key methodological approach to the complexity of the interrelationship between material culture and farming is provided by an important new development in bioarchaeological method, which is the focus of the second part of this chapter. Until recently, agricultural spread was discernible only indirectly, through various components of material culture in conjunction was plant and animal macrofossils. It is now theoretically feasible to examine the spread of the crops and animals directly through their biomolecular composition. Of particular interest in this respect is the survival of ancient DNA in these tissues. At a conceptual level, the prin-ciple of using DNA to understand the particular patterns of origin and spread of a spe-cies is broadly similar in the case of crops as in the more familiar example of humans. We can take the better known study of human origins and spread as a baseline against which to consider the particular issues of a DNA-based analysis of early agriculture.

In both research fields, the assumption is that a dendrogram of similarity will mir-ror the origins and spread of a genotype, and that a molecular clock may be assembled on the basis of global similarity to provide a very rough timescale. The agricultural case differs both in the length of that timescale, shorter by a factor of 10 or 20, and the scale of questions being addressed. The much reduced timescale, of around 10,000 years, brings into question the utility of a molecular clock, which in its simplest form assumes an unmodified random mutation rate for non-coding DNA regions, consider-ably constraining both its precision and its accuracy. Although in principle such a clock could be greatly refined for particular well known non-coding regions, and is no more intrinsically problematic than a wide range of stochastic clocks used in archaeology, in practice the short timescale of agricultural origins and spread may well continue to limit its applicability. It follows that bioarchaeological specimens, dated radiometrically, are likely to play a role in agricultural studies more central than they do currently in studies of human origins. In terms of the scale of questions being addressed, there are indeed some that are similar in general form to the "Out of Africa" question in the study of human origins. The issue of whether our principal cultivars became domesticated in genetic terms once or on several occasions is still central to understanding that transformation (cf. Harris, Blumler and Zohary in Chs 1, 3 and 9 in this volume). We are also unclear whether agriculture moved out of its heartlands once or as a repeated pulse, an issue that has been discussed by Sherratt and Zvelebil in their developments of Renfrew's hypothesis (see above). We may also hope to pen-etrate the finer details of agricultural spread. To illustrate this, we can take as a base-line a hypothetical dendrogram based on an ideal DNA region (one in which base replacement is simple and stochastic) and the most elementary demic-diffusion concept for the wave-of-advance model (cf. Ammerman & Cavalli-Sforza 1973).

In an idealized dendrogram, each branch division will correspond to a random mutation (i.e. a DNA replacement) in the particular non-coding region being examined, such that the overall dendrogram will correspond to a particular phylogenetic tree. The scale of resolution of that tree depends on the particular replacement rate in that region: a slow-changing region might generate the phylogeny of flowering plants, whereas a fast-changing region that generates a subspecific phylogeny is of greater relevance here. A hypothetical demic-diffusion spread that is even in space and in time will evenly disperse the branches of such a dendrogram, so that the branch tips correspond directly and evenly to the "front" resulting from that diffusion. Within the dendrogram, the only expected variability will be in branch length, normally distributed according to the random nature of DNA replacement.

Any deviations from idealized demic diffusion will result in deviations from this idealized dendrogram, and looking for such deviations provides the methodological basis for tracking the spread of early crops and early farmers across the world's surface. Any departure from that hypothetical dendrogram, be it that the spread is sporadic in space and time or composed of a succession of pulses, to follow the alternatives discussed by Sherratt & Sherratt (1988) and by Zvelebil & Zvelebil (1988), would *in principle* modify either of these dendrogram characteristics in a predictable manner. Whether or not such fine-scale variations will be detectable *in practice* will depend on how biomolecular archaeology progresses, and to what degree the many practical obstacles are successfully overcome. It is important to emphasize that such phylogenetic analysis is by no means straightforward in living, let alone in archaeological, specimens.

A further distinction between human and agricultural species is the scale of onslaught, conscious and unconscious, on the genetic range of agricultural species that has taken place over the past two centuries. The extent of genetic extinction can only be surmised, and may only ever be revealed through biomolecular archaeology. We also suspect that crop genotypes were impoverished, although to a lesser extent, in Europe in the previous 1500 years, when a general intensification of agriculture and narrowing of cereal taxa in use can be charted in the bioarchaeological record (cf. van Zeist et al. 1991). In contrast to the human case, a genetic range suitable to elucidate longer-term phylogenies may not fully survive in contemporary material. Only through examining subfossil material can we attempt an informed assessment of the extent to which surviving land races and tissue banks (e.g. herbariums, seed stores) embrace the previous genetic range of our principal economic species. Once again, the archaeological specimens are paramount.

In the first part of this chapter, we argued that the significance of agriculture cannot be elucidated in terms of its origins alone, but involves a more detailed understanding of the emergent structure of its continuing spread. We also anticipate that the methods of ancient-DNA analysis applied to agricultural plants and animals may have great potential in that elucidation. Against that background, we now report briefly on the start we have made to exploring the potential of those methods in practice, with reference to studies of wheat, and what we see as future directions of research.

First, considering the survival of archaeological DNA, some of the key work conducted by Paabo and his colleagues was conducted on soft animal tissues preserved in rather unusual environments (Paabo 1985, Paabo et al. 1988). The potential for a more general archaeological applicability came with the extension of these analyses to such ubiquitous materials as vertebrate bone (Hagelberg et al. 1989) and charred seeds (Allaby et al. 1994). Some initial success has been achieved in amplifying ancient DNA from domestic animal bones, and although the problems of contamination are less intractable than in the case of human bone, the inherent porosity and openness to the soil environment of bone tissue is invariably a constraint on analyses.

In morphological terms, the two principal materials of archaeobotany, seeds and pollen, approach closed systems within the soil, which reflects an evolutionary design specifically to restrict interaction with their surroundings. Work on DNA detection has proceeded with both these types of material, and has made significant progress with the former, in particular in the work of Goloubinoff et al. (1993), Rollo et al. (1991), and the present authors (Allaby et al. 1994). As with all archaeological DNA, the strands are heavily fragmented, reduced to lengths of a few hundred base pairs, and may have been subject to partial oxidation and transformation of side chains. In our own work on wheat, we have targeted those preservation categories that are most commonly encountered in archaeological contexts, i.e. charring or carbonization, desiccation, mineralization and waterlogging. In each case, wheat DNA has been successfully identified in specimens of between 1,000 and 3,300 years old (Brown et al. 1993). Intuitively, we would expect the most favourable preservation conditions to be desiccation and waterlogging, in which biochemical transformation is most severely restricted. This may indeed be the case, and will be of considerable value in exploring the above issues, for example in Anatolia and elsewhere in the dry environments of Southwest Asia, or around the lakes of Switzerland. However, a realization of the aims outlined at the start of this chapter does significantly depend upon the more ubiquitous process of charring, which still accounts for the bulk of the archaeobotanical dataset. In our pilot studies, it came as something of a surprise to learn that DNA survived at all in what we have tended to think of as heavily combusted material, but this perhaps highlights how little we understand of the process of carbonization in archaeological terms. What are referred to as charred or carbonized grains have, in some instances at least, now been shown, by several researchers working independently, to retain a range of biomolecules that dispose of the conjecture that they survive through being fully thermally reduced to elemental carbon (information from the present authors, R. Evershed and F. McClaren).

In the laboratory at the University of Manchester Institute of Science and Technology we have worked further on charred specimens of wheat and have amplified and sequenced particular regions of nuclear DNA from the first millennium bc spelt wheat from the Iron Age hillfort at Danebury in Hampshire (Jones 1984). The region we have been exploring to date is a 246 base-pair segment that lies immediately before the open reading frame of a gene responsible for the production of glutenin, a protein that plays a central role in the structural properties of bread. This gene is repeated twice on each member of each of the three pairs of chromosome sets that make up the hexaploid genome of *Triticum spelta*. The copy number of 12 genes per genome thus magnifies the chance of detection correspondingly. A fuller account of the detection of this gene has been published separately (Allaby et al. 1994), and we confine ourselves here to a summary comment. Extracts were prepared from grain samples from two separate archaeologial contexts, and the DNA amplified and sequenced. The sequences matched their closest modern allele with one and eight nucleotide differences respectively.

In other words, without developing the interpretation of these particular nucleotide variations, we seem to have a basis for moving along the research path outlined in the earlier part of this chapter. We shall need to continue methodological refinement, and to continue assessing the suitability of different areas of the published wheat genome to meet these aims. We are also in the process of assessing plastid DNA, and in addition the nuclear DNA that we suspect is trapped within pollen grains. As the methods are currently destructive, we do not want to move along that path at a faster rate than those methodological refinements allow, and have instead chosen a sequential path of research goals appropriate to the availability of archaeobotanical material.

In this first stage, we have chosen to work on a relatively local aspect of crop movement, chosen in relation to the availability of plentiful, well sealed, cereal assemblages. This is the inclusion of much of northwestern Europe within the Roman Empire, and the question we are addressing is whether greater genetic similarity is encountered in assemblages of *T. spelta* organized regionally, or chronologically, before and after the Roman conquest. We intend subsequently to conduct an investigation on a larger temporal and spatial scale, to examine whether later prehistoric *T. dicoccum* (i.e. before the intense restriction of crop genotypes in the historic period) clusters genetically on a continental or macroregional scale. This will move us in the direction of addressing the goals discussed at the start of this chapter, although we should emphasize that the first two stages of research are essentially vehicles for methodological refinement and exploring the potential of the technique. If our results to date are anything to go by, that potential is indeed great.

References

Allaby, R. G., M. K. Jones & T. A. Brown 1994. DNA in charred wheat grains from the Iron Age hillfort at Danebury, England. *Antiquity* **68**, 126–32.

Ammerman, A. J. & L. L. Cavalli-Sforza 1973. A population model for the diffusion of early farming in Europe. In *The explanation of culture change: models in prehistory,* A. C. Renfrew (ed.), 343–57. London: Duckworth.

Barker, G. 1985. *Prehistoric farming in Europe.* Cambridge: Cambridge University Press.

Bell, M. & M. J. C. Walker 1992. *Late Quaternary environmental change: physical and human perspectives.* London: Longman.

Binford L. R. 1968. Post-Pleistocene adaptations. In *New perspectives in archeology* S. R. Binford & L. R. Binford (eds), 313–41 Chicago: Aldine.

Bottema, S. & H. Woldring 1990. Anthropogenic indicators in the pollen record of the eastern Mediterranean. In *Man's role in the shaping of the eastern Mediterranean landscape,* S. Bottema, G. Entjes-Nieborg, W. van Zeist (eds), 231–64. Rotterdam: Balkema.

Brown, T. A., R. G. Allaby, K. A. Brown, M. K. Jones 1993. Biomolecular archaeology of wheat: past, present and future. *World Archaeology* **25**, 64–73.

Childe V. G. 1936. *Man makes himself.* London: Watts.

Delcourt, H. R. & P. A. Delcourt 1991. *Quaternary ecology: a paleoecological perspective.* London: Chapman & Hall.

Dennel, R. W. 1983. *European economic prehistory: a new approach.* London: Academic Press.

Ellen, R. F. 1982 *Environment, subsistence and system: the ecology of small-scale social systems.* Cambridge: Cambridge University Press.

Goloubinoff, P., S. Paabo, A. C. Wilson 1993. Evolution of maize inferred from sequence diversity of an adh2 gene segment from archaeological specimens. *Proceedings of the National Academy of Sciences USA* 90, 1997–2001.

Graham, R. W. & E. L. Lundelius Jr 1984. Coevolutionary disequilibrium and Pleistocene extinctions. In *Quaternary extinctions: a prehistoric revolution*, P. S. Martin & R. G. Klein (eds), 233–49. Tucson: University of Arizona Press.

Hagelberg, E., B. Sykes, R. Hedges 1989. Ancient bone DNA amplified. *Nature* 342, 485.

Harris, D. R. & G. C. Hillman 1989. Introduction. In *Foraging and farming: the evolution of plant exploitation*, D. R. Harris & G. C. Hillman (eds), 1–8. London: Unwin Hyman.

Hillman, G. C. & M. S. Davies 1990. Domestication rates in wild-type wheats and barley under primitive cultivation. *Botanical Journal of the Linnean Society* 39, 39–78.

Hodder, I. R. 1990. *The domestication of Europe.* Oxford: Basil Blackwell.

Huntley, B. 1990. Dissimilarity mapping between fossil and contemporary pollen spectra in Europe for the last 13,000 years. *Quaternary Research* 33, 360–76.

Huntley, B. & H. J. B. Birks 1983. *An atlas of past and present pollen maps for Europe 0–13,000 years ago.* Cambridge: Cambridge University Press.

Jones, M. K. 1984. The plant remains. In *Danebury: an Iron Age hillfort in Hampshire*, B. Cunliffe (ed.), 483–95. Research Report 52, Council for British Archaeology, London.

Lewthwaite, J. G. 1982. Acorns for the ancestors: the prehistoric exploitation of woodlands in the West Mediterranean. In *Archaeological aspects of woodland ecology*, M. Bell & S. Limbrey (eds), 217–30. Oxford: British Archaeological Reports, International Series 146.

Paabo, S. 1985. Molecular cloning of ancient Egyptian mummy DNA. *Nature* 314, 644–5.

Paabo, S., J. A. Gifford, A. C. Wilson 1988. Mitochondrial DNA sequences from a 7,000-year old brain. *Nucleic Acids Research* 16, 9775–87.

Renfrew, A. C. 1987. *Archaeology and language: the puzzle of Indo–European origins.* London: Jonathan Cape.

Rindos, D. 1984. *The origins of agriculture: an evolutionary perspective.* New York: Academic Press.

Rollo, F., F. M. Venanzi, A. Amici 1991. Nucleic acids in mummified plant seeds: biochemistry and molecular genetics of pre-Columbian maize. *Genetical Research* 58, 193–201.

Sherratt, A. & S. Sherratt 1988. The archaeology of Indo–European, an alternative view. *Antiquity* 62, 584–95.

Willis, K. J. & K. D. Bennett 1994. The Neolithic transition – fact or fiction? Palaeoecological evidence from the Balkans. *The Holocene* 4, 326–30.

Wright Jr, H. E. 1993. Environmental determinism in Near Eastern prehistory. *Current Anthropology* 34, 458–69.

van Zeist, W., K. Wasylikowa, K. E Behre (eds) 1991. *Progress in Old World palaeoethnobotany: a retrospective view on the occasion of the International Work Group for Palaeoethnobotany.* Rotterdam: Balkema

Zvelebil, M. (ed.) 1986. *Hunters in transition.* Cambridge: Cambridge University Press.

Zvelebil, M. & K. V. Zvelebil 1988. Agricultural transition and Indo–European dispersals. *Antiquity* 62, 574–83.

—1990. Agricultural transition, "Indo–European origins", and the spread of farming. In *When worlds collide: the Bellagio papers*, T. L. Markey & J. A. C. Greppin (eds), 237–66. Ann Arbor, Michigan: Karoma.

CHAPTER SEVEN

The impact of diseases upon the emergence of agriculture

Les Groube

The excitement of recovering earlier and earlier Pleistocene dates for human emergence and settlement of various parts of the world must be tempered by an awareness that early dates can pose a host of explanatory problems, not the least of which is accounting for the apparently small human population at the end of the Pleistocene. It is now axiomatic, but still inexplicable, that the growth of the population of modern humans was *on average* minuscule during the Palaeolithic. It is axiomatic because of the great time depth that we can now ascribe to the emergence of modern humans (*c.* 100,000 years?); it is inexplicable because of the undoubted fecundity and breeding efficiency of the human female. I look at the implications of this great time depth first and return to the issue of fecundity later.

The Pleistocene inheritance

It is obvious that over a period of 100,000 years average population growth must have been close to stationary or the population would have exploded into ludicrously high numbers by the end of the Pleistocene. Table 7.1 illustrates this problem, which can be most simply expressed as "the tyranny of the exponent". Allowing 5,000 years for the "maturation" of an original pair to a stable population of 25 we have:

Table 7.1 The tyranny of the exponent. Population outcome at the end of the Pleistocene from three small rates of (annual) natural increase, starting with a nominal founding pair 100,000 years ago.

$[25] \times 1.0001^{85000}$	$= 122,817$	
$[25] \times 1.00015^{85000}$	$= 8,605,565$	
$[25] \times 1.0002^{85000}$	$= 602,848,242$	

Such bold figures as in Table 7.1 can, however, hide a multitude of problems that the hypothetical growth curves in Figure 7.1 attempt to expose. On the timescale of 90,000 years from the initial emergence of *Homo sapiens* to the end of the Pleistocene

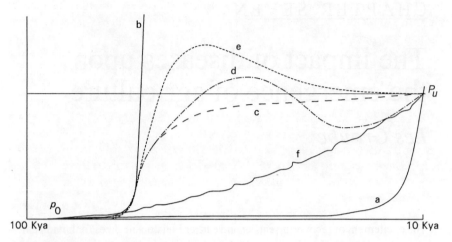

Figure 7.1   Some hypothetical trajectories for population growth from 100,000 years ago to the end of the Pleistocene (for explanation see text).

there is almost an infinity of possible trajectories for population growth from P_0 (the stable foundation population) to P_u (ultimate population at the end of the Pleistocene).

The curves in Figure 7.1 are hypothetical and smoothed; real population progress in the Pleistocene would have oscillated far more. Curves (a), (b) and (c) are mathematically predictable; the first two are simple exponential curves, the third, (c), is a logistic (or sigmoid) curve. Curves (d), (e) and (f) are compound curves involving more than purely mathematical considerations, but are not entirely speculative. It is obvious also that many more bizarre population curves could connect P_0 and P_u, particularly within the extremes defined by curves (a) and (e). We will never know the actual shape of population growth during this period, but by the end of the Pleistocene, despite 90,000 years of expansion by a redoubtable and adaptable animal able to colonize almost all the accessible land on Earth (from the Tropics to the Arctic Circle, from Africa to northern Europe and via Asia to South America and Tasmania), population densities appear to have been low, with the total world population measured only in a few millions.

If we generously assume that P_u was 10 million, then curve (a) in Figure 7.1 (a steady-rate natural increase curve) represents an annual growth of 1.000152 (0.0152%). Even the most extreme growth represented by the initial phase of curve (e) is only 1.000646 (0.0646%), but this does mean a doubling of the population every 1,000 or so years, which is evident from its continuation with curve (b) where P_u is achieved early in the Pleistocene. This doubling time looks quite dramatic by the standards of prehistorians but is trivial biologically. In northern Europe during 1970–5, with the lowest natural increase in the modern world, doubling time was 231 years; for most countries in the developing world doubling time is less than 30 years (UNSO 1979: table 1). Thus, according to Figure 7.1, one of the highest hypothetical rates we can reasonably allow for population growth during the Pleistocene is nearly five times slower than the slowest (regional) rates today, although this comparison is seriously imperilled by the improving mortality patterns in most Western countries that register a positive (short-term) natural increase when in fact there is often long-term demographic decline.[1]

Curve (c) follows the form of a logistic curve and was calculated by the equation recommended in Bodmer & Cavalli-Sforza (1976: 736). In such a curve the initial rate of natural increase progressively declines as the population approaches a "maximum" determined by some independent restraint. Such a pattern is called "logistic growth" in contrast to the "exponential growth" of curves (a) and (b). Curves (d) and (e) are initially logistic and then move into a slow decline with (e) showing recovery towards the end of the Pleistocene. Curve (f), which is close to a straight line between the exponential and the logistic curves, incorporates the additional factor of Pleistocene colonization and is probably the most plausible of the growth patterns, as the following discussion explains.

Curve (b) can be rejected outright and the remaining five curves have different levels of credibility. With a steady-rate growth the result can only be the simple exponential curve (a), where it is obvious that, for the bulk of the 90,000 years, there were too few people on Earth to initiate the colonization that clearly took place. For example, if the colonization of Sahuland (New Guinea–Australia) was c.50,000 years ago, as recent dates suggest (Groube et al. 1986, Roberts et al. 1990), there would have been – according to curve (a) based on a world population of 10 million at the end of the Pleistocene – only about 50,000 people anywhere on Earth, let alone in southern East Asia whence the human settlement of Sahuland originated. Certainly demographic factors could not have given any incentive for the risky, open-sea voyaging required to colonize Sahuland.

The more recent settlement of the Americas is more harmonious with curve (a). By about 20,000 years ago (a plausible date for the initial settlement of North America), the same arithmetic would recommend a population of at least two million on Earth, of which a small proportion in northeastern Asia could well have initiated the colonization of the Americas. A larger world population would make it even more plausible, but this would require a different growth rate.

Curve (a), however, is extremely attractive to advocates (e.g. Boserup 1965, Cohen 1977) of the hypothesis that a population crisis in the late Pleistocene and/or early Holocene initiated the remarkable worldwide trends towards intensification in the food quest. Although a rate such as 1.000152 is incredibly low by modern standards, it would result in a doubling of *world* population every 4,561 years. Thus, between 12,000 and 7,500 years ago – critical years in the emergence of agriculture – the world population may have doubled. But the populations in many *long-settled regions* (fundamentally those closest to Africa, thus including many of the regions of concern in this book), may already have stabilized to much smaller rates of increase, as will be seen below. But, combined with the crisis of climatic amelioration in the terminal Pleistocene, this curve obviously gives credibility to many interlocking arguments that find in ecological pressures the genesis of agriculture. Unfortunately, evidence that man was successfully colonizing areas remote from Africa by at least 60,000 years ago recommends that, although there may well have been a population crisis towards the end of the Pleistocene, its origin was not in growth *per se* in the form of curve (a), nor indeed need it have been caused at all by population growth. The equally plausible claims for bio-system collapses, coastal changes, land and faunal loss, and increasing desertification with the climatic amelioration, could well have induced a population crisis. Other population growth curves can be constructed (such as (d) in Fig. 7.1) that are more harmonious with evidence of early expansion/colonization and a terminal Pleistocene population crisis.

If we reject curve (a) as being, on the whole, implausible, then we must accept that any other curve we may construct connecting P_0 to P_u must be, either initially or later, logistic in shape. It is essential, therefore, to examine the nature of logistic growth, particularly *how* the "maximum" or "threshold" restrains growth. Before doing this I will briefly examine the credibility of the remaining logistic or partly logistic curves, (c), (d) and (e). Curve (c), a formal logistic growth curve, remains comfortably below the magic threshold of 10 million. It suffers, together with curves (d) and (e), an obvious weakness, at least to my reading of Pleistocene prehistory, in that it predicts far too many people too early in man's Pleistocene existence. That *Homo sapiens* may have been as numerous as 8 million (curve c) or 12 million (curve e) as early as 60,000 years ago will stretch the faith of even the most excitable archaeologist. With such numbers around for over 20,000 or 30,000 years, the belated appearance of modern man in Europe is a little odd, as is the late colonization of the Americas. Logistic growth of this form, however, gives ample demographic credibility to the risky early settlement of Sahuland.

Curves (d) and (e) explore the biologically legitimate case of "overshoot" reaching a peak during one of the milder phases of the last glaciation *c.*60–40,000 years ago, with population declining steadily in the case of (e) but recovering with (d) after the peak of the final glaciation *c.*20,000 years ago. Other logistic growth patterns could be suggested, one starting its steep ascent somewhat later than curve (c) is plausible, but once again the evidence that man was in Asia and presumably in northern Asia as well by about 60,000 years ago is troublesome. Discussion of curve (f) will be suspended until we have examined further aspects of logistic growth.

The logistic (or sigmoid) curve has held a special place in demography and population biology since the demonstration that Malthus's "geometric" growth was seldom witnessed outside the laboratory (e.g. Verhulst 1847, Pearl & Reed 1920). Finite limitations in food resources, territory, nesting sites and so forth – generally bundled together into the concept of "carrying capacity" (a phrase first coined in 1936: Andrewartha 1963) – impose restrictions upon growth, as populations increase. As there are many types of logistic curve, there are also many ways of calculating this gradually tightening restraint upon growth, but they all share a common concept of a population threshold, a "maximum" to which, in the end, all reproductive efforts must respond.

These issues are not simply of arithmetic; they strike at a central nerve in our understanding of prehistory – the fecundity of the human female. Without exception, all textbooks in human biology and physical anthropology note the breeding efficiency and potential fertility of the human female. Thus, we must assume, to envisage such low population growth, one or more of the following: extraordinary restraint in sexual congress throughout the late Pleistocene or some form of efficient contraception; cultural controls such as regulation of age at marriage; extremely high foetal, infant and adult mortality; or the constraints of resource limitation within the carrying-capacity model. The latter tends to be the favourite solution.

Thus, population stagnation during the late Pleistocene is usually seen to have two related causes: (a) that the available technology limited the success of the food quest and restricted growth to thresholds determined by local resource availability, and/or (b) population expansion led to over-exploitation of accessible large game followed by population decline to a stable equilibrium between the hunter and the hunted. Either pattern could result in the logistic growth and low rates of natural increase implied in the above figures. The general equations for logistic growth, however, do not explain *how* the restraint affects birth rate or mortality, the two crucial variables in establishing natural increase. But it is not difficult to envisage as resource thresholds are approached, a medically acceptable growth restraint with increasing malnutrition delaying menarche, lowering fertility, increasing mortality (particularly of vulnerable pregnant women) and so forth. Close to the threshold, the medically compromised, the aged and children would be increasingly at risk. Equally persuasive and dynamic variants of the carrying-capacity model can be devised to explain the paradox of high fecundity and low fertility over such a long period.

Despite the logical force of the carrying-capacity model, it is inappropriate to apply it on a *world* scale to a highly adaptable omnivorous animal such as *Homo sapiens* able to expand into and colonize almost all the rest of the (terrestrial) world. From the time of their appearance, humans had no serious competitors in the vast range of environments they could occupy. Obviously, increasing ecological pressures would promote emigration into "empty" areas, each requiring adjustment to new food resources, climates and new local perils in the form of macropredators (e.g. carnivores) or micropredators (e.g. the agents of infectious diseases).[2]

When a population can migrate in this manner, the restraints of a maximum in the standard equations for logistic growth do not apply. When colonization (emigration) ceases – when all accessible land has been settled – the equations once again become valid. It is improbable, in my opinion, at least on a world scale, that emigration and colonization had ceased by the end of the Pleistocene; the Americas were probably still infilling, and although the rising sea levels of the terminal Pleistocene may have deprived coastal populations of favourable environments (particularly in terms of vegetation responses, cf. Chappell 1993), there were vast land and hunting gains in the higher latitudes as the ice sheets and glaciers retreated.

But in those regions such as North Africa, Southwest Asia and the Mediterranean littoral, which were among the first areas to be colonized in man's expansion out of tropical Africa, the situation could have been very different from the overall world picture. Emigration northwards to relieve any population pressure would have been possible only during temporary interstadials and after the final retreat of the ice that began about 20,000 years ago. Elsewhere, to the south and east, the land would have long been colonized and the frontier of expansion of *Homo sapiens* would have been many thousands of kilometres away.

The demographic consequences for this region of increasing aridity and desertification as the Pleistocene drew to an end are obvious, as Childe (1941) pointed out, but it is also obvious that population constraints must have been in operation long before these climatically induced changes occurred. Otherwise, as argued for the world population, the population of this region would have exploded into enormous numbers before the end of the Pleistocene. This is not supported by the archaeological evidence. Once again, as on the larger world scene, the evidence that *Homo sapiens* (e.g. in the guise of Cro-Magnon man in western Europe) was actively colonizing out of this region, denies a simple exponential growth; the pattern must have been wholly or partly logistic, and the populations in this region, particularly if they were as low on the eve of the neolithic revolution as the 50,000 to 100,000 claimed by Carniero & Hilse (1966), must have been close to stationary for tens of thousands of years. This has important consequences for what happened during the millennia of final adjustment to the changed climate.

Thus, in general, logistic growth resulting from an approaching threshold in carrying capacity is appropriate only on a local scale, particularly in regions close to initial human expansion. But as local thresholds were approached, population would have spilled into adjoining unsettled areas: colonization would be under way. Figure 7.2 is a speculative exploration of this compounding regional expression of logistic growth, which results in the growth of world population shown in curve (f) in Figure 7.1.

Figure 7.2 can be interpreted solely in terms of the impact of local resource limitations after adjoining regions had been settled and emigration was no longer possible. This "compound-logistic" model gains some support from the independent evidence of faunal loss and species reduction during this period. The hypothesis, favoured by many (e.g. Martin & Wright 1967), that man's hunting activities were partially responsible for the late Pleistocene faunal impoverishment, not only supports logistic growth but also a rapid approach to a threshold, in this case that determined by the availability of readily hunted larger game. In contrast, exponential growth would result in too few hunters for most of the late Pleistocene to have any impact upon

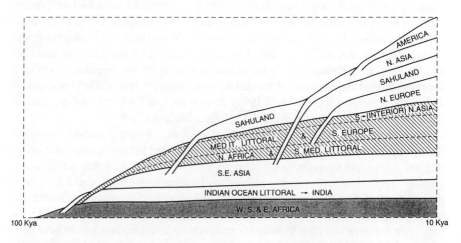

Figure 7.2   Compound logistic population growth curves for different regions of active human colonization during the Pleistocene. The overall shape is that of curve (f) in Figure 7.1, but for each region growth is initially logistic, with extremely low growth thereafter.

fauna, let alone the worldwide reduction in populations of large mammals that has been hypothesized.

Alternatively, the hominid ancestors of modern humans, during millions of years of increasingly efficient hunting, may have been largely responsible for the faunal collapse, with *Homo sapiens* merely completing the task in the past 100,000 years and extending the pattern into new regions such as Sahuland and the Americas. But even if Pleistocene faunal loss was independent of human activities, it would have resulted in an unstable threshold and a shrinking "maximum" carrying capacity, thus bringing on the resource crisis all the more rapidly. However, man's undoubted adaptive flexibility suggests that a *slow* switch to hunting smaller game and collecting a broader range of foods would have posed few problems. Because the loss of the larger animals will almost certainly have benefited smaller animals, the switch in hunting strategies may have been far less an act of desperation than an obvious work-effort gain. As nothing happened very fast in the Palaeolithic, there was plenty of time for these changes to be implemented.

Indeed, the trend in archaeology to seek in the carrying-capacity model so much of the explanatory burden of change in prehistory shows a lack of faith in the very stuff of human evolution; lack of faith in the large brains of the developing hominids, in the efficiency of their stone tools, in their command of fire, and in the utility of emerging social systems with the inestimable advantage of continuity of experience over generations gained through language. The words of Ashley Montagu (1956: 9) bear repetition:

> As an animal man is the most plastic, the most adaptable, the most educable of all living creatures. Indeed, the single trait that is alone sufficient to distinguish man from all other creatures is the quality of educability – it is the species character of *Homo sapiens*.

But if this capable and highly fecund animal was able to adapt to the changing circumstances of the Pleistocene, what possible restraints could maintain human population growth close to stationary for such long periods? What was the "maximum" of the logistic growth equation and what were the regulatory mechanisms? In the next three sections I will seek an answer to these questions by examining the role of infectious diseases during the Palaeolithic.

Mortality in the Palaeolithic

Mortality in most natural populations occurs in five ways:
- from macropredation: being the victim of the food quest of (large) predators (e.g. the carnivores)
- from food-quest failures: malnutrition and starvation
- from micropredation: being victim of the food quest of the micro-organisms of infectious diseases
- from accidents: traumatic deaths during life-experience but including, in the

case of humans, deaths from intra-specific competition or warfare
* from senescence, the failures of ageing, non-infectious diseases such as cancers, cardiac problems, etc.

Of these, death from macropredation is so rare in human populations as to be included in the category of accidental death. Food-quest failure, of course, is the central focus of carrying-capacity models of human populations (other limitations, such as the availability of nesting sites, do not apply). If limitations in food supply (or dietary essentials such as proteins) are the underlying causes of the regional logistic-growth curves shown in Figure 7.2, there are two ways in which this could be translated into population numbers. These are shown in Figure 7.3.

The first possibility (Fig. 7.3a) represents the overshoot/crash strategy of some natural populations (e.g. lemmings). Cemetery evidence of this would be high birth and death rates, with poor survivorship at all ages and with skeletal evidence of malnutrition and other related stress, that is, an unhealthy population. The second possibility (Fig. 7.3b) represents a population responding to diminishing food resources *before* reaching the threshold. There are two main ways in which this could happen:
* A "natural" response with: lower protein intake delaying menarche and increasing foetal wastage (i.e. reduced parity); higher child mortality through inefficient lactation and/or poor weaning foods; and additional stress at child-birth – all of which would be compounded by an increased workload as readily won resources become exhausted. The cemetery evidence of this process would reveal lower overall birth rates and death rates than from the overshoot strategy but with a higher proportion of deaths in the reproductive sector and among children. Adult mortality on the other hand (with the possible exception of females of breeding age) would be reduced. Skeletal evidence of malnutrition could be expected in infants.
* An "artificial" or "cultural" response that would include cultural constraints on age at marriage, birth interval, parity, etc., perhaps supplemented by some form

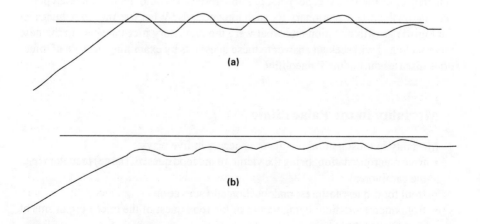

(a)

(b)

Figure 7.3   Alternative resolutions of the carrying-capacity model (for explanation see text)

of contraception and/or infanticide. The cemetery evidence of this type of pal-aeolithic population at equilibrium with local resources would show low parity, much lowered birth rate and death rate, with reduced infant mortality (except where there was infanticide) and few signs of malnutrition. This population, in contrast to that from the overshoot strategy, would appear to be extremely healthy.

Unfortunately, the small amount of cemetery evidence from the Palaeolithic is late and this reflects the climatic stresses of the terminal Pleistocene (Acsádi & Nemeskéri 1970, Nemeskéri 1972; Hassan 1981: ch. 7), but it certainly does not favour the option of cultural controls on reproduction. Mortality rates are high, particularly in the early years, suggesting that mortality was a principal constraint on population growth. Indeed, the "lemming option" with high mortality at all ages (Fig. 7.3a) appears not unrealistic from some of the available cemetery evidence. However, direct evidence of malnutrition is lacking, so it is not possible to establish whether these high mortality patterns were attributable to diminishing food resources or some other cause.

Of the remaining causes of mortality listed above, micropredation, trauma and senescence, the last is assumed to be least important during the Palaeolithic. Ageing, with cardiac problems, cancers and senility, as well as eyesight, hearing and mobility failures, would affect only the very few who achieved old age. However, traumatic death could have been relatively important. Accidents during hunting, drownings, burns and falls, many with healing complications, would have been fairly frequent but essentially would form part of the background "noise" of mortality. Homicide and warfare, also, may have been more important in the Palaeolithic than we tend to assume, although direct mortality during fighting (in contrast to dying from compli-cations such as septicaemia from injuries), judging from ethnographic evidence, would probably have been low. Nevertheless, Livingstone (1968) seems confident that up to 15 per cent of any male cohort of Australian Aboriginal hunters may have been lost in warfare.

Micropredators, however, as the agents of infectious diseases, are by far the most important cause of death in *Homo sapiens* in the past as well as today. As the demog-rapher Coleman (1986: 25) writes "Human populations used to be thought unique in the animal kingdom because their high burden of mortality from infectious disease had undoubtedly caused the majority of human deaths up to the present." This state-ment reflects the human advantage (through tools, fire and other aspects of culture) in controlling and in most cases eliminating mortality from macropredation, which is responsible for a large proportion of deaths in less favoured species. Coleman (ibid.), however, admits that "[recent] Studies of populations of insects, birds and small mam-mals have all revealed cyclical changes in antibody rates, infestation rates of parasites, and population numbers . . .".

Recognition that the role of infectious diseases in evolutionary history may well have been underestimated is now a current issue among biologists (Keymer & Read 1990, Rennie 1992); archaeologists, concerned with what was, until recently, the most disease-ridden animal of all, should be alert to these trends. As ecology (fundamen-tally the economics of living organisms) has as its central pivot the food quest, all eco-logical explanations of regularities (and oddities) in the prehistoric record (including carrying capacity) concern the food quest in one way or another. Thus, it is surprising that those questing after humans as food – the parasites of infectious diseases – and their impact are, with a few exceptions, not included in our models.[3]

The principal reason for ignoring the impact of disease comes from the observation of medical biologists, epidemiologists and geneticists that the *high-mortality epidemic*[4] infectious diseases such as measles, mumps, diphtheria, typhus, smallpox and so forth, which have afflicted mankind during the past few millennia, could not have existed (at least in their present form) during the Palaeolithic (Haldane 1932, Motulsky 1960). It is obvious that there would have been few opportunities during the Palaeolithic for any "crowd" diseases that required, for continuity of infection, high densities and/or large numbers of hosts (i.e. density-dependent diseases or DDD); the high-mortality epidemic diseases were artefacts of civilization. This theme was reinforced by the work of Black (1966) on measles, which demonstrated convincingly that this highly contagious viral infection could not persist in small isolated communities; populations approaching 300,000 were required for it to be maintained as an endemic childhood disease. Many other diseases have been identified as by-products of crowding into villages and cities and/or close association between agriculturalists and their domesticates. These claims, central to the prehistory of the emergence of agriculture, have been closely studied by some prehistorians, notably in a series of papers by Cohen, Armelagos and others, which culminated in Cohen's seminal *Health and the rise of civilization* (1989). The principal thesis of that book, however, is not that of this chapter (the impact of infectious diseases upon prehistory), but the reverse theme favoured by epidemiologists, that is, the impact of prehistoric developments such as the Neolithic Revolution or the emergence of civilization upon infectious diseases. Cohen's argument that health deteriorated (i.e. morbidity increased) with changes in diet, increased sedentarism and crowding cannot be doubted, but his more serious claims that mortality increased and life-expectancy was reduced by these same developments is less acceptable, particularly because it depends on the notoriously difficult interpretation of prehistoric cemeteries (see Groube in press).

Because of the great mutability of most micropredators, it is quite reasonable to assume that less lethal ancestors of many of the "crowd" diseases were about during the late Pleistocene (Motulsky 1960); indeed the lack of crowds during the Palaeolithic may be exaggerated. "Singsings", where several small groups gather together for initiation ceremonies, marriages, funerals and to settle disputes may have occurred several times in the lifetime of the average hunter–gatherer. Seasonal flushes of food (e.g. in rivers, lakes or on the sea coast) or, in bad seasons, retreat to areas of famine foods, can also bring isolated bands into close contact. But more importantly it is simply naïve to assume that diseases such as measles or cholera were lurking about (sustaining themselves on what?) awaiting human population growth before emerging with their present high mortality pattern. Certainly, the remarkably efficient way the individual immune system copes with measles suggests long familiarity with the virus or a closely related form. It is not improbable, as I argue elsewhere, that measles mortality may have increased with population because of the relatively inefficient method of mucous transmission (Groube n.d.a).

The professional focus of epidemiologists upon "spectacular" high-mortality diseases, inevitable in a science dedicated to controlling or eliminating epidemics of any form, has also diverted attention from the myriad low-mortality infections (e.g. the common cold) or the rare high-mortality infections (e.g. rabies, tetanus) that may have been as important during prehistory as epidemics have been in recent history. Thus, despite the 150 years that have passed since the publication of Lyell's *Principles of geology*, catastrophes in the form of epidemics are still an important explanatory device in demography, epidemiology and history. Low-mortality childhood infections that are always with us (i.e. are *endemic*),[5] attract neither historians nor medical research funds, but are as important to the prehistorian as were the slow incremental processes of erosion and sedimentation to Lyell. They are the real and unseen culprits in man's poor demographic performance before the Holocene. Each of these (now mostly benign) infectious diseases was probably first experienced during expansion into new territories as an epidemic: a new disease that the individual immune system had to recognize and learn to combat. Because everyone in such a (virgin soil) epidemic lacks experience of the disease, everyone would be infected, a few, perhaps, with serious effects. These traumatic experiences with micropredators in the past may have left little record except in our remarkably efficient immune system, which, if we could interpret it, may carry a prehistory of disease confrontation along the following lines:

(a) In leaving the homeland of mankind, the humid tropical rainforests, our primate ancestors were able to escape from the richest and most prolific natural habitat for parasites into more sterile landscapes such as the semi-arid deserts and eventually into colder regions. This must have been a tremendous demographic asset that more than compensated for any additional hazards encountered in their travels. The falling temperatures of the final glaciation would have reduced parasite numbers, and, although the colder and drier environments were more sterile, the human food quest was often less productive, so that population densities did not improve.

(b) Despite leaving behind many tropical parasites specifically adapted to the early hominids and to anatomically modern humans, it was not possible for man to escape entirely from micropredators; everywhere there were different micro- and macroparasites[6] adapted to different primary hosts and conditions. Some of these, particularly associated with the hunt, may have posed temporary threats by accidental invasion of man (zoonosis). Others, after hundreds of years of contact (and tens of millions of parasite generations) changed sufficiently to transfer permanently to the newcomer (see (d) below).

(c) In addition to the peril of new microbes, many of those that humans brought with them, with their huge potential mutability, were able to adapt as quickly as their hosts to new climates and conditions. Some parasites, of course, were poor travellers, unable to maintain themselves in the small host populations involved in colonization. Thus, it is likely that only micropredators requiring low-population thresholds for continuity of infection would have been transported great distances during initial colonization. Low threshold diseases are necessarily low mortality diseases, so few of the passengers brought from their homeland would have been very lethal; in addition, the individual immune system would already have been inured to them. More lethal higher threshold diseases may have caught up with their hosts later. Many vector-dependent parasites, such as those of malaria (*Plasmodium* spp.), which are dependent on temperature/humidity-sensitive vectors (anophelene mosquitoes), or the schistosomes (the parasite of bilharzia), which require certain species of *Bulinus* snails as vectors, also found it more difficult to follow their hosts out of the rainforests. These awaited the rising temperatures of the terminal Pleistocene to escape from their tropical homeland – and then played a prominent role in the prehistory of Southwest Asia during the Holocene.

(d) In addition to wandering so far from home and accidentally encountering new micropredators, humans had the unfortunate habit, through the hunting efficiency gained from the use of tools and by the accidental misuse of fire, of narrowing the faunal variability around them, and thus forcing many parasites, deprived of their former hosts, to focus upon this new meat source. Throughout the Pleistocene and well into the Holocene, man slowly became a "mono-crop" for many micropredators that successfully adapted to the new animal; indeed, many of the most important human diseases, such as malaria, smallpox, epidemic typhus, and syphilis (congenital and epidemic), lack alternative animal reservoirs. In turn, man's highly efficient immune system learned to recognize and combat each new invader, but not without a cumulative toll, which, I believe, is the principal cause of the apparently low natural increase of the human population during the Pleistocene.

(e) Throughout this long period of human expansion, the opportunities for further migration diminished as the frontiers of colonization moved farther away and populations stabilized within long-established regions. This stability favoured certain parasites of disease that require critical host numbers and/or population concentrations (density) for efficient transmission (the "density-dependent" diseases or DDD). Thus began a domination of human demographic history that has not yet come to an end: DDDs cause the majority of recurrent epidemics. Indeed, *under certain conditions that depend critically upon the lethality of the disease, the existing natural increase of the host population and the immune response, they can bring population growth to a standstill, although generally not into decline* (see below).

Density-dependent diseases, however, may not have been the principal culprits in disease mortality in the Palaeolithic. For example, septicaemia and tetanus, which are occupational hazards for hunter–gatherers, or even rabies, none of which is technically density-dependent, may have claimed more lives more frequently than any DDD. Diseases from contaminated food or from poor preparation and storage must have claimed many victims. However, few infectious diseases of man are not to some extent density dependent. Macroparasites such as worm infections, which reproduce (through eggs) outside the hosts and expand by accumulation rather than duplication within the host, are obviously density dependent in that the opportunity for re-infection depends on host numbers and availability. Most vector-borne diseases, although they have an additional constraint from fluctuations in the numbers/density of vectors, require large host numbers for efficient transmission. Only epidemics of the rare zoonotic diseases such as the plague, which is dependent upon rat rather than human population size, escape the generalization that most human epidemics are caused by density-dependent diseases through the dynamics of host population growth determined by the classical interplay of fertility and mortality.

It is clear that, throughout the Palaeolithic, the expanding population of *Homo sapiens* will have occasionally encountered some relatively high-mortality diseases, particularly by zoonotic transfer from parasites with animal reservoirs. High fertility may sometimes have been cancelled out by infrequent episodes of high mortality, but like almost everyone who has looked at this issue I am confident that such encounters were too rare to have much long-term effect. High-mortality diseases provoke effective (and rapid) immune responses and tend therefore to regulate themselves. We must seek a more convincing explanation than appeal to unknown catastrophes, in the form of high mortality epidemics, to explain low fertility in the Palaeolithic. Unless we understand this, the rapid improvement in fertility in the early Holocene, heralded by worldwide trends towards intensification, makes little sense.

The role of infectious diseases

It is impossible to discuss the crucial role of infectious diseases, particularly that of DDDs, without recourse to some numbers. I have no desire to halve the readership of this book with each new equation, as Hawking's anonymous friend warned (Hawking 1988: vi), but prehistorians need to heed the sentiments of demographers who admit that "In the end, demography without numbers is waffle, an amiable kind of social natural history" (Schofield & Coleman 1986: 4). I include in the next two sections sufficient mathematical detail to avoid being too amiable. More detailed discussion, including the derivation of many of the expressions discussed below, will be published elsewhere (Groube n.d.a); some details, including notation, can be found in Groube (in press).

The most serious infectious diseases are *recurrent*, of epidemic or endemic occurrence. First contact between an infectious disease and a population lacking immunity is generally an epidemic provoked by a rapid proliferation of the parasite because of the plenitude of food in the form of "susceptible" hosts. The epidemic ends when the number/density of susceptibles falls below a transmission threshold characteristic of the parasite. The epidemic will recur if the parasite can maintain itself after the loss of its food supply. The parasite may be able to persist, for example, at a low infective level within the population, or by infecting other nearby (still susceptible) populations of the same host or in a different (reservoir) host. When the number/density of susceptibles recovers in the original population and rises above the transmission threshold, an epidemic will recur. The speed of recovery, which determines the interval to a second and subsequent epidemics, depends on the nature of the immune response, whether imparting protection for life (as with measles) or only a few months (as with the common cold). The impact of the epidemic depends on the lethality of the organism and the individual immune responses of the host/victim.

If a disease does have a number/density transmission requirement, it is density dependent. *If the disease is density dependent and the population continues to grow after the initial outbreak, it will slowly "progress" from epidemic to endemic occurrence, with regular shortening of the intervals between the outbreaks.* The distinction between endemic and epidemic (cf. *n.* 4 and *n.* 5) is not of kind (the same organism can be endemic or epidemic in occurrence) but of frequency of invasive activity. Any epidemic disease can become endemic under certain (commonly occurring) conditions: when the disease provokes an individual immune response that gives partial or complete immunity to re-infection and/or mortality (*acquired immunity*); and when the *initial* epidemic interval (from the first to the second epidemic) is less than the effective life of the acquired immunity. Thus, the gain from population growth over the epidemic interval is greater than the loss from epidemic mortality, and at the time of the second epidemic there are some survivors of the first epidemic with acquired immunity.

If these conditions are fulfilled, then the disease will, as the population continues to grow, "progress" from epidemic to endemic occurrence, with the epidemic interval [ei, the years between peaks of infectivity], slowly reducing. The initial epidemic interval and the succeeding epidemic intervals are specific to a disease, particularly to its cohort-mortality (m_e), to the nature and longevity of the immune response to it, to the original natural increase (ni_0) and to the age-specific mortality schedule before the disease was introduced. The subsequent pattern of epidemics with diminishing epidemic intervals is discussed elsewhere (Groube n.d.a). Some of the more important issues for archaeologists are the following.

(a) There is an important (indeed axiomatic) condition of all exponential (natural) growth that *the time interval for any magnitude of increase (or decrease) in a population (e.g. ×0.5, ×2, ×3, etc.) must be a **constant** such as, for example, the 25 years claimed by Malthus for the doubling (×2) of the (White) population in North America in the late eighteenth and early nineteenth centuries.*[7] As a consequence, during the progression of a DDD from epidemic to endemic occurrence, population growth *can never be (strictly) exponential* because, with systematically reducing epidemic intervals, the magnitude of increase cannot be at a constant interval; indeed as the *ei* reduces the time interval for any specified magnitude of growth *increases.*

(b) It is characteristic, also, of a DDD progression that *the rate of reduction in* ei *declines systematically as the population grows, with the eis becoming closer and closer to equal,* and, *the overall population gain (*nI = incremental increase) *from epidemic to epidemic, will keep falling as long as the ei keeps reducing.* Thus, during a disease progression the original exponential growth curve "bends" towards a logistic growth pattern. This bending will continue until epidemic intervals stabilize or the difference becomes so small as to have no detectable impact on the overall shape of the growth.

(c) There are several important interrelated equations that determine the outcome of a disease progression:

$$1 - (nI/ni_0)^{\beta-1} > {}_\beta m_e \qquad \text{(Eq. 7.1)}$$

where:

nI = incremental increase, = population growth from epidemic peak to epidemic peak after the introduction of the disease. (Note: nI is exponential only when eis are equal.) In contrast, ni_0 is the pre-epidemic natural increase and the reciprocal of the expression within the brackets is the rate of recovery *between* each epidemic (from an epidemic aftermath to the onset of the next).

β = average age of the mother at the birth of her last child. β as a subscript before m_e means cohort mortality of the disease to age β (see *n.* 14 below).

When, as in this equation, the gain from the existing reproductive effort is greater than the disease mortality, there are two possible outcomes:

(i) The ei will continue reducing close to or less than one year with the population continuing to grow but at a *less* than exponential rate. As the eis approach annual, the growth curve will "flatten" (become more linear) with the slope determined by the robustness of the original natural increase. For most infections, at least of the placental mammals, reduction in the ei will be halted by the maternal immunity "acquired" by the infant (through placental transfer or in the mother's milk). This interval of maternal protection varies (e.g. about 6 months for malaria or 14 months for measles). When all the DDDs infecting a particular population have "progressed" to the intervals set by maternal immunity, growth can be fully exponential (see (ii) below).

(ii) The ei can become "fixed" at an interval greater than one year ($ei(f)$), for climatic or other reasons independent of host numbers or immune response, while the population is still growing. Thus, the relatively inefficient transmission of the measles virus (via aerosol mucous drops) requires a sufficient number of susceptible hosts to be "herded" together, which in modern societies tends to occur only in schools, so that epidemic regularity is determined by school starting age (as well as other factors).[8] The most common restraint upon ei reduction is the seasonal summer/winter or wet/dry annual cycles; disease occurrence, particularly if vectors or intermediate hosts are involved, can be severely affected by seasonal variations. Many DDDs, therefore, will halt at annual or close to annual recurrence (as infant diseases) regardless of the level of maternal immunity provoked by the disease. As most micropredators have their own population and transmission limitations, a frequent result is that the reduction in ei halts at a frequency determined by these limitations. With a *constant* epidemic interval there will also be a *constant* interval for any magnitude of growth that will thus be exponential ((a) above). The host population will continue to grow at a reduced exponential rate adjusted to the disease mortality of those aged from $x_0 - x_{ei(f)}$ which can be calculated from:

$$nI = [(1 - {}_\beta m_e)\,(ni_0^{\beta-1})]^{1/\beta - 1} \qquad \text{(Eq. 7.2)}$$

(d) Stabilization of ei can also occur by an equilibrium being established between ni_0 and m_e, when the population will become stationary ($nI = 1.0$):

$$1 - (nI/ni_0)^{\beta-1} = {}_\beta m_e \qquad \text{(Eq. 7.3)}$$

Thus, when a population reaches a certain size (P_{max}, see Eq. 7.4 below), the gain from natural increase is exactly cancelled out by the mortality from the disease, and the *equilibrium* established will keep the population stationary, unless either cohort mortality from the disease is reduced or reproductive effort is improved. Thus, if the mortality is particularly high during one epidemic when the population is at equilibrium, growth will become negative (< 1.0), but with a constant reproductive effort the interval to the next epidemic will be longer and the equilibrium will be restored.

Obviously, this equilibrium is more likely to occur when ni_0 is low and *reproductive effort is not or cannot be improved.* The establishment of such equilibria may have been quite frequent in the Pleistocene, when natural increase, as already discussed, appears on the average to have been very low and if, as I argue in the next section, ni_0 was relatively low among hunter–gatherers because of requirements for widely spaced births, which itself constrained additional reproductive effort. Thus, many of the relatively innocuous DDDs that would have dogged the expansion of *Homo sapiens* out of Africa, could have had a far more dramatic effect on population growth than their modest mortalities superficially suggest. What is clear is that the human skills that had given rise to tools, language and culture could not cope with micropredators; indeed, their very existence was not even suspected until the seventeenth century, when van Leeuwenhoek first saw microbes under a primitive microscope.

Under these circumstances a density-dependent disease of relatively low mortality can bring growth to a halt at a constant (average) epidemic interval. This will result in a full logistic curve with a "maximum" population so that the standard methods of calculating logistic growth are appropriate; the only difference is that the "maximum" is determined by the disease presence, not by resource limitation.

In addition, when both m_e and ni_0 are modest (as we must assume for the bulk of the Pleistocene), this reduction in growth rate towards a stable ei will continue for hundreds of years and, even before one disease has become stabilized as an endemic infant infection, another may have taken its place at epidemic occurrence, thus inhibiting full recovery of exponential growth. The resulting *compound* growth curve, incorporating incremental disease loadings during human expansion in the Pleistocene, would be logistic, in its initial stages at least, eventually assuming the close-to-linear shape of curve (f) in Figure 7.1 and in Figure 7.2. Thus, it is possible to model linear population growth during the Pleistocene without appeal to "resource limitations" or even the concept of "carrying capacity", although both were very important.

A disease progression that results in a population standstill is obviously of great interest to archaeologists puzzled by the apparently slow population growth during the Pleistocene. The mortality (m_e) required to halt population growth at a specified rate of natural increase (ni_0) can be calculated from Equation 7.3 above. It is also possible to estimate the population size at equilibrium (P_{max}), at an epidemic interval of one year (infant mortality), from the next equation when life-table data are available:

$$P_{max} = [th \times e_0 + m_e]$$
(Eq. 7.4)

where:

e_0 = life-expectancy at birth from the life-table for the population[9] and
th = threshold (number of susceptibles) required to initiate an epidemic.

If we return to Figure 7.1 and take our theoretical original Pleistocene colonists with a natural increase of 1.000152 (curve (a), with a doubling time of 4,561 years), using Equation 7.3 and with β at 30 years, a disease of only 0.44 per cent would halt population growth. But with a healthy hunting–gathering population with vital statistics such as those of the Dobe !Kung (Howell 1979: table 11.1) we have a different resolution. With the relatively handsome natural increase of 1.0026, and β at 34 years, it is clear that only a disease of 8.2 per cent cohort mortality would bring the population growth to a standstill. Thus, a likely Pleistocene parasite such as *Plasmodium vivax* (malaria: Groube 1993) with a (cohort) mortality of 2.5 per cent, would barely slow down the growth of the Dobe !Kung:

$$nI = [(1-0.025)\,(1.0026^{33})]^{1/33} = 1.00183$$

If our late Pleistocene hunters and gatherers differed little from the Dobe !Kung except in higher mortality (from infanticide and fighting), resulting in a growth closer to zero, the presence of a parasite of such modest mortality as *P. vivax* (labelled "benign" by the medical profession today[10]), would halt all growth if the existing natural increase (ni_0) were <1.0008, which is higher than the most extreme growth rate given in Figure 7.1.

From these examples, the extreme vulnerability of populations of low natural increase to diseases of only modest mortality should be clear. To have this effect, however, infection must be targeted at those of breeding age or younger ($<x_\beta$). Density-dependent diseases that provoke effective individual immune responses "progress" from population-wide epidemics to age-specific diseases of the young as the population grows. They are the diseases that have greatest impact upon natural increase; diseases of senescence, in contrast, have no such impact, and many other infections (e.g. septicaemia, tetanus, botulism) will not progress in the same manner. Similarly, rare epidemics of *irregular* occurrence, no matter how catastrophic in short-term impact, have little lasting effect on natural increase, and, most importantly, recurrent diseases of severe mortality tend to be self-regulating and leave little long-term imprint except in the immune system.

If the disease mortality is higher than 2 per cent, there will usually be sufficient selective pressure within the population to promote the conservation of any genetic traits that improve individual immune defences against the disease, and m_e will decline with natural (exponential) growth restored. This result, *which occurs only when the* m_e *is high*, follows the promotion/conservation of any and all inherited defences against the disease. This changes all the preceding arguments. The crucial numbers of immune expand at a rate greater than the mere accumulation of those with acquired immunity; the reduction in epidemic intervals will slow down, stabilize and even reverse, with epidemic intervals lengthening as the number of those genetically protected approaches 100 per cent. Natural selection would systematically remove the more vulnerable throughout the disease progression. With high-mortality epidemics, the survivors would tend to be increasingly dominated by those with some level of genetic advantage. Another closely related factor would also come into play as the disease progressed towards the younger age-groups: the greater ease with which younger children handle most infections (Burnet & White 1972: 100) with consequent lower mortality. There is some evidence, also, that many parasites of disease become less dangerous during a lengthy disease progression (ibid.), thus lessening the chances of an equilibrium being established and the population becoming stationary.

(e) The equilibria described above, where population growth comes to a halt at certain (low) levels of disease mortality and reproductive effort, assume a "closed system" where the only source of fresh susceptibles to the disease are from within the population itself (i.e. those born after the last epidemic and therefore lacking immunity). *It is important to note that, when the system is "closed" in this manner, DDDs cannot, of themselves, cause population decline; equilibrium will always be re-established at zero growth* (Eq. 7.3). The long-term population growth curve of a disease progression finishing at equilibrium will be logistic, with the ultimate outcome a stationary population. If equilibrium is not established and epidemic intervals continue to shrink (as with the !Kung case above), the population will continue to grow, but at an ever-diminishing (non-exponential) rate.

Even when a population is a closed breeding system, reproductive effort may vary between various subpopulations within it. Although significant internal variations in reproductive effort are unlikely in hunting–gathering populations, the emergence of class, caste and professional elites in post-Neolithic societies is often accompanied by shifts in reproductive patterns. If the parasite has equal access to all such subpopulations, those with lower reproductive effort will become proportionately smaller as the disease progresses because the timing of epidemics is determined by the *average* birth-rate (i.e. the average production of susceptibles). As nI can vary between subpopulations, it is possible for the nI of an elite to be *negative* in violation of the conditions of equilibria that deny the possibility of decline being initiated by DDDs (Eq. 7.3 above), and:

$$1 - (nI_{sub}/ni_{sub})^{1/\beta-1} < {}_\beta m_e \qquad \text{(Eq. 7.5)}$$

Obviously, among breeding elites, protection against other forms of mortality, such as from malnutrition and poor hygiene, tends to compensate for any reduction in reproductive effort, but the above equation makes it clear that a DDD can imperil the demographic security of breeding elites.

The impact of Equation 7.5 is even more ominous if the system is *not* closed and there is another source of fresh susceptibles such as immigrants, indentured labour or slaves. Obviously, epidemic intervals will be determined by the rate and number of alternative susceptibles entering the system, as well as by the "native" birth rate. If the average age of immigrants (i.e. fresh susceptibles) is close to x_β and they themselves breed, the initial immigrant generation length (from arrival to x_β) will be very short. Combined with the low mortality of adults, this will result in, for the initial generation only, phenomenally high rates of natural increase (Groube n.d.b). It is not unlikely for a newly arrived *adult* immigrant population to double itself within ten years of arrival even though their actual reproductive effort differs little from that of the native population. Although the children of the immigrants obviously revert to a normal genera-tion length and survivorship to x_β, if immigration continues, these initial high rates of increase in numbers of susceptibles will provoke epidemics at shorter intervals than the native birth rate can cope with, thus promoting the demo-graphic success of the migrants at the expense of the native/resident population, which will decline relatively and could be entirely replaced by the incoming populations. They, in turn, by becoming the new "natives", will suffer the same fate if immigration persists or is revived. In the migration of people from dis-ease-low regions to disease-high regions (as from the high-altitude steppes to the river civilizations of Southwest Asia), we see a natural mechanism for the constant ethnic and language replacements that appear to typify the civilizations in this region (Mallory 1989, Groube n.d.b).

The fact that DDDs can frequently result in logistic growth has escaped comment because there was no need to look beyond resource limitation and inter-species com-petition through macropredation for a growth restraint for most animal (or plant) pop-ulations. However, *Homo sapiens* is (and was) an extremely resourceful and adaptable animal, able to survive on a vast range of foods and, through the use of fire and tools, able to tolerate extremes in temperature and withstand challenges from competitors with great efficiency. Even the huge climatic changes of the later Pleistocene probably occurred too slowly to threaten such a resourceful animal able to follow, with great persistence, shifting animal and plant resources (cf. Coleman 1986: 23). But ability to use fire and make tools, adaptability, resourcefulness and persistence were no defence against the unseen foe, the micropredators causing sickness and occasionally death (ibid.).

A final and most important issue remains. Mortality from epidemic diseases in any cohort (from x_0-x_β) is "incremental" in that no single high-mortality disease need be present, but rather several DDDs, each with more modest lethality. Thus, ten relatively benign diseases of *c.* 0.5 per cent mortality would result in a lowering of potential breeders at x_β by 5 per cent ($(1-0.005)^{10} = 0.95$) that would have a major impact upon natural increase. Similarly, if the acquired immunity of a disease is only short-lived, it can revisit the same cohort with the same penalty in mortality several times before x_β. The vast number of relatively benign infectious diseases humans acquired during their Pleistocene wanderings could compound into mortality of considerable signifi-cance. Thus, the high-threshold/high-mortality diseases of classic epidemiology need not be invoked; catastrophes are not essential, indeed they are very unlikely. High-mortality infectious diseases either provoke strong immune responses with high lev-els of resistance in the population or they are unable to maintain themselves.

But each of the diseases hovering around a case mortality of about 1 per cent or less is below the threshold where we can expect natural selection to conserve advantageous genes. Nevertheless, they can add up to a considerable burden of mortality for the population, which, *if it had been caused by a single disease,* would have been neutralized through natural selection. Thus, these diseases slip through the long-term protection of natural selection with only the individual immune system and good luck for defence. But it is with these otherwise unavoidable deaths that apparently trivial differences in behaviour can alter the survival prospects of different populations. Thus, the development of the cooking of meat and fish would eliminate deaths caused by many different diseases through contamination and food poisoning. Improvements in hygiene, hand-washing and so forth (perhaps for religious reasons) could reduce mortality from another suite of diseases transmitted through the oral–faecal route. Prohibition on the eating of pork would be similarly beneficial. Populations with these forms of behaviour would prosper in contrast with those that did not have them. This suggests rather oddly that cultural selection operates on what is left over by, or inaccessible to, natural selection; it operates on the trivial rather than the spectacular.

Fecundity and fertility

The preceding arguments show that density-dependent diseases could have played a significant role in maintaining low growth rates during the Palaeolithic, *but only if pre-epidemic natural increase preceding disease intervention was already low.* This is obviously a circular argument: low natural increase begets low natural increase. Thus, we must return to the opening paragraphs of this chapter and ask why was fecundity not translated into fertility during the 90,000 years or so of sapient expansion? To answer this question we must look at the "motor" of reproduction, the "breeding group".

The "breeding group" is defined here as that subpopulation alive between the average age of the mother at the birth of her first child (x_α) and the average age of the mother at the birth of her last child (x_β).[11] Within that subpopulation there is the obvious division between male and female and within the latter, the crucial incubators, we have:

- a population-specific average involvement in breeding
- a medically determined individual breeding capacity or potential, usually called fecundity.

These are combined here into a single expression (sx).[12]

I have elsewhere established (Groube in press) that the following simple expressions can be derived from ethnographic and cemetery life-table data.[13]

$$pt_{(ni = 1.0)} = \frac{sx}{sc_\beta} \tag{Eq. 7.6a}$$

$$t_{(ni > 1.0)} = \frac{sx}{sp_\beta} \tag{Eq. 7.6b}$$

$$pt_{(ni > 1.0)} = \frac{sx}{sc_\beta} \times ni_0^{\beta - 1} \tag{Eq. 7.6c}$$

where:

pt = parity, or number of births\woman\lifetime

sx = breeding ratio or the proportion of *actual* mothers in any cohort.[12]

sc_β = cohort survival to age β. This is usually called "survivorship"; the more complex notation is to distinguish it from sp_β (below).[14]

sp_β = population survival at age β: p_β/p_0. This is not the same as survivorship (above).[14]

Parity is important to archaeologists because, when preservation conditions are suitable, it can be estimated with a fair degree of accuracy from cemetery remains (Angel 1969, 1971, Stewart 1970, Houghton 1975, 1980), but we can never know how far parity is influenced by cultural factors such as preferences in child-spacing, numbers of children, age-at-marriage, and so on, and how much is attributable to medical factors such as the normal ageing sterility or individual failings in fecundity. The proportion of women of the requisite ages actually involved in breeding (sx), also, has the same cemetery reflection, but as so few palaeodemographic analyses incorporate reliable estimates of sex or parity, the above expression employing sx (derived from ethnographic sources) is the most useful approach.

Parity can also be estimated from ethnographic and demographic sources (Pt):

$$Pt = \frac{x_\beta - x_\alpha}{bs} + 1 \qquad \text{(Eq. 7.7)}$$

where:

bs = birth spacing/interval

This expression is useful to archaeologists who struggle with inadequate cemetery data, because, for each of the terms in the equation, reasonable estimations are available from ethnography and demography, particularly from the work of Lee (1980), Howell (1979) and others on relict hunter–gatherer populations. The observations of Howell (ibid.) on the !Kung with $Pt = 4.7$, $x_\beta-x_\alpha = 15$ years and $bs = 4.1$ could have been calculated from the equation above with only two of the variables known. Obviously, being derived from field observations, Pt incorporates the rate of natural increase so that:

$$\frac{\text{(Eq. 7.7)}}{\text{(Eq. 7.6a)}} \quad \text{or} \quad \frac{Pt\,(ni > 1.0)}{pt\,(ni = 1.0)} \qquad \text{(Eq. 7.8)}$$

from which a sensitive estimation of *potential* ni can be derived from Equations 7.6a and 7.7:

$$ni^{\beta-1} = \frac{sc_\beta}{sx} \times \left[\frac{x_\beta - x_\alpha}{bs} + 1\right] \qquad \text{(Eq. 7.9)}$$

Of crucial importance is the identification by Lee (ibid.) and others of a threshold in birth spacing of about 3–4 years (depending on the density of local resources) for mobile hunter–gatherer groups. More frequent births (<3 years) can provoke physiological stress upon mothers and children in populations where adult women are also expected to be involved in the food quest. The existence of such a threshold gives us an immediate and ideal biological restraint upon fertility. The increasing likelihood of foetal wastage resulting in greater intervals between live births and of child/mother malnutrition would have a strong braking effect upon natural increase in mobile groups.

For the well documented !Kung the above equation requires an estimate only of sx (in bold below) to restore the natural increase identified by Howell (1979: table 11.1). This is an efficient breeding ratio, lower than that of 2.3 derived from the estimations given in Note 12.

$$ni = \left[\frac{0.51}{2.18} \times \left(\frac{15}{4.1} + 1\right)\right]^{1/33} = 1.0026$$

If we introduce the additional mortality of *vivax* malaria (2.5%), cohort survivorship to x_β (sc_β) will fall to 0.497 and nI will be reduced to 1.0018, the same result as that gained from Equation 7.2 quoted above. But the terms in Equation 7.9 are very subtly interrelated; because the increased mortality lowers life-expectancy, fewer women will survive to x_β, which will become a little younger, and as malaria is particularly severe on first pregnancies (Groube 1993: 174), frequently resulting in foetal loss (as well, sometimes as the loss of the mother), x_α will be older, probably by several months. The effect of both is to reduce the years of breeding. As there is ample opportunity, with a bs of 4.1 years, to replace the foetal wastage characteristic of malaria, this term does not change, but the value for sx will slightly increase as fecundity (f^*) reduces and maternal mortality (m^*) increases. The equation might now look like this, with only bs unchanged:

$$ni = \left[\frac{0.497}{2.22} \times \left(\frac{14.4}{4.1} + 1\right)\right]^{1/32.5} = 1.0031$$

If the population attempted to restore the original natural increase of 1.0026, birth spacing would have to be reduced to 3.73 years (a 10% reduction), which is equivalent to an even greater loss of available adult women's labour.

It is perhaps fortunate that malaria, along with many other noxious tropical diseases, was safely locked up in the shrunken tropical zones of the late Pleistocene; this was one bonus of the cold conditions. This is particularly true if one considers the cemetery evidence from late-Pleistocene sites; epipalaeolithic Taforalt, for example, assuming $x_\alpha = 16$ and $x_\beta = 30$ years, with survivorship to x_{30} of only 0.312 (Hassan 1981: table 7.8), if additionally afflicted with *vivax* malaria, would require a birth spacing of 2.14 years just to remain stationary. The mobility of a hunting–gathering group would certainly be compromised by such a short birth interval. But we cannot be certain that malaria mortality is not already included in the original cemetery survivorship figures, so that this sort of exercise is pointless without palaeopathological evidence of cause of death.

Because I have argued elsewhere (Groube in press) that much cemetery analysis is flawed by the failure to take account of emigration/immigration and/or the possibility of natural increase, it is pointless to re-examine such inadequate data too rigorously. Nevertheless, from what little cemetery evidence is available, it is clear that survivorship to x_β was poor by the end of the Pleistocene and that these populations were not only close to zero growth but extremely vulnerable to any additional mortality.

By the end of the Pleistocene we can expect long-settled regions such as Southwest Asia, the Mediterranean littoral and North Africa to support stable but nearly stationary populations, a pattern that could have been in existence for many tens of thousands of years. It is probable that, in this vast and rich area, actual numbers were in the hundreds of thousands, thinly dispersed, but relatively healthy and successful. The population ceilings in the many diverse regions would have been determined by different suites of micropredators balanced by reproductive effort within the larger envelope of carrying capacity. The gradually changing climate and associated floral and faunal changes of the terminal Pleistocene were probably sufficiently slow to be accommodated by the highly educable population of *Homo sapiens*, but, by the beginning of the Holocene, with world temperatures perhaps a little higher than today, another crisis emerged: the invasion of formerly temperate and cooler regions by micropredators from the tropics.

Conclusion: the return of the bugs

The last millennia of the Pleistocene and the early Holocene would have caused little more than a minor hiccup to a relatively stable demographic pattern were it not for the expansion of many micropredators that had long been left behind in their tropical homeland. Many parasites responded very rapidly to the improving world temperature; "coming down like the wolf on the fold" they expanded out of the humid tropics. The climatic amelioration during the terminal Pleistocene was a bonanza for many temperature- and humidity-sensitive micropredators and/or their vectors. Coastal changes, particularly swamp formation with the rising sea levels (cf. Chappell 1993) created ideal conditions for anophelene mosquitoes, the vector of *vivax* malaria, which, as we have already seen, would have punished any hunting groups wavering near zero growth. Along the protein-rich coasts of western and northern Europe there were many potential hosts for *Plasmodium vivax*. Everyone living near saline swamps would have been particularly at risk. It is probable that *P. vivax* was already on the move before the formal end of the Pleistocene, invading northern Europe to reach the present limits of its distribution (Norway, Sweden and northern Russia) within a few centuries of the onset of warmer conditions. The regions earliest affected would have been those closest to Africa; as the world temperatures slowly recovered from the peak of the last glacial, intermittent invasions of *P. vivax*, bringing epidemic malaria, would have become increasingly frequent in Southwest Asia and the Mediterranean region. Stable endemic malaria (the least destructive form) would have taken longer to develop, requiring not only relatively high host densities near the swamps but uniform temperatures. Coastal mesolithic settlements would have been severely hit, but, with the speed with which communal immunity can develop (premunition: Groube 1993: 171), the establishment of endemic malaria would have been rapid after temperatures stabilized; mesolithic demography would have been transformed by this efficient parasite.

In other regions, less damaging but more numerous viral, bacterial, protozoal, fungal and helminthic parasites would have made less spectacular but significant inroads into regions from which they had long been excluded. It is impossible to review in this chapter the extent of the damage they could have wrought; indeed it would be largely guesswork, but few human hunting communities close to the centres of disease dispersal could have remained unaffected by the invasion of these new but *unseen* foes. Many such groups, following the animals they hunted northwards, moved beyond the newly extended range of these micropredators. Others, unable to move, and forced with the increasing aridity into the better-watered areas, were trapped in increasingly unhealthy environments. (This launches a medical version of Childe's famous oasis theory of the origins of agriculture and pastoralism.)

This was a demographic crisis determined not by resource limitation but by the speed of the parasitic invasion and the inertia of the response of populations adjusted for millennia to near zero growth. There are many reasons for this inertia: the basic conservatism of breeding and rearing practices, where change occurs over generations not years, is obviously important, particularly as such demographic crises are largely invisible. But the essential reason is that there can be only one way to respond to increased mortality: by increased reproductive effort, which means *reduced birth intervals*. We have already seen that birth intervals of less than three years, for medical and physiological reasons, are incompatible with a highly mobile hunting–gathering way of life. A population already close to zero growth, such as is suggested by the Taforalt cemetery for example, would suffer severely if any disease or combination of diseases approaching 2–3 per cent mortality was introduced. Natural increase could be restored only by *reducing mobility* to allow higher fertility or by moving away permanently from areas of infection.

Malaria is not the only serious disease that would have invaded Southwest Asia and the Mediterranean region in the early Holocene; schistosomiasis would also have moved out of Africa (the snail vector was probably already present in the swamps of the Nile), and hook-worm, similarly, would have expanded with the improving climatic conditions. These three diseases together formed a terrible trinity for populations in or near the swamps of lower Mesopotamia and the Nile Delta. The high mortality was balanced by immigration that made inevitable the consequences of Equation 7.5: continuous ethnic and language replacements over millennia.

It is only too obvious, if earlier marriage was impossible, that many terminal Pleistocene and early Holocene populations would have had to reduce their mobility and increase their food resources if short birth spacing was not to lead to serious stress on the infant and/or mother. Initially the shift would have been very small, with only minor adjustments in mobility – a little more intensive hunting and a small shift in the burden of women from collecting to child rearing. But, as argued above, each new micropredator would add incrementally to the mother's burden and the pressure for a more sedentary way of life. However, each slowing down in the landscape would increase the risk that other parasites, kept at bay by the mobility of hunting groups, could now target *Homo sapiens*. Temporary high-density groupings would become more common, with regular visits, often seasonal, to the most productive areas, thus increasing micropredatorial penetration. This is the beginning of the escalator that led eventually to food-quest intensification, agriculture and even to the development of cities. At each stage, from initial intensification to urbanism, it is significant, although rarely mentioned, that females were the most important passengers on this escalator, becoming more and more specialized incubators for an increasingly unhealthy population. Powering this escalator were an army of micropredators, which gained, with increasing ease, access to the expanding but increasingly sedentary host population. Each step towards fully sedentary life attracted further micropredators, aided by failing sanitation, crowding and malnutrition.

I have described here only the bottom steps of the escalator. Cohen, in his remarkable book *Health and the rise of civilization* (1989), has documented the next stages: my version of the later events would differ little from his, apart from the consequences of Equation 7.5, which is the subject of another paper (Groube n.d.b). It is only concerning the *motive* to climb upon the escalator in the first instance that I beg to differ, and I do so because of unease with the case presented by Cohen. To me, and I suspect to most evolutionary biologists as well, it is biologically absurd that any animal would or could select a strategy where increased mortality and reduced life-expectancy endangered the efficiency of breeding. Biological evolution is powered by the selection of strategies for improved success in breeding; strategies that threaten breeding will not be selected even if, in the long term, such strategies would improve efficiency. As evolutionary biologists keep insisting, selection is blind. It does not and cannot "plan"; it merely responds to immediate breeding success. If we admit the Cohen case, which requires some remarkably percipient human groups to choose to intensify the food quest despite greater mortality, increased morbidity and lowered life-expectancy, we must be able to answer two crucial questions: "Why bother if there is no immediate gain?" and "How could a strategy that decreased breeding success be selected?". One must ask of the first group or groups who chose to intensify – *and* tolerate increased mortality, morbidity and lowered life-expectancy – how they survived in competition with groups who did not? And if they were not in competition with other groups, "Why bother?" To make the case, as does Cohen, that a serious health burden was incurred in the development of civilization, requires addressing the above questions. I believe that the argument presented in this chapter provides some answers.

Perversely, therefore, I would claim that agriculture and eventually cities were the consequences of micropredatorial pressure initiated by the warming climate at the end of the Pleistocene, and that when the escalator of intensification started it was almost impossible to stop or get off it – reproductive effort had to be constantly improved to keep ahead of diseases. This micropredatorial pressure sustained the impetus of intensification, diversification and subsequent developments in productivity that resulted in agriculture and pastoralism. Perhaps we owe more to bugs than we dare admit.

Notes

1. In modern populations there have been vast improvements, because of medical advances, in mortality in infants and the elderly. The former improves natural increase, the latter does not. This impact has not yet stabilized and when it does the statistics of many modern nations will show demographic decline; long-term survival prospects are disguised by the reducing mortality of those beyond the years of reproduction.
2. "Macropredation" in the sense used here is what is usually referred to as "predation", such as the hunt-

ing for food by the big cats and other carnivores. Because of control of fire, the use of tools and group protection, macropredation was of little concern to Pleistocene man. "Micropredation" refers to the invasion of *Homo sapiens*, through a variety of routes, by micro-organisms that utilize some part of the human body for food and/or reproduction. During the Pleistocene, when human population densities and natural increase were low, it is unlikely that many of these invasive micro-organisms caused death and, for those that did, human mortality rates would be very low. Most micropredators would have mildly toxic effects on humans for short periods during infection, with occasional individuals more seriously affected, particularly if they were malnourished or their immune system was compromised. Micropredators can be divided into micro- and macroparasites (see *n.* 6).

3. V. G. Childe, to the best of my knowledge, did not accept any role for human diseases in prehistory. Hassan, in his influential pioneering book *Demographic archaeology* (1981) barely mentions the role of diseases either in population regulation or as a consequence of prehistoric developments. Only one of his "models" (fig. 13.6), supported by a few lines of text (p. 227), even admits that epidemics may be a consequence of large populations; as with so much to do with mortality in prehistory, the existence of diseases is taken for granted and thereafter ignored. Only Cohen (1989) and his associates, although with a very different emphasis from that given here, recognize that diseases have great importance in prehistory.

4. An epidemic is merely a sudden intensification of activity of an invading micro-organism. In severe epidemics, conditions in the target population must favour efficient (usually rapid) disease transmission; an essential requirement is sufficient food for the parasite in the form of accessible, susceptible hosts.

5. "Endemic" is used here in its epidemiological sense as being a continuous or nearly continuous infection of childhood and infancy, with older members of the population having *acquired immunity* from their childhood experience with the disease. Endemic is also used (correctly) to refer to a disease that is native or aboriginal to a region; more loosely to any disease that does not occur in sudden epidemic-like intensifications, such as tuberculosis, diarrhoea and many respiratory illnesses (e.g. Kunitz 1968); and even more loosely to mean common or commonly occurring diseases. Endemic is not used in these broader senses here.

6. Apart from the obvious difference in size and cell complexity – with microparasites such as bacteria or protozoa the parasite load comes from multiplication *within* the host (in this case man), whereas with macroparasites such as helminths (worms) that live within their host but discharge their eggs *outside* their hosts – parasite load is determined by the frequency and success of re-infestation (see also Anderson & May 1979: 362).

7. When the rate of increase is not large the time required (T) for any magnitude of exponential increase can be calculated from:

$$T = \frac{\log nM}{r}$$

where M = magnitude of increase and r = rate (exponential).

8. When a relatively high mortality disease such as measles that should keep "progressing" to at least annual regularity is halted in this way, then the (number) threshold for initiating an epidemic (th) rises with the continuing population increase (Groube n.d.a).

9. During a disease progression, population increases by *accumulation* of survivors of earlier epidemics (i.e. those with acquired immunity), which depends on the existing mortality schedule. The size for any ei can be calculated from column Tx in a standard life-table by some arithmetical manipulations too complex to describe here (Groube n.d.a). Fortunately, for the crucial one-year epidemic interval, e_0 (derived from column Tx) $\times th$ will give a sound estimate of the number in the population with acquired immunity. Note also, $e_0 = 1000$/birth rate (=BR) when population is stationary, so that BR is also implicit in the equation.

10. *Vivax* malaria may not have been so "benign" before the appearance of *P. falciparum*, a late intruder in most malarial areas. The conservation of abnormal haemoglobins as powerful inherited defences against the highly lethal *falciparum* malaria (*c.*25 per cent cohort mortality) such as sickle-cell anaemia, the thalassaemias, G6PD deficiency and so on, may have reduced the lethality of *vivax* malaria during the past 2,000 years (Groube 1993: 173–4).

11. The validity of this definition (in contrast, for example, to taking the biological menarche to menopause interval) is discussed in Groube (in press, n.d.a). Fortunately, a substantial amount of comparative data is available on x_α and x_β for modern and ethnographic populations allowing sound estimates for prehistory to be made.

12. This expression is discussed in Groube (in press), but because of its importance in this text it is summarized here. Values in {} are estimations for late Pleistocene hunter–gatherers derived from many factors (Groube n.d.a):

$$sx = [sr \times m* \times i* \times w* \times rm]$$

where:

sr = sex ratio at birth expressed as

$$sr = \frac{m+f}{f} \quad \{2.05\}$$

$m*$ = relative survivorship of females (S_f) to completion of fertility where there is sex-biased mortality (female infanticide, male mortality in war, maternal mortality, etc.):

$1/S_f$ {1.05}

$f*$ = fecundity (potential fertility, male and female):

1 + average fertility {1.05}

This is a measure of average infertility during the breeding years. It includes ageing-sterility and all other medical and genetic impediments to fertility (both sexes).

$w*$ = proportion of women actively involved in reproduction expressed as:

1 + average rate of withdrawal {1.00}

This measure is obviously only relevant where women are able to exercise choice (for personal, religious or professional reasons). In terms of reproduction it is equivalent to induced sterility or a change of sex.

rm = impact of speed of re-marriage upon the death of either partner, expressed as relative loss of reproductive time between marriages. This index is affected by customs and mortality during the ages of breeding:

1 + % loss of breeding time {1.02}

Thus, if the mourning lasts one year, for example, a significant proportion of the effective (female) breeding period is lost. If there is no re-marriage, then, obviously, mortality during the breeding year would have to be incorporated into sx. From ethnographic evidence $rm*$ is assumed to be low for most hunter–gatherer societies during prehistory.

13. This expression and those developed from it, including those in Groube (in press), make an assumption that the decline in population number between age-intervals is linear, which is the standard assumption in constructing life-tables and cannot be avoided in palaeodemography where skeletal age cannot be closely estimated and where age-intervals as low as five years are of dubious validity.

14. By the mean age of her last birth (β), the average mother should have completed her breeding commitments to replace herself and a male, to contribute her share to the replacement of women unable or unwilling to breed, or those, male and female, who are partially or wholly sterile. In addition, she must contribute her share of the surplus births required for a stable natural increase. Thus, a sound first approximation of a breeding generation would be:

$$g = \alpha + ni(1-sc_\beta)(\beta-\alpha) + sx - 1$$

If we look at the !Kung (Howell 1979: tables 4.4 and 11.1) we have:

$$g = 19 + 1.0026(1-0.51)(15) + 1.05 = 27.419$$

which is the same as that calculated by well established demographic methods by Howell (ibid.: table 11.1) of 27.42 years. This is confirmation of the robustness of β as a measure of reproductive span (Groube in press, n.d.a).

References

Acsádi, G-Y. & J. Nemeskéri 1970. *History of human lifetime and mortality*. Budapest: Ackademiai Kiado.

Anderson, R. M. & R. M. May 1979. Population biology of infectious diseases, Part I. *Nature* **280**, 361–7.

Andrewartha, H. G. 1963. *Introduction to the study of animal populations*. Chicago: University of Chicago Press.

Angel, J. L. 1969. The bases of palaeodemography. *American Journal of Physical Anthropology* **30**, 427–37.

— 1971. Early neolithic skeletons from Çatal Hüyük: demography and pathology. *Anatolian Studies* **20**, 77–98.

Black, F. L. 1966. Measles endemicity in insular populations: critical community size and its evolutionary implications. *Journal of Theoretical Biology* **11**, 207–11.

Bodmer, W. F. & L. L Cavalli-Sforza 1976. *Genetics, evolution, and man*. San Francisco: W. H. Freeman.

Boserup, E. 1965. *The conditions of agricultural growth*. Chicago: Aldine.

Burnet, MacF. & D. White 1972. *Natural history of infectious diseases*. Cambridge: Cambridge University Press.

Carniero, R. L. & D. F. Hulse 1966. On determining the probable rate of population growth during the Neolithic. *American Anthropologist* **68**, 177–81.

Chappell, J. 1993. Late Pleistocene coasts and human migrations in the Austral region. In *A community of culture: the people and prehistory of the Pacific*. M. Spriggs, D. E. Yen, W. Ambrose, R. Jones, A. Thorne, A. Andrews (eds), 43–8. Occasional Papers in Prehistory 21, Department of Prehistory, Research School of Pacific Studies, Australian National University.

Childe, V. G. 1941. *Man makes himself*. London: Watts.

Cohen, M. N. 1977. *The food crisis in prehistory*. New Haven, Connecticut: Yale University Press.

— 1989. *Health and the rise of civilization*. New Haven, Connecticut: Yale University Press.

Coleman, D. 1986. Population regulation: a long-range view. In *The state of population theory*, D. Coleman & R. Schofield (eds), 14–41. Oxford: Basil Blackwell.

Groube, L. M. 1993. Contradictions and malaria in Australian and Melanesian prehistory. In *A community of culture: the people and prehistory of the Pacific*. M. Spriggs, D. E. Yen, W. Ambrose, R. Jones, A. Thorne, A. Andrews (eds), 164–86. Occasional Papers in Prehistory 21, Department of Prehistory, Research School of Pacific Studies, Australian National University.

— In press *The geometry of the dead*. In *Pacific culture history: essays in honour of Roger Green*. J. Davidson, G. Irwin, D. Brown, A. Pawley (eds). Auckland: The Polynesian Society.

— n.d.a. *Micropredation in world prehistory*. [The completion of this book awaits publication of several papers already in press or in preparation.]

— n.d.b. *Ethnic replacement and Indo–European origins: the role of infectious diseases*. [This paper discusses the impact of immigration from low-disease (high altitude and high latitude) regions upon a disease equilibrium established in a high-disease region such as the river civilizations of Southwest Asia.]

Groube, L. M., J. Chappell, J. Muke, D. Price 1986. A 40,000 year-old occupation site at Huon peninsula, Papua New Guinea. *Nature* **324**, 453–5.

Haldane, J. B. S. 1932. *The inequality of man*. London: Chatto & Windus.

Hassan, F. A. 1981. *Demographic archaeology*. London: Academic Press.

Hawking, S. W. 1988. *A brief history of time*. London: Bantam.

Houghton, P. 1975. The bony imprint of pregnancy. *Bulletin of the New York Academy of Medicine* **51**, 655–61.

— 1980. *The first New Zealanders*. Auckland: Hodder & Stoughton.

Howell, N, 1979. *The demography of the Dobe !Kung*. New York: Academic Press.

Keymer, A. E. & A. F. Read 1990. The evolutionary biology of parasitism. Symposia of the British Society of Parasitology, vol. 27. *Parasitology* **100** (Supplement), 1–115.

Kunitz, S. J. 1968. Mortality since Malthus. In *The state of population theory: forward from Malthus*, D. Coleman & R. Schofield (eds), 279–302. Oxford: Basil Blackwell.

Lee, R. B. 1980. Lactation, ovulation, infanticide and women's work: a study of hunter–gatherer population regulation. In *Biosocial mechanisms of population regulation*, M. N. Cohen, R. Malpass, H. Klein (eds), 321–48. New Haven, Connecticut: Yale University Press.

Livingstone, F. B. 1968. The effects of warfare on the biology of the human species. In *War: the anthropology of armed conflict and aggression*, M. Fried, M. Harris, R. Murphy (eds), 3–15. New York: Natural History Press.

Mallory, J. P. 1989. *In search of the Indo–Europeans; language, archaeology and myth*. London: Thames & Hudson.

Martin, P. S. & H. E. Wright (eds) 1967. *Pleistocene extinctions: the search for a cause*. New Haven, Connecticut: Yale University Press.

Montagu, A. 1956. *The biosocial nature of man*. New York: Grove Press.

Motulsky, A. G. 1960. Metabolic polymorphisms and the role of infectious diseases in human evolution. *Human Biology* **32**, 28–62.

Nemeskéri, J. 1972. Some comparisons of Egyptian and early Eurasian demographic data. *Journal of Human Evolution* **1**, 171–86.

Pearl, R. & L. J. Reed 1920. On the rate of growth of the population of the United States since 1790 and its mathematical representation. *Proceedings of the National Academy of Sciences of the USA*, **6**, 275–88.

Rennie, J. 1992. Living together (trends in parasitology). *Scientific American* **266**(1), 104–13.

Roberts, R. G., R. Jones, M. A. Smith 1990. Thermoluminescence dating of a 50,000 year-old human occupation site in northern Australia. *Nature* **345**, 153–6.

Schofield, R. & D. Coleman 1986. Introduction: the state of population theory. In *The state of population theory: forward from Malthus*, D. Coleman & R. Schofield (eds), 1–13. Oxford: Basil Blackwell.

Stewart, T. D. 1970. Identification of the scars of parturition in skeletal remains of females. In *Personal identification in mass disasters*, T. D Stewart (ed.), 127–35. Washington DC: Smithsonian Institution Press.

UNSO (United Nations Statistical Office), Department of Economic and Social Affairs, 1979. *1978 Demographic Yearbook*. New York: United Nations.

Verhulst, P. F. 1847. Deuxième mémoire sur l'accroissement de la population. *Nouveaux Mémoires de l'Académie Royale des Sciences et Belles Lettres de Bruxelles* **20**, 1–32.

Weiss, K. M. 1973. Demographic models for anthropology. *American Antiquity* **38**, Part 2, Memoir 7.

CHAPTER EIGHT

Plate tectonics and imaginary prehistories: structure and contingency in agricultural origins

Andrew Sherratt

To anyone with imagination, there are few more fascinating subjects than plate tectonics. There is a tantalizing arbitrariness about the way in which continental masses move around and collide. To realize that the Weald of southern England is a remote echo of the creation of the Alps, caused by the collision of the Eurasian and North African plates, is to raise the question: what would have happened if it had struck somewhere else? Or missed altogether? Or if the Indian plate had struck Asia farther east, and the Himalayas been created in Indonesia? These questions are not altogether idle. For the movements of the continents exercised a decisive influence on evolution and not least on the history of the human species; and the realization that the present disposition of the continental masses is the result of a series of accidents brings home what Stephen Jay Gould (1990) has said about the inhabitants of the Burgess Shale: that what exists today is but an arbitrary selection from a whole range of evolutionary possibilities. I want to apply these thoughts to the more recent history of our species, by using them as a springboard for some controlled speculations. They were prompted by the well known fact that Madagascar, although only 400 km off the African mainland at its nearest point (and only a short hop away from the first documented appearance of *Homo erectus*), was not colonized until the early centuries AD, and then from the other side of the Indian Ocean, from Indonesia. Now for the greater part of its length, the Mediterranean is in fact wider than the Mozambique Channel. Were it not for Gibraltar, the central Mediterranean islands, and the isthmus of Suez, then Africa and Eurasia would be isolated by a comparable distance; and when the East African and Erythraean rift systems develop further, they may well come to be so. Had the Tethys not been obliterated, Europe could have been effectively an island. And so on.

Idly ruminating on these points, it occurred to me to wonder what European prehistory would have been like if Europe had been literally isolated in this way. Given our current knowledge of world prehistory, could one in the imagination sketch out what might have happened? When would it have been discovered and colonized by

Near Eastern seafarers, given that the Near East (Southwest Asia) retained sufficient similarity to its historic form to generate a Neolithic and then an Urban Revolution? And what would these seafarers have found? Intoxicated by a new-found sense of power, I then began to imagine what might happen if one could create seas and land-bridges at will – interactive prehistory at the push of a button, with different outcomes depending on the chosen continental configuration – Europe isolated after the intro-duction of the Neolithic, developing in isolation; or after the beginning of the Bronze Age; or whatever. At that point I began to realize that such brainstorming was actually an essential part of the historical imagination: the ability to envisage alternative out-comes, and thus to trace the causal links between the different parts of what actually happened. If one area influenced another, then things would have been different had that link not existed; and we can mentally gauge how important that link was by imag-ining what would have happened had it not existed. Why not, then, conduct the exper-iment more systematically, by asking the question at regular intervals, and by varying the extent of the separation?

I cannot claim to have thought through all the possibilities; but the mental exercise has left me feeling more supple, and less certain of the categories within which we work. It is rather like what the evidence of pollen analysis did to plant sociology in showing that what we think of as somehow "natural" associations (such as mixed oak forest) were much more like shifting configurations, thrown together often by chance. The boom in hazel that was so prominent a feature of early Holocene Europe, for example, did not inevitably occur in earlier interglacial cycles, because it was the product not of a simple vegetational succession but of differential colonization rates, themselves largely determined by the size and location of refuge areas. In short, it was very much a matter of chance.

Plate tectonics and the genesis of *Homo*

This sense of the accidental can be discerned in palaeontology as well. Instead of what might be called an autonomist interpretation of evolution, there is a new cata-strophism, with mass extinctions caused by the impact of extraterrestrial objects of various kinds. The most famous is, of course, the end of the dinosaurs in the Late Cre-taceous terminal catastrophe (although this is by no means the only example). The mammalian opportunity was, in that sense, an accident; and the conference in London that gave rise to this book might otherwise have taken place among a group of brainy bipedal dinosaurs (literally, that is, not just metaphorically). Even the purely terres-trial processes of biological evolution have an accidental component, however, in so far as they were influenced by the chance configuration of continental masses. Indeed, the whole human story – the emergence of the human species and the pattern of faunal evolution of which it was part – was to a large extent controlled by accidents of plate tectonics: on the one hand by their effects on climate, and on the other hand because of their effects on biogeography.

In the first place, the constant wandering of patches of continental crust, and their assembly into supercontinents and dispersal as smaller ones, has a powerful effect on global climate, depending on whether major continental masses come to be positioned over the poles. Thus, the whole climatic history of the Cenozoic has been largely determined by the fact that Antarctica came to be positioned over the South Pole, where the consequent accumulation of ice caused a gradual cooling, which eventually passed the threshold of sensitivity to Milankovich fluctuations in the phase that we separate off as the Pleistocene. The evolution of the hominid line – like that of other ground-living primates – critically depended on the creation of open habitats as a consequence of this cooling (and its effects on precipitation), accelerated at times by further effects of plate movement such as the joining of North and South America, which affected oceanic circulation patterns.

The second aspect of plate tectonics that is relevant to the human story is the movement of the continental masses in relation to each other, and particularly the convergence of those that came to make up the Old World – the collision of Africa with Eurasia, and India with East Asia. It was this process that led to the creation of the Alps and the Himalayas – and the obliteration of the Tethys Sea – as a result of the prolonged impact. This provided the opportunity for movement between landmasses: the exchange of African and Eurasian fauna, with the spread of horses and bovids *to* Africa, and the dispersal of elephants and primates *from* Africa, in which the spread of the human species was a minor chapter. The pattern that was produced by the Cenozoic was an "Old" World and a "New" World – terms that reflect the experience of the sixteenth century AD, but are also symptomatic of a deeper structure: a set of "joined up" continental masses constituting Eurasia with a pendant Africa, and a loosely attached or completely separated Pacific periphery of Australia, Oceania and the Americas. This continental configuration, and the population movements it permitted, was the topological foundation for the emergence and spread of successive species of *Homo*.

Why should this concern us, as archaeologists? In a sense, these are the "givens", the preconditions of our subject. But it is salutary to be reminded of the fact that they were, in a sense, accidents – events rather than processes, in the rhetoric of the 1960s – and thus *historical* in that they could have happened otherwise. In a subject where constant, cumulative change sometimes comes to seem inevitable, it is as well to be reminded of the chapter of accidents that forms the background to the processes we want to explain. It is the same message as that of the Burgess Shale: that what actually happened was only a haphazard selection from a wider set of possible outcomes. The point is not merely a philosophical one, however, but also a practical one, because it suggests that important – even unique – changes take place not on the regular surfaces of large and predictable processes, but in the cracks and interstices in the pattern: the historically unusual conjunctions of spatial and temporal circumstances that generate unique opportunities for novelties to arise.

The two sets of processes outlined above – the Cenozoic cooling and the convergence of continents – exercised a critical influence on human development in the period that we traditionally term the "Ice Age", in one of whose brief warmer episodes we are still living. Geologically speaking, the modern world came into existence in the Pleistocene, when the Milankovich rules came into play. Small fluctuations in insolation were reflected in global climatic changes of increasing magnitude, culminating in the continental glaciations of the middle and later Pleistocene. What are seen from a northern perspective as glaciations must more relevantly be described, however, as desiccation phases in the tropics, which were of even greater significance for early hominid and human populations. Both Brian Fagan (1990: 65) and I have hit on the same metaphor to describe part of this process: what we have called the "Saharan pump", by which populations were repeatedly sucked into the great landmass of North Africa during episodes of high rainfall and vegetation growth, and successively expelled in periods of desiccation. This was a major engine of population dispersal, propelling hominids across the land-bridge of the Levant to seek their fortune in Eurasia. The importance of glaciation in this process, as a phenomenon of high latitudes remote from where the main biological action was taking place, was paradoxically therefore less through the geological and vegetational changes it induced (although much of our Quaternary research budget is devoted to elucidating their minor fluctuations), and more through the effects on global sea levels of the amount of water locked up as ice. In synchrony with the terrestrial spasms, areas of continental shelf were alternately revealed and covered by the sea. These provided further pumps, where extensive areas of land were temporarily exposed and flooded, and sometimes provided fluctuating land-bridges between alternately joined and separated landmasses. Glaciation itself, once human populations had become adapted to cold conditions during the last glaciation, exercised a further propellant effect, forcing (or giving a competitive advantage to) the Eurasian Neanderthals who moved south into areas such as the Levant after 100,000 bp, before themselves giving way to anatomically modern populations from the south in the latter half of the last glaciation.

These random stirrings of the pattern of human populations were important not only in their general character but also in their specific effects, in that they were constrained by the layout of continental masses and the climatic conditions that affected them. It was in the bottlenecks and funnels of the humanly inhabited world that these processes were at their most intense. It is important to preserve this Pleistocene perspective when considering the events that followed.

Plate tectonics and the genesis of agriculture

There are two aspects of this set of processes, therefore, that relate to the focus of interest in this volume on the origins and spread of farming. One is the cycle of pressures and opportunities that it gave rise to; the other is how these were actually configured on the ground. Together, these produced the properties that characterize the past 10,000 years, which were otherwise just another brief warm episode in a series of climatic cycles. What made the Holocene so different – when in other respects it was just another interglacial – was the fact that certain areas emerged as "hot spots" that were consistent foci of change. Certain unusual conjunctions of features produced conditions that were not widely replicated. These gave rise to population density gradients far steeper than anything that had existed in the Pleistocene: in a word, "nuclear" areas. What lay behind the emergence of such nuclearity? Unlike the kinds of climatically induced population pressures of the Pleistocene, these areas created *endogenous* pressure; within a few millennia of the onset of the Holocene, they were regions that generated their own patterns of population growth, which in turn affected much of the surrounding continental masses. Such demographic transitions took place only in extremely localized circumstances, and completely independently only in perhaps three places on the Earth's surface – the classic areas of the origins of farming. Because farming was so rapidly adopted during the Holocene, we tend to view it as in some sense inevitable. This disguises what ought to be the real surprise: the rarity of the conjunction of conditions that actually gave rise to it. It is this aspect that relates to my theme of accidental conjunction.

Of course, early "agriculture" was only one of a set of more differentiated and locally intensive food-getting practices that emerged around the world as modern human populations explored the potential of a range of new and old habitats; but it had a set of emergent properties with fundamental consequences in the places where it emerged. These had to do with two things: a concentration on vegetable foods with specialized storage organs, and a process of habitat-switching that transferred plants adapted to seasonal stress (and thus restricted to marginal habitats) into habitats of much greater primary productivity. The necessary conditions to trigger this process were twofold: first, situations where marked ecological contrasts occurred within a restricted area (and perhaps even within the social territory of an individual group or set of groups); and secondly conditions of demographic pressure that rendered alternatives unattractive or impossible. The kinds of contrasts where such developments might occur most rapidly were not the gently graded series of habitats that characterize homogeneous temperate areas, but stark juxtapositions of hills, desert and alluvium. The kinds of pressures that forced the pace were precisely the rapid environmental changes that characterized the shift from glacial to interglacial conditions – but most especially in situations where populations had little opportunity to escape.

Let us try to design such a set of circumstances. A uniform forest zone offers few opportunities: the specialized food-storage organs are nuts, which are uniformly distributed and hard to increase within a localized area. A coast offers shellfish, already localized, but hard to transfer to new areas (and in any case difficult to store, increase, etc.). A range of mountains offers some possibilities, but within a uniform climatic zone the changes are generally too gradual. What is really needed is the addition of a desert. The conjunction of all these aspects maximizes the contrasts, and multiplies the number and size of ecotones. It provides the two critical elements: the existence both of plants with specialized storage organs and of new habitats to which they can be transferred. To this one can add a set of environmental fluctuations, to stir things up a bit and provide an incentive – a sort of micro-Saharan pump, to tempt populations in, then push them out. Fluctuating rainfall conditions would be one mechanism, perhaps with rising sea levels to give a bit of consistent directionality.

But what we also need to build in is something to stop people escaping, something that precludes a simple solution of out-migration. It is here that we should continue to think in Pleistocene terms, and not just shrink to a Holocene space-frame. In the middle of a continent, there are opportunities to escape environmental pressure by moving in many different directions. People can migrate outwards from high-density areas, and pressure builds up only where such movements are funnelled and con-

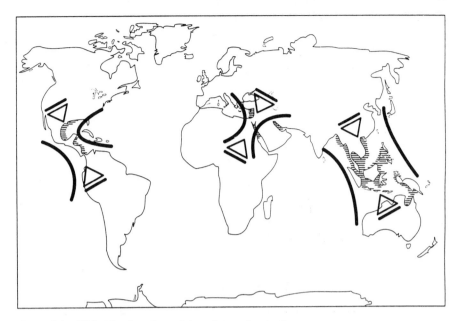

Figure 8.1 Global bottlenecks and the origins of agriculture.

stricted. In such narrow strips of habitable land, however, pressure can build up very quickly – especially if they link two continental systems that are both liable to shed population by out-migration into a corridor between them. What we need to build in, therefore, is a *bottleneck*, an isthmus of some kind between growing systems. A glance at a global map (Fig. 8.1) suggests some likely areas: the narrow strips of land separating North and South America, Africa from western Eurasia, and Australia from the East Asian mainland. The last of these is, of course, much broader than the other two; but it also has a very much greater proportion of flooding continental shelf. Gratifyingly, it was precisely in such locations that agriculture first appeared.

This is not, of course, intended as a rigorous demonstration, but it does point out the kinds of factors involved and why they were relatively localized. It emphasizes the need to continue thinking in Pleistocene terms about large-scale flows of population, and the background framing that they provide to local situations. If we now look specifically at the Levantine isthmus (Fig. 8.2), we can see that it combines almost all of the features mentioned: a bottleneck configuration, and constraints of sea and desert on either side, with an axial mountain chain or parallel chains. Rising sea levels and fluctuating desert margins provide the pressures and prevent lateral out-migration; the double funnel provides resistance at either end; within the isthmus, the intimate juxtaposition of coastal plain, montane, rift valley and desert habitats provide maximum opportunities for switching plants from one habitat to another – in this case the wild, rainfed cereals of the hills (watered by westerly winds penetrating along the Mediterranean and falling on higher ground) to well watered lowland habitats, where they could be maintained artificially. Here, pinpoints of locally dense population were possible at oases within the rift, at places such as Jericho.

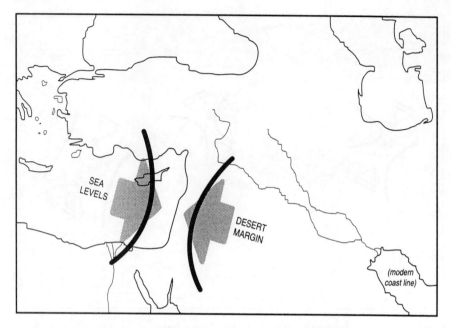

Figure 8.2   Pressures on the Levantine bottleneck in the early Holocene.

If we now step back a moment and ask why this unusual conjunction of conditions exists (Fig. 8.3), the answer combines the geo-history of the region with the zonal properties of global climate under late Cenozoic conditions. Latitudinally (but to the east displaced by the disposition of the continental masses) the arid zone created by descending air and high evaporation rates occupies northern Africa and swings up into central Asia. Also extending east/west, but crossing over the arid zone in the Levant, the chain of Tertiary fold-mountains created by the meeting of the African and Eurasian continental masses swings across southern Europe and then southeastwards as the Taurus–Zagros arc, to join the Himalayas in the Pamir Knot. Occupying the basin between them in the west is the truncated remnant of the Tethys Sea, the Mediterranean, with its outliers forming the Black Sea, the Caspian and the Aral Sea (or as much of it as still exists). Westerly winds, penetrating along the Mediterranean, drop their moisture on the mountains as they cross the arid belt at the eastern end of the Mediterranean, creating the zonally atypical conditions of the Fertile Crescent – a kind of macro-oasis with runoff from the hills supporting springs, wadis and the great perennial rivers of Mesopotamia. In a further complication, Mediterranean climates themselves are created by seasonal shifts between tropical desert and temperate rainfall regimes; and Egypt, otherwise desert, is supported by the waters of the Nile, fed by tropical rainfall.

It would be hard to imagine a more unusual conjunction of conditions; and it is this highly unusual mixture that explains the unique historical role of Southwest Asia throughout the Holocene – in the genesis of farming, then in the origins of urban life (through the contrast between its irrigable plains and their resource-rich hinterlands), and then in the spread of maritime urban trading systems, first in the Mediterranean,

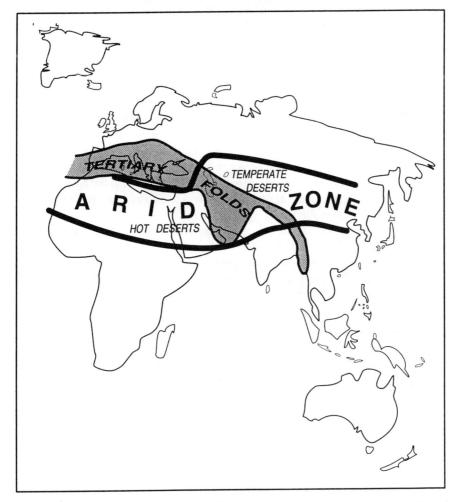

Figure 8.3 The unique conjunction: the Near East (Southwest Asia) as the intersection of the arid zone, the Tertiary fold chain and the Tethys axis.

and afterwards in the Indian Ocean. By contrast, the much more homogeneous stretches of temperate and boreal forest that make up the rest of western Eurasia had a far slower dynamic, and were therefore constantly transformed by inputs from the faster-developing region to the south. So, too, was northern Africa (although sub-Saharan Africa was more intermittently influenced because of the desert barrier, which became more extensive in the middle Holocene). In broad perspective, then, both Europe and Africa were margins: areas that were transformed from outside. Southwest Asia, on the other hand, was destined by nature to be nuclear.

Non-nuclear regions

If so, then what would have happened if Europe, or northern Eurasia, had been an island? If wild cereals had not grown there, it would have lacked one of the essential preconditions for farming; and with a relatively homogeneous vegetation cover, switching would have been less likely to occur. Would cultivation have been worth-while, with only poppies, pulses or cabbages? And even if it had, would we call it farming, by comparison with cereal-based village farming on the Near Eastern pattern, with its explosive properties? And what of local domestic animals? If an inde-pendent northern Eurasia had been linked to the Americas, there would have been horses. Would these horses ever have come to be domesticated, in the absence of the model provided by cattle domestication, which was itself a product of the sedentari-zation caused by cereal cultivation?

The point is a fundamental one, because economies such as pastoralism were argu-ably regional adaptations of a unitary primitive farming. They were in large part cre-ations stimulated by what had already happened in Southwest Asia. Indeed, the whole complex of secondary agriculture can be modelled (Fig. 8.4) as a set of interactions and knock-on effects within the developing primary complex. Even reindeer pasto-ralism seems to have been a knock-on effect of steppe pastoralism, itself ultimately a consequence of primary farming. Had the chain of latitudinal links been broken at any point, then the causal chain, too, would have been ruptured. No steppe, horse-based pastoralism in Eurasia, then; and no domestic reindeer. And what about Africa, if, after the dispersal of *Homo sapiens*, its links to Eurasia had been severed? Would tropical millets have been brought into cultivation, or iron-working spread across Africa? Surely not, within the timescale that they did, without the western Asiatic model. Agriculture as a practice would presumably have arrived in the same way as the banana eventually did, as a result of Indian Ocean maritime contacts. So, too, with an isolated Europe: farming would have been brought by the Phoenicians, to an epi-Mesolithic continent. Similar questions can be raised concerning other parts of the world. What would North America have looked like if the continent ended at Texas? Where would Japan be without China? What would India's history have been, were it still an island in the ocean? At one level, such thoughts are idle speculation. Yet all

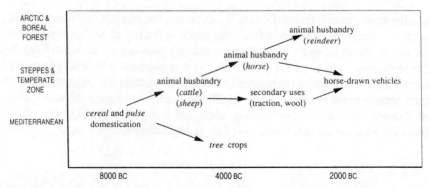

Figure 8.4   Interactions and knock-on effects in the development of Old World farming.

the present configurations are to some extent accidental. They could not have been predicted from a map of the globe at the end of the Cretaceous, or even in the Miocene. They *could* have been different, and if so the history of the human species would have been different too.

Nuclear regions and their margins

Of course to imagine alternative histories can only be a mental exercise. But it is a useful antidote to unthinking assumptions, such as that of local autonomism. Most prehistorians active today have grown up in an atmosphere of reaction to the grand reconstructions of an earlier generation, whether Gordon Childe in Europe or Robert Heine-Geldern in the Pacific. When less was known about world prehistory, it was easier to postulate waves of horsemen overwhelming Europe, or successive waves of seafarers crossing the Pacific. We now know better: we have filled in much of the detail. The processes look infinitely more complex. But what we have lost in this wealth of new information is the sense of interconnectedness, a consciousness of the structural settings of the regions we study. I believe that it is time to recapture some of this sense of connectivity. One symptom of it is the interest in world-systems theory; but this is to start from the wrong end, to work backwards from capitalism to prehistory. There is much centricity in pre-urban systems, perhaps more than we suspect, but the language of core and periphery is too specifically tailored to recent history to capture this larger sense. That is why the terms "marginal" and "nuclear" have the right resonance; and why it is worth the effort of trying to imagine what margins would look like without their nuclear areas.

Let me give one final example of such potential interconnectedness. At first sight, the Eskimo spread into the Arctic, or the Polynesian spread into outer Oceania, seem to have little to do with the contemporary spread of urbanism in the heartlands of world population, from the Mediterranean to China. Yet some element of pressure seems to be a necessary component of both these movements on the outer edges of the inhabited world. Over what area was such demographic pressure generated? How large a demographic hinterland must one postulate? Was it just a narrow adjacent strip; or was the demographic differential between heartland and margin, between the urban areas and the still uninhabited regions, so steep that one can postulate a constant outward pattern of migration of continental proportions, whose knock-on effect reached to the outer limits of Eurasia and beyond? I ask the question only to point up how primitive our concept of demographic pressure really is (cf. Cavalli-Sforza and Groube in Chs 4 and 7 in this volume). By comparison with the sophistication with which meteorologists model variations in barometric pressure, we have hardly begun. But does not demography, too, have its highs and lows, its fronts and its cyclones? Having thrown out migration as an unthinking model of cultural change, should we not begin to reintegrate it as an essential element of demographic reality?

Conclusion

I hesitate to call any of this a paradigm shift, but I do think that it is more than just a set of pipe-dreams. Such thinking is possible because we now know enough about different parts of the world to have a truly comparative prehistory: we can do more than simply describe what was there, we can predict what might have happened in other conditions, by mobilizing insights from one area and deploying them in another. It goes along with other symptoms of maturity: we can grow out of knee-jerk reactions to such words as "migration" or even "diffusion", to examine some of the phenomena that might lurk beneath the labels, and need to be brought back into our explanations. But if my instincts are correct, prehistory is unified not only at a *comparative* level but also at a *structural* level, in that developments in different parts of the world are related in rather fundamental ways. Prehistorians are beginning to recognize this once again, and there is an increasing readiness to accept the importance of evolution at the centre, as well as adaptation at the edge. I have argued this for the Bronze Age (Sherratt 1993), but it works for earlier periods too. After all, what is the "out of Africa" model but a global core–periphery paradigm for the Palaeolithic?

In its most abstract terms, what I am advocating is a move away from the idea of general successions – the universal stages-of-culture model that we have inherited from Enlightenment and Victorian system-builders – towards the idea that structure can be the outcome of a chapter of rare but important accidents. And the eventful arbitrariness but structured outcomes of plate tectonics give us just the mental flexibility we need in order to approach the finer detail of the Holocene. There is, then, no such thing as *pre*history: only a seamless transition from one kind of history to another.

References

Fagan, B. 1990. *The journey from Eden: the peopling of our world*. London: Thames & Hudson.
Gould, S. J. 1990. *Wonderful life: the Burgess Shale and the nature of history*. London: Hutchinson.
Sherratt, A. 1993. What would a Bronze Age world system look like? Relations between temperate Europe and the Mediterranean in later prehistory. *Journal of European Archaeology* 1, 1–51.

PART TWO
Southwest Asia

CHAPTER NINE

The mode of domestication of the founder crops of Southwest Asian agriculture

Daniel Zohary

Introduction

A major problem yet to be solved in crop-plant evolution is the mode of domestication of the various cultivated plants. For each crop the question can be asked: was its wild progenitor taken into cultivation only once? If so, the cultivated derivative is a product of a single domestication event and thus the result of "monophyletic evolution" under cultivation. Alternatively, the wild progenitor could have been introduced into cultivation many times and in different places. If that is the case, one is faced with multiple events of domestication and with "polyphyletic evolution".

Discrimination between these two modes of domestication can be of considerable help when one wishes to reconstruct the early history of cultivated plants. It has extra significance when applied to key crops known to have founded agriculture in a given region. If the mode of origin of such founder crops is elucidated, it can help to answer the basic question: how (and perhaps where) did agriculture begin?

In a previous paper (Zohary 1989) I suggested that genetic comparisons between cultivars and their wild progenitors provide clues for the evaluation of single versus multiple domestications. It was argued that several lines of evidence indicate that at least some of the crops associated with the beginnings of food production in Southwest Asia were taken into cultivation only once or very few times. Since then the mode of domestication of the Southwest Asian founder crops has been further explored by both Blumler (1992) and myself. This chapter considers the available evidence, and the conclusions that can be drawn from the information now available.

Background

The early neolithic crop assemblage

Plant remains that have been expertly identified and radiocarbon dated are now available from hundreds of neolithic sites in Southwest Asia, Europe and the Nile Valley (for recent reviews see van Zeist et al. 1991, Zohary & Hopf 1993). This rich archaeobotanical documentation demonstrates the following facts:

- Three cereal crops: emmer wheat *Triticum turgidum* subsp. *dicoccum*, barley *Hordeum vulgare*, and einkorn wheat *Triticum monococcum* were (in this order of importance) the principal founders of neolithic agriculture in this part of the world. Definite signs of their cultivation first appear in the Near Eastern "arc" in Pre-Pottery Neolithic B (PPNB) contexts dated to the eighth and seventh millennia bc (uncalibrated radiocarbon time) (Fig. 9.1).

- The domestication of these cereals went hand-in-hand with the introduction into cultivation of several companion plants. Most common – in the PPNB farming villages – are the remains of two pulses: lentil *Lens culinaris* and pea *Pisum sativum*; and of a single oil-and-fibre crop, flax *Linum usitatissimum* (Fig. 9.1). Less frequent – but obviously part of the crop assemblage – are two other grain legumes: bitter vetch *Vicia ervilia* and chick pea *Cicer arietinum*. These five com-

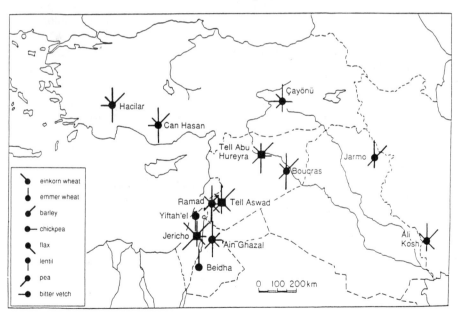

Figure 9.1   Crop assemblage in the early neolithic farming villages in Southwest Asia before 6000 bc (uncalibrated radiocarbon dates). ■: Earliest sites, with deposits containing remains of crops dated to the eighth millennium bc. ●: Somewhat later sites, dated to the seventh millennium bc. A short whisker indicates that the crop is relatively rare and a long whisker that it is relatively common among the excavated plant remains. (Adapted from Zohary & Hopf 1993: 37).

panion crops were very probably domesticated simultaneously with the wheats and barley, or were taken into cultivation just a short time later.

• The subsequent expansion of neolithic agriculture to Europe, Caucasia, Central Asia, the Nile Valley and the Indus basin was also based on this crop assemblage. The plants with which food production started in the Southwest Asian "nuclear area" were transported (already as domesticated crops) to initiate agriculture all over these vast territories.

The claims for early neolithic domestication of additional plants are less convincing, although some finds hint that faba bean (broad bean) *Vicia faba* (Kislev 1985), grass pea *Lathyrus sativus* (Zohary & Hopf 1993: 115) and rye *Secale cereale* (Hillman 1978, de Moulins 1994) might also belong to the early neolithic crop assemblage. But for these three additional crops the published evidence from archaeology and/or from the living plants is still insufficient. For this reason they are not included in the present assessment.

The wild progenitors of the neolithic founder crops

The relationships between the founder crops and their wild relatives have also been intensively studied (for recent reviews see Zohary 1989, Smartt 1990, Zohary & Hopf 1993). In each of the eight founder crops, crossing experiments (frequently accompanied by protein or by DNA comparisons) have clarified the genetic affinities between the cultivars and their related wild species. In each, the wild progenitor from which the crop could have evolved is now satisfactorily identified (Table 9.1). Furthermore, the geographical distribution, ecological specificities, and the ranges and structuring of genetic variation in most of these wild relatives have been explored.

Finally, comparisons between the wild progenitors and their cultivated derivatives have also established the main domestication traits that evolved in these crops in response to selection (frequently unconscious selection) under cultivation. Thus, the

Table 9.1   The Southwest Asian neolithic founder crops and their wild progenitors.

Cultivated crop	Wild progenitor
1. Emmer wheat: *Triticum turgidum* subsp. dicoccum	Wild emmer wheat: *Triticum turgidum* subsp. *dicoccoides* (= *T. dicoccoides*)
2. Einkorn wheat: *Triticum monococcum*	Wild einkorn wheat: *Triticum monococcum* subsp. *boeoticum* (= *T. boeoticum*)
3. Barley: *Hordeum vulgare*	Wild barley: *Hordeum vulgare* subsp. *spontaneum* (= *H. spontaneum*)
4. Pea: *Pisum sativum*	Wild pea: *Pisum sativum* subsp. *humile* (= *P. humile*)
5. Lentil: *Lens culinaris*	Wild lentil: *Lens culinaris* subsp. *orientalis* (= *L. orientalis*)
6. Chickpea: *Cicer arietinum*	Wild chickpea: *Cicer arietinum* subsp. *reticulatum* (= *C. reticulatum*)
7. Bitter vetch: *Vicia ervilia*	Wild bitter vetch: wild forms of Vicia ervilia
8. Flax: *Linum usitatissimum*	Wild flax: *Linum usitatissimum* subsp. *bienne* (= *L. bienne*)

search for the wild ancestry of these eight founder crops is more or less completed. It is unlikely that their wild ancestry will have to be revised, or that any additional wild-types, involved in their domestication, will be discovered in the future.

Pollination systems and speciation patterns in the wild relatives

The wild progenitors (as well as most other closely related wild relatives) of the founder crops are all predominately self-pollinated (autogamous) annual plants. As previously pointed out (Zohary 1969), the fact that all eight crops arose from autogamous wild ancestors is not surprising, because self-pollination conferred major advantages ("pre-adaptation") at the start of domestication. More important – for the present considerations – is the fact that this pollination system considerably affects speciation patterns in the wild. Among other things, selfing – because it isolates to a large extent the various inbred lines from one another – allows for the establishment of chromosomal rearrangements (translocations, inversions, etc.), whereas in cross-pollinated populations such chromosomal mutations are usually quickly eliminated because heterozygous individuals are semi-sterile. Indeed, quite a few autogamous wild species in Southwest Asia and the Mediterranean basin have been found to be chromosomally polymorphic, that is, they contain two or several chromosomal arrangements. Similarly, selfing allows for a quick build-up of reproductive isolation barriers such as cross-incompatibility, hybrid inviability or hybrid sterility between diverging populations; and speciation in selfers is frequently sympatric. The same geographical area can harbour several taxonomically closely related autogamous species. (In cross-pollinated plants the *closest* species usually occupy separate geographical areas.) Another outcome of the quick build-up of reproductive isolation barriers is the relatively frequent occurrence of reproductively isolated but morphologically almost indistinguishable sibling species. As elaborated in the next section, all these features can be of help when one attempts to trace the mode of origin of the founder crops.

Kinds of evidence

Clues for discriminating between the two modes of domestication (single event versus multiple events) have been obtained from the following comparisons between the Southwest Asian crops and their wild relatives:

Genetic polymorphism

The available information on genetic polymorphisms in the crops and their wild progenitors has been used to evaluate what population geneticists call "founder effects". In other words, comparisons have been made between the range of genetic diversity in the wild progenitor and the amount of this diversity present in its cultivated derivative. The richer the genic or chromosomal polymorphism in the wild and the poorer its representation under cultivation, the stronger is the suspicion that the crop concerned is a product of a single or very few introductions into cultivation and ensuing domestication. Situations in which the wild background contains *several* distinct genetic variants, whereas under domestication we find only *one* of these types are unambiguous. Such uniformity in the cultivars, particularly if it repeats itself, suggests single-event domestication. In contrast, when a cultivar contains a large amount of the genetic polymorphism that occurs in the wild, the chances are that the wild ancestor was introduced into cultivation not once but many times; although one also has to bear in mind that introgression caused by secondary hybridization between cultivars and their wild and weedy relatives could also enrich the variability in the crop.

Chromosome polymorphism As already pointed out, cytological studies have revealed that Mediterranean self-pollinated annual species are frequently chromosomally polymorphic, that is, they contain several chromosomal types. The wild ancestors of lentil and pea follow this trend. They have both been found to contain more than one chromosome arrangement.

Rich chromosomal polymorphism has been detected in the wild lentil *Lens culinaris* subsp. *orientalis*. Fifteen accessions of this progenitor, collected in Southwest Asia (Fig. 9.2), were tested cytogenetically (Ladizinsky et al. 1984) and were found to represent six distinct chromosome races. Six accessions contained what was dubbed the "standard" karyotype. The other nine collections differed from this chromosome type (and frequently also from one another) by one or two reciprocal translocations (in one case also by a paracentric inversion). In contrast, the cultivated lentil *L. culinaris* is chromosomally uniform: its karyotype was found to be identical with

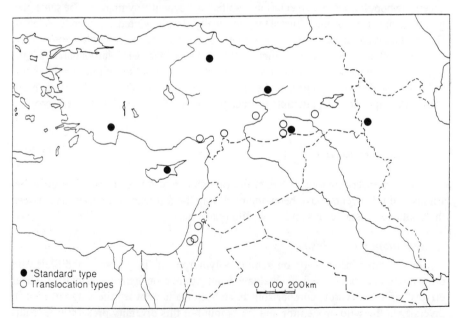

Figure 9.2   Known sites of the various chromosomal races of wild lentil *Lens culinaris* subsp. *orientalis* (= *L. orientalis*) in Southwest Asia (excluding populations in Central Asia). Solid circles represent locations harbouring the "standard" chromosome type; open circles represent locations harbouring the five additional chromosomal types. (Compiled from Ladizinsky et al. 1984).

the "standard" chromosome arrangement in *orientalis*. Assuming that the 15 tested wild accessions are representative, the frequency of the "standard" race in Southwest Asia is about 0.4. At such a frequency, the chances of picking up the "standard" karyotype twice is 0.160, three times 0.064, and four times in a row 0.026. Admittedly, the number of the tested collections is limited. However, the chromosomal uniformity in the cultivars seems to indicate that in Southwest Asia, lentil was introduced into cultivation only once or very few times.

Cytogenetic tests have also revealed (Ben Ze'ev & Zohary 1973) that the wild progenitor of the cultivated pea, namely *Pisum sativum* subsp. *humile*, is chromosomally polymorphic, although less so than the highly variable wild lentil. Only six collections of this wild pea have been tested and they were found to fall into two chromosomal races. Chromosomes in two samples, one from the Golan in northern Israel and the other from central Turkey, were found to be identical to the "standard" arrangement characteristic of almost all pea cultivars. Four other accessions obtained from southern and central Israel differed from this karyotype by a single (and the same) reciprocal translocation. Compared to lentil, the cytological data on pea are obviously much more fragmentary. Yet they point to the same conclusion.

Isozyme, seed-protein and DNA polymorphisms Several molecular techniques have been used since the mid-1970s to assess genetic polymorphisms in crops and their wild relatives. Earlier studies centred on electrophoretically discernible variation in proteins (particularly enzymes and seed-storage proteins). More recently these tests were augmented by even more sensitive analyses of DNA variation, particularly the cleaving of DNA by restriction enzymes (RFLP = restriction fragment-length polymorphisms). These surveys revealed considerable genetic variation in many crops. They also showed that very frequently crops are much less variable than their wild progenitors. In terms of protein polymorphism and DNA variation, wheats, barley, pea and lentil rank among the better studied crops. In all of them the cultivated varieties have been found to contain only a fraction of the genetic polymorphisms encountered in their wild counterparts. Although such differences between the crops and their wild progenitors are rightly interpreted as signs of founder effects in evolution under domestication, they usually lack the resolution power to distinguish unequivocally between single and multiple domestications. This inability stems from the fact that, although cultivars are commonly less variable, they still contain a considerable portion of the genetic polymorphism found in their wild progenitors. As I have previously pointed out (Zohary 1989), such variation (in the crops) need not represent multiple domestications. The wild progenitors of wheats, barley, lentil and pea frequently display a considerable amount of intra-population polymorphism. The intensive studies of wild emmer wheat in Amiad, eastern Galilee (Nevo et al. 1991), and of wild barley in several locations in Israel (Nevo et al. 1979, 1986) have already demonstrated how extensive such diversity can be, even in one place. Thus, even if the domestication of each of these founder crops happened in a single location, the initial sample taken into cultivation could have been quite variable. In addition, the variation in the domesticates could have been enriched by secondary hybridization with the wild relatives.

In spite of these limitations, protein and/or DNA polymorphisms already provide relevant clues, particularly when the wild progenitor varies geographically and can be subdivided in molecular terms into distinct geographical races, each with its specific isozymes or with differently cleaved DNA segments. In such cases, comparison of the geographical differentiation (in the wild) with the variation encountered in the crop can lead to a more precise delimitation of the place (or places) of origin. For example, evidence from isozyme and ribosomal DNA implicates only subspecies *strangulata* of *Aegilops squarrosa* (restricted geographically to the southern Caspian Sea belt) as the contributor of the D genome to the hexaploid bread wheat *Triticum aestivum* (Nishikawa 1983, Lagudah et al. 1993). Similarly, isozyme comparisons (Doebley 1990) reveal the close genetic similarities between cultivated maize and one subspecies of wild teosinte (*Zea mays* subsp. *parviglumis*), and exclude the isozymically more distant races of wild teosinte as candidates for the ancestry of the crop. Thus, the molecular data assembled help to pinpoint geographically the origins of both cereals. They indicate that hexaploid wheat could not have originated everywhere in the vast distribution area of *A. squarrosa,* but only in a definable part of it, and that cultivated maize evolved from recognizable populations of wild teosinte native to a very restricted area in Mexico. For both crops the putative area of origin has been considerably reduced. So has the expectation of many independent domestication events.

For the present assessment, the patterns of chloroplast DNA (cpDNA) revealed in pea and in its wild relatives are also meaningful. Palmer et al. (1985) found that the wild forms of *Pisum sativum* are polymorphic in their cpDNA. Significantly, the pattern characteristic of the cultivars was found only in the two accessions of wild *P. sativum* subsp. *humile,* which were also characterized by the "standard" pea chromosome arrangement. Admittedly, the number of wild *humile* collections tested by these authors is small. Yet the available evidence on cpDNA polymorphism corroborates the earlier information on chromosome polymorphism (Ben Ze'ev & Zohary 1973), and further supports a single domestication of the pea rather than multiple ones.

Similarly, Clegg et al. (1984) examined cpDNA variation in barley, *Hordeum vulgare,* testing 11 accessions of wild barley *H. vulgare* subsp. *spontaneum* (obtained from Israel, Iran and Morocco) and 9 accessions of cultivated barley. They found that wild *spontaneum* plants showed polymorphism in restriction sites and could be divided into three chloroplast lineages, only one of which was present in the cultivated material tested. These finds were later confirmed by more comprehensive tests made by Neele et al. (1988). A much larger sample of wild barley (245 accessions from 25 populations in Israel and 5 populations in Iran) was examined by them; and a very representative collection (62 accessions) of cultivated barley (*vulgare, distichum, deficiens* and *irregulare* forms) was also tested. The three lineages [− − −], [− − +] and [+ + −] first detected by Clegg et al. (1984) in wild *spontaneum* were re-identified by Neele et al. (1988). All three chloroplast families were richly represented in the wild samples tested by them. In fact many of the wild barley populations contained two or even three chloroplast types. In contrast, with only two exceptions, all the cultivated material tested was found to be uniform and belonged to the [− − −] chloroplast family. Again, such uniformity suggests single or very few events of domestication.

Species diversity

The rationale used in the comparisons of genetic polymorphism can also be applied to species diversity. If the Southwest Asian "nuclear area" harbours not only the wild progenitor but also additional related wild species, the question can be asked: how many of these wild, equally attractive species have derivatives under cultivation? Situations where the wild background contains *several* very similar candidates, whereas in cultivation one finds derivatives of only *one* of them, support a single domestication.

Closely related wild species with similar potential for domestication   Several of the founder crops are represented in Southwest Asia not only by their wild progenitors. As pointed by Blumler (1992), this region harbours additional wild species that closely resemble the progenitors in their general habit, in their reproductive biology, and – most importantly – in their attractiveness for domestication. Such a pattern of species diversity is particularly developed among the legumes. In three (out of the four) founder pulse crops (i.e. pea, lentil and chickpea) the "nuclear area" harbours a *group* of taxonomically closely related (but reproductively well isolated) wild species.

The genus *Pisum* contains two species, both native to Southwest Asia (Davis 1970, Smartt 1990: 178: Zohary & Hopf 1993: 95) (Fig. 9.3). The first is the crop species *P. sativum*, which is represented in this region by its two wild races, subsp. *humile* and subsp. *elatius*. The second is wild *P. fulvum*, with its characteristic mauve-

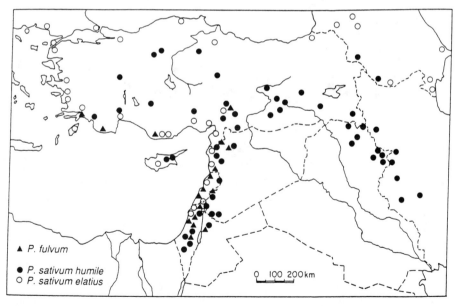

Figure 9.3   Distribution of the wild members of the genus *Pisum* in Southwest Asia, showing representative sites of the two wild subspecies of *P. sativum* – the "steppe type" *humile* pea and the "maquis type" *elatius* pea – and of wild *P. fulvum*. (Compiled from Davis 1970, Mouterde 1972; Zohary & Hopf 1993: 98; and unpublished data of D. Zohary.)

coloured flowers, which is a common annual legume in the Mediterranean vegetation belt of the Levant and of southwestern Turkey. Also *P. fulvum* is a selfer, with sweet pods and tasty seeds. It is as productive and as attractive for cultivation as the wild forms of *P. sativum*. Yet there are no signs of its having been domesticated.

The genus *Lens* comprises four wild species: *L. culinaris* subsp. *orientalis* (= *L. orientalis*), *L. odemensis*, *L. ervoides* and *L. nigricans* (Ladizinsky 1989, Zohary & Hopf 1993: 89). All occur in Southwest Asia (Fig. 9.4) and all are annual selfers with similar general habit and seeds. Yet only subsp. *orientalis* has been taken into cultivation, despite the fact that in the Mediterranean belt of the Levant and southwestern Turkey *L. ervoides* and *L. odemensis* occur as well, and the fourth species of wild lentil, *L. nigricans*, which is widely distributed over the central and western parts of the Mediterranean basin, also extends to western Turkey.

The group pattern repeats itself in *Cicer* (Fig. 9.5). Southwest Asia harbours five taxonomically closely related wild annual species of chickpea: *C. arietinum* subsp. *reticulatum*, *C. echinospermum*, *C. judaicum*, *C. pinnatifidum* and *C. bijugum* (van der Maesen 1972, 1987, Ladizinsky & Adler 1976, Zohary & Hopf 1993: 102). All are selfers, and have similar growth habit, seeds and taste. All have been placed (together with the crop) in series *Arietina*, sect. *Monocicer* of the genus *Cicer* (van der Maesen 1972, 1987). Yet only *C. arietinum* subsp. *reticulatum* – which is very

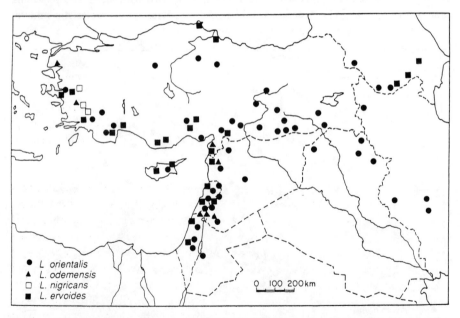

Figure 9.4   Distribution of the four wild members of the genus *Lens* in Southwest Asia. Note that in the Levant *L. ervoides* and *L. odemensis* occur sympatrically with the wild progenitor of the cultivated lentil *L. culinaris* subsp. *orientalis* (= *L. orientalis*). In southwestern Turkey they are joined also by *L. nigricans*. (Compiled from Mouterde 1972, Ladizinsky et al. 1984, Ladizinsky 1989, Hoffman et al. 1986; Zohary & Hopf 1993: 91; and unpublished data of D. Zohary.)

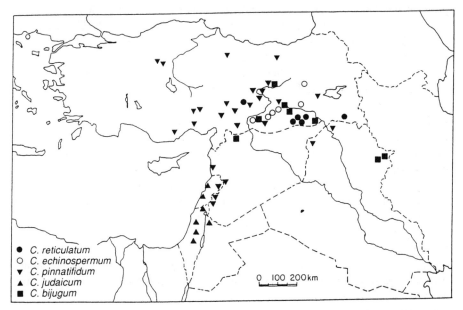

Figure 9.5 Distribution of the five closely related annual wild species of *Cicer*. Note that only one of these species, namely *C. arietinum* subsp. *reticulatum* (= *C. reticulatum*), has been domesticated; and that this wild progenitor is known only from a restricted area in southeastern Turkey. (Compiled from van der Maesen 1972 and Ladizinsky & Adler 1976).

restricted in its geographical distribution – has been taken into cultivation.

All in all, many species of wild legumes native to Southwest Asia seem to have the potential for development as pulse crops, and yet again and again only a *single* wild progenitor has been selected from among a *series* of closely related and equally attractive wild candidates. This pattern is hard to explain by a model of multiple introductions into cultivation.

Sibling species A special case of species diversity is provided by "sibling species", that is, taxa so similar morphologically that it is very difficult – or even impossible – to distinguish between them by their appearance; yet crossing experiments and cytogenetic tests reveal that they are already effectively separated from one another by reproductive isolation barriers such as cross-incompatibility, hybrid inviability, or hybrid sterility. Such a pattern of speciation has been discovered in the tetraploid wheats. One wild-type, *Triticum turgidum* subsp. *dicoccoides*, is genomically identical and fully interfertile with all the tetraploid cultivated wheats grouped under *T. turgidum* (genomic constitution: AABB). It is identified as the wild progenitor of cultivated emmer, *T. turgidum* subsp. *dicoccum*, and its more advanced free-threshing durum-type derivatives (Zohary & Hopf 1993: 40). The second wild-type, *T. timopheevii* subsp. *araraticum* (genomic constitution: AAGG), is intersterile with the first wild-type as well as with the tetraploid cultivated emmer and durum wheats, and it played no part in their domestication (ibid. 1993: 54). It is affiliated only to tetraploid *T. timopheevii* subsp. *timopheevii* (genomic constitution: AAGG), a rare half-weed–half-cultivated plant endemic to the Republic of Georgia in the Caucasus.

It is practically impossible to distinguish between *dicoccoides* and *araraticum* wheats morphologically, either in herbarium collections or during field excursions. However, many seed samples of tetraploid wild wheats have been collected in Southwest Asia and cytogenetically tested to establish their genomic constitution. The results have clarified the distribution of the two sibling species. Both wild wheats are characteristic annual constituents of the oak park-forest belt in the central and eastern parts of the Near Eastern "arc" (Fig. 9.6), and occasionally they even form mixed stands. Moreover, in this area *araraticum* wheat seems to be as common as (or even more common than) *dicoccoides* wheat. In addition, wild *dicoccoides* (AABB) forms grow alone in the southern Levant whereas *araraticum* (AAGG) extends to Armenia and Azerbaijan (Fig. 9.6). In spite of this extensive geographical overlap, only the *dicoccoides* AABB genomic combination is present in the thousands of tetraploid (as well as hexaploid) wheat cultivars. There are no cultivated derivatives having the *araraticum* AAGG genomic constitution. The only exception is the very local Georgian *T. timopheevii*, which is, probably, not an old relic crop but a more recent, secondary domesticate. Assuming that *dicoccoides* and *araraticum* forms are equally common

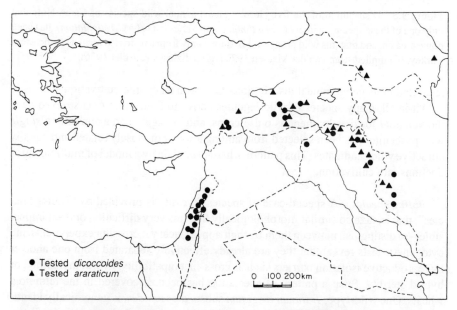

Figure 9.6 Distribution of the two wild "sibling species" of tetraploid (2n=28) wheats. The symbols represent the localities of the cytogenetically tested collections of wild emmer wheat *Triticum turgidum* subsp. *dicoccoides* (= *T. dicoccoides*) (●) and of wild Timopheev's wheat *T. timopheevii* subsp. *araraticum* (= *T. araraticum*) (▲). Note that in the central and eastern parts of the Near Eastern arc wild Timopheev's wheat is as common or even more common than wild emmer wheat. (Based on Zohary & Hopf 1993: 41; compiled from Rao & Smith 1968, Dagan & Zohary 1970, Tanaka & Ishii 1973, Mann 1973 and Tanaka et al. 1979).

in the central and eastern parts of the Near Eastern "arc", the chances (in this region) of picking *dicoccoides* twice is 0.25, three times 0.125 and four times in a row only 0.063.

Also, in the diploid einkorn wheat *Triticum monococcum* we are apparently faced, in the wild, with similar species diversity. There is a growing body of evidence to suggest that in the Near Eastern arc wild einkorn wheat *T. monococcum* subsp. *boeoticum* (which is fully interfertile with the crop) does not exist alone. It is frequently accompanied by a second diploid wild-type, which is morphologically very similar to wild einkorn, but which is intersterile both with the *monococcum* cultivars and with the *boeoticum* wild forms (Waines & Barnhart 1992). The crossing experiments are not as extensive as in the wild tetraploid wheats. Yet some wheat geneticists (e.g. Miller 1987, Waines & Barnhart 1992) already regard this intersterile type as a separate wild diploid wheat species (*T. urartu*) and stress that it has nothing to do with the domestication of einkorn wheat.

In summary, in the wheats, as in the legumes, species divergence in the wild when compared with the uniformity in the crops, suggests single rather than multiple domestications. This is particularly true of the tetraploid wheats, where available data are hard to explain by multiple events.

The genetic architecture of domestication traits

Clues for discriminating between single and multiple domestications can also be obtained by elucidating the genetic basis of traits that evolved soon after the plants were introduced into cultivation; that is, by examining the genetic nature of traits that have low fitness under wild conditions, and which were strongly advantaged and promptly (and automatically) selected for when the wild progenitor was introduced into the system of sowing, reaping and threshing. (For details on "domestication traits" that evolved in the founder crops see Zohary & Hopf 1993: 17–18, 87, 120.) Well recognized traits of this kind are the breakdown of the wild mode of seed dispersal and the loss of seed dormancy. When, throughout the crop, such a change is governed by mutation in the *same* gene (or *same* genes), the uniformity suggests single origin. In contrast, when in different cultivars such a trait is governed by mutations in *different* genes, one should suspect independent domestications in different places.

The rationale behind such considerations is parallel evolution. Evolutionists have long been aware of the fact that similar selection pressures, applied independently to separate populations, very frequently result in similar gains. However, in different populations such changes are achieved not only by re-occurrence of mutation in the same gene-locus but also by mutations in *different* genes. In other words, the breakdown of a wild-type adaptation, or the acquisition of new specialization under domestication, need not necessarily be governed by the same specific gene (or by the same combination of genes). Mutations in *different* genes can *each* bring about very similar functional changes. Examples of parallel effects caused by mutations in different genes abound in crops. In fact they are the rule rather than the exception. Thus, dozens of non-allelic genes, *each* causing male sterility, have been detected by breeders in barley, in tomato, in maize, and in many other crops (Kaul 1988); and recessive mutations causing a shift from two rows to six rows were induced in barley in four additional gene-loci (v_2, v_3, v_4, v_5), each located on a different chromosome (Fukuyama et al. 1982; Hockett & Nilan 1985: 207).

The significance of such parallel effects is clear: it is safe to assume that in the wild progenitors of the Southwest Asian founder crops, the potential for causing a breakdown of a wild adaptation exists not in one gene-locus but in several different gene-loci. Assuming similar rates of mutation, and the presence of only two potential gene-loci, the chances that two domestication events will end up with mutation in the same gene-locus is 0.50, and for three events 0.25. If more than two gene-loci can independently cause the change, the probabilities are, of course, much lower. Therefore, if a wild progenitor has been taken into cultivation many times, one would expect to stumble – quite often – on parallel evolution and detect different non-allelic major genes, each controlling the same domestication trait, in different groups of cultivars of the crop. In contrast, uniformity in the genetic background of the tested domestication trait (the same gene, or genes, in all cultivars) points to a single origin.

An obvious advantage of domestication traits is that they evolved only under cultivation and are strongly selected against and absent in the wild. In tracing the genetic nature of such traits one is not concerned with contributions from the wild background but rather with new developments under domestication. In other words, domestication traits are free from "contaminations" caused by secondary hybridization and introgression from the wild gene pool.

Breakdown of the wild mode of seed dispersal   This is the easiest-to-spot and the best-studied domestication trait in the Southwest Asian crops. It involves the change from the shattering ears or dehiscent pods characteristic of the wild progenitors to non-shattering ears or non-dehiscent fruits in the cultivated derivatives. (For a comprehensive examination of this trait in wheat and barley see Hillman & Davies 1990.) In emmer wheat (Love & Craig 1924), einkorn wheat (Sharma & Waines 1980), barley (Takahashi 1964, 1972), pea (Zohary, unpublished data) and lentil (Ladizinsky 1985), crosses between the wild progenitors and the cultivars have shown that this shift is brought about by a recessive mutation in one major gene or (more rarely) by a joint effect of two such genes. In all these crops, breeders have also performed many intra-crop crosses (between cultivars). Except for barley, none of these within-crop crosses has been reported to produce wild-type brittle or dehiscent F_1 hybrids or F_2 segregants. Such results (for geneticists they constitute tests for allelism) indicate that, within emmer wheat, einkorn wheat, pea and lentil, the *same* major gene (or the *same* combination of two genes) is responsible for the breakdown of the wild-type adaptation. Only in barley have some crosses between non-brittle cultivars resulted in F_1 hybrids with wild-type brittle ears indicating the presence of two independent recessive genes, bt and bt_2 (Takahashi 1964, 1972).

Loss of seed dormancy   A second development under domestication, common to all the Southwest Asian founder crops, is the loss of the wild-type inhibition of germination. The information available on this trait is less extensive than on the loss of the wild-type seed dispersal. Moreover, genetic analysis of a physiological trait is more complex than tests of morphological characters. Fortunately, in many pulses the loss of wild-type germination inhibition seems to be associated with morphological changes in the seed coat (thicker, harder, more impermeable testa in the wild forms; thinner, more permeable testa in the cultivars). This structural change is particularly clear in the pea (Werker et al. 1979, Butler 1989), where it can serve as a reliable, visible marker for the breakdown of the wild-type physiological adaptation – also recognizable in archaeological remains (Butler 1989, and pers. comm.). In lentil, crosses between modern cultivars and wild *orientalis* forms showed that the loss of the wild-type thick seed coat is governed by a single recessive mutation (Ladizinsky 1985). Also in the pea (Zohary unpublished data), and very probably in the two other founder pulses, this loss seems to be controlled mainly by a single major gene or by a combination of two complementary genes. Significantly, breeders have already carried out many inter-varietal crosses in the cultivated pea, lentil and chickpea, and there are no reports of the appearance of individuals with wild-type seed coat among the F_1 or F_2 hybrid derivatives of such crosses. This situation suggests that, throughout each of these three cultivated pulses, the genetic basis for the breakdown of the wild-type seed dormancy is uniform and it points to single domestications.

Discussions and conclusions

Genetic tests that are sufficiently comprehensive and specifically planned to throw light on the mode of origin of the Southwest Asian founder crops have not yet been attempted. The genetic evidence cited in this chapter consists mainly of facts extracted from experiments designed to answer totally different questions. Inevitably, these are just fragments of information, frequently in need of further confirmation and additional support from intentionally designed tests. In spite of these limitations, the available evidence leads to the following conclusions:

- The mode of domestication of the Southwest Asian founder crops (as well as other cultivated plants) need not remain an open question. Several kinds of genetic tests can be proposed for obtaining critical evidence. If carried out on a sufficient scale, such examinations could provide firm evidence for discriminating between "monophyletic" and "polyphyletic" origins.
- Some of the available genetic evidence (such as chromosome polymorphism in lentil, chloroplast DNA polymorphism in barley, sibling species in tetraploid wheats, the nature of the loss of wild-type seed dispersal and germination inhibition) already appear to be highly indicative. Taken together with the floristic information on species composition, they suggest that at least emmer wheat – the most important crop of Southwestern Asian and European neolithic agriculture – as well as pea and lentil (the main grain legumes) were each taken into cultivation only once, or at most only very few times. Evidence pertaining to the mode of origin of einkorn wheat, chickpea, bitter vetch and flax is much more meagre, yet the data seem to be compatible with the notion of a single origin in each case. Only in barley, where two different non-shattering genes (bt and bt_2) have been discovered (Takahashi 1964), is there an indication that this important crop has been taken into cultivation more than once. Yet even here the chloro-

plast DNA data suggest that only very few events have occurred.

In conclusion, the available data – fragmentary as they are – appear to support the hypothesis that the development of grain agriculture in Southwest Asia was triggered (in each crop) by a single domestication event or at most by very few such events. However, although such mode of origin is indicated for the majority of the founder crops, the data tell us very little about the way the Southwest Asian neolithic crop "package" was assembled. It remains an open question whether these crops were taken into cultivation together in the same place, or whether different crops were domesticated (perhaps each only once) in different places. Yet once the technology of crop cultivation was invented, and the domesticated forms of wheats, barley, pulses and flax first appeared, they probably spread over the Near Eastern arc in a manner similar to the way in which they later spread into Europe: not by additional domestications in each species but by diffusion of the already existing domesticates. In other words, soon after the first non-shattering and easily germinating cereals, pulses and flax appeared, their superior performance under cultivation became decisive, and there was no need for repeated domestication of the wild progenitors. Moreover, because this new system of crop cultivation expanded rapidly, there was little chance for grain agriculture to develop independently elsewhere in Southwest Asia or Europe. This is apparently true not only for the neolithic founder crops but also for the first Southwest Asian domesticated herd animals: sheep and goat (cf. Uerpmann, Legge and Hole in Chs 12, 13 and 14 in this volume).

References

Ben-Ze'ev, N. & D. Zohary 1973. Species relationships in the genus *Pisum* L. *Israel Journal of Botany* **22**, 73–91.

Blumler, M. K. 1992. Independent inventionism and recent genetic evidence on plant domestication. *Economic Botany* **46**, 98–111.

Butler, A. 1989. Cryptic anatomical characters as evidence of early cultivation in the grain legume (pulses). In Harris & Hillman (1989: 390–407).

Clegg, M. T., A. H. D Brown, P. R. Whitfeld 1984. Chloroplast DNA diversity in wild and cultivated barley: implications for genetic conservation. *Genetical Research* **43**, 339–43.

Dagan, J. & D. Zohary 1970. Wild tetraploid wheat from West Iran cytogenetically identical with Israeli *T. dicoccoides*. *Wheat Information Service (Kyoto)* **31**, 15–17.

Davis, P. H. 1970. Pisum. In *Flora of Turkey* (vol. 3), P. H. Davis (ed.), 370–3. Edinburgh: Edinburgh University Press.

de Moulins, D. M. 1994. *Agricultural intensification in Southwest Asia during the Aceramic Neolithic: evidence from charred remains of crops and their weeds*. PhD dissertation, Institute of Archaeology, University College London.

Doebley, J. 1990. Molecular evidence and the evolution of maize. In *New perspectives on the origin and evolution of New World domesticated plants*, P. K. Bretting (ed.), 6–28 [supplement to *Economic Botany* **44**].

Fukuyama, T., R. Takahashi, J. Hayashi 1982. Genetic studies on the induced six-rowed mutants in barley. *Berichte Ohara Institut Landwirtschaft und Biologie*, Okayama University, **18**, 99–113.

Harris, D. R. & G. C. Hillman (eds) 1989. *Foraging and farming: the evolution of plant exploitation*. London: Unwin Hyman.

Hillman, G. C. 1978. On the origins of domestic rye – *Secale cereale*: the finds from aceramic Çan Hasan III in Turkey. *Anatolian Studies* **28**, 157–74.

Hillman, G. C. & M. S. Davies 1990. Measured domestication rates in wild wheats and barley under primitive cultivation, and their archaeological implications. *Journal of World Prehistory* 4, 157–222.

Hockett, E. A. & R. A. Nilan 1985. Genetics. In *Barley*, D. C. Rasmusson (ed.), 187–230. Madison: American Society of Agronomy.

Hoffman, D. L., D. E. Soltis, F. J. Muehlbauer, G. Ladizinsky 1986. Isozyme polymorphism in *Lens* (Leguminosae). *Systematic Botany* 11, 392–402.

Kaul, M. L. H. 1988. *Male sterility in higher plants* [Monographs in Theoretical and Applied Genetics 10]. Berlin: Springer.

Kislev, M. E. 1985. Early Neolithic horsebean from Yiftah'el, Israel. *Science* 228, 319–20.

Ladizinsky, G. 1985. The genetics of hard seed coat in the genus *Lens. Euphytica* 34, 539–43.

— 1989. Origin and domestication of Southwest Asian grain legumes. In Harris & Hillman (1989: 374–89).

Ladizinsky, G. & A. Adler 1976. Genetic relationships among the annual species of *Cicer* L. *Theoretical and Applied Genetics* 48, 196–203.

Ladizinsky, G., D. Braun, D. Goshen, F. J. Muehlbauer 1984. The biological species of the genus *Lens* L. *Botanical Gazette* 145, 253–61.

Lagudah, E. S., R. Appels, D. McNeil, D. P. Schachtman 1993. Exploiting the diploid D genome chromatin for wheat improvement. In *Gene conservation and exploitation, 20th Stadler genetics symposium*, J. P. Gustafson, R. Appels, P. Raven (eds), 87–107. New York: Plenum Press.

Love, H. H. & W. T. Craig 1924. The genetic relation between *Triticum dicoccum dicoccoides* and a similar morphological type produced synthetically. *Journal of Agriculture Research* 28, 515–19.

Mann, S. S. 1973. Cytoplasmic and cytogenetic relationships among tetraploid *Triticum* species. *Euphytica* 22, 287–300.

Miller, T. E. 1987. Systematics and evolution. In *Wheat breeding*, F. G. H. Lupton (ed.), 1–30. London: Chapman & Hall.

Mouterde, P. 1970. *Nouvelle flore du Liban et de la Syrie*, vol. 2. Beirut, Lebanon: Dar El-Machreq.

Neele, D. B., M. A. Saghai-Maroof, R. W. Allard, Q. Zhang, R. A. Jorgensen 1988. Chloroplast DNA diversity in populations of wild and cultivated barley. *Genetics* 120, 1105–110.

Nevo, E., A. H. D. Brown, D. Zohary 1979. Genetic diversity in the wild progenitor of barley in Israel. *Experientia* 35, 1027–9.

Nevo, E., A. Beiles, D. Zohary 1986. Genetic resources of wild barley in the Near East: structure, evolution and application in breeding. *Biological Journal of the Linnean Society* 27, 355–80.

Nevo, E., I. Noy-Meir, A. Beiles, T. Krugman, M. Agami 1991. Natural selection of allozyme polymorphisms: micro-geographical, spatial and temporal ecological differentiations in wild emmer wheat. *Israel Journal of Botany* 40, 419–49.

Nishikawa, N. 1983. Species relationship of wheat and its putative ancestors as viewed from isozyme variation. *Proceedings of the 6th International Wheat Genetics Symposium, Kyoto, Japan*, 53–63.

Palmer, J. D., R. A. Jorgensen, W. F. Thompson 1985. Chloroplast DNA variation and evolution in *Pisum*: patterns of change and phylogenetic analysis. *Genetics* 109, 195–213.

Rao, P. S. & E. L. Smith 1968. Studies with Israeli and Turkish accessions of *Triticum turgidum* L. emend. var. *dicoccoides* Korn. Bowden. *Wheat Information Service, Kyoto* 26, 6–7.

Sharma, H. C. & J. G. Waines 1980. Inheritance of tough rachis in crosses of *Triticum monococcum* and *T. boeoticum. Journal of Heredity* 71, 214–16.

Smartt, J. 1990. *Grain legumes: evolution and genetic resources*. Cambridge: Cambridge University Press.

Takahashi, R. 1964. Further studies on the phylogenetic differentiation of cultivated barley. *Barley Genetics* 1 [Proceedings of the 1st International Barley Genetic Symposium, Wageningen], 19–26.

— 1972. Non-brittle rachis 1 and non-brittle rachis 2. *Barley Genetics Newsletter* 2, 181–2.

Tanaka, M. & H. Ishii 1973. Cytogenetic evidence on the speciation of wild tetraploid wheats collected in Iraq, Turkey and Iran. *Proceedings of the 4th Wheat Genetics Symposium*, 115–21. Columbia: University of Missouri.

Tanaka, M., T. Kawahara, J. Sano 1979. The origin and the differentiation of the B and G genomes of tetraploid wheats. *Report of the Plant Germ-plasm Institute*, Kyoto University 4, 1–11.

van der Maesen, L. J. G. 1972. Cicer *L., a monograph of the genus, with special reference to the chick-*

*pea (*Cicer arietinum *L.), its ecology and cultivation.* Communication 72/10, Agricultural University Wageningen.

van der Maesen, L. J. G. 1987. Origin, history and taxonomy of chickpea. In *The chickpea*, M. C. Saxena & K. B. Singh (eds), 11–34. Cambridge: CAB International.

van Zeist, W., K. Wasylikowa & K-H. Behre (eds) 1991. *Progress in Old World palaeoethnobotany.* Rotterdam: Balkema.

Waines, J. G. & D. Barnhart 1992. Biosystematic research in *Aegilops* and *Triticum*. *Hereditas* **116**, 207–12.

Werker, E., I. Marbach, A. M. Mayer 1979. Relation between the anatomy of the testa, water permeability and the presence of phenolics in the genus *Pisum*. *Annals of Botany* **43**, 765–71.

Zohary, D. 1969. The progenitors of wheat and barley in relation to domestication and agricultural dispersal in the Old World. In *The domestication and exploitation of plants and animals*, P. J. Ucko & G. W. Dimbleby (eds), 47–66. London: Duckworth.

— 1989. Domestication of the Southwest Asian Neolithic crop assemblage of cereals, pulses, and flax: the evidence from the living plants. In Harris & Hillman (1989: 355–75).

Zohary, D. & M. Hopf 1993. *Domestication of plants in the Old World: the origin and spread of cultivated plants in West Asia, Europe, and the Nile Valley*, 2nd edn. Oxford: Oxford University Press.

CHAPTER TEN

Late Pleistocene changes in wild plant-foods available to hunter–gatherers of the northern Fertile Crescent: possible preludes to cereal cultivation

Gordon Hillman

Introduction

The apparent near-synchroneity of the beginnings of cultivation in different parts of the world has led many to invoke a climatic trigger (e.g. Byrne 1987) or the involvement of "intermediate-scale changes in the physical environment" (Harris 1977: 189–97). The effects of climatic change on the plant-based components of the subsistence economy were mediated principally by changes in the distribution and composition of vegetation, and by concomitant changes in the plant-food resource base. Several recent models now offer ecologically explicit hypotheses for precisely how specified changes in climate might have resulted in shifts in resource base and subsistence that culminated in cultivation. In the Southwest Asian arena, examples of such recent models include Henry (1985, 1989), McCorriston (1992), McCorriston & Hole (1991).

However, these particular models are concerned primarily with the adoption of emmer and barley cultivation in the southern Levant. Indeed, one of them (McCorriston 1992, and McCorriston & Hole 1991) suggests that the rapid spread of cultivation from the Jordan Valley would probably have pre-empted any independent beginnings of cultivation elsewhere. This is true, it could; but only if the climatic changes that triggered these events in the southern Levant occurred earlier there than equivalent changes farther north. McCorriston & Hole (1991) interpret the pollen data as indicating precisely this, as do others such as Wright (1993).

By contrast, the model presented here argues that the key climatic changes occurred almost synchronously in both the southern Levant and farther north, and that, although climatic changes were leading to cultivation in the southern Levant, they were simultaneously having an equally dramatic impact on subsistence in the northern Fertile Crescent (Fig. 10.1).[1] I attempt to model first the nature and timing of climat-

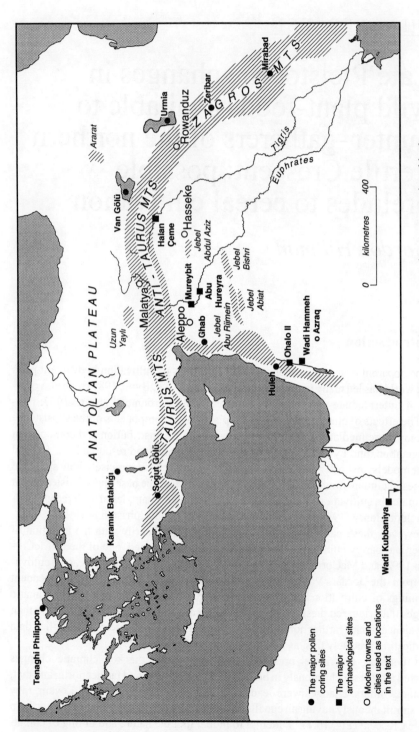

Figure 10.1 Location of archaeological sites, pollen coring sites and mountain ranges mentioned in the text.

ically induced changes in vegetation distribution in the northern Fertile Crescent and, secondly, concomitant changes in the availability of those plant-foods (particularly wild cereals and other caloric staples) likely to have been used by local pre-agrarian hunter–gatherers. A separate paper (to be published elsewhere), then models:

- the seasonal components of these changes in resource base
- the possible effects of these altered seasons of availability (and inter-annual unpredictability) on the food storage practices of local hunter–gatherers and their patterns of mobility
- ways in which these extensions of sedentism and storage are likely to have led to accelerated population growth
- how the resulting stress on carrying capacity is likely to have led to attempts to increase returns from wild plant resources, with eventual resort to the cultivation of amenable annuals, particularly the local wild cereals: principally einkorn wheat, annual rye and barley. The effect of the Younger Dryas climatic episode in exacerbating the stress on carrying capacity in some areas is also considered. That cultivation and domestication of the rye, at least, occurred independently in the northern Fertile Crescent is supported by finds of domestic rye from Abu Hureyra that currently pre-date the earliest domesticates of the southern Levant by some 500 years.[2]

In discussing the changing patterns of availability of wild plant-foods after the Glacial Maximum, the present model assumes that broad-spectrum subsistence was already practised well before the end of the Middle Palaeolithic (Edwards 1989a, Hillman 1989, Hillman et al. 1989b, Kislev et al. 1992), and it therefore excludes any role for a "broad-spectrum revolution" as a forerunner to cultivation (cf. Flannery 1969). Correspondingly, although this chapter acknowledges that systematic burning was probably applied to help maintain (or even increase) the diversity of wild plant-foods during the Epipalaeolithic, if only in Levantine woodland and park-woodland (Bar-Yosef & Belfer-Cohen 1989: 488; Lewis 1972; McCorriston 1992: e.g. 95–7; McCorriston & Hole 1991: 57; Naveh 1984), it also accepts that the controlled use of burning almost certainly began much earlier.

In modelling changes in plant-food availability I have particularly targeted the wild cereals, because their increased availability appears to have been relatively abrupt, to have had a profound effect on local hunter–gatherer subsistence, and to have triggered increases in food storage and sedentism that were key precursors to the eventual adoption of cultivation. The wild cereals most likely to have become available as extensive stands to Late Pleistocene hunter–gatherers in the *northern* Fertile Crescent are wild einkorn wheat, *Triticum monococcum* subsp. *boeoticum*, wild annual rye, *Secale cereale* subsp. *vavilovii*, and wild barley, *Hordeum spontaneum*. (Wild emmer, *T. dicoccoides*, would probably have been present as only a minor admixture in the einkorn stands.) It may be no coincidence that it is in this same area that we encounter the earliest finds of the domestic derivatives of the first two of these cereals, namely domestic einkorn, *T. monococcum* subsp. *monococcum,* and domestic rye, *S. cereale* subsp. *cereale*, although finds are still sparse (van Zeist 1972, Hillman 1975, 1978, Moore et al. in press, Colledge 1994, de Moulins 1994).

For convenience, a second species of wild einkorn, *T. urartu*, is here grouped with

T. monococcum subsp. *boeoticum*, because the two species are very similar and appear to have been utilized by Late Pleistocene hunter–gatherers in exactly the same way (Hillman et al. 1993: 101), although present evidence suggests that only *boeoticum* was eventually taken into cultivation and domesticated (Miller 1987; Zohary in Ch. 9 in this volume). Also, because our knowledge of the ecology of wild annual rye is still relatively limited, common wild einkorn, *T. monococcum* subsp. *boeoticum*, is used as the working example throughout this chapter.

Changes in the availability of plant-food resources (particularly wild einkorn) during the Late Pleistocene

Present-day distribution and habitat affiliations of wild einkorn

The present-day regional distribution of wild einkorn is clearly illustrated in the maps of Daniel Zohary (1989 & this volume and cf. Zohary & Hopf (1993). They show primary (non-weedy) stands established right around the Fertile Crescent and across much of Anatolia (Fig. 10.2).

As for specific habitat affiliations, dense stands of wild einkorn are characteristic of open areas within what is potentially the oak–Rosaceae park-woodland belt of M. Zohary's (1973) "sub-Mediterranean zone" or my "xeric woodland zone" (Moore et al. in press). They often reach their greatest extent where the oak–Rosaceae park-woodland begins to open out into what is today treeless steppe. However, the work

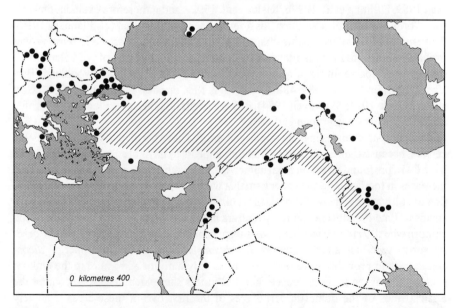

Figure 10.2   Present-day distribution of wild einkorn wheat (*Triticum boeoticum*). The shaded area represents areas of massive stands, often in primary habitats; the dots represent additional areas supporting mainly weedy populations. (Redrawn from Zohary & Hopf 1993: 34, map 1).

of Blumler (1984, 1991a, 1993, 1994) and Naveh (1967) indicates that annual grasses such as the wild cereals could (and do) extend beyond the potential frontier of oak–Rosaceae park-woodland in many areas with deep fine-textured soils where the establishment of tree seedlings is prevented by reduced access to soil moisture. This penetration by the annual grasses takes them into a drier vegetation zone, which today is classified by Zohary (1973) as the first zone of primary steppe and by Pabot (1957) as a moist zone of secondary steppe. In the absence of deforestation, cultivation and heavy grazing by domestic animals, however, this "penetration zone" abutting the boundary of oak–Rosaceae park-woodland would support terebinth–almond woodland–steppe (Hillman, in Moore et al. in press). But although this woodland–steppe zone would potentially extend many kilometres before finally giving way to open steppe, the stands of wild cereals and other annual grasses would probably penetrate favourable areas of only the proximal parts of the zone. Certainly, our fieldwork indicates that einkorn is today unable to grow in the few surviving islands of terebinth–almond woodland–steppe that represent *distal* extensions of the zone and which can still be found in remote parts of the steppe on isolated ranges of hills such as the Jebel Abdul Aziz, Jebel Abu Rijmein and Jebel Bishri (Hillman et al. 1989a, Hillman in Moore et al. in press) (see Fig. 10.1).

The oak–Rosaceae park-woodland and proximal parts of terebinth–almond woodland–steppe are now extremely degraded or eliminated altogether, so before attempting to define where einkorn would have grown in the Late Pleistocene, it is first necessary to model the *potential* distribution of xeric woodland under modern climatic conditions, in the absence of deforestation, cultivation and heavy grazing by domestic animals. I have assembled such a model in Moore et al. (in press; see in particular fig. 3.7). The model proposes that oak–Rosaceae park-woodland could potentially extend eastwards from the northern Levant to within 50 km of the middle Euphrates bend near Mureybit (see Fig. 10.1), and south from the central Anti-Taurus almost to Hasseke. This would take it beyond the present-day secondary steppe formations classified by Zohary (1973) as *"Ballotetalia undulatae"* and well into Pabot's (1957) "partie est de la zone syrienne". And under these same conditions, terebinth–almond woodland–steppe would, even today, extend to within 30 km of the site of Abu Hureyra.

Despite the fact that the acute disequilibrium conditions of the Late Pleistocene will have seen dramatic dislocations of prior patterns of association between wild cereals and the arboreal components of oak–Rosaceae park-woodland and terebinth–almond woodland–steppe, the probable past limits of the major trees and shrubs of these two formations provide a useful starting point for assessing the ancient distribution of wild einkorn and the other wild cereals.

General models of the distribution of xeric woodland in Southwest Asia in the Late Pleistocene and Early Holocene

Van Zeist & Bottema (1982, and in their dauntingly comprehensive study of 1991) have greatly aided understanding of ancient vegetation by publishing models in the form of maps of the possible past distribution of major vegetation formations ranging from forest to desert–steppe. These maps are reproduced here as Figures 10.3–10.5.

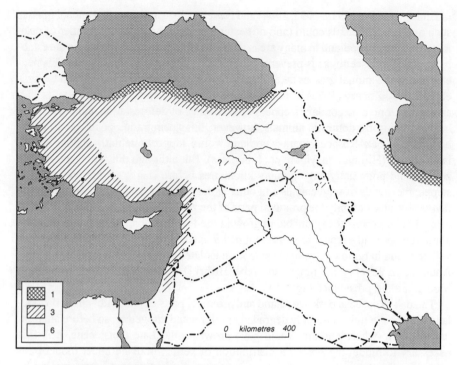

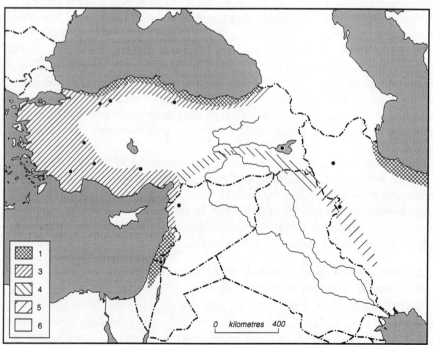

The first map (Fig. 10.3) indicates that, at 16000–14000 bc, arboreal vegetation of the Fertile Crescent survived only in the form of "woodland and/or forest–steppe", and was restricted to the western Levant with, perhaps, an isolated refuge or two in the northern Zagros, and possibly one near present-day Malatya. Under these cold dry conditions, the rest of the area was steppe or desert–steppe.

The second map (Fig. 10.4) suggests that, by 10000–9000 bc, warmer, moister conditions had allowed the development of dense forest in the southern Levant; the spread of some form of "forest–steppe" across the Anti-Taurus Mountains; and the spread of a thinner scatter of trees down the Zagros Mountains at elevations otherwise dominated by steppe. The authors do not specify a date for the *start* of this spread, but in view of the dates assigned to the successive maps, it has to be some time between 14000 and 10000 bc. The differences between the vegetation of the northern

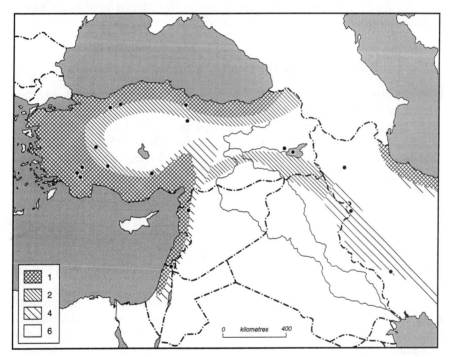

Figure 10.5   Inferred distribution of the palaeo-vegetation of Southwest Asia and southeast-ernmost Europe at *c.* 6000 bc. (Redrawn from van Zeist & Bottema 1991: 124, Fig. 44.) Van Zeist & Bottema propose that: 1 = "forest"; 2 = "woodland"; 4 = "forest–steppe"; and 6 = "steppe & desert–steppe".

Figures 10.3 and 10.4 (opposite page)   Inferred distribution of the palaeo-vegetation of Southwest Asia and southeasternmost Europe during the periods 16000–14000 bc and 10000–9000 bc respectively. (Redrawn from van Zeist & Bottema 1991: 122–3, Figs 42–3.) Van Zeist & Bottema propose that: 1 = "forest"; 3 = "woodland and or forest–steppe"; 4 = "forest–steppe"; 5 = "steppe with very scattered tree stands"; and 6 = "steppe & desert–steppe".

and southern Levant proposed on this second map are based on opposing trends indicated by the pollen diagrams from Ghab and Hula respectively. Whether or not these differences are real is discussed below.

The authors suggest that the spread of woodland–steppe across the northern and eastern sectors of the Fertile Crescent could have started from one or more woodland refugia, most obviously from the northern end of the major Levantine woodland refuge and the adjacent (eastern) end of the Taurus refuge in south-central Turkey, but also from one of the tentatively postulated small refugia farther east, such as the one near Rowanduz, and possibly even from additional small pockets of trees that might have survived in occasional sheltered spots located below the depressed upper (low-temperature) limits of tree growth, protected from the desiccating winds, and provided with extra water from runoff.

The third map (Fig. 10.5) shows what is essentially a further infilling of these areas by denser forms of woodland, and further extension into adjacent areas of steppe.

The problem of dating the start of woodland expansion

Despite the indisputable utility of these maps of past vegetation distribution, they are no more than models and, of the several problems besetting their compilation mentioned by the authors, perhaps the greatest is the uncertainty attaching to the date of the start of Late Pleistocene woodland spread across the northern Fertile Crescent and down the Zagros. The uncertainty arises from the fact that the date traditionally suggested (e.g. by van Zeist & Bottema 1982) for the start of woodland spread (*c.* 10000 bc) is based on a single contentious radiocarbon date for a major episode of Late Pleistocene woodland expansion visible in the Ghab pollen diagram (see Figs 10.2, 10.7). This date was obtained from mollusc shells that are quite likely to have incorporated fossil carbon from limestone carbonates during their growth, which would make the date artificially early (Niklewski & van Zeist 1970, van Zeist 1980, van Zeist & Bottema 1982). The trends in woodland advance/retreat visible in the Ghab diagram (as currently dated) also conflict with trends observed at other sites.

In this model I propose a date of *c.* 13000 bc for the start of woodland expansion in and from the northern Levant, as well as in the southern Levant – a date substantially earlier than that traditionally accepted. The reasons for adopting this early date are outlined in the sections that follow, together with a summary of alternative interpretations of the evidence.

Dating the start of Late Pleistocene woodland expansion in the southern Levant

The new pollen diagram from Hula in northern Israel (Baruch & Bottema 1991, Baruch 1994) is reproduced in Figure 10.6. It indicates that, during the cold dry conditions of the Glacial Maximum, oak woodland continued to survive in the area, but that, from about 13000 bc, there was a steady expansion (and no doubt infilling) of the woodland. This process accelerated from about 11000 bc and reached a climax around 9500 bc. The authors comment:

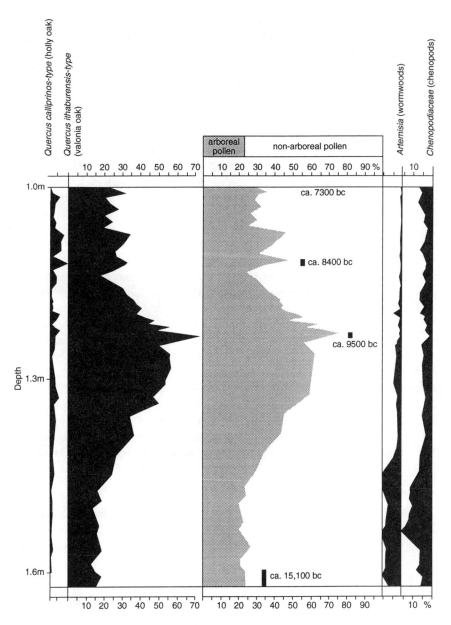

Figure 10.6 Part of the Hula pollen diagram. (Redrawn from Baruch & Bottema 1991: 15, fig. 3.) The dates are in uncalibrated radiocarbon years bc.

The marked rise in humidity in the Hula area, during this time-period, must have resulted from a considerable increase in precipitation [at least during the spring to early summer growing period: GCH], as this was also a period of substantial rise in global temperatures; this is especially true of the later part of this stage, which coincides with the early stages of the Allerød [Interstadial]. (Baruch & Bottema 1991: 17)

From 9500 to about 8500 bc, the diagram shows a sharp reduction in woodland, although until 9000 bc, at least, woodland cover nevertheless appears to have remained extensive. During the second part of this period (which coincides with peak of the Younger Dryas) temperatures were much lower, so there must have been sharply increased aridity during the season of active growth.[3] Thereafter, the diagram indicates some re-expansion of woodland, marking the onset of moister, but also warmer, conditions with the start of the Holocene.

The start of woodland expansion in the southern Levant can therefore be dated to around 13000 bc, with a sharp reversal coinciding with the Younger Dryas. This broadly accords with trends identifiable (albeit with less certainty) in the earlier Hula diagram by Tsukada (in Bottema & van Zeist 1981, van Zeist & Bottema 1982) and the as yet sparsely dated diagram from Weinstein-Evron (1983).

Evidence from charred remains of food plants from early sites in the southern Levant also supports the pollen evidence in suggesting uninterrupted survival of woodland across much of the southern Levant, which cannot therefore have been limited to a narrow coastal strip below 300m as proposed by Henry (1985). The abundant remains of food plants from the 17000 bc site of Ohalo II by the Sea of Galilee reveal that the occupants gathered woodland (or woodland–steppe) foods such as acorns and almonds, together with the grain of wild emmer and barley – grasses that today characterize the steppic (lower) fringe of woodland in the Jordan Valley (Kislev et al. 1992). And 6,000 years later the occupants of Wadi Hammeh in the middle Jordan Valley were continuing to gather food plants characteristic of the woodland fringe (Colledge, in Potts et al. 1985).

Dating the start of Late Pleistocene woodland expansion from the northern Levant

The most direct evidence for dating the start of Late Pleistocene woodland expansion in the northern Levant comes from:

- the upper sections of the first pollen core (core I) from Ghab (Niklewski & van Zeist 1970, thereafter summarized by van Zeist & Woldring 1980, Bottema & van Zeist 1981, van Zeist & Bottema 1982, 1991, Baruch & Bottema 1991)
- studies of pollen preserved in dry deposits of some epipalaeolithic sites (e.g. Leroi-Gourhan 1979, 1981a,b,c, van Zeist & Woldring 1980, Leroi-Gourhan & Darmon 1991)
- remains of wood charcoal from epipalaeolithic sites in the area
- charred remains of food plants from the same sites.

Evidence from wetland pollen cores   The upper section of the Ghab I pollen diagram (part of which is reproduced here as Fig. 10.7) indicates the following:

- a major episode of woodland expansion (or infilling) in zone Y1, which the authors suggest could be dated (by interpolation) to 23000–18000 bc;
- a continuation of this extended woodland (albeit with some fluctuations) in zones Y2–Y4 with interpolated dates of 18000–12000 bc;
- a dramatic woodland retreat in Y5 with interpolated dates of 12000–9000 bc;
- and an equally dramatic expansion of woodland in zones Z1 and Z2 dated to *c.* 9000–6000 bc on the basis of a radiocarbon date of 10040 ±55 bp (GrN 5810) (= roughly 8000 bc) that coincides with the peak of woodland expansion (Niklewski & van Zeist 1970, Bottema & van Zeist 1981, van Zeist & Woldring 1980, van Zeist & Bottema 1982, 1991, Baruch & Bottema 1992).

However, this radiocarbon date is the only one determined for the entire upper part of the Ghab sequence, and it was obtained from mollusc shells that could theoretically have incorporated fossil carbon (from limestone carbonates) during their growth, which would make the date excessively early (Niklewski & van Zeist 1970, van Zeist & Woldring 1980, van Zeist & Bottema 1982).

As it stands, this dating of the episodes of woodland expansion and contraction at Ghab (with the associated interpolated dates) makes them almost the exact obverse of those in Baruch & Bottema's (1991) pollen diagram from Hula, as they themselves stress (ibid.: 17). With the existing date, the trends at Ghab also conflict with those observed at other pollen-core sites in the region, such as Tenaghi–Phillipon in Greece (Wijmstra 1969), and arguably Karamik–Bataklığı in southwestern Turkey (van Zeist et al. 1975) and Zeribar in Iran (van Zeist & Bottema 1977). The trends at each of these sites are much closer to those at Hula (see below), and can be identified despite the fact that:

- the cores suffer from the usual shortage of dates
- tree cover was relatively sparse at Karamik–Bataklığı relative to present-day levels
- tree cover had barely begun to establish at Zeribar by the time of the Younger Dryas, such that parallel trends have to be sought in the spectra for some of the steppe taxa. With its existing date, the Ghab sequence also conflicts with the more global changes (e.g. in temperature) indicated by work outside the region, even at the Glacial Maximum when most workers suggest that the same sort of cold, dry conditions prevailed throughout Southwest Asia.

Thus, for periods when almost all other pollen sites with usable data indicate cold, dry conditions and widespread woodland retreat (e.g. the periods coinciding with the Glacial Maximum and the Younger Dryas), the Ghab diagram, as presently dated, shows woodland expansion; and for a period when the other diagrams indicate moist warm conditions and woodland expansion, the Ghab diagram shows the most dramatic woodland retreat in the entire sequence.

Evidence from archaeological-site pollen   Leroi-Gourhan (1974, 1979, 1980, 1981a,b,c, 1984) and Leroi-Gourhan & Darmon (1991) have undertaken extensive studies of the relatively scant pollen preserved in aerobic deposits on archaeological

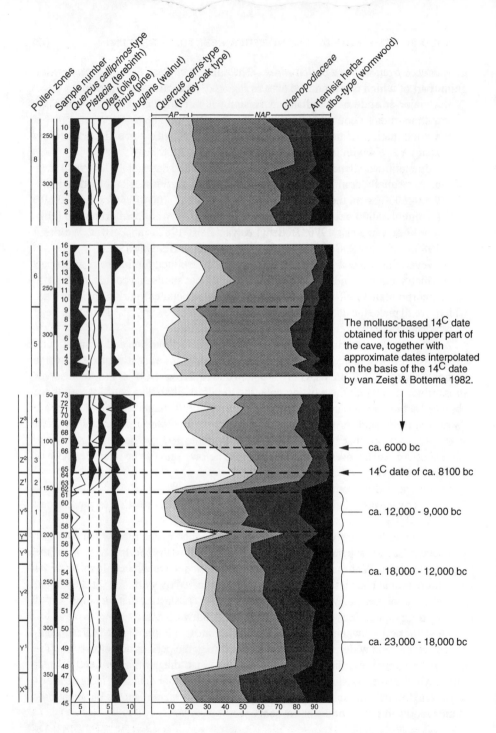

The mollusc-based 14C date obtained for this upper part of the cave, together with approximate dates interpolated on the basis of the 14C date by van Zeist & Bottema 1982.

← ca. 6000 bc

← 14C date of ca. 8100 bc

ca. 12,000 - 9,000 bc

ca. 18,000 - 12,000 bc

ca. 23,000 - 18,000 bc

Figure 10.7 The uppermost section of the pollen diagram from Ghab in northwestern Syria. (Redrawn from van Zeist & Bottema 1982: 303, fig. 14.5.) AP = arboreal pollen; NAP = non-arboreal pollen.

sites in the Levant such as Hayonim, 'Ain Mallaha, Mureybet and Aswad. They have further combined these data to produce a collective pollen curve for southwestern Asia considered as a unit (Fig. 10.8). This seems to suggest a pattern that closely parallels that traditionally associated with northern Europe, with episodes identified as correlating with the Allerød Interstadial, the Younger Dryas, and the ensuing, rapid woodland advance. Thus, it appears to reinforce the view that the Ghab sequence, as currently dated, is anomalous.

However, the spectra present some problems. Leroi-Gourhan's original pollen data for Mureybet could be interpreted as implying woodland retreat at the very point at which her combined diagram indicates the start of woodland spread (Leroi-Gourhan 1974; also the primary data and summaries of her work presented in van Zeist & Woldring 1980 and van Zeist & Bottema 1991). On the other hand, the frequency of tree pollen in the Mureybet samples was so low that it was clearly impossible to reach firm conclusions. This is particularly frustrating, as the site occupies a critical position just 175 km east-northeast of Ghab. The matter remains open.

Evidence from wood charcoals   Many of the uncertainties concerning the chronology and spatial distribution of woodland spread in the northern Levant and northern Fertile Crescent could be resolved by studies of wood charcoal from a scatter of early sites in these areas. Preliminary studies of the wood charcoals from the key sites of Abu Hureyra and Mureybet are now being greatly expanded by George Willcox and Caroline Cartwright, and equivalent studies will shortly be undertaken at Qermez Dere (Mark Nesbitt), M'lefaat (Nesbitt) and Hallan Çemi (Nesbitt) (Fig. 10.1). Willcox (pers. comm.) has already identified oak charcoal from early epipalaeolithic levels at Abu Hureyra, and the pattern of identifications through the well dated 1,500-year epipalaeolithic sequence there could confirm whether or not the woodland was in retreat at this critical time, which coincides with the Younger Dryas.

Evidence from remains of food plants   Charred remains of seeds of wild food plants from epipalaeolithic levels at Abu Hureyra indicate precisely the opposite set of trends to those at Ghab during the period of overlap, yet Abu Hureyra lies just 180 km due east of Ghab, and could reasonably be expected to have experienced the same climatic trends. More specifically, the Abu Hureyra remains indicate the survival of xeric woodland within reach of the site from the start of occupation at 9500 bc until 9000 bc. At that point, the effects of desiccation, which may well already have begun by 9500 bc, apparently started to "bite" and took the woodland out of foraging range of the site (Hillman et al. 1989a, Moore & Hillman 1992). This desiccation trend "bottomed" around 8400 bc, with no clear sign of woodland re-expanding into the area before the end of epipalaeolithic occupation around 8000 bc.

By contrast, the equivalent period at Ghab (with the Ghab date as it stands, this embraces the end of zone Y5 through to the end of zone Z1 – see Fig. 10.7) shows a dramatic change from maximum woodland retreat at 9500 bc, to maximum woodland expansion at 8000 bc, precisely the reverse of Abu Hureyra. (The chronology of the Abu Hureyra sequence is unlikely to be in error, because it rests on 14 radiocarbon dates, 11 of which are AMS dates based on samples of bone and grain (Moore et al.

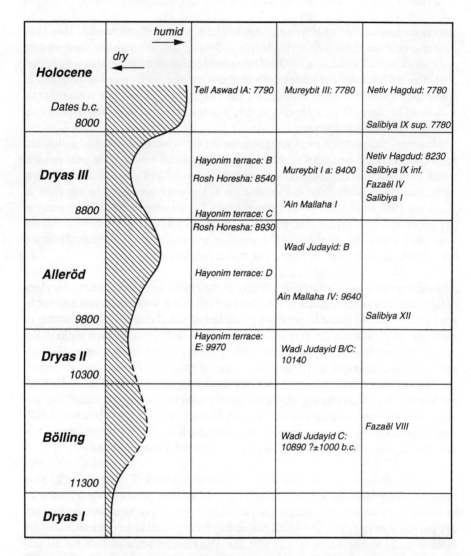

Figure 10.8 The combined results of analyses by Leroi-Gourhan & Darmon of pollen from aerobic deposits on a range of epipalaeolithic sites in the Levant and Euphrates Valley, showing a pattern of vegetation changes which corresponds closely with those established for Europe. (Redrawn from Leroi-Gourhan & Darmon 1991: 23, fig. 1.) All the dates are in uncalibrated radiocarbon years bc. (*Note:* Leroi-Gourhan (1981a: 109) has also recorded a similar pattern of changes farther east at Zarzi, Zawi–Chemi and Shanidar, all in the Zagros Mountains.)

1986).) Significantly, the trends at Abu Hureyra match those at Hula in the southern Levant very closely indeed.

Having outlined some of the evidence pertinent to dating the start of woodland spread from the northern Levant, we can now consider some explanations of the apparent contradictions.

EXPLANATION 1   One of the three possible explanations for Ghab and Hula producing opposite trends, which is offered by Niklewski & van Zeist (1970), Bottema & van Zeist (1981), van Zeist & Bottema (1982, 1991) and Baruch & Bottema (1991), is that the Ghab area experienced climatic events analogous to those experienced elsewhere (e.g. the Allerød Interstadial and Younger Dryas), but that these events had different effects here. Thus, during cold, dry periods such as the Glacial Maximum and the Younger Dryas, the low temperatures reduced evapotranspiration enough to more than compensate for the reduction in precipitation, thus allowing woodland to expand. Conversely, when other sites in the area indicate a widespread shift to moister warmer conditions, especially during the time of the Allerød Interstadial of northern Europe (10000–9000 bc), the increase in precipitation in the Ghab area (unlike anywhere else) was insufficient to compensate for increased evapotranspiration, and the woodland therefore contracted. This explanation is difficult to accept: not only are these effects improbable in themselves, but, if they occurred, there is no apparent reason why they should have been restricted to this one area of the northern Levant.

EXPLANATION 2   The second explanation for the anomalous pattern of the Ghab sequence is that the radiocarbon date of *c.* 8100 bc for the sharp peak in woodland expansion in the upper part of the Ghab core is erroneous. This was first advanced by those directly involved with the pollen studies (Baruch 1994, Baruch & Bottema 1991, Bottema & van Zeist 1981, Nikelwski & van Zeist 1970). To quote Baruch (1994: 111): "a dating error in the Ghab diagram should be seriously considered". The argument was further developed by Bar-Yosef & Belfer-Cohen (1992), and also by Moore & Hillman (1992), who drew attention to the additional evidence from Abu Hureyra and also identified trends in the Zeribar and other pollen diagrams that are the exact opposite of those in the Ghab core – with the date as it stands. The proposal, therefore, is that:

- the single, mollusc-based date for the upper part of the Ghab sequence is several centuries too early
- that the date of 8100 bc would better fit the end of the preceding trough of woodland contraction or the very early stages of the ensuing re-expansion (probably the terminal phase of the Younger Dryas)
- that the dramatic contraction of forest (zones Y4 and Y5) started around 9500 bc, rather than around the published interpolated date of 12000 bc (Fig. 10.7 above); and, more uncertainly
- that the preceding period of expanded (but fluctuating) woodland possibly covers the period from only 13000 to 9500 bc, rather than the published 23000 to 12000 bc. [Sytze Bottema & Willem van Zeist have now kindly sent me the relevant part of the core to arrange AMS radiocarbon dating of any solid, non-molluscan, carbonaceous matter that may survive: GCH.]

If the proposed 500 to 1,000 year adjustment of the Ghab radiocarbon date (and, more importantly, the major adjustments of associated interpolated dates of the preceding phases) are accepted, the Late Pleistocene pattern of woodland advance and retreat seen at Ghab immediately accords with the trends seen at Hula (Baruch & Bottema 1991), at Abu Hureyra (Hillman et al. 1989a) and at Tenaghi–Phillipon (Wijmstra 1969), and we also see a greatly improved fit with the trends recorded at Zeribar (van Zeist & Bottema 1977), Karamik–Bataklığı (van Zeist et al. 1975), and Sögüt Gölü (ibid.), as well as with trends apparent in the pollen record at archaeological sites such as Hayonim and 'Ain Mallaha (Leroi-Gourhan 1981a,b, Leroi-Gourhan & Darmon 1991).

The date-adjusted trends at Ghab also broadly coincide with broad regional or global trends recorded outside Southwest Asia, including events such as the Younger Dryas and the Allerød Interstadial, which were initially identified in northern Europe. Indeed, the authors of the Southwest Asian palynological studies used here all cite the obvious parallels with these and the other major northern hemispheric events, and it certainly seems improbable that Southwest Asia remained immune to their effects. Garrard (1993) similarly cites evidence for the impact of the Younger Dryas extending down to the southern Levant, causing a dramatic fall in the level of Lake Lisan at precisely this time (Begin et al. 1985, Macumber & Head 1991, both as cited by Garrard 1993). Further evidence of the Younger Dryas affecting the southern Levant comes from the geological studies of Yechieli et al. (1993) of deposits from the Dead Sea.

The fact that episodes such as the Younger Dryas appear to have impacted on the entirety of Southwest Asia does *not*, however, preclude a southerly monsoon circulation also having had some influence in, for example, possibly amplifying the effect of the northerly interstadials such that they were manifested somewhat earlier in the southern Levant than they were farther north, for instance at Abu Hureyra.

If we accept this argument for broadly similar vegetation trends having occurred at roughly the same time throughout the Levant during this period, then the start of Late Pleistocene expansion of woodland in the northern Levant can tentatively be dated to about the time of its inception in the Hula diagram, namely *c.* 13000 bc. We can also assume that there was a sharp reversal starting around 9500 bc (with much of the woodland surviving for a century or two, but probably not reproducing) and bottoming around 8600–8400 bc, followed by some measure of recovery, which in some areas (including Ghab) was seemingly very vigorous. This recovery appears to date to a few centuries after the trough bottom, perhaps to between 8200 and 8000 bc, although this event is of less concern to the present model.

EXPLANATION 3   Wright (1993) offers an entirely different explanation for the differences between the Ghab and Hula diagrams, and some similar ideas are advanced by Rognon (1987) and Weinstein-Evron (1983 and pers. comm.). Wright proposes that the atmospheric circulation patterns of the Late Glacial, which brought cold, dry conditions to most of Southwest Asia, would have persisted in the northern Levant until 9500 bc, but in the southern Levant would have been "replaced by monsoonal circulation between about 13000 and 9500 bc, involving increased summer rains as well as warmer summer temperatures" (Wright 1993: 465). This, he suggests, would account for the florescence of woodland at Hula between these dates, and the prevention of any woodland expansion around Ghab. The cold, dry conditions in the-northern Levant were replaced around 9500 bc by the Mediterranean pattern of wet warm winters and dry, hot summers, similar to those of the present day, which allowed the belated expansion of woodland in this area. The model appears to preclude any significant impact of the Younger Dryas anywhere in the region (cf. Wright 1989).

Evidence that could be argued to support this model comes from the paucity of occupation sites so far identified in the northern Levant during the period coinciding with the Hula woodland advance, when, in the southern Levant, there was an apparent florescence of Natufian sites exhibiting features normally associated with year-round sedentism (Bar-Yosef 1983, 1987). Although this evidence may seem persuasive, Edwards (1989b) rightly stresses the need for more reliable information before we assume extended sedentism at any of the Natufian sites, particularly those in the Jordan Valley.

On the other hand, the Wright model fails to account for the survival of trees from an earlier moist phase at Abu Hureyra from 9500 until 9000 bc, and sharp desiccation becoming manifest by 9000 and bottoming around 8400 bc, namely, the opposite trend to that seen at Ghab as currently dated. He attempts to circumvent this problem by grouping Abu Hureyra with sites of the Natufian heartland in the southern Levant (Wright 1993: 465–6). However, the reality is that Abu Hureyra sits squarely in the northern Levant, over 400 km from the Natufian heartland, but just 180 km due east of Ghab.

Conclusions on dating the start of woodland expansion from the northern Levant

There are difficulties with all three of the above explanations. For example, the cold, dry conditions of the Pleniglacial do not square with the evidence for high lake levels in some areas during the same period (Roberts & Wright 1993). Maybe it was not drought that limited tree growth, but low levels of CO_2 (Blumler: pers. comm.), which have recently been proposed to have peaked at the Glacial Maximum causing an obverse of the "greenhouse effect".

Nevertheless, "explanation 2" currently seems to fit the available data best, and for the purpose of this model, I have therefore adopted a date of $c.$ 13000 bc for the start of woodland expansion from the northern Levant (and, indeed, from any other refugia in the region), with a brief reversal during the Younger Dryas, followed in turn by some measure of woodland recovery and continued spread. It has to be hoped that results from the new studies of wood charcoals will reveal whether or not "explanation 2" is correct, although more pollen studies to fill the yawning gaps separating the coring sites are also badly needed, as has been repeatedly stressed by van Zeist & Bottema.

Steppe vegetation in the northern Fertile Crescent before 13000 bc

The models of palaeovegetation constructed by van Zeist & Bottema (1982, 1991, and Figs 10.3–10.5 above) indicate that, for some millennia during and after the Pleniglacial, almost all the interior of Southwest Asia was dominated by steppe and desert–steppe. This included the northern Fertile Crescent where the only possible exceptions might have been occasional pockets of trees in the favoured locations mentioned above. The steppic components of their models are based principally on the detailed pollen spectra from Lakes Zeribar and Mirabad in the northern Zagros (van Zeist & Bottema 1977, thereafter summarized in Bottema & van Zeist 1981, van Zeist & Bottema 1982, 1991; see also Wright et al. 1967; part of one of the Zeribar pollen diagrams is reproduced as Fig. 10.9). Although the oak (*Quercus*) and terebinth (*Pistacia*) curves on the left of the Zeribar diagrams Ia and Ib show small, brief inputs of pollen of both types throughout the Pleniglacial, van Zeist & Bottema (1977: 66) attribute this to long-distance transport from remote refugia.[4]

The impossibility of precisely identifying pollen from grasses and other potentially diagnostic taxa inevitably hampers attempts to model the composition of this upland steppe flora and the food resources it offered, and we are forced to incorporate studies of present-day steppe, particularly the steppe in areas protected from heavy grazing by domestic animals such as nature reserves, reservoir enclosures and military training grounds.[5] In so doing, we clearly have to guard against unwarranted uniformitarian assumptions regarding the composition of ancient plant communities, particularly during periods of acute ecological disequilibrium such as prevailed at the end of the Pleistocene (Blumler in Ch. 3 in this volume, Davis 1983, Huntley 1991, Huntley & Webb 1989, Webb 1986). In later sections of this chapter I have therefore attempted to model specific dislocations of plant associations, for example the penetration of certain wild cereals into what, by then, was moist upland steppe, from their assumed erstwhile "equilibrium" associations in the ecotone between park-woodland and woodland–steppe.

The status of grasses in the pre-13000 bc steppe

Southwest Asian steppe is generally termed "*Artemisia*–Chenopodiaceae steppe" in both the modern and ancient settings. This reflects the abundance of wormwoods such as *Artemisia herba-alba* and a wide variety of chenopods – not the leafy annuals such as "fat hen" or "goose-foot", but perennial shrublets growing knee-high and with small fleshy leaves. However, the term "*Artemisia*–Chenopodiaceae steppe" tends to obscure the fact that grasses are a conspicuous component of most undegraded forms of present-day steppe, and were probably a significant component of the local Pleniglacial steppe as well.

Today, the most abundant grasses are perennials such as the viviparous *Poa bulbosa* and *P. sinaica* characterized by miniature, 5 cm tall tussocks of glaucous, wiry leaves that can form a near-continuous cover resembling a grey-green lawn.[6] However, this level of abundance is generally attributed to heavy grazing (Zohary 1973), although it is equally clear that very heavy grazing by sheep does eventually kill them (and everything else that is not inedible) and turns steppe into desert (Hillman, unpublished field notes).[7] On the other hand, as soon as grazing pressures are reduced, additional, much taller perennial grasses appear, assuming that viable seed still survives in the soil and the soil itself has not become too degraded in the meantime. These are the feather grasses, *Stipa* and *Stipagrostis* (formerly *Aristida*) species, which produce tall tussocks and a sea of silvery plumes that billow in the wind, obscuring all other vegetation. Several feather grass species thrive in even the driest zones of steppe. In Central Asia, similar vegetation prompted Pasternak (1922) to evocative descriptions of the "breathing of the feather grass steppe" blowing in billows and "as boundless as a seascape".

Annual grasses are also common in present-day steppe, mostly dwarf taxa such as *Nardurus*, *Psilurus* and *Trachynia*, together with a range of small bromes and taller "wall barleys" of the *Hordeum murinum* complex. The latter often form dense stands in damp hollows.

In the Zeribar pollen diagram, prior to *c.* 13000 bc we find not only the expected high pollen input from the wormwoods and chenopods, but also a consistent 5–20 per cent input from grasses. Van Zeist & Bottema (1977: 63) suggest that the grasses therefore represented "a rather modest part of the Pleniglacial vegetation". However, the grasses most likely to have thrived in this cool, dry steppe are the perennials described above, and these particular grasses are likely to have been grossly under-represented in the pollen record. There are three reasons for this: the perennial *Stipa* species are relatively poor pollen producers; the perennial *Poa* species are viviparous, and so produce practically no pollen; and the steppe species of wall barley are cleistogamous (i.e. the florets remain closed and fail to shed most of their pollen). The 5–20 per cent of grass pollen could therefore be interpreted as suggesting that grasses were a significant component of the steppe vegetation, even at the altitude of Lake Zeribar, where low temperatures at this time might have been a limiting factor for many plants.

Prior to *c.* 13000 bc, therefore, the northern Fertile Crescent was covered by many thousands of square kilometres of steppe dominated not only by wormwoods and various shrubby chenopods, but almost certainly also by grasses such as perennial feather grass. Nevertheless, there can be no doubt that the grasses were a smaller component of the steppe than they became later on (see below). In particular, some of the large-seeded species of tussocked feather grass, such as *S. barbata*, would probably have achieved high densities only in areas with enhanced soil water, for instance, at breaks in slopes. On the other hand, regular burning (every 1–3 years, perhaps) of these particular areas after grain harvest in mid-summer could have eliminated many competing plants, cleared away old growth, released nutrients via the ashes, and encouraged tillering of the perennial tussock grasses (in this case, *Stipa* or *Stipagrostis* species), thereby allowing them to form almost pure stands and significantly increasing grain yields relative to transport costs (McCorriston 1992: 34, 53; Naveh 1974, 1984) – certainly, burning seems to have been applied to this end by indigenous peoples of California and the North American Great Basin (Steward 1938, Lewis 1972, Thomas 1981).

Other herbs of the pre-13000 bc steppe

Even the driest zones of steppe are remarkably rich in species, and the three dominants – wormwoods, chenopods and grasses – would have been accompanied by literally hundreds of species of the leguminous, spiney, cushion-tragacanths (*Astragalus* spp.), sainfoins (*Onobrychis* spp.), *Cousinia* thistles, knapweeds (*Centaurea* spp.), scattered clumps of tall wild fennels (*Ferula* spp.) and many other plants that in late spring would have formed a carpet of colour.

Plant-foods of the pre-13000 bc steppe

A huge number of these steppe plants produce edible seeds or fruits, "roots", leaves, shoots or flowers that have been used as food by recent hunter–gatherers, pastoralists or cultivators. Even in the Azraq Desert Basin in eastern Jordan, with a mere 100mm annual rainfall, I found that 70 per cent of the plants growing in "islands" of desert–steppe vegetation produced some sort of human food. (The survival of so many palatable plants on these "islands" reflects the fact that they were located too far beyond the limits of unbroken steppe to be regularly grazed by domestic animals.) The success of many of these same plants (including precisely the same species of feather grass) in secondary steppe at high elevations in Anatolia (e.g. on the mountains around the high plateau of Uzun Yayla east of Kayseri) further suggests that the cool conditions before 13000 bc would also not have prevented such plants growing in some abundance at lower elevations on the "hilly flanks" of the northern Fertile Crescent. During even the most arid and cold episodes of the Pleniglacial, therefore, the steppe vegetation is likely to have offered local foragers a diverse array of wild plant-foods that could have provided not only carbohydrates, oils and proteins, but also vitamins, minerals and those miriad "secondary compounds" that are coming to be recognized as essential for complete human health (Fellows 1993a,b).

In what follows, examples are given of some of the more obvious plant-foods indicated by "ethno-ecological modeling applied to hunter–gatherers of the pre-13000 bc steppe of the northern Fertile Crescent".[8] However, references to ethnographic observations of recent usages of these plants are too numerous to cite, and I include one or two only for those plant-foods whose role in human diet may seem surprising.

The relatively low energy costs of processing starch-rich, lowish-fibre **"root" foods** would have made them prime targets (see Cane 1989 for the relative advantages of "root" foods over small-seeded grain foods). Indeed, many of them are still gathered by the Bedouin today. Obvious examples of root foods that grow well in conditions as xeric as those of the pre-13000 bc northern Fertile Crescent include the large root tubers of the cream-flowered cranesbill (*Biebersteinia multifida*), the hairy storksbill (*Erodium hirtum*), and several species of wild salsify (*Scorzonera* spp.); the fleshy first-year tap-roots of wild parsnips; and the swollen stem-bases of giant broomrapes such as the dazzling yellow *Cistachne tubulosa*. Throughout several zones of steppe in spring, it would also have been possible to gather huge quantities of a truffle (Arabic *kâmâ*).

Although seed foods incur higher processing costs, they can nevertheless provide good energy returns, especially when they are rich in oils, and many seed foods are very palatable. The most universally available seed food across the Fertile Crescent as a whole before 13000 bc would probably have been the **seeds of the broad range of perennial chenopod shrublets**. Our studies of return-rates of seed foods from a range of different perennial chenopods of the dry zones of steppe through to full desert indicate that they would have offered a very attractive resource in the dry steppe of Late Pleistocene Southwest Asia. Their special attractions include the following:

(a) Different combinations of the many taxa grow prolifically in each of the zones of steppe and desert–steppe, even when it is too dry for the wormwoods (*Artemisia* spp).

(b) Their seeds mature in winter, when most other seed foods are scarce. (For a few examples of their seasons of seed shed, see table 14.1 in Hillman et al. 1989a.)

(c) The chenopods of any one species in any one area shed all their seeds within a couple of days, allowing efficient scheduling of harvesting effort.

(d) On being shed, the wings of their persistent perianths ensure that the seeds are blown into piles in and around the bottoms of bushes, or accumulate in small hollows, allowing them to be bulk-harvested with minimal energy expenditure.

(e) Unlike the wild cereals, de-husking the chenopod seeds (to remove the persistent perianth) involves simple rubbing and winnowing.

(f) The seeds are very oil-rich, and therefore provide a compact and relatively light source of energy. This is important in minimizing transport costs.

(g) Although, like all seeds, they must be roasted and ground to make them digestible (and thence ensure efficient energy returns during gut transit), few of the taxa need detoxification and, even for those with toxins (e.g. *Anabasis syriaca* and *A. setifera*), a single leaching of the flour from roasted seeds seems to be sufficient to eliminate the irritant effect (Hillman, unpublished field and laboratory notes). The one major exception to (c–e), above is *Cornulaca setifera*, a spiney shrublet much favoured by camels but less attractive to humans.

The tiny, parachuted **seeds of the wormwoods**, the second steppe dominant, might seem an improbable source of food, and yet the equally small seeds of related species of *Artemisia* were gathered and pounded to an edible pulp by some native Americans (Bean & Saubel 1972: 43; Kirk 1975: 141). A similar role in the diet of hunter–gatherers of Southwest Asian steppe cannot therefore be excluded, although the seeds (pounded or intact) are unlikely often to survive preservation by charring in archaeological deposits in identifiable form.

A more obvious example of a palatable seed-food from "grassland–wormwood–chenopod steppe" is the **grain of wild grasses**, particularly the perennial feather grasses (*Stipa* and *Stipagrostis* spp.), although the distribution of really dense stands would probably have been patchy and concentrated at the breaks of slopes and other locations with enhanced soil moisture (see above). As noted above, however, grain yields from stands of these grasses could perhaps have been significantly enhanced by regular burning (Naveh 1974, 1984; McCorriston 1992: 34), assuming that the mobile hunter–gatherers were there in late summer. Ethnographic records from three continents reveal that the grain of both (*Stipa* and *Stipagrostis* spp.) has regularly served as food for recent hunter–gatherers and pastoralists (e.g. Steward 1938, Harlan 1989), and ancient parallels of this practice are indicated by an abundance of charred grains of at least three species of *Stipa* throughout the epipalaeolithic occupation at

Abu Hureyra (Hillman 1975, Hillman et al. 1989a, Moore et al. in press). One of the species identified was *S. gigantea*, a spectacular plant with plumes reaching well over 2m, which no longer grows anywhere in the Fertile Crescent. Damp hollows in the steppe would also have produced useful yields of the edible grains of the wall barley grasses that are also amply represented among the food remains from epipalaeolithic Abu Hureyra. It should nevertheless be remembered that grasses are widely regarded as ranking "near the bottom of the optimal diet in an arid environment" (Layton et al. 1991: 260).

Other seeds foods likely to have abounded in the dry cool steppe of the pre-13000 bc northern Fertile Crescent include the clusters of huge seeds of the perennial thistle-like *Gundelia tournefortii*; the oily seeds of the many species of steppe and desert–steppe storksbills (*Erodium* spp.); the tiny, prolifically produced and easily gathered seeds of the small succulent *Aizoon hispanicum* (Bailey & Danin 1981 report that the Bedouin of the Sinai and Negev gather and grind the seeds of a very close relative to make bread); the nutlets of joint-pine (*Ephedra* spp.) – at least in some areas such as Lake Van at a somewhat later date (van Zeist & Woldring 1978), although seemingly not around Zeribar (see diagrams Ia & Ib in van Zeist & Bottema 1977); the oil-rich seeds of various poppies, mainly in moister areas; seeds of a wide range of steppic mallow, in green and ripe states; seeds from the violently bitter-fleshed colocynth melon (*Citrullus colocynthus*), which grows abundantly in even the most minor wadis; the seeds of a vast array of legumes, including the large-seeded sainfoins (*Ono-brychis* spp.) and the small-seeded relatives of fenugreek (*Trigonella* spp.); and the seeds of several steppe crucifers (members of the mustard family). However, flour from the roasted seeds of most wild legumes and crucifers would need to have been leached to detoxify it.

The spiney caper bush (*Capparis* spp.) is best known in Europe and America for its edible flower buds, rich in nutritious pollen, but its large pendulous fruits with leathery green skins enclosing sweet red flesh can also be eaten, complete with their bitter seeds if roasted and ground. The plants of dry steppe could also have provided a wide array of edible leaves, shoots and flowers, too numerous to detail here.

Low resource density in steppe before 13000 bc

It must be stressed that, despite the enormous diversity of potential plant-foods in steppe, before 13000 bc many of them would probably have been restricted to moister soils, for example at breaks of slopes. Overall, therefore, the mean energy yield per unit area of this dry, cool steppe is likely to have been relatively low compared with that available from:

- the moister forms of steppe that developed later (see below)
- terebinth–almond woodland–steppe with its areas of annual grasses
- oak–Rosaceae park-woodland
- wetlands of the sort likely to have occupied parts of the middle Euphrates and Tigris Valleys (Hillman, in Moore et al. in press).

These relatively low caloric yields from dry steppe may appear to conflict with Keeley's (1991: 182, 188) conclusion that "open terrain" provides richer yields than forests, even under strongly continental conditions. Although his conclusion is true if we compare certain forms of forest with certain types of open habitat, it has universal validity *only* if food-yields from different vegetation types are compared using the *percentage of the total biomass* that is edible by humans. On this basis, herbaceous vegetation (with a low biomass) tends to attract high scores compared with forest (with a very high biomass). But although such a basis of comparison is used in many modern ecological studies, it is irrelevant to understanding resource potential as it affects hunter–gatherers. For them, what matters is the net digestible caloric return per hectare and, on this basis, some forms of forest offer a vastly better "deal" than any open habitat (other than wetlands). Indeed, when processing costs are added, the predominantly small-seed foods of steppe and other dryland habitats offer *even poorer* returns when compared with nuts from forest trees (Mason 1992, 1995a,b, Simms 1987).

However, it should also be remembered that the net caloric returns of many "root" foods exceed those of both nuts and small-seed foods, whether the "roots" come from wetlands, dry forest glades, steppe or desert. Certainly, Cane (1989) reports that the Alyawara of Australia found that the energy costs of processing small-seed foods were so high that they were prepared to travel only half the distance to gather such seeds compared with the distance they would travel for roots. The advantages of certain root foods are particularly apparent when yields are measured in terms of digestible caloric returns, that is, in terms of calories absorbed through the gut wall.

13000 bc and the start of increased yields from plant-foods of steppe

The date 13000 bc is the start of woodland expansion around Hula, and the date adopted in this model for woodland expansion from the northern Levant and the improvement of conditions for plant growth throughout the region. Evidence from marine oxygen-isotope studies shows a rise in temperatures around this time (Bard et al. 1990: 405), but the resulting increases in evapo-transpiration must have been more than compensated by increased precipitation during the spring and/or summer when temperatures were high enough for active plant growth. From 11000 bc this trend became stronger and finally peaked around 9500 bc.

There are three pollen sites in the steppe with cores covering this period: Lake Zeribar at 1,300m in the central-northern Zagros Mountains (van Zeist & Bottema 1977: cores Ib and II), Lake Mirabad at *c.* 800m in the south-central Zagros Mountains (van Zeist & Bottema 1977), and the saline Lake Urmia at 1280m on the northern Iranian Plateau (Bottema 1986), although the Urmia core starts only at *c.* 11200 bc, and the Mirabad core even later at *c.* 10400 bc. The pollen record at all three sites indicates that they were a long way from major woodland refugia, and the increases in moisture availability in such locations is reflected primarily in increases in what the summary pollen diagrams record as "other herbs" (i.e. herbaceous plants including grasses, but excluding taxa such as Umbelliferae plotted separately in the summary diagram – Fig. 10.9, below). The Zeribar diagrams Ib and II show just such an increase in the pollen of "other herbs" starting around 13000 bc and peaking around 9500 bc, after which date there is a sharp reduction coinciding with the start of the Younger

Dryas. The separate curves for grasses ("other Gramineae") show the same trend. In the Urmia diagram, a slow rise in grass pollen and, later, its more rapid decline (correlating inversely with the curve for the more drought-tolerant wormwood) appears to coincide closely with these changes.

The increase in "other herbs", including grasses, certainly represents an overall improvement in plant-food yields. Having started around 13000 bc, this enrichment became still more pronounced between c. 11000 and 9500 bc. The yields of chenopod seeds were probably reduced only slightly, whereas yields of wormwood seeds (if they were used by local hunter–gatherers) would have declined because, compared with most perennial chenopods, wormwood competes poorly with tall perennial grasses. But from most of the other steppe foods, significant *increases* could be expected. Several plants with edible bulbs that would hitherto have been relatively scarce would probably now have abounded in moister areas, for example, the purple-blue tatar lily (*Ixiolirion tartaricum*), various wild tulips (*Tulipa* spp.), crocuses (*Crocus* spp, see Zohary 1973 for reference to their edibility), star-of-Bethlehem (*Ornithogalum* spp.), grape hyacinths (*Muscari* and *Bellevalia* spp.) and, around moisture-retaining crevices of rocks, bulbs of one of the barley grasses, *Hordeum bulbosum*.

Grain from wild grasses would also have become more plentiful: because the dominant grasses are likely to be underrepresented in pollen spectra (see above), the modest increases in the pollen diagrams probably represent significant increases in grain yield. Increased densities would probably have been particularly apparent in the large-grained species of perennial feather grass (e.g. *Stipa lagascae, S. hohenackeriana* and *S. barbata*). Indeed, in some localities, densities might have matched those cited above for present-day exclosures in the moister zones of steppe, although yields could perhaps have been increased still further by burning, which would reduce competition from some other plants, clear old growth and release nutrients. Enhanced seed yields would also have become available at this time from the wall barleys (forming almost pure stands in many damp hollows) and from the crucifers, poppies and wild legumes.

Several centuries later, around 9000 bc, many of these same food plants were still being used by epipalaeolithic hunter–gatherers at Abu Hureyra, on the lowland (southern) fringe of the northern Fertile Crescent, even though, by then, the steppe had been invaded by attractive additional foods such as wild cereals (see below; Hillman et al. 1989a). Indeed, evidence for utilization of some of these foods is also now beginning to emerge from even later epipalaeolithic sites in the northern Fertile Crescent such as Hallan Çemi, Qermez Dere and M'lefaat (Nesbitt: pers. comm.).

Effect of increasing climatic seasonality and unpredictability during the Late Pleistocene on the abundance of steppe food plants

Although the Glacial Maximum (c. 16000 bc) was characterized by cool, dry conditions, differences between winter and summer were not dissimilar to those in the region today. After 16000 bc there was a trend towards increased seasonality (continentality), and more specifically (in Southwest Asia) towards colder, wetter winters, and hotter drier summers. It was conditioned primarily by increased summer insolation and reduced winter insolation resulting from the Milankovich effect, and the trend peaked around 8000 bc (Byrne 1987: 24–5; COHMAP 1988). Wright (1993: 464) suggests that these effects were further exacerbated by a northward expansion of the tropical high-pressure cell that brought "the summer drought and strong seasonality that have been characteristic ever since". Byrne (1987: 27) further argues that the sharpening of inter-season variation during the Late Pleistocene was accompanied by increased fluctuations between years, resulting in greater unpredictability in rainfall and temperature, and irregular droughts. The existence of sharp inter-annual fluctuation between the Glacial Maximum and the start of the Younger Dryas is now also clearly indicated by evidence from the Greenland ice cores (Taylor et al. 1993).

The effect of these trends would have been to favour geophytes (herbaceous perennials with underground storage organs) and annuals, particularly larger-seeded annuals such as the wild cereals (Blumler 1984, 1991a,b, and in Ch. 3 in this volume; Byrne 1987: 28). Out in the steppe, the food plants that would have been advantaged would therefore have included all the "root" foods noted above, and the many annuals with edible seeds, including a wide range of crucifers, poppies and wild legumes, the annual chenopod *Chenolea arabica*, and the potentially prolific barley grasses. By contrast, other potential providers of seed foods, such as the perennial chenopods, wormwoods and the perennial feather grasses, would have been progressively disadvantaged. Nevertheless, the fact that grain from perennial feather grasses was still being heavily used at Abu Hureyra around 9000 bc (Hillman et al. 1989a) suggests that at least these particular perennials survived in significant numbers.

The spread of woodland across the northern Fertile Crescent

The most widely acknowledged effect of increased soil moisture in the Late Pleistocene is the expansion of woodland. The principal trees involved in its spread within or across the northern Fertile Crescent are likely to have included the following: xeric oaks such as *Quercus brandtii* and *Q. boissieri*, which today continue to abut onto the steppe in the northern Fertile Crescent; two terebinth species, *Pistacia atlantica* and *P. khinjuk*; and xeric members of the rose family (Rosaceae), particularly wild almonds such as *Amygdalus orientalis* and *A. webii*, but also the yellow-fruited hawthorn (*Crataegus aronia*), and perhaps the Syrian pear (*Pyrus syriaca*). They were probably also accompanied by a maple (*Acer monspessulanum*), a buckthorn shrub (*Rhamnus palaestina*), and Christ's thorn (*Paliurus spina-christi*). However, the rosaceous trees are insect-pollinated, as are the maple, hackberry, buckthorn and Christ's thorn, so their pollen will not be represented in the pollen diagrams. Terebinth pollen, too, is much more poorly disseminated than oak pollen, and is therefore substantially underrepresented in the pollen diagrams (van Zeist: pers. comm.).

Most of our evidence for the pattern of woodland spread across the Northern Fertile Crescent comes from the remarkable set of pollen diagrams from Lakes Zeribar and Mirabad cited above (see Fig. 10.9). As noted above, van Zeist & Bottema (1977, 1982, 1991) suggest that the spread of woodland started not only from the northernmost end of the Levantine woodland ("forest") refuge, but perhaps also from smaller refugia farther east, such as those tentatively indicated in Figure 10.3 near Malatya and Rowanduz. There may also have been small pockets of trees in other favourable locations. The diversity and dissected nature of the terrain in the northern Fertile Crescent makes this inherently probable.

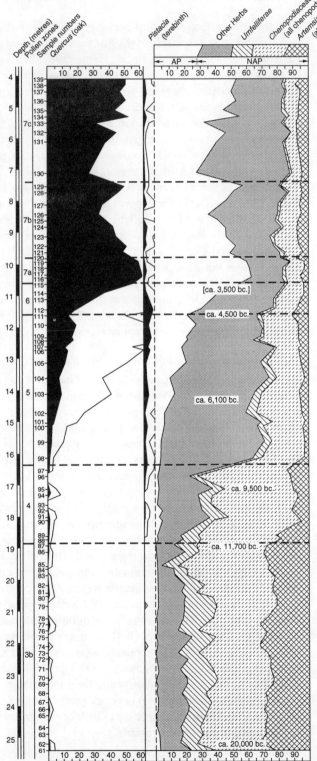

Figure 10.9 A small section of the Zeribar pollen diagram Ib. (Redrawn from van Zeist & Bottema 1977: Fig. 23.) The core was taken from Lake Zeribar in the northern Zagros Mountains, at an altitude of 1300 m. The dates are in uncalibrated radiocarbon years bc, all from the Groningen Laboratory, but with the date of *c.* 4500 bc interpolated by van Zeist & Bottema (1977; 1982: 279). In the curves for oak and terebinth, the open, unshaded curves represent a multiple of the frequencies actually recorded (for which the curves are shaded black), and have been added to allow the pattern of changes to be visible even when the frequencies are very low.

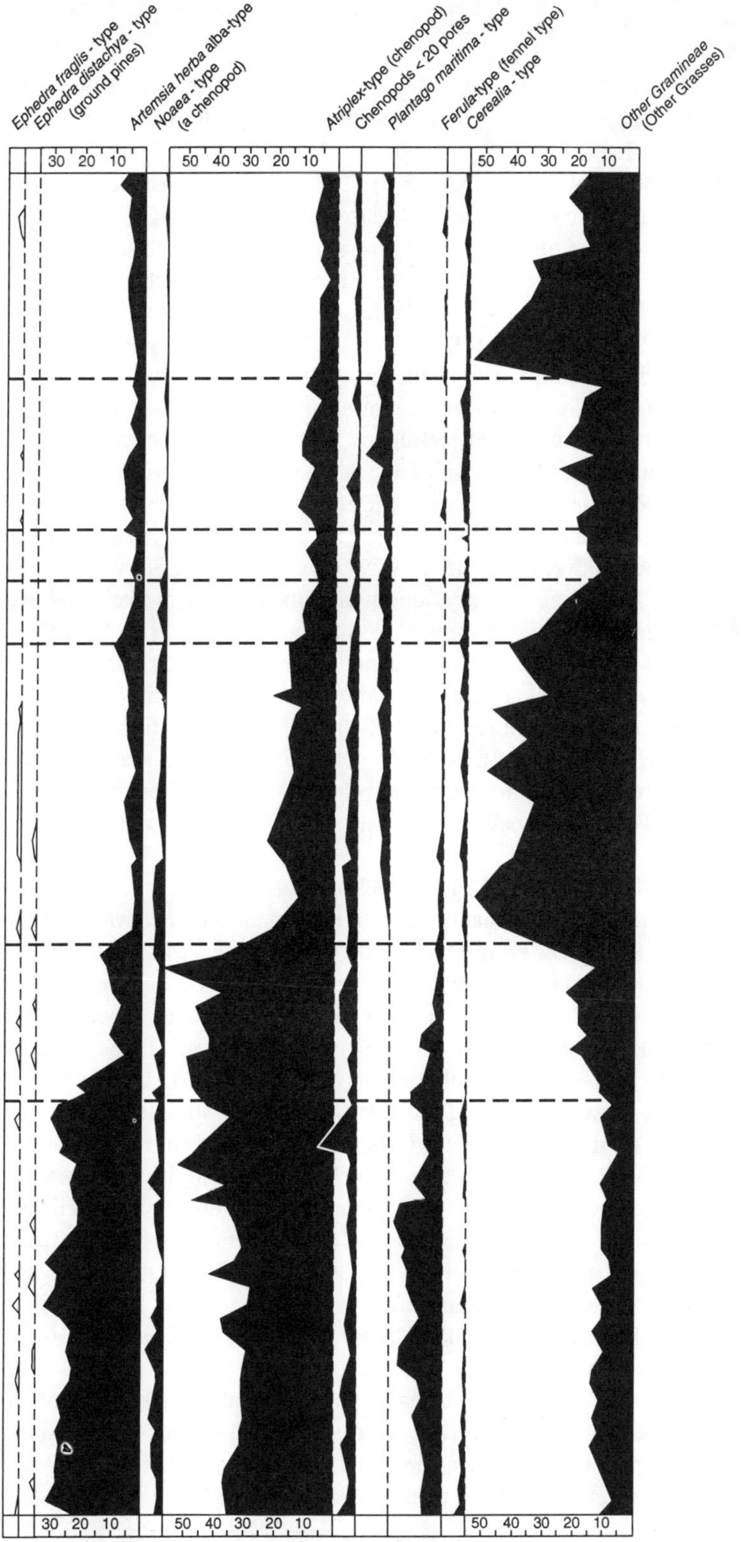

Ephedra fraglis - type
Ephedra distachya - type
(ground pines)
Artemsia herba alba-type
Noaea - type
(a chenopod)
Atriplex-type (chenopod)
Chenopods < 20 pores
Plantago maritima - type
Ferula-type (fennel type)
Cerealia - type
Other Gramineae
(Other Grasses)
30 20 10
50 40 30 20 10
50 40 30 20 10

But how quickly could oak–terebinth–Rosaceae woodland be expected to have spread into what, by then, was moist steppe? Useful clues come from isopoll studies from Late Pleistocene Europe, North America and Japan (Huntley & Birks 1983, Huntley 1988, 1991, Webb 1988, Huntley & Webb 1989). Regardless of the continent and the species involved, all oaks appear to have expanded at a rate of 75–500m per year, with the vast majority of observed examples falling in the range 150–200m per year, that is, around 150–200km per millennium (Huntley & Birks 1983: table 6.13; Huntley 1988: 362). Their estimates for the rates of spread of terebinth suggest a slightly faster rate of 200–300km per millennium.

The distance from the northernmost Levant across the northern Fertile Crescent to Zeribar is 1,200km. *If*, therefore, there were no mini-refugia in the central section of the northern Fertile Crescent of the sort mentioned above, then oaks spreading from the northeastern Levant could theoretically have taken anything between 2,400 and 16,000 years to reach Zeribar, but with a most probable migration time a millennium or so either side of 6,000 years. And if the Younger Dryas interposed, it is reasonable to suppose that woodland advance would have been interrupted for a few centuries coinciding with the "trough" of cold dry conditions. (In fact, this is likely to have affected only the later stages of the spread.) Assuming, therefore, that woodland advance began around 13000 bc as proposed, then oaks migrating from the northeast Levant would have reached Zeribar some time after 10000 bc, with the most likely date of arrival a millennium or so either side of 7000 bc. Terebinth could be expected to arrive a millennium or so earlier. If, however, oak and terebinth migration started from refugia not far from Zeribar, for example from the suggested Rowanduz mini-refuge (Figs 10.1, 10.3), then both oak and terebinth should have reached Zeribar very much sooner.

In fact, the Zeribar diagram (Fig. 10.9) indicates that oak arrived in the Zeribar area about 8000 bc, and terebinth somewhat (perhaps a millennium) earlier (van Zeist & Bottema 1977, 1982, 1991). The point at which they are assumed to have arrived in the Zeribar area is the point in the diagram when the frequency of their pollen significantly exceeds the low-level inputs of preceding periods when the presence of their pollen was attributable to long-distance wind-transport (see *n.* 4.) These dates of arrival are close to those predicted, on the assumption of migration having started from the northeastern Levant, and using the oak and terebinth migration rates that Huntley (1988: table 3) and Huntley & Birks (1983: table 6.13) indicate to be the most probable. These dates of arrival clearly do not exclude the possibility of migration having started from a refuge that van Zeist & Bottema suggest might have existed near Malatya, just 200km from the northeastern edge of the Levantine refuge (Fig. 10.3). However, it does suggest that there is only a very low probability that the oaks and terebinth spread from the suggested mini-refuge near Rowanduz. If such a refuge existed, then it probably lacked oaks and terebinths, even though other, insect-pollinated trees could theoretically have been present.

From *c.* 8500 to 4800 bc we see a slow, steady increase in oak and terebinth pollen, which van Zeist & Bottema (1977: 69) see as an increasing density of terebinth–almond woodland–steppe with some oak trees, although with terebinth definitely the dominant. (It should be remembered that terebinth pollen tends to be relatively underrepresented.) The "peak" of terebinth pollen before the eventual steep rise in oak pollen probably reflects the relatively drought-tolerant terebinth–almond woodland preceding the eventual establishment of woodland dominated by oaks (Freitag 1977: 94; van Zeist & Bottema 1977: 67).

There are three reasons for this first "wave" of woodland–steppe having been dominated not by oaks but by terebinth, probably together with wild almonds, hawthorns and buckthorn. First, the terebinth, at least, is likely to have migrated slightly faster (Huntley 1988: 362). Secondly, each of these dryland trees and shrubs is likely to have had a "head start" because, back in the woodland refugia, they would have dominated the outermost steppe-abutting zone. Thirdly, as conditions became moister, they would have started migrating sooner because of the apparent ability of their seedlings to establish themselves at lower levels of soil moisture. During the migration, however, the original patterns of association between even these more drought-resistant trees and shrubs could well have been dislocated (Davis 1983, Huntley 1991, Huntley & Webb 1989, Webb 1986).

The spreading woodland–steppe should therefore be pictured as a very thin scatter of trees dominated by terebinth and dryland almonds, shrubs such as buckthorn and Christ's thorn, and with the occasional hawthorn and perhaps some Syrian pear. In appearance, this probably resembled woodland–steppe surviving today on ranges such as the Jebel Abdul Aziz (Fig. 10.1; and see photos in Moore et al. in press: fig. 3.5). However, even this thin scatter of trees and shrubs would have provided important new plant-foods for the steppic hunter–gatherers.[9]

At 4500 bc the Zeribar diagram shows a sharp increase in oak pollen, with a corresponding percentage decrease in grass pollen, a decline in terebinth pollen, and a continuation of the decline in chenopods and wormwoods. Van Zeist & Bottema (1977; 1982: 279) interpret this as increased net humidity allowing replacement of the woodland–steppe by much denser oak woodland or even full oak forest. Such a scenario also fits Byrne's (1987) and the COHMAP (1988) model, which suggests full dissipation by this point of the extreme seasonality that had peaked during the Pleistocene/Holocene transition. However, the woodland is still likely to have been patchy, because seedling establishment by woody plants is apparently difficult on the fertile basaltic and terra rossa soils found in many parts of the Fertile Crescent (Blumler 1984, 1991a,b).

The spread of wild einkorn across the northern Fertile Crescent

The same conditions that permitted the spread of woodland also allowed the spread of wild cereals and other herbaceous annuals, which hitherto probably achieved their highest concentrations in the broad woodland–steppe ecotones discussed above. However, their spread (individually and collectively) has to be modelled separately from the spread of trees, on account of the inevitable dislocation of any pre-existing associations that characterized earlier climatic conditions (cf. Davis 1983, Huntley 1991, Huntley & Webb 1989, Webb 1986). Unfortunately, the difficulty of distinguishing the different grasses by their pollen precludes any possibility of using isopoll studies to calculate migration rates, as has been done for some of the trees. Nevertheless, it is often argued that, even though acorns and other fruits can be carried considerable distances by members of the crow family and in the unvoided faeces of some large mammals (Huntley: pers. comm. 1995), the relatively small seeds of grasses are disseminated still farther and faster. There are two reasons for this expectation:

- fertile grass florets are more readily carried by the wind
- their barbed awns allow them to adhere to the coats of wide-ranging large mammals such as onager, gazelle and wolf.[10,11]

In fact, the Zeribar pollen diagram (Fig. 10.9) suggests that migrating grasses spread together with (or slightly behind) the first terebinths: the dramatic increase in the pollen of "other herbs", particularly grasses ("other Gramineae" in Fig. 10.9) starts around 9000 bc, and this roughly coincides with the first of more significant increases in terebinth pollen. Van Zeist & Bottema (1977: 71–2) attribute the grass pollen increase to dryland grasses (in the steppe) rather than to grasses of the lake fringe or peatlands, and propose (p. 76) that grasses also then played a more prominent role in the drier lower altitude steppe at Mirabad. This steep rise in grasses and other herbs is unprecedented in the Zeribar pollen sequence and is unlikely to be attributable merely to enhanced local water availability – after all, the increases in grass pollen as a result of enhanced regional moisture levels between c. 13000 and 9500 bc are relatively modest, as is their subsequent decrease coinciding with the onset of the Younger Dryas (see above). Another factor must be involved, and the obvious candidate is the arrival of a rich flora of annual grasses and other herbs migrating with the terebinths. These grasses are likely to have included both the wild einkorns (*Triticum monococcum* subsp. *boeoticum* and *T. urartu*), wild barley (*Hordeum spontaneum*) and perhaps wild annual rye (*Secale cereale* subsp. *vavilovii*).

But where was the starting point of this migration of annual grasses? It was concluded above that the delayed arrival of terebinth and oaks at Zeribar suggests that they most probably originated from the Levantine refuge, or possibly from an adjacent mini-refuge near Malatya. It was also concluded that this did not exclude the possible survival of certain insect-pollinated trees such as wild almonds and hawthorn in mini-refugia closer to Zeribar (e.g. at Rowanduz, and perhaps in even smaller refugia elsewhere. However, present-day distribution patterns of wild einkorn suggest that it is unlikely to have survived in any such oak-free refugia: we have yet to find any einkorn in woodland–steppe in Syria lacking oaks and dominated by drought-resistant taxa such as wild almonds and hawthorn, and it is similarly absent from arid-zone terebinth woodland, at least where this represents the outer drier parts of this zone (Hillman: unpublished field notes). It is therefore probable that the wild einkorn that spread across the northern Fertile Crescent originated *not* from any such xeric mini-refugia, but rather from the northeastern edge of the Levantine woodland refuge.

By contrast, the same studies revealed that wild barley can grow in arid-zone almond and terebinth woodland, if only on north-facing slopes, and so could probably have survived in any such refugia – provided that it was not grazed out by herbivores such as onager or gazelle targeting isolated clusters of trees as browse and shelter. On the latter point, our field studies in *Pistacia vera* woodland–steppe in the Batkhyz reserve of southeastern Turkmenistan have revealed that gazelle and onager are unlikely to have completely eliminated wild barley, especially where it grows in the spiny *Ephedra ciliata* thickets around the bases of the trees. The wild barley that probably invaded the northern Fertile Crescent might therefore have spread, not only from the northern Levant, but also from xeric mini-refugia farther east, if any such existed.

The place of these wild cereals among the annuals generally was probably that of a conspicuous (and possibly dominant) component in even the first "bow-wave" of invaders. This is suggested by their invasive tendencies and related ability to out-compete other annuals by virtue of the fact that their large seed size allows rapid early seedling growth, and the flag leaf and other photosynthetic surfaces responsible for "grain fill" overtop most other herbaceous vegetation. These same abilities have also allowed wild einkorn and wild barley to become very effective weeds of crops of domestic cereals. Limbrey (1990) has further noted that invasive plants such as these would have been particularly advantaged on naturally disturbed, "self-mulching" soils, such as vertisols, that today occur at many points in the Fertile Crescent, although they also compete effectively on other basaltic soils and often on terra rossas as well.

Despite their probable predominance, however, the arrival of wild wheat and barley in the Zeribar area will not be manifest in the "cerealia-type" pollen curve in the Zeribar diagram, because both cereals are effectively cleistogamous, that is, their pollen is rarely released and so remains largely unrepresented in any pollen diagram.[12] The probable pattern of spread of wild cereals across the northern Fertile Crescent is summarized in Figure 10.10.

Massive increases in combined yields of wild food plants

In the absence of dense tree cover, wild einkorn in particular tends to form dense stands, and its yields per square metre often match those of cultivated wheats under traditional management (Harlan 1967, Zohary 1969, Hillman 1973, Russell 1988; Hillman & Davies 1990: table I; Willcox 1992, 1995). In addition, wild einkorn seems able to establish itself over a much broader range of edaphic conditions than, say, wild emmer wheat, and this capacity perhaps accounts for its ability to produce fairly consistent yields year-on-year, especially when yields are averaged across areas as large as those probably exploited by any one band of hunter–gatherers (Hillman: unpublished field observations 1969–92).[13] It is therefore possible to envisage a vast expanse of wild einkorn expanding across erstwhile steppe, and resembling a seemingly limitless, if patchy, field – laced with a thin scatter of terebinth trees, almonds and hawthorns. Similarly, huge dense stands can be produced by wild barley and wild annual rye. Whereas the productivity of several of the existing plant-foods of the steppe is likely to have been reduced by competition from these invaders, the addition of seed and grain foods from the new annuals, particularly from wild cereals such as einkorn and barley, must have offered massive net increases in combined caloric returns.

As large-seeded annuals, the relative abundance of the wild cereals such as einkorn will have been further enhanced, even relative to other grasses, by the increasing climatic seasonality discussed above (Blumler 1984, 1987, 1991a, 1994, and in Chapter 3 in this volume; Byrne 1987: 28). This increased seasonality peaked around 8000 bc, so concomitant increases in grain yields will have been amplified as the cereals spread eastwards, until the onset of the period of desiccation that coincided with the Younger Dryas. (By this time, the wild cereals had probably almost reached Zeribar; see Fig. 10.10b.)

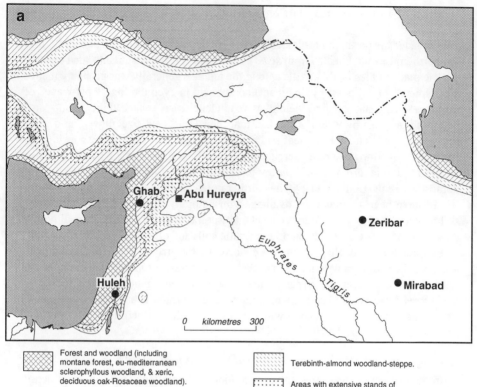

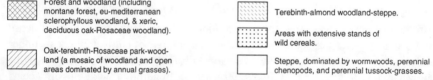

Forest and woodland (including
montane forest, eu-mediterranean
sclerophyllous woodland, & xeric,
deciduous oak-Rosaceae woodland).

Oak-terebinth-Rosaceae park-woodland (a mosaic of woodland and open
areas dominated by annual grasses).

Terebinth-almond woodland-steppe.

Areas with extensive stands of
wild cereals.

Steppe, dominated by wormwoods, perennial
chenopods, and perennial tussock-grasses.

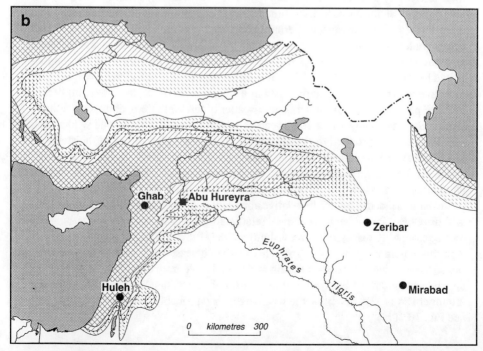

Figure 10.10   Models of the possible distribution of forest, woodland, wild cereals, woodland–steppe and steppe in the northern Fertile Crescent at two points in time during the spread
of vegetation from the northeastern Levant and/or a possible mini-refuge near Malatya. (a) The
situation at *c.* 11000 bc, i.e. 2,000 years after the beginning of the expansion of woodland–
steppe and annual grasses. (b) The situation at *c.* 9000 bc, i.e. 4,000 years after the beginning
of the expansion of woodland–steppe and annual grasses, and at a point when the dry, cold
conditions of the Younger Dryas would probably have just started to interrupt their spread for
a few centuries.

The subsequent arrival of oaks and other woodland trees will not have obliterated
the wild cereals. Even though tree cover slowly increased, the eventual oak-dominated woodland will have remained open for a long time, and on the deeper basaltic
and terra rossa soils, where wild einkorns, wild rye and wild barley thrive in particularly dense stands, Blumler (1984, 1991a,b, 1993, and in Ch. 3 in this volume) has
noted that seedling establishment of many woody plants is often poor. (I am not convinced that this limitation applies equally to *Pistacia atlantica*, which often appears
to thrive on such soils, albeit only in its usual sparse stands.) Vast populations of wild
cereals are therefore likely to have remained an important feature of the resource environment for a very long time. Indeed, such stands could potentially continue to thrive
today, extending beyond the limits of oak-dominated park-woodland and into the
proximal parts of the much sparser terebinth–almond woodland–steppe,[14] although
not into the more remote ranges where the last pockets of terebinth woodland–steppe
survives today (Hillman, in Moore et al. in press).

Once woodland was well established, Lewis (1972) and Naveh (1974, 1984) have
suggested that the use of fire by hunter–gatherers could, in any case, have opened it
up to allow the re-establishment of stands of wild cereals. However, the burning of
pre-existing wild stands of cereals immediately after harvest would *not* have provided
an effective means of eliminating competition and increasing their yields, as suggested by Lewis (1972). There are two reasons for this. First, Blumler (1991b) has
found that the grains of wild barley and emmer, at least, are killed by burning (except
for emmer spikelets wedged in cracks around rock outcrops). The morphology and
implanting behaviour of einkorn and rye spikelets (not yet studied by Blumler) further
lead me to suggest that they, too, would suffer the same fate in areas of fine-grain soils,
although they might just survive on cracked vertisols where spikelet penetration is
probably deeper. Secondly, McCorriston (1992), McCorriston & Hole (1991) and
Naveh (1974, 1984) have found that fire generally disadvantages annuals relative to
perennials such as the tussock grasses. Despite these limitations, the extent of wild
stands of wild cereals could doubtless have been increased by sowing gathered grain
onto burnt areas, rather as described for some indigenous hunter–gatherers of the
Great Basin by Steward (1938) and Thomas (1981). Certainly, Naveh (1984: 56) has
found that wild barley is a particularly effective colonizer of recently burnt areas, even
though any of its grains already present during the burning would be killed.

But regardless of the effectiveness of any landscape management aimed at maintaining areas of wild cereals once woodland developed, it is clear that the initial invasion of wild cereals and other annual grasses into erstwhile steppe will have

enormously increased caloric yields per unit area, and correspondingly increased carrying capacity. Although the northern Fertile Crescent had already experienced improvements in food yields since 13000 bc, the increases accompanying the invasion of wild cereals were unprecedented: not only were the increases themselves likely to have been far greater than anything experienced in the area since well before the Glacial Maximum, but they also occurred relatively abruptly.

As indicated above, available evidence currently suggests that this massive and abrupt increase in carrying capacity started at the western end of the northern Fertile Crescent around 13000 bc and progressed slowly eastwards, thereafter to spread southeast down the Zagros and reach the Zeribar area around 9000 bc. The effects on hunter–gatherer socio-economy are likely to have been profound, although responses may have been somewhat different among hunter–gatherers of the eastern parts of the Fertile Crescent, for whom the change came at a time closer to peak climatic seasonality and inter-annual unpredictability. Also, for those in the southern Zagros, the change would probably have been preceded (and delayed) by the cold, dry conditions of the Younger Dryas.

Impacts on local hunter–gatherers

The effects of these increases in carrying capacity on the hunter–gatherers of the northern Fertile Crescent are analyzed in detail in a forthcoming paper. It draws not only on field ecological studies, but also on the archaeobotanical and artefactual record from pre-agrarian sites in the area, and even more on ethnographic studies (including cross-cultural studies such as those of Thomas 1981, Layton et al. 1991, and Keeley 1988, 1991, 1992) of the response of recent hunter gatherers to different resource environments and the seasonal availability of storable foods. What follows is a necessarily simplistic outline of some of the arguments of that paper.

Storage and sedentism   Analysis of the seasonal distribution of the increases in potential starch–protein staples during the Late Pleistocene suggests that, whereas the piecemeal regional changes after 13000 bc would have allowed small incremental increases in any existing practices of food storage and winter sedentism, the abrupt changes accompanying the invasion by wild cereals and other annuals would have prompted hunter–gatherer groups in some areas to increase massively their storage of plant-foods (and perhaps also some animal foods) and greatly to extend their periods of sedentary settlement. It is suggested that in ecologically favourable areas where potential staples were available from different ecosystems with different cycles of seasonal availability of key foods, sedentism could quickly have increased to the point where at least the pregnant woman, young children and a proportion of the other band members could remain year-round in just one base camp. This shift would in some cases have marked the start of other cultural changes that characterized many "delayed-return" hunter–gatherers of recent times (cf. Woodburn 1980, Hoffman 1984). The core of these changes could have occurred quite rapidly (cf. Keeley 1991).

Birth rates and food stress   Once pregnant woman and a proportion of other band members, including some of the other young women of child-bearing age, could be based around a single camp for much of the year, several factors (including the relaxation of certain cultural controls) would have allowed birth rates to increase sharply. However, the high potential net return rates from key resources in and around favourable locations would have allowed several generations to elapse before any concomitant stress on carrying capacity would be experienced. At that point, one of several trajectories could have been followed (cf. Harris 1990: 16–28 and fig.2; Layton et al. 1991). However, for many of those now heavily dependent on storage and occupying particularly favourable locations in a region where both water supplies and (initially, at least) woody fuel were concentrated in well separated locations, an obvious response would have been to try to increase yields from local stands of key staples. The paper explores several options, but none seems likely to have produced caloric returns that could have kept pace with rapid population growth.

Cultivation   There was, however, a device that allowed more food to be extracted from less land. This involved selecting one, two, three or more food plants, destroying the natural vegetation in areas where these plants were normally unable to compete but where they could grow prolifically if competition were eliminated, breaking up the soil, and sowing the seeds of the selected plants (or planting their stocks). This was cultivation, which although ecologically destructive, eventually irreversible, probably requiring restructuring of understandings of human relationships with the rest of the living and non-living world (cf. Ingold 1988, and in this volume), and probably ethically and spiritually unacceptable to many groups (cf. McLuhan 1973), nevertheless offered an immediate solution to the pressing problem of too many humans to feed from too small an area. (Ironically, the cultivation "solution" has, of course, ensured that the problem has continued in ever more exacerbated form ever since). The cultivation option was further favoured by the fact that sedentary hunter–gatherers occupying the more productive locations in the Fertile Crescent already had perfect candidates for both cultigens and cultivated land. The wild cereals met all the requirements of effective cultigens; and the moisture-enhanced soils on small terraces and at other breaks of slope around the lower reaches of the major wadi systems, which characterized most of the favoured locations, would have made possible yields far greater than in the drier locations where the cereals grew naturally – once native vegetation was eliminated (Hillman, in Moore et al. in press).

In this trajectory, therefore, it is suggested that cultivation began among hunter–gatherer groups who had recently shifted from a significant level of dependence on immediate returns, to heavy dependence on delayed returns.

Timing and detection   Because the model suggests that these events were triggered by the invasion of wild cereals, and because this invasion appears to have started from the northeastern Levant around 13000 bc and reached Zeribar only around 9000 bc, the model prediction is that archaeologists working in the northern Fertile Crescent are likely to encounter the earliest local cases of the beginnings of cereal cultivation in the *western* part of the northern Crescent. Here, some cereal cultivation probably started as early as 12000 bc (as, indeed, it probably did in parts of the Jordan Valley). The model correspondingly proposes that the earliest instances of the adoption of cultivation farther east in the Fertile Crescent are likely to be progressively later.

However, detecting the start of cultivation will, as ever, be problematic. First, cultivation prior to domestication can currently be recognized only from indirect evidence, not from the remains of the crops themselves (Hillman et al. 1989a, Hillman & Davies 1990: 199-210). Secondly, the nature of the processes involved ensures that domestication itself is often difficult to detect. The experimentally based models of Hillman & Davies (1990, 1992) suggest that, once the wild-type cereals were under cultivation, morphologically altered domestic forms could have "taken over" the crops within a couple of centuries or even sooner. However, this occurs only if the cultivators used harvesting methods favouring the domestic mutants, and, while these methods would have offered the cultivators some immediate advantages, some groups may well have used methods which left their crops in the wild-type state for centuries or millennia. (This has been termed "non-domestication cultivation".) And even when domestication-inducing methods *were* applied, the models indicate that a range of factors such as unripe harvesting, and heavy introgression (genetic infiltration) of wild-type genes from nearby populations of wild cereals, could have caused domestication to take much longer than two centuries, and resulted in a correspondingly protracted period of "pre-domestication cultivation". Indeed, even with the most rapid domestication, it is inevitable that "modifier genes" would have ensured that the crops continued to contain an admixture of wild forms for many centuries, e.g. right through the Pre-Pottery Neolithic (Hillman & Davies 1990: 193, 194, fig. 11; 1992: 139, figs 13, 14). This effect, combined with the inherent problems of distinguishing wild and domestic cereals from charred remains (ibid. 1992: appendix pp. 157–8), ensures that detection of domestication in the archaeological record will continue to be extremely difficult. The recent work of Willcox (1995) underlines the possibility that domestication was, indeed, retarded in this way, and that mixtures and wild and domestic types continued for centuries. But although archaeobotanists have already spent years researching alternative methods of detecting both domestication and non- and pre-domestication cultivation (Colledge 1988, Butler 1989, Hillman et al. 1989a, Kislev 1989, 1992, Hillman & Davies 1990, 1992, McLaren et al. 1991, Hillman et al. 1993), progress is slow and piecemeal.

Other trajectories   As the Late Pleistocene progressed and climatic seasonality and unpredictability neared its peak, hunter–gatherer groups following other trajectories would have encountered increasing problems of fluctuating yields of the wild cereals on which they had become increasingly dependent. (Even the yields of wild einkorn from the entire territory of a hunter–gatherer group would have been affected; see above.) One way of stabilizing yields fluctuating because of water stress is to sow the cereals in areas fed by permanent springs and duly cleared of competing vegetation. Suitable springs can be found scattered right across the Fertile Crescent, and they could have been used for small-scale cultivation by a number of groups. Finally, it could be argued that the dry conditions during the "trough" of the Younger Dryas (*c.* 8700 to 8200 bc) similarly drove yet more groups to cultivate just such "oasis" locations (cf. McCorriston & Hole 1991). And if this were so, then it is inevitable that cases of fairly early cultivation and domestication such as those now tentatively identified at epipalaeolithic Abu Hureyra in levels dated to *c.* 8400 bc (see *n.* 2) will eventually be encountered at many other sites. In these last scenarios, cultivation could *theoretically* have preceded shifts to year-round sedentism and provided an additional "delayed return" component for an economy otherwise heavily dependent on *immediate* returns. In practice, however, several factors make such a progression improbable.

Details of the ecological constraints and possible mechanisms for each of these trajectories are not presented here, but will be published in full elsewhere, together with due discussion of parallels among recent hunter–gatherers.

Conclusions

This chapter has sought to establish the chronology of major changes in vegetation cover in the northern Fertile Crescent during the Late Pleistocene, and to outline the resulting changes in the plant-food resource base available to local hunter gatherers. Existing evidence suggests that steppe vegetation throughout Southwest Asia started to become richer from about 13000 bc, and that this significantly enhanced the availability of potential starch–protein staples, albeit incrementally. Woodland spread also began at 13000 bc, not only in the southern Levant, but also from the northern Levant across the northern Fertile Crescent. This spread of oak-dominated park-woodland was apparently preceded by a thin scatter of terebinth-dominated woodland–steppe, including, in many areas, swathes of annuals, particularly annual grasses dominated by wild cereals. This invasion across the northern Fertile Crescent appears to have started (around 13000 bc) primarily from the northeastern Levant or nearby "mini-refugia". From here, the terebinths and annual grasses (probably with certain almonds and hawthorns) appear to have reached Zeribar by 9000 bc, followed within a millennium by the oaks and eventually by other members of oak–Rosaceae park-woodland.

The effect of this invasion was to increase dramatically the gross yields of plant-foods per unit area, particularly potential starch–protein staples, and correspondingly to increase carrying capacity. It is suggested (in outline only here) that these increases prompted significant extensions both in the storage of plant-foods and in sedentism, and that the ensuing increases in birth rate eventually produced stresses on carrying capacity, which, in certain locations, led to the cultivation of cereals. It is proposed that these shifts could have been under way by 12000 bc in northwestern parts of the Fertile Crescent, that they occurred progressively later farther east, and that increasing climatic seasonality and unpredictability coupled with the dry conditions coinciding with the Younger Dryas produced further shifts to cereal cultivation during the mid-ninth millennium bc. Given this pattern of events, it could fairly be claimed that climatically induced changes in the plant-food resource-base available to hunter–gatherers in the northern Fertile Crescent during the Late Pleistocene were, indeed, preludes to the start of local cereal cultivation.

Notes

1. The model outlined in this chapter is based on presentations first given in 1977 at the Department of Archaeology, University College Cardiff, and at the Conference of the Association of Environmental Archaeology held in Cardiff in 1986. In this chapter, the term "Fertile Crescent" is defined as the crescent of relatively fertile terrain embracing most of the Levant, the southern foothills of the Anti-Taurus Mountains, and the western foothills of the Zagros Mountains, and it approximates to Braidwood's "Hilly Flanks". The *"northern Fertile Crescent"* denotes the southern foothills of the Anti-Taurus Mountains stretching from the northern Levant northwest of present-day Aleppo, to the northwestern foothills of the Zagros (see Fig. 10.1).

2. Charred grains of a fully domestic form of rye and a hexaploid wheat have been identified from two deposits (so far) of the later stages of the Late Epipalaeolithic at Abu Hureyra dated to between 8600 and 8400 bc. Because they are so early, several of the grains will be radiocarbon dated by the AMS method at the Oxford Laboratory which has already dated 11 grains of *wild* einkorn and *wild* rye from these and other epipalaeolithic levels. Remains of both rye and free-threshing wheats tend to be underrepresented on archaeological sites (Hillman 1978), so the finds of these two domesticates could well indicate that either or both were cultivated in the area as crops in their own right.

   If the early date is confirmed, it will be necessary to revise aspects of the interpretation of the Abu Hureyra plant remains offered for the final phases of the Epipalaeolithic in Hillman et al. (1989a). However, the central conclusions still stand, namely that the *wild type* cereals identified in all levels of the Epipalaeolithic, including the uppermost, were almost certainly gathered from wild stands. The one exception might be wild annual rye, *Secale cereale* subsp. *vavilovii*, the charred grains of which from these final phases of the Epipalaeolithic could have come either from wild stands or from wild types infesting the domestic crops (Moore et al. in press). As noted elsewhere in this chapter, little is known of its ecology, in particular whether, under conditions prevailing at the time, it could have grown in mixed stands with wild einkorn, as does its cousin, perennial mountain rye, *S. montanum*. However, when studying massive stands of wild annual rye in one of its final refugia on the slopes of Mount Ararat in 1992, we did not observe any wild einkorn.

3. Throughout this chapter, vegetation changes are generally related to changes in water availability *during the growing season* rather than to the changes in *annual* rainfall cited by many authors. On most terrain in the region, the only precipitation that contributes to tree growth is the snow that melts during the spring, and the rain that falls from early spring to late summer, i.e. the precipitation that provides soil moisture during the seasons when air and soil temperatures are high enough for active plant growth. The often considerable rainfall in autumn and early winter might recharge deeper underground reserves, but these are largely unavailable for plant growth.

4. That such oak pollen could have been blown all the way from even the Levantine refuge is attested by the presence in the Zeribar Pleniglacial pollen sequence of small numbers of olive pollen grains, which are much less effectively dispersed than oak pollen but must nevertheless have originated from the Mediterranean zones of either the Levant or the Black Sea coasts (van Zeist & Bottema 1977).

5. Useful studies of present-day (or recent) steppe in Southwest Asia are available in Louis (1939), Walter (1956), Pabot (1957, 1967), Birand (1970), the remarkable two tomes of Zohary (1973), Sankary (1977) and Frey & Kurschner (1989). I have also assembled detailed reconstructions of *potential* vegetation, including steppe, in the northern Fertile Crescent, under modern climatic conditions but in the absence of cultivation, deforestation and heavy grazing by domestic animals (in Moore et al. in press). These reconstructions are based on aspects of the published studies cited above and on 20 years of personal fieldwork in the area. Reconstructions of potential vegetation of Southwest Asia as a whole are also offered in van Zeist & Bottema (1991, see in particular their fig. 4).

6. A viviparous grass is one in which the florets produce no seeds, and instead sprout a miniature plant in which the early stages of growth are already complete. Vivipary is an adaptation to short growing seasons, and is also found in the sub-Arctic, e.g. in the northern fescue (*Festuca vivipara*).

7. The impact of grazing on the grass flora is complex, and the literature is laced with apparent contradictions. For example, Blumler (1993) notes that grazing eliminates annual grasses, and Pabot (1967), Hillman (1975) and McCorriston (1992: 102) have observed that heavy grazing eliminates perennial tussock grasses (bunch grasses). Both observations are correct. Heavy grazing in late spring can quickly

eliminate most (but rarely all) of the taller annual grasses, particularly in drier areas where there is little possibility of producing replacement ears before the upper layers of the soil, where most annual grasses root, dry out completely. Even in southern England, all but the shortest annual grasses can be largely eliminated from permanent pasture simply by letting sheep graze it hard in late spring and early summer. Early cuts of hay can similarly eliminate most of the taller annuals from hay meadows. In dry climates, exceptions include grasses such as the small bromes, e.g. *Bromus squarrosus*, the dwarfed forms of which produce well awned ears (complete with grains) so rapidly that they can often achieve an unpalatable (and fertile) state between successive grazings.

On the other hand, heavy grazing that is year-round and is continued year-on-year eventually eliminates the perennial grasses too, although prostrate mini-tussocks, e.g. those of *Stipagrostis*, can "hang-on" for several years. The only grasses that survive this long-term overgrazing are dwarf perennials such as *Poa bulbosa* and *P. sinaica*, and stunted forms of dwarf annuals such as *Nardurus subulatus* and *Psilurus incurvus*. But eventually even these are grazed out, leaving, in areas such as Abu Hureyra, only those plants toxic to herbivores such as *Andrachne telephoides*, *Fagonia olivieri*, *Peganum harmala* and various species of *Euphorbia* (Hillman 1975) or, in areas with less than *c*. 120mm rainfall, desert.

8. "Ethno-ecological modeling" of the plant-based components of past hunter–gatherer subsistence involves combining ecological models of the composition of ancient vegetation (based, in turn, on several submodels), with ethnographic models based on cross-cultural common denominators in the recorded patterns of preference and resource scheduling among recent hunter–gatherers subsisting in equivalent resource zones (Hillman 1989, Hillman et al. 1989b).

9. Although the edible nutlets of the terebinths offer nothing approaching a starch staple, the wild almonds, although laced with cyanogenic glycocides, can be detoxified by grinding and roasting or by fermentation (McLaren 1995), and they then offer an invaluable source of plant oils and starch. The equally starch-rich acorns of *Querus brandtii* and *Q. boissieri* were still eaten in recent years with appropriate processing, which, for small-scale consumption by adults, was only minimal (Mason 1992: 92–3); indeed, *Q. boissieri* was still on sale in the early 1970s in the (then) small market town of Karaman in Anatolia (Hillman: pers. obs.). The fruits of the yellow hawthorn are not only very palatable (even without exposure to frost), but are probably as rich in vitamins B and C as the western European species (cf. Lanska & Zilak 1992). And although the fresh, bullet-hard fruits of the Syrian pear are packed with stone cells offering culinary delights akin to eating dry gravel, the fruits become soft and sweet once they are bletted.

10. An obvious arid-zone exception to the often slower spread of trees and shrubs is the Christ's thorn bush (*Paliurus spina-christi*), which has large discoid fruits with wide wings that would possibly have allowed it to be dispersed even faster than terebinth and many of the grasses.

11. Wind dissemination of small to medium-size seeds is still further enhanced when they are shed onto frozen snow (Huntley: pers. comm. 1995). It is therefore significant that, once wild cereals have shed all their brittle-rachised spikelets (in early summer), the 2–4 basal spikelets of each ear are retained on the straw well into the winter and are released only when the decomposing top of the straw finally breaks off in the winter winds (Hillman & Davies 1990, 1992). In the erstwhile mountain steppe of the northern Fertile Crescent, it is inevitable that this sometimes happened when there was a cover of frozen snow, thus allowing the cereal straw and spikelets to be blown by the wind for considerable distances. Indeed, it is possible that there has been a strong selective advantage for plants producing not only the promptly shed self-implanting spikelets but also a few spikelets that are retained on the straw for dispersal during the winter.

12. By contrast, wild annual rye (*Secale cereale* subsp. *vavilovii*) is an outbreeder (Kobyljanskij 1989, but contra Hammer et al. 1987, whose description probably applies to another species, *Secale iranicum* Kobyl.) and, as rye pollen can be distinguished from that of other grasses, its demonstrable absence in the Zeribar diagram must imply that it did not grow around Zeribar at this time. However, if wild ryes, wheats and barley are thus unrepresented in the "cerealia-type" pollen curve of the Zeribar diagram, the reader might well ask what other plants produce pollen of this type. The answer is the goat-face grasses, *Aegilops* spp. (van Zeist et al. 1975: 117), and it is presumably the pollen from certain outbreeding species of this genus that is represented here.

13. Blumler (in Ch. 3 in this volume) notes that the extreme species diversity found in dense stands of wild

emmer growing in the Jordan Valley is maintained only by virtue of the periodic "collapses" of the emmer component. The reason that even the densest stands of wild einkorn maintain reasonable species diversity in the *absence* of such collapses is probably that the stands are never quite as dense as those of some emmer populations, and the species diversity is seemingly never as great anyway, although published studies are largely lacking.

14. I know of just one such example of a population of wild einkorn growing beyond the potential limits of oak woodland and which survived into the 1970s. It grew on the lower northeast facing slopes of Karadag in south-central Turkey, and reached its maximum density immediately beyond (below) the limit of the oaks. It was interspersed with a thin scatter of wild almonds, hawthorns and terebinths, although in this case it was only the small species of terebinth (*Pistacia terebinthus* subsp. *palaestina*) that survived, and the formation could not properly be rated as an altogether typical example of tere-binth–almond woodland–steppe.

References

Bailey, C. & A. Danin 1981. Bedouin plant utilization in Sinai and the Negev. *Economic Botany* **35**, 145–62.

Bard, E., B. Hamelin, R. G. Fairbanks, A. Zindler 1990. Calibration of the ^{14}C timescale over the past 30,000 years using spectrometric U–Th ages from Barbados corals. *Nature* **345**, 405–10.

Bar-Yosef, O. 1983. The Natufian of the southern Levant. In *The hilly flanks and beyond*, C. Young, P. E. L. Smith, P. Mortensen (eds), 11–42. Chicago: The Oriental Institute, University of Chicago Press.

— 1987. Late Pleistocene adaptations in the Levant. In *The Pleistocene Old World*, O. Soffer (ed.), 219–36. New York: Plenum Press.

Bar-Yosef, O. & A. Belfer-Cohen 1989. The origins of sedentism and farming communities in the Levant. *Journal of World Prehistory* **3**, 447–97.

— 1992. From foraging to farming in the Mediterranean Levant. In *Transitions to agriculture in prehistory* [Monographs in World Archaeology 4], A. B. Gebauer & T. D. Price (eds), 21–48. Madison, Wisconsin: Prehistory Press.

Baruch, U. 1994. The Late Quaternary pollen record of the Near East. In *Late Quaternary chronology and palaeoclimates of the Eastern Mediterranean*, O. Bar-Yosef & R. S. Kra (eds), 103–19. Tuscon: Radiocarbon (Dept. of Geosciences, University of Arizona).

Baruch, U. & S. Bottema 1991. Palynological evidence for climatic changes in the Levant ca.17000–9000 BP. In *The Natufian Culture in the Levant*, O. Bar-Yosef &F. Valla (eds), 11–20. Ann Arbor, Michigan: International Monographs in Prehistory.

Bean, L. J. & K. S. Saubel 1972. *Temalpakh: Cahuilla Indian knowledge and usage of plants*. Banning, California: Malki Museum.

Begin, Z. B., W. Broecker, B. Buchbinder, Y. Druckman, A. Kaufman, M. Margaritz, D. Neef. 1985. *Dead Sea and Lake Lisan Levels in the last 30,000 years* Jerusalem: Geological Survey of Israel Report 29/85.

Birand, H. 1970. Die Verwüstung der *Artemisia*-Steppe bei Karapinar in Zentralanatolien. *Vegetatio* **20**, 21–47.

Blumler, M. A. 1984. *Climate and annual habit*. MA thesis, Department of Geography, University of California, Berkelcy.

— 1987. Large-seededness in the Gramineae and agricultural origins. Paper presented at the Glynn Isaac Memorial Colloquium, Berkeley, April 1987.

— 1991a. *Seed weight and environment in mediterranean-type grasslands in California and Israel*. PhD dissertation, Department of Geography, University of California, Berkeley.

— 1991b. Fire and agricultural origins: preliminary investigations. In *Fire and environment: ecology and cultural perspectives*, S. G. Nodvin & T. A. Waldron (eds), 351–8. Asville, North Carolina: United States Department of Agriculture.

— 1993. Successional pattern and landscape sensitivity in the Mediterranean and Near East. In *Land-*

scape sensitivity, D. S. G. Thomas & R. J. Allison (eds), 287–305. Chichester, England: John Wiley.

— 1994. Evolutionary trends in the wheat group in relation to the environment, Quaternary climate change and human impacts. In *Environmental change in drylands*, A. C. Millington & K. Pye (eds), 253–69. Chichester, England: John Wiley.

Bottema, S. 1986. A Late Quaternary pollen diagram from Lake Urmia (northwestern Iran). *Review of Palaeobotany and Palynology* **47**, 241–61.

Bottema, S. & W. van Zeist 1981. Palynological evidence for the climatic history of the Near East, 50,000–6,000 BP. In *Préhistoire du Levant: chronologie et organisation de l'espace depuis les origines jusqu'au VIᵉ Millenaire*, 111–32. Paris: Editions du CNRS, Colloques Internationaux du CNRS No 598: (Maison de l'Orient, Lyon, 10–14 juin 1980).

Butler, A. 1989. Cryptic anatomical characters as evidence of early cultivation in the grain legumes (pulses). In Harris & Hillman (1989: 390–407).

Byrne, R. 1987. Climatic change and the origins of agriculture. In *Studies in the Neolithic and Urban Revolutions: the V. Gordon Childe Colloquium*, L. Manzanilla (ed.), 21–34. Oxford: British Archaeological Reports, International Series 349.

Cane, S. 1989. Australian Aboriginal seed grinding and its archaeological record: a case study from the Western Desert. In Harris & Hillman (1989: 99–119).

COHMAP 1988. Climatic changes of the last 18,000 years: observations and model simulations. *Science* **241**, 1043–51.

Colledge, S. M. 1988. Scanning electron microscope studies of the pericarp layers of some wild wheats and ryes. In *Scanning electron microscopy in archaeology*, S. Olsen (ed.), 225–36. Oxford: British Archaeological Reports, International Series 452.

— 1994. *Plant exploitation on Epipalaeolithic and early Neolithic sites in the Levant*. PhD dissertation, Department of Archaeology and Prehistory, University of Sheffield.

Davis, M. 1983. Climatic instability, time lags and community ecology. In *Communityecology*, J. Diamond & T. J. Chase (eds), 269–84. New York: Harper & Row.

de Moulins, D. M. 1994. *Agricultural intensification in Southwest Asia during the Aceramic Neolithic: evidence from charred remains of crops and their weeds*. PhD dissertation, Institute of Archaeology, University College London.

Edwards, P. C. 1989a. Revising the broad spectrum revolution: and its rôle in the origins of Southwest Asian food production. *Antiquity* **63**, 225–46.

— 1989b. Problems of recognising earliest sedentism: the Natufian example. *Journal of Mediterranean Archaeology* **2**, 5–48.

Fellows, L. E. 1993a. Plant chemicals and the needs of tomorrow. *In Traditional medicine*, B. Muckherjee, A. Patra, S. K. Tripathi, S. K. Bhunia (eds), 192–204. New Delhi: Oxford & IBH Publishing.

— 1993b. What can higher plants offer the industry? *Pharmaceutical Journal* (May 1993), 658.

Flannery, K. V. 1969. Origins and ecological effects of early domestication in Iran and the Near East. In *The domestication and exploitation of plants and animals*, P. J. Ucko & G. W. Dimbleby (eds), 73–100. London: Duckworth.

Freitag, H. 1977. The Pleniglacial, Late-Glacial and early Postglacial vegetations of Zeribar and their present-day counterparts. *Palaeohistoria* **19**, 87–95.

Frey, W. & H. Kurschner 1989. *Vorderer Orient. Vegetation 1: 8 000 000, Karte A VII*. Wiesbaden: Tübinger Atlas der Vorderer Orients.

Garrard, A. N. 1993. Recent research on the Epipalaeolithic and early Neolithic of the southern Levant. *Palaeolithic–Mesolithic Newsletter* **1**, 9–11.

Hammer, K., E. Skolimowska, H. Knüpffer 1987. Vorarbeiten zur monographischen Darstellung von Wildpflanzensortimenten: *Secale* L. *Die Kulturpflanze* **35**, 135–77.

Harlan, J. R. 1967. A wild wheat harvest in Turkey. *Archaeology* **20**, 197–201.

— 1989. Wild-grass seed harvesting in the Sahara and Sub-Sahara of Africa. In Harris & Hillman (1989: 79–98).

Harris, D. R. 1977. Alternative pathways toward agriculture. In *Origins of agriculture*, C. A. Reed (ed.), 179–243. The Hague: Mouton.

— 1990. *Settling down and breaking ground: rethinking the Neolithic Revolution*. Twaalfde Kroon-

Voordracht. Amsterdam: Stichting Nederlands Museum voor Anthropologie en Prehistorie.

Harris, D. R. & G. C. Hillman (eds) 1989. *Foraging and farming: the evolution of plant exploitation*. London: Unwin Hyman.

Henry, D. O. 1985. Preagricultural sedentism: the Natufian example. In *Prehistoric hunter–gatherers: the emergence of cultural complexity*, T. Douglas Price & J. A. Brown (eds), 365–84. Orlando: Academic Press.

— 1989. *From foraging to agriculture: the Levant at the end of the Ice Age* Philadelphia: University of Pennsylvania Press.

Hillman, G. C. 1973. Agricultural productivity and past population potential at A_van: an exercise in the calculation of carrying capacities. *Anatolian Studies* **23**, 225–39.

— 1975. The plant remains from Abu Hureyra: a preliminary report. In "The excavation of Tell Abu Hureyra in Syria: a preliminary report", A. M. T. Moore. *Proceedings of the Prehistoric Society* **41**, 70–3.

— 1978. On the origins of domestic rye – *Secale cereale*: the finds from aceramic Can Hasan III in Turkey. *Anatolian Studies* **28**, 157–74.

— 1989. Late Palaeolithic plant foods from Wadi Kubbaniya in Upper Egypt: dietary diversity, infant weaning, and seasonality in a riverine environment. In Harris & Hillman (1989: 207–39).

Hillman, G. C., S. M. Colledge, D. R. Harris 1989a. Plant food economy during the Epipalaeolithic period at Tell Abu Hureyra, Syria: dietary diversity, seasonality, and modes of exploitation. In Harris & Hillman (1989: 240–68).

Hillman, G. C., E. Madeyska, J. G. Hather 1989b. *Wild plant foods and diet at Late Palaeolithic Wadi Kubbaniya: the evidence from charred remains. In The prehistory of Wadi Kubbaniya*, vol. 2: *Palaeoeconomy, environment and stratigraphy*, F. Wendorf, R. Schild, A. Close (eds), 162–242. Dallas, Texas: Southern Methodist University Press.

Hillman, G. C. & M. S. Davies 1990. Measured domestication rates in wild wheats and barley under primitive cultivation, and their archaeological implications. *Journal of World Prehistory* **4**, 157–222.

— 1992. Domestication rates in wild wheats and barley under primitive cultivation: preliminary results and archaeological implications of field measurements of selection coefficient. In *Préhistoire de l'agriculture: nouvelles approches expérimentales et ethnographiques* [Monographie 6, Centre de Recherches Archéologiques 6], P. C. Anderson (ed.), 113–58. Paris: Editions du CNRS.

Hillman, G. C., S. Wales, F. S. McLaren, J. Evans, A. E. Butler 1993. Identifying problematic remains of ancient plant foods: a comparison of the role of chemical, histological and morphological criteria. *World Archaeology* **25**, 94–121.

Hoffman, C. L. 1984. Punan foragers in the trading networks of Southeast Asia. In *Past and present in hunter–gatherer studies*, C. Schrire (ed.), 123–49. London: Academic Press.

Huntley, B. 1988. Glacial and Holocene vegetation history: Europe. In *Vegetation history*, B. Huntley & T. Webb III (eds), 341–83. Dordrecht: Kluwer.

— 1991. How plants respond to climate change: migration rates, individualism and the consequences for plant communities. *Annals of Botany* **67** (supplement), 15–22.

Huntley, B. & H. J. B. Birks 1983. An atlas of past and present pollen maps for Europe: 0–13000 BP. Cambridge: Cambridge University Press.

Huntley, B. & T. Webb III. 1989. Migration: species' response to climatic variations caused by changes in the earth's orbit. *Journal of Biogeography* **16**, 5–19.

Ingold, T. 1988. Notes on the foraging mode of production. In *Hunters and gatherers: history, evolution and social change*, T. Ingold, D. Riches, J. Woodburn (eds), 269–85. Oxford: Berg.

Keeley, L. H. 1988. Hunter–gatherer economic complexity and "population pressure": a cross-cultural analysis. *Journal of Anthropological Archaeology* **7**, 373–411.

— 1991. Ethnographic models for late glacial hunter–gatherers. In *Late glacial industries in Northwest Europe: human adaptation and environmental change at the end of the Pleistocene* [Report 77], N. Barton, A. J. Roberts, D. A. Roe (eds), 179–90. London: Council for British Archaeology.

— 1992. The use of plant foods among hunter–gatherers: a cross-cultural survey. In *Préhistoire de l'agriculture: nouvelles approches expérimentales et ethnographiques* [Monographie 6, Centre de Recherces Archéologiques], P. C. Anderson (ed.), 29–38. Paris: Editions du CNRS.

Kirk, D. R. 1975. *Wild edible plants of western North America*. Happy Camp, California: Naturegraph.

Kislev, M. E. 1989. Pre-domesticated cereals in the Pre-Pottery Neolithic A period. In *Man and culture in change*, I. Hershkovitz (ed.), 147–51. Oxford: British Archaeological Reports, International Series 508.

— 1992. Agriculture in the Near East in the VIIth millennium bc. In *Préhistoire de l'agriculture: nouvelles approches expérimentales et ethnographiques* [Monographie 6, Centre de Recherches Archéologiques], P. C. Anderson (ed.), 87–93. Paris: Editions du CNRS.

Kislev, M. E., D. Nadel, I. Carmi 1992. Epipalaeolithic (19000 BP) cereal and fruit diet at Ohalo II, Sea of Galilee, Israel. *Review of Palaeobotany and Palynology* 73, 161–6.

Kobyljanskij, V. D. 1989. *Flora of cultivated plants of the USSR*, vol. II, Part 1: *Rye* [in Russian]. Leningrad: Agropromizdat.

Lanska, D. & P. Zilak 1992. *The illustrated guide to edible plants*. London: Chancellor. (Translated from the Czech original by D. Coxon.)

Layton, R., R. Foley, E. Williams 1991. The transition between hunting and gathering and the specialized husbandry of resources: a socio-ecological approach. *Current Anthropology* 32, 255–74.

Leroi-Gourhan, A. 1974. Etudes palynologiques des derniers 11,000 ans en Syrie semi-désertique. *Paléorient* 2, 443–51.

— 1979. Analyses polliniques de Tell Aswad. *Paléorient* 5, 170–6.

— 1980. Les analyses polliniques au Moyen-Orient. *Paléorient* 6, 79–91.

— 1981a. Diagrammes polliniques de sites archéologiques au Moyen-Orient. *Beihefte sum Tübingen Atlas der vorderen Orients*, Reihe A, 8, 121–33.

— 1981b. Palynological investigations. In D. O. Henry, A. Leroi-Gourhan, A. M. J. Davis, The excavation of Hyonim Terrace. *Journal of Archaeological Science* 8, 42–6.

— 1981c. Le Levant à la fin du Pleistocene et à l'Holocene d'après lapalynologie. In *Préhistoire du Levant: chronologie et organisation de l'espace depuis les origines jusqu'au VIe Millénaire*. Paris: Editions du CNRS, Colloques Internationaux du CNRS N° 598 (Maison de l'Orient, Lyon, 10–14 juin 1980).

— 1984. L'environnement de Mallaha (Eynan) au Natoufiein. *Paléorient* 10, 101–5.

Leroi-Gourhan, A. & F. Darmon 1991. Analyses polliniques de stations natoufiennes au Proche Orient. In *The Natufian Culture in the Levant*, O. Bar-Yosef & F. Valla (eds), 21–6. Ann Arbor: International Monographs in Prehistory.

Lewis, H. T. 1972. The role of fire in the domestication of plants and animals in southwest Asia. *Man* 7, 195–222.

Limbrey, S. 1990. Edaphic opportunism? A discussion of soil factors in relation to the beginnings of plant husbandry in south-west Asia. *World Archaeology* 22, 45–52. Louis, H. 1939. *Das natürliche Pflanzenkleid Anatoliens, geographisch gesehen*. Stuttgart: Pencke. (Geographische Abhandlungen 3/12).

Louis, H. 1939. *Das natürliche Pflanzenkleid Anatoliens, geographisch gesehen* [Geographische Abhandlungen 3/12]. Stuttgart: Pencke.

Macumber, P. G. & M. J. Head 1991. Implications of the Wadi al-Hammeh sequences for the terminal drying of Lake Lisan, Jordan. *Palaeogeography, Palaeoclimatology, Palaeoecology* 84, 163–73.

Mason, S. L. R. 1992. *Acorns in human subsistence*. PhD dissertation, Institute of Archaeology, University College London.

— 1995a. Acorn utopia? Determining the role of acorns in past human subsistence. In *Food in antiquity*, J. Wilkins, D. Harvey, M. Dobson (eds), 12–24. University of Exeter Press.

— 1995b. Acorn-eating and ethnographic analogies: a reply to McCorriston.*Antiquity* 69, 1025–9.

McCorriston, J. 1992. *The early development of agriculture in the ancient Near East: an ecological and evolutionary study*. PhD dissertation, Department of Anthropology, Yale University.

McCorriston, J. & F. Hole 1991. The ecology of seasonal stress and the origin of agriculture in the Near East. *American Anthropologist* 93, 46–69.

McLaren, F. S. 1995. Plums from Doura Cave, Syria: the chemical analysis of charred fruit stones. In *Res archaeobotanicae*, H. Kroll & R. Pasternak (eds), 195–218. Kiel: Institut für Ur- und Frühgeschichte der Christian-Albrecht Universität.

McLaren, F. S., J. Evans, G. C. Hillman 1991. Identification of charred seeds from Southwest Asia. In *Archaeometry '90: Proceedings of the 26th International Symposium on Archaeometry, Heidel-*

berg, 1990, E. Pernicka & G. Wagner (eds), 797–806. Basel: Birchäuser.

McLuhan, T. C. (compiler) 1973. *Touch the earth: a self-portrait of Indian existence*. London: Abacus.

Miller, T. E. 1987. Systematics and evolution. In *Wheat breeding: its scientific basis*, F. G. H. Lupton (ed.), 1–30. London: Chapman & Hall.

Moore, A. M. T., J. A. J. Gowlett, R. E. M. Hedges, G. C. Hillman, A. J. Legge, R. A. Rowley-Conwy 1986. Radiocarbon accelerator (AMS) dates for the epipalaeolithic settlement of Abu Hureyra, Syria. *Radiocarbon* **28**, 1068–76.

Moore, A. M. T. & G. C. Hillman 1992. The Pleistocene to Holocene transition and human economy in Southwest Asia: the impact of the Younger Dryas. *American Antiquity* **57**, 482–94.,

Moore, A. M. T., G. C. Hillman, A. J. Legge in press. *Abu Hureyra and the beginnings of agriculture*. New York: Oxford University Press.

Naveh, Z. 1967. Mediterranean ecosystems and vegetation types in California and Israel. *Ecology* **48**, 445–59.

— 1974. The effects of fire in the Mediterranean region. In *Fire and ecosystems*, T. T. Kozlowski & C. E. Ahlgren (eds), 401–34.

— 1984. The vegetation of the Carmel and Sefunim and the evolution of the cultural landscape. In *Sefunim prehistoric sites, Mount Carmel, Israel*. A. Ronen (ed.), 23–63.

Niklewski, J. & W. van Zeist 1970. A Late Quaternary pollen diagram from northwestern Syria. *Acta Botanica Neerlandica* **19**, 737–54.

Pabot, H. 1957. *Rapport au gouvernement de Syrie sur l'écologie végétale et ses applications*. Rome: United Nations, Food and Agriculture Organisation.

— 1967. *Pasture development and rangeland improvement through botanical and ecological studies: report to the Government of Iran*. Report TA 2311, United Nations, Food and Agriculture Organisation, Rome.

Pasternak, B. L. 1922. *My sister, life: summer 1917*. Moscow: Pevetz. (Unpublished English translation by Richard McKane of selected poems.)

Potts, T. F., S. M. Colledge, P. C. Edwards 1985. Preliminary report on a sixth season of excavation by the University of Sydney at Pella in Jordan (1983/84). *Annals of the Department of Antiquities of Jordan* **29**, 181–210.

Roberts, N. & H. E. Wright Jr 1993. The Near East and Southwest Asia. In *Global climatic change since the last glacial maximum*, H. E. Wright Jr, J. E. Kutzbach, T. Webb III, W. F. Ruddiman, F. A. Street-Perrott, P. J. Bartlein (eds), 194–220. Minneapolis: University of Minnesota Press.

Rognon, P. 1987. Relations entre phases climatiques et chronologiques au Moyen Orient de 16000 a 10000 BP. In *Chronologies in the Near East. Relative and absolute chronology 16000–4000 BP*, O. Aurenche, J. Evin, F. Hours (eds), 189–206. Oxford: British Archaeological Reports, International Series 379.

Russell, K. W. 1988. *After Eden: the behavioural ecology of early food production in the Near East and North Africa*. Oxford: British Archaeolgical Reports, International Series, 391.

Sankary, M. N. 1977. *Ecology, flora and range management of arid and very arid zones of Syria: conservation and development* [in Arabic]. Aleppo: University Press.

Simms, S. 1987. *Behavioural ecology and hunter–gatherer foraging: an example from the Great Basin*. Oxford: British Archaeological Reports, International Series 381.

Steward, J. 1938. *Basin–plateau aboriginal socio-political groups*. Bureau of American Ethnology Bulletin 120, Smithsonian Institution, Washington DC.

Taylor, K. C., G. W. Lamorey, G. A. Doyle, R. B. Alley, P. M. Grootes, P. A. Mayewski, J. W. C. White, L. K. Barlow 1993. The "flickering switch" of Late Pleistocene climatic change. *Nature* **361**, 432–6.

Thomas, D. H. 1981. Complexity among Great Basin Shoshoneans: the world's least affluent hunter–gatherers? In *Affluent foragers: Pacific coasts east and west* [Senri Ethnological Series 9], S. Koyama & D. H. Thomas (eds), 19–52. Osaka: National Museum of Ethnology.

van Zeist, W. 1972. Palaeobotanical results of the 1970 season at Çayönü, Turkey. *Helinium* **12**, 3–19.

— 1980. Holocene vegetation of northwestern Syria. *Palaeohistoria* **22**, 111–25.

van Zeist, W. & S. Bottema 1977. Palynological investigations in Western Iran. *Palaeohistoria* **19**, 19–85.

— 1982. Vegetational history of the Eastern Mediterranean and the Near East during the last 20,000 years. In *Palaeoclimates, palaeoenvironments and human communities in the Eastern Mediterranean region in later prehistory*, J. L. Bintliff & W. van Zeist (eds), 277–321. Oxford: British Archaeological Reports, International Series 133.

— 1991. *Late Quaternary vegetation of the Near East* [Beihefte zum Tübinger Atlas des Vorderen Orients, Reihe A (Naturwissenschaften) 18]. Wiesbaden: Reichert.

van Zeist, W., H. Woldring, D. Stapert 1975. Late Quaternary vegetation and climate in Southwestern Turkey. *Palaeohistoria* **17**, 55–143.

van Zeist, W. & H. Woldring 1978. A postglacial pollen diagram from Lake Van in East Anatolia. *Review of Palaeobotany and Palynology* **26**, 249–76.

Walter, H. 1956. Vegetationsgliegerung Anatoliens. *Flora, oder Allgemeine Botanischen Zeitschrift* **143**, 295–326.

Webb, T. III 1986. Is vegetation in equilibrium with climate? How to interpret Late Quaternary pollen data. *Vegetatio* **67**, 75–91.

— 1988. Glacial and Holocene vegetation history: eastern North America. In *Vegetation history*, B. Huntley & T. Webb III (eds), 385–414. Dordrecht: Kluwer.

Weinstein-Evron, M. 1983. The palaeoecology of the early Wurm in the Hula Basin, Israel. *Paleorient* **9**, 5–19.

Wijmstra, T. A. 1969. Palynology of the first 30m of a 120m deep section in northern Greece. *Acta Botanica Neerlandica* **18**, 511–27.

Willcox, G. 1992. Archaeobotanical significance of growing near eastern progenitors of domestic plants at Jalès (France). In *Préhistoire de l'agriculture: nouvelles approches expérimentales et ethnographiques* [Monographie 6, Centre de Recherches Archéologiques], P. C. Anderson (ed.), 159–77. Paris: Editions du CNRS.

— 1995. Wild and domestic cereal exploitation: new evidence from early neolithic sites in the northern Levant and south-eastern Anatolia. *ARX World Journal of Prehistoric and Ancient Studies* **1**, 9–16.

Woodburn, J. 1980. Hunter–gatherers today and reconstructions of the past. In *Soviet and Western anthropology*, E. Gellner (ed.), 115–40. New York: Columbia University Press.

Wright Jr, H. E. 1989. The amphi-atlantic distribution of the Younger Dryas climatic fluctuation. *Quaternary Science Reviews* **8**, 295–306.

— 1993. Environmental determinism in Near Eastern prehistory. *Current Anthropology* **34**, 458–69.

Wright Jr, H. E., J. H. McAndrews, W. van Zeist 1967. Modern pollen rain in western Iran and its relation to plant history and Quaternary vegetation history. *Journal of Ecology* **55**, 425–43.

Yechieli, Y., M. Magaritz, Y. Levy, U. Weber, U. Kafri, W. Woelfli, G. Bonani 1993. Late Quaternary geological history of the Dead Sea area, Israel. *Quaternary Research* **39**, 59–67.

Zohary, D. 1969. The progenitors of wheat and barley in relation to domestication and agricultural dispersal in the Old World. In *The domestication and exploitation of plant and animals*, P. J. Ucko & G. W. Dimbleby (eds), 47–66. London: Duckworth.

— 1989. Domestication of the Southwest Asian Neolithic crop assemblage of cereals, pulses, and flax: the evidence from the living plants. In Harris & Hillman (1989: 358–73).

Zohary, D. & M. Hopf 1993. Domestication of plants in the Old World: the origin and spread of cultivated plants in West Asia, Europe, and the Nile Valley, 2nd ed. Oxford: Oxford University Press.

Zohary, M. 1973. *Geobotanical foundations of the Middle East*. Stuttgart: Fischer.

CHAPTER ELEVEN

The emergence of crop cultivation and caprine herding in the "Marginal Zone" of the southern Levant

Andrew Garrard, Susan Colledge,
Louise Martin

Introduction

Southwest Asia is regarded as the earliest centre of extensive plant and animal domestication in the world. Since the late 1940s a succession of projects have looked at the archaeological and ecological background to the domestication process. During the early years, fieldwork was undertaken in the eastern and western wings of the "Fertile Crescent". More recently, as a result of changing circumstances, research has focused on sites in the northern and western sectors. In ecological terms, most of the work has been undertaken in the present zone of moist steppe and woodland (which receives over 200 mm rainfall per annum), in the oases of the Levant and along the terraces of the Euphrates (Fig. 11.1). However, an important complementary body of field research has been undertaken in the dry steppe and subdesert belt of the southern Levant, particularly in eastern Jordan (Fig. 11.2). This region is of particular significance for two reasons. First, although closely adjacent, it does not appear to have lain within the natural habitat zone of most of the plant and animal species that were domesticated; therefore, when they appear in the archaeological record, one is provided with a clear *terminus ante quem* for the process of domestication. Differentiating between wild and domestic forms in the natural distribution areas of the wild ancestors is far more problematic. Secondly, early models for the origins of food production based on the concept of population–resource imbalance stressed the potential significance, in initial moves to domestication, of the areas lying around the margins of the resource-rich habitats of Southwest Asia (Binford 1968, Flannery 1969). Although these models have been modified as a result of subsequent developments in theory, the significance of the "Marginal Zone" in the emergence of cultivation and pastoralism has, until recently, never been tested through systematic field research.

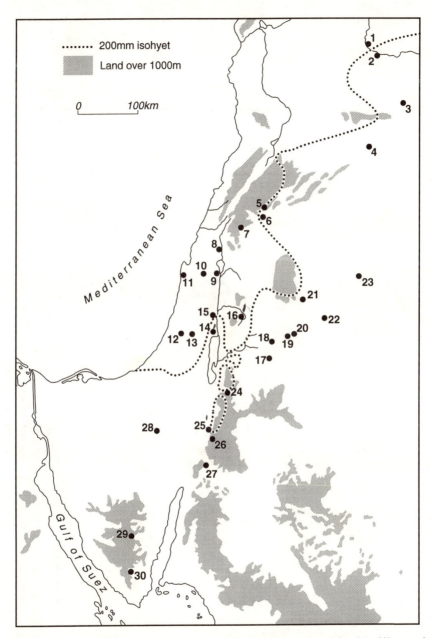

Figure 11.1 Sites and study areas mentioned in the text. Areas west of the dotted line receive over 200mm rainfall per annum. The numbered localities are: 1 Mureybet; 2 Tell Abu Hureyra; 3 El Kowm; 4 Palmyra; 5 Ghoraifé; 6 Tell Aswad; 7 Tell Ramad; 8 'Ain Mallaha, Beisamoun; 9 Ohalo; 10 Yiftah'el; 11 Atlit, Nahal Oren; 12 Hatoula; 13 Abu Gosh; 14 Jericho; 15 Netiv Hagdud, Gilgal; 16 'Ain Ghazal; 17 Wadi Jilat; 18 Kharaneh; 19 Uwaynid; 20 Azraq; 21 Khallat Anaza; 22 Dhuweila; 23 Burqu; 24 Wadi Hasa; 25 Beidha; 26 Basta; 27 Wadi Judayid, Tor Hamar; 28 Abu Salem, Rosh Horesha; 29 Wadi Tbeik; 30 Abu Madi, Ujrat el Mehed.

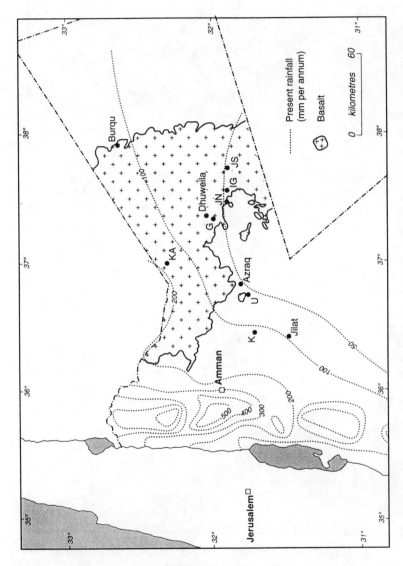

Figure 11.2 Epipalaeolithic and neolithic sites and study areas in eastern Jordan (the "Marginal Zone"). Dashed lines indicate rainfall isohyets. Site codes are: K = Kharaneh; U = Uwaynid; KA = Khallat Anaza; G = El Ghirqa; JN = Jebel Naja; IG = Ibn el Ghazzi; JS = Jebel es Subhi.

In order to place the evidence for the beginnings of food production derived from the present dry steppe and subdesert of the southern Levant into its wider context, it is helpful first to review what is known of the process from the better-watered areas of the "Levantine Corridor".

The emergence of crop cultivation and caprine herding in the Levantine Corridor

Plant domestication

Within Southwest Asia, the first plants to show evidence of domestication[1] were carbohydrate- and protein-rich cereals and pulses. The physical characteristics used in determining domestication include the breakdown of the wild mode of seed dispersal, the loss of wild-type regulation of germination, and increases in seed size and yield potential. The finding of species outside their natural habitats is used to lend support to domestication hypotheses (Zohary & Hopf 1988: 13–16, 83–4; Zohary 1992).

Within the Levantine Corridor, van Zeist & Bakker-Heeres (1982) have argued for the presence of domestic emmer wheat at Tell Aswad near Damascus by 7800 bc (all dates cited are uncalibrated). This claim is based on the finding of enlarged grains and the location of the site in an area beyond the presumed natural habitat of wild emmer. The area receives less than 200 mm direct rainfall, but it is located close to the marshes of the former Lake Aateibé. The earliest postulated evidence for domestic einkorn wheat is rather later, coming from levels at Jericho dated to 7300–6500 bc. Hopf (1983) based her characterization on grain size and the location of the site far south of the present natural distribution of einkorn in southern Turkey (for further discussion of the latter see below). Kislev et al. (1986) claimed evidence for domestic barley from levels dated to 8000–7800 bc at Gilgal and Netiv Hagdud in the Jordan Valley. This was based on the presence of "tough" rachis fragments. However, more recently Kislev (1989), Hillman & Davies (1992: 157–8) and others have demonstrated that low proportions of tough rachises can occur in assemblages of wild barley and one has to be cautious in using their presence as an indicator of domestication. Naked wheat and barley appear in the Damascus Basin and Jordan Valley in the early seventh millennium bc.

There is circumstantial evidence for pulse cultivation in the eighth millennium bc (Kislev & Bar-Yosef 1988, Kislev 1992). Lentils are found at virtually every site, and pea is known from the 7800 bc levels at Tell Aswad (van Zeist & Bakker-Heeres 1982). The finding of a hoard of over 1.4 million lentils, together with a traditional weed of lentil fields, in a context dated to 6800 bc at Yiftah'el in Galilee, is regarded as confirming early cultivation (Garfinkel et al. 1988). However, morphological evidence for the domestication of legumes in the form of changes in seed coat and size is only apparent from the late seventh and early sixth millennia bc (Zohary & Hopf 1988: 83–112).

Explanations for the shift to plant cultivation and domestication have been the subject of many articles and volumes. There is substantial evidence for a harsh environmental episode in the eastern Mediterranean in the ninth millennium bc coinciding with the period of the Younger Dryas in Europe (Baruch & Bottema 1991, Moore & Hillman 1992; and cf. Hillman and Hole in Chs 10 and 14 in this volume). This would undoubtedly have affected the resources available to semi-sedentary late Natufian populations. There have also been increasingly sophisticated demographic-pressure models proposed in recent years such as the "packing model" of Binford (1983: 208–13) and that of Harris (1990). Bender (1978) and Hayden (1990) have countered such arguments by pointing to the potential demands of alliance systems and status competition that may have led hunter–gatherer groups to intensify their means of production.

Animal domestication

The first evidence for the domestication of ungulates in Southwest Asia[2] occurs several hundred years after agriculture (in the sense of crop cultivation: Harris 1989) is thought to have developed. The features used to demonstrate a close human–animal relationship include changes in bone size and morphology, dramatic diachronic changes in the spectra of species present, the finding of species outside their natural range, changes in slaughter patterns indicative of stock management, and increased incidence in bone diseases indicative of husbandry (Davis 1987: 126–54; Meadow 1989). Goat and sheep were the first ungulates to be domesticated (cf. Uerpmann, Legge and Hole in Chs 12, 13 and 14 in this volume), and a brief discussion follows here concerning their wild distribution and domestication in the fertile areas of the Levantine Corridor.

Wild goats (*Capra aegagrus*) appear to have inhabited the craggy terrain of the Levant through the late Pleistocene and early Holocene. Bones are known from epipalaeolithic and aceramic neolithic sites in Lebanon, Syria, Jordan and Israel as far south as Beidha near Petra (Uerpmann 1987). At that latitude their distribution appears to have overlapped with the ibex (*Capra ibex*), which is thought to have inhabited the Negev, Sinai and southern Jordan. Remains of both ibex and wild goat were found at Beidha (Hecker 1975, 1982).

The earliest strong evidence for goat management in Southwest Asia comes from levels dated to 7000 bc at Ganj Dareh in western Iran (cf. Legge and Hole in Chs 13 and 14 in this volume). A comparison of the slaughter pattern of goat relative to other species at the site, and to faunal assemblages from earlier sites in the region, indicates an increased focus on the slaughter of young males. This is highly suggestive of a herding strategy (Hesse 1978, 1984). Within the Levant, evidence for goat domestication before 6500 bc is very limited. A dramatic swing from gazelle to goat in the middle Pre-Pottery Neolithic B (PPNB) at Jericho in the Jordan Valley (7200–6500 bc), and the finding of a high incidence of foot pathology in goats from the same period at 'Ain Ghazal near Amman, does however hint strongly at herd management (Clutton-Brock 1979, Köhler-Rollefson et al. 1988). Legge argues (in this volume) that the small size of middle-PPNB goat bones from Beidha suggests domestication. In the late PPNB (6,500–6000 bc), there was an extension in the geographical distribution of goat exploitation in the Levant. Thus, whereas gazelle was the dominant species in the middle PPNB at sites such as Nahel Oren and Yiftah'el in northern Israel (Legge 1973, Horwitz 1987), goat was common in the late PPNB at Abu Gosh,

Beisamoun and Atlit, which are located in adjacent areas (Davis 1978, Ducos 1978a, Horwitz & Tchernov 1987). Farther north, at Tell Abu Hureyra on the Euphrates, there was a dramatic shift from gazelle to goat and sheep exploitation at about 6300 bc (Legge & Rowley-Conwy 1987), although Legge argues (in this volume) that domestic goats were present there from early in the PPNB.

There is slightly less agreement about the distribution of wild sheep (*Ovis orientalis*) in the late Pleistocene and early Holocene. Sheep bones are known from several epipalaeolithic and aceramic neolithic sites in northern Syria and in northern and eastern Iraq (Uerpmann 1987, Legge & Rowley-Conwy 1986; Legge in Ch 13 in this volume). They have also been found at contemporary sites in southern Jordan (Wadi Judayid: Henry & Turnbull 1985), the Negev (Abu Salem and Rosh Horesha: Davis et al. 1982) and as far north as Hatoula (Davis 1985) and Jericho (Clutton-Brock 1979) in central Israel. However, in spite of extensive excavations of terminal Pleistocene and early Holocene sites in northern Israel, central and northern Jordan and southern Syria, no remains of wild sheep have been found that date to before 6500 bc.[3] This suggests that the wild sheep population of the southernmost Levant was probably separated from the more extensive population in northern Syria, northern and eastern Iraq, Turkey and Iran (cf. Ducos 1993b).

Bones of wild sheep represent approximately half the animal remains recovered from ninth millennium bc levels at M'lefaat, Zawi Chemi and Shanidar in northeastern Iraq, and Perkins (1964) argued for domestication at the last two sites. However, his reasoning has been heavily criticized by other authors and is no longer regarded as valid (e.g. Bökönyi 1969, Uerpmann 1979). Helmer (1988) argues that the earliest evidence for size-change in sheep resulting from domestication occurs in the middle of the seventh millennium bc at sites such as Çayönü in southeastern Turkey. In the northern and southern extremities of the Levant, where there were wild sheep populations, there is no evidence for their large-scale use prior to 6500 bc. They account for 13.9 per cent of the fauna in the Natufian levels at Wadi Judayid in southern Jordan (Henry & Turnbull 1985) and for about 12 per cent, in combination with goat, in the aceramic neolithic levels at Tell Abu Hureyra (Legge in Ch. 13 in this volume). In both regions there is a dramatic increase in their use in the late PPNB (*c.* 6300 bc). Sheep and goat, between them, account for about 80 per cent of the fauna at Basta in southern Jordan (Becker 1991) and 70 per cent at Tell Abu Hureyra where sheep outnumber goats by about 3:1 (Legge 1975, and Ch. 13 in this volume). In the central Levant, sheep make their first appearance in the Damascus region at *c.* 6500 bc and increase greatly in numbers over the following 200–300 years (Ducos 1993a,b). Farther south, at 'Ain Ghazal near Amman, there is no evidence of sheep before 6500 bc, but they are abundant after 6000 bc. The faunal record from the period in between is very poor (Wasse 1994).

Explanations for the beginnings of animal domestication have been broad and varied. Appreciating that the earliest domestic animals appeared to have been kept by agriculturalists, Flannery (1969) noted that domestic animals provided a "walking larder" and security against crop failure. They were also available for exchange. Cohen (1977) argued that animal domestication would have been forced on increasingly sedentary farmers living in restricted territories. The areas around settlements would have gradually become depleted of game. Legge & Rowley-Conwy (1987) have suggested that overkill of migratory gazelle may have led to the substantial rise in the use of domestic sheep and goat evident at late PPNB Abu Hureyra. Hesse (1984) has argued that, by eliminating competitors for pasturage, by careful culling of the flock and by selective breeding, herders would have been able to obtain more animal products from a given area than they could from exploiting a wild herd. If dairying was involved in early domestic animal economies, this would certainly have been true. So far, there is no clear evidence that milk products were being exploited before the Chalcolithic or Early Bronze Age in Southwest Asia (Sherratt 1981, Davis 1984, Horwitz & Smith 1991), but it should be borne in mind as a possibility. Hayden (1990) has discussed the role that social competition may have played in the domestication or acquisition of livestock as well as plant cultivars, and Hodder (1990) has described the potential symbolic importance of taming the wild.

By the late seventh or early sixth millennium bc, when mixed herds of sheep and goat were being kept in parts of Southwest Asia, it is clear that sheep were commonly the dominant species in the flocks. At Gritille, Abu Hureyra and Bouqras on the Euphrates, at Ghoraifé 2 and Tell Ramad near Damascus, and at 'Ain Ghazal near Amman, sheep outnumbered goat by c. 3:1 (Legge 1975, Clason 1979–80, Stein 1989, Ducos 1993b, Wasse 1994). Lancaster & Lancaster (1991) have argued that the keeping of mixed herds of sheep and goat must undoubtedly relate to their complementary feeding behaviour and different climatic tolerances. Sheep prefer to graze herbaceous annuals and are more tolerant of cold and wet conditions, whereas goats prefer to browse perennial plants and are better able to withstand heat and drought. Keeping mixed herds provides an insurance against climatic variability as well as an effective way of utilizing available forage. However, as Köhler-Rollefson (1988: 90) notes, goats are capable of degrading landscapes through their browsing behaviour and this may prove a disincentive to keeping them in large numbers. They also have a more independent character, which makes them more difficult to control. One must also assume that differences in carcass products, hair and milk (if it was being exploited) affected herd structure.

The emergence of crop cultivation and caprine herding in the Marginal Zone of the southern Levant

The database

The foregoing discussion of the emergence of crop cultivation and caprine herding in the Levantine Corridor was based on evidence gleaned from sites in the moist steppe and woodland zone, the Jericho and Damascus oases, and the upper Euphrates Valley. During the 1980s, two projects were undertaken in eastern Jordan that looked closely at chronologically contemporary developments in the present dry steppe and subdesert regions, lying to the east of the fertile corridor. The first was directed by Garrard and it focused on the Epipalaeolithic and Neolithic of the Azraq area and the limestone steppe to its southwest (Garrard et al. 1994a). The second was directed by Betts and investigated the same period in the basalt steppe to the northeast of Azraq

(Betts 1993) (Fig. 11.2). In the course of the two projects, faunal assemblages were obtained from 21 sites (Table 11.1 & Martin 1994) and macrobotanical material from four sites (Table 11.2 & Colledge 1994a). Relevant faunal material was also obtained from the epipalaeolithic site of Kharaneh 4, to the west of Azraq, excavated by Muheisen (1988).

Although extensive studies have also been made of the Epipalaeolithic of the dry steppe and subdesert of southern Jordan, the Negev and Sinai (Marks 1976, 1977, Bar-Yosef & Phillips 1977, Goring-Morris 1987, Clark et al. 1988, Henry 1988), the Neolithic has been less thoroughly investigated (Bar-Yosef 1981, Goring-Morris 1993). No macrobotanical assemblages have so far been retrieved from terminal Pleistocene and early Holocene sites in these regions, and significant faunal collections have been reported only from seven: five of epipalaeolithic date (Butler et al. 1977, Henry & Turnbull 1985, Henry & Garrard 1988, Clark et al. 1988) and two from the PPNB (Tchernov & Bar-Yosef 1982, Dayan et al. 1986). Unfortunately, no assemblages have been obtained from the early sixth millennium bc, which was probably a formative period in the development of caprine herding in the more arid regions. With the exception of the very significant work being undertaken by the Cauvins and Stordeur in the El Kowm Basin (Cauvin & Coqueugniot 1988, Stordeur 1989, Cauvin & Stordeur 1994), and the limited surveys and excavations of Suzuki & Kobori (1970) and Hanihara & Akazawa (1979) in the Palmyra area, very little is known of the Epipalaeolithic and Neolithic of the Syrian steppe and desert to the south of the Euphrates. So far, no assemblages of animal and plant remains have been published from these regions.

The environment and settlement history of eastern Jordan

As has been indicated, most of the archaeozoological and archaeobotanical information on the emergence of crop cultivation and caprine herding in the Marginal Zone of the Levant has been obtained from the Jordanian plateau, extending from the Jordanian Highlands in the vicinity of Amman eastwards to the Iraqi frontier (Fig. 11.2). The central part of this area is covered by an extensive canopy of late Tertiary basalts, which rise from c. 500m at Azraq to over 1,800m in Jebel Druze in southern Syria. Substantial areas of these lava fields are strewn with boulders and the drainage channels are often craggy. To the south and east of the basalt, the terrain is less severe, being surfaced by Cretaceous and early Tertiary limestones, marls and cherts or by late Tertiary and Quaternary sedimentary formations. The annual rainfall over the eastern plateau varies from around 200mm to less than 50mm. Remnant steppe vegetation is found in the higher rainfall areas (>100mm rainfall per annum), but elsewhere the surface is actively deflating into reg or hammada. The only major springs are at Azraq, which is at the centre of a 12,000km^2 drainage basin, but smaller seepages are found around the perimeter of the basalt flows, at localities such as Burqu. At the present time, much of this region is suited only for seasonal goat, sheep or camel pastoralism, although small-scale opportunistic cereal cultivation is attempted along wadi courses in the north and west. Irrigation farming is being developed at Azraq (Nelson 1973).

Our knowledge of terminal Pleistocene and early Holocene environments in this region is still very limited and stems largely from the faunal and floral record, which

Table 11.1 Percentage representation of species at epipalaeolithic and neolithic sites in eastern Jordan.

Site and period	Ovis/Capra	Gazella	Equus	Bos	Sus	Camelus	Lepus	Carnivores	Aves	Testudo	Total bones
Epipalaeolithic 18000–8500 bc											
Kharaneh 4		88.4	6.6	0.2			1.9	2.7	0.2	X	4351
Uwaynid 18	0.2	83.2	14.1	1.0		0.2	1.0	0.2	0.2	X	518
Jilat 6		85.7	9.0	0.3			2.4	0.9	1.5	X	2726
Jilat 22	0.1	64.7	18.4		0.2		3.5	4.2	9.1	X	1330
Azraq 18		23.6	37.2	36.6			0.4	0.8	1.2		246
Khallat Anaza	59.4	21.9	6.3				9.4	3.1			32
Early and Middle PPNB 7500–6500 bc											
Jilat 7		54.9		0.1			36.3	7.9	0.8	X	1563
Jilat 32		3.7					94.4	2.8			107
Late PPNB 6500–6000 bc											
Azraq 31 – PPNB	3.6	39.3	25.0	21.4			10.7				56
Dhuweila – PPNB	0.2	96.6	1.1				1.4	0.6	0.1		2693
Late Neolithic 6000–5000 bc											
Jilat 25	71.2	6.2					19.2	2.1	1.4	X	146
Jilat 13	27.3	24.9	0.2	0.2			33.8	10.4	3.4	X	2973
Azraq 31 – LN	19.3	52.3	5.6				10.3	3.4	9.1	X	409
Dhuweila – LN	0.5	96.7	0.7				1.7	0.3	0.2	X	8192
Burqu	54.7	9.0	11.9				20.9	3.5			201

Notes:

Percentages are based on the total number of bones identified to genus (subfamily in the case of *Ovis/Capra*) within groups indicated. The figures exclude *Testudo* (presence indicated by X), rodents and insectivores (the last two groups were insignificant).

Sources of the above data:

Kharaneh 4: Garrard (unpublished ms.) based on material from 1981 excavations; Khallat Anaza: Garrard (1985); Uwaynid 18, Jilat 6, Azraq 18: Garrard et al. (1988a); Jilat 32, Azraq 31-PPNB: Martin (1992a); Burqu: Martin (1992b); Jilat 7, Jilat 13, Jilat 25: Martin et al. (1994); Jilat 22, Azraq 31-LN, Dhuweila-PPNB, Dhuweila-LN: Martin (1994)

Faunal assemblages have also been obtained from six other epipalaeolithic and neolithic sites in eastern Jordan, but the sample sizes were very small and the details are not given here. For information on Jilat 9, Jilat 10 & Uwaynid 14, see Garrard et al. (1988a); for Jebel Naja & Ibn el-Ghazzi, see Garrard (1985); for Jilat 26, see Martin et al. (1994).

Table 11.2   Cereals and legumes from neolithic sites in eastern Jordan.

		Jilat 7 Early PPNB	Jilat 7 Middle PPNB	Jilat 13 Late Neolithic	Azraq 31 Late PPNB	Dhuweila Late PPNB
Cereals						
Triticum boeoticum	grains		X	X		X
Triticum monococcum	grains	X	X	X		
Triticum dicoccum	grains		X	X		
Triticum spp. (glume wheat)	chaff		X	X		
Hordeum spontaneum	grains	X	X	X		X
Hordeum spontaneum	chaff	X	X	X		
Hordeum sativum	grains	X	X	X	X	
Hordeum sativum	chaff	X	X	X	X	
Hordeum sativum naked	grains			X		
Culm nodes		X	X	X		
Basal culm fragments		X	X	X		
Legumes						
Lens sp.			X	X		
cf. *Cicer sp.*			X			
Vicia cf. *ervilia*			X			
Vicia/Lathyrus spp.		X	X	X		
Legume indet. (large)		X	X	X		

Sources: Colledge & Hillman 1988, Colledge 1994a,b.

is discussed in more detail below. The large-mammal fauna was essentially steppic, comprising species such as *Gazella subgutturosa, Equus hemionus* and *Lepus* sp. *Capra* cf. *aegagrus* occurred in the lava country and particularly in the higher terrain to the north, and *Bos primigenius* in the marshlands around Azraq (Garrard et al. 1988a, 1994a). The neolithic botanical assemblages from the Jilat region indicate that *Pistacia atlantica* (an element of the Irano–Turanian flora) extended into the western wadis, and the occurrence of seeds of *Ficus carica* suggests that there may have been more spring activity in this region. Geological evidence for spring activity was also found at the epipalaeolithic site of Jilat 22, in levels dating to 11000 bc (Garrard & Byrd 1992). The environmental information obtained from the more fertile lands to the west, and particularly from the well dated Huleh pollen core in the northern Jordan Valley, suggests that the period when there was maximum effective moisture was between 13000 and 9500 bc. This was followed first by an intensely cool and dry epi-sode between 9500 and 8500 bc (= the Younger Dryas) and then by renewed climatic amelioration in the early Neolithic (Baruch & Bottema 1991, Bar-Yosef 1991, and cf. Hillman in Ch. 10 in this volume). Although limited, the environmental data from southern Jordan, the Negev and Sinai support this general model of climatic change (Goldberg 1986, Goring-Morris 1993).

Archaeological survey and excavation in eastern Jordan, reinforced by over 60 radiocarbon dates, has revealed sites from much of the Epipalaeolithic and Neolithic (Betts 1993, Garrard et al. 1994a). However, there are significant gaps in the record, of which the most conspicuous is that coinciding with the PPNA (8300–7500 bc). With the exception of Abu Madi 1, archaeologists have also failed to find settlements of this period in southern Jordan, the Negev and Sinai (Bar-Yosef & Belfer-Cohen 1989, Goring-Morris 1993). This is intriguing, as there is evidence from the Levantine Corridor for climatic amelioration and this is the episode from which the earliest domesticated cereals have been identified from areas such as the Damascus Basin. Evidence for early PPNB settlement (7500–7200 bc) is also rare in these regions, but increasing numbers of sites from the seventh and sixth millennia bc are being found. The PPNB and early late neolithic sites in eastern Jordan are much smaller than many contemporary settlements in the Levantine Corridor, and the structures more lightly built. The PPNB structures are usually circular and semi-subterranean and they are suggestive of seasonal rather than permanent occupation (Garrard et al. 1994b). The dwellings have more in common with contemporary neolithic structures from the Negev and Sinai than with those at major farming villages such as 'Ain Ghazal and Jericho to the west. The early late neolithic structures are similar in design to those from the PPNB, but the individual dwellings are generally larger, suggesting use by larger co-resident groups or by humans and livestock (see below).

The emergence of crop cultivation in eastern Jordan

Plant remains are very scarce from epipalaeolithic contexts in Southwest Asia, but a small assemblage was obtained from levels dated to 14000 bc at Jilat 6, which is located in the limestone steppe 55km southwest of the Azraq oasis (Fig. 11.2) (Colledge & Hillman 1988, Garrard & Byrd 1992). The assemblage is dominated by chenopod seeds typical of the present-day habitat and it is possible that these were collected for human consumption. There was no hint of the wild cereals known from the mesic locality of Ohalo 2 (17000 bc), which is located beside the Sea of Galilee (Kislev et al. 1992).

As was discussed above, no PPNA settlements have been found, but seed assemblages were recovered from early, middle and late PPNB and early late-neolithic contexts at four sites. The larger collections were from Jilat 7 (*c.* 7500–6500 bc) and Jilat 13 (6000–5500 bc) and the smaller from the late PPNB levels at Azraq 31 (6500–6000 bc) and Dhuweila (6500–6000 bc). The latter site lies in the basalt steppe 60km east of the Azraq oasis (Fig. 11.2). The assemblages from the Jilat sites contained wild and domestic-type einkorn (*Triticum boeoticum* and *T. monococcum*), domestic-type emmer (*T. dicoccum*), wild and domestic-type barley (*Hordeum spontaneum, H. sativum*), lentil and probable chickpea (Table 11.2). The collection from Azraq contained domestic-type barley and that from Dhuweila wild-type barley and einkorn. Given that these areas presently lie well outside the habitat of wild cereals and large-seeded pulses, and also outside the range of rainfed agriculture, it is particularly interesting that these species were found. The obvious question is: were they growing locally or imported from a distance?

The wild cereals may have grown as weeds of cultivation and need not have come from sources separate from the domestic grain. Although it cannot be proved, local cultivation seems likely at Jilat, because small quantities of cereal chaff were found in each of the samples, suggesting that processing was undertaken nearby. There are also several plant species in the assemblages (e.g. fig) that suggest that conditions may have been slightly moister than at present (for a full species list see Colledge 1994b).

Today cereal cultivation is occasionally attempted in drainage channels upstream from the Jilat sites, and if there was slightly higher rainfall in the Neolithic, cultivation may have been practised in the vicinity of the settlements. Such cultivation has also been seen close to Dhuweila, and irrigation is possible at Azraq.

The presence of einkorn in the early PPNB samples from Jilat is intriguing, because, prior to its discovery, the middle PPNB einkorn seeds from Jericho (Hopf 1983) were the earliest known from the southern Levant. Today the nearest non-weedy wild-forms of einkorn are found in Turkey and Kurdistan (Zohary & Hopf 1988: 28–36). However, it is possible that its early Holocene distribution included southern Syria and north-central Jordan because einkorn is thought to be more drought-tolerant than emmer and it particularly favours basaltic soils (Gordon Hillman: pers. comm.).

The emergence of caprine herding in eastern Jordan

Faunal assemblages have been recovered from 21 of the epipalaeolithic and neo-lithic sites investigated in eastern Jordan and they are providing a rich dataset on sub-sistence developments through the late Pleistocene and early Holocene. As has already been mentioned, the fauna is essentially steppic throughout the period. The proportional representation of species from the main sites discussed in the text are dis-played in Table 11.1 and Figure 11.3. The latter is divided both chronologically and by major habitat. The sample sizes from two of the illustrated site contexts were very small (Khallat Anaza and the late PPNB of Azraq 31), but they have been included because they are from periods and areas that are otherwise poorly represented. The faunal sequence is best discussed by chronological stage.

Epipalaeolithic (18000–8500 bc).   Gazelle (with some horn cores identifiable as *Gazella subgutturosa*) very much dominates the assemblages from sites in the lime-stone steppe, representing 80–90 per cent of the fauna at three of the localities (Jilat 6, Kharaneh 4, Uwaynid 18). Equids (with some teeth identifiable to *Equus hemionus/ asinus* and *E. hydruntinus*) were also significant in terms of meat weight, and tortoise (*Testudo*) remains are common. The latter are mainly represented by carapace frag-ments and have not been included in percentages based on total number of identifiable osteological units, because of the lack of comparability of body parts. It is possible that some of the carapaces had been used as containers. Sheep/goat (*Ovis/Capra*) bones represented less than 0.2 per cent of the total faunal remains from sites in the limestone steppe and, given the sample sizes, the wide timeframe and the varying location of the sites, this strongly suggests that caprines did not inhabit this region at this time (see the earlier discussion of the distribution of wild sheep). Goat bones were however found at the Natufian site of Khallat Anaza, which is located in the craggy basalt terrain 60 km north of Azraq (Fig. 11.2). The assemblage from the Natufian site of Azraq 18 contained many bones of cattle (*Bos primigenius*) as well as of equid and gazelle. The cattle probably inhabited the extensive marshland around the oasis, as do feral water buffalo today.

Early and Middle PPNB (7500–6500 bc).   As has been mentioned, no evidence has been found for PPNA settlement on the Jordanian plateau, but faunal assemblages

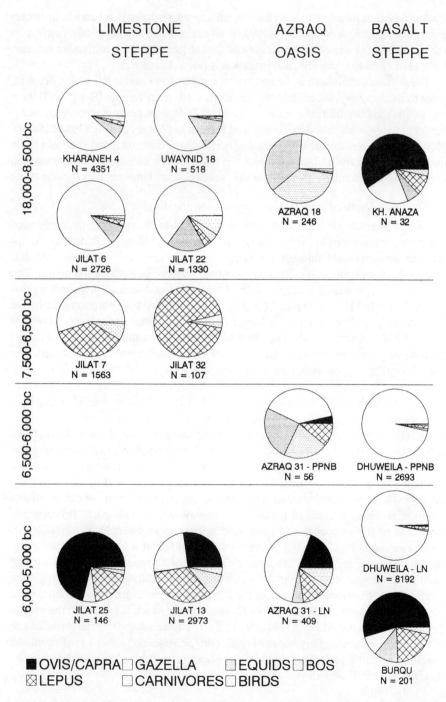

Figure 11.3 Pie charts showing the proportions of various species represented by bones at epipalaeolithic and neolithic sites in eastern Jordan (based on data in Table 11.1).

have been recovered from the early and middle PPNB sites of Jilat 7 and Jilat 32 in the limestone steppe. These differ in two striking ways from earlier assemblages in the region. First, by the absence of equids, although they occur in later sites to the east. Secondly, by the considerable increase in the use of hare (*Lepus* sp). These changes coincide with the appearance of crop cultivars in the area, which has already been discussed.

Significant reductions in equids have been noted at other early neolithic sites in Southwest Asia, particularly at Mureybet and Abu Hureyra on the Euphrates (Legge 1975, Ducos 1978b) and at sites in the Zagros (Hesse 1978). Hesse has suggested that early Holocene habitat changes may have been responsible for their disappearance in western Iran. Although this is possible in the Jordanian context, other factors may have been significant. It is possible that the beginnings of cultivation on the western steppe led to changes in the catchment areas being exploited for hunting, or perhaps in the season or timing of hunting expeditions. It is also possible that an expansion of human population in this region led to increased predation pressure on the equids or to increasing disturbance of this portion of their range.

The dramatic increase in the exploitation of hare during the early and middle PPNB may be linked to the disappearance of the equids and to other factors described above. Hare accounts for 36 per cent of the animal remains at Jilat 7 and 94 per cent in the small sample from Jilat 32, which may have been a specialized settlement. It continues to be significant in later periods. Hares live at low densities in the wild and their routine exploitation may have required nets or other equipment not used with the larger mammals. The only other Southwest Asian site of this period with a high proportion of hare is the middle PPNB settlement at Wadi Tbeik in southern Sinai (Tchernov & Bar-Yosef 1982).

Late PPNB (6500–6000 bc)   No late PPNB sites have been found in the limestone steppe, but animal remains of this period have been obtained from the oasis site of Azraq 31, and from Dhuweila, which lies in the basalt steppe to the east. Two bone samples were obtained from the former: one of which is very small but from undisturbed contexts radiocarbon dated to 6400±120 bc, and the second of which is larger but may be contaminated (Martin 1992a: 26). Although the species proportions are similar in each, only the undisturbed sample is presented in Table 11.1 and Figure 11.3. The two assemblages closely resemble the collection from the nearby Natufian site of Azraq 18. The main differences relate to the increased importance of hare and the presence of a few caprine bones (3.5%). Given that (as already noted) domestic sheep and goat are known from late PPNB sites in the more fertile lands to the west, it is possible that the bones derive from an early introduction of domestic livestock to Azraq. However, the presence of wild goat in the assemblage from the Natufian site of Khallat Anaza to the north indicates that this species could have inhabited the craggy basalt terrain close to Azraq (Fig. 11.2).

The late PPNB faunal assemblage from Dhuweila, to the east of Azraq, consists almost entirely of gazelle, and Betts (1988) has argued that it may have been a hunting-drive site. This is based on the finding of stone-built "desert kites" or hunting traps in the region (Helms & Betts 1987). Although a possible kite wall overlays the late neolithic deposits at Dhuweila, no stratified evidence has been found in Southwest Asia to indicate that these structures were in use during the Neolithic. Nevertheless, it remains an intriguing possibility and it is hoped that further survey and excavation will throw light on this.

Late Neolithic (6000–5000 bc)   No data are available on late PPNB subsistence in the limestone steppe, but two early late-neolithic sites with radiocarbon dates ranging between 6070±80 and 5880±90 bc have been excavated at Wadi Jilat (Jilat 13 and 25: Garrard et al. 1994b). Both contain substantial proportions of sheep and goat as well as gazelle, hare and fox. Given the almost complete absence of caprine bones from earlier sites in this habitat, it is assumed that the caprines were introduced by humans during the late seventh millennium bc. It was mentioned above that a very small number of caprine bones, which might be of domestic or wild origin, were found in the levels dated to 6400 bc at Azraq 31. Following a stratigraphic break, many sheep and goat bones were found in early sixth millennium bc contexts (Martin 1992a, 1994). Caprine bones also represent over half of an assemblage from the late sixth millennium bc site of Burqu 27,140 km east of Azraq (Martin 1992b). Meanwhile, gazelle and hare continued to be exploited at each of these localities, and in late sixth millennium bc levels at Dhuweila gazelle still accounts for over 96 per cent of the fauna. As was mentioned above, Betts (1988) has argued that this was a specialized drive site.

Domestic sheep and goats may well have been introduced into eastern Jordan as mixed herds, the one species complementing the other in terms of feeding behaviour and climatic tolerance (Lancaster & Lancaster 1991). At each of the sites containing caprines, sheep substantially outnumber goats. As has already been pointed out, this is also the case at many other late seventh and early sixth millennium bc sites in Southwest Asia, and it was argued that it may relate to differences in their browsing/grazing behaviour and ease of control as well as to differences in their products. A study of caprine slaughter patterns at Jilat 13 (Mylona 1992, Powell 1992) found that the majority of animals were killed in the first few years of life, which might suggest that they were culled for meat rather than other products (Payne 1973). It is necessary, however, to be very cautious in the interpretation of such data from this period.

Two models have been proposed for the introduction of domestic livestock into eastern Jordan. To discuss the first, it is necessary to explain events that occurred in the Levantine Corridor. During the mid- to late seventh millennium bc, many villages appear to have been abandoned in the southern Levant (e.g. Jericho, Yiftah'el), although a few survived (e.g. 'Ain Ghazal, Tell Ramad) and new ones were founded (e.g. Basta, Beisamoun). Early researchers sought climatic explanations, but no direct evidence of climatic change was found. Rollefson & Köhler-Rollefson (1989, 1993) have suggested that ecologically ill conceived early agricultural and pastoral activities, including the maintenance of goat herds close to villages, may have led to environmental degradation and forced a relocation of settlement. They believe that this may have been alleviated by a separation of the agricultural and pastoral sectors of the economy at the end of the seventh millennium bc. This would have involved the development of a mobile herding system, in which livestock were removed from the agricultural areas for substantial portions of the year. They argue that the first live-stock in eastern Jordan may have been introduced by village herders from the Levan-tine Corridor.

Detailed studies of the architectural and technological traditions through the Neo-lithic in the survey areas covered in eastern Jordan show strong local continuity and suggest that the inhabitants of the steppe had a distinct identity different from groups to the west (Baird et al. 1992, Baird 1993, Garrard et al. 1994b). Thus, there is no clear evidence for the presence of herders from the Levantine Corridor. Nevertheless, it is likely that there was extensive contact and trading/exchange of materials such as gazelle meat, hides, and the greenstone widely used in bead manufacture. At present, the data support the notion that the first livestock were adopted to serve the needs of the indigenous steppic groups.

A second model has been proposed by Byrd (1992), who suggests that both crop cultivation and caprine herding may have developed in the steppe in response to an increasing imbalance between population and resources. He argues that this may have been induced by a steady influx of hunter–gatherers from the west, displaced by the expansion of farming communities. This may certainly have been a factor.

Once domestic sheep had been introduced into the central and southern Levant and had begun to be maintained in mixed herds with goats, it is likely that the "pastoral package" became increasingly attractive as a buffer against risks of crop failure. This would have been particularly true in the marginal lands, where slight changes in rainfall regime would have had a dramatic effect on the potential for cultivation. It is interesting that plant processing equipment is less frequent and diverse in early sixth millennium bc sites, suggesting that caprine herding and hunting and gathering may have been more attractive options (Wright 1993). Once dairying was incorporated into the econ-omy, large-scale animal herding is likely to have become an attractive strategy. It is also important not to underestimate the potential prestige that may have accrued from the procurement of livestock and the availability of their products (Hayden 1990).

The emergence of crop cultivation and caprine herding in the Negev and Sinai

As has already been indicated, no archaeobotanical and very little archaeozoolog-ical data are presently available on neolithic subsistence strategies in other areas of the Marginal Zone to the east and south of the Levantine Corridor. The only well pub-lished faunal assemblages are from the middle PPNB of Wadi Tbeik (Tchernov & Bar-Yosef 1982) and the late PPNB of Ujrat el-Mehed (Dayan et al. 1986) in southern Sinai. In both cases ibex is the dominant species. In neither case is there evidence for domes-tication, although it is argued that selective culling of males may have occurred at Wadi Tbeik. The earliest direct evidence for animal domesticates is from the Early Bronze Age (c. 3000 bc; Rosen 1988). However, as Goring-Morris (1993: 77) has noted, a "package" of domesticates had reached the Nile Valley from the Levant by 5000 bc and these must have crossed the western Negev and northern Sinai. It is there-fore likely that caprine herding and perhaps localized crop cultivation were being practised along this corridor in the sixth millennium bc.

Conclusions

In this chapter the evidence relating to the origins of crop cultivation and caprine herding in the Marginal Zone (the present dry steppe and subdesert belt) of the southern Levant has been reviewed. Most of the archaeobotanical and archaeozoological information derives from two field projects undertaken in eastern Jordan through the 1980s: one of which focused on the limestone steppe and the Azraq oasis (Garrard et al. 1994a) and the other on the basalt steppe to the east (Betts 1993).

There is no evidence from Jordan or elsewhere in the Levant to support models that propose that plant and animal domestication first developed in the Marginal Zone. Where data are available, there seems to have been a timelapse between the first occurrence of crop cultivars and domestic livestock in the Levantine Corridor and their appearance in the more arid tracts to the east and south.

PPNA settlement (8300–7500 bc) is virtually unknown from the marginal territories, although evidence from more mesic localities indicates that this was a period of climatic amelioration following the cool and dry conditions of the period of the Younger Dryas. It was during the PPNA that the first cereals showing morphological evidence of domestication appeared in the Levantine Corridor.

Early PPNB sites (7500–7200 bc) are also scarce, but a settlement from this period has been excavated at Jilat 7 in eastern Jordan and has yielded domestic-type einkorn and barley. This is in an area that presently lacks springs and receives only half the rainfall necessary for reliable rainfed agriculture. The presence of cereal chaff suggests local processing and probably also local cultivation. This is supported by the presence of other species indicative of moist habitats. Coinciding with the appearance of cultivars, there were changes in animal exploitation in this region. Although gazelle continued to be an important staple, equids disappeared from assemblages. In their place, there was an increased emphasis on hare. It is possible that the disappearance of equids related to the changing catchments being exploited by early cultivators, but it is also possible that over-predation, habitat changes or range disturbance were significant factors.

In terms of numbers of sites, the middle PPNB (7200–6500 bc) is much better represented in eastern Jordan. Excavations in the upper levels of Jilat 7 have yielded domestic-type emmer and large-seeded pulses in addition to domestic-type einkorn and barley. The associated animal remains are similar to those from the earlier Neolithic. No late PPNB (6500–6000 bc) sites have been found in this immediate area, but the oasis settlement of Azraq 31, farther east, has yielded a faunal assemblage that includes a very small percentage of caprine bones, which could derive from wild or domestic animals.

Sites relating to the early Late Neolithic (*c.* 6000 bc) in this region contain many sheep and goat bones, the former being the dominant species. Meanwhile, gazelle and other steppic mammals continued to be exploited; for instance, in levels dated to 5500–5000 bc at Dhuweila east of Azraq, gazelle accounts for 96 per cent of the animal remains. This suggests that the site was used as a specialized hunting station, perhaps involving drives, as has been postulated by Betts (1988).

It is thought that the mixed herds of sheep and goats were adopted by the indigenous inhabitants of the steppe and that the "pastoral package" would have provided a useful risk-buffer for those engaged in marginal farming and hunting. However, it is uncertain how far environmental, demographic or social factors may account for the initial appearance of the domestic caprines. Once dairying was established, large-scale animal herding would have become an increasingly attractive option in the Marginal Zone.

As Goring-Morris (1993) notes, very little direct evidence relevant to the origins of crop cultivation and caprine herding has been retrieved from the Negev and Sinai regions, but it is assumed, on the basis of the appearance of West Asian domesticates in the Nile Valley at 5000 bc, that caprine herding and perhaps limited cultivation was being practised in the western Negev and northern Sinai in the preceding centuries.

Acknowledgements

The authors are very grateful to their field colleagues for much support and many valuable discussions: in particular to Douglas Baird, Alison Betts, Brian Byrd, William Lancaster and Katherine Wright. They would also like to thank Dimitri Mylona, Adrienne Powell and Alex Wasse for the use of information contained in their dissertations. This work would not have been possible without the co-operation of the Department of Antiquities in Jordan and generous grants from the British Academy, the British Institute at Amman for Archaeology and History, the British Museum, the Leverhulme Trust, the Palestine Exploration Fund, the Science and Engineering Research Council and the Wainwright Fund.

Notes

1. For "plant domestication" see the definition of Hillman & Davies (1992: 114). For a discussion of the diversity and range of levels of plant manipulation see Harris (1989 and Ch. 1 in this volume).
2. For "animal domestication" see the definition of Clutton-Brock (1989: 7). For a discussion of the diversity and range of levels of animal manipulation, see Horwitz (1989) and Harris (Ch. 1 in this voume).
3. Ducos (1968) reported sheep bones from the Natufian levels at Nahel Oren and 'Ain Mallaha, and the middle-PPNB levels at Munhata. However, this is refuted in a more recent publication (Ducos 1993b: 154). Legge (1973) and Bouchud (1987) did not find any sheep bones in their analysis of more recently excavated samples from Nahel Oren and 'Ain Mallaha.

References

Baird, D. 1993. *Neolithic chipped stone assemblages from the Azraq Basin, Jordan and the significance of the Neolithic of the arid zones of the Levant.* PhD dissertation, Department of Archaeology, University of Edinburgh.
Baird, D., A. Garrard, L. Martin, K. Wright 1992. Prehistoric environment and settlement in the Azraq Basin: an interim report on the 1989 excavation season. *Levant* **24**, 1–31.
Bar-Yosef, O. 1981. Neolithic sites in Sinai. In *Bëitrage zur Umweltgeschichte des Vorderens Orients,* W. Frey & H-P. Uerpmann (eds), 217–35. Beihefte zum Tübinger Atlas des Vorderen Orients, Reihe A (Naturwissenschaften) 8. Wiesbaden: Dr L. Reichert.

— 1991. The Early Neolithic of the Levant: recent advances. *The Review of Archaeology* 12, 1–18.
Bar-Yosef, O. & A. Belfer-Cohen 1989. The origins of sedentism and farming communities in the Levant. *Journal of World Prehistory* 3, 447–98.
Bar-Yosef, O. & J. L. Phillips 1977. *Prehistoric investigations in Gebel Maghara, northern Sinai*. Jerusalem: Institute of Archaeology, Hebrew University, Qedem 7.
Baruch, U. & S. Bottema 1991. Palynological evidence for climatic change in the Levant ca.17,000–9,000 B. P. In *The Natufian Culture in the Levant*, O. Bar-Yosef & F. Valla (eds), 11–20. Ann Arbor, Michigan: International Monographs in Prehistory.
Becker, C. 1991. The analysis of mammalian bones from Basta, a Pre-Pottery Neolithic site in Jordan: problems and potential. *Paléorient* 17, 59–76.
Bender, B. 1978. Gatherer–hunter to farmer: a social perspective. *World Archaeology* 10, 204–22.
Betts, A. V. G. 1988. 1986 excavations at Dhuweila, eastern Jordan. *Levant* 20, 7–21.
— 1993. The Neolithic sequence in the east Jordan Badia: a preliminary overview. *Paléorient* 19, 43–54.
Binford, L. R. 1968. Post-Pleistocene adaptations. In *New perspectives in archeology*, S. R. Binford & L. R. Binford (eds), 313–41. Chicago: Aldine.
— 1983. *In pursuit of the past*. London: Thames & Hudson.
Bökönyi, S. 1969. Archaeological problems and methods of recognizing animal domestication. In *The domestication and exploitation of plants and animals*, P. J. Ucko & G. W. Dimbleby (eds), 219–29. London: Duckworth.
Bouchud, J. 1987. *La faune du gisement natoufien de Mallaha (Eynan) Israel*. Mémoires et Travaux 4, Centre de Recherches Préhistoriques Français de Jérusalem, Paléorient Association, Paris.
Butler, B. H., E. Tchernov, H. Hietala, S. Davis 1977. Faunal exploitation during the late Epipalaeolithic in the Har Harif. In *Prehistory and paleoenvironments in the central Negev, Israel* (vol. 2), A. E. Marks (ed.), 327–46. Dallas: Southern Methodist University Press.
Byrd, B. F. 1992. The dispersal of food production across the Levant. In *Transitions to agriculture in prehistory* [Monographs in World Archaeology 4], A. B. Gebauer & T. D. Price (eds), 49–61. Madison: Prehistory Press.
Cauvin J. & D. Stordeur 1994. Radiocarbon dating El-Kowm: Upper Paleolithic through Chalcolithic. In *Late Quaternary chronology and paleoclimates of the eastern Mediterranean*, O. Bar-Yosef & R. Kra (eds), 201–4. Radiocarbon, Department of Geosciences, University of Arizona.
Cauvin, M-C. & E. Coqueugniot 1988. L'oasis d'el Kowm et le Kébarien Géométrique. *Paléorient* 14, 270–82.
Clark, G. A., J. Lindly, M. Donaldson, A. Garrard, N. Coinman, J. Schuldenrein, S. Fish, D. Olszewski 1988. Excavations at Middle, Upper and Epipalaeolithic sites in the Wadi Hasa, west-central Jordan. In Garrard & Gebel (1988b: 209–85).
Clason, A. T. 1979–80. The animal remains from Tell es Sinn, compared with those from Bouqras. *Anatolica* 7, 35–53.
Clutton-Brock, J. 1979. The mammalian remains from the Jericho Tell. *Proceedings of the Prehistoric Society* 45, 135–57.
— (ed.) 1989. *The walking larder: patterns of domestication, pastoralism, and predation*. London: Unwin Hyman.
Cohen, M. 1977. *The food crisis in prehistory*. New Haven: Yale University Press.
Colledge, S. M. 1994a. *Plant exploitation on Epipalaeolithic and early Neolithic sites in the Levant*. PhD dissertation, Department of Archaeology and Prehistory, University of Sheffield.
— 1994b. The botanical remains. In "Prehistoric environment and settlement in the Azraq Basin: an interim report on the 1987 and 1988 excavation seasons", A. N. Garrard, D. Baird, S. Colledge, L. Martin & K. Wright. *Levant* 26, 100–5.
Colledge, S. M. & G. C. Hillman 1988. Plant remains. In "Environment and subsistence during the Late Pleistocene and Early Holocene in the Azraq Basin", A. N. Garrard, S. Colledge, C. Hunt, R. Montague. *Paléorient* 14, 44–7.
Davis, S. J. M. 1978. Etude de la faune. In *Abu Gosh et Beisamoun*, M. Lechevallier (ed.), 195–7. Mémoires et Travaux 2, Centre de Recherches Préhistoriques Français de Jérusalem, Paléorient

Association, Paris.
— 1984. The advent of milk and wool production in west-central Iran. In *Animals and archaeology, 3: early herders and their flocks*, J. Clutton-Brock & C. Grigson (eds), 265–78. Oxford: British Archaeological Reports, International Series 202.
— 1985. A preliminary report of the fauna from Hatoula: a Natufian–Khiamian (PPNA) site near Latroun, Israel. In *Le site Natoufien–Khiamien de Hatoula, près de Latroun, Israël*. M. Lechevallier & A. Ronen (eds), 71–98. Cahiers 1, Centre de Recherche Français de Jérusalem, Jerusalem.
— 1987. *The archaeology of animals*. London: Batsford.
Davis, S. J. M., A. N. Goring-Morris, A. Gopher 1982. Sheep bones from the Negev Epipalaeolithic. *Paléorient* **8**, 87–93.
Dayan, T., E. Tchernov, O. Bar-Yosef & Y. Yom-Tov 1986. Animal exploitation in Ujrat el-Meked, a Neolithic site in southern Sinai. *Paléorient* **12**, 105–15.
Ducos, P. 1968. *L'origine des animaux domestiques en Palestine*. Mémoire 6, Institut de Préhistoire, Université de Bordeaux [Bordeaux: Delmas].
— 1978a. La faune d'Abou Gosh; proto-élevage de la chèvre au néolithique pré-céramique. In *Abu Gosh et Beisamoun*, M. Lechevallier (ed.), 107–20. Mémoires et Travaux 2, Centre de Recherches Préhistoriques Français de Jérusalem, Paléorient Association, Paris.
— 1978b. *Tell-Mureybet: étude archéozoologique et problèmes d'écologie humaine 1*. Paris: Editions du CNRS.
— 1993a. Some remarks about *Ovis*, *Capra* and *Gazella* remains from two PPNB sites from Damascene, Syria, Tell Aswad and Ghoraifé. In *Archaeozoology of the Near East*, H. Buitenhuis & A. T. Clason (eds), 37–45. Leiden: Universal Book Services/Dr W. Backhuys.
— 1993b. Proto-élevage et élevage au Levant sud au VIIe millénaire BC. Les données de la Damascène. *Paléorient* **19**, 153–74.
Flannery, K. V. 1969. Origins and ecological effects of early domestication in Iran and the Near East. In *The domestication and exploitation of plants and animals*, P. J. Ucko & G. W. Dimbleby (eds), 73–100. London: Duckworth.
Garfinkel, Y., M. E. Kislev, D. Zohary 1988. Lentil in the Pre- Pottery Neolithic B Yiftah'el: additional evidence of its early domestication. *Israel Journal of Botany* **37**, 49–51.
Garrard, A. N. 1985. Appendix 1: faunal remains. In "Black Desert survey, Jordan: third preliminary report", A. Betts. *Levant* **17**, 39–49.
Garrard, A. N., R. Montague, B. West 1988a. Animal remains. In "Environment and subsistence during the Late Pleistocene and Early Holocene in the Azraq Basin", A. N. Garrard, S. Colledge, C. Hunt, R. Montague. *Paléorient* **14**, 46–8.
Garrard, A. N. & B. F. Byrd 1992. New dimensions to the Epipalaeolithic of the Wadi el-Jilat in central Jordan. *Paléorient* **18**, 47–62.
Garrard, A. N. & H-G. Gebel (eds) 1988b. *The prehistory of Jordan*. Oxford: British Archaeological Reports, International Series 396 i and ii.
Garrard, A. N., D. Baird, B. Byrd 1994a. The chronological basis and significance of the Late Paleolithic and Neolithic sequence in the Azraq Basin, Jordan. In *Late Quaternary chronology and paleoclimates of the eastern Mediterranean*, O. Bar-Yosef & R. Kra (eds), 177–99. Radiocarbon, Department of Geosciences, University of Arizona.
Garrard, A. N., D. Baird, S. Colledge, L. Martin, K. Wright 1994b. Prehistoric environment and settlement in the Azraq Basin: an interim report on the 1987 and 1988 excavation seasons. *Levant* **26**, 73–109.
Goldberg, P. 1986. Late Quaternary environmental history of the southern Levant. *Geoarchaeology* **1**, 225–44.
Goring-Morris N. 1987. *At the edge: terminal Pleistocene hunter–gatherers in the Negev and Sinai*. Oxford: British Archaeological Reports, International Series 361.
— 1993. From foraging to herding in the Negev and Sinai: the Early to Late Neolithic transition. *Paléorient* **19**, 65–90.
Hanihara, K. & T. Akazawa 1979. *Paleolithic site of Douara Cave and paleogeography of Palmyra Basin in Syria*, part II. Bulletin 16, University Museum, University of Tokyo.

Harris, D. R. 1989. An evolutionary continuum of people–plant interaction. In *Foraging and farming: the evolution of plant exploitation*, D. R. Harris & G. C. Hillman (eds), 11–26. London: Unwin Hyman.
— 1990. *Settling down and breaking ground: rethinking the Neolithic Revolution.* Twaalfde Kroon-Voordracht, Stichting Nederlands Museum voor Anthropologie en Praehistorie, Amsterdam.
Hayden, B. 1990. Nimrods, piscators, pluckers and planters: the emergence of food production. *Journal of Anthropological Archaeology* **9**, 31–69.
Hecker, H. M. 1975. *The faunal analysis of the primary food animals from Pre-Pottery Neolithic Beidha (Jordan)* [PhD dissertation, Department of Anthropology, Columbia University]. Ann Arbor, Michigan: University Microfilms.
— 1982. Domestication revisited: its implications for faunal analysis. *Journal of Field Archeology* **9**, 217–36.
Helmer, D. 1988. Les animaux de Cafer et des sites précéramiques du Sud-Est de la Turquie: essai de synthèse. *Anatolica* **15**, 37–48.
Helms, S. W. & A. V. G. Betts 1987. The desert "kites" of the Badiyat esh-Sham and North Arabia. *Paléorient* **13**, 41–67.
Henry, D. O. 1988. Summary of prehistoric and palaeoenvironmental research in the northern Hisma. In Garrard & Gebel (1988b: 7–37).
Henry, D. O. & A. N. Garrard 1988. Tor Hamar: an Epipalaeolithic rockshelter in southern Jordan. *Palestine Exploration Quarterly* **120**, 1–25.
Henry, D. O. & P. F. Turnbull 1985. Archaeological and faunal evidence from Natufian and Timnian sites in southern Jordan. *Bulletin of the American Schools of Oriental Research* **257**, 45–64.
Hesse, B. C. 1978. *Evidence for husbandry from the Early Neolithic site of Ganj Dareh in western Iran* [PhD dissertation, Department of Anthropology, Columbia University]. Ann Arbor, Michigan: University Microfilms.
— 1984. These are our goats: the origins of herding in West Central Iran. In *Animals and archaeology, 3: early herders and their flocks*, J. Clutton-Brock & C. Grigson (eds), 243–64. Oxford: British Archaeological Reports, International Series 202.
Hillman, G. C. & M. S. Davies 1992. Domestication rates in wild wheats and barley under primitive cultivation. In *Préhistoire de l'agriculture: nouvelles approches expérimentales et ethnographiques* [Monographie 6, Centre de Recherches Archéologiques], P. C. Anderson (ed.), 113–58. Paris: Editions du CNRS.
Hodder, I. 1990. *The domestication of Europe: structure and contingency in neolithic societies.* Oxford: Basil Blackwell.
Hopf, M. 1983. Jericho plant remains. In *Excavations at Jericho* (vol. 5), K. M. Kenyon & T. A. Holland (eds), 576–621. London: British School of Archaeology in Jerusalem.
Horwitz, L. K. 1987. Fauna from the PPNB site of Yiftah'el: new perspectives on domestication. *Mitekufat Haeven* **20**, 181–2.
— 1989. A reassessment of caprovine domestication in the Levantine Neolithic: old questions, new answers. In *People and culture in change*, I. Hershovitz (ed.), 153–81. Oxford: British Archaeological Reports, International Series 508(i).
Horwitz, L. K. & P. Smith 1991. A study of diachronic change in bone mass of sheep and goats from Jericho (Tel es-Sultan). *Archaeozoologia* **4**, 29–38.
Horwitz, L. K. & E. Tchernov 1987. Faunal remains from the PPNB submerged site of Atlit. *Mitekufat Haeven* **20**, 72–8.
Kislev, M. E. 1989. Pre-domesticated cereals in the Pre-Pottery Neolithic A period. In *People and culture in change*, I. Hershkovitz (ed.), 147–52. Oxford: British Archaeological Reports, International Series 508(i).
— 1992. Agriculture in the Near East in the VIIth millennium bc. In *Préhistoire de l'agriculture: nouvelles approches expérimentales et ethnographiques* [Monographie 6, Centre de Recherches Archéologiques], P. C. Anderson (ed.), 87–94. Paris: Editions du CNRS.
Kislev, M. E. & O. Bar-Yosef 1988. The legumes: the earliest domesticated plants in the Near East. *Current Anthropology* **29**, 175–9.

Kislev, M. E., O. Bar-Yosef & A. Gopher 1986. Early Neolithic domesticated and wild barley from the Netiv Hagdud region in the Jordan Valley. *Israel Journal of Botany* **35**, 197–201.

Kislev, M. E., D. Nadel, I. Carmi 1992. Epipalaeolithic (19,000 bp) cereal and fruit diet at Ohalo II, Sea of Galilee, Israel. *Review of Palaeobotany and Palynology* **73**, 161–6.

Köhler-Rollefson, I. 1988. The aftermath of the Levantine Neolithic Revolution in the light of ecological and ethnographic evidence. *Paléorient* **14**, 87–93.

Köhler-Rollefson, I., W. Gillespie, M. Metzger 1988. The fauna from Neolithic 'Ain Ghazal. In Garrard & Gebel (1988b: 423–30).

Lancaster, W. & F. Lancaster 1991. Limitations on sheep and goat herding in the eastern Badia of Jordan: an ethnoarchaeological enquiry. *Levant* **23**, 125–38.

Legge, A. J. 1973. The fauna. In "Recent excavations at Nahal Oren, Israel", T. Noy, A. J. Legge, E. S.Higgs. *Proceedings of the Prehistoric Society* **39**, 90–91.

— 1975. The fauna of Tell Abu Hureyra: preliminary analysis. *Proceedings of the Prehistoric Society* **41**, 74–6.

Legge, A. J. & P. A. Rowley-Conwy 1986. New radiocarbon dates for early sheep at Tell Abu Hureyra, Syria. In *Archaeological results from accelerator dating*, J. A. J. Gowlett & R. E. M. Hedges (eds), 23–35. Monograph 11, Committee for Archaeology, University of Oxford.

— 1987. Gazelle killing in Stone Age Syria. *Scientific American* **257**, 88–95.

Marks, A. E. 1976, 1977. *Prehistory and paleoenvironments in the central Negev, Israel,* vols 1 & 2. Dallas: Southern Methodist University Press.

Martin, L. 1992a. The faunal remains. In "Prehistoric environment and settlement in the Azraq Basin: an interim report on the 1989 excavation season", D. Baird, A. Garrard, L. Martin, K. Wright. *Levant* **24**, 25–6.

— 1992b. Faunal remains. In "Preliminary report of the 1989 excavations at Site 27 of the Burqu/Ruweishid Project", C. J. McCartney. *Levant* **24**, 50–1.

— 1994. *Hunting and herding in a semi-arid region: an archaeological and ethological study of the faunal remains from the Epipalaeolithic and Neolithic of eastern Jordan.* PhD dissertation, Department of Archaeology and Prehistory, University of Sheffield.

Martin, L., D. Mylona, A. Powell 1994. The faunal remains. In "Prehistoric environment and settlement in the Azraq Basin: an interim report on the 1987 and 1988 excavation seasons", A. N. Garrard, D. Baird, S. Colledge, L. Martin, K. Wright. *Levant* **26**, 95–100.

Meadow, R. H. 1989. Osteological evidence for the process of animal domestication. In *The walking larder: patterns of domestication, pastoralism, and predation*, J. Clutton-Brock (ed.), 80–90. London: Unwin Hyman.

Moore A. M. T. & G. C. Hillman 1992. The Pleistocene to Holocene transition and human economy in Southwest Asia: the impact of the Younger Dryas. *American Antiquity* **57**, 482–94.

Muheisen, M. S. 1988. The Epipalaeolithic phases of Kharaneh IV. In Garrard & Gebel (1988b: 353–67).

Mylona, D. 1992. *Late Neolithic economy in Wadi el Jilat, north-west Jordan.* MSc thesis, Department of Archaeology and Prehistory, University of Sheffield.

Nelson, B. 1973. *Azraq, desert oasis.* London: Allen Lane.

Payne, S. 1973. Kill-off patterns in sheep and goats: the mandibles from Aşvan Kale. *Anatolian Studies* **23**, 281–303.

Perkins, D. 1964. Prehistoric fauna from Shanidar, Iraq. *Science* **144**, 1565–6.

Powell, A. 1992. *An analysis of the animal bones from Area B, Wadi el-Jilat 13, a Late Neolithic site from northeast Jordan.* MSc thesis, Department of Archaeology and Prehistory, University of Sheffield.

Rollefson, G. O. & I. Köhler-Rollefson 1989. The collapse of early Neolithic settlements in the southern Levant. In *People and culture in change,* I. Hershovitz (ed.), 73–89. Oxford: British Archaeological Reports, International Series 508i.

— 1993. PPNC adaptations in the first half of the 6th millennium BC. *Paléorient* **19**, 33–42.

Rosen, S. A. 1988. Notes on the origins of pastoral nomadism: a case study from the Negev and Sinai. *Current Anthropology* **29**, 498–506.

Sherratt, A. 1981. Plough and pastoralism: aspects of the Secondary Products Revolution. In *Patterns of the past*, I. Hodder, G. Isaac, N. Hammond (eds), 261–305. Cambridge: Cambridge University Press.

Stein, G. 1989. Strategies of risk reduction in herding and hunting systems of Neolithic southeast Anatolia. In *Early animal domestication and its cultural context*, P. J. Crabtree, D. Campana & K. Ryan (eds), 87–97. Philadelphia: University of Pennsylvania.

Stordeur, D. 1989. El Kowm 2 Caracol et le PPNB. *Paléorient* **15**, 102–10.

Suzuki, H. & I. Kobori 1970. *Report of the reconnaissance survey on Palaeolithic sites in Lebanon and Syria*. Bulletin 1, University Museum, University of Tokyo.

Tchernov, E. & O. Bar-Yosef 1982. Animal exploitation in the Pre-Pottery Neolithic B period at Wadi Tbeik, southern Sinai. *Paléorient* **8**, 17–38.

Uerpmann, H-P. 1979. *Probleme der Neolithisierung des Mittelmeerraums* [Beihefte zum Tübinger Atlas des Vorderen Orients, Reihe B (Geisteswissenschaften) 28]. Wiesbaden: Dr L. Reichert.

— 1987. *The ancient distribution of ungulate mammals in the Middle East* [Beihefte zum Tübinger Atlas des Vorderen Orients, Reihe A (Naturwissenschaften) 27]. Weisbaden: Dr L. Reichert.

van Zeist, W. & H. A. H. Bakker-Heeres 1982. Archaeobotanical studies in the Levant, 1: neolithic sites in the Damascus basin: Aswad, Ghoraifé and Ramad. *Paleohistoria* **24**, 165–256.

Wasse, A. 1994. *Pastoral adaptations in the central and southern Levant during the Neolithic: the sheep and goat bones from 'Ain Ghazal, Jordan*. BA Report, Institute of Archaeology, University College London.

Wright, K. I. 1993. Early Holocene ground stone assemblages in the Levant. *Levant* **25**, 93–111.

van Zeist, W. & J. A. H. Bakker-Heeres 1982. Archaeobotanical studies in the Levant 1. Neolithic sites in the Damascus Basin: Aswad, Ghoraifé and Ramad. *Paleohistoria* **24**, 165–256.

Zohary, D. 1992. Domestication of the Neolithic Near Eastern crop assemblage. In *Préhistoire de l'agriculture: nouvelles approches expérimentales et ethnographiques* [Monographie 6, Centre de Recherches Archéologiques], P. C. Anderson (ed.), 81–86. Paris: Editions du CNRS.

Zohary, D. & M. Hopf 1988. *Domestication of plants in the Old World: the origin and spread of cultivated plants in West Asia, Europe, and the Nile Valley*. Oxford: Oxford University Press.

CHAPTER TWELVE

Animal domestication – accident or intention?

Hans-Peter Uerpmann

In the year 1979 a print of the photograph now reproduced as Figure 12.1 was given to the author as a birthday present. The print was entitled: *The Neolithic Revolution?* and the gift was a response to the publication of a book on the origins of the neolithic economy (Uerpmann 1979). The picture – taken at the Stuttgart Zoo – shows a Hamadryas baboon riding on a North African barbary sheep. It was received as a joke rather than a contribution to science, and its deeper meanings were only recognized many years later during the preparation of the present chapter. The organizer of the conference for which this chapter was prepared invited me to consider "biological perspectives on animal domestication", and the question I then asked myself was whether there actually were biological perspectives on this process beyond size reduction, twisted horns, checkered colourations and reduced brain-sizes.

Figure 12.1 shows two animals interacting in a way that provokes the question: did the baboon domesticate the barbary sheep in order to sit on it? And, beyond that: are there relationships between different animal species comparable to human animal husbandry and the whole complex of keeping domestic livestock? Usually, of course, we consider the management of animals by humans as a cultural achievement particular to mankind.

Symbiosis and the niche concept

The relationship between humans and domesticates can, in general, be described as symbiotic, although it is a very special symbiosis for which there are no close parallels in the animal kingdom. However, we should be wary of considering ourselves as special in comparison to animals, because much of what we call culture is generically the same as what we call behaviour in animals, and many features that we think to be special in man are only special because we know and appreciate ourselves much more than any other living beings. We should recognize that the complex relationships between humans and domestic animals are really special forms of symbiosis, as Zeuner suggested over thirty years ago (Zeuner 1963: 36–64).

The photograph of the young baboon and the barbary sheep obviously shows some

Figure 12.1   The Neolithic Revolution? A Hamadryas baboon on the back of a North African Barbary sheep, Stuttgart Zoo. (Photograph from the author.)

form of playful symbiosis. The monkey has its fun and the sheep takes advantage of the grooming that is extended to it now and then. But any serious biologist will be appalled if this is called an example of symbiosis. He or she will say that this is a completely artificial situation, that the Hamadryas baboon and the barbary sheep never meet each other in the wild, because their natural ranges are far apart, and that even if they did meet they would never get acquainted enough for this sort of interspecific interaction.

There is no doubt that the animals in the photograph live in the unnatural environment of a zoo enclosure. The behaviour shown here is not natural in so far as it is never seen in the wild. But it is not wholly artificial either, because it developed by itself and was not induced by training by the zoo-keepers. What we can see here is that the repertoire of mammalian behaviour towards other species includes extra-ordinary possibilities that will become evident only – if at all – under very special conditions. Before we assume that animal domestication could only have been the result of rational human interference with animals, we must, therefore, exclude natural circumstances that might have created a situation comparable to that in a zoo enclosure, or any other very special set of preconditions.

The first thing that comes to mind in this context is the well known "oasis hypothesis" for the explanation of animal (and plant) domestication. This hypothesis, which seems to go back to Pumpelly,[1] was proposed and popularized by Childe (1928: 42–5, 1936: ch. v). It postulated that a mutual approach between humans and animals happened in oasis situations in Southwest Asia at the end of the last glacial period when oases shrank as a result of increasingly arid conditions in the early Holocene. We now realize that this hypothesis is ecologically naïve, and we also know that the direction of climatic change at the end of the Pleistocene was not from moist to dry but the reverse. The Late Pleistocene was a hyper-arid period in Southwest Asia and North Africa, and conditions became much more favourable in the Early Holocene. Thus, the "enclosure element" of the example illustrated in Figure 12.1, as paralleled in the "oasis hypothesis", cannot be invoked to explain the beginnings of animal domestication in Southwest Asia. We should anyway be on our guard against simplistic approaches to the problem, regardless of the fact that any written explanation of complex historical developments requires some simplification.

In evolutionary biology the niche concept has been successfully applied to explain biological diversification. It is also helpful in the present case. We can conceive the zoo enclosure of our example as a particular niche where the ranges of Hamadryas baboon and barbary sheep overlap, for whatever reasons, and where – because of the particular circumstances of the niche – they developed an interspecific relationship not seen anywhere outside the niche. However, although such a physical enclosure is conceivable as a niche, the niches we have to imagine as effective during early animal domestication were "circumstantial" rather than physical.

Domestication of the dog

In order to elaborate this concept, it is helpful first to consider the domestication of the dog, although this has nothing directly to do with the origins of the neolithic economy. The wolf is the ancestor of the dog. Ever since man entered Eurasia about 1.5 million years ago, the ranges of humans and wolves overlapped geographically. Except for the past few millennia, when hunting became insignificant for human subsistence, the two species demonstrated remarkable parallels in their patterns of behaviour. In both species, social hunting of large prey animals was an important part of the subsistence strategy. Parallel evolution of social structures and means of vocal and visual communication in humans and wolves can, among other features, be explained on this basis.

Some of the factors influencing the interspecific relationships between wolf and man are listed in Figure 12.2. Factors such as the mutual fear of predation keep the two species apart, but there are also relatively strong attractions between them. Of particular importance is the fact that communication is quite easy between man and wolf. Signs of aggression, fear, submission, joy, and other kinds of behaviour are mutually

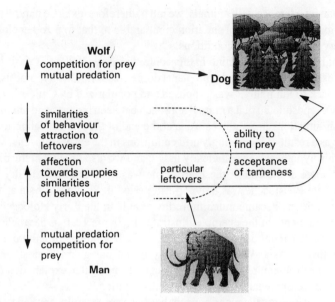

Figure 12.2   Wolf domestication in terms of the niche concept.

understood. One should remember Romulus and Remus – the legendary founders of Rome – in this context. Wolves are the only animals to which several old legends accredit the ability to raise human offspring.

Evidence for a mutual approach of man and wolf exists from Upper Palaeolithic sites in eastern and central Europe, where environmental circumstances and techno-logical developments enabled humans to prey on animals that were beyond the capa-bilities of wolves, and which produced sufficient edible material to allow the successful hunter to tolerate some scavenging by the local wolf population – although, no doubt, many wolves paid with their skins for attempts to participate in a mammoth feast. In these circumstances, some young wolves seem to have been adopted by human hunters. Because of the extraordinary size of the principal prey – mammoths – the wolves had a chance to survive for some time in the companionship of people. There are finds of intermediate dog-wolves from the Upper Palaeolithic of central and eastern Europe, which indicate that a "circumstantial niche" existed for these animals that separated them from the rest of the wolf population to the extent that dental anomalies and a slight reduction of tooth size could become manifest – changes known to start to occur very fast in captive wolf populations. Apparently the niche remained "shallow" throughout the Upper Palaeolithic. Genetic isolation between tame and wild wolves does not seem to have been strict or regularly maintained over several generations.

The situation changed and the niche became "deeper" at the end of the Pleistocene when forests started to cover most of the formerly open steppes of Europe. Human hunters, with their poorly developed sense of smell, had a serious handicap now in finding their prey. The occasional tame wolf puppy that had a chance to demonstrate its superior capabilities of remote sensing would now have found acceptance and appreciation as a hunting companion. The relationships between the two species thus acquired a new quality, and genetic isolation between wild and tame wolves could thenceforth increase to the point where the dog as a distinct animal starts to become visible in the zooarchaeological record at mesolithic sites in Denmark, in England at Star Carr and in other parts of the northern hemisphere (for further details on dog domestication see Clutton-Brock 1981: 34–45).

Domestication of herbivores

If we now try to apply this explanatory approach to the domestication of herbivores, we see immediately that the basic relationships between the species involved are completely different. In Figure 12.3 the factors that determine man/animal relationships are compared for wild sheep and wolves. The fundamental differences are easy to recognize. There is nothing that attracts wild herbivores to their human hunters, and there is only our nursing instinct for animal babies that might provide a reason for a temporary symbiosis between humans and wild sheep or other young herbivores. The idea – favoured by Eric Higgs and his followers (e.g. Higgs 1972) – that specialization by hunters on a particular species of prey finally led to its domestication is nothing but a theoretical concept. Ecological reality tells us that specialization by a predator results in refined avoidance strategies by the prey. For example, intense hunting pressure can cause a species to become completely nocturnal. Animals from hunted wild populations can be taken hostage, and perhaps, to some extent, can be "brain-washed" by an experienced animal keeper, but the so-called "herd following" of specialized hunters will only have made the animals even shyer and will certainly not have turned them into domesticates – not to speak of the fact that it is physically impossible for human hunters to follow a herd of wild sheep or goats closely in their

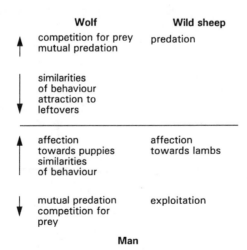

Figure 12.3 Wolf, sheep and man: factors influencing interspecific relations.

extremely broken natural habitats in Southwest Asia. Only a very young animal can become acquainted with humans under friendly circumstances and will then not see them as potential predators for the rest of its life. Both the monkey and the barbary sheep in Figure 12.1 are young. Only the young of the two populations kept together in the enclosure developed a special kind of interspecific relationship; the older ones remained indifferent to each other.

For herbivore domestication one has to assume that this very special relationship between man and animal had its origin in the nursing of very young individuals of the respective species (Galton 1865, Serpell 1989). This is the only plausible way to produce tame animals that then could be founders of a domestic herd. It is important, however, to stress that a tame animal is not automatically a domestic animal. A certain degree of tameness is necessary for domestication, but further steps in animal management are required to complete the process. By definition, the transformation from wild to domestic cannot happen within the generation of the individuals originally taken from the wild. Domestication is a process that requires sustained breeding of tame animal populations. From the beginning, these populations should be genetically isolated from the populations of their wild relatives. Most animal species can be tamed, but only a few have become domesticated.

The simplicity of what can be called the "nursing hypothesis" of herbivore domestication is however contradicted by the obvious complexity of the actual historical processes that brought it about. Although it is possible to imagine a natural, unconcious approach between man and wolf leading to the domestication of the dog, it seems very unlikely that something similar should happen with a herbivore. It appears that herbivore (sheep and goat) domestication occurred spontaneously only once (in Southwest Asia), which must be considered as statistical evidence for the low probability of such a process occurring. And it is also evidence against the assumption that the first domestication of a herbivore was a conscious process. If herbivore domestication had happened as a deliberate, rational response to protein shortage (for whatever reason), then it would surely have happened much earlier, at many places in the world, and to more species than just sheep and goat, which – to our present knowledge – were the first domestic herbivores. We must continue, therefore, to look for a constellation of circumstances that made the improbable possible, such as the constellation of circumstances that allowed the baboon to ride on a barbary sheep.

The search for the constellations of circumstances in which early herbivore domestication took place must be guided by the actual knowledge of this process, which has accumulated over the past hundred years. Geographically we know the general area in which sheep and goats must have been domesticated. The wild bezoar, *Capra aegagrus* – the progenitor of the domestic goat – is endemic to the mountains of Southwest and western Central Asia (Uerpmann 1987: 113–8; 1989a). Its range at the time of its first domestication was more extensive than today, but we can be sure that it did not extend into Europe or North Africa. It is more difficult to establish the natural distribution of sheep (Uerpmann 1987: 124–32; 1989a), mainly because wild mouflons exist on islands in the western Mediterranean, but we now have good evidence that these animals are not really wild but feral, having been introduced there as domesticates early in the Neolithic. The natural range of wild sheep has its centre in the moun-

tain steppes of Central Asia and extends, in such habitats, westwards across Iran to
Asia Minor. Formerly it ended at the edge of the Mediterranean forests in western and
southern Anatolia, and extended southwards along the same vegetational border into
the hinterland of the Levantine coast. To the east the range of wild sheep extends
through Siberia and reaches western North America from Alaska to Mexico. Chromosomal research in the 1960s and 1970s has shown, however, that only the western
Asiatic mouflon of Southwest Asia, the group called *Ovis orientalis* by the present
author, is ancestral to domestic sheep (Uerpmann 1987: 126). Therefore, the area
where sheep and goat could have been domesticated extends from western Turkey to
Baluchistan and from the Caucasus to Sinai. It is within these biogeographical limits
that we have to look for evidence of this process.

There is no need here to discuss the biological evidence for domestication in sheep
and goat, but most researchers in this field accept the view that a reduction in average
animal size early in the Neolithic is due to the beginning of economically significant
animal husbandry (Uerpmann 1979). This is thought to have occurred by the time of
the Pre-Pottery Neolithic B (PPNB) and its chronological equivalents. The so-called
Pre-Pottery Neolithic A (PPNA) lacked animal husbandry and is here included in the
Proto-Neolithic (Uerpmann 1989b).

By the time of the PPNB there were domestic goats in Israel and Jordan, and its chronologically equivalent cultures farther north also had domestic sheep. Therefore, we
must look at the conditions during the immediately preceding proto-neolithic period
if we want to study the circumstances of early herbivore domestication. Important features of the full Neolithic developed during this period, the most obvious of which is
architecture. The oldest known villages in the world belong to the proto-neolithic
period in Southwest Asia, and if they are plotted on a map we see a striking congruence
between their distribution and that of the dense stands of wild barley shown by Harlan
& Zohary (1966) (cf. Uerpmann 1980). However, there is not only biogeographical
evidence to connect the proto-neolithic settlements to the distribution of wild cereals.
Harvesting tools, mortars, and silos are other features indicating a dominant role of
grain and perhaps pulses in the economy of this period. And this grain-based economy
must have influenced the attitude of the proto-neolithic people towards animals.

The proto-neolithic people had essentially to obtain their meat by hunting. As usual
in hunter–gatherer populations, the only impetus to keep live animals for a certain
time was the nursing of animal babies. In Figure 12.4 some of the factors that influence the lifetime of animals raised for this reason by unspecialized hunter–gatherers
are compared to those characteristic of proto-neolithic hunters and cereal gatherers/
cultivators. The sedentary, grain-based way of life of the proto-neolithic people would
have increased the chances that young animals would become sexually mature and
start to produce offspring in captivity, and there would then be an increased probability that their captors would realize the economic potential of this domestic production of offspring.

However, in reality, the increased probabilities of animal companions having a
longer life-span cannot have been very high. The proto-neolithic period lasted for
about two millennia and there are no indications that animal husbandry replaced hunting as a means of providing protein during this period. Sedentary life and a hunting

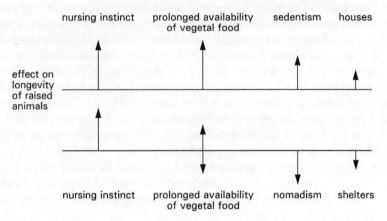

Proto-neolithic hunters and cereal gatherers/cultivators

nursing instinct   prolonged availability   sedentism   houses
of vegetal food

effect on
longevity
of raised
animals

nursing instinct   prolonged availability   nomadism   shelters
of vegetal food

Unspecialized hunters and gatherers

Figure 12.4 Some factors affecting man–animal relationships.

economy are to some extent mutually exclusive and at some of the proto-neolithic settlements there are suggestions of severe protein shortage, such as evidence that people
may have started to eat snails, frogs and foxes. Protein shortage would certainly not
favour the longevity of young animals raised in captivity. Nevertheless, a few successive years of good cereal harvests in only a few of the proto-neolithic villages may
have been sufficient to establish some productive flocks of captive herbivores – and
if there was a general shortage of protein it would have encouraged acceptance of the
new method of meat production. In any case, there are elements in the particular circumstances of the Proto-Neolithic that would have increased the chances of herbivore
domestication happening as a natural process. Human ingenuity is only needed in this
hypothesis to the extent that someone had to realize the potential of what was going
on among the animals raised in the settlements – probably by the women and children
– and had to transform it into an economic practice.

So far, we have only considered longevity as a factor favouring the reproduction
of sheep and goats in captivity, but theoretically Figure 12.4 applies to all herbivores
that were in contact with proto-neolithic people. The following species are known to
have been exploited by proto-neolithic hunters (listed from the largest to the smallest):

aurochs	*Bos primigenius*
red deer	*Cervus elaphus*
onager/ass	*Equus hemionus/africanus*
wild boar	*Sus scrofa*
fallow deer	*Dama mesopotamica*
wild goat	*Capra aegagrus*
wild sheep	*Ovis orientalis*
roe deer	*Capreolus capreolus*
gazelles	*Gazella gazella/subgutturosa*

Not all of them will stimulate the human nursing instinct, at least not for a lengthy period. We can therefore exclude some species from an unconcious process of domestication simply on the base of their size and rate of growth. This is true for the aurochs, whose calves would have become unmanageable after a few weeks. Red deer, especially the large subspecies living in Southwest Asia, would have been much the same, and also the equids, which are anyway difficult to control. Young wild boar make nice pets and the females remain manageable well into sexual maturity, although the males do not. Their rude behaviour would have restricted the length of time their companionship would have been tolerated in a proto-neolithic village to less than the time necessary for unplanned reproduction. The first five species – aurochs, red deer, onager, ass and wild boar – can therefore be excluded as candidates for self-domestication.

Of the remaining species, gazelles were most important as a source of food for many proto-neolithic settlers in the Levant. There has been much speculation about their possible domestication (e.g. Zeuner 1963: 434–5). Young gazelles can become very tame and even the adults remain attractive to people. They could be regarded as prime candidates for lasting companionship with man, but no convincing evidence for the domestication of any species of gazelle has been discovered. This becomes understandable if we consider the difficulties that zoos have even nowadays in trying to establish gazelle populations. Gazelles are difficult to breed in captivity because they have a complex pattern of territorial behaviour during the rutting season. They must, therefore, also be excluded as candidates for self-domestication.

Roe deer is also well known as a species that cannot be kept close to man for lengthy periods. It is much more difficult to domesticate than fallow deer, which species is just now becoming a full domesticate kept as a farm animal in many parts of Europe. With regard to a possible unplanned start of reproduction in a population of young roe or fallow deer kept as pets, their patterns of rutting behaviour may, as in other species of deer, have been too complex.

Sheep and goats remain on the list as the only animals suited to companionship with humans as lambs or kids, a companionship that could potentially last long enough for reproduction to start and continue under the restricted conditions of life in a proto-neolithic village. This is attributable particularly to the mountainous character of their natural habitat, where rutting often takes place on a few square metres of flatter ground on a mountain crest. These animals are also used to taking shelter in caves. They would therefore have accepted houses more easily than the other animals on the list. Thus, the circumstances prevalent in proto-neolithic villages did not create a niche for herbivore domestication in general; the niche suited only sheep and goats. It must be seen as a rare chance that these animals occurred just at the place where this niche opened in the early Holocene.

In summary, the first domestication of herbivorous animals can be explained as a natural process that resulted from a rare constellation of environmental, biological and social factors that occurred together only in a very restricted area of the world, namely western Southwest Asia, during a short span of geological time, namely the beginning of the present interglacial period. Conscious human action was not required, only reaction and transformation when the process was already well under way.

Following the establishment of a full neolithic economy, including sheep and/or goat husbandry, new criteria must be applied to the consideration of animal domestication. After the invention of the steam engine it was only a matter of time before the petrol engine followed. When the basic techniques of animal management had been learned with sheep and goats, a more difficult species could be approached consciously and domesticated in due course. It is significant that cattle domestication cannot be pinpointed on the map. There seem to have been at least three independent centres: one in the southern Levant, one in Anatolia, and one on the eastern margins of Southwest Asia. The beginnings of pig domestication must have followed a similar pattern, but this process is still poorly understood by zooarchaeologists.

With four domesticated species of herbivore – sheep, goat, cattle and pig – and the dog in addition, the neolithic economy was fully equipped to spread over Eurasia and Africa. It is remarkable that little "domestication euphoria" broke out, which might have incorporated other suitable species, especially among the African ruminants. A few additional herbivores were domesticated when new niches opened early in the metal ages. The domestication of the donkey and the horse are probably responses to the increased need for means of transportation when it became necessary to bring ores and fuel to the smelting centres and to distribute their products. In the case of the horse, and probably also the donkey, domestication was multicentric (Uerpmann 1990) and for the horse certainly not restricted to southern Russia – if it happened there at all in early times.

Domestication of other animals

Finally, taking the niche concept a little further, it should be mentioned that a niche opened for the domestication of small animals, such as rabbit and chicken, when people started to live in cities and were unable to stock their own farmyards with a complete set of the larger domestic animals. We should also recognize that we are now witnessing the domestication of many new species in fish-tanks and terraria all over the civilized world. This niche results from our alienation from nature, which also makes it difficult for many of us to perceive interspecific relationships between mankind and other mammals as biological rather than cultural features.

Note

1. According to a comment made by Richard H. Meadow after the conference that gave rise to this book, Pumpelly went to Anau in order to test the oasis hypothesis, which seems to have been discussed already in the nineteenth century. [*Editor's comment*: I can find no reference in Pumpelly's account (1908) of his work in Central Asia to his having gone to Anau in order to test the oasis hypothesis, but he does introduce the concept of "progressive desiccation" in the Preface (p. xxiv), and he suggests that the post-glacial trend towards aridity "continued through thousands of years" and caused "related peoples [to become] isolated in oases" (p. 64). That Childe was familiar with Pumpelly's work is clear from a reference in *The most ancient East* (1928: 223), but this refers to "trade" goods at Anau and bears no relation to the oasis hypothesis.]

References

Childe, V. G. 1928. *The most ancient East: the oriental prelude to European prehistory.* London: Kegan Paul, Trench, Trubner.

— 1936. *Man makes himself.* London: Watts.

Clutton-Brock, J. 1981. *Domesticated animals from early times.* London: Heinemann & British Museum (Natural History).

Galton, F. 1865. The first steps towards the domestication of animals. *Transactions of the Ethnological Society of London* (NS) **3**, 122–38.

Harlan, J. R. & D. Zohary 1966. Distribution of wild wheats and barley. *Science* **153**, 1074–80.

Higgs, E. S. (ed.) 1972. *Papers in economic prehistory.* Cambridge: Cambridge University Press.

Pumpelly, R. (ed.) 1908. *Explorations in Turkestan: expedition of 1904: prehistoric civilizations of Anau* [2 vols]. Publication 73, Carnegie Institution, Washington DC.

Serpell, J. 1989. Pet-keeping and animal domestication: a reappraisal. In *The walking larder: patterns of domestication, pastoralism, and predation.* J. Clutton-Brock (ed.), 10–21. London: Unwin Hyman.

Uerpmann, H-P. 1979. *Probleme der Neolithisierung des Mittelmeerraumes* [Beihefte zum Tübinger Atlas des Vorderen Orients, Reihe B (Geisteswissenschaften) 28]. Wiesbaden: Dr L. Reichert.

— 1980. *Middle East: Protoneolithic period* [Tübinger Atlas of the Middle East, map B I 6]. Wiesbaden: Dr L. Reichert.

— 1987. *The ancient distribution of ungulate mammals in the Middle East* [Beihefte zum Tübinger Atlas des Vorderen Orients, Reihe A (Naturwissenschaften) 27]. Wiesbaden: Dr L. Reichert.

— 1989a. *Middle East: ancestral forms of domestic animals and early domestication* [Tübinger Atlas of the Middle East, map A VI 16]. Wiesbaden: Dr L. Reichert.

— 1989b. Animal exploitation and the phasing of the transition from the Palaeolithic to the Neolithic. In *The walking larder: patterns of domestication, pastoralism, and predation.* J. Clutton-Brock (ed.), 91–6. London: Unwin Hyman.

— 1990. Die Domestikation des Pferdes im Chalkolithikum West- und Mitteleuropas. *Madrider Mitteilungen* **31**, 109–53.

Zeuner, F. E. 1963. *A history of domesticated animals.* London: Hutchinson.

CHAPTER THIRTEEN

The beginning of caprine domestication in Southwest Asia

Tony Legge

Introduction

The bones of wild sheep (*Ovis orientalis*) and wild goats (*Capra aegagrus*) are known from rather few sites in Southwest Asia before the neolithic period, a situation that is in marked contrast to the later abundance of those species as domesticates. Bones of wild sheep and goat have been recovered from fewer than 20 late palaeolithic and mesolithic sites, and in only a few instances have both species been identified at the same site. Uerpmann (1987) lists six pre-neolithic sites with unquestionable identifications of both sheep and goat, to which list can be added the site of Wadi Judayid (Henry & Turnbull 1985). Further, even where caprine bones are found, they usually represent a minor food resource relative to the more abundant bones of deer, cattle, and pig, or, especially in steppe habitats, of gazelle and onager.

The natural habitats of wild sheep and goats are somewhat different. Goats typically occupy steep and rocky habitats. Although they are good climbers, their slow gait on level ground makes them vulnerable to predation and thus restricts their distribution. Sheep are good runners and can live in more undulating terrain, giving them a wider distribution in the wild (Legge & Rowley-Conwy 1986, Uerpmann 1987).

The local distribution and comparative rarity of pre-neolithic caprines contrasts with their great abundance and wide dispersal during the later Aceramic Neolithic, the period during which it is accepted that these species were domesticated in Southwest Asia. The assumption is easily made that caprines were wild when their remains constitute a small part of the fauna of a site, and domestic when they constitute a large proportion. This is probably correct in most instances, even if this is an oversimplified view of a complex process. It is important therefore to try to determine the status of the caprines found in some aceramic neolithic settlements, where they constitute a small part of an otherwise wild fauna; for example at Tepe Asiab (Bökönyi 1977), in the Pre-Pottery Neolithic A (PPNA) levels at Tell es-Sultan (Clutton-Brock 1971, 1979, Clutton-Brock & Uerpmann 1974) and Tell Abu Hureyra (Legge 1975, 1977, Legge & Rowley-Conwy 1987), and in the earlier levels at Çayönü (Lawrence 1982).[1] Were the caprines at these settlements domesticated while still a minor part of a fauna of otherwise wild mammals?

In the following discussion, archaeological sites are attributed to the periods published by the *Maison de l'Orient* (Aurenche et al. 1987); most belong to Periods 2 (10,300–9600 bp) and 3 (9600–8600 bp).

The recognition of early mammal domestication

The criteria used in the recognition of mammal domestication have been widely reviewed (e.g. Bökönyi 1969, 1989, Davis 1987, Meadow 1989). Those that bear most directly upon the recognition of the earliest mammal domestication can be summarized as:

- *A change in species abundance*   A marked increase in the proportion of a species within the sequence at one site, or at the sites of one region, can be taken as evidence for domestication.
- *The introduction of a new species*   Where a new species enters the archaeological record it may be assumed to have been introduced as a domestic mammal if the cultural setting is appropriate and the species is one that is domestic now.
- *Morphological and body size change*   Most mammal species have been changed in body size or other morphological traits by domestication. A sample of the wild species from the same locality is needed against which to measure such changes. Such samples are seldom available.
- *Population structure*   In a domestic herd or flock, the age and sex structure is manipulated by its owners in order to maximize outputs by the conservation of females and the selective slaughter of sub-adult males for consumption. It is problematic to argue that a given population structure differs from a wild norm, in that none such exist. The identification of a high frequency of sub-adult bones in the sample *and* an adult herd in which females are the majority is evidence for domestication.

Other criteria that have commonly been suggested, such as the finding of artefacts associated with domestication or of artistic representations that depict domestication (Bökönyi 1969), are seldom relevant when interest focuses on the earliest stages of domestication.

These methods for recognizing early domestication all suffer from limitations, and no single test can provide an unequivocal answer. Difficulties are encountered because of low numbers of bones in many archaeological samples, sometimes made worse by poor methods of recovery in excavation, and also by the sparsity of the evidence that we have about the body size and morphology of pre-domestic caprines. The archaeological sequence in Southwest Asia also shows a break in occupation between the Mesolithic and the Neolithic at most sites. Those sites where the economy was based on hunting and gathering seldom used the same land resources as early farming settlements (Legge 1977), which introduces a further environmental variable into the study of domestication processes. Consequently mammals can seldom be studied in both their pre-domestic and domesticated forms at one site.

In the study of mammal domestication, interest has also focused on definition of the stages through which this process may have gone; much has been written about "incipient" and "proto" domestication, suggesting a looser relationship than that usually envisaged with herded animals (see, for example, Hecker 1982, Horwitz 1989, 1993). Given the problems associated with the recognition of early domestication, it seems improbable that the material available for study can yet be used to determine such finer gradations of the process, even supposing they correspond to reality. For the purposes of this chapter a narrow view is taken of domestication: the evidence for change in species distribution, body size and manipulated population structures is taken to reflect the degree of population isolation and transformation indicative of human control.

Size change under domestication

Meadow (1989) has focused attention on the work of Widdowson (1980, Widdowson & Lister 1991) as a means of explaining size reduction under domestication. In her work, Widdowson showed that a low level of maternal nutrition will give rise to smaller offspring. By this process, reduced body size can represent a rapid phenotypic change that would be manifest in a single generation. Genetic selection would result in further modification. There may be some evidence for this practice in the available bone measurements. For example, at Ganj Dareh (Period 3) Hesse (1978: fig. 60) has demonstrated the selective cull of sub-adult male goats for meat production but it is notable that those males culled before their bones were fused commonly show *larger* bone measurements than do the males that were retained into adult life. The same phenomenon has been observed during study of the goat bones from Tell Abu Hureyra (see below). It is possible that this reflects a deliberate selection of the smaller males as breeding stock. Both these sites are discussed further below.

The use of size change in the study of caprine domestication

Much recent work has focused on the observation of size change as a means of identifying early domestication (Uerpmann 1979, Meadow 1984, Helmer 1989), although the scarcity of sheep and goat bones at most early neolithic sites in Southwest Asia raises obvious difficulties for the determination of body size and the detection of size change. Many samples do not have enough specimens of any one bone for the measurements to yield much information about the body size of the population. To compensate for this difficulty, Uerpmann (1979: figs 2, 3) introduced to archaeology a method by which measurements from different bones (humerus, radius, metapodials, etc.) can be combined in one histogram. Measurements of these bones taken from a modern "standard animal" of the same species provide a baseline against which the archaeological specimens may be compared by the proportion that they are larger or smaller than the standard, now usually calculated by the log-ratio method (Meadow 1984). Although this method is now quite widely used as a test for early domestication, it may be noted that there are potential technical problems that bear on its use, as well as the limitation of relying on a single test for the recognition of domestication.

By the use of this method, Uerpmann has shown that sheep and goats in Southwest Asia show no significant size change through the later Palaeolithic, Mesolithic and "Proto-Neolithic", but became significantly smaller in the Aceramic Neolithic. Although this analysis provided a valuable overview of the process of caprine domestication, it cannot be accepted without reservation, because it combines several smaller bone samples into larger units based on their cultural association with the Aceramic Neolithic, and there are consequently some uncertainties in the chronological groupings of the samples employed.

The caprine bone samples utilized by Uerpmann come from sites very widely spread in space and time. The bone measurements for mesolithic goats (Uerpmann 1979) are from two sites (one in Iraq, one in Lebanon: 49 bones); the proto-neolithic sample is from four sites (one in Jordan, two in Iraq, one in Iran: 67 bones) and the Aceramic Neolithic is represented by four sites (Asikli Höyük, Çayönü and Çan Hasan III in Turkey and Ganj Dareh in Iran: 357 bones). The aceramic neolithic sample shows a significant size reduction from sites of the previous few millennia. However, two problems can be identified. First, from the published evidence it is evident that most bone measurements in the aceramic neolithic sample come from Ganj Dareh and, secondly, it is probable that the sample combines both wild and domestic goats; it is likely, on the basis of their large size, that the goat bones from Asikli Höyük and Çayönü (early levels) are from wild animals, whereas those from Ganj Dareh are domestic (see below). By the same method, the sheep bones also show a marked size reduction with the Aceramic Neolithic. In Uerpmann's samples, all mesolithic sheep-bone measurements are from Palegawra Cave in Iraq (47 bones), whereas the proto-neolithic bone measurements are from four sites (one in Syria, two in Iraq, one in Iran: 98 bones) and the aceramic neolithic specimens are from four sites (three in Turkey and one in Syria: 284 bones). Again, very different parts of the Fertile Crescent are represented in these samples.

Helmer (1989) approached the investigation of early domestic caprines by following Uerpmann's method, but treating the bone measurements from each site separately. Although this approach may require working with uncomfortably small samples, there is a consistency in the patterns that have emerged in Helmer's study. From a study of 12 sites, he shows a significant size reduction in sheep *during* the Aceramic Neolithic; the sheep bones from the Period 2 sites of Tell Mureybet and Tepe Asiab, and the early Period 3 sites of Cafer Höyük, Asikli Höyük, and Ganj Dareh are of large body size, whereas those from seven later Period 3 sites in his sample are significantly smaller. The goat shows the same pattern, although only at Cafer Höyük in Turkey and Tepe Asiab in Iran are large goats found, and at nine sites from later Period 3 the goats are significantly smaller than these.

The degree of size-change observed in these samples, and its timing, makes it probable that domestication was the cause. However, problems remain in the use of comparisons based on size alone, especially by the log-ratio method (see also Ducos 1991). For example, the processes of taphonomy and post-depositional destruction remove many bones from the archaeological record, usually those of the lowest density. For the limb bones, these are obviously the unfused specimens. In caprines the different limb bones fuse in a sequence that begins at about 6–8 months of age and this continues to more than 36 months of age. Early fusion confers a significant advantage for bone survival in archaeological samples. Consequently, many bone assemblages contain a large proportion of early-fusing bones, such as the distal humerus, or bones that have no fusion point, such as the astragalus. These bones also have well defined measurement points, and their good survival means that they comprise a significant part of published lists of bone measurements. Yet it is now evident that these bones grow significantly *after* fusion, or, in the case of the astragalus, for some time after the bone has developed an apparently adult form (Legge & Rowley-Conwy 1988). Measurements of such bones are thus age-dependent and the resulting size distribution is partly a reflection of the adult body size of the population, and partly of the age structure of the population. Thus, the combination of different bones in a log-ratio diagram will show a distribution and range that is, to an unknown degree, age-dependent.

The representation of the sexes may also have a significant effect upon the results. As noted above, domestication can be recognized where a bone sample shows a selected age profile; in goats, a species with marked sexual dimorphism, this conclusion is reinforced by a bias towards adult females among the bones. In both sheep and goat the sexes spend much of the year apart in different habitats. Seasonal hunting episodes might therefore result in a marked bias towards one sex or the other; indeed, this was argued by Hesse (1984) in his interpretation of the caprine bones from Level E at Ganj Dareh in Iran. In this case, a sample of few bones would not reflect the entire *range* of population size (Legge 1981, Meadow 1984), leading to only a partial view and the possibility of a wrong interpretation about the status of the specimens, especially where low sample numbers have been compensated by the use of log-ratio diagrams.

A further limitation in this method will be apparent to any who have made use of it. The different bones that are combined in a sample commonly show different degrees of variation from the standard measurement. For example, astragalus measurements may be larger than the standard that is used, whereas metacarpal measurements may be found to be smaller than the standard. This raises the possibility that the pattern that emerges will be dependent upon which bones have most often survived, which may not be in the same proportions from site to site.

The restricted nature of the material available thus presents several difficulties. First, wild caprines are obviously found at sites that were within their natural habitat, whereas most sites with domestic caprines were probably outside those areas. A significant local environmental change is therefore associated with the process of domestication (cf. Uerpmann and Hole in Chs 12 and 14 in this volume). When evidence for apparently small caprines is found, it cannot be assumed that the putative domestic population is being measured against its ancestral population when the samples come from widely dispersed sites. As Uerpmann (1978) has noted, modern wild sheep differ in size according to the environment in which they are found; in the wetter uplands of Turkey and Iraq they are today larger than in more arid regions, which would also hold for archaeological specimens from many sites to the east and the west of the Tigris–Euphrates basin.

Secondly, the major change in caprine abundance occurs *within* the Aceramic Neolithic at some sites (Legge 1972, 1977). Most mammal bones from earlier aceramic neolithic sites are of wild species (gazelles and onagers, or, in wetter areas, wild cattle, pigs and deer), whereas later aceramic neolithic sites have abundant caprines and few wild mammals. It has been suggested that this change was related to the destruction of the local wild fauna during the Aceramic Neolithic (Legge 1977, Legge & Rowley-Conwy 1987) and the replacement of this lost protein by the appearance of domestic stock. The use of a generalized aceramic neolithic grouping masks this major change.

There is a third problem that also bears on the study of these bone samples. The most commonly used system of bone measurements was published nearly 20 years ago (von den Driesch 1976), but even now the alphabetical codes that designate each measurement are far from commonly employed in publications. For example, in the von den Driesch system the distal humerus can be measured either as the articular width BT (smaller) or the total epiphysis width Bd (larger), but without the appropriate designation it is not always possible to be sure which measurement was taken from the descriptions given in many publications. The most commonly published measurement of this bone appears to be Bd, which is the *maximum* width dimension of the trochlea, including the lateral epicondyle on the lateral surface of the trochlea. Measurements of the fused distal humeri from aceramic neolithic caprines at Abu Hureyra show that the Bd measurement is between 1 per cent and 9 per cent greater than BT on the same specimen. Bearing in mind the probability that the epicondyles develop more with advancing age in mammals, it seems likely that this measurement too is significantly age-dependent. Thus, an already limited set of data is rendered more uncertain still.

The evidence for early caprine domestication at sites in different regions of Southwest Asia can now be reviewed, concentrating on those sites where some body of published data is available.

Turkey

Cafer Höyük (Period 3)

The site of Cafer Höyük is dated to the early ninth millennium bp and has a fauna of caprines (53–63%), with some cattle, pig and deer. Both sheep and goats are identified, although goats make up 85–90 per cent of the identified caprine bones. Helmer (1989: figs 6 & 7) used the log-ratio method to show that the sheep bones from Cafer are as large as those from Tell Mureybet, and the goats are as large as those from Tepe Asiab (Bökönyi 1977, and see below). On this basis he interpreted them as representing wild populations. For the more abundant goat bones this conclusion is further supported by the measurements of the distal humerus (Fig. 13.1), which do not show the numerical bias towards adult females that may be anticipated in a domestic population (Helmer 1989: fig. 9).

Asikli Höyük (Period 3)

Payne (1985) found that the small sample of bones from Asikli Höyük (early ninth millennium bp) included both sheep and goat. Their status is not clear. The bones come from large animals, although Payne notes that the mandibles are from young animals and fall into his D and E age classes (1–3 years). Helmer (1989: fig. 6) shows

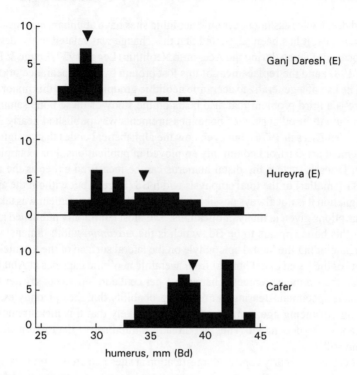

Figure 13.1 Goats: distribution of the distal humerus BT measurement; the arrow marks the mean of each population.

Sources of bone measurements used in Figures 13.1–13.10
Abu Hureyra (Legge & Rowley-Conwy: unpublished), 'Ain Ghazal (Köhler-Rollefson 1989: fig. 1), Tepe Asiab (Bökönyi 1977), Basta (Becker 1991: fig. 3), Beidha (Hecker 1984), Cafer (Helmer 1989: fig. 9), Çayönü (Lawrence 1980; U = upper levels, E = early levels), Ganj Dareh (Hesse 1978). The single capital letters in parentheses in Figures 13.1–13.10 refer to site levels.

that the eight sheep bones from Asikli are as large as those from Cafer and Mureybet. However, this is not a wholly reliable comparison, as the small Asikli sample includes measurements of three bones that were only referred to sheep (Payne 1985: Table 4) and one distal humerus where the published BT measurement is compared with the larger Bd measurement published for the Mureybet sheep (illustrated in Ducos 1968, 1978: measurement DTD). The five radiocarbon dates from Asikli all fall within the earlier half of the ninth millennium bp, and thus match the earlier part of the Cafer sequence. The chronological evidence supports the probability that the Asikli caprines were wild.

Çayönü Tepesi (Period 3)

The site of Çayönü is dated to the late tenth to early ninth millennia bp and has a fauna in which cattle, pig and red deer comprise the larger part. Caprines comprise about 10 per cent in the earlier "AD area" and 26 per cent in the later "H area" (Lawrence

1980, 1982). By the later phases of occupation at Çayönü, caprines had risen to over 80 per cent of the large mammals. In the earlier publication Lawrence concluded that the sheep were domestic, but that evidence for goat domestication was uncertain. A combined sample of mandibles showed that approximately 35 per cent came from animals that had not completed their adult dentition, but no further data on the age structure are given. More recently, Lawrence (1982) has suggested that the caprines were wild in the lower levels at Çayönü and that both species were domestic in the upper levels. The report gives some bone measurements, but only as sample number, mean and range.

The distal humerus and astragalus of goat are fairly numerous from both the early and later phases. Both sets of measurements differ mainly at the larger end of the range, where the earlier sample has more large specimens (Figs 13.2, 13.3). For the sheep, there is also a size reduction between these levels, although this is most evident in the distal humerus measurement (Figs 13.4, 13.5). Uerpmann (1979: fig. 5) has shown that the Çayönü sheep are considerably smaller than a combined sample from Asikli and Çan Hasan III, although in the light of more recent stratigraphic divisions at Çayönü it is uncertain how this information relates to the earlier and later phases at the site. However, the limited data suggest that the later Çayönü caprines are of a similar size to other samples within this area that are interpreted as domestic. The sheep from the "West area" at Çayönü are also small (Fig. 13.6).

There is also a shift from predominant goats to a larger proportion of sheep through the occupation at the site. Lawrence's data (1982: table 3) show that goats outnumbered sheep by about 4:1 in the earlier levels, but that the two species were more nearly equal in the later levels. This change is paralleled in the Abu Hureyra sequence and at other sites (see below), that also show a progressive shift to a larger proportion of sheep through the archaeological sequence. This is interpreted as a response to

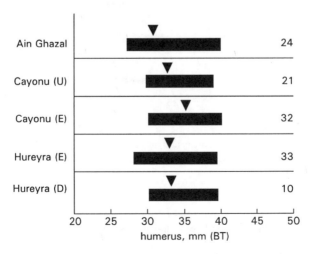

Figure 13.2 Goats: mean and range of the distal humerus BT measurement; number of bones in the sample shown in right-hand column.

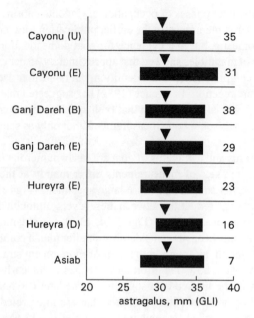

Figure 13.3   Goats: mean and range of the astragalus GLI measurement; number of bones in the sample shown in right-hand column.

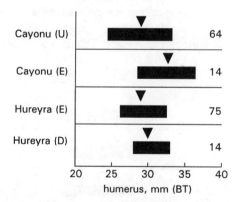

Figure 13.4   Sheep: mean and range of the distal humerus BT measurement; number of bones in the sample shown in right-hand column.

landscape changes, with a preferential grazing species replacing a browsing species as the woody vegetation receded under herding pressure. Thus, the increased proportion of caprines in the later phases at Çayönü, and the greater proportion of sheep at the same time, can also be taken as indicative of their husbandry.

Helmer (1985: 120) notes that the sheep and goat bones from Cafer are larger than

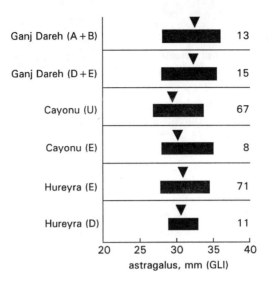

Figure 13.5 Sheep: mean and range of the astragalus GLI measurement; number of bones in the sample shown in right-hand column.

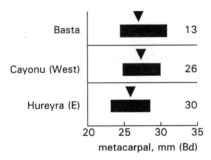

Figure 13.6 Sheep: mean and range of the metacarpal Bd measurement; number of bones in the sample shown in right-hand column.

those from Çayönü. However, the only published measurements that correspond between the two sites are those of the distal humerus of goats (Lawrence 1982: table 2; Helmer 1985: table III). In Lawrence's description of her measurements, it seems evident that the humerus is defined by BT, whereas Helmer's measurement of the same bone appears to be Bd. Bearing in mind the greater size of the Bd measurement, comparison between the two sites can at best be oblique.

It seems probable that the caprines from the upper levels at Çayönü were domestic, although until the bone data are published in full uncertainties remain, especially with regard to the caprines in the lower levels of the site.

Gritille (Period 4)

The site of Gritille is dated to the later ninth millennium bp. By this time, caprines amounted to 76 per cent of the identified bone sample (Stein 1989). Of the caprine bones that were identified to species, sheep outnumber goats by nearly 3:1. Stein suggests that the caprines were domesticated by this time, based upon the age structure of a combined mandible sample for the two species, in which 65 per cent were killed before 36 months of age. Measurements of the distal humerus are also given for an undifferentiated caprine sample (Stein 1989: fig. 4), although the large specimens shown in that diagram do not necessarily represent hunted wild goats, as was suggested, and are more likely to derive from domestic males. Large male goats from the later Aceramic Neolithic at Abu Hureyra are of this size and come from a time and place where it is highly unlikely that wild males would have been encountered.

In summary, the pattern from excavated sites in Turkey suggests that the caprines from Cayönü (lower levels), Cafer and Asikli were wild, or probably so (a conclusion based mainly on their large size), whereas those from the upper levels at Cayönü, and those from Gritille, were probably domestic.

Iraq and Iran

To the east of the Tigris–Euphrates Basin, wild caprines are better known from late palaeolithic and mesolithic cave (Period 1) sites (see Uerpmann 1987 for a review of these, and cf. Hole in Ch 14 in this volume). The neolithic settlements so far excavated in Iraq and Iran do not have the extensive mesolithic occupations that were found at the base of Tell es-Sultan and Tell Abu Hureyra.

Tepe Asiab (Period 2)

Tepe Asiab is situated near Kermanshah in Iran, and has been dated to about 9755–8700 bp (Bökönyi 1977). The fauna shows considerable diversity, with cattle, sheep, goat, pig, onager, red, roe and fallow deer and gazelle. Goat and, less commonly, sheep bones amount to 36 per cent of those identified, and red deer, at 38 per cent, are unusually abundant for a site in Southwest Asia. Pig make up a further 18.6 per cent, and cattle 6.5 per cent. This contrasts markedly with the fauna from the later neolithic (Period 5) site of Tepe Sarab, which is located nearby. Here sheep and goat bones comprise almost 85 per cent of those identified, with gazelle bones at 12.3 per cent. Cattle, pig and deer are uncommon.

The goats at Tepe Asiab are large (Fig. 13.7), and were regarded by Bökönyi (1977: 20–22) as wild but with some "transitional" forms. Three horn cores (ibid.: 17–19) show slight twisting – a feature that has often been associated with early domestication – but this is at best slender evidence, even for a postulated "incipient" stage of the process. The goats are mainly adult, with only 18 per cent killed before maturity, which contrasts with the situation seen at the nearby site of Tepe Sarab, where 33–40 per cent were killed before maturity. The Sarab goats are also small (Bökönyi 1977: figs 3, 16) and certainly domestic.

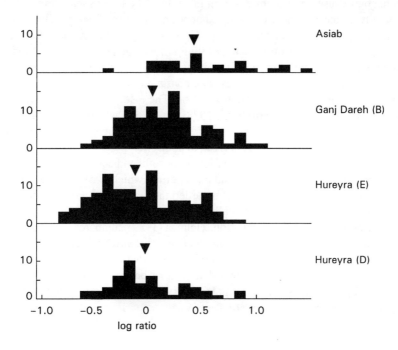

Figure 13.7   Goats: combined measurements of different bones compared by
the log-ratio method; the arrows mark the mean of each distribution

There are few measured sheep bones from Tepe Asiab, but the measurements suggest that the animals were large. The measurements from the adjacent but later site
of Tepe Sarab are significantly smaller. At Tepe Asiab, goats outnumber sheep by
rather more than 2:1, whereas at Tepe Sarab sheep are much more common than goats
(4:1). There is no evidence to suggest that the sheep and goats were other than wild
at Tepe Asiab.

Ganj Dareh (Period 3)

The 18 conventional radiocarbon dates for the Ganj Dareh sequence and the four
AMS radiocarbon dates (Hedges et al. 1990) almost all come within the first half of
the ninth millennium bp, although there are a few that are conspicuously earlier or
later. Ganj Dareh is one of the few early neolithic sites in Southwest Asia for which
the fauna has been comprehensively published. Caprines comprise more than 90 per
cent of the identified fragments, with goats outnumbering sheep by almost 9 to 1
among the bones fully identified to these species.

In his study, Hesse (1978, 1984) argued, on the basis of their population structure,
that the goats in Levels A to D were domesticated. He particularly concentrated on
the proportion of the sexes that were culled in relation to the age classes, determined
both by tooth eruption and bone-fusion patterns. The high degree of sexual dimor-

phism in goats causes measurements from the unfused bones of subadult males to be substantially larger than those of the fused bones from mature females. This effect is apparent even from 12 months or so of age (Davis 1987), and Hesse used this fact to infer a preferential cull of juvenile males with unfused bones, whereas the females were retained beyond the age at which their metatarsals were fused (Hesse 1978: fig. 60; 1982). He argued that most females were conserved for breeding and most males were killed at an effective size for consumption. The evidence for a selective cull is supported by the slaughter pattern (Hesse 1978: figs 53, 54), where the combined sample of sheep and goat mandibles shows a heavy mortality among young individuals: only about 30 per cent of the herd survived to adult life.

These data represent good evidence for a purposeful and controlled cull, intended to maximize both breeding potential and meat output, which is wholly characteristic of a domestic herd. Hesse (1984: 315) regarded the Ganj Dareh goat population as "... husbanded, though morphologically wild ...". This understates the degree of size reduction evident in the population. Helmer (1989) compares the Ganj Dareh goat-bone measurements with those from other neolithic sites in Southwest Asia. The measurements are as small as those from other sites at which the goats were domesticated; for example, Figure 13.7 shows that the goat-bone measurements from Ganj Dareh and Abu Hureyra are from animals of very similar size, and both populations are significantly smaller than those of Tepe Asiab.

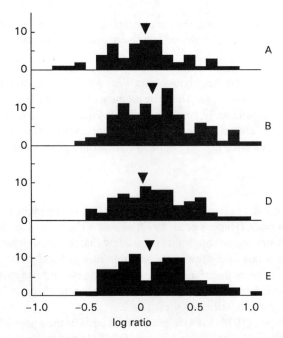

Figure 13.8 Ganj Dareh goats: combined measurements of different bones from Levels A, B, D and E compared by the logratio method; the arrows mark the mean of each distribution.

Uncertainty has surrounded the status of the goats from Level E, the earliest at Ganj Dareh (Hesse 1978, 1984). The apparently early dates for this level, and the lack of architectural features, has led to the interpretation that the caprines from Level E were not domestic. Helmer (1989: figs 8, 9) compared the goat bones from Level E (earliest) and Level A (latest) at Ganj Dareh, and showed that the two samples cannot be separated on the basis of body size; both are significantly smaller than those from the nearby site of Tepe Asiab. The samples from Levels A, B, D and E are good, and these data are further plotted here (Fig. 13.8). There is no evidence for size change through the sequence; the sample means are almost identical, as is the range of each sample, with only occasional specimens that fall at the extreme dimensions. The goat distal humerus measurements (Bd) from Ganj Dareh are rather smaller than those from Abu Hureyra (Fig. 13.1), and also show a marked numerical bias towards the smaller females. On the basis of the above evidence, it is probable that the Ganj Dareh goats were domestic throughout the archaeological sequence at the site.

The sheep is a species showing a lower degree of sexual dimorphism than the goat, so that the bone dimensions of smaller adult males overlap with those of the larger females; a plot of sheep-bone measurements seldom allows a clear distinction to be made between the sexes. The sample of sheep bones from Ganj Dareh is also smaller than that of goat bones, but if the sheep bones from all levels are combined the sample suggests that the species was large (Figs 13.5, 13.9). Hesse (1984: 314) concluded

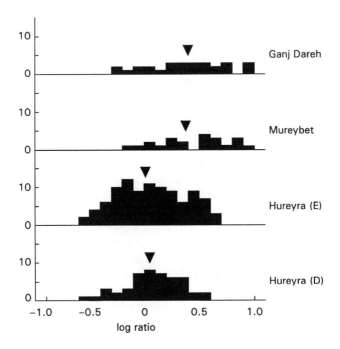

Figure 13.9   Sheep: combined measurements of different bones compared by the log-ratio method; the arrows mark the mean of each distribution.

that "There is no evidence to suggest that sheep were being culturally controlled". Their large size in relation to other archaeological samples was demonstrated by Helmer (1989), and it is probable that the Ganj Dareh sheep were wild. The sequence at Ganj Dareh shows that there is no morphological evidence for the simultaneous domestication of sheep and goat at the site, even though both species have been identified from the earlier sites of Tepe Asiab and Warwasi within 30 km of Ganj Dareh (Uerpmann 1987).

The Levant

Wadi Judayid (Period 1)

This site of the Natufian Culture has radiocarbon dates of 11,950 ±800 bp, 12,090 ±800 bp and 12,793 ±659 bp. Both sheep and goat have been identified in a small fauna that otherwise includes onager, gazelle and wild cattle. Although the number of identified bones is rather small, sufficient measurements are available to show that, by the log-ratio method, both sheep and goats were large-bodied. The mean of the goat-bone measurements is the same as that from Tepe Asiab, although the size range is small. The sheep bones are also from large animals, and the mean is close to that of Tepe Asiab and Ganj Dareh.

Natufian caprines would normally be interpreted as wild, even in the absence of a sufficient sample for this proposition to be fully tested. This expectation is supported by the large size of both the sheep and the goat bones. Although the sample is small, it is an important addition to our information on wild caprines near the southern limits of the Fertile Crescent.

The Damascus region: Tell Aswad, Ghoraifé and Tell Ramad (Final Period 2 and Period 3)

Ducos (1993) has reported the faunal sequence from three closely adjacent sites near the modern city of Damascus in Syria. The earliest of these sites, Tell Aswad, has a fauna in which goats are the most common of the larger mammals, whereas sheep are absent except for a very small percentage found in the latest PPNB levels. Radiocarbon dates suggest that the settlement at Aswad was occupied between about 9800 and 8800 bp, i.e. from the end of the PPNA through the earlier part of the PPNB. Ducos shows that the Aswad goats are rather small-bodied, and that the size distribution and population mean compares closely with those of Tell es-Sultan PPNB and Abu Gosh. The population distribution also shows a bias towards the smaller females (ibid.: figs 4, 5). According to Ducos, the age structure also shows a low mortality of infant goats, but a significant peak of killing in the 1–2 year age-class. He concludes that the inhabitants of Aswad were practising some form of loose herding or "proto-elevage", although the small size and age structure of the goat population could be interpreted as indicative of a fully domestic herd.

The fauna from the later (middle and late PPNB) site of Ghoraifé shows significant changes between Phases I and II. In Phase I both sheep and goat are found, and the caprines together comprise rather more than half of the large mammals that were identified (Ducos 1993: table 2). Goats outnumber sheep by about 3 to 1. In Phase II, the situation is reversed and sheep outnumber goats by rather more than 3 to 1. The proportion of caprines within the fauna is also significantly larger. The mammal fauna from Phase I at Tell Ramad, a late PPNB site, also shows a high sheep-to-goat ratio of rather more than 3 to 1. Mammal species other than caprines now only comprise some 28 per cent of the identified sample. There seems no reason to doubt that both sheep and goats were fully domesticated throughout this sequence. It is unlikely that such a high proportion of goats would be found at Tell Aswad unless they were under human control, bearing in mind the location of this settlement. This is supported by the evidence for small body-size and the age and sex structure of the population. The appearance of sheep – probably, like the goats, introduced as domestic animals – as a significant proportion of the Ghoraifé and Ramad faunas is a good indication of the intensification of this process.

Tell es-Sultan (Jericho) (Periods 2 and 3)

Evidence for the domestication of caprines at Tell es-Sultan is limited by the small bone sample. Zeuner (1955) described goat horn-cores with an incipient spiral from the PPNB, but the best evidence comes from change within the faunal sequence. There are only four bones from the mesolithic levels at the site, and none is caprine. In the protoneolithic and PPNA levels caprines comprise less than 5 per cent of the identified bones in a fauna that is otherwise composed of pig, wild cattle, gazelle and fox, although both goats and, more rarely, sheep have been identified (Clutton-Brock 1971, 1979, Clutton-Brock & Uerpmann 1974).

In the PPNB levels caprine bones account for some 60 per cent of the identified bones of the large mammals. Goat bones greatly outnumber those of sheep, and their abundance indicates that they were domestic. The goats, judging by the few published measurements, were small. Only seven bones have been confidently identified as sheep, with a further five specimens attributed to that species (Clutton-Brock & Uerpmann 1974). Five sheep bones could be measured, one from the PPNA and four from the PPNB. When compared with sheep-bone measurements from other sites in the region, the bones appear to be from small animals. The specimens all fall at or below the population mean from Abu Hureyra, and four specimens are also smaller than any from Tell Mureybet. Although this might suggest that the sheep at Tell es-Sultan were also domestic, the small sample precludes further interpretation.

This pattern can be seen at other Levantine sites where caprines are usually uncommon in PPNA sites but then become abundant in PPNB sites. In addition to Tell es-Sultan, Davis (1985) has demonstrated the presence of a few caprine bones (probably sheep) at the PPNA site of Hatoula, and, at Nahal Oren, Legge (1973) identified a small percentage of goat bones in the PPNA levels. Bar Yosef et al. (1991) found the ibex, *Capra nubiana*, at the PPNA site of Netiv Hagdud near Tell es-Sultan in the Jordan valley, but other caprines were absent. On the other hand, the late PPNB sites of Beisamoun and Abu Gosh (Davis 1978) have faunas in which caprines constitute 60–70 per cent of the large mammal bones. In the southern Levant the archaeological record suggests that the caprines found in Period 3 sites were all goats, and that sheep appear only in the final part of the PPNB.

'Ain Ghazal (Period 3)

The site dates from the late tenth to the late eighth millennium bp, the aceramic neolithic occupation being dated to between 9200 and 8000 bp (Rollefson et al. 1992). Half of the fauna is reported to consist of caprines, all of which are goats in the earlier occupation (Köhler-Rollefson 1989). The other half of the fauna consists of wild mammals. Most of the goats were killed when immature. From the published bone measurements, it is evident that the goats were quite small. Figure 13.2 shows that the humerus BT measurements are close in size to goats from Abu Hureyra and other Southwest Asian sites. This measurement also shows a very marked bias towards females. The high proportion of goats found at 'Ain Ghazal, in a setting where the natural habitat for wild goats is limited, further supports the interpretation that they were domestic.

Beidha (Period 3)

The fauna from the PPNB levels at Beidha presents a particular problem in its analysis, in that two species of caprines are reported from pre-neolithic faunas both at Beidha and from the nearby epipalaeolithic site of Madamagh. At the latter site, both the ibex, *Capra nubiana,* and the wild goat, *Capra aegagrus*, were identified by Perkins (1966), but in the results reported from a more recent excavation at Madamagh the presence of *C. nubiana* is listed as questionable, whereas *C. aegagrus* is definitely identified (Uerpmann 1987: tables 25a, 26b). The difficulty of distinguishing between the postcranial bones of these two species is widely acknowledged, and identifications are usually based on the horn cores alone. The natufian levels at Beidha yielded a sample of 136 bones, of which 90 (66%) were identified as *Capra*. Four horn-core fragments of *Capra* are recorded in the sample Perkins identified from the same levels (Hecker 1984: 385), of which three were identified as *nubiana* and one as *aegagrus*. In the PPNB levels at Beidha 80 per cent of the caprine horn cores were identified by Hecker as *aegagrus*.

Hecker (1982) interpreted the caprine bones as showing at most "cultural control" rather than full domestication. The dimensions of the *Capra* bones are described by Hecker (1982: 229) as ". . . a bit smaller than those from Jericho PPN levels". However, from the figures given for the range of metacarpal measurements (Hecker 1982: table 3), the difference is greater than this might imply, with the goat bones from PPNA Jericho being much larger than those from Beidha. The measurements of fused goat metapodials are given as the mean and range (Hecker 1982: 230), but these fall within the size of populations that are usually interpreted as domestic; for example, the metacarpals are rather smaller than those found at other later Period 3 sites (Fig. 13.10). The age structure of the goat population at Beidha, in so far as this is reflected by the proportions of fused and unfused bones, also shows that a high proportion were slaughtered as sub-adults (60% by 24 months of age). The rather small size of the goats and their age profile can readily support the interpretation that the specimens of *C. aegagrus* at Beidha came from a fully domestic population; indeed, it is quite possible that *C. aegagrus* was present *only* as a domestic mammal during the PPNB at Beidha. Although this species has been identified in the nearby epipalaeolithic site of Madamagh, and possibly in the natufian levels at Beidha, there is little evidence for the coexistence of both species of *Capra* prior to the PPNB levels at Beidha.

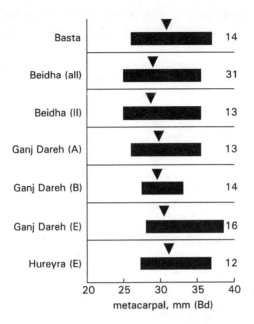

Figure 13.10   Goats: mean and range of metacarpal Bd measurement; number of bones in the sample shown in the right-hand column.

Basta (Period 3)

The site of Basta is dated to the latter part of the PPNB, with two dates that fall into the late ninth millennium bp. The large mammal bones are predominantly of caprines, amounting to 76 per cent of those identified, with both sheep and goat reported (Becker 1991). Goats outnumber sheep in the ratio of 3:2. Other species are uncommon except for gazelle, which accounts for 10 per cent of the sample. The metacarpal and metatarsal dimensions are plotted for the sheep and goat (Becker 1991: fig. 3), and these show that both species were small (Figs 13.6, 13.10) and close in size to those from other later aceramic neolithic sites. No data on the age profile of the cull at Basta are yet available. The site is only 18 km from Beidha, in a setting of low rolling hills (Andrew Garrard: pers. comm.). Although wild sheep might be expected in such terrain, it would be unsuited to wild goats. The presence of a large proportion of goats at Basta is good evidence that this species was under human control. The small size of both sheep and goat at Basta further suggests that both species were domestic.

Azraq

Caprine bones are rare from upper palaeolithic and epipalaeolithic sites in the Azraq Basin, in faunas largely composed of gazelle, equids and hare (Baird et al. 1992, Garrard et al. 1994 and Ch. 11 in this volume). The early to middle PPNB site of Jilat 7 (earlier Period 3), dated at 8810 ±110 and 8520 ±110 bp, also lacks caprines, in a fauna similar to that of the epipalaeolithic sites. The site of Jilat 13 has been dated to the beginning of the Late Neolithic, between 7920±100 bp and 7830±100 bp. The fauna has about 30 per cent caprines in each of three levels, including both sheep and goat. This rise in caprines has, reasonably, been interpreted as marking their appearance as domesticates.

Recent results from Tell Abu Hureyra, Syria (Periods 1, 3 and 4)

Full use was made of proper methods for the recovery of mammal bones in the excavations at this site. Consequently the sample is large and complete. The faunal sequence spans several millennia, from the Mesolithic to the Ceramic Neolithic. The extensive occupation in the Aceramic Neolithic begins at about 9700 bp, but most of the faunal material comes from levels dated to 9400 bp and later (Period 3).

Gazelles are abundant in the mesolithic fauna, with some onager, and fewer bones of deer, cattle and pig. Six per cent of the bones are identified as caprine. Those that can be identified to species level have all been determined as sheep, and direct dating of the bones by the AMS radiocarbon method has confirmed that sheep were part of the mesolithic fauna (Legge & Rowley-Conwy 1987). The aceramic neolithic fauna is similar in most respects to that of the Mesolithic, except that caprines show a significant increase, to 12–14 per cent, and among these the first identified goat bones are found – in Abu Hureyra Period 2A, which is dated to 9400–8300 bp.

By means of tooth-wear and bone-growth studies it has been shown that the gazelles, and probably the onager too, were culled only in a short season in early summer whereas the caprines were present at the site throughout the year (Legge & Rowley-Conwy 1987). In the later Aceramic Neolithic there was a rapid faunal change in which the gazelles rapidly declined, probably as a result of over-exploitation, and their numbers were replaced by abundant sheep and goat. This transition is dated to about 8300 bp. Thus, the proportion of caprines increases through the sequence in two stages: a moderate increase to 12–14 per cent, associated with the first aceramic neolithic occupation at the site (Abu Hureyra 2A), and a more dramatic increase, to 65–75 per cent of the fauna, later in the Aceramic Neolithic (Abu Hureyra 2B). The recognition of domestic mammals at Abu Hureyra rests on several lines of evidence.

The appearance of new species   Earlier work (Legge 1972, 1977) reported the presence of both sheep and goats in the mesolithic fauna at Abu Hureyra. Since then, a full study of the stratification has shown that a small amount of material from the overlying Aceramic Neolithic had been included in this first analysis of the mesolithic fauna, and that the identified goat bones came from these levels. The rather scarce mesolithic caprines are now identified as sheep. This conclusion is reinforced by the setting of Abu Hureyra, which, at the junction of the Euphrates floodplain and undulating steppe, is unsuited to wild goats. With the beginning of the Aceramic Neolithic, caprines increase to 12–14 per cent of the large mammal bones, and the first bones of goats are found. Goats represent a new species in the archaeological sequence, and their presence is interpreted as the result of the introduction of a domestic population. An alternative view might be that caprines increased as a result of more intensive hunting, but this cannot be supported because the goat is absent in the mesolithic fauna and because the settlement at Abu Hureyra increased greatly in size at that time. The wild, non-migratory species (cattle, pig and deer) show a marked decline, as a consequence, presumably, of the growth in the human population.

Size change   The presence of mesolithic levels at the base of the tell provides an important opportunity to monitor body size in the common species such as gazelles. There was a decrease in the body size of mammals at the end of the last glacial period in Southwest Asia (Kurten 1965, Davis 1981, 1987). Davis has shown that the size decrease in *Gazella gazella* occurred at about 12,000 bp, a little before the first settlement at Abu Hureyra. The gazelles at Abu Hureyra provide no evidence for size change throughout the archaeological sequence.

Comparisons of the sheep and goat bones from Abu Hureyra have been made by the log-ratio method (Figs 13.7, 13.9) both between the earlier Aceramic Neolithic (with 12% caprines) and the later Aceramic Neolithic (65–75% caprines), and with other samples from Southwest Asian sites. It is clear that the sample mean and the size range for both species in the earlier and later samples are identical. The goat bones from both periods also show the typical skewed distribution towards the smaller female size, in spite of the obscuring effects of the log-ratio method of plotting. Comparisons of other bone measurements, between the two periods and with other sites (Figs 13.1, 13.3–13.5), all further demonstrate the absence of size change as well as the small size of the populations.

Proportions of the sexes   For the goat, the combined sample plotted by the log-ratio method (Fig. 13.7) shows a bias towards the smaller females, and this is still more evident in the BT and Bd measurements of the distal humerus from several sites (Fig. 13.2). It has been noted above that sheep bones are less sensitive to this type of analysis.

Age structure of the population   The slaughter pattern of mammal populations is calculated by tooth eruption and by bone fusion. This latter approach was utilized by Hole et al. (1969) in the study of caprine bones from Ali Kosh, and later by Hesse (1978) in his study of the bones from Ganj Dareh. In each sample most of the earlier-fusing bones were found to be fused, whereas the later-fusing bones were mostly unfused. In other words, a large proportion of the caprines passed through their juvenile life to be killed as sub-adults, showing a selective cull of those animals that were approaching maturity.

The pattern of bone fusion at Abu Hureyra compares closely with Hesse's data from Ganj Dareh. Bones thought to fuse in the 18–24 month period (distal metacarpal, distal tibia) are 60–70 per cent fused, showing that most animals lived beyond that age, and only about 35 per cent of animals lived beyond 36 months of age, as shown by the later-fusing bones. An important point is that the patterns of caprine mortality in the earlier and later Aceramic Neolithic at Abu Hureyra are virtually identical, and both can be interpreted as showing a structured cull with selective juvenile mortality.

The earlier and later populations of both sheep and goat at Abu Hureyra cannot be separated on the basis of body size, size range, or in the manner of the cull. Further, there is strong supporting evidence for the introduction of the domestic goat at the beginning of the Aceramic Neolithic at the site. Thus, caprines may be domestic when they comprise even only a minor part of a fauna that is otherwise composed of wild species. The conclusion is that domesticated caprines appeared at Abu Hureyra at the same time as the first domesticated plants (i.e. early in the Aceramic Neolithic).

The chronology of caprine domestication

If the limited caprine bone samples present a problem in the recognition of early domestication, the published radiocarbon dates offer a similar challenge in establishing its chronology. Yet this is an important aspect of the study of domestication, because the process can only be calibrated by this means. The history of archaeological thought on the nature of early domestication has been diverse, and different popular theories have offered contrasting points of view. The process of domestication has been variously argued as rapid or gradual, and it has been seen as an innovation that occurred at particular centres or throughout wide regions. Only closely dated archaeological sequences can resolve these issues.

Many aceramic neolithic sites in Southwest Asia now have large numbers of radiocarbon dates (Aurenche & Evin 1987), although the dates do not always present a clear picture of the chronology of a site (Gascó 1987). Dates from a defined cultural sequence may show a large overlap between phases (Aurenche et al. 1987). Date lists for the same site but including dates determined by different laboratories, and recent as opposed to more "historic" radiocarbon dates, often disagree, and the archaeologist has difficulty in processing this information in a way that is detached from chronological expectations. However, it is possible to see a pattern of events in the presently available data, albeit with many uncertainties.

In Turkey, the sites of Cafer, Asikli and the lower levels at Çayönü have caprines that have been interpreted as wild. Radiocarbon dates from Cafer fall between 8980 and 8400 bp, and are very similar to those from Asikli. The settlement at Çayönü begins a little earlier, although the radiocarbon dates suggest that the upper levels, with putative domestic caprines, postdate 9000 bp. The radiocarbon dates from Gritille fall between 8600 and 7770 bp and there is little doubt that the caprines there were domestic.

In Iran, the few dates from Tepe Asiab span a millennium, from 9755±85 bp to 8700±100 bp, and they are broadly contemporary with the lower levels at Çayönü, Asikli and Cafer. The goat bones at Tepe Asiab come from very large individuals that are usually interpreted as wild. Sheep bones are less common, although they too appear to be large. The radiocarbon dates from Ganj Dareh cluster between 9000 and 8450 bp (19 dates), with only three that are significantly earlier or later than these. The goats are regarded as domestic throughout the life of the settlement, whereas the sheep appear to be wild.

In the Levant, caprines are present in the PPNA sites, but they are represented by few bones, except in the earliest levels at Tell Aswad. The early PPNB fauna at Tell Aswad also contains a high proportion of goats that Ducos (1993) has interpreted as herded. It is possible that Jericho too had domestic goats at that time. The aceramic neolithic settlement at Abu Hureyra is dated from 9400 bp, and both sheep and goat can be identified as domestic. Caprines initially comprised only a small part of the aceramic neolithic fauna, but they are interpreted as having been domestic throughout the neolithic occupation of the site.

There is also good evidence to regard the caprines at Ramad, 'Ain Ghazal (goat only in the earlier phases), Beidha (goat only), and Basta as domestic. Most radiocarbon dates for 'Ain Ghazal postdate 9000 bp, although a few suggest that the settlement may have begun a little earlier. Dates for Beidha and Basta indicate that these sites belong to the later PPNB, as do the sites with caprine bones in the Azraq basin.

Thus, there is evidence of domestic goats in the earlier PPNB sites of the Levant, and perhaps from the early tenth millennium bp, whereas the absence of sheep from Levantine sites suggests that their origin as domesticates lay to the north or east. Sites in the Damascus region show that sheep were introduced only by about 8600 bp, by which time they were domestic at Abu Hureyra and probably at other sites to the north and east. Shortly after this, the spread of both species as domesticates was rapid, extending to the more marginal habitats.

The dating evidence suggests that a timespan of less than one millennium can encompass the appearance of domestic caprines at sites throughout the Fertile Crescent. With our present limited knowledge these events are difficult to interpret with any confidence. Few sites have evidence for domestic mammals before 9000 bp, which suggests that early domestication was a very local phenomenon, although one that is likely to have occurred at more than one place. Whether the sheep was separately domesticated or whether this followed from goat domestication remains an open question. Once caprine domestication was achieved, their adoption and dispersal was very rapid.

This synopsis is problematic, and clearly fraught with difficulties of sample size, bone-measurement data, inconsistencies within radiocarbon dates and differences in interpretation. Some of these problems should be resolved with the full publication of sites now under study, and others may be eliminated through further excavation. It must be hoped that future work will be supported by the standardization both of recovery methods in excavation and in the publication of bone measurements.

There have been many attempts to explain the reasons that underlie the beginnings of mammal and plant domestication, and much work remains to be done before the process is well understood. This remarkable phenomenon had unparalleled consequences for the human species, and, if for this reason alone, it deserves the most careful and rigorous investigation.

Acknowledgements

Part of the work on the mammal remains from Tell Abu Hureyra was supported by the Science-based Archaeology Committee of the Science and Engineering Research Council (Research Assistant: Peter Rowley-Conwy), and by many years of voluntary help from John and Phoebe Williams. Andrew Garrard and Andrew Moore made helpful comments on an earlier draft of this chapter, but the responsibility for its contents lies with the author.

Note

1. The location of most of the archaeological sites mentioned in this chapter is shown elsewhere in this volume on the distribution maps in Chapters 11 and 14 by Garrard et al. and by Hole.

References

Aurenche, O. & J. Evin 1987. List of the ^{14}C dates from the archaeological sites of the Near East from 14000 to 5700 BP. In *Chronologies in the Near East*, O. Aurenche, J. Evin, F. Hours (eds), 151–76. Oxford: British Archaeological Reports, International Series 379 i.

Aurenche, O., J. Evin, O. Gascó 1987. Une séquence chronologique dans le Proche Orient 12000 á 7000 BC et sa relation avec les données du radiocarbon. In *Chronologies in the Near East*, O. Aurenche, J. Evin, F. Hours (eds), 683–744. Oxford: British Archaeological Reports, International Series 379 ii.

Baird, D., A. Garrard, L. Martin, K. Wright 1992. Prehistoric settlement and environment in the Azraq Basin: an interim report on the 1989 excavation season. *Levant* **24**, 1–31.

Bar-Yosef, O., A. Gopher, E. Tchernov & M. Kislev 1991. Nativ Hagdud; an early Neolithic site in the Jordan Valley. *Journal of Field Archaeology* **18**, 405–24.

Becker, C. 1991. The analysis of bones from Basta, a pre-pottery Neolithic site in Jordan: problems and potential. *Paléorient* **17**, 59–75.

Bökönyi, S. 1969. Archaeological problems and methods of recognising animal domestication. In *The domestication and exploitation of plants and animals*, P. J. Ucko & G. W. Dimbleby (eds), 219–29. London: Duckworth.

— 1977. *The animal remains from four sites in the Kermanshah Valley, Iran: Asiab, Sarab, Dehsavar and Siahbid*. Oxford: British Archaeological Reports, Supplementary Series 34.

— 1989. Definitions of animal domestication. In *The walking larder: patterns of domestication, pastoralism, and predation*, J. Clutton-Brock (ed.), 22–7. London: Unwin Hyman.

Clutton-Brock, J. 1971. The primary food animals of the Jericho tell from the proto-Neolithic to the Byzantine period. *Levant* **3**, 41–55.

— 1979. The mammalian remains from the Jericho Tell. *Proceedings of the Prehistoric Society* **45**, 135–57.

Clutton-Brock, J. & H-P. Uerpmann 1974. The sheep of early Jericho. *Journal of Archaeological Science* **1**, 261–74.

Davis, S. J. M. 1978. Etude de la faune. In *Abu Gosh et Beisamun, deux gisements du VIIe millénaire avant l'ere Chrétienne en Israel*, M. Lechevallier (ed.), 195–7. Memoires et Travaux 2, Centre de Recherches Préhistoriques Français de Jerusalem, Jerusalem.

— 1981. The effects of temperature change and domestication on the body size of late Pleistocene to Holocene mammals of Israel. *Palaeobiology* **7**, 101–14.

— 1985. A preliminary report of the fauna from Hatoula: a Natufian–Khiamian (PPNA) site near Latroun, Israel. In *Le site Natoufien–Khiamien de Hatoula, près de Latroun, Israël*, M. Lechevallier & A. Ronen (eds), 71–98. Cahiers 1, Centre de Recherche Français, Jerusalem.

— 1987. *The archaeology of animals*. London: Batsford.

Ducos, P. 1968. *L'origine des animaux domestiques en Palestine*. Mémoire 6, Institut de Préhistoire de l'Université de Bordeaux, Bordeaux.

— 1978. *Tell Mureybet: étude archéozoologique et problèmes d'écologie humaine*. Paris: Editions du CNRS.

— 1991. *Bos, Ovis* et *Capra* dans les sites néolithiques du Proche-Orient. *Paléorient* **17**, 161–8.

— 1993. Proto-élevage et élevage au Levant sud au VIIe millénaire BC. Les données de la Damascène. *Paléorient* 19, 153–74.

Garrard, A. N., D. Baird, S. College, L. Martin, K. Wright 1994. Prehistoric environment and settlement in the Azraq Basin: an interim report on the 1987 and 1988 excavation seasons. *Levant* 26, 73–109.

Gascó, J. 1987. Traitements graphiques des dates radiocarbone: application du Proche Orient. In *Chronologies in the Near East*, O. Aurenche, J. Evin, F. Hours (eds), 21–37. Oxford: British Archaeological Reports, International Series 379 i.

Hecker, H. 1982. Domestication revisited: its implications for faunal analysis. *Journal of Field Archaeology* 9, 217–36.

— 1984. *The faunal analysis of the primary food animals from Pre-Pottery Neolithic Beidha (Jordan)* [PhD dissertation, Department of Anthropology, Columbia University]. Ann Arbor, Michigan: University Microfilms.

Hedges, R. E. M., R. A. Housley, C. R. Bronk, G. J. van Klinken 1990. Radiocarbon dates from the Oxford AMS system: archaeometry date list 11. *Archaeometry* 32, 211–37.

Helmer, D. 1985. Etude préliminaire de la faune de Cafer Höyük (Malatya-Turquie). *Cahiers de l'Euphrate* 4, 117–20.

— 1989. Le développement de la domestication au Proche-Orient de 9500 à 7500 BP: les nouvelles données d'el Kowm et de Ras Shamra. *Paléorient* 15, 111–21.

Henry, D. O. & P. F. Turnbull 1985. Archaeological and faunal evidence from Natufian and Timnian sites in southern Jordan. *Bulletin of the American Schools of Oriental Research* 257, 45–64.

Hesse, B. 1978. *Evidence for husbandry from the Early Neolithic site of Ganj Dareh in western Iran* [PhD dissertation, Department of Anthropology, Columbia University]. Ann Arbor, Michigan: University Microfilms.

— 1984. These are our goats: the origins of herding in West Central Iran. In *Animals and archaeology 3: early herders and their flocks*, J. Clutton-Brock & C. Grigson (eds), 243–64. Oxford: British Archaeological Reports, International Series 202.

Hole, F., K. V. Flannery, J. Neely 1969. *Prehistory and human ecology of the Deh Luran Plain*. Memoirs of the Museum of Anthropology 1, University of Michigan, Ann Arbor.

Horwitz, L. K. 1989. A reassessment of caprovine domestication in the Levantine Neolithic: old questions, new answers. In *People and culture in change*, I. Hershkovitz (ed.), 153–81. Oxford: British Archaeological Reports, International Series 508 i.

— 1993. The development of ovicaprine domestication during the PPNB of the southern Levant. In *Archaeozoology of the Near East*, H. Buitenhuis & A. T. Clason (eds), 27–36. Leiden: Universal Book Services/Dr W. Backhuys.

Köhler-Rollefson, I. 1989. Changes in goat exploitation at 'Ain Ghazal between the early and late Neolithic: a metrical analysis. *Paléorient* 15, 141–5.

Kurten, B. 1965. Carnivora of the Palestine caves. *Acta Zoologica Fennica* 107, 1–74.

Lawrence, B. 1980. Evidences of animal domestication at Cayonu. In *The joint Istanbul–Chicago Universities' prehistoric research in southeastern Anatolia*, H. Çambel & R. J. Braidwood (eds), 285–312. Istanbul: Edebiyat Fakültesi Basimevi.

— 1982. Principal food animals at Cayonu. In *Prehistoric village archaeology in south east Turkey*, L. S. Braidwood & R. J. Braidwood (eds), 175–99. Oxford: British Archaeological Reports, International Series 138.

Legge, A. J. 1972. Prehistoric exploitation of the gazelle in Palestine. In *Papers in economic prehistory*, E. S. Higgs (ed.), 119–24. Cambridge: Cambridge University Press.

— 1973. The fauna. In "Recent excavations at Nahal Oren, Israel", T. Noy, A. J. Legge & E. S. Higgs, 90–1. *Proceedings of the Prehistoric Society* 39, 75–99.

— 1975. The fauna of Tell Abu Hureyra: preliminary analysis. *Proceedings of the Prehistoric Society* 41, 74–6.

— 1977. The origins of agriculture in the Near East. In *Hunters, gatherers and first farmers beyond Europe*, J. V. S. Megaw (ed.), 51–67. Leicester: Leicester University Press. Legge, A. J. 1981. Aspects of cattle husbandry. In *Farming practice in British prehistory*, R. Mercer (ed.), 169–81. Edinburgh: Edinburgh University Press.

Legge, A. J. & P. A. Rowley-Conwy 1986. New radiocarbon dates for early sheep at Tell Abu Hureyra, Syria. In *Archaeological results from accelerator dating,* J. A. J. Gowlett & R. E. M. Hedges (eds), 23–35. Monograph 11, Oxford University Committee for Archaeology, Oxford.

— 1987. Gazelle killing in Stone Age Syria. *Scientific American* **257**(2), 76–83.

— 1988. *Star Carr revisited; a re-analysis of the large mammals.* London: Birkbeck College, University of London, Centre for Extra-Mural Studies.

Meadow, R. 1984. Animal domestication in the Middle East; a view from the eastern margin. In *Animals and archaeology 3: early herders and their flocks,* J. Clutton-Brock & C. Grigson (eds), 309–37. Oxford: British Archaeological Reports, International Series 202.

— 1989. Osteological evidence for the process of domestication. In *The walking larder: patterns of domestication, pastoralism, and predation,* J. Clutton-Brock (ed.), 80–90. London: Unwin Hyman.

Payne, S. 1985. Animal bones from Asikli Huyuk. *Anatolian Studies* **35**, 109–22.

Perkins, D. 1966. The fauna from Madamagh and Beidha; a preliminary report. *Palestine Exploration Quarterly* **98**, 8–61.

Rollefson, G., A. Simmons, Z. Kafafi 1992. Neolithic cultures of 'Ain Ghazal, Jordan. *Journal of Field Archaeology* **19**, 443–70.

Stein, G. 1989. Strategies of risk reduction in herding and hunting systems of Neolithic southeast Anatolia. In *Early animal domestication and its cultural context,* P. Crabtree, D. Campana, K. Ryan (eds), 87–97. MASCA Research Papers in Science and Archaeology, vol. 6, supplement. The University Museum of Archaeology and Anthropology, University of Pennsylvania, Philadelphia.

Uerpmann, H-P. 1978. Metrical analysis of faunal remains from the Middle East. In *Approaches to faunal analysis in the Near East,* R. H. Meadow & M. A. Zeder (eds), 41–5. Harvard: Peabody Museum, Harvard University.

— 1979. *Probleme der Neolithisierung des Mittelmeerraums.* [Beihefte zum Tübinger Atlas des Vorderen Orients, Reihe B (Geisteswissenschaften) 28]. Weisbaden: Dr L. Reichert.

— 1987. *The ancient distribution of ungulate mammals in the Middle East.* [Beihefte zum Tübinger Atlas des Vorderen Orients, Reihe A (Naturwissenschaften) 27]. Weisbaden: Dr L. Reichert.

von den Driesch, A. 1976. *A guide to the measurement of animal bones from archaeological sites.* Harvard: Peabody Museum, Harvard University.

Widdowson, E. M. 1980. Growth in animals. In *Growth in animals,* T. L. J. Lawrence (ed.), 1–9. London: Butterworth.

Widdowson, E. M. & D. Lister 1991. Nutritional control of growth. In *Growth regulation in farm animals,* A. M. Pearson & T. R. Dutson (eds), 67–101. London: Elsevier.

Zeuner, F. E. 1955. The goats of early Jericho. *Palestine Exploration Quarterly* April, 70–86.

CHAPTER FOURTEEN

The context of caprine domestication in the Zagros region

Frank Hole

Introduction

It is widely accepted now that agriculture originated in the "Levantine Corridor", probably close to the permanent lakes in the Jordan valley some 12,000 years ago (calibrated) as a result of plausible circumstances and processes (McCorriston & Hole 1991). Persuasive arguments suggest that agriculture arose in one locale as a single development and gradually spread northwards with branches extending both east and west. Within 2,000 years, animal domestication had spread rapidly through the zones of agriculture and it provided the basis for the true Neolithic Revolution. Although these basic facts are widely accepted, no definitive identification has been made of where and under what circumstances livestock were domesticated. This chapter addresses that problem, but until requisite fieldwork can be carried out, its conclusions must remain hypothetical.

It is generally agreed that the dog was the first domesticate and that it was kept as a pet, hunting companion or camp guard, rather than as a staple food (cf. Uerpmann in Ch. 12 in this volume). The first edible domesticates were goats and/or sheep (the caprines), followed shortly by pigs and cattle. This discussion concentrates on the caprines (cf. Legge in Ch. 13 in this volume). Can we identify circumstances that were necessary and sufficient for livestock domestication to occur? I argue that several plausible candidate circumstances can be identified. As with agriculture, one of these must have been "cultural": the new ability and propensity of people to enter into husbanding relationships with animals, because any imaginable external factor (all of which start with hunger) must have existed many times during the long course of human history, yet none of these prior events resulted in domestication. At the end of the Pleistocene, a combination of circumstances evidently gave people "the incentive to keep animals in a controlled manner" (Clutton-Brock 1981: 190), but domestication occurred initially among few species and was highly localized, implying that most species were not suitable as domesticates and that the necessary cluster of triggering factors – cultural and environmental – were not present everywhere.

Following reasons discussed elsewhere (Hole 1989), I regard the region where Iraq, Turkey and Iran intersect as the most likely locale for the domestication of the caprines. An outline of the reconstructed scenario follows.

As early as 13000 BP (all dates cited are calibrated) in the northeastern part of Southwest Asia (the Near East) villages appear, featuring houses and a variety of grinding tools, but without evidence of either domestic animals or cultivated plants. There is no evident transition from the preceding epipalaeolithic hunting–gathering tradition. These villages are part of an area-wide phenomenon that occurred towards the end of the Bolling–Allerød phase of warming. The trajectory of climatic changes occurring in different regions of Southwest Asia during the time of the Younger Dryas are debated, but in deposits from Lake Zeribar a noticeable reduction in cereal-type pollen occurs, implying drier conditions. It is possible that these conditions affected overall biotic productivity and restricted the movements of hunter–gatherers to highly localized, sheltered refugia where forest products could be secured. Following the Younger Dryas, a climatic amelioration allowed forests to spread, segmenting formerly open ranges into smaller units and arranging the niches for different species by altitude and type of vegetation (cf. Hillman's interpretation of these environmental changes in Ch. 10 in this volume [ed.]). Sedentism and the reduction of open range encouraged territoriality. People began to protect and propagate local herds, a pre-domestication practice that can be referred to as food resource management (FRM) and which led ultimately to domestication. Belatedly, when cereal grasses reached this region, perhaps at about the same time as the practice of cultivation, there was opportunity for people to establish villages based on herding, collecting and agriculture outside the forest zone.

Figures 14.1 and 14.2 illustrate the spatial–temporal framework discussed in this chapter. In essence they show the following:

- epipalaeolithic sites occur at elevations between 700 m and 1400 m
- a significant temporal gap may exist between the epipalaeolithic and the oldest proto-neolithic sites
- the proto-neolithic sites lie at lower elevations, between 300 m and 800 m; these settlements occurred first during the time of the Younger Dryas
- only after the climatic optimum had reached its peak, around 10000 BP, did occupation of the higher mountain valleys of the Zagros resume
- agriculture and animal domestication are documented as early as 10000 BP
- sites of these early agricultural settlements occurred at higher elevations that any known epipalaeolithic site (up to 1860 m)
- after 9000 BP, agricultural villages are present in all zones utilized today. These facts imply that climatic and other environmental changes were powerful forces in the spread of agriculture and possibly in the inception of animal domestication.

The timing of domestication

This section deals with chronology, because the specific time that domestication took place (if we can imagine that it happened only once), as well as the rate at which it occurred, relate to climate and environment. Fortunately, there is now a means of

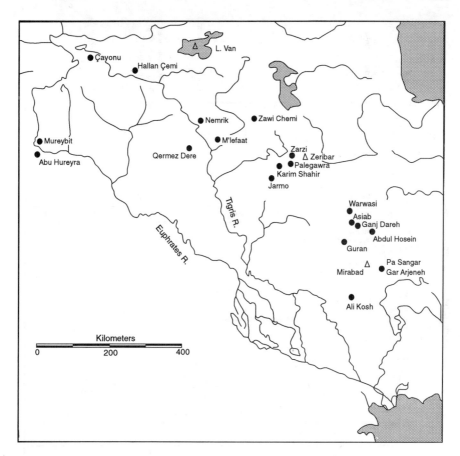

Figure 14.1   Map of the Zagros and northern Mesopotamia showing the locations of epipal-aeolithic and proto-neolithic sites. Triangles indicate lakes from which pollen cores have been taken.

calibrating radiocarbon dates back to the end of the Last Glacial, using a combination of methods from studies of tree-rings, marine corals, ice cores and lake varves (Stuiver & Reimer 1993). The calibration makes it possible to relate the cultural changes to synchronous changes in climate and environment, although problems still exist in reconciling calibrations derived from the different methods and on different sets of data (Becker et al. 1991, Kromer & Becker 1992, Lotter et al. 1992).

The dates cited in this chapter were calculated with CALIB 3.0.3A, a computer program produced by the Quaternary Isotope Laboratory of the University of Washington (Stuiver & Reimer 1993). One major effect of the new calibrations is to push the ages of sites back further in *calendar* time and to spread the duration of the transition to agriculture, as well as its subsequent dispersals, over a much longer period: in short, the rate of adoption of agriculture and animal domestication was slower than heretofore supposed, although the order of events remains the same. The oldest radiocarbon-dated cereals are from Netiv Hagdud, Gilgal and Jericho in the Jordan Valley (Hopf

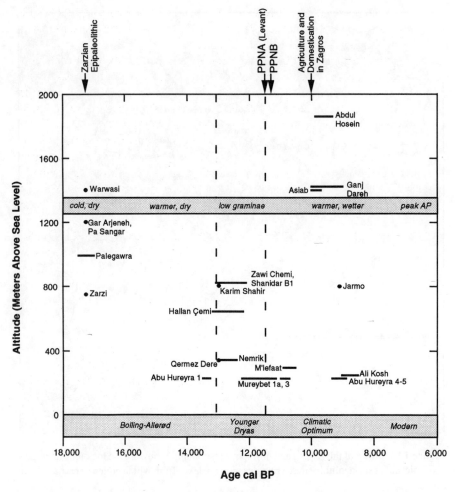

Figure 14.2   A spatial-temporal framework for the Zagros and northern Mesopotamia related to significant climatic episodes (lower shaded bar) and vegetation revealed by the Zeribar pollen cores (upper shaded bar). Initial dates for sites for which reliable radiocarbon dates are available are shown with two sigma error bars; other sites are placed on the basis of typological comparisons. All dates are calibrated.

1983) and from Aswad in the Damascus Basin (van Zeist 1982 (1985), Zohary 1992). These dates range from 12500 to 10500 BP, but the spread of agriculture, as evidenced by Pre-Pottery Neolithic B (PPNB) settlements in the Levant and by contemporary villages in the Zagros, begins shortly before 11000 BP and continues for another 2500 years before the advent of pottery making. By 9000 BP domestic sheep and goats were available to most villagers, and herding had replaced or supplemented hunting at many sites. The transformation from a hunting and collecting economy, perhaps beginning with the *cultivation* of wild cereals, to the establishment of permanent villages and a mixed agricultural economy with fully domesticated races of plants and animals, took place over at least 3000 years. This makes the process comparable with the rate of adoption of agriculture seen in other parts of the world, despite differences in environments, crops and time of onset of domestication.

A second implication of the longer timescale is that it places the onset of domestication shortly after the Younger Dryas phase, conventionally dated to 11000–10000 bp (maximum spread 13000–11500 BP), but considerable uncertainty exists over its duration and local effects (Wright 1989, Hajdas et al. 1993, Mayewski et al. 1993, Taylor et al. 1993). Although Wright (1993) questions whether the Younger Dryas actually affected Southwest Asia, most hold that it resulted in increased aridity (e.g. Moore & Hillman 1992). There seems little doubt, however, that the time assigned to the Younger Dryas was one of substantial climatic change in Southwest Asia, both in the Levant and the Zagros. For example, Bottema has demonstrated a virtual absence of cereal-type pollen during that interval in lake-core pollen spectra (Bottema 1992a: fig. 3).

The Younger Dryas ended just after the beginning of a period of increased solar insolation resulting from changes in the Earth's orbital parameters. Temperatures gradually warmed in the summer and decreased in the winter, and precipitation increased (COHMAP 1988). When these new conditions set in, we find the first evidence of domesticated cereals. With these lines of evidence we can hardly ignore that there may have been several climatically related causal factors involved in the process of domestication.

Despite these indications, the patterns of climate and of climatic change in Southwest Asia are not well understood. Bintliff (1982) noted that it is a highly complex region affected by two dominant weather systems, and that changes throughout the region may be asynchronous as well as different. The critical issues are timing and the specific regional effects of changing weather systems. When attempting to reconstruct conditions at the time of domestication, we must recognize that they were continually changing – *none of the climatic conditions prevailing at the time of domestication exists today anywhere in Southwest Asia.*

The Zagros region

In contrast with the southern Levant, where there is a seamless transition from Natufian to Pre-Pottery Neolithic A (PPNA) and PPNB, a completely satisfactory transition has not been established from the Epipalaeolithic Zarzian to the oldest villages of the Zagros. It not possible at this time to determine whether a transition exists, but I argue below that there are good reasons to think that the upper elevations of the Zagros were effectively abandoned for some millennia. If true, this has implications for the origin of the oldest villages and for their relations with those in the Levant.

The Late Epipalaeolithic of the Zagros

Zarzian sites are rarer than either upper palaeolithic (Baradostian) or middle palaeolithic sites, possibly because the period was comparatively short-lived The only dates for the period are from Palegawra and they imply an occupation of the cave between 17300 and 17000 BP, exactly contemporary with the Kebaran sites of the Levant with which it shares typological similarity. My research indicates that the Zarzian developed directly from the Baradostian and underwent some changes before it disappeared (Hole & Flannery 1967, Hole 1970). Olszewski estimates that the Zarzian began by 22000 and perhaps ended around 14000 BP (Olszewski 1993a: 211), although there are no dated sites to support these estimates. In the Zagros, following the Zarzian there is no counterpart to the Natufian, and as yet only a few sites outside caves and rockshelters have been reported (Braidwood & Howe 1960: 28, 55–7, Mortensen 1975). Faunal remains, as well as the transitory nature of the sites, imply that the Zarzians were hunters and gatherers (Hole & Flannery 1967, Hole 1970). The next evidence chronologically consists of a small series of "aceramic neolithic" or "proto-neolithic" sites both inside and outside caves, with some traces of architecture, at elevations below 800m. The oldest of these are approximately 13000–12500 BP, at the beginning of the Younger Dryas. The higher mountain valleys are not occupied again until about 10000 BP, after which most sites have indications of cereal agriculture and animal domestication.

There are two things to account for: first, the possible temporal gap between the Zarzian and the oldest villages, a gap reflected in the lithic technology; secondly, the shift in pattern of occupation from upland caves and rockshelters to the establishment for the first time of villages with substantial buildings at lower elevations. The possible temporal gap, and the shift to lower elevations, may have had a climatic stimulus, but the construction of houses could be an independent invention or a diffusion of practices first seen in the Levant, either adopted by locals or introduced by immigrants.

A temporal gap and the shift to lower elevations could be accounted for by climatic conditions that were inimical to the hunting–gathering way of life in the uplands. The climatic evidence derives from several sources: pollen from Lake Zeribar, and fauna and pollen from epipalaeolithic sites. Traditionally, pollen provides the regional climatic indicators. At Lake Zeribar in the central western Zagros and Lake Van in eastern Anatolia, the pattern of change from dry steppe to forest is similar, but the timing of the changes is quite different. Pollen profiles for Lakes Van and Zeribar show few changes in the ratios of trees to non-arboreal vegetation before 13500 BP, but Bottema finds a decided interruption in cereal-type pollen in the range 15000–13000 BP (Bottema 1992a: 103–4), implying that conditions became noticeably drier and/or colder just before the turn for the better. Such conditions may have forced trees back into the refugia that they had probably occupied during the late glacial period. In summary, this broad region appears to have remained largely treeless during the Bolling–Allerød phase, and the increasing temperatures merely accentuated the prevailing dry conditions. As Bottema observed, "the critical factor for many plant species, especially trees, was moisture" (Bottema 1992b: 31). At Lake Zeribar the incursion of trees took place by 12500 BP and the forest reached modern conditions by 6300 BP, whereas at Van the change took place between 7300 BP and 3700 BP. Because of wide sampling intervals, these dates may contain some inaccuracies, but they imply that there was a decided south-to-north lag in the re-establishment of the forest in the Van region (van Zeist & Bottema 1982: 280), an inference that is supported by pollen at

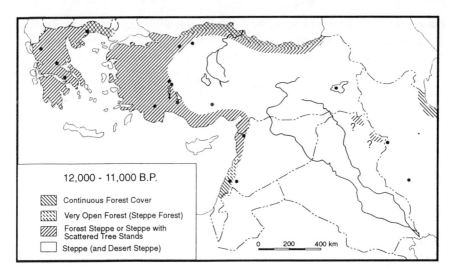

Figure 14.3   Palaeo-vegetation map 12000–11000 BP, showing the possible location of an area of relict forest near the intersection of Iran, Iraq and Turkey. Essentially the same distribution is seen at the end of the late Glacial, 18000–16000 BP, but by 8000 BP there was continuous tree cover from the Levant, across the Taurus and down the Zagros to near the Gulf. The locations of pollen cores at Lakes Van, Zeribar and Mirabad are shown by dots. (Map based on van Zeist & Bottema 1982.)

Lake Mirabad, south of Zeribar, where the transition is seen first. van Zeist & Bottema (1982: 293) speculate that the difference in precipitation between these two lakes may have been related to an eastward shifting of the depressions generated by low-pressure systems in the eastern Mediterranean. Because neither lake is particularly close to the early villages, we turn now to pollen derived from archaeological sediments.

The upper palaeolithic layers at the site of Zarzi (altitude 760m) lacked arboreal pollen, whereas a small amount occurred in the later Zarzian layers. At Shanidar B2, the Zarzian layer, "a scrub savanna had already begun to develop and oak had reached 6 per cent; Oleaceae and Pistachio are also found" (Oates 1982: 361). At Zarzian Palegawra (990m), charcoal of oak, tamarisk, poplar and a conifer has been identified (Braidwood & Howe 1960: 59). Although contemporary lake pollen (at 1300m) suggests a dry steppe, clearly trees were available in some, perhaps very restricted locales, during the Bolling–Allerød phase. In this regard it is interesting that van Zeist and Bottema (1977: figs 30, 81) identified precisely the region of Zarzi and Zawi Chemi as the most likely forest refuge in the Zagros because of its elevation and rainfall (Fig. 14.3). The pollen supports this interpretation but, of course, cannot specify the limits of any relict forest.

The final source of climatic information is fauna from the epipalaeolithic sites. The rodents found throughout the occupation of Warwasi (1400m), from the Mousterian through the Zarzian, were not forest dwellers and they lived in colder, drier conditions than today (Turnbull 1975: 142). Although fauna are not as sensitive to climatic changes as is stationary vegetation, the distribution of wild species provides a general view of regional environmental conditions. Hesse found a marked change from onager and red deer at epipalaeolithic sites to the caprines in the Proto-Neolithic and Neolithic. He remarked (Hesse 1978: 49), "At no site in the Zagros is there a continuum of equid specialization crossing the Pleistocene/Holocene boundary" (see also Bököny 1982). The contrast with sites on the low steppe is striking, for at Mureybet, Bouqras and Abu Hureyra, steppe species such as onager and gazelle predominate, although some aurochs and deer indicate the presence of forests along the Euphrates River. Moore & Hillman (1992) argue for an interruption in settlement at Abu Hureyra during the Younger Dryas, and infer considerably drier conditions even along the Euphrates (Moore in press).

One must bear in mind, however, that the Zagros is highly complex topographically and might have supported a wide diversity of vegetation in niches whose altitude, exposure and latitude resulted in substantial differences in temperature and precipitation. Freitag (1977: 89) reminds us that the western side of the Zagros will have received up to twice as much precipitation as Lake Zeribar, and that oaks on northern exposures can survive with half the precipitation normally expected. These differences may explain the localization of forest refugia and consequently the locations of the earliest villages in the piedmont zone on the western slopes of the Zagros.

No known sites in either eastern Anatolia or Iran bridge the transition from Zarzian occupation to village settlements (Algaze et al. 1991, Rosenberg & Togul 1991), nor are such sites known from the lowland Jezireh where extensive surveys have been carried out in the Sinjar region of Iraq (Oates 1982), in the Khabur (by Hole) and in the Balikh (Copeland 1979). Only the merest hints of an Epipalaeolithic have been reported and there is no evidence for upper palaeolithic occupation. This contrasts with the middle Euphrates where several early villages, including Mureybet and Abu Hurerya, are known. The special nature of this riparian niche for sustaining hunter–gatherers must be stressed, for it is not at all typical of northern Mesopotamia. As Oates (1982) noted, the Jezireh lies along the 200mm precipitation isohyet today and its vegetation is extremely sensitive to even small shifts in rainfall. Because the flat, open Jezireh receives far less rain that the western slopes of the Zagros, an actual absence of sites would be expected if the climate had been colder and drier before 12500 BP. The archaeological coverage of the northern steppe is far better than for the mountains so that the absence of such sites between the Euphrates and the Zagros is believable, with the caveat that sites may be buried and therefore unseen (Hole 1993).

In sum, the chronology and distribution of known Zarzian sites, along with their faunal contents and indications from vegetational reconstructions, suggest that epipalaeolithic hunter–gatherers in the mountains were few and engaged in hunting onagers, red deer and some caprines. Following the late glacial, the Boreal–Allerød warming may have reduced even the sparse biomass of the upper valleys in the millennia before forests began to colonize from their refugia at lower elevations. During this interval, hunters may have developed techniques for efficiently exploiting tree fruits, as well as a broader spectrum of fauna. During the Younger Dryas, they established villages in sheltered lowland locations, which they continued to occupy throughout this colder, dry interval. Once warmer and wetter conditions resumed, the caprines, as well as hunters and pastoralists, began to spread into the higher eleva-tions, whereas the onagers remained chiefly on the lowland steppe.

Early villages

From the Levant to the edge of the Zagros, sedentary settlement occurs just before or at the time of the Younger Dryas, apparently before agriculture, in a wide variety of geographical settings. Rosenberg suggests (pers. comm.) that there is a "round house horizon" coterminous with the first sedentism across the northeastern region, beginning around 13000 BP. As would be expected on climatic grounds, somewhat older structures of this type are found in the southern Levant, but the pattern extends into the Zagros. In each region, round houses appear before there is demonstrable evi-dence for domestication. The fact that houses appear first during this interval suggests that the preceding warmer climate was an enabling factor in the shift of settlement to lower elevations and the shift in diet towards the use of more plant foods. However, the more severe conditions of the Younger Dryas may have stimulated intensive uti-lization of these foods and perhaps given impetus to new techniques for managing or husbanding food resources. Among these would be an increasing ability to harvest, store and process plant foods, but they might also include stimulating the growth of desired species, and perhaps controlling and protecting herds of caprines. The partic-ular plants consumed varied with the region; only in the Levantine Corridor did the harvesting of grasses assume overriding importance and lead to agriculture. In that region, hunted gazelle continued to supply much of the meat protein. In regions out-side the early distribution of cereals, tree fruits may have dominated the vegetable diet (McCorriston 1992, Olszewski 1993b) and the availability of caprine herds and their amenability to human domination may have encouraged experiments in husbandry.

Referring to the same cultural horizon, Howe characterized "a hypothetical central Zagros intermontane–piedmont culture province of both shifting and semi-anchored hunter–gatherers who were in a state of transition toward being somewhat more set-tled, and possibly toward being incipient food producers, during a period extending either side of 8000 BC" (Howe 1983: 132). The older sites in this group, Karim Shahir, Zawi Chemi, Shanidar B1, M'lefaat and Gird Chai, are in the piedmont zone within a radius of 150km, whereas the later sites, Asiab and Ganj Dareh, are at twice the ele-vation of the former, considerably farther south and, we now know, probably as much as 2,000 years younger. Howe cites the similarities in cultural inventory among these sites: round houses, use of grinding and pounding implements (mortars, handstones, pestles), celts and clay figurines. The fauna in these sites (except for Ganj Dareh) are predominantly morphologically wild sheep and goats.

Qermez Dere and Nemrik 9 in Iraq and Hallan Çemi in Turkey add considerably to this picture, although highly variable radiocarbon dates make precise correlations among all these sites impossible. That all the piedmont sites are archaeologically con-temporary is clear from comparisons of artifacts, but evidence for long-term relatively continuous occupation is strongest for the sites at the lowest elevations. This suggests the possibility of a two-fold system, with permanent winter sites and a pattern of sum-mer transhumance. Such a system neither implies nor excludes the herding of caprines, but does imply patterns of movement compatible with herding. These low-elevation

sites also extend the distribution observed by Howe farther on to the upper Mesopotamian plain, a region that has demonstrable connections at this time through lithics
with the Euphrates and the Levant (Kozlowski 1990, 1992, Rosenberg & Davis 1992).

Qermez Dere, a village on the upper Mesopotamian plain just south of the Jebel
Sinjar at 340m, was occupied during the Younger Dryas. The biological remains
imply at least a spring-through-autumn occupation, apparently not one of summer
transhumance, a pattern one might have predicted for this interval. Rather, the site is
situated in an ecotone where a rich variety of plants and animals would have been
available year round. The plants include einkorn, barley, legumes and pistachio nuts,
and the hunted animals include wild cattle, equids, gazelle, sheep, goat, hare and birds
(Watkins 1990a).

At Hallan Çemi, 640m above sea level, also occupied during the Younger Dryas,
the villagers consumed quantities of almonds, pistachios, plums and pulses, but apparently no cereals. Although oak charcoal was found in the site, there are no reported
remains of acorns (Rosenberg pers. comm.). These findings suggest that the lower
edge of the oak forest may have been close to the site as early as 12500 BP. Rosenberg
& Davis (1992) and Rosenberg (1994) also report that large quantities of animal bones
have been recovered, all of them apparently wild species, including sheep, deer and
pigs. The presence of quantities of clams harvested in the spring implies starvation
food during the leanest months. The plant remains, representing summer and autumn
harvest, include many almonds, pistachios, plums and pulses. In sum, the pattern suggests year-round occupation. As at Qermez Dere, highly localized rich food resources
enabled settlement to be permanent and apparently based on hunting and gathering.

Curiously, at neither Hallan Çemi nor Qermez Dere are fireplaces or hearths evident inside the houses, despite ostensible seasonal need for warmth (Kozlowski &
Kempisty 1990, Watkins 1990b). At Qermez Dere the houses were dug partly into
the ground and may have had substantial roofs supported on pillars. Hallan Çemi
reportedly contains abundant evidence of burned daub. Thus, a combination of semi-
subterranean construction and heavy roofs may have been sufficient to protect against
the extremes of weather, perhaps supplemented with fires in portable braziers.

What remains is to determine whether and how these early villages may fit into a
picture of emerging domestication or the spread of agriculture. Agriculture spread initially into a very restricted niche, as argued by Sherratt (1980). Briefly, this niche is
characterized by standing water, lake, marsh or riverside locales where seasonal
flooding would renew soil moisture and curtail weeds, making planting easy and
ensuring the growth of crops. This is not the classic "dry-farming" zone; rather it
makes use of intensely local, unusually wet locales, wherever they might be situated.
Such locales also provided reeds and perhaps trees, aquatic fauna and birds; no doubt
they attracted wild fauna. In short, these were ideal places for hunters and gatherers,
but only for short-term visits if foods could not be stored. Because many of these
favourable niches may have lain outside the natural distribution of cereals and pulses,
and because the annual inundation would kill seeds left in the ground, deliberately
planting crops annually was necessary. Not coincidentally, this planting is the one
essential requirement for domestication.

How do these locales compare with those of the early piedmont villages? According to present evidence, none is situated in the kind of environment just described. Rather, most are in regions with well drained slopes where cereals and pulses might grow naturally today. However, at the time the sites were occupied, there is no evidence that cereals had yet arrived in the region (cf. Hillman in Ch. 10 in this volume). The sites are on or close to rivers and streams, but there is little or no floodplain that would have provided a suitable seedbed for early farmers. It may be that these people, with satisfactory wild resources and little population pressure, had no need to enhance production through extending any plants beyond their natural ranges. Indeed, unless cereals or legumes were present, there were no likely candidate species because trees were already available and probably beginning to expand their distribution naturally when climate ameliorated.

There is, however, a strong possibility that the resources available on the plain during the summer began to diminish, whereas those of the mountains, as at Karim Shahir, became more attractive. When the climate ameliorated after 11500 BP (perhaps very quickly), with the climatic optimum augmenting normal summer insolation, as well as lowering winter temperatures, there may have been a new incentive to practice vertical transhumance. Today, mean July temperatures in Mosul (close to Qermez Dere) are 43°C, and the January minimum is 2°C, but the extremes are 51°C and −11°C (Ruffner & Bair 1984: 341) – conditions that were exacerbated during the climatic optimum. Because of intense summer desiccation, little fresh food would have been available at the lower elevations except in the late winter and spring. Under such conditions it is likely that the ungulates and people migrated between mountain valleys and piedmont if routes were open. This climate, with attendant shifts in vegetation zones, may have led to the eventual abandonment of sites such as Nemrik and Hallan Çemi and the subsequent dramatic shift to sites in the higher mountain valleys.

The process of domestication

We can only speculate on how livestock came to be incorporated into the domestic system because there is no direct evidence of the process taking place *in situ* at any site. At none of the villages discussed do the faunal assemblages display morphological indicators of domestication, and there are only tenuous hints of domestication in age:sex ratios, as at Zawi Chemi. The first unequivocal evidence for sheep/goat domestication is found in villages, such as Ganj Dareh, where there is also evidence of cereal agriculture. Thus, any reconstruction must be based on principles and reasonable inference. Because cereal agriculture arose in the Levant without animal husbandry, and evidence for intensive use of the caprines is oldest in the Zagros–Taurus region, I have argued for independent centres of domestication (Hole 1984, 1989).

I discussed above the possibility of "permanent" villages in the lower oak–pistachio zone of the Zagrosian piedmont and suggested that a combination of forests expanding out of their refugia, and intense seasonality brought about during the climatic optimum, may have encouraged seasonal utilization of upland valleys and led to the demise of lowland villages. The important implications are of developing opportunity for renewed exploitation of the mountain valleys and the need for transhumance, for I believe that these factors triggered the move to caprine domestication.

During the Epipalaeolithic, most human groups in Southwest Asia were mobile, despite the existence of a few sites in the Levant with substantial architecture and investment in non-portable facilities. By the time of the earliest villages, however, seasonal mobility may have essentially ceased for those few groups living in locales where food was available the year round. Therefore, for domestication of livestock to succeed in these locales it had to be compatible with sedentary life. Alternatively, if domestication occurred among mobile peoples, animal husbandry had to fit into a logical routine of resource procurement rather than replace a large element of it. Because the evidence for the existence of mobile people at the time of the Proto-Neolithic is sparse, it is most likely that domestication occurred first among the more sedentary groups. Sedentism in itself would exert some pressure on local fauna among people who continued to hunt, but the faunal remains at Hallan Çemi and Qermez Dere give no hint of depletion; therefore, it is probable that those people lived well below the potential carrying capacity in so far as game is concerned, for a considerable length of time. But time eventually ran out when the climate ameliorated, as outlined above. Given stressful circumstances, animals that might be worthy of management had to be good to eat and amenable to human dominance, and they had to be able to reproduce under captivity and not compete with humans for food. These factors exclude many species as potential domesticates (Clutton-Brock 1981, Davis 1987, Horwitz 1989; Uerpmann in Ch. 12 in this volume).

We cannot know in detail what the behaviour of either the hunter–gatherers or the caprines was at the time of domestication, but ethological studies of similar herbivores today give some clues. The most detailed and useful of these is Geist's remarkable field study of mountain sheep in America (Geist 1971). He stresses two traits of sheep that render them particularly amenable to human control: a strict dominance hierarchy and territoriality. Sheep bands follow leaders, normally the largest ram or ewe, but they can also imprint on humans if they are exposed to them in the first days of their lives. Sheep are gregarious and genetically disposed to follow leaders, a disposition that is reinforced by various patterns of behaviour. Secondly, sheep are rigidly terri-torial, apparently "inheriting" territories and consequently are reluctant, except under strong leadership, to move to new ones. Ordinarily, sheep move seasonally through their territories, occupying minimally one each in summer and winter to ensure adequate forage. There is good reason to think that, at least in these traits, all sheep are similar (Clutton-Brock 1981: 55; Tani 1989).

It is possible that goats, which are very closely related biologically to sheep and generally occur in the same territories, display similar behaviour, although they have not been studied in equivalent detail. Where these species occur together, "goats occupy the broken, rocky terrain while sheep keep to the open, rolling mountain uplands" (Geist 1971: 352). In archaeological sites goats and sheep, whether wild or domestic, commonly occur together, suggesting that their behaviour has not changed much over the millennia.

In order to reconstruct the possible use of seasonal pasture by the caprines and humans, we must assess the distribution and quality of vegetative resources available at the time of domestication. We can roughly assess the impact of the various climatic changes on the vegetation by observing their modern analogues. The type of *Artemisia* steppe found at the end of the Pleistocene is today characterized by cool summers and cold winters, with up to 300mm of winter rainfall. The warm piedmont steppe is characterized by cool winters, warm summers and precipitation in the range of 300–400mm. The oak woodland requires upwards of 500mm precipitation. Botanists have calculated that biomass production in the mediterranean complex is approximately a linear function of precipitation. Thus, twice the precipitation produces twice the weight of vegetation and animal production (Houérou 1981: fig 25.6), although the slope of the regression depends on local minimum temperatures and the seasonal distribution of precipitation. Another important factor is the lapse rate, which in this region is 0.7°C per 100m. Today, the minimum temperature at Mosul is 1.8°C, with an annual range of 40.5° and an annual precipitation of 392mm (Nahal 1981: 77, 81). Applying the lapse rate, the minimum temperature at Tabriz (the analogue for the *Artemisia* steppe), would be –6°, close to actual weather records that give –5.5° as the actual average minimum in February (Takahashi & Arakawa 1981: 234).

An analogue for the warm savanna with *Plantago maritima*, which developed during the Bolling–Allerød, is Baghdad where the mean minima are 4.3°C and 25.3°C and the mean maxima 10.0°C and 34.8°C for January and July respectively. These calculations imply that there was a temperature increase at the elevation of Lake Zeribar of about 10°C between 14500 and 11000 BP, essentially the same as the estimate for the depression of temperatures at the peak of the most recent glaciation (Wright 1983: 506).

During the late Pleistocene, with snowlines depressed as much as 600m, most of the higher elevations may have been beyond exploitable limits even for goats. As the climate warmed, the vast regions of pasturage enjoyed by the caprines in the mountains today would have just been opening to potential colonization around 11000 BP. It might seem plausible that animals would readily move into new territory, but in the few cases studied it has been repeatedly observed that sheep are highly territorial and not given to exploration. Geist speculated that younger rams may have explored new territories and then colonized them when they were followed later by young ewes, but the process has never actually been observed. There are no observational data of which I am aware that informs on goat behaviour, but the two species are commonly thought to be similar. Whatever the process, following the initial emplacement into newly opened pastures (assuming that it happened before human intervention), the development of the oak forests would slowly and inexorably have segregated the previously open habitat by "interfering with migratory routes" (Hesse 1978: 328). Where once there had been vast open expanses with only topographic impediments, now pastures were becoming circumscribed by encroaching forests. All authors agree that neither sheep nor goats willingly travel into forests, despite the fact that both can be taught to travel *through* them on defined paths, and goats are well known to eat arboreal vegetation and even climb trees. We must infer, therefore, that any territorial instincts that may already have resided in these creatures were enhanced by the new realities.

With circumscription, and with higher evapotranspiration during the climatic optimum, forage would have died off sooner in the summer, reducing the quality of the pastures, and it would have been more difficult for herds to escape the heavier snows in winter through transhumance. These new conditions may have had a deleterious effect upon the overall caprine biomass and must have led periodically to the extinction of local populations, as happens even today during blizzards or droughts. Hesse (ibid.: 335) concludes that "in the early Holocene local sheep and goat populations were subject to wide fluctuations in density over the short term". Under such conditions, hunters depending on these animals may have embarked on a strategy of food resource management (FRM), that is, an effort to ensure that resources are available when needed. Managed resources are protected and/or enhanced in order to ensure continued or increased availability. Elimination of predators, culling of non-productive animals, enhancing the growth of pasturage, providing supplementary forage, and implanting animals into depleted or vacant habitats (ibid.: 336) are methods of FRM that can be carried out with wild populations, and which mimic behaviour typically expended upon domesticates. FRM thus may be a prerequisite to domestication and it represents a cultural threshold induced by a developing awareness of the relationships between cause (human actions) and effects (viability of herds).

As Hesse reconstructed it, one place where this may have occurred is Ganj Dareh Tepe, one of the highest early agricultural sites in the Zagros. A date of c. 12200 BP has been attributed to the basal layer E, but I have argued that a date for the site between c. 10000 and 9400 BP is more likely (Hole 1987). This supposition is strengthened by the fact that the earlier date would put Ganj Dareh well within the time of the Younger Dryas, when climate probably was the most severe since the late Pleistocene. However, the argument is clinched by the fact that agriculture is attested in the basal layer (van Zeist et al. 1984). My interpretation is that Ganj Dareh represents one of the first movements of livestock under the control of humans into the upland pastures. Because agriculture is also attested at Ganj Dareh, it is appropriate to ask whether it was an essential prerequisite for animal domestication.

It is often stated that hunters cannot have been directly involved in the domestication process, but this plays upon the stereotype of "Man the Hunter", too enthralled by the chase and inured to death, to care for nature's creatures. It is asked, how can a man trained from childhood as an efficient and selective killer turn into a husbandman? After writing off the probability of any male-induced transition that was not forced by the dire alternative of starvation, the argument proceeds, young girls or women must first have taken animals in as cuddly pets, perhaps successfully raising some in captivity, before men would learn to appreciate their advantages. Although such scenarios play powerfully on human sentiments, they give little insight into the process of domestication, and I argue that they are false analogies.

The more useful and realistic analogy is with food collectors whose subsistence is based on plants. The ethnographic literature is replete with examples of hunter–gatherers burning vegetation, scattering seeds, and diverting water to stands of wild grass. Harris (1989) has conveniently characterized a continuum of more intensive plant-exploitation activities that may be paralleled by humans who were attempting similarly to enhance their vegetative environment in the Zagros and, at least initially, inadvertently raising the carrying capacity for the ungulates. The literature leaves no doubt that modern hunters are well aware of the advantages of burning, and we may surmise that similar perceptions existed among the late Pleistocene hunters of Southwest Asia (Lewis 1972). Nevertheless, the limits inherent in arguing from the perspective of modern hunter–gatherers should be evident, and it remains to be demonstrated that *any* hunter–gatherers at the time of early domestication engaged in *any* kinds of resource "management". However, it is virtually certain that *normal* activities produced occasional *inadvertent* effects that would have been perceived and might later have developed into deliberate management.

Less speculative is how climatic shifts – from cold, dry, to warm, dry, to cold, dry, to warmer, wetter and more seasonal – affected the ungulates and the humans. In response to the spreading of forests from refugia, around 13000 BP humans began to cluster at sites where almonds, pistachios, acorns and fruits could be harvested in bulk. When the climate worsened again, people adopted more intensive means of exploiting these local foods. Then, after the Younger Dryas, as the climate warmed but seasonality increased, the lowland locations became less desirable and seasonal mobility resumed. The forests began to recolonize higher elevations, and the ungulate populations increased and altered their distribution patterns. The onagers and gazelles, which had previously frequented the higher mountain valleys, were now largely relegated to the drier, open, lowland steppe, whereas sheep and goats proliferated in the more upland regions. But, because of encroaching forests, isolated populations of these animals in the mountain plains were subject to catastrophic losses through either hunting or adverse weather, because they were unable to follow their former routes of transhumance and interaction.

Under such conditions, as Hesse has speculated (1978), human intervention in the herds would ensure access to livestock that hunting alone might no longer accomplish. As he and others have pointed out, it is not difficult to tame wild goats and sheep, because they bond quickly to humans when they are taken shortly after birth (Reed 1986, Tani 1987). Although herds could be propagated in this manner by protecting them from predators and provisioning them during the lean season, they also could be substantially augmented through expanded exploitation of mountain pastures under the leadership of human herders.

The scenario that emerges from a reconsideration of the Zagros Proto-Neolithic is one of a focus on storable resources in a very limited zone where trees remained in refugia, and a continued emphasis on hunting. As aridity became more intense, the biomass was reduced and it became more difficult to secure game all year round solely through hunting. In order to ensure adequate animal protein and products, the semi-sedentary gatherers of nuts and other plant foods seized control of nursery herds, nurtured the offspring, and eventually implanted managed herds (either seasonally or permanently) into formerly under-utilized mountain pastures. We do not yet know precisely when this happened, or even whether goats or sheep were the first domesticates, but the process is most likely to have occurred between 11000 and 10000 BP. Even at this time, however, it seems that there still were hunters practising transhumance, as at Asiab, whereas nearby, at Ganj Dareh, agriculturalist-herders were settling.

In sum, caprine domestication may have occurred a thousand years or so later than cereal agriculture began in the Levant, in response to similar climatic/environmental conditions. The practical implication of this conclusion is that further archaeological exploration should take place in northeastern Iraq, southeastern Turkey, and north-western Iran, preferably in the lower mountain valleys where herds might first have been implanted along the relatively easy routes of transhumance or migration that are still in use today (Hole 1980). The region that should be investigated is bracketed by the piedmont villages below 600 m, and the upland sites at 1300 m and above. As trees, shrubs and herbs recolonized the area, the first new territories must have been either within or just above the expanding forests and grasslands.

It is unlikely that an obviously "transitional" site will be found in which there is a replacement of morphologically wild with morphologically domestic fauna without apparent break in continuity. Indeed, unless sites were occupied over a considerable span, as was the case at Ali Kosh (Hole et al. 1969), such changes could not be placed in a true sequence. However, there is another problem: the speed at which mor-phological change may have taken place once herds were under human control and isolated from interbreeding with their wild relatives. This may have been an archae-ologically instantaneous change (Horwitz 1989). At the moment, because of political problems in the region concerned, such investigations cannot be carried out. How-ever, it may be possible to test the idea presented here, that environmental depletion, resulting from increasing seasonality, led to the abandonment of the piedmont vil-lages. Currently, archaeological data from three of these villages, Hallan Çemi, Nem-rik and Qermez Dere, are under examination. Because each village was occupied for a considerable length of time, analysis of the animal and plant remains in sequence should indicate whether there are noticeable changes in the composition of these remains, and whether the evidence for seasonal uses of the sites changes.

This leaves the final question. When and under what circumstances did cereal agri-culture arrive in this region? All the dates currently available imply that it did so dur-ing the PPNB, a thousand years or so after it began in the southern Levant. This lag allows for the natural expansion of grasslands as climate ameliorated from south to north and west to east (cf. Hillman in Ch. 10 in this volume). It cannot now be deter-mined whether the process of animal domestication was proceeding relatively inde-pendently of agriculture or occurred only after agriculture reached the region. Whatever the precise sequence may have been, once the connections were estab-lished, both the spread of agriculture eastwards and of animal domestication west-wards were rapid. And the fact that obsidian from the Van region begins to appear in Levantine sites, at about the same time as the introduction of livestock, suggests that it may have been spread by the herders.

Acknowledgements

I would like to thank Bonnie Hole for useful editorial suggestions and both she and Nicholas Kouchoukos for help with figures and the calibration of radiocarbon dates. Michael Rosenberg kindly provided unpublished information about Hallan Çemi, and I benefited from discussions with participants in the Prehistoric Society Conference about the general problems discussed in this chapter. However, the conclusions reached are mine.

References

Algaze, G., R. Breuninger, C. Lightfoot & M. Rosenberg 1991. The Tigris–Euphrates archaeological reconnaissance project: a preliminary report of the 1989–1990 seasons. *Anatolica* **17**, 175–240.

Becker, B., B. Kromer, P. Trimborn 1991. A stable isotope tree-ring time scale of the Late Glacial/ Holocene boundary. *Nature* **353**, 647–9.

Bintliff, J. L. 1982. Palaeoclimatic modelling of environmental changes in the east Mediterranean region since the last glaciation. In Bintliff & van Zeist (1982: 485–527).

Bintliff, J. L. & W. van Zeist (eds) 1982. *Palaeoclimates, palaeoenvironments and human communities in the eastern Mediterranean region in later prehistory.* Oxford: British Archaeological Reports, International Series 133

Bököny, S. 1982. The climatic interpretation of macrofaunal assemblages in the Near East. In Bintliff & van Zeist (1982: 149–63).

Bottema, S. 1992a. Cereal-type pollen in the Near East as indicators of wild or domestic crops. In *Préhistoire de l'agriculture: nouvelles approches expérimentales et ethnographiques* [Monographie 6, Centre de Recherches Archéologiques], P. C. Anderson (ed.), 95–106. Paris: Editions du CNRS.

— 1992b. Prehistoric cereal gathering and farming in the Near East: the pollen evidence. *Review of Palaeobotany and Palynology* **73**, 21–33.

Braidwood, R. J. & B. Howe (eds) 1960. *Prehistoric investigations in Iraqi Kurdistan* [Studies in Ancient Oriental Civilization 31, Oriental Institute]. Chicago: University of Chicago Press.

Clutton-Brock, J. 1981. *Domesticated animals from early times.* London: Heinemann and British Museum (Natural History).

— 1989. Introduction. In Clutton-Brock (1989: 1–3).

— (ed.) 1989. *The walking larder: patterns of domestication, pastoralism, and predation.* London: Unwin Hyman

COHMAP 1988. Climatic changes of the last 18,000 years: observations and model simulations. *Science* **241**, 1043–52.

Copeland, L. 1979. Observations on the prehistory of the Balikh valley, Syria, during the 7th to 4th millennia BC. *Paléorient* **5**, 251–75.

Davis, S. J. M. 1987. From hunter to herder: the origin of domestic animals. In *The archaeology of animals,* S. J. M. Davis, 126–54. London: Batsford.

Freitag, H. 1977. The pleniglacial, late glacial and early postglacial vegetations of Zeribar and their present-day counterparts. *Palaeohistoria* **19**, 87–95.

Geist, V. 1971. *Mountain sheep: a study in behavior and evolution.* Chicago: University of Chicago Press.

Hajdas, I., S. D. Ivy & J. Beer. 1993. AMS radiocarbon dating and varve chronology of Lake Soppensee: 6000 to 12000 ^{14}C years BP. *Climate Dynamics* **9**, 107–16.

Harris, D. R. 1989. An evolutionary continuum of people–plant interaction. In *Foraging and farming: the evolution of plant exploitation,* D. R. Harris & G. C. Hillman (eds), 11–26. London: Unwin Hyman.

Hesse, B. C. 1978. *Evidence for husbandry from the Early Neolithic site of Ganj Dareh in western Iran.* [PhD dissertation, Department of Anthropology, Columbia University]. Ann Arbor, Michigan: University Microfilms.

Hole, F. 1970. The paleolithic culture sequence in western Iran. In *Proceedings of the VII International Congress of Prehistoric and Protohistoric Sciences, Prague,* 286–92. Prague: Institut d'Archéologie de l'Academie Tchecoslovaque des Sciences à Prague.

— 1980. The prehistory of herding: some suggestions from ethnography. In *L'archéologie de l'Iraq du début de l'époque néolithique à 333 av. n/ère: perspectives et limites de l'interpretation anthropologique des documents,* M. Barrelet (ed.), 119–30. Paris: Editions du CNRS.

— 1984. A reassessement of the Neolithic Revolution. *Paléorient* **10**, 49–60.

— 1987. Chronologies in the Iranian Neolithic. In *Chronologies in the Near East,* O. Aurenche, J. Evin, F. Hours (eds), 353–79. Oxford: British Archaeological Reports, International Series 379 i.

— 1989. A two-part, two-stage model of domestication. In Clutton-Brock (1989: 97–104).

— 1991. Feyda, Kuran. *American Journal of Archaeology* **94**, 687–8.

— 1993. The prehistory of the Khabur. In *La Djezire et l'Euphrate syriens de la protohistoire à la fin*

du second millenaire av. J. C.: tendances dans l'interpretation historique des donées nouvelles,
O. Rouault & M. Wäfler (eds), Paris: ADPF, Ministère des Affaires Etrangères.

— 1994. Khabur Basin PPN and early PN lithic industries. In *Studies in early Near Eastern production, subsistence and environment 1*, H. G. Gebel & S. K. Kozlowski (eds), 331–48. Berlin: Ex Oriente.

Hole, F. & K. V. Flannery 1967. The prehistory of western Iran: a preliminary report. *Proceedings of the Prehistoric Society* 33, 147–206.

Hole, F., K. V. Flannery, J. A. Neely 1969. *Prehistory and human ecology of the Deh Luran plain: an early village sequence from Khuzistan, Iran.* Memoir 1, Museum of Anthropology, University of Michigan.

Hopf, M. 1983. Jericho plant remains. In *Excavations at Jericho,* K. M. Kenyon & T. A. Holland (eds), 576–621. London: British School of Archaeology at Jerusalem.

Horwitz, L. K. 1989. A reassessment of caprovine domestication in the Levantine Neolithic: old questions, new answers. In *People and culture in change,* I. Hershkovitz (ed.), 153–81. Oxford: British Archaeological Reports, International Series 508 i.

Houérou, H. N. le 1981. Impact of man and his animals on mediterranean vegetation. In *Ecosystems of the world* I: *terrestrial ecosystems, 11 – Mediterranean-type shrublands,* F. di Castri, D. W. Goodall, R. L. Specht (eds), 479–521. Amsterdam: Elsevier.

Howe, B. 1983. Karim Shahir. In *Prehistory archeology along the Zagros flanks,* L. S. Braidwood, R. J. Braidwood, B. Howe, C. A. Reed, P. J. Watson (eds), 23–154. Publication 105, Oriental Institute, University of Chicago.

Kozlowski, S. K. 1990. *Nemrik 9: Pre-Pottery Neolithic site in Iraq: (General Report – Seasons 1985–1986).* Warsaw: University of Warsaw.

— 1992. *Nemrik 9: Pre-Pottery Neolithic site in Iraq, vol.2: House No.1/1A/1B.* Warsaw: University of Warsaw.

Kozlowski, S. K. & A. Kempisty 1990. Architecture of the pre-pottery neolithic settlement in Nemrik, Iraq. *World Archaeology* 21, 348–62.

Kromer, B. & B. Becker 1992. Tree-ring ^{14}C calibration at 10000 BP. In *The last deglaciation: absolute and radiocarbon chronologies,* E. Bard & W. S. Broecker (eds), 3–11. Berlin: Springer.

Lewis, H. T. 1972. The role of fire in the domestication of plants and animals in Southwest Asia: a hypothesis. *Man* 7, 195–222.

Lotter, A. F., B. Ammann & J. Beer 1992. A step towards an absolute time-scale for the Late Glacial annually laminated sediments from Soppensee (Switzerland). In *The last deglaciation: absolute and radiocarbon chronologies,* E. Bard & W. S. Broecker (eds), 45–68. Berlin: Springer.

Mayewski, P. A., L. D. Meeker, S. Whitlow 1993. The atmosphere during the Younger Dryas. *Science* 261, 195–7.

McCorriston, J. 1992. *The early development of agriculture in the ancient Near East: an ecological and evolutionary study.* PhD dissertation, Department of Anthropology, Yale University.

McCorriston, J. & F. Hole 1991. The ecology of seasonal stress and the origins of agriculture in the Near East. *American Anthropologist* 93, 46–69.

Moore, A. in press. Abu Hureyra and the beginning of agriculture and village life. In *La Djezire et l'Euphrate syriens de la protohistoire à la fin du second millenaire av. J. C.: tendances dans l'interpretation historique des donées nouvelles,* O. Rouault & M. Wäfler (eds), . Paris: ADPF, Ministère des Affaires Etrangères.

Moore, A. M. T. & G. C. Hillman 1992. The Pleistocene to Holocene transition and human economy in Southwest Asia: the impact of the Younger Dryas. *American Antiquity* 57, 482–94.

Mortensen, P. 1975. Survey and soundings in the Holailan Valley 1974. In *Proceedings of the IIIrd Annual Symposium on Archaeological Research in Iran,* 1–12. Tehran: Iranian Centre for Archaeological Research.

Nahal, I. 1981. The mediterranean climate from a biological viewpoint. In *Ecosystems of the world* I: *terrestrial ecosystems, 11 – Mediterranean-type shrublands,* F. di Castri, D. W. Goodall, R. L. Specht (eds), 63–86. Amsterdam: Elsevier.

Oates, J. 1982. Archaeological evidence for settlement patterns in Mesopotamia and eastern Arabia in relation to possible environmental conditions. In Bintliff & van Zeist (1982: 359–93).

Olszewski, D. I. 1993a. The Zarzian occupation at Warwasi Rockshelter, Iran. In *The Paleolithic prehistory of the Zagros–Taurus*, D. I. Olszewski & H. L. Dibble (eds), 207–36. Philadelphia: The University Museum, University of Pennsylvania.

— 1993b. Subsistence ecology in the Mediterranean forest: implications for the origins of cultivation in the Epipaleolithic southern Levant. *American Anthropologist* **95**, 420–35.

Reed, C. A. 1986. Wild animals ain't so wild, domesticating them not so difficult. *Expedition* **28**, 8–15.

Rosenberg, M. 1994. Hallan Çemi Tepesi: some further observations concerning stratigraphy and material culture. *Anatolica* **20**, 121–40.

Rosenberg, M. & M. K. Davis 1992. Hallan Çemi Tepesi, an early aceramic Neolithic site in eastern Anatolia. *Anatolica* **18**, 1–18.

Rosenberg, M. & H. Togul 1991. The Batman River archaeological site survey, 1990. *Anatolica* **17**, 241–54.

Ruffner, J. A. & F. E. Bair (eds) 1984. *The weather almanac*. Detroit: Gale Research.

Sherratt, A. 1980. Water, soil and seasonality in early cereal cultivation. *World Archaeology* **11**, 313–30.

Stuiver, M. & P. J. Reimer 1993. Extended ^{14}C data base and revised CALIB 3.0 ^{14}C age calibration program. *Radiocarbon* **35**, 215–30.

Takahashi, K. & H. Arakawa (eds) 1981. *Climates of southwestern and western Asia*. Amsterdam: Elsevier.

Tani, Y. 1987. Two types of human interventions into the sheep flock: intervention into the mother–offspring relationship, and raising the flock leader – their geographic distribution and meanings among southwest Eurasian pastoralists. In *Domesticated plants and animals of the southwest Eurasian agro-pastoral culture complex*, vol. II: *pastoralism*, Y. Tani (ed.), 1–42. Kyoto: The Research Institute for Humanistic Studies, Kyoto University.

— 1989. The geographical distribution and function of sheep flock leaders: a cultural aspect of the man-domesticated animal relationship in southwestern Eurasia. In Clutton-Brock (1989: 185–99).

Taylor, K. C., G. W. Lamorey, G. A. Doyle 1993. The "flickering switch" of late Pleistocene climate change. *Nature* **361**, 432–6.

Turnbull, P. F. 1975. The mammalian fauna of Warwasi rock shelter, west-central Iran. *Fieldiana* **33**, 141–55.

van Zeist, W. & J. A. H. Bakker-Heeres 1982 (1985). Archaeobotanical studies in the Levant. I. Neolithic sites in the Damascus Basin: Aswad, Ghoraifé, Ramad. *Palaeohistoria* **24**, 165–256.

van Zeist, W. & S. Bottema 1977. Palynological investigations in western Iran. *Palaeohistoria* **19**, 19–85.

— 1982. Vegetational history of the eastern Mediterranean and the Near East during the last 20,000 years. In Bintliff & van Zeist (1982: 277–321).

van Zeist, W., P. E. L. Smith, R. M. Palfenier-Vegter 1984. An archaeobotanical study of Ganj Dareh Tepe, Iran. *Palaeohistoria* **26**, 201–24.

Watkins, T. 1990a. Qermez Dere. *American Journal of Archaeology* **94**, 285–6.

— 1990b. The origins of house and home? *World Archaeology* **21**, 336–47.

Wright, H. E., Jr 1983. Climatic change in the Zagros Mountains – revisited. In *Prehistoric archaeology along the Zagros flanks*, L. S. Braidwood, R. J. Braidwood, B. Howe, C. A. Reed, P. J. Watson (eds), 505–10. Chicago: Oriental Institute Publications, vol. 105.

— 1989. The amphi-Atlantic distribution of the Younger Dryas climatic fluctuation. *Quaternary Science Reviews* **8**, 295–306.

— 1993. Environmental determinism in Near Eastern prehistory. *Current Anthropology* **34**, 458–69.

Zohary, D. 1992. Domestication of the Neolithic Near Eastern crop assemblage. In *Préhistoire de l'agriculture: nouvelles approches expérimentales et ethnographiques* [Monographie 6, Centre de Recherches Archéologiques], P. C. Anderson, (ed.), 81–6. Paris: Editions du CNRS.

CHAPTER FIFTEEN

The one-humped camel in Asia: origin, utilization and mechanisms of dispersal

Ilse Köhler-Rollefson

Introduction

The dispersal of the one-humped camel or dromedary (*Camelus dromedarius*) in Eurasia occurred in historical times. This process began at the end of the second millennium BC with the emergence of the Midianites from the Arabian peninsula and probably was not concluded before the fourteenth century AD when the one-humped camel apparently reached its present most easterly distribution in the continent, in India (Köhler-Rollefson 1993). The eastward spread of the camel is documented through historical records and artistic representations rather than through osteological finds from archaeological sites. Because the camel was, in comparison with other domestic animals, a late arrival in Asia, the process of its dispersal affords an excellent opportunity for focusing on one dimension of human–animal relationships that is rarely touched upon by prehistorians and zooarchaeologists. Scientific efforts usually concentrate on establishing the temporal and locational contexts of domestication, whereas the factors that determine the *function* or *position* that an animal species comes to occupy in a particular culture are seldom considered. Yet the latter aspects have far-reaching ecological and socio-economic implications. They have the potential to influence the interaction of a culture with its natural environment far into the future and to shape its social structure fundamentally.

Attitudes to animal domestication and domesticates

When pondering the reasons and incentives for the first domestication of a new taxon, or the dissemination of an already domesticated species to another culture, scholars tend to be influenced by their own cultural backgrounds. Thus, it is often a foregone conclusion for observers with Western cultural backgrounds that sheep and goats were brought under human control to serve as "livestock", that a crucial motive of cattle and horse domestication was their physical power, and that dogs were integrated into human society to act as guards or hunting companions. However, as even a cursory glance at cross-cultural human–animal relationships amply demonstrates, most animals singled out for domestication have the potential to serve a very wide variety of purposes. Furthermore, the function of animals in human societies is usually not restricted to utilitarian purposes; they often fulfil important and culturally distinct symbolic and ritual roles. Their position can range from being a pet or even an object of religious veneration to being shunned and declared ritually unclean. Among the better known examples are the cow figuring as an object of religious devotion in Hindu culture, but rather unsentimentally considered exclusively as a source of food in Western culture, and the dog who became the closest friend of humans in the West, while being regarded as a culinary delicacy in eastern Asia and classified unclean in Muslim culture. Attitudes can vary even among neighbouring and closely related cultural groups; for instance, horse-meat consumption is socially acceptable in France and Belgium, but rejected in Germany and Britain.

These examples may suffice to demonstrate that the ways in which cultures interact with individual animal species are highly specific and quite frequently develop into hallmarks of identity. The attitude shown towards particular animals can provide an emblem for community identification and, in extreme cases, can become a rallying point against others. The Indian Mutiny of 1857, which was kindled by rumours that bullets had been greased with fat from cows and pigs and had thereby become ritually unclean to both Hindus and Muslims, provides an excellent illustration of this point.

Only rarely have the factors that were responsible for shaping a society's relationship with a domestic animal been reconstructed, and in many cases very little evidence is available. Yet this is a question that is of more than just academic interest. Human–animal relationships, whether they are preferences or avoidances, can have far-reaching consequences for the interaction of a society with its environment. Heavy economic and dietary reliance on goat and sheep husbandry in Southwest Asia contributed to degradation of rangeland and deforestation, probably already in prehistoric times (Köhler-Rollefson 1991a), whereas social restrictions on sheep and goat breeding based on explicit ecological considerations among the communities of India's Thar Desert may have deferred similar processes there until the early part of the twentieth century (Mohnot pers. comm.). On the other hand, the ban on cow slaughter in India, which according to some anthropologists (e.g. Harris 1975) may have initially represented a sound response to local conditions, is rejected by most economists and animal scientists as economically and ecologically destructive in the current context of population pressure and depleted vegetation cover (Lodrick 1981). Yet, there is no indication that the attitude that regards the cow as sacrosanct will change.

Variations in cultural attitudes towards animals can sometimes be traced back to separate centres of domestication, for instance in the case of the dog, which may have been domesticated independently in several different parts of Eurasia (cf. Uerpmann in Ch. 12 in this volume). The Southeast Asian tradition of regarding this animal as a food source is already evident there in early times (Herre & Röhrs 1990), in China apparently since the Neolithic (Ben-Shun 1984). Arguably, the Western companion relationship with this species may already be reflected in the Natufian "puppy burial" from 'Ain Mallaha (Davis & Valla 1978).

Although the details are still hazy, the one-humped camel seems to be among those animals that were domesticated within one geographically well defined area, in this case the Arabian peninsula (Mikesell 1955, Compagnoni & Tosi 1978, Hoch 1979; Uerpmann 1987: 48–52). From this area of origin it was dispersed over all of northern Africa, parts of East Africa, and Asia as far east as India. More recent attempts to introduce it to other parts of the globe, including Australia and the Americas, did not meet with lasting success. Despite originating from a single "hearth", camels are used in a wide variety of ways, and a remarkable range of socioreligious relationships with this species has developed in pastoral societies. The purpose of this chapter is to try to reconstruct how these evolved, with special reference to India. There, at the eastern margin of its distribution, the one-humped camel has come to occupy a unique social role for the pastoral societies that breed it, and it is used there in a way that is very much at variance with patterns prevailing elsewhere in the world.

Utilization of the dromedary in India

A detailed description of camel utilization in India and of the Indian brand of camel pastoralism illustrates the multi-faceted and differentiated role animals can play in a people's economic and social life. With 1.1 million dromedaries, India has the third largest camel population in the world. They are concentrated in its western states, Rajasthan and Gujarat, to some extent also in Haryana and, formerly, in the Punjab (Khanna et al. 1990). Other parts of India are climatically unsuitable for camels. The economic role of camels is largely restricted to providing draught power for carts, for ploughs and for lifting water. Their extensive use for traction is a recent development that postdates the Second World War, and can be linked to the invention of the current type of cart that is equipped with used aeroplane tyres (Kothari pers. comm.). This vehicle provides transport regardless of the presence or condition of roads, and has effectively revolutionized rural transport in Rajasthan. Previously, camels were used mainly as beasts of burden and were preferred to ox carts only in sandy desert. Because the loading and unloading of camels at overnight stops was very time-consuming, ox carts had a comparative advantage on the main traffic arteries, but this has changed with the introduction of the new camel carts, which, because of their larger size, are much more efficient than ox carts.

Whereas small-scale ownership is widespread and not restricted to any particular caste, the large- scale breeding and supply of camels is in the hands of a Hindu caste called the Raikas or Rebaris (Köhler-Rollefson 1992a,b). Numbering about 200,000 families, the Raikas usually specialize in either sheep or camel breeding, in addition to serving as hired herders for livestock owners belonging to other castes. The camel-breeding Raikas own sizeable herds of camels, averaging 20–50 head in the more humid parts of Rajasthan and 50–200 head in the sparsely populated zone of the extreme west. The present rationale of their breeding system is to produce camels for the market in draught animals. They sell all their young male camels at large markets such as Pushkar or Tilwara. Male animals are preferred on account of their superior strength. Female animals are much less sought after as work animals; in addition, their sale is not condoned by caste conventions.

Other camel products are of little significance. The Raikas observe an absolute taboo against the slaughter of camels and the consumption of camel meat. Hindu beliefs in vegetarianism and *ahimsa* (i.e. the sanctity of all life) present no satisfactory explanation for this phenomenon, because at least some Hindus consume mutton and produce sheep for sale as slaughter animals. In addition, certain Muslim camel-breeding groups in the border areas between India and Pakistan, including the Sindhi Muslims of the Jaisalmer area, and the nomads of the Cholistan desert, also abhor the consumption of camel meat.

The Raikas do sporadically milk their camels to augment the domestic milk supply from their goats or buffaloes, and migrant herdsmen may on occasion even subsist exclusively on camel milk for periods lasting several weeks. However, it is always only a very small percentage of lactating females that is milked, and most of the milk potential remains unexploited.

One of the cultural tenets of the Raikas holds that camel milk should always be consumed fresh; it is not supposed to be heated or processed into curd. The reasons given for this avoidance are not consistent. A minority of Raikas considers that camel milk does not have the right properties to be processed into curd, an explanation that is questionable because African and Arabian camel nomads successfully manufacture it. More frequently, prohibition by local deities and gods, such as Pabuji and Shakti-mata, are alluded to. The Raikas also view the sale of camel milk with contempt, an attitude that they share with other camel pastoralists. At the same time it is common practice to give away camel milk free to members of the village community.

Camel wool is a scarce product that is kept for the manufacture of domestic articles, such as shawls, blankets, ropes, string-beds, and so on. The Raikas commonly profess that camel wool should not be sold, but this attitude seems to be changing. Camel dung is sold by certain sedentary camel breeders as fertilizer. The Raikas do not use the products that can be obtained from the dead animal (skin and bones), even though there is a market for them.

The role of the camel in Raika society transcends purely utilitarian aspects. According to their myths of origin, the first Raika was created by Lord Shiva for the express purpose of looking after the first camel that the goddess Parvati had just shaped from clay. The camel is an essential component of wedding rituals, and female camels are always part of the dowry, even today when sons may no longer engage in camel herding but take up wage labour instead. On memorial stelae, Raika ancestors are often depicted as riding on a camel. Camel-mounted female deities are worshipped by the Rebaris of Gujarat (Westphal-Hellbusch & Westphal 1974).

The dromedary in other pastoral societies

A brief survey of the economic and sociocultural role of the dromedary in modern pastoral societies demonstrates the unique nature of the Indian human–camel relationship and puts it into a wider perspective.

From an ecological viewpoint, camel pastoralism can be termed the ultimate human arid-land adaptation (Köhler-Rollefson 1992a). Camel pastoralists are the only human groups in a position seasonally to exploit arid regions that receive less than 200mm of annual rainfall. The range of the one-humped camel extends from Mauritania in the west to the Indian Thar Desert in the east, and thus overlaps almost exactly the Old World arid-zone belt. The factors that inhibit the wider dispersal of the camel include humidity and temperature. One-humped camels are not well adapted to low temperatures and especially cannot withstand cold dampness. In humid tropical areas camels succumb to the insect-transmitted disease, trypanosomiasis (cf. Wilson 1984).

Camels can be put to myriad different uses. The economic productivity of the camel can be summarized as follows: camels can produce up to 10kg of milk per day or 4000 litres per lactation period, even under traditional methods of pastoral management; their meat is tasty, with live weights of up to 600kg and carcass weights of around 300kg; they can be bled to provide about 5 litres of blood per month; wool yields are 1–1.5kg per camel per year; their dung is an excellent fuel and has fertilizing effects; they can carry burdens of up to 200kg at a pace of 2–3km/hour; and as riding animals they can cover distances of 65–80km per day over extended periods, or 112km per day for two days, or 144km in one day (Wilson 1984, Köhler-Rollefson 1991b). However, camel pastoral societies tend to make use of only a limited range of the products that are theoretically available. Concentrating on one aspect often entails trade-offs on other products. For instance, if there is a heavy emphasis on milk production, this will affect meat output; different breeds of camels are used for riding and as beasts of burden; blood is taken only from non-milking animals.

Three broad patterns can be distinguished in the geographical distribution of camel utilization (Köhler-Rollefson 1993):

- Subsistence-orientated systems prevail in the Horn of Africa, which has the largest concentration of camels. Cushitic-speaking groups, such as the Somalis, Rendille, Gabra, and Turkana, place heavy emphasis on milk utilization, and camel milk represents a crucial part of their diet, with all other considerations taking second place. Camels are not used for riding, although to some extent they serve as pack animals and provide meat; these groups are also the only ones who bleed their camels to obtain food (bleeding is prohibited in Islam). Interaction with camels is dominated by rituals. Milking of camels can be undertaken only by celibate males; twice a year there are large gatherings at which castrated male camels are ritually killed and feasted on; and many camel-related transactions can only take place on certain days of the week (Sato 1980, Schlee 1989, Stiles 1992).

- The Arabian Bedouins and North African camel pastoralists of Arab descent practise a multi-purpose utilization, making the most complete and pragmatic use of their camels, with few ingrained taboos (cf. Hitti 1981). In the past they used the camel as source of food and also provided large numbers of camels for the market in transport animals, although they maintained separate breeding populations for these purposes. These groups used camel milk, but it did not represent the mainstay of their diet, with some exceptions (Cole 1975). Today the market for caravan animals is being replaced by an emerging demand for camel meat among the poorer people of the large urban centres.

- (c) In Asia, camel utilization is largely restricted to transportation. With the exception of the Raikas of Rajasthan (Köhler-Rollefson 1992a,b) and the Jats of the Indus Delta (Westphal-Hellbusch & Westphal 1964), no specialized camel pastoralists have been described. But many sheep/goat pastoralists in Afghanistan, Iran, and Pakistan keep a few camels as pack animals to transport their belongings on migrations (Tapper 1985). [*Editor's comment*: the one-humped camel is bred, and milked, by at least some pastoralists in Central Asia, e.g. in the Kara Kum Desert in southern Turkmenistan (personal observation 1989).]

Early historical evidence for the dromedary in western Southwest Asia

Although we still know very little about the initial stages of domestication of the camel in the Arabian peninsula (Köhler-Rollefson 1990), it is clear that when the camel first appeared in the Levant it was as a fully domesticated animal with attendant pastoral populations. Biblical references imply that the camel arrived here with a vengeance, in the guise of hordes of camel-mounted tribes such as the Midianites who spilled out of northern Arabia into the eastern Mediterranean area and wreaked havoc on the agricultural fields of its settled population. According to Judges (6:5), these groups and their camels "were without number" and inflicted devastating damage on the cultivated fields of the Israelites. Although the Midianites who occupied the Hisma and the coastal mountains of northern Arabia in the twelfth and thirteenth centuries BC should probably be regarded as the earliest camel breeders to whom we can attach a name, Knauf (1988) depicts them in a much more balanced manner, concluding that they were agro-pastoralists who combined terraced agriculture with camel breeding, as well as mining and trading activities. From the ninth century BC onwards, these tribes are referred to only as "Aribi" (Arabs). The first time the Arabs are mentioned in written historical records, it is in connection with camels. This is in reference to a sheikh called Gindibu who supported the Aramean king of Damascus in a battle in 833 BC at Qarqar in Syria against the Assyrian king Shalmaneser III. Gindibu reportedly had 1,000 camels (Eph'al 1982). In 733 BC Samsi, the queen of the Arabs, engaged in a fight with the Assyrian king Tiglat-Pileser III. The booty he took from her included 30,000 camels, in addition to captives, sheep, and spices. She later paid tribute that included camels, she-camels, and their young. Literary sources indicate that, besides controlling desert pasturage, she also had a share in the spice trade (ibid.).

In summary, the existing historical and archaeological data make it evident that the first camel pastoralist societies that evolved in the Arabian peninsula entered the core area of Near Eastern civilizations at the transition from the second to the first millennium BC. The historical records also indicate that, at that time, the prime use of camels was for raiding and warfare, and that camel-mounted warriors could gain military and thus political strength. This advantage was quickly realized by major powers such as the Assyrians, who entered into alliances with the camel pastoralists who had initially threatened their security and integrated them into their armies. Thus, Esarhaddon deployed camel troops during his second Egyptian campaign at Thebes in 671

BC. A century later the Persian king Cambyses relied on camels to carry water on his foray into Egypt. Other Persian kings also employed dromedaries in warfare. In the battle of Sardes in 546 BC, Cyrus purposefully deployed dromedaries to frighten the horses of his enemy Croesus, king of Lydia, a tactic that worked; and in 480 BC his descendant Xerxes also employed a corps mounted on dromedaries during his campaign in Greece (Zeuner 1963: 347–8).

In spite of references to the use of the dromedary by the Achaemenids, even under their successors, the Parthians, two-humped camels appear to have been more prevalent than one-humped camels. Only under the Sasanians do the depictions of one-humped camels start to predominate in seal impressions and on silver plates showing Bahram Gur (Bulliet 1975). Bulliet concluded that the one-humped camel slowly displaced the two-humped camel in Central Asia as a vehicle for trade along the Silk Roads, and he credited the Parthians with recognizing the superior load-carrying abilities of hybrids between Bactrians and dromedaries, but the military use of the dromedary for both logistic and strategic purposes may have been an equally or even a more important factor in this dispersal. The practice of cross-breeding the two species continued, however, at least until AD 1000 in the Indus Valley, as is testified by Al Idrisi, and eleventh-century Arab traveller (Eliot & Dowson 1867).

The arrival of the dromedary in India

The time of the first occurrence of the one-humped camel in the Indian subcontinent is a subject of controversy (Sathe & Atre 1988–9, and cf. Meadow in Ch. 22 in this volume). There are claims for the presence of the camel in the Indus Valley civilization of the third millennium BC, and several Harappan sites have produced camel bones (Sewell & Guha 1931, Prashad 1936, Nath 1962, Thapar & Lal 1969), some of which were described as derived from *Camelus dromedarius*. A photograph of a camel skeleton from Sir Mortimer Wheeler's excavations at Mohenjo Daro has been published (Meadow 1984). However, artistic representations strongly suggest that it was the two-humped Bactrian camel that was represented at these early sites in Pakistan and India. Excavations at Pirak in the Kachi Plain of Pakistan produced clay figurines of two-humped camels from levels dating to the second and first millennium BC (Meadow 1979); and the two-humped camel is also evidenced by figurines found at sites in the Yamuna-Ganges Valley from AD 300 to 600 (Prakash 1985).

The first definite reference to the dromedary in the Indian subcontinent appears to be in connection with the Muslim conquest. On his invasion of Sind in AD 717, Muhammed bin Qasim was accompanied by troops including 6,000 soldiers mounted on dromedaries and a baggage train of 3,000 Bactrian camels (Elliot & Dowson 1867). The lack of definite earlier evidence suggests that the dromedary arrived in the Indian subcontinent as part of Islamic culture. But it is not impossible that it had already been introduced into Sind with the conquests of Darius (525 BC) or Alexander (326–325 BC), both of whom are known to have employed dromedary-mounted troops on their campaigns elsewhere. In either case there is little doubt that the function of the dromedary when it entered the subcontinent was as an adjunct to military operations.

However, there is a big difference between the incidental arrival of an animal in a new area and its active adoption by the local population, even more so the development of a pastoral society specializing in its production. Evidence for these advanced stages in the integration of the camel into the local socio-economic system comes considerably later. According to local folklore and a frequently recited oral epic, the camel was popularized in Rajasthan by the Rajput hero Pabuji, an historical figure who lived at the beginning of the fourteenth century. The Rajputs composed Rajasthan's ruling elite of maharajahs, feudal lords and lesser landowners. Pabuji, who ruled over a small estate in western Rajasthan, is said to have abducted herds of female camels belonging to a Muslim ruler in Lankia, a village near Umarkot in Sind, relying on the help of a Raika named Harmel (Smith 1991).

Scholars insist that the camel was known in Rajasthan prior to Pabuji's time, and they refer to isolated artistic representations of the camel that predate Pabuji, including stone carvings at the ninth-century temple of Bardoli and at Kiradu that are thought to date to the twelfth century (Srivastava 1981). Historical sources also attest that the Muslim invaders, Mahmud of Ghazni (AD 997–1030) (Nazim 1931) and Ala-ud-din Khilji (AD 1296–1316) (Srivastav 1981) employed large numbers of burden camels as logistical support on their forays into Hindustan. But there is no indication that the camel was actively adopted and bred by Rajasthan's local population prior to the fourteenth century, and a careful scrutiny of historical references suggests that the camel population of India began to expand shortly after the exploits of Pabuji. A fourteenth-century Arab writer stated that in India camels were owned only by kings and potentates (Spies 1936), and for the Delhi ruler, Muhammed ibn Tuluq, who ruled from AD 1325 to 1351, the camel presented to him by Ibn Battuta was apparently still something of an oddity (Ibn Battuta 1971). By contrast, his successor Firuz Shah Tuluq (AD 1351–1388) is reported to have had a "thriving camel establishment in the district of Dublahan where whole villages were appropriated to them and their keepers" (Elliot & Dowson 1871: 356–7). It thus seems reasonable to deduce that although camels may have made an occasional appearance in Rajasthan/India prior to the fourteenth century, camel pastoralism did not develop until after that date.

Apart from the mythical Raika named Harmel, who is said to have helped bring camels to Rajasthan, the first historical mention of the Raika/Rebari caste dates to the time of the Mughal emperor Akbar (AD 1566–1605). In a description of court life in Delhi, the Rebari are characterized as "a class of Hindus who are acquainted with the habits of the camel", who served as camel-mounted messengers and were put in charge of herds of breeding camels (Abu'l Fazl Allami 1965: 155). Another reference indicates that they came to the Mughal court from Rajasthan together with Rajput brides betrothed to Mughal princes. "They were skilled camel-keepers, which the Muslims were not, and a story goes that once, when camel milk was prescribed for a Jodhpur princess at Akbar's court, no one could milk a she-camel except a Rahbari" (Ibbetson et al. 1970: 269).

There are few historical sources for Rajasthan predating Akbar's reign that could elucidate the beginnings of the relationship between Rajputs and Raikas. But for Mughal and later periods a clear picture can be pieced together. During the Mughal period (AD 1526–1707) the Rajput kings of Rajasthan established camel corps for use in warfare, and in order to have a steady supply of camels available they also maintained herds of breeding camels (Saxena 1989). For the specific purpose of looking after these herds they employed Raikas, a relationship that continued until the beginning of this century (Srivastava 1991).

Summarizing the historical evidence, it is clear that the dromedary arrived in India as a military animal linked with kings and feudal lords rather than the rural population. The Raika/Rebari pastoralists did not adopt camel breeding for subsistence purposes, but were appointed to take care of the camel herds owned by royalty and nobility. In the beginning of the twentieth century the requirements of Rajput rulers for camels to fulfil military functions petered out, and since the 1950s they have been replaced by a demand for draught animals by the rural population.

Cultural and ecological factors

The historical context in which the camel was introduced to India can account for some facets of the Indian system of camel utilization. The fact that the dromedary was introduced into Rajasthan as a means of military transportation must have shaped local perceptions about possible ways of using this animal, and it was adopted solely in that function by Rajput feudatories. Because Rajasthan already supported a wide spectrum of domestic animals that provided a full range of livestock products, there was no impetus for using the camel for any purpose other than transportation.

However, several sociocultural and ecological factors probably also contributed to the development of restrictions on camel utilization. Being entrusted with supervising the herds of breeding camels of the royalty and nobility, the Raikas had an opportunity to become intimately aware of the camel's potential uses. Their relationship to the camel was probably influenced by the fact that they initially did not own camels, but acted only as caretakers. This would have acted as a powerful constraint on the slaughter or killing of camels. The Raikas may also have consciously or subconsciously transferred the special status that Rajputs confer on the horse as a mount and in wedding rituals to their relationship with the camel.

An ecological explanation can be proposed for the various rules of Raika society that prevent intensive utilization of milk, such as the prohibition against the sale and the processing of milk. In a pastoral system geared towards the production of calves, milk exploitation is counterproductive. Intensive milking of camels significantly depresses their reproductive rate by interfering with conception, slowing down rates of calf growth and causing high rates of calf mortality. The milk-orientated systems of camel pastoralism in East Africa have rates of calf mortality of about 30 per cent (Schwartz & Walsh 1993). By contrast, the Raikas report hardly any losses among their camel calves.

The remaining idiosyncracies of the camel-utilization practices of the Raika, such as the refusal to sell wool or parts of the carcass, can be explained as an outcome of the traditional *jajmani* village economic system that was based on the exchange of services and products between different castes rather than cash transactions (Lewis

1958). For instance, the utilization of the carcass for leather is the traditional prerogative of a special caste, the Chamars.

Comparison with dispersal of the dromedary in Africa

The forces behind the dispersal of the dromedary throughout Asia differed starkly from those that obtained for its spread in northeastern Africa, the area where it is presently of greatest economic importance. There is strong ethnographic evidence, summarized by Bulliet (1975), that the dromedary was introduced into Africa from Arabia via two different routes. It arrived in North Africa via the Sinai, but apparently was not widely used in the area until around the second or third century AD, when it became popular for pulling ploughs as well as being used for transportation (Brogan 1954).

In the Horn of Africa, where the camel's potential value as a source of food is the prime consideration, its expansion can be linked to increasing desiccation. Although no date can be attached to the event, it is generally assumed that the camel was introduced to the Horn of Africa from southern Arabia across the Strait of Bab el Mandab (Bulliet 1975, Wilson 1984). Possibly this feat can be attributed to the Sabaeans, a southern Arabian people who colonized parts of northern Ethiopia in the first millennium BC. Archaeological and historical evidence for the area is scanty, but there appears to have been a gradual southward spread of pastoral groups towards Kenya, and it has been suggested that, between the tenth and the thirteenth centuries AD, some camel pastoral groups moved into the Chalbi region of northern Kenya (Stiles 1984). The continuing southward spread of the camel in Kenya during the nineteenth and twentieth centuries is well documented. The originally cattle-breeding Turkana obtained camels through raids in the nineteenth century. With the aim of improving the drought tolerance of their herds, other formerly cattle-orientated groups, such as the Samburu (Sperling 1987), the Pokot (Bollig 1992), and even some Maasai groups, are now following suit. These groups are supported in this economic transformation by Western and local aid agencies who acknowledge that the camel is the ideal means of sustainably utilizing arid lands, affording its owners a greater degree of economic security and drought survival than any other domestic animal. In West Africa a similar southward expansion of the camel is also in process. Here the camel is adopted mainly by farmers to carry harvested grain from the fields to storage facilities (rim 1992).

Conclusions

Human–animal relationships are often remarkably constant through the ages. Once established, a certain manner of interaction usually becomes so deeply ingrained into the cultural make-up and ideology of a group that it is virtually impossible to change, even if an alteration of the ecological or economic context of their lives would render this sensible. Animals that were originally adopted as pets will not become sources of food, and vice-versa. Just as the cow is unlikely to lose its sacred status among Hindus, dogs or cats will never appear on Western menus, and pigs will probably not advance to membership of Western households, even if they could make an important contribution to the disposal of organic garbage in urban environments. It seems that only changes in religious adherence have the power to override the prevailing attitudes of human groups to particular animals. In ancient Egypt, cats were venerated and they occupied almost god-like positions, but they lost this special status for the local population with the advent of Christianity (Herre & Röhrs 1990). In Jordan, pork consumption was substantial during Byzantine times, but lost significance when the area came under Islamic rule. Because of this apparent power of religious persuasions to shape human attitudes towards animals, a detailed reconstruction of the cultural process by which the camel, as an Islamic instrument of warfare, was integrated into the local Hindu social structures of western India promises to be a fascinating line of enquiry. And, although it occurred in relatively recent times, the dispersal of the dromedary is a process that is of interest and relevance also to prehistorians, because it demonstrates archaeologically invisible aspects of the spread of animal domesticates.

Acknowledgements

Field and archival research in India was supported by the American Institute of Indian Studies, New Delhi, and the National Geographic Society, Washington DC. It was conducted in affiliation with the National Camel Research Centre in Bikaner and the Rupayan Sansthan in Jodhpur to whose respective directors, Dr N. D. Khanna and Padamshree Komal Kothari, I am grateful for guidance. Field investigations about the Raika camel pastoralists benefited substantially from the help of Dr D. R. Dewasi, Mr H. S. Rathore, and Dr V. K. Srivastava, and Dr G. O. Rollefson provided helpful input into the writing process. I would like to express my sincere thanks to all of the above.

References

Abu "l-Fazl Allami 1965. *Ain-i Akbari* [translated into English by H. Blochmann]. Delhi: Aadiesh Book Depot.
Ben-Shun, C. 1984. Animal domestication in Neolithic China. In *Animals and archaeology, 3: early herders and their flocks*, J. Clutton-Brock & C. Grigson (eds), 363–69. Oxford: British Archaeological Reports, International Series 202.
Bollig, M. 1992. East Pokot camel husbandry. *Nomadic Peoples* 31, 34–50.
Brogan, E. 1954. The camel in Roman Tripolitania. *Papers of the British School at Rome* 9, 126–31.
Bulliet, R. W. 1975. *The camel and the wheel*. Cambridge, Mass.: Harvard University Press.
Cole, D. 1975. *Nomads of the nomads: the Al-Murrah Bedouin of the Empty Quarter*. Arlington Heights: AHM Publishing.
Compagnoni, B. & M. Tosi 1978. The camel: its distribution and state of domestication in the Middle East during the third millennium BC in the light of finds from Shar-i-Sokhta. In *Approaches to faunal analysis in the Middle East*, R. H. Meadow & M. A. Zeder (eds), 91–103. Cambridge, Massachusetts: Harvard University, Peabody Museum Bulletin 2.
Davis, S. & F. R. Valla 1978. Evidence for the domestication of the dog 12,000 years ago in the Natu-

fian of Israel. *Nature* **276**, 608–10.

Elliot, H. M. & J. Dowson 1867. *The history of India, as told by its own historians*, vol. 1. London: Truebner.

Elliot, H. M. & J. Dowson 1871. *The history of India, as told by its own historians*, vol. 3. London: Truebner.

Eph'al, I. 1982. *The ancient Arabs*. Leiden: Brill.

Harris, M. 1975. *Cows, pigs, wars, and witches*. New York: Vintage.

Herre, W. & M. Röhrs 1990. *Haustiere – zoologisch gesehen*. Stuttgart: Gustav Fischer.

Hitti, P. 1981. *History of the Arabs*. London: Macmillan.

Hoch, E. 1979. Reflections on prehistoric life at Umm an-Nar (Trucial Oman) based on faunal remains from the third millennium BC. In *South Asian Archaeology 1977*, M. Taddei (ed.), 589–638.

Ibbetson, D., E. MacLagan, H. A. Rose 1970. *A glossary of the tribes and castes of the Punjab and North-West Frontier Province*, vol. 3. Lahore: Languages Department, Punjab.

Ibn Battuta 1971. *The travels of Ibn Battuta ad 1325–1354*. Cambridge: Cambridge University Press.

Khanna, N. D., A. K. Rai, S. N. Tandon 1990. Population trends and distribution of camel population in India. *Indian Journal of Animal Sciences* **60**, 1093–101.

Knauf, E-A. 1988. *Midian. Untersuchungen zur Geschichte Palästinas und Nordarabiens am Ende des 2. Jahrtausends v. Chr.* Wiesbaden: Otto Harrassowitz.

Köhler-Rollefson, I. 1990. An update on domestication and dispersal of the dromedary. In *Proceedings of the International Conference on Camel Production and Improvement, 10–13 December, 1990, Tobruk, Lybia*, 49–53.

— 1991a. Resolving the revolution: Late Neolithic refinements of economic strategies. *Archaeozoologica* **3**, 201–8.

— 1991b. Camelus dromedarius. *Mammalian Species* **375**, 1–8.

— 1992a. The Raika camel pastoralists of western India. *Research and Exploration* **8**, 117–9.

— 1992b. The Raika dromedary breeders of Rajasthan: a pastoral system in crisis. *Nomadic Peoples* **30**, 74–83.

— 1993. Camels and camel pastoralists in Arabia. *Biblical Archaeologist* **56**, 180–8.

Lewis, O. 1958. *Village life in northern India*. New York: Vintage Books.

Lodrick, D. 1981. *Sacred cows, sacred places. Origin and survival of animal homes in India*. Berkeley: University of California Press.

Meadow, R. H. 1979. A preliminary note on the faunal remains from Pirak. In *Fouilles de Pirak*, J. F. Jarrige, J-F. Enault & M. Santoni (eds), 334. Paris: Diffusion de Boccard.

Meadow, R. H. 1984. A camel skeleton from Mohenjo-Daro. In *Frontiers of the Indus civilization*, B. B. Lal & S. P. Gupta (eds), 133–9. New Delhi: Books & Books.

Mikesell, M. W. 1955. Notes on the dispersal of the dromedary. *Southwestern Journal of Anthropology* **11**, 231–45.

Nath, B. 1962. Remains of horse and Indian elephant from prehistoric site of Harappa. *Proceedings of the 1st All India Congress of Zoology* **2**, 1–14.

Nazim, M. 1931. *The life and times of Sultan Mahmud of Ghazna*. Cambridge: Cambridge University Press.

Prakash, P. 1985. *Terracotta animal figurines in the Ganga Yamuna valley (600 BC – 600 AD)*. Delhi: Agam Kala Prakashan.

Prashad, B. 1936. Animal remains from Harappa. *Memoirs of the Archaeological Survey of India* **51**, 1–62.

rim 1992. *Nigerian national livestock resource survey* [6 vols]. Report by Resource Inventory and Management Limited (rim), Abuja, Nigeria.

Sathe, V. G. & S. Atre 1988–89. The problem of the camel in the Indus civilization. *Bulletin of the Deccan College Postgraduate and Research Institute* **47–48**, 301–6.

Sato,.S. 1980. Pastoral movement and the subsistence unit of the Rendille of northern Kenya. *Senri Ethnological Studies* **6**, 1–78.

Saxena, R. K. 1989. *The army of the Rajputs*. New Delhi: Munshiram Manoharlal.

Schlee, G. 1989. *Identities on the move: clanship and pastoralism in northern Kenya*. Manchester: Manchester University Press.

Schwartz, H. J. & M. G. H. Walsh 1993. Improving reproductive performance in the dromedary: consequences to production systems. In *Actes de l'atelier "Peut-on améliorer les performances de reproduction des camelins?"*, G. St. Martin (ed.), 409–25. Paris: CIRAD-EMVT.

Sewell, R. & B. S. Guha 1931. Zoological remains. In *Mohenjo-daro and the Indus civilization*, J. Marshall (ed.), 649–72. London: Probsthain.

Smith, J. 1991. *The epic of Pabuji: a study, transcription, and translation*. Cambridge: Cambridge University Press.

Sperling, L. 1987. The adoption of camels by Samburu cattle herders. *Nomadic Peoples* **23**, 1–18.

Spies, O. 1936. *An Arab account of India in the 14th century*. Stuttgart: Bonner Orientalistische Studien.

Srivastav, A. K. 1981. *Khalji sultans in Rajasthan*. Buxipur: Purvanchal Prakashan.

Srivastava, V. K. 1991. Who are the Raikas/Rabaris? *Man in India* **71**, 279–304.

Srivastava, V. S. 1981. The iconography of the ustravahini devi. In *Cultural contours of India* V. S. Srivastava (ed.), 178–87. New Delhi: Abhinav Publications.

Stiles, D. 1984. Stopping the desert spread with a camel. *The Ecologist* **14**, 38–43.

— 1992. The Gabbra: traditional social factors in aspects of land-use management. *Nomadic Peoples* **30**, 26–40.

Tapper, R. 1985. One hump or two? Hybrid camels and pastoral cultures. *Production Pastorale et Société* **16**, 55–69.

Thapar, B. K. & B. B. Lal 1969. Excavations at Kalibangan, District Ganganagar. In *Indian Archaeology 1964–65 – a review*, A. Ghosh (ed.), 35–9. New Delhi: Archaeological Survey of India.

Uerpmann, H-P. 1987. *The ancient distribution of ungulate mammals in the Middle East* [Beihefte zum Tübinger Atlas des Vorderen Orients, Reihe A (Naturwissenschaften) 27]. Wiesbaden: Dr L. Reichert.

Westphal-Hellbusch, S. & H. Westphal 1964. *The Jat of Pakistan*. Berlin: Duncker & Humblot.

— 1974. *Hinduistische Viehzüchter im nordwestlichen Indien*, vol. 1. *Die Rabari*. Berlin: Duncker & Humblot.

Wilson, R. T. 1984. *The camel*. Harlow, England: Longman.

Zeuner, F. E. 1963. *A history of domesticated animals*. London: Hutchinson.

PART THREE
Europe

CHAPTER SIXTEEN

The development of agriculture and pastoralism in Greece: when, how, who and what?

Paul Halstead

Research into the development of agriculture and pastoralism in Greece has been as much a story of changing questions as of accumulating answers. In this case, the questions have often been implicit rather than explicit, but "when", "how", "who" and "what" have successively dominated most research over the past four decades. Current answers to these four questions are here reviewed in turn.

When?

During the 1950s and 1960s, soundings at open sites such as Argissa (Boessneck 1962, Hopf 1962), Knossos (Evans 1968, Jarman & Jarman 1968), Lerna (Gejvall 1969) and Nea Nikomedeia (Higgs 1962, van Zeist & Bottema 1971) established that the earliest known neolithic settlements in Greece (Fig. 16.1), of seventh millennium bc date, used a range of cereal and pulse cultigens and domestic animals. Evidence for the use of gathered wild plants or hunted wild animals was extremely sparse and the full "package" of cereals and pulses, together with domestic sheep, goat, cow and pig, appears more or less ubiquitous on early neolithic settlements (Halstead 1992a). Compared with west Mediterranean Europe (Lewthwaite 1986), these sites suggest a rapid substitution of domesticates for wild resources.

The process of adoption of domesticated plants and animals has been investigated in most detail at Franchthi cave (Fig. 16.1), the only site in Greece with a published bioarchaeological sequence spanning the mesolithic–neolithic transition. Here the uppermost mesolithic levels, dating to the eighth millennium bc, are characterized by bones (Payne 1975, 1985) of red deer (*Cervus elaphus*) and (presumably wild) pig (*Sus scrofa*) and by a range of gathered plants (Hansen 1991) including oat (*Avena* sp.), wild barley (*Hordeum spontaneum*) and lentil (*Lens* sp.). From *c.* 7000 bc, the succeeding "aceramic neolithic" levels are characterized by remains of sheep (*Ovis aries*), goat (*Capra hircus*), pig, emmer (*Triticum dicoccum*), two-row barley (*H.*

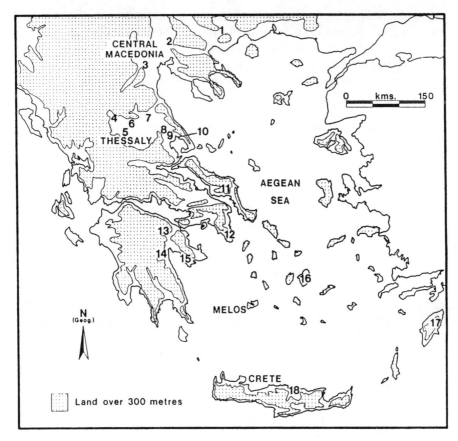

Figure 16.1   Map of Greece, showing sites and regions referred to in the text.
1. Sitagroi; 2. Assiros Toumba; 3. Nea Nikomedeia; 4. Theopetra; 5. Prodromos; 6. Zarko; 7. Argissa; 8. Sesklo; 9. Dimini; 10. Pevkakia; 11. Skoteini; 12. Kitsos; 13. Nemea; 14. Lerna; 15. Franchthi; 16. Zas; 17. Kalythies; 18. Knossos

distichum) and larger-seeded lentil. From *c.* 6000 bc, the ceramic-neolithic levels also include remains of cattle (*Bos* sp.) and einkorn (*T. monococcum*).

At Franchthi, it is possible that the adoption of domesticates took place piecemeal over a period of several centuries. After the appearance of sheep/goat, which defines the beginning of the Neolithic, pig is first documented towards the end of the Aceramic Neolithic and cattle in the Ceramic Neolithic – although the existing preliminary report (Payne 1975) does not indicate that the earliest specimens of pig and cattle were domesticated. Crops too may have been introduced several centuries after the appearance of sheep and goat. The evidence for domesticated plants in the aceramic neolithic levels is restricted to 27 specimens of emmer, 8 of lentil and 5 of barley (from Hansen's Zone VI and Interzone V/VI), and these might have been introduced by later cuttings and burrows, as has been argued for a few pieces of pottery found in the same levels (Perlès 1990). Even if these specimens are not intrusive, the domesticated status of lentil and barley is not beyond question. The mesolithic and neolithic lentils differ only in the slightly larger size of the latter, and the aceramic neolithic specimens fall within the overlap zone between the two periods and so cannot be categorized as either small/wild or large/domesticated (Hansen 1991). In the case of barley, it is not clear how secure was the identification of the five aceramic neolithic grains to domestic two-row barley rather than the wild barley represented in the mesolithic levels.

On the other hand, Franchthi cave may well be unrepresentative of the early farming economy on open settlements. The associated open settlement known as Franchthi "Paralia" was not founded until the Ceramic Neolithic (Wilkinson & Duhon 1990), and finds of shed deciduous teeth show that, during the Aceramic Neolithic, sheep and goats were corralled in the cave (Payne 1985). The absence at Franchthi cave of the "sickle blades" so characteristic of early neolithic open sites also suggests some functional specialization (Perlès 1988). On available radiocarbon dating evidence (Jacobsen & Farrand 1987), aceramic neolithic Franchthi may be no earlier than ceramic early neolithic levels at open sites with a wide range of animal and plant domesticates and so may have been no more than a "satellite" herding camp of a mixed farming settlement elsewhere (Payne 1975).

Although domestic animals and plants seem, in contrast with west Mediterranean Europe, to have been adopted as an integrated "package" in Greece, the spread of this "package" was apparently a very gradual process. The earliest, seventh-millennium bc farming sites are strongly concentrated in the fertile lowlands of eastern mainland Greece and in particular in Thessaly (Theochares 1973, Wijnen 1982, Halstead 1994). In the western mainland, in much of the northeastern and southeastern mainland and in the smaller islands, recognizable farming settlements are either absent or rare before the later Neolithic or Early Bronze Age, that is, the fifth to third millennia bc (Theochares 1973, Zachos 1987, Cherry 1981, 1990, Halstead 1994). In the mountains of northwestern Greece, widespread evidence of agricultural colonization is as yet known only from the Late Bronze Age to Early Iron Age transition, that is, the late second to early first millennium bc (Kilian 1973, Vokotopoulou 1986).

How?

The question of when domesticates appeared in Greece is usually a prelude to considering how they came to be there. In the case of early neolithic Knossos on Crete, the entire suite of domestic animals was apparently absent from the indigenous fauna and so must have been deliberately introduced by human colonists (Sondaar 1971, Jarman in press), whether from mainland Greece or from farther east. In mainland Greece, cattle and pigs were hunted at mesolithic Franchthi and so might have been domesticated locally. Suggestions of reduced size in these two species, even in the earliest known neolithic levels at open settlements (Boessneck 1962, Jarman & Jarman 1968, von den Driesch 1987, Payne & Bull 1988), are compatible with the introduction of already domesticated stock, but might equally reflect the failure to find earlier sites where initial domestication took place. Goat, however, and the commonest domestic animal, sheep, were almost certainly introduced from farther east (Payne

1985). Lentil and barley were also exploited at mesolithic Franchthi, and populations of wild lentil (Ladizinsky 1989), einkorn (Zamanis et al. 1988) and barley (Efthimiadis et al. 1985) are widespread in Greece today. Cytogenetic studies suggest that modern domesticated lentils are derived from wild populations in Southwest or Central Asia (Ladizinsky 1989), but the same need not be true of neolithic lentils, so local domestication in Greece cannot as yet be excluded (but see Zohary in Ch. 9 in this volume, for a contrary view). There is no evidence for local wild progenitors of emmer, apparently the most important cereal in neolithic Greece, or of bread wheat. Therefore, at least some of the domesticates must have been introduced to Greece, and the same may be true for the remainder.

However, Franchthi does provide some evidence for local pre-adaptation to the adoption of domesticated cereals (cf. Dennell 1983: 167; Zvelebil 1986). Seeds of wild oat are among the most abundant and most regularly encountered plant remains in the upper mesolithic levels at Franchthi, but disappear from the record at the beginning of the Neolithic. If wild oat ceased to be collected because its place was taken by domesticated cereals, this perhaps implies that the mesolithic inhabitants were already dependent on the seeds of wild cereals as a major source of carbohydrates and so may have been predisposed to adopt cultivated cereals when these became available.

Who?

Partly because at least some of the domesticates seem to have been introduced to Greece, the "how" question is often rephrased as a "whodunnit": immigrants from farther east or mesolithic inhabitants of Greece? This simple opposition between immigrants and natives may be a false dichotomy: for ecological, demographic and social reasons, foraging groups in Greece are likely to have been fairly sparse, mobile and fluid in composition, and may have formed part of a single interbreeding population with similar groups in western Turkey (cf. Wobst 1974, Wiessner 1982; Binford 1983: 204–8). The appearance in mesolithic levels at Franchthi of obsidian from Melos, one of a chain of islands linking mainland Greece and Turkey, underlines the feasibility of pre-neolithic interaction across the Aegean (Renfrew & Aspinall 1990). Nonetheless, several lines of evidence have been used in attempts to choose between the immigrant and indigenous alternatives.

- Archaeobotanical and archaeozoological evidence is ambiguous. The introduction to Greece of at least some domesticates has been thought suggestive of immigrant farmers, but hints in the Franchthi plant remains of mesolithic pre-adaptation to the use of cultigens reinforce the case for indigenous adoption.
- The extreme rarity of recognizable mesolithic sites in Greece (Perlès 1990), particularly in areas of dense neolithic settlement such as Thessaly, has been cited as evidence for the immigration of farmers (e.g. Hansen 1991), but in this case absence of evidence is surely not evidence of absence. The human group that used Franchthi cave during the Mesolithic probably amounted to no more than a "minimum band" of 25 or so persons (Jacobsen 1981) and, simply to ensure demographic viability, must have formed part of a larger breeding unit of at least

175–475 (Wobst 1974). The implication is that further mesolithic sites await discovery in Greece, for instance, the recently excavated Theopetra cave (Fig. 16.1) in Thessaly (Fakorellis et al. in press).

• Cultural evidence is also problematic. For most of Greece, the material traces of any mesolithic inhabitants are more or less unknown, precluding assessment of local (dis)continuity. The earliest chipped stone assemblages from neolithic open settlements in Thessaly (e.g. Argissa: Fig. 16.1), have little in common with mesolithic Franchthi, in tool types or basic production strategies, but this may be the result of comparing sedentary farming villages with a seasonal foraging camp. Even if contrasting production strategies cannot be explained in "functional" terms (Perlès 1988), "stylistic" traits should not be seen as a passive reflection of biological genealogy, but as an active statement of cultural affiliation (e.g. Conkey & Hastorf 1990) and as such are unlikely to have remained unaffected by the radical social and demographic changes that accompanied the spread of farming. This is particularly clear in the case of neolithic Crete, where material culture reveals the isolation of the island's human population rather than their origins (Broodbank 1992).

At Franchthi, continuity can be examined more directly. The aceramic neolithic chipped-stone assemblage includes a few new elements, but the major break occurs at the beginning of the Ceramic Neolithic (Perlès 1990). This new industry has more in common with neolithic open settlements in Thessaly than with mesolithic Franchthi. The aceramic neolithic assemblage from Franchthi is extremely small, but the same picture emerges from Shackleton's (1988) study of the marine molluscs from the cave. These exhibit striking continuity through the upper mesolithic and aceramic neolithic levels, which share an assemblage dominated by *Cerithium vulgatum*. A change to a more mixed assemblage occurs in the Ceramic Neolithic. Thus, change in both lithic industry and marine molluscan assemblage does not coincide with the introduction of domestic animals and perhaps crops in the Aceramic Neolithic, but with the founding of the open "Paralia" settlement outside the cave and with the unambiguous presence of cereal and pulse crops in the Ceramic Neolithic. If the Paralia settlement represents the first appearance at Franchthi itself of a sedentary, mixed-farming community, this is likely to have influenced the lithic assemblage both directly, by imposing new tasks, and indirectly, by occasioning shifts in patterns of mobility and time scheduling which affected the acquisition and working of lithic raw materials. Shifts in mobility are also likely to have affected the "embedded procurement" of shellfish (Shackleton 1988). Conversely, the lack of change at the beginning of the Aceramic Neolithic suggests that the introduction of domestic animals was not disruptive to existing patterns of stone tool production or shellfish procurement. This continuity between the Mesolithic and Aceramic Neolithic has been interpreted as an expression of cultural identity: Perlès (1990) again emphasizes basic strategies of lithic production, while Shackleton (1988) persuasively argues that the molluscan assemblage represents human selection among the species available near Franchthi.

The safest conclusion is that the types of evidence presently available are incapable of resolving the geographical and biological origins of the first farmers in Greece. The most economical interpretation of Franchthi is as a site peripheral to the inception of arable farming, but more suggestive of the adoption of domesticates by indigenous foragers than of their introduction by immigrant farmers. Although the discontinuity between the Aceramic and Ceramic Neolithic might be explicable in purely "functional" terms, this is far less plausible for the continuity between the Mesolithic and Aceramic Neolithic.

The hypothesis of indigenous adoption also receives some circumstantial support from the spatial pattern of agricultural colonization in Greece. The apparent absence of early farming settlements from the smaller islands, from much of the southeastern mainland and from the high mountains, can plausibly be explained in terms of the increased risk of farming in areas of low rainfall, limited ecological diversity, or poor soils (Cherry 1981, Halstead 1981, 1990). The absence of early farming sites in the well watered and fertile southwestern mainland, however, and their rarity in much of lowland central Macedonia, with its exceptional wealth of large rivers, cannot readily be explained in terms of ecological impediments to farming. If future research reveals that populations of foragers persisted in these two areas through the earlier Neolithic, the distribution of seventh millennium bc farming settlements may reflect the adoption of domesticates by foragers under stress.

What?

Research to date on early farming in Greece has tended to neglect arguably the most basic question – "What?". In practice, research has concentrated on the spread of cereal and pulse cultigens and "farmyard" animals, with the tacit assumption that the presence of such species is evidence of a new agricultural or pastoral economy. The terms "agriculture" and "pastoralism", in turn, implicitly conjure up visions of recent Mediterranean rural economy, dominated by extensive cereal cultivation in alternation with bare fallow, by local specialization in olives or vines, and by the transhumant movement of sheep flocks between summer pastures in the mountains and winter pastures on lowland fallow fields. Each of these elements of "traditional" land use has been seen as a response to the Mediterranean environment, specifically to the climate of mild wet winters and hot dry summers and to the mountainous terrain (Grigg 1974: 123–7), and so has been widely extrapolated to later prehistory (e.g. Renfrew 1972, Jarman et al. 1982, Sampson 1993).

It is now clear, however, that "traditional" mediterranean land use is not simply a timeless response to the regional environment (Halstead 1987):

- Extensive cereal agriculture is characteristic of large landholdings, which rely on labour-saving crops (cereals rather than pulses), labour-saving methods of cultivation (ploughing with animals rather than hand-tillage) and labour-saving husbandry practices (fallowing rather than weeding, manuring, etc.) to supply cheap grain to urban dwellers and the rural poor, who in turn provide the essential seasonal labour force at harvest time. Extensive agriculture is thus dependent on marked inequality of land ownership, whereby some have more land than they can themselves cultivate and others have too little land to sustain themselves (Halstead 1992a).

- Local specialization in olives and vines is dependent on the shifting opportunities of a global market economy, with such perennial crops being grubbed out in favour of staple grain crops during periods of economic instability.
- Transhumant pastoralism tends to be practised only by flocks too large to be fed perennially in either the lowlands or uplands and is dependent on large-scale clearance in both lowlands and uplands, on large lowland estates which maintain extensive blocks of fallow land suitable for winter grazing, and on an urban market or comparable outlet for pastoral produce (Lewthwaite 1981, Cherry 1988, Halstead 1990).

It is arguable that in Greece these preconditions of "traditional" land use existed, at the earliest, from the second millennium bc, when there is evidence of regional redistributive centres and marked social inequality (Killen 1985) and of extensive clearance at least in the lowlands (Bottema 1982). Significantly, even at this late date, there are indications that extensive agriculture, local specialization in olives and vines, and extensive sheep herding may have been characteristic only of land use under the direct control of the late Bronze Age palaces (Halstead 1992a, cf. Jones 1992).

If "traditional" patterns of extensive land use did not begin to emerge until the second millennium bc or even later, what was the nature of neolithic farming? In many parts of mediterranean Europe, extensive agriculture co-existed until a few decades ago with holdings too small to justify the costs of maintaining plough animals (e.g. Delille 1977 [Italy], Psikhoyios 1987 [Greece]). Such small holdings were instead cultivated by hand and were often farmed under an intensive "horticultural" regime, rather than a scaled-down version of plough agriculture: cereal–pulse rotations were favoured over the alternation of cereal with fallow, and crops were regularly manured and weeded (e.g. Halstead & Jones 1989). Several lines of evidence provide more or less indirect support for such a horticultural regime in neolithic Greece:

- The first indications of animal traction in Greece, a yoked oxen figurine from Nemea (Pullen 1992) and the keeping of adult male cattle at Pevkakia (Jordan 1975, Amberger 1979) (Fig. 16.1), are of third millennium bc date (broadly contemporary with early evidence for ox-traction and the plough in other parts of Europe – Sherratt 1981); such sparse evidence should not be pushed too far, but is consistent with small-scale cultivation and manual tillage in neolithic Greece.
- The existing archaeobotanical record of cleaned crop products suggests that, in sharp contrast to recent extensive agriculture, the labour-intensive pulses were grown as commonly as cereals in neolithic Greece (Halstead 1994).
- The extreme difficulty of detecting agricultural clearance in the palynological record until the later Bronze Age (Bottema 1982) is compatible with small-scale neolithic cultivation, although existing lowland cores are from large catchments in which clearance might easily be masked.
- The overwhelming predominance of sheep at early neolithic settlements (Halstead 1992b), in a relatively wooded landscape well suited to cattle, pigs and goats, perhaps indicates that stock husbandry was also small scale and was closely integrated with cleared land, thus helping to maintain the fertility of arable plots.
- The decrease in size of domestic cattle and pigs during the Neolithic (von den Driesch 1987) suggests that these animals were effectively isolated from inter-

breeding with their larger wild relatives and so also implies close supervision near the settlement rather than extensive herding in the surrounding woods.

For neolithic Central Europe and for late Bronze Age Assiros Toumba in northern Greece (Fig. 16.1), an intensive, horticultural regime is suggested by crop weeds (Jones 1992) and it is to be hoped that, in the future, the nature of crop husbandry in neolithic Greece will also be clarified by the recovery of adequate weed assemblages.

The proposed regime of small-scale farming, both arable and pastoral, implies that cereal and pulse crops were the mainstays of subsistence. The typical early neolithic "village" settlement of perhaps 50–300 persons was too large for a significant contribution to be made to energy requirements by livestock, unless these were managed intensively for milk production – and the evidence of mortality patterns suggests that this was not the case, at least for the commonest domestic animal, the sheep (Halstead 1989).

Livestock may, nonetheless, have played a vital role in subsistence. Greece is climatically similar to (if not indeed part of) the broad Southwest Asian source area of early plant and animal domesticates. The fertile lowlands of eastern mainland Greece, where known early neolithic settlements are concentrated, offered a favourable environment for early farmers, although staple crops would have faced occasional hazards from rainless winters, late frosts and so on. To some extent, farmers can cushion themselves against the risk of failure by growing a range of crops with different growth requirements and tolerances, and neolithic farmers in Greece grew a strikingly wide range of cereals and pulses (Halstead 1989). Although extensive archaeobotanical work on early neolithic sites in Central Europe has produced little firm evidence for crops other than emmer or an emmer–einkorn maslin (Willerding 1980), a mere handful of early neolithic sites in Greece (Argissa, Knossos, Nea Nikomedeia, Prodromos and Sesklo, Fig. 16.1) has yielded caches of emmer, einkorn, bread/macaroni wheat (*T. aestivum / T. durum*), naked barley (*H. vulgare var. nudum*), lentil, pea (*Pisum sativum*), grass pea (*Lathyrus sativus*) and bitter vetch (*Vicia ervilia*). In the event of more pervasive crop failure, wild resources would have offered limited succour to village communities and there is little bioarchaeological evidence for their use. However, livestock may have offered a significant alternative source of food, and the emphasis on sheep, which store fat well, and the management of flocks according to a low-risk "meat" strategy, may have ensured a reliable supply of energy (Redding 1981, Halstead 1992b).

During the later Neolithic and Early Bronze Age, the colonization of the agriculturally marginal hills of the southeastern mainland and the arid Cycladic islands is likely to have further boosted the importance of livestock, as has been argued for marginal colonization in temperate Europe (Legge 1981, Halstead 1989). At the same time, the widespread prevalence of small "hamlet" settlements will have reduced the degree of obligatory dependence on arable farming for subsistence. To varying degrees, livestock husbandry at the cave sites of Kitsos on the mainland (Jullien 1981) and Skoteini (Kotjabopoulou & Trantalidou 1993), Kalythies (Halstead & Jones 1987) and Zas in the islands (Fig. 16.1) placed far higher reliance on goats than at the earlier villages. At about the same time, there is evidence from several lowland areas in the eastern mainland of major episodes of erosion, implying substantial destabilization of the landscape (van Andel et al. 1990, Zangger 1991), while increases in the pollen of the hornbeams (*Carpinus ostrya* (= *Ostrya carpinifolia*) and *C. betulus*) may reflect increasing levels of browsing (cf. Turrill 1929). The chronological and spatial resolution of both the geoarchaeological and palynological evidence is as yet coarse, but, combined with the increasing relative importance of goats, it may indicate more extensive livestock husbandry in agriculturally marginal areas from as early as the later Neolithic (Halstead 1981, cf. Sampson 1993).

Land use during at least the earlier Neolithic, however, is likely to have been small scale, intensive and stable, so that the availability of human labour rather than land would have been the limiting factor in farming. Recognition of the key importance of labour directs attention to the nature of early farming society.

What society?

As has already been noted, the typical early farming settlement was a village, of perhaps 50–300 inhabitants. Such large aggregations placed severe constraints on subsistence, more or less forcing reliance on stored cereal and pulse crops. Dependence on stores of highly seasonal crops, with heavy labour requirements around planting and harvesting time, favours the isolation of a family labour force and the establishment of obstacles to wider sharing (Flannery 1972). In common with similar early farming villages in Mesoamerica, Southwest Asia and the southern Balkans (Tringham 1971, Flannery 1972), Greek neolithic villages are characterized by substantial rectangular houses, enclosing some form of family household. These houses contrast sharply with the small, one- or two-person huts that characterize some pre- or proto-neolithic settlements in Southwest Asia (Flannery 1972) and the Balkans (Srejovic 1972) – and they are reported from some of the earliest neolithic habitation-levels in Greece (e.g. Protonotariou-Deïlaki 1992).

The subsistence strategies of individual domestic units in neolithic Greece have received very little attention, but there is some evidence that individual households grew a range of crops and kept a range of livestock, so reducing the risk of subsistence failure (Halstead 1992b). Nonetheless, as Sahlins (1974: 41–148, esp. 86) has observed, the Achilles' heel of the neolithic "domestic mode of production" is the dependence of individual households on periodic assistance from the wider community. Individual households would have been vulnerable to fluctuations in the numbers of both consumers and workers, and the death or incapacity of a key worker at a critical point in the domestic cycle, or at a time when stores had been depleted by a poor harvest, would have been particularly threatening to the survival of the household. Two interrelated responses are, first, overproduction and the storage of the resulting surplus (which increases stress on the labour force) and, secondly, the cultivation of social relationships which can be mobilized to provide labour or food in time of need. Such social relationships tend to be created and maintained through hospitality, thus adding a further incentive for overproduction.

In practical terms, reliance on neighbours for help in times of need would have been facilitated by the prevailing early neolithic pattern of village settlement. The crowded nature of these neolithic villages, in comparison with rural settlements in modern Greece, would have maintained social pressure against domestic hoarding (cf. Whitelaw 1983) and it is possible that the remarkable residential stability which gave rise to the distinctive "tell" settlements in the lowlands of eastern Greece reflects the high premium placed on maintaining ties of neighbourliness.

Perhaps as a consequence of this interdependence between neighbours, the architectural isolation of the family household was a very gradual process. In early and middle neolithic villages, such as Sesklo (Fig. 16.1), cooking facilities were commonly located outdoors in the open spaces between houses (Theochares 1980), inviting the sharing of cooked food. At late neolithic villages such as Dimini (Fig. 16.1), external facilities still occur, but sharing was constrained by walls or ditches that subdivided the settlement into smaller residential areas (Hourmouziadis 1979). By the Final Neolithic and Early Bronze Age, the isolation of the family household was completed with the building of internal "kitchen extensions", as at Sitagroi (Renfrew 1970), or the enclosing of the house within a walled courtyard, as at Pevkakia (Milojcic 1972) (Fig. 16.1).

The recurrent labour crises of the neolithic household and the inevitable tensions between domestic isolation and collective security, between hoarding and sharing, perhaps found expression in material culture – in painted house models and human figurines (Hourmouziadis 1973) and even in a model family apparently deposited as a foundation offering under a late neolithic house at Zarko (Gallis 1985) (Fig. 16.1). Such figurines, and elaborately decorated tableware underlining the social significance of food and drink, largely disappeared during the Final Neolithic and Early Bronze Age with the ultimate architectural isolation of the family household.

Conclusions

In the lowlands of the east-central mainland, the neolithic "package" of domestic plants and animals was adopted more or less wholesale in the seventh millennium bc. In other regions of Greece, marginal to farming or perhaps favourable to foraging, the spread of this package seems to have been delayed by up to several millennia. How these domesticates spread is uncertain, but adoption by indigenous foragers remains a strong possibility.

Even more gradual than the spread of the domesticates was the development of extensive farming systems akin to traditional "agriculture" and "pastoralism". In prehistory, such extensive husbandry practices may have been restricted to arable estates and flocks managed directly by the late Bronze Age palatial authorities.

Neolithic farming may have more closely resembled recent intensive horticulture than agriculture, and this, *inter alia*, focuses attention on human labour as a critical constraint on survival and thus on the nature of early farming society. The isolation of the family household as the basic unit of production and consumption appears to have been a very gradual process, taking place over three to four millennia. The tension between the managerial simplicity of domestic self-sufficiency, and the long-term necessity for mutual help between neighbouring households, may account for the architectural isolation of the house, the symbolic emphasis on human figurines, and the decorative elaboration of vessels suitable for the provision of hospitality.

In the early farming communities of the Balkans, a very similar material culture has been interpreted in terms of a wide-ranging concern with the opposition between "domus", representing the domestication of both nature and society, and "agrios", its wild counterpart (Hodder 1990: 44–99). It is by no means impossible that the westward movement of domesticates was accompanied by the spread of such an ideology, but nor is there any reason to believe that early farmers did, conveniently, share the prehistorian's obsession with the domestication of nature or society. The interpretation advanced here is that this distinctive material culture reflects the tension between the neolithic household and the wider village community (cf. Sahlins 1974). This interpretation is more contextually sensitive than Hodder's highly generalized model, arising as it does from an attempt to identify the social and economic problems posed for early farmers in Greece by the conjuncture of particular patterns of residence (the family household), settlement (the village community) and land use (intensive horticulture with small-scale stock husbandry).

The question "Why?" has not been explicitly addressed here for two reasons. First, the answer to this question is often built into the answer to the question "how": immigrant farmers are carried to Greece on a demographic "wave of advance" originating in Southwest Asia, or, local development and adoption of farming are stimulated by subsistence stress in mesolithic Greece. Secondly, and more critically, the answer to the question "Why?" depends on what is to be explained. In Greece, the "origins and spread of agriculture and pastoralism" embraces several related but different processes, spanning several millennia, and following distinctive regional and local trajectories that are as yet very imperfectly perceived. As Kotsakis (1992) has argued, the establishment of farming in Greece was no less dependent on the neolithic social formation, and the symbolic mediation of the internal contradictions between the household and the village, than on the availability of appropriate plant cultigens and livestock. With recognition of the complexity of the problem of early farming, a variety of "Why?" questions may be posed and a corresponding diversity of answers may be expected.

Acknowledgements

I am grateful to Yannis Hamilakis, Nina Kiparissi-Apostolika and Vasso Rondiri for providing copies of relevant papers, to Kostas Kotsakis for stimulating discussions on this subject, and to Glynis Jones for critical scrutiny of an earlier draft of this paper.

References

Amberger, K-P. 1979. *Neue Tierknochenfunde aus der Magula Pevkakia in Thessalien, 2: die Wiederkäuer.* Inaugural dissertation, University of Munich.
Binford, L. R. 1983. *In pursuit of the past.* London: Thames & Hudson.
Boessneck, J. 1962. Die Tierreste aus der Argissa-Magula vom präkeramischen Neolithikum bis zur Mittleren Bronzezeit. In *Argissa-Magula 1*, V. Milojcic, J. Boessneck, M. Hopf, 27–99. Bonn: Habelt.

Bottema, S. 1982. Palynological investigations in Greece with special reference to pollen as an indicator of human activity. *Palaeohistoria* **24**, 257–89.

Broodbank, C. 1992. The neolithic labyrinth: social change at Knossos before the Bronze Age. *Journal of Mediterranean Archaeology* **5**, 39–75.

Cherry, J. F. 1981. Pattern and process in the earliest colonisation of the Mediterranean islands. *Proceedings of the Prehistoric Society* **47**, 41–68.

— 1988. Pastoralism and the role of animals in the pre- and proto-historic economies of the Aegean. *Cambridge Philological Society* **14** (supplementary volume), 6–34.

— 1990. The first colonization of the Mediterranean islands: a review of recent research. *Journal of Mediterranean Archaeology* **3**, 145–221.

Conkey, M. & C. Hastorf 1990. Introduction. In *The uses of style in archaeology*, M. Conkey & C. Hastorf (eds), 1–4. Cambridge: Cambridge University Press.

Delille, G. 1977. *Agricoltura e demografia nel regno di Napoli nei secoli 18 e 19*. Naples: Guida.

Dennell, R. W. 1983. *European economic prehistory: a new approach*. London: Academic Press.

Efthimiadis, P., A. Zamanis, E. Skorda 1985. Two-rowed wild barley from four islands of Greece. *Sveriges Utsädesförenings Tidskrift* **95**, 63–70.

Evans, J. D. 1968. Knossos Neolithic part 2: summary and conclusions. *Annual of the British School at Athens* **63**, 267–76.

Fakorellis, G., G. Maniatis, N. Kiparissi in press. *Khronoloyisi me radioanthraka digmaton apo to spilaio Theopetras, Kalabakas*. B Symposio Arkhaiometrias, 1993, Thessaloniki.

Flannery, K. V. 1972. The origins of the village as a settlement type in Mesoamerica and the Near East. In *Man, settlement and urbanism*, P. J. Ucko, R. Tringham, G. W. Dimbleby (eds), 23–53. London: Duckworth.

Gallis, K. J. 1985. A late neolithic foundation offering from Thessaly. *Antiquity* **59**, 20–4.

Gejvall, N-G. 1969. *Lerna 1: the fauna*. Princeton: American School of Classical Studies at Athens.

Grigg, D. B. 1974. *The agricultural systems of the world*. Cambridge: Cambridge University Press.

Halstead, P. 1981. From determinism to uncertainty: social storage and the rise of the Minoan palace. In *Economic archaeology*, A. Sheridan & G. Bailey (eds), 187–213. Oxford: British Archaeological Reports, International Series 96.

— 1987. Traditional and ancient rural economy in mediterranean Europe. *Journal of Hellenic Studies* **107**, 77–87.

— 1989. Like rising damp? An ecological approach to the spread of farming in southeast and central Europe. In *The beginnings of agriculture*, A. Milles, D. Williams, N. Gardner (eds), 23–53. Oxford: British Archaeological Reports, International Series 496.

— 1990. Present to past in the Pindhos. *Rivista di Studi Liguri* **56**, 61–80.

— 1992a. Agriculture in the bronze age Aegean. In *Agriculture in ancient Greece*, B. Wells (ed.), 105–16. Stockholm: Swedish Institute at Athens.

— 1992b. From reciprocity to redistribution: modelling the exchange of livestock in neolithic Greece. *Anthropozoologica* **16**, 19–30.

— 1994. The north-south divide: regional paths to complexity in prehistoric Greece. In *Development and decline in the Mediterranean Bronze Age*, C. Mathers & S. Stoddart (eds), 195–219. Sheffield: Collis.

Halstead, P. & G. Jones 1987. Bioarchaeological remains from Kalythies cave, Rhodes. In *I Neolithiki Periodos sta Dodekanisa*, A. Sampson (ed.), 135–52. Athens: Ministry of Culture.

Halstead, P. & G. Jones 1989. Agrarian ecology in the Greek islands. *Journal of Hellenic Studies* **109**, 41–55.

Hansen, J. M. 1991. *Excavations at Franchthi Cave, Greece, fascicle 7: the palaeoethnobotany of Franchthi Cave*. Bloomington: Indiana University Press.

Higgs, E. S. 1962. Fauna (in R. J. Rodden, Excavations at the early neolithic site at Nea Nikomedeia, Greek Macedonia [1961 season]). *Proceedings of the Prehistoric Society* **28**, 271–4.

Hodder, I. 1990. *The domestication of Europe*. Oxford: Basil Blackwell.

Hopf, M. 1962. Bericht über die Untersuchungen von Samen und Holzkohlenresten von der Argissa-Magula aus den prakeramischen bis mittlerebronzezeitlichen Schichten. In *Argissa-Magula 1*. V. Milojcic, J. Boessneck, M. Hopf (eds), 101–19. Bonn: Habelt.

Hourmouziadis, G. 1973. *Ta neolithika idolia tis Thessalias*. Volos: Society for Thessalian Studies.
— 1979. *To neolithiko Dimini*. Volos: Society for Thessalian Studies.
Jacobsen, T. W. 1981. Franchthi cave and the beginning of settled village life in Greece. *Hesperia* **50**, 303–19.
Jacobsen, T. W. & W. R. Farrand 1987. *Excavations at Franchthi Cave, Greece, fascicle 1: Franchthi Cave and Paralia: maps, plans, and sections*. Bloomington: Indiana University Press.
Jarman, M. R. in press. Human influence in the development of the Cretan fauna. *The Pleistocene and Holocene fauna of Crete and its first settlers*, D. Reese (ed.). Madison: Prehistory Press.
Jarman, M. R. & H. N. Jarman 1968. The fauna and economy of early neolithic Knossos. *Annual of the British School at Athens* **63**, 241–64.
Jarman, M. R., G. N. Bailey, H. N. Jarman (eds) 1982. *Early European agriculture*. Cambridge: Cambridge University Press.
Jones, G. 1992. Weed phytosociology and crop husbandry. *Review of Palaeobotany and Palynology* **73**, 133–43.
Jordan, B. 1975. *Tierknochenfunde aus der Magula Pevkakia in Thessalien*. Inaugural dissertation, University of Munich.
Jullien, R. 1981. La faune des vertébrés. In *La grotte préhistorique de Kitsos (Attique), 2*, N. Lambert, 569–90. Paris: French School at Athens.
Kilian, K. 1973. Zur eisenzeitlichen Transhumanz in Nordgriechenland. *Archäologisches Korrespondenzblatt* **3**, 431–5.
Killen, J. T. 1985. The Linear B tablets and the Mycenaean economy. In *Linear B: a 1984 survey*, A. Morpurgo Davies & Y. Duhoux (eds), 241–305. Louvain: Louvain University Press.
Kotjabopoulou, E. & K. Trantalidou 1993. Faunal analysis of the Skoteini cave. In *Skoteini Tharrounion*, A. Sampson (ed.), 392–434. Athens: A. Sampson.
Kotsakis, K. 1992. O neolithikos tropos paragoyis: ithayenis i apoikos? In *Diethnes sinedrio yia tin Arkhaia Thessalia: sti mnimi tou D. R. Theokhari*, 120–35. Athens: Ministry of Culture.
Ladizinsky, G. 1989. Origin and domestication of the Southwest Asian grain legumes. In *Foraging and farming: the evolution of plant exploitation*, D. R. Harris & G. C. Hillman (eds), 374–89. London: Unwin Hyman.
Legge, A. J. 1981. The agricultural economy. In *Grimes Graves excavations 1971–72*, R. J. Mercer (ed.), 79–103. London: HMSO.
Lewthwaite, J. G. 1981. Plains tails from the hills. In *Economic archaeology*, A. Sheridan & G. Bailey (eds), 57–66. Oxford: British Archaeological Reports, International Series 96.
— 1986. The transition to food production: a mediterranean perspective. In *Hunters in transition*, M. Zvelebil (ed.), 53–66. Cambridge: Cambridge University Press.
Milojcic, V. 1972. Neue deutsche Ausgrabungen in Demetrias/Thessalien, 1967–72. *Jahrbuch der Heidelberger Akademie der Wissenschaften*, 61–74.
Payne, S. 1975. Faunal change at Franchthi Cave from 20,000 BC to 3,000 BC. In *Archaeozoological studies*, A. T. Clason (ed.), 120–131. Amsterdam: Elsevier.
— 1985. Zoo-archaeology in Greece: a reader's guide. In *Contributions to Aegean archaeology: studies in honor of William A. McDonald*, N. C. Wilkie & W. D. E. Coulson (eds), 211–44. Minneapolis: University of Minnesota.
Payne, S. & G. Bull 1988. Components of variation in measurements of pig bones and teeth. *Archaeozoologia* **2**, 27–66.
Perlès, C. 1988. New ways with an old problem: chipped stone assemblages as an index of cultural discontinuity in early Greek prehistory. In *Problems in Greek prehistory*, E. B. French & K. A. Wardle (eds), 477–88. Bristol: Bristol Classical Press.
— 1990. *Excavations at Franchthi Cave, Greece, fascicle 5: les industries lithiques taillées de Franchthi, 2: les industries du mésolithique et du néolithique initial*. Bloomington: Indiana University Press.
Protonotariou-Deïlaki, E. 1992. Paratirisis stin Prokeramiki (apo ti Thessalia sta Dendra tis Argolidos). In *Diethnes sinedrio yia tin Arkhaia Thessalia: sti mnimi tou D. R. Theokhari*, 97–119. Athens: Ministry of Culture.

Psikhoyios, D. K. 1987. *Proikes, foroi, stafida kai psomi: oikonomia kai oikoyenia stin agrotiki Ellada tou 19 aiona.* Athens: Ethniko Kentro Koinonikon Erevnon.

Pullen, D. J. 1992. Ox and plough in the early bronze age Aegean. *American Journal of Archaeology* **96**, 45–54.

Redding, R. W. 1981. *Decision making in subsistence herding of sheep and goats in the Middle East* [PhD dissertation, Department of Anthropology, University of Michigan]. Ann Arbor: University Microfilms.

Renfrew, C. 1970. The burnt house at Sitagroi. *Antiquity* **44**, 131–4.

— 1972. *The emergence of civilisation: the Cyclades and the Aegean in the third millennium* BC. London: Methuen.

Renfrew, C. & A. Aspinall 1990. Aegean obsidian and Franchthi Cave. In Perlès (1990: 257–70).

Sahlins, M. 1974. *Stone age economics.* London: Tavistock.

Sampson, A. 1993. *Skoteini Tharrounion.* Athens: A. Sampson.

Shackleton, J. 1988. *Excavations at Franchthi Cave, Greece, fascicle 4: marine molluscan remains from Franchthi Cave.* Bloomington: Indiana University Press.

Sherratt, A. G. 1981. Plough and pastoralism. In *Pattern of the past: studies in honour of David Clarke.* I. Hodder, G. Isaac, N. Hammond (eds), 261–305. Cambridge: Cambridge University Press.

Sondaar, P. Y. 1971. Paleozoogeography of the Pleistocene mammals from the Aegean. *Opera Botanica* **30**, 65–70.

Srejovic, D. 1972. *Europe's first monumental sculpture: new discoveries at Lepenski Vir.* London: Thames & Hudson.

Theochares, D. R. 1973. *Neolithic Greece.* Athens: National Bank of Greece.

— 1980. To neolithiko spiti. *Anthropoloyika* **1**, 12–14.

Tringham, R. 1971. *Hunters, fishers and farmers of eastern Europe 6000–3000* BC. London: Hutchinson.

Turrill, W. B. 1929. *The plant-life of the Balkan peninsula.* Oxford: Oxford University Press.

van Andel, T., E. Zangger, A. Demitrack 1990. Land use and soil erosion in prehistoric and historical Greece. *Journal of Field Archaeology* **17**, 379–96.

van Zeist, W. & S. Bottema 1971. Plant husbandry in early neolithic Nea Nikomedeia, Greece. *Acta Botanica Neerlandica* **20**, 524–38.

Vokotopoulou, J. 1986. *Vitsa: ta nekrotafia mias Molossikis Komis, 1.* Athens: Ministry of Culture.

von den Driesch, A. 1987. Haus- und Jagdtiere im vorgeschichtlichen Thessalien. *Prähistorische Zeitschrift* **62**, 1–21.

Whitelaw, T. M. 1983. People and space in hunter–gatherer camps. *Archaeological Review from Cambridge* **2**, 48–66.

Wiessner, P. 1982. Risk, reciprocity and social influences on !Kung San economics. In *Politics and history in band societies*, E. Leacock & R. Lee (eds), 61–84. Cambridge: Cambridge University Press.

Wijnen, M. 1982. *The Early Neolithic I settlement at Sesklo.* Leiden: Leiden University Press.

Wilkinson, T. J. & S. T. Duhon 1990. *Excavations at Franchthi Cave, Greece, fascicle 6: Franchthi Paralia: the sediments, stratigraphy, and offshore investigations.* Bloomington: Indiana University Press.

Willerding, U. 1980. Zum Ackerbau der Bandkeramiker. In *Beiträge zur Archäologie Nordwestdeutschlands und Mitteleuropas*, T. Krüger & H-G. Stephan (eds), 423–56. Hildesheim: August Lax.

Wobst, H. M. 1974. Boundary conditions for palaeolithic social systems. *American Antiquity* **39**, 147–78.

Zachos, C. L. 1987. *Ayios Dhimitrios, a prehistoric settlement in the southwestern Peloponnesos: the Neolithic and Early Helladic Periods* [PhD dissertation, Department of Archaeology, University of Boston]. Ann Arbor: University Microfilms.

Zamanis, A., S. Samaras, N. Stavropoulos, J. E. Dillé 1988. *Report of an expedition to rescue germplasm of wild species of wheat and relatives in Greece, June 1988* (Greek Gene Bank Scientific Bulletin 5). Thessaloniki: North Greece Agricultural Research Center.

Zangger, E. 1991. Prehistoric coastal environments in Greece: the vanished landscapes of Dimini Bay and Lake Lerna. *Journal of Field Archaeology* **18**, 1–16.

Zvelebil, M. 1986. Mesolithic societies and the transition to farming: problems of time, scale and organisation. In *Hunters in transition: mesolithic societies of temperate Eurasia and their transition to farming.* M. Zvelebil (ed.), 167–88. Cambridge: Cambridge University Press.

CHAPTER SEVENTEEN

The cultural context of the first use of domesticates in continental Central and Northwest Europe

Julian Thomas

Introduction

This contribution is intended as a commentary upon, and an extension of, some of the other arguments presented in this volume. Several other chapters (e.g. Zvelebil in Ch. 18) emphasize the importance of the immediate context (whether social, cultural or ecological) within which domesticates may have been adopted. I build upon this point by focusing on the specific local conditions surrounding the first appearance of domesticated plants and animals around the northwestern fringe of Europe. It is unquestionably the case that, in Eurasia, species that were initially domesticated in western Asia were later introduced into areas to which they were alien. Nonetheless, I argue that no single explanatory mechanism can adequately cover the whole of this process of expansion. It is conventional for studies of the European Neolithic to attempt to isolate a single causal motor for the spread of agriculture, whether demographic (Renfrew 1976) or ideological (Hodder 1990). To this tendency we can link the imperative to conceive of the Neolithic as an unchanging entity that can be identified by a fixed set of traits (Zvelebil 1989). This in turn enables Zvelebil (in Ch. 18 in this volume) to recognize agro-pastoral farming as "the signature of the Neolithic". What I contest is that we can distinguish such a set of economic and cultural practices in the abstract, which together constitute an integrated package that logically precedes the contexts in which it was manifested (Thomas 1993).

It was this understanding of the Neolithic as a unified phenomenon marching its way across Europe that enabled Ammerman & Cavalli-Sforza (1971, 1973) to present their "wave of advance" model for the expansion of agriculture into Europe. Their account relied upon a series of then newly available radiocarbon determinations for neolithic activity across the continent. By plotting each date on the map, they were able to construct a series of arcs, radiating outwards from Jericho, and representing the spatial diffusion of farming at a constant temporal rate (Fig. 17.1). Only major irregularities of topography were argued to have interfered with the unbroken process of advance, which was generated by rising population levels continually ejecting peo-

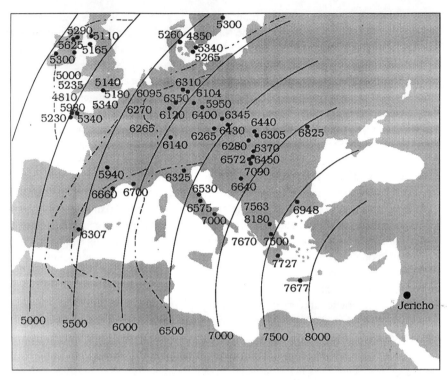

Figure 17.1 Ammerman & Cavalli-Sforza's "wave of advance" model for the spread of agriculture into Europe. The radiocarbon dates are expressed in years bp (redrawn from Ammerman & Cavalli-Sforza 1971: 685). The broken lines represent probable regional variations in the rate of spread.

ple forwards into uncultivated territory. What is striking about Ammerman & Cavalli-Sforza's map is that, whereas some of these radiocarbon dates relate to fully agricultural settlements, where communities relied upon domesticated plants and animals for their subsistence, others document the isolated appearance of domesticated resources, or simply of formally neolithic material culture. It seems to have been assumed that because the Neolithic was an integrated package, the appearance of any one element was a manifestation of the presence of the whole. Because the only point at issue was the presence or absence of this "neolithic package", the social or cultural processes involved were conceived of as being essentially unidirectional. First a given area was not used for agriculture, and then it was.

As Price argues (in Ch. 19 in this volume), more recent perspectives have emphasized that the "neolithic revolution" was a slow and gradual process, rather than a dichotomous shift from one monolithic state to another. In addition, I suggest that the different changes portrayed as being bound together in a unified process may not always have proceeded at a uniform rate. The introduction of food plants and of domesticated mammals, the use of pottery and of ground and polished stone tools, the emergence of sedentary villages, the first construction of earth and stone monuments and the development of new funerary practices might each have had a separate temporality. Yet the use of the term "the Neolithic" implies that these phenomena can be rolled together into a seamless whole. Demonstrably, the evidence from prehistoric Europe shows that a range of very different processes was at work, generating considerable variability. In some regions, all of the elements appeared at roughly the same time, whereas in others there were major timelags, or particular changes failed to manifest themselves altogether. Mesolithic/neolithic Europe is consequently best perceived as a complex mosaic of ecological, social and cultural conditions, giving rise to a series of radically different contexts into which domesticates might be introduced in quite different ways. Since Ammerman and Cavalli-Sforza's day, there has been a growing recognition that farming did not spread into all parts of Europe by means of population movement. In the western Mediterranean, it is probable that the Cardial-Ware network initially established connections between hunter–fisher–gatherer communities, which later facilitated the dispersal of domesticated species (Lewthwaite 1981: 296). In Scandinavia, the gradual adoption of non-local plants and animals by indigenous populations is well documented (see Price in Ch. 19 in this volume).

These points imply that one of the most important factors conditioning the extent to which farming or pastoralism might become established in a given region would have been the character and organization of the indigenous inhabitants. In some cases, hunter–fisher–gatherers may have been driven out, or may have found their way of life disrupted by incoming farming groups. In other areas, the aboriginal population may simply have been absorbed by farming communities. Yet, as Zvelebil & Rowley-Conwy (1984, 1986) have argued, Scandinavian foragers were able to resist both displacement and assimilation for many centuries. Their argument relies upon an assumption that farming and foraging were inherently incompatible ways of life (ibid.: 105), a point that appears to be supported by ethnographic evidence. In contemporary observations, the uses of the landscape and the scheduling of time and resources implicit in mobile hunting and sedentary farming often prove difficult to reconcile. However, I argue that in this case ethnographic parallels are of limited utility. Although general anthropological theory is of the greatest possible help in understanding the European Mesolithic and Neolithic, it may be that the particular societies that existed at this time were historically and culturally unique. Domestication involves above all a change in the social relationships between people, and between people, plants and animals (Ingold 1980, and Ch. 2 in this volume; Bender 1978: 204). The use of domesticates entails not simply a change in the range of resources and economic strategies that people have at their disposal: it involves a change in the way in which people engage with their world. Zvelebil & Rowley-Conwy's model implies that the hunter–fisher–gatherer communities of northern and western Europe were condemned *eventually* to adopt farming because their economic base was inherently more prone to disruption and resource crisis than the superior way of life that would eventually engulf them. They might hold off their own adoption of agriculture, but this was only a postponement.

I wish to suggest that the indigenous peoples of Northwest Europe were more active in the social and economic changes that took place in the fifth to third millennia bc than this perspective would allow. The mesolithic communities of Europe were already dynamic and changing societies, with a range of different sets of social relationships and economic practices, when they first encountered agriculturalists. So not only did the farming groups of Central Europe impose themselves upon or interact with foraging bands in a range of different ways, but the responses of those foragers will not have been uniform. Some may have been disrupted or assimilated, but it seems that many groups adopted aspects of the neolithic way of life in a fashion that was both novel and inventive. At the risk of labouring the point, the variation in the adoption of domesticates and other cultural traits by mesolithic groups in Northwest Europe was preconditioned by the already existing variations in social relations and historical trajectories. Although in some cases the resilience of these communities relied upon an outright rejection of the new, more often innovations were seized upon enthusiastically – and transformed. For, rather than a wholesale transformation to agriculture, communities in Scandinavia, Britain and Ireland, the Low Countries, northern France and the North European plain used individual aspects of what they could take from the Neolithic in order to create something new. What emerged in subsequent centuries was a series of social and economic forms that cannot easily be pigeon-holed as "hunter–gatherer" or "agricultural", and for which we would be hard put to find direct analogues in the contemporary world. Moreover, it is impossible to understand the developments of this period in terms of Ammerman & Cavalli-Sforza's unidirectional framework. The adoption of domesticates was here meshed into a very complex series of social changes, where economic developments may sometimes have played a causal role, whereas in other contexts they may have been a side-effect of other processes entirely. Whereas in some cases mesolithic groups were the recipients of innovations acquired from neolithic communities, I argue that at some points the opposite was the case. In particular, in the last quarter of the fourth millennium bc, new forms of organization began to appear in both the Atlantic fringe and the Central European loess country, which owed as much to mesolithic as to neolithic traditions.

Native transformations

Because the introduction of domesticates into Europe involved a series of different social processes, it is possible at a gross level of generality to define several overall stages or phases. These may be said to begin with the first agricultural presence north of the Alps and the Carpathians, the Linearbandkeramik (LBK). Although some might argue for an indigenous origin for these communities, most authorities agree that the LBK is a rare example of the rapid colonization of a large area by a distinct population (Modderman 1988, Milisauskas & Kruk 1989). Although the whole area from Hungary to the Low Countries shows signs of having been occupied by groups who practised a relatively uniform subsistence strategy (cattle herding with small-scale cultivation) and maintained a uniform material culture (timber-framed longhouses, band-decorated pottery and stone adzes), it seems likely that within this overarching unity there was considerable diversity of practice (Modderman 1988, Coudart 1991). Moreover, once the initial explosive expansion of population was succeeded by standstill and settlement nucleation, a process of gradual regionalization of cultural form and social practice appears to have set in (Starling 1985: 49; Bogucki & Grygiel 1993: 404).

From the period when LBK communities ceased their expansion across the loess country, and into that when the Danubian cultural entity devolved into the Rössen, later Lengyel, Bischeim and Cerny cultural groups, some form of contact was maintained with foraging bands around the fringes of the settled area. Indeed, it seems possible that seasonal cattle transhumance periodically took individuals or groups from LBK settlements down into the hunting lands in the North European lowlands, where they left behind traces of temporary camps (Bogucki 1987: 7; Bogucki & Grygiel 1993: 413). The outcome of this contact is best documented in the case of the Ertebølle groups of Denmark and southern Sweden, who can be shown to have adopted innovations from neolithic communities. Ertebølle people made pottery, in distinctive "point-butted" forms, but using a basic technology that appears to have been derived from the LBK (Midgley 1992: 398). At sites such as Löddesborg, such Ertebølle pots sometimes contain the impressions of cereal grains, also presumably acquired from the south (Nielsen 1986: 241). Other sites, such as Store Åmose in West Zealand, have produced Danubian shafthole stone adzes from closed Ertebølle contexts (Fischer 1982: 7). Moreover, bones of domestic pig from some shell-middens demonstrate that Ertebølle communities were able to integrate some measure of animal husbandry into an intensive foraging way of life (Rowley-Conwy 1981). Jennbert (1985) has suggested that these artefacts and domesticates may have been acquired through a network of prestige exchange between Ertebølle and LBK groups, which would have had the effect of enhancing the social position of those among the foraging bands who were in a position to pass on valued items as gifts. Thus, although shafthole adzes would have been technologically inferior to mesolithic flint axes (Midgley 1992: 400), their principal significance might have been as tokens of alliance and indebtedness. The escalating social competition that access to exotic goods and domesticates may have engendered might in turn have promoted a greater willingness to adopt more intensive forms of material production, enabling still more competitive consumption to develop.

Although the favourable preservational conditions of the south-Scandinavian kitchen middens, and a strong history of field research there, have meant that we know a great deal about the adoption of exotic traits within the late Ertebølle (cf. Price in Ch. 19 in this volume), it may be that some of these developments are common to a wider group of later mesolithic societies. The distribution of LBK and Rössen shafthole adzes beyond the loess country extends over much of the North European plain (Sherratt 1990), and point-butted pottery was common to a number of different mesolithic cultural groupings. There is no hard and fast line that divides the Ertebølle from the Ellerbeck and Lietzow cultural groups, or even from those of Boburg, Nollheide and Wistka, which extend the distribution into the Polish lowlands (Midgley 1992: 11). These in turn are connected to the pottery-using "Forest Neolithic" communities of the southern Baltic: Jühnsdorf, Chojnice and Pienki (Zvelebil & Dolukhanov 1991: 247). Louwe-Kooijmans (1976: 247) may thus have been correct to postulate the existence of a broad band of "half-neolithic communities" running continuously across the North European plain. Bogucki (1987: 4) argues that all these late-

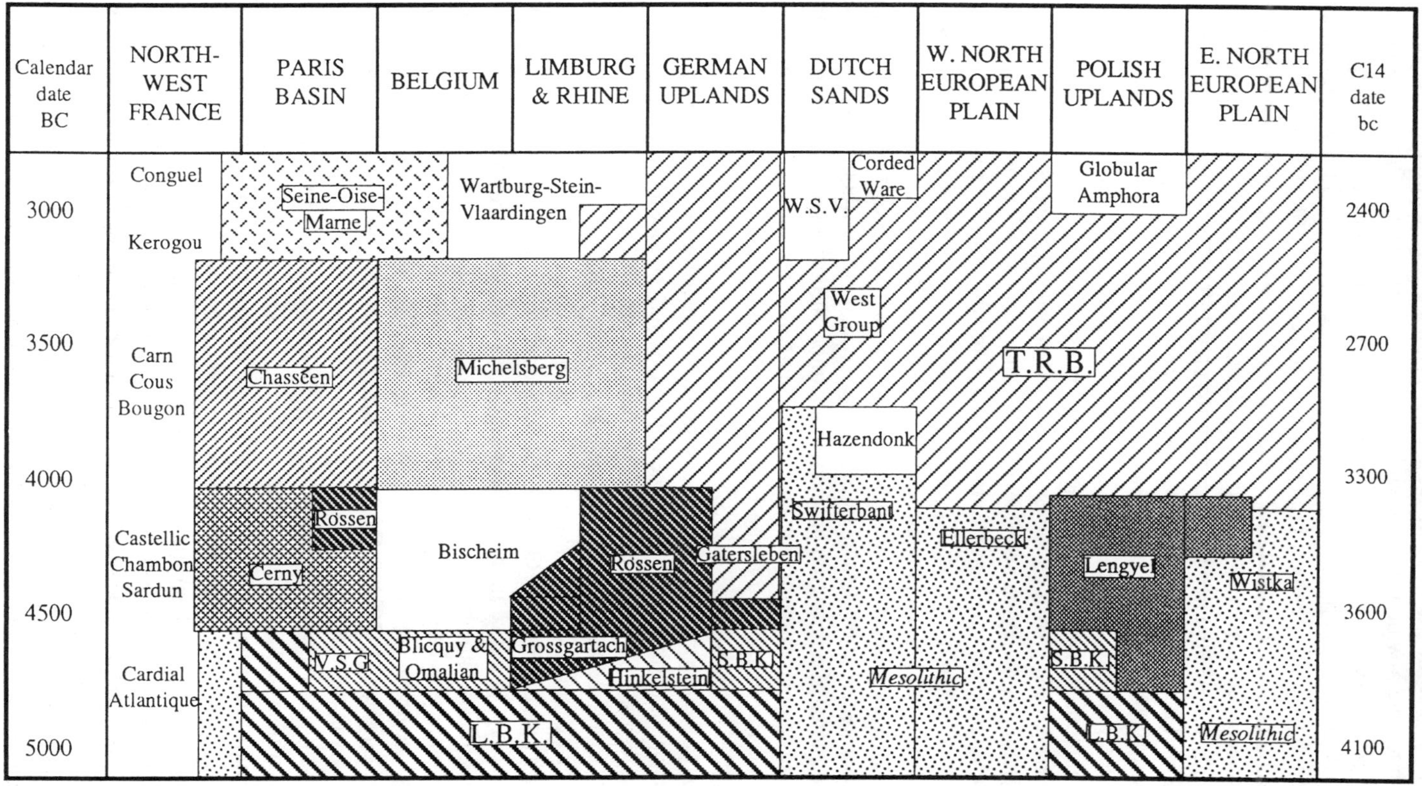

Figure 17.2 Major cultural groups in continental Central and Northwest Europe in the fifth and fourth millennia bc, from the end of the LBK to the end of the TRB.

Calendar date BC	NORTH-WEST FRANCE	PARIS BASIN	BELGIUM	LIMBURG & RHINE	GERMAN UPLANDS	DUTCH SANDS	W. NORTH EUROPEAN PLAIN	POLISH UPLANDS	E. NORTH EUROPEAN PLAIN	C14 date bc
3000	Conguel / Kerogou	Seine-Oise-Marne	Wartburg-Stein-Vlaardingen			Corded Ware / W.S.V.	T.R.B.	Globular Amphora		2400
3500	Carn / Cous / Bougon	Chasséen	Michelsberg			West Group				2700
4000	Castellic / Chambon / Sardun	Cerny / Rossen	Bischeim	Rossen / Gatersleben		Hazendonk / Swifterbant	Ellerbeck	Lengyel / Wiska		3300
4500	Cardial / Atlantique	V.S.G.	Blicquy & Omalian	Grossgartach / Hinkelstein	S.B.K.	Mesolithic	Mesolithic	S.B.K. / LBK	Mesolithic	3600
5000		LBK								4100

mesolithic groups may have practised complex forms of logistic mobility, enabling them to integrate a wide range of wild and domestic resources. There is certainly widespread evidence to suggest that elements of neolithic culture were adopted by other mesolithic communities contemporary with the Ertebølle. In the Polish low-lands, late-mesolithic sites have produced isolated vessels of LBK and TRB (Trichter-beckerkultur or Funnel-necked Beaker Culture) pottery, as well as bones of domestic pig and sheep (Domańska 1990). Similarly, foragers of the Rhine–Meuse–Schelde group made use of bone-tempered pottery (Keeley 1992: 87). In the southwestern Netherlands, late mesolithic sites have repeatedly produced flint points of LBK/Rössen style (Arts 1990: 303). The Swifterbant groups of the Dutch coastal lowlands used point-butted pots that have been described as "Dutch Ertebølle" (de Roever 1979). These communities certainly exploited both domestic and wild animals, and barley seems to have been grown on the Swifterbant levee sites (Louwe-Kooijmans 1987: 237; Zvelebil & Rowley-Conwy 1986: 77). An interconnected group of later meso-lithic communities on the North European plain, of which the Ertebølle are merely the most archaeologically visible, thus appear to have selectively appropriated material culture, animals and plants acquired from LBK, Rössen and Lengyel agricul-turalists. This development should be seen in the broader context of northern and western European hunter–fisher–gatherers in general, many of whom appear to have been using intensified material production and more structured patterns of mobility to facilitate complex ritual activity and more elaborate social relationships. This ten-dency is clearly manifested in the Breton coastal cemeteries of Téviec and Hoëdic (Bender 1981: 154; Kirk 1991: 113).

Although the late mesolithic groups dispersed between the Low Countries and the Polish lowlands form a relatively coherent unit, it may be that native communities were involved in interaction with the LBK from its earliest incursion into temperate Europe. Around the western fringe of the loess country, ceramic styles have been rec-ognized that occur both as elements of LBK assemblages and on their own, in areas beyond the LBK distribution. Of these, the La Hoguette pottery is contemporary with the earliest LBK presence in the northwest, and the type site in Normandy is remote from areas of LBK settlement (Bogucki & Grygiel 1993: 407; Lüning et al. 1989). The Limburg pottery is later, but repeats the pattern of being quite distinct from LBK ceramics, occurring on LBK sites and also alone, as at Kesseleyk on the Limburg sands (Louwe-Kooijmans 1976: 238, Keeley 1992: 82). Given the suggestion that these tra-ditions, as well as the Blicquy pottery of the Belgian Hainault, may have mixed together traits drawn from a range of sources, including the Cardial Ware of western France as well as the LBK (Louwe-Kooijmans 1993: 125), an interesting cultural proc-ess appears to have been at work. For although the LBK itself may have been rather conservative, using a relatively unchanged repertoire of animals, plants, pottery styles, stone tools and domestic architecture for hundreds of years, among the sur-rounding groups of hunter–fisher–gatherers innovations in both subsistence economy and forms of material culture were experimented with and recombined in striking new ways. This suggests a process very like that described by Bhabha (1994): the emer-gence of "cultural hybridity" at the edges and in the interstices of contemporary cul-tural formations. By recontextualizing aspects of the neolithic way of life, foraging peoples were able to transform them into something new and distinctive (for a more extensive discussion of this process, see Thomas 1996).

Compared with the farming communities on the loess land, the hunter–fisher–gatherers of the Atlantic and Baltic coastal areas may have been characterized by relatively open social relationships, a high degree of mobility (particularly by sea, even allowing for a growing tendency towards sedentary living), and the exchange of personnel between groups. Given these circumstances of enhanced interaction and circulation of cultural knowledge, it might be to these later mesolithic groups, rather than to the primary neolithic farmers, that one should look for evidence of radical social and cultural change. Consequently, it is unsurprising that the emergence of new cultural traditions in the mid-fourth millennium bc, with Cerny in northern France and the early TRB on the North European plain, has been attributed to interaction between foragers and farmers, or just to the appropriation of neolithic traits by mesolithic people (Midgley 1992, Cassen 1993). In the case of the early TRB, Bogucki (1987: 8) argues for an economic strategy involving a selective incorporation of domesticates into a mobile way of life. I am suggesting that this judicious adoption of aspects of what the Neolithic had on offer was a more general phenomenon that extended to material culture as well as to domesticates.

A new kind of Neolithic

It has been pointed out before that, following some centuries of standstill in which the LBK, Rössen and Lengyel peoples made only minor inroads into the lands beyond the loess, the later fourth millennium bc saw a sudden expansion of neolithic settlement (Zvelebil & Rowley-Conwy 1986, Thomas 1988). It has been recognized that this new phase involved a decisive shift from colonization to acculturation. The picture I am presenting here implies rather more: that an entirely different *kind* of Neolithic had emerged, involving a fundamentally different relationship between people and domesticates. As Price points out (in Ch. 19 in this volume), the earliest TRB presence in southern Scandinavia is documented by earthen long barrows, bog deposits and flint mines, while traces of permanent settlement appear much later. This presents a vivid contrast with the LBK expansion on to the loess country some centuries earlier, where all aspects of the primary Neolithic were in place from the start. My argument is that the Cerny and initial TRB zones represent contexts within which the Neolithic was reformulated, in that the individual elements that had been held together by custom and tradition within the LBK were here drawn upon selectively by native North European communities. Areas such as Britain, Ireland and southern Scandinavia were not "acculturated" by existing agricultural populations: their mesolithic groups actively chose to engage in new networks of contact and new social and economic practices, which first emerged in the early TRB and Cerny contexts. As Sherratt (1990: 152) has pointed out, it was in precisely these two cultural contexts that earthen long barrows and long enclosures were constructed for the first time. Both the Kujavian long mounds of the early TRB and the long enclosures of the Paris Basin and Normandy generally occur in clusters, which may echo the layout of primary neolithic longhouse settlements (Midgley 1985, Kirk 1995). Effectively, the native peoples of these areas had adopted the longhouse form (which was still in use among late Lengyel communities when the TRB was first established: Bradley 1994), but had transformed it into a "house of the dead", which formed a landscape focus for a still mobile way of life (Hodder 1984). Significantly, though, the burials placed inside these mounds and enclosures were of diagnostically mesolithic type: extended inhumations in Kujavia and cist burials in northern France (Midgley 1985: 197; Kirk 1996).

Just as Northwest European funerary practice involved the appropriation and transformation of elements drawn from the primary Neolithic of Central Europe, so too changes in subsistence practice involved the recontextualization of domesticated resources. This point perhaps demonstrates the drawbacks of separating "the economy" from other aspects of culture and social relations, as if subsistence practice developed purely in response to environmental conditions. In the case of Northwest Europe, changes in resource use followed a parallel course to other cultural changes. This can best be demonstrated in the case of Britain. Traditionally, archaeologists working on the British Neolithic have tended to look for a pattern of adoption similar to that in Central Europe. Thus, Case (1969: 177) wrote of a mature and integrated system of mixed farming introduced to Britain by an incoming continental population. Such a system would supplant the use of wild resources entirely and at a stroke. However, as Zvelebil & Rowley-Conwy (1986: 85) point out, the first use of domesticates within a society may be quite distinct from a wholesale shift to dependence on agriculture. This is the basis for their three-stage model of availability, substitution and consolidation. Under this rubric, I would argue that the "substitution phase" in some areas of Northwest Europe was very long indeed. Increasingly, the British evidence is starting to suggest that domesticated species were introduced as one element of a broad-spectrum hybrid economy, which moreover showed considerable variation from one region to another. Clearance and arable cultivation may have been more extensive on the Wessex chalklands than elsewhere (Entwistle & Grant 1989). Sites such as the extensive waterlogged settlement at the Stumble, in the Blackwater estuary of Essex, have produced traces of cereals, but also hazelnut shells, rosaceous fruits such as sloes, and root and rhizome fragments (Murphy 1990: 23). It seems that, while some cereals were being cultivated, the collecting of wild plant foods continued to be of importance throughout the Neolithic. The subsoil pits that have often been regarded as traces of eroded settlements (e.g. Field et al. 1964) appear rarely to have held cereals for storage. Further, there is very little substance to claims that neolithic cultivation caused marked pedological changes (Entwistle & Grant 1989: 204–5). Charred seed assemblages, too, give little indication that extensive arable farming was established in neolithic Britain. Arable weed floras are almost entirely absent, and the majority of assemblages are rich in wild species, particularly wild fruit- and nut-bearing trees and shrubs (Moffet et al. 1989: 246).

It is possible that in many cultural settings around the world, cultivated plants were not introduced initially as staple crops, but were adopted because of their prestigious or symbolic importance (Farrington & Urry 1985: 146). This process could include medicinal or narcotic plants, or plant foods that were eaten only by prestigious individuals or on special occasions. In this respect, it may be that the LBK example of a fully agricultural society rapidly becoming established in a particular region may be the exception rather than the rule. In the British context this is implied by the charred plant remains from the main causewayed enclosure on Hambledon Hill, in Dorset. This site appears not to have been permanently occupied, but was used for activities that included the formal deposition of artefacts in pits and the elaborate treatment of the remains of the dead (Mercer 1980, 1988). In the pits, deposits of barley, wheat and hazelnut shells were encountered, without traces of weed seeds or other processing residues (Legge 1989: 218–9). Similarly, although many of the faunal samples from both earlier and later neolithic contexts in Britain are dominated by domestic species, the locations from which they have been recovered are predominantly ceremonial monuments, including barrows, causewayed enclosures and henges (Thomas 1991: 7–28). At these sites, large-scale feasting seems often to have taken place, and entire joints of meat were sometimes deliberately deposited, suggesting conspicuous consumption. The possibility thus exists that the contribution of domestic animals to everyday diet has been overestimated, and that, as with plant foods, a mixture of indigenous and introduced species was used over a long period.

Conclusion

The introduction of domestic animals and cultivated plants into the northwestern extremities of Europe is best understood as having been enmeshed in a complex series of social and cultural processes. The fifth and fourth millennia bc were characterized by very intense interaction between late mesolithic foraging groups, which facilitated the exchange of cultural knowledge, including the awareness of the potentials of crop-cultivation and livestock herding. The outcome of this circulation of knowledge, of artefact styles and of plants and animals was the gradual emergence of "hybrid" social–cultural–economic formations, in which native communities were able to assimilate aspects of neolithic and mesolithic traditions. This process culminated in the establishment of the Cerny and early TRB traditions, the first "native Neolithics" of Northwest Europe. It was because this new form of Neolithic was flexible – a set of material and symbolic resources to be drawn upon rather than a closed tradition – that other indigenous groups were able to adopt and adapt it for themselves, resulting in the Scandinavian TRB, the northern Chasséen and the British early Neolithic. In each of these areas, domesticated resources may have been used in markedly different ways, from broad-spectrum foraging to cattle pastoralism supplemented by plant gathering, to stable agriculture. What is important is that the other elements of the Northwest European Neolithic, particularly material culture, provided a framework for social integration and interaction between communities practising diverse subsistence strategies. Funerary monuments, polished stone axes, plain bowl pottery and ditched enclosures may not have amounted to the shared system of meanings that Hodder (1990) attributes to them, but they may have represented a "material language" through which communities were able to construct their own identities and to negotiate alliances.

I began this chapter by arguing that the spread of agriculture into Europe has been perceived as a one-way process, in which a dynamic economic system overwhelmed groups of static and "timeless" hunter–fisher–gatherers. The alternative view that I have presented suggests that mesolithic communities were active in the changes of the fourth millennium bc, that they creatively drew upon and transformed the "agricultural package". Moreover, it seems that not all of the changes spread from southeast to northwest. If the Cerny and early TRB zones represented a crucible in which new relationships between people, material culture, plants and animals were forged, this new pattern spread not only into the Atlantic fringe but also onwards to the loess country of Central Europe. Here, the stable, nucleated longhouse settlements of the LBK, Rössen and Lengyel were succeeded by more mobile and ephemeral settlement patterns of the Michelsberg and the later TRB. Seemingly, more use was made of wild resources, the exchange of artefacts took on a greater significance, and the later LBK trend towards greater differentiation between groups in terms of artefact styles was reversed (Nielsen 1986: 242; Wansleben & Verhardt 1990; Midgley 1992: 322). In a sense, although we have long thought of the fourth millennium bc as the period of "neolithization" of Northwest Europe, it would be just as accurate to talk of the "mesolithization" of Central Europe.

References

Ammerman, A. J. & L. L. Cavalli-Sforza 1971. Measuring the rate of spread of early farming in Europe. *Man* **6**, 674–88.

Ammerman, A. J. & L. L. Cavalli-Sforza 1973. A population model for the diffusion of farming into Europe. In *The explanation of culture change: models in prehistory*, A. C. Renfrew (ed.), 343–58. London: Duckworth.

Arts, N. 1990. Archaeology, environment, and the social evolution of later band societies in a lowland area. In Bonsall (1990: 291–312).

Bender, B. 1978. Gatherer–hunter to farmer: a social perspective. *World Archaeology* **10**, 204–22.

— 1981. Gatherer–hunter intensification. In *Economic archaeology*, A. Sheridan & G. Bailey (eds), 149–58. Oxford: British Archaeological Reports, International Series 96.

Bhabha, H. K. 1994. *The location of culture*. London: Routledge.

Bogucki, P. 1987. The establishment of agrarian communities on the North European plain. *Current Anthropology* **28**, 1–24.

Bogucki, P. & P. Grygiel 1993. The first farmers of central Europe: a survey article. *Journal of Field Archaeology* **20**, 399–426.

Bonsall, C. (ed.) 1990. *The Mesolithic in Europe*. Edinburgh: John Donald

Bradley, R. J. 1994. From the house of the dead. Paper presented at the conference of the Theoretical Archaeology Group, Bradford.

Case, H. J. 1969. Neolithic explanations. *Antiquity* **43**, 176–86.

Cassen, S. 1993. Material culture and chronology of the middle Neolithic of western France. *Oxford Journal of Archaeology* **12**, 197–208.

Coudart, A. 1991. Social structure and relationships in prehistoric small-scale societies: the Bandkeramik groups in Neolithic Europe. In *Between bands and states*, S. A. Gregg (ed.), 295–420. Carbondale, Illinois: Southern Illinois University Press.

de Roever, J. P. 1979. The pottery from Swifterbant – Dutch Ertebølle? *Helenium* **19**, 13–36.

Domańska, L. 1990. Elements of a food-producing economy in the late Mesolithic of the Polish lowland. In Bonsall (1990: 447–55).

Entwistle, R. & A. Grant 1989. The evidence for cereal cultivation and animal husbandry in the southern British Neolithic and Bronze Age. In Milles et al. (1989: 203–15).
Farrington, I. & J. Urry 1985. Food and the early history of cultivation. *Journal of Ethnobiology* **5**,
143–57.
Field, N. H., C. L. Matthews, I. F. Smith 1964. New Neolithic sites in Dorset and Bedfordshire, with
a note on the distribution of Neolithic storage-pits in Britain. *Proceedings of the Prehistoric Society*
30, 352–81.
Fischer, A. 1982. Trade in Danubian shaft-hole axes and introduction of Neolithic economy in Den-
mark. *Journal of Danish Archaeology* **1**, 7–12.
Hodder, I. R. 1984. Burials, houses, women and men in the European Neolithic. In *Ideology, power
and prehistory*, D. Miller & C. Tilley (eds), 51–68. Cambridge: Cambridge University Press.
— 1990. *The domestication of Europe: structure and contingency in neolithic societies.* Oxford:
Blackwell.
Ingold, T. 1980. *Hunters, pastoralists and ranchers: reindeer economies and their transformations.*
Cambridge: Cambridge University Press.
Jennbert, K. 1985. Neolithisation – a Scanian perspective. *Journal of Danish Archaeology* **4**, 196–7.
Keeley, L. H. 1992. The introduction of agriculture to the western north European plain. In *Transitions
to agriculture in prehistory* [Monographs in World Archaeology 4], A. B. Gebauer & T. D. Price
(eds), 81–95. Madison: Prehistory Press.
Kirk, T. 1991. Structure, agency and power relations *"chez les derniers chasseurs-cueilleurs"* of north-
west France. In *Processual and postprocessual archaeologies: multiple ways of knowing the past,*
R. W. Preucel (ed.), 108–25. Carbondale: Southern Illinois University Press.
— 1996. Constructions of death in the early Neolithic of the Paris Basin. In *Understanding the Neolithic of North-West Europe*, M. Edmonds & C. Richards (eds), 102–27. Glasgow: Cruithne Press.
Legge, A. 1989. Milking the evidence: a reply to Entwistle and Grant. In Milles et al. (1989: 217–42).
Lewthwaite, J. 1981. Ambiguous first impressions: a survey of recent work on the early Neolithic of
the west Mediterranean. *Journal of Mediterranean Anthropology and Archaeology* **1**, 292–307.
Louwe-Kooijmans, L. P. 1976. Local developments within a borderland. *Oudheidkundige Mededelin-
gen* **57**, 226–97.
— 1987. Neolithic settlement and subsistence in the wetlands of the Rhine/Meuse delta of the Netherlands. In *European wetlands in prehistory*, J. Coles & A. Lawson (eds), 227–51. Oxford: Oxford
University Press.
— 1993. The Mesolithic/Neolithic transformation in the lower Rhine basin. In *Case studies in European prehistory*, P. Bugucki (ed.), 95–145. Boca Raton, Florida: CRC Press.
Lüning, J., V. Kloos, S. Albert 1989. Westliche nachbarn der Bandkeramischen Kultur: La Hoguette
und Limburg. *Germania* **67**, 355–420.
Mercer, R. J. 1980. *Hambledon Hill: a neolithic landscape.* Edinburgh: Edinburgh University Press.
— 1988. Hambledon Hill, Dorset, England. In *Enclosures and defences in the Neolithic of western
Europe,* C. Burgess, P. Topping, C. Mordant, M. Madison (eds), 89–106. Oxford: British Archae-
ological Reports, International Series 403.
Midgley, M. S. 1985. *Origin and function of the earthen long barrows of northern Europe.* Oxford:
British Archaeological Reports, International Series 259.
— 1992. *TRB Culture: the first farmers of the North European Plain.* Edinburgh: Edinburgh University
Press.
Milisauskas, S. & J. Kruk 1989. Neolithic economy in central Europe. *Journal of World Prehistory* **3**,
403–46.
Milles, A., D. Williams, N. Gardner (eds) 1989. *The beginnings of agriculture.* Oxford: British Archae-
ological Reports, International Series 496.
Modderman, P. J. R. 1988. The Linear Pottery Culture: diversity in uniformity. *Berichten Van de Rijks-
dienst voor het Oudheidkundig Bodermonderzoek* **38**, 63–139.
Moffett, L., M. A. Robinson, V. Straker 1989. Cereals, fruit and nuts: charred plant remains from Neolithic sites in England and Wales and the Neolithic economy. In Milles et al. (1989: 243–61).
Murphy, P. 1990. *The Stumble, Essex (Blackwater Site 28): carbonised neolithic plant remains.* London: Ancient Monuments Laboratory Report 126/90.

Nielsen, P. O. 1986. The beginning of the Neolithic – assimilation or complex change? *Journal of Danish Archaeology* **5**, 240–3.

Renfrew, C. 1976. Megaliths, territories and population. In *Acculturation and continuity in Atlantic Europe,* S. de Laet (ed.), 198–220. Bruges: De Tempel.

Rowley-Conwy, P. 1981. Mesolithic Danish bacon: permanent and temporary sites in the Danish Mesolithic. In *Economic archaeology*, A Sheridan & G. Bailey (eds), 51–5. Oxford: British Archaeological Reports, International Series 96.

Sherratt, A. 1990. The genesis of megaliths: monumentality, ethnicity and social complexity in Neolithic north-west Europe. *World Archaeology* **22**, 147–67.

Starling, N. 1985. Colonisation and succession: the earlier Neolithic of central Europe. *Proceedings of the Prehistoric Society* **51**, 41–58.

Thomas, J. S. 1988. Neolithic explanations revisited: the Mesolithic–Neolithic transition in Britain and south Scandinavia. *Proceedings of the Prehistoric Society* **54**, 59–66.

— 1991. *Rethinking the Neolithic.* Cambridge: Cambridge University Press.

— 1993. Discourse, totalisation and "the Neolithic". In *Interpretative archaeology,* C. Tilley (ed.), 357–94. London: Berg.

— 1996. *Time, culture and identity: an interpretive archaeology.* London: Routledge.

Wansleben, M & L. B. M. Verhart 1990. Meuse valley project: the transition from the Mesolithic to the Neolithic in the Dutch Meuse valley. In *Contributions to the Mesolithic in Europe,* P. M. Vermeersch & P. van Peer (eds), 389–42. Leuven: Leuven University Press.

Zvelebil, M. 1989. On the transition to farming in Europe, or what was spreading with the Neolithic: a reply to Ammerman (1989). *Antiquity* **63**, 379–83.

Zvelebil, M. & P. Dolukhanov 1991. Transition to farming in eastern and northern Europe. *Journal of World Prehistory* **5**, 233–78.

Zvelebil, M. & P. Rowley-Conwy 1984. Transition to farming in northern Europe: a hunter–gatherer perspective. *Norwegian Archaeological Review* **17**, 104–28.

— 1986. Foragers and farmers in Atlantic Europe. In *Hunters in transition: mesolithic societies of temperate Eurasia and their transition to farming,* M. Zvelebil (ed.), 67–93. Cambridge: Cambridge University Press.

CHAPTER EIGHTEEN

The agricultural frontier and the transition to farming in the circum-Baltic region

Marek Zvelebil

Introduction

The purpose of this chapter is to outline the transition to farming in the lands adjoining the Baltic Sea, with special reference to the impact of the agricultural frontier. For two reasons, this is a key area for our understanding of the process of "neo-lithization" in Europe and of the agricultural transition in general: first, the transition in the Baltic region was slow and relatively recent, allowing us to investigate it at a finer degree of resolution than elsewhere; secondly, it involved to a greater or lesser degree indigenous hunter–gatherers of the Mesolithic. In this area, therefore, we should allow for the persistence of dynamic and evolving mesolithic societies, which did not constitute a mere periphery to the Southwest Asian core area, but made their own contribution to the subsequent development of European society.

Ostensibly, the transition to farming is an economic process involving a shift from dependence on biologically wild to biologically domesticated resources. However, this process cannot be separated from the cultural, social and historical contexts in which it occurred. The change in economy may be a cause of, or perhaps a consequence of, changes in ideology, material culture or the social organization of participant groups, changes often collectively referred to as neolithization. It is not clear whether these changes were broadly simultaneous and whether, in Europe, the shift from dependence on undomesticated local resources to *agro-pastoral* farming can be regarded as a signature for the sociocultural developments of the Neolithic (see, for example, Ammerman & Cavalli-Sforza 1984, Zvelebil 1986a, 1989, Thomas 1987, 1988, Ammermann 1989). In my opinion, the shift in the mode of subsistence to agro-pastoral farming remains the only process that is relatively clearly defined, geographically widespread, and sufficiently archaeologically detectable to act as the signature of the Neolithic (Zvelebil 1996). The question of whether this change in the mode of subsistence corresponded to changes in social structure, ideology and other features of the mode of production (cf. Woodburn 1988, Ingold 1988, Thomas 1991) should be examined within individual regional and historical contexts.

It has been common to regard the adoption of farming in Europe as a case of replacement of the indigenous hunter–gatherers by farmers spreading from Southwest Asia, and, over the generations, colonizing hitherto unfarmed areas in Europe (Piggott 1965, Case 1969, Ammerman & Cavalli-Sforza 1984, Renfrew 1987). Although this may have occurred in the continental interior of Europe – in the area of the first Balkan Neolithic and Linear Pottery Ware or Linearbandkeramik (LBK) cultures and their derivatives (Zvelebil & Zvelebil 1988) – it did not do so in other parts of Europe, particularly the circum-Baltic region, where there is evidence of continuities in material culture and settlement pattern between the Mesolithic and the Neolithic. There, a strong case can be made for the local adoption of farming by the indigenous hunter–gatherers (Zvelebil & Rowley-Conwy 1984, 1986). However, local adoption does not preclude individual migration between the hunter–gatherer and farmer communities. Gene flow probably did occur through intermarriage or hypergyny, or by "infiltration" (Neustupný 1982): the arrival of itinerant specialists in the communities of either farmers or foragers. If the spread of farming involved gene exchange between neolithic and mesolithic populations, it is more likely to have occurred through such processes rather than as a result of demic diffusion; and the concept of an agricultural frontier-zone provides the social context within which such genetic exchanges may be identified. It also serves to reduce the gap in the often polarized discussion about human migration at the mesolithic/neolithic transition (cf. Ammerman 1989, Zvelebil 1989) and allows us to contemplate *gradual* changes in the gene pool of the first farmers in Europe, as the adoption of farming moved from the Balkans to northern Europe in the course of some 5,000 years.

Mapping the spread

The shift to agro-pastoral subsistence can therefore serve as a useful point of departure for considering the mesolithic/neolithic transition and as the basis for mapping the spread of farming. In order to counter the traditional notion of a rapid transition to farming, and as an alternative to its most recent and elaborated version – the wave of advance model (Ammerman & Cavalli-Sforza 1984) – we have developed a model of the agricultural transition that describes the process in three stages: availability, substitution and consolidation (Zvelebil & Rowley-Conwy 1984, Zvelebil 1986a). Each stage is defined by the economic evidence, considered at a regional scale (Fig. 18.1). The model operates within the broader sociocultural context of an agricultural frontier: a zone of interaction between foragers and farmers, marked by various forms of contact and exchange (Alexander 1978, Leacock & Lee 1982, Schrire 1984, Dennell 1985, Ingold et al. 1988, Spielman 1991).

During the availability phase, farming is known to the foraging groups and there is an exchange of materials and information between foragers and farmers, without the adoption of farming. Farmers and foragers develop contacts, but the two societies operate as culturally and economically independent units. The availability phase ends with the adoption of at least some major elements of farming by the foragers. I suggest that, in the archaeological record, domesticates will form less than 5 per cent of the

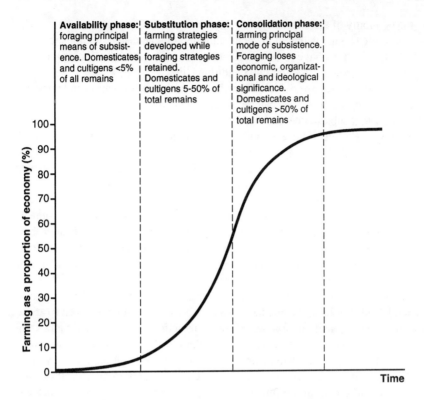

Figure 18.1 The three-stage availability model of the transition to farming (after Zvelebil 1986b: 6).

faunal sample (excluding dogs) at sites in the availability phase.

During the substitution phase, farming practices replace hunting and gathering strategies, although agro-pastoral farming still remains embedded within an overall foraging–farming economy. This phase is most often regarded as the time of the presumed neolithization. In the archaeological record, this phase can be said to include sites with less than 50 per cent of domesticates in the faunal samples on a regional scale.

The consolidation phase marks the shift to full dependence on agriculture. Economically, this is the first stage of a predominantly neolithic economy, marked by both the extensive and intensive growth of food production: the secondary colonization of sub-optimal habitats and more intensive farming practices, with domesticates constituting 50–100 per cent of the faunal samples on a regional scale.

This three-stage availability model allows us to monitor the agricultural transition at a finer level of resolution than was previously possible. But it is an heuristic device developed principally to examine the prevailing notion of a rapid introduction of farming (Ammermann & Cavalli-Sforza 1984, Renfrew 1987, Neustupný 1987, Aurenche & Cauvin 1989; but see also Dennell 1983, Barker 1985, Price 1987 and Ch. 19 in this volume, Zvelebil & Dolukhanov 1991). It contains two implicit assumptions, that:

- archaeologically recovered animal and plant remains on a regional scale reflect

the economy of a community
• economic change is linked to social and ideological change within society.

These assumptions have to be taken into account in the evaluation of the model. The first assumption is based on two conditions, that:
• taphonomic processes, which affect the deposition, preservation and retrieval of animal and plant remains, can be understood and used to calibrate the raw data to represent subsistence more accurately
• the regional scale of the economic reconstruction will reduce the local variation in animal and plant samples and give a more accurate account of subsistence.

These conditions can rarely if ever be met in full, and so, as a rule, we can only obtain a relative and coarse picture of a subsistence change from foraging to farming (Grayson 1979, Hastorf & Popper 1988).

The second assumption recognizes the fact that there is commonly some link between subsistence change and socio-ideological factors, although the latter factors should be examined independently. Even without making any explicit assumptions about the nature of the social organization of the societies in question, the model is structured as a progression to farming through three phases, and as such it assumes the final outcome; one that is inevitably contingent on ideology and social structure in general. The lengths of the availability and subsistence phases themselves are seen as linked to the intensity of forager–farmer interactions, and to the organization of labour in farming and foraging economies (Zvelebil & Rowley-Conwy 1984, Zvelebil 1986b); and so involve a relationship between social organization, ideology and the model. These links limit the scope of the model: it does not account for the cases of "reverse" transitions from farming to foraging, nor can it adequately describe societies where the substitution phase extended for a very long time, in other words where a mixed foraging–farming economy became part of an established way of life rather than a phase in a transition. On the other hand, the model allows for the existence of such societies, and it is through its application that their persistence in the prehistory of Europe has been established and described in outline (Zvelebil & Rowley-Conwy 1986, Dolukhanov 1986, Zvelebil & Dolukhanov 1991).

According to our three-stage model, the substitution phase will in typical cases be relatively short, because of scheduling problems and the labour costs of maintaining a balanced hunting–farming economy. Ethnographic sources support this argument: subsistence societies tend either to depend heavily on agriculture or to engage in it only to a negligible extent. A survey of 200 such societies shows a remarkable lack of cases where agriculture forms 5–45 per cent of subsistence, although this is not the case with herding (Fig. 18.2). The substitution phase, as a signature for the shift to agro-pastoral farming, is then a relatively rare occurrence in the ethnographic record, on a synchronic scale. This implies that it tends to be short in duration, and provides some justification for the sigmoid curve of the "typical" course of agricultural transition (Fig. 18.1).

Analogous reasoning, and the same bi-modal distribution of the dependence on agriculture, led Hayden (1990) to suggest that societies with low dependence on farming used agricultural products mainly to acquire social prestige, which was linked to the extra labour needed to produce them, whereas those that depended more heavily

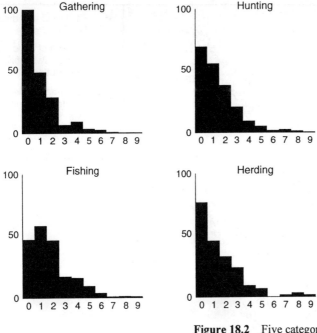

Figure 18.2 Five categories of subsistence as defined in Murdock's *Ethnographic Atlas* for a representative sample of 200 of the world's societies (reproduced with permission from Hunn & Williams 1982: 6). The horizontal axes represent Murdock's estimate of the percentage of dependence of the society on the mode of subsistence (0 = 0–5%, 1 = 6–15%, thereafter at 10% intervals to 9 which = 86–100%). The vertical axes = the number of societies assigned a given level of dependence. Note the anomalous bimodal distribution of dependence on agriculture.

on agriculture had solved the problem of the higher labour costs of farming (relative to hunting and gathering), and were therefore able to shift rapidly to economic dependence on agriculture.

Bearing these arguments in mind, we can now turn to the evidence from northern Europe. The position of the agricultural frontier illustrated in Figure 18.3 denotes the boundary between the availability and substitution zones. From this map we see that:

- the transition to farming was slow and lasted, in the circum-Baltic region as a whole, some three thousand years
- it was marked by the existence of stationary frontiers, such as the Ertebølle/middle neolithic frontier, or the late neolithic frontier in the eastern Baltic
- it was also marked by reverse transitions from farming to foraging in south-central Sweden in the mid-third millennium bc.

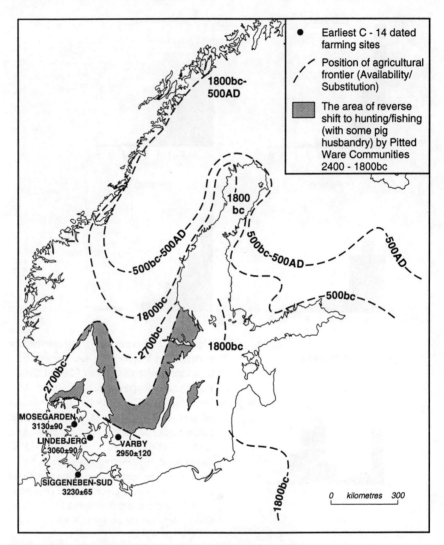

Figure 18.3   The spread of farming in the circum-Baltic region.

However, the agricultural frontier is more than a boundary. It is a far-reaching phenomenon, covering a wide geographical space, within which contacts between foragers and farmers occur, and which is occupied by communities in different stages of the transition. Viewed in this perspective, the process of the transition to agriculture involved communities in one or another part of circum-Baltic Europe between about 4000 and 500 bc (Fig. 18.4). Consequently, two other features of the transition in the circum-Baltic region emerge:

- the long persistence of hunter–gatherer societies in the availability phase, marked by evidence for the exchange of goods with farming communities
- the existence of mixed hunting-farming groups, characterized by an extended

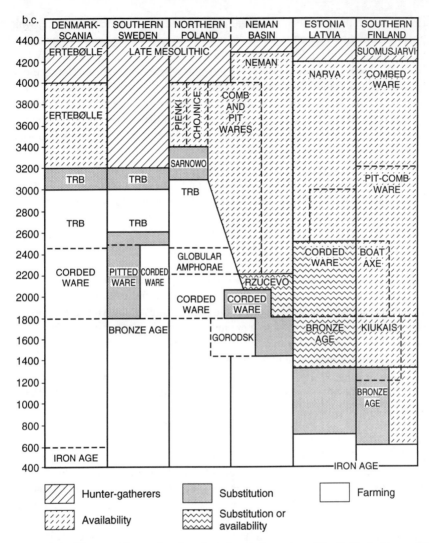

Figure 18.4   The transition to farming along the southern rim of the Baltic in terms of the three-stage availability model. In the eastern Baltic, the proportion of domesticates at the Corded Ware and early Bronze Age settlements was very variable, ranging from 0% to 14%; hence this period could be characterized as either availability or substitution, depending on the region.

substitution phase, a situation not common in the ethnographic record.

This is particularly the case in the eastern part of the Baltic, where the substitution phase may have lasted 700–1500 years (Zvelebil & Rowley-Conwy 1986, Zvelebil & Dolukhanov 1991, Zvelebil 1993).

Data from southern Finland serve to emphasize this point. Despite an active search for early traces of domestication, neither archaeobotanical nor archaeozoological evidence indicates the existence of farming prior to the late Kiukias to early Bronze Age period, dated to the mid-second millennium bc. The palynological evidence, which is, thanks mainly to Vuorela's work, the most comprehensive record for the agricultural transition in Finland (Vuorela 1970, 1972, 1975, 1986, in press, Vuorela & Lempiainen 1988, Gronlund et al. 1990), shows that whereas human interference dates back to the fourth millennium bc, there is no evidence for cereal cultivation until the beginning of the Bronze Age, while the development of an agricultural landscape, maintained by field cultivation, does not occur until the early first millennium AD. Even after that, the extent of permanent agricultural settlement was limited to southwestern Finland, so that even in the mid-sixteenth century AD large parts of the northeastern Baltic remained occupied by forest farmers, reindeer herders and commercial hunters, whose lifestyle had more to do with hunting and gathering than with farming. The last agricultural frontier in Europe is only a few hundred years old.

The cultural and historical context

The spread of farming should not be considered outside its cultural and historical context. Prehistoric societies are defined by their material culture contained in the archaeological record. Individual archaeological cultures of the Mesolithic and Neolithic have often been regarded, to a greater or lesser extent, as representing "ethnic groups", "tribes" or "folk" with a shared sense of belonging and a shared gene pool, and with a common material culture, socio-economic organization, ideology and even language (e.g. Piggott 1965, Kivikoski 1967, Case 1969, Neustupný 1982, 1987, Ammerman & Cavalli-Sforza 1984, Vencl 1986, Renfrew 1987, Mallory 1989, Cavalli-Sforza 1991).

This is still the case despite the 30 years of arguments which have shown such a normative view of archaeological culture to be inadequate (e.g. Binford 1965, Clarke 1968, Neustupný 1971, Schiffer 1976, Shennan 1989) and contrary to ethnographic evidence, which in fact shows that it does not hold true in general (e.g. Hodder 1978, 1982, Shennan 1989). It has often been shown that we cannot assume coincidence between gene flow (migration) and material-culture patterning, between material and non-material aspects of culture, and between material culture and economy (Hodder 1978, 1982, Ehret 1988, Olsen 1988). A wide array of variables – the availability of raw materials, artefact function (both practical and symbolic), technological competence, exchange patterns, descent and residence rules, marriage patterns, sexual division of labour, social context of production, status and prestige, mobility patterns, subsistence strategies, population dynamics, ideology, discard patterns and taphonomic factors – all contribute to the creation of interlocking patterns of cultural variation and graduated, rather than discrete, patterns of spatial variation in attributes of material culture. Rather than being signatures for self-defined separate units of society ("ethnic groups"), major archaeological cultures, defined as geographically discrete co-occurring sets of artefacts, are more likely to represent socio-economic changes and symbolic innovations in prehistoric societies that include individual "ethnicities", which we as archaeologists should perceive to be "signals of behavioral, economic and symbolic distinctness" (Dolukhanov 1993: 122).

The implications of the above for the present study are: (a) the link between foraging and farming economies and the social and ideological character of their respective societies, which is at the core of our definition of "mesolithic" and "neolithic", remains an assumption to be examined with case studies; (b) because shared elements in material culture do not necessarily correspond to a shared economy, an archaeological culture can include several distinct groups practising different subsistence strategies, for example, this may have been the case with the "Boat Axe culture" groups who farmed in Sweden, hunted and gathered in southern Finland and engaged in either itinerant trading or foraging with small amounts of stock-keeping in the eastern Baltic (Malmer 1962, Edgren 1970, Zvelebil 1981, Zvelebil & Dolukhanov 1991); and (c) population movements may occur independently of material-culture patterning and, conversely, changes in material culture may not signal migrations.

Bearing this in mind, the transition to farming in the Baltic region can be said to have occurred in the historical context of three phenomena: (a) developing complexity among circum-Baltic hunter–gatherer communities between 5000 and 2000 bc; (b) increasing impact of the agricultural frontier between c. 4000 and 1000 bc; and (c) deteriorating ecological conditions for the adoption of farming arising from the Atlantic–Suboreal climatic change which took place around 3000 bc.

The notion of complexity among circum-Baltic hunter–gatherers is now a familiar topic of discussion (e.g. Madsen 1986, Larsson 1990, Zvelebil & Dolukhanov 1991, Price & Gebauer 1992). Despite the growing awareness of regional variation in degrees of complexity, and of different forms of complexity recognizable in the ethnographic record (Zvelebil 1996), the late mesolithic communities in the coastal regions of the Baltic can claim most of the attributes of a complex hunter–gatherer society: these include a degree of sedentism, high population density, more intensive food procurement, technological elaboration, development of exchange networks, social differentiation, and the emergence of territorial claims. Such complex hunter–gatherer communities would have been more productive and capable of supporting higher population densities than the more mobile, dispersed communities of the continental interior of central and western Europe. Their economy was based on the exploitation of a wide range of resources, arranged in seasonal schedules, and included specialized use of seasonally available resources, such as waterfowl, fish, seals, and plant foods (Dolukhanov 1979, 1993, Rowley-Conwy 1983, Price 1985, 1987, Rowley-Conwy & Zvelebil 1989, Larsson 1990, Zvelebil & Dolukhanov 1991, Price & Gebauer 1992, Zvelebil 1992).

From this economic basis, a form of local husbandry or resource management may have emerged between c. 4000 and 2000 bc. We cannot prove that the resources in question – nuts (especially water chestnut and hazelnut), aquatic foods and pigs (Zvelebil 1995) – were domesticates, but their intensive use as a package makes sense nutritionally and as insurance against economic failure.

Dominance of pig and seal or other aquatic resources occurs frequently on mesolithic sites from Ireland to the eastern Baltic. There is clear evidence for specialization in seal hunting between about 4000 and 1500 bc. There is circumstantial evidence of pig taming, and widespread evidence for the specialized exploitation of water chestnut at circum-Baltic sites (Zvelebil 1994: 39–40). These resources complement each other, with the pig in the role of a tame scavenger around base camps, and a source of protein and fat, with nuts as sources of carbohydrate and fodder for the pigs, and with seal and fish as food sources for people and pigs at times of seasonal abundance. In this way, wild-pig management could become a highly productive element of an integrated subsistence system, which would have encouraged more intensive control of pig and nut resources: a situation that some scholars would view as incipient domestication.

The notion of indigenous pig management receives further, conditional support from the terminology for "pig" in Old Irish, Old Germanic and Lithuanian within northern Europe. Hamp (1987) has argued that five northern European, substratum terms can be identified, denoting pig/pig-nut (*keul*), pig (*mokku*), piglet (*suku*), young pig (*banu*) and boar (*turko*), showing that "the pig had a special value that went back to a North or Central European pre-IE substratum" (1987: 186). This evolved terminology may possibly reflect pig-management strategies by the local non-Indo–European speakers of the Mesolithic, prior to their contact with the neolithic farmers, who are thought by some to have spoken Indo–European languages (Renfrew 1987 and Ch. 5 in this volume, Zvelebil & Zvelebil 1988).

The Ertebølle/Ellerberg foragers of the coastal areas of the southern Baltic represent the best example of such social and economic complexity among the mesolithic hunter–gatherers (Rowley-Conwy 1983, Madsen 1986, Bogucki 1987, Larsson 1990, Price & Gebauer 1992). The logistic and specialized procurement of resources, the investment in mass-capture facilities and other labour-intensive technology, the evidence for food processing and storage, and the indications of management of woodland and its resources (Welinder 1989, Mithen 1990, Zvelebil 1993, 1995), all suggest the operation of a system of delayed return, as defined by Woodburn (1988). Such a system would be embedded within social relations based on kinship and affinity, and operated by men through the exchange of women and other (material) assets within a cognitive framework where the egalitarian ideology was in abeyance (ibid.).

The social system and social structure of the Ertebølle hunter–gatherers goes some way to support these expectations. While Ertebølle is still regarded as a "band society" (Newell 1984), there is evidence for status differentiation (Clark & Neeley 1987, Constandse-Westermann & Newell 1989, Larsson 1990, Neeley & Clark 1990, Meiklejohn & Zvelebil 1991), linked, perhaps, to the control of material assets: food resources and exotic artefacts (O'Shea & Zvelebil 1984, Price & Gebauer 1992). Evidence for differences in limb laterization between men and women at cemeteries such as Skateholm (Constandse-Westermann & Newell 1989) suggests that women gained their status through means other than physical labour, one of which may have been association with the high-status men. Hodder (1990: 180–1) found that symbolic activity emphasized the dominance of the male in hunting and trading: the "agrios", with little or no traces of the "domus". All this suggests the delayed-return male-dominated social structure presented by Woodburn (1988) on the basis of ethnographic data. Yet there are indications that the situation was more complex. Judging by the variation in grave goods, females gained high status, and signatures of domus/household (other than elaborate domestic architecture, cf. Hodder 1990) do in fact occur in Ertebølle contexts. Formalized burial of dogs at Skateholm (Larsson 1990) – the only fully domesticated animal in the society – suggests that its members distinguished between the tame and the wild. In summary, Ertebølle society was probably organized along lines similar to "complex" hunter–gatherers in the ethnographic record: it retained the hunter–gatherer mode of subsistence, but was socially too differentiated to fit within the hunter–gatherer "mode of production" (cf. Ingold 1988).

The structure of such hunter–gatherer society must have influenced its relationship to agro-pastoral farming. Investment in the existing technology and economy would raise the cost of the structural change required by the adoption of farming (Zvelebil & Rowley-Conwy 1984, Hayden 1990). At the same time, the complex hunter–gatherer system was, through storage and higher productivity, more capable of coping with short-term fluctuations in resources. From these perspectives then, complex hunter–gatherers can be expected to resist the adoption of farming.

In contrast, hunter–gatherer socio-economic organization was vulnerable to long-term resource variation and to sociodemographic pressures latent in the society as a result of increased sedentism and increased capacity for social differentiation. On the basis of ethnohistorical analogies, sociospatial mobility appears fundamental to the persistence of hunter–gatherer societies who are in contact with farmers (Woodburn 1982, 1988, Olsen 1988). Increase in sedentism renders hunter–gatherers more vulnerable to interference by farmers and to the imposition of social control by farming groups (Olsen 1988). In such a situation, the impact of the agricultural frontier may have played a crucial role in the adoption of farming.

Forager–farmer interactions

Contact between mesolithic hunter–gatherers and neolithic farmers occurred within the agricultural frontier zone, which conceptually can be divided into mobile and stationary frontiers (Alexander 1978, Green & Perlman 1985). Mobile frontiers develop during periods of agricultural expansion and are typically associated with models of agricultural colonization by demic diffusion. On the basis of ethnohistorical data, agricultural communities in such rapidly shifting frontier zones share several special features: rapid population growth, extensive land-use patterns, frequent relocation of settlement, low subsistence and high labour costs, preponderance of males and younger people over females and the old. Dennell (1985) has questioned the application of some of these features to the prehistoric case of the mesolithic/neolithic transition.

Stationary frontiers develop in stable or slowly changing situations, allowing for the development of contact and exchange between foragers and farmers. Judging by the rate of spread of farming in the circum-Baltic region, stationary frontiers marked long periods of stability (the availability phase) followed by shorter periods of rapid adoption of farming (the substitution phase, mobile frontier) in the western Baltic, whereas in the eastern Baltic the availability and substitution phases were both long, and the conditions of the stationary frontier prevailed.

Within the contact zone of a stationary frontier, four types of developments were common: exchange of technological innovations and imports, exchange of mates, transmission of diseases and ecological change. Ethnographic evidence for different types of exchange in subsistence societies shows that social and geographical distance (kin and tribal boundaries) are the two main factors specifying the nature of the exchange. Malinowski (1950) specified six forms of exchange among the Trobrianders, whereas Sahlins (1974) used social distance to outline his model of generalized, balanced and negative reciprocity. Also inspired by the ethnohistorical evidence, Dennell (1985) elaborated on the notion of mobile and stationary frontiers to illustrate the range of forager–farmer interactions possible, and to show how farming could have spread through Europe by contact rather than by demic diffusion (and cf. Thomas in Ch. 17 in this volume).

Using this information, we can begin to build a more concrete model of forager–farmer interaction in the circum-Baltic region. Let us consider the Ertebølle/middle neolithic frontier. The role of contact between foragers and farmers across this frontier could have been both supportive (Bogucki 1988, Gregg 1988), and disruptive for the foragers (Moore 1985, Keeley 1992). I suggest that in the early phase of the forager–farmer contact, co-operation would have prevailed. At this stage, the effect of the frontier would have been largely supportive: the exchange of foodstuffs across the frontier would reduce stochastic variation in food supply and the risk of failure for both the hunting and farming communities. This would be especially true for farmers who had recently adopted farming, or who had recently moved into a new area. In terms of local adoption, there may have been kin relations between foragers and farmers, with the result that balanced, rather than negative reciprocity, would occur. In addition to foodstuffs, other forms of exchange, including information, partners, prestige items and raw materials may have played a role equal to or greater than food exchange (Fig. 18.5).

In a broader context, the movement of livestock may have been of major importance in regional exchange systems. In the later Neolithic of the North European plain, which was marked by a shift to greater animal husbandry and by acephalous, lineage-orientated social structure, exchange in cattle would have occurred, along the lines suggested by Sherratt (1982: 23) "as transactions between acephalous groups linked by alliance in conditions of general insecurity. A characteristic of such systems was the elaboration of many kinds of competitive prestige items within the range of utilitarian artifacts." Such a system is represented diagrammatically in Figure 18.5.

There is a growing body of evidence for such exchange in the Ertebølle-neolithic context (Fig. 18.6) (Fischer 1982, Jennbert 1984, Madsen 1986, Solberg 1989, Larsson 1990, Sherratt 1990, Midgley 1992, Price & Gebauer 1992, Hedges et al. 1995; Price in Ch. 19 in this volume). The imports from farming societies include the technology of pottery making and the pots themselves, such as the Baalberg and Michelsberg pottery at Rosenhof (Schwabedissen 1981). They also include shoe-last adzes and other stone-axe imports, while T-shape antler axes, bone combs, and rings appear to be Ertebølle imitations of the neolithic artefacts (Solberg 1989, Price & Gebauer 1992). Bones of cattle, found in small quantities on late mesolithic sites in Denmark, Scania and northern Poland, are also probably the results of trade (Rowley-Conwy 1980, Zvelebil & Rowley-Conwy 1986, Tomaszewski 1988, Kabacinski 1992). As Jennbert has argued (1984), cattle may have been traded as prestige items as well as food. These products may have been exchanged for furs, seal fat, and forest products such as honey. The evi-

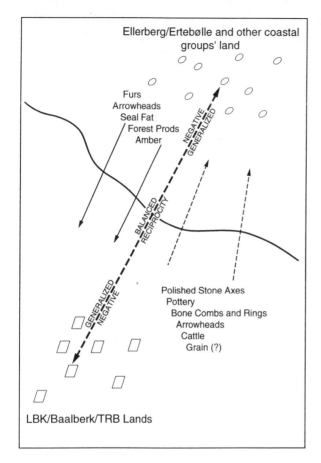

Figure 18.5
Forager–farmer contacts
expected during the earlier
part of the availability
phase, when co-operation
prevails over competition.

dence for the specialized exploitation of fur animals, and their use for fur rather than for meat, at such sites as Tybrind Vig and Ringkloster (Andersen 1975, 1987, Rowley-Conwy 1980) offers at least some support for this suggestion.

A similar exchange system must have existed within the frontier zone in the eastern Baltic in the fourth and third millennia bc, where there is clear evidence for trade in amber (Vankina 1970) and other prestige items (axes, pots), and possibly also agricultural imports (Dolukhanov 1979, 1993) as well as trade in seal fat (Zvelebil 1981, Rowley-Conwy & Zvelebil 1989) (Fig. 18.7). Local pottery shows the influence of ornamental motifs from the early neolithic sites in the Dnieper basin (Zvelebil & Dolukhanov 1991) and from the western Baltic (Dolukhanov 1979, Timofeev 1987, 1990), giving rise to hybrid ceramic traditions in northeastern Poland and Lithuania (Timofeev 1987). Such contact and exchange network reached out over a wide area of the Baltic and eastern Europe, creating a pathway for new ideas and cultural innovations, which, in the later stages, may have been manifested archaeologically in the Corded Ware/Boat Axe horizon (Zvelebil 1993).

With the increasing duration of the agricultural frontier, disruptive effects gained the upper hand (Fig. 18.8). This was probably marked by the following developments:

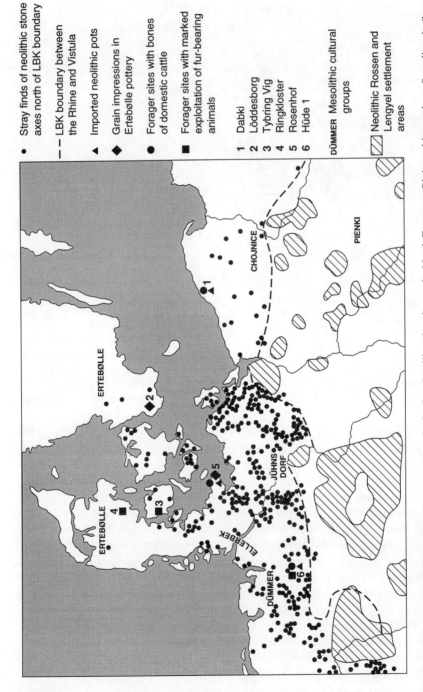

Figure 18.6 Evidence for forager–farmer contacts in the fourth millennium bc on the North European Plain and in southern Scandinavia (based on data in Andersen 1975, 1987, Bogucki 1988, Jennbert 1985, Kabacinski 1992, Schwabedissen 1981 and Sherratt 1990).

- internal disruption of the social fabric among hunter–gatherers arising from increased circulation of prestige items and increased social competition
- opportunistic use of hunter–gatherer lands by farmers, which, as Moore (1985) has shown, can seriously interfere with hunter–gatherer foraging strategies and information exchange and initiate disruptive ecological changes
- direct procurement of raw materials and wild foods by farmers who establish their own "hunting lands" in hunter–gatherer territories as part of secondary agricultural expansion
- increased exploitation of export commodities by hunter–gatherers to the long-

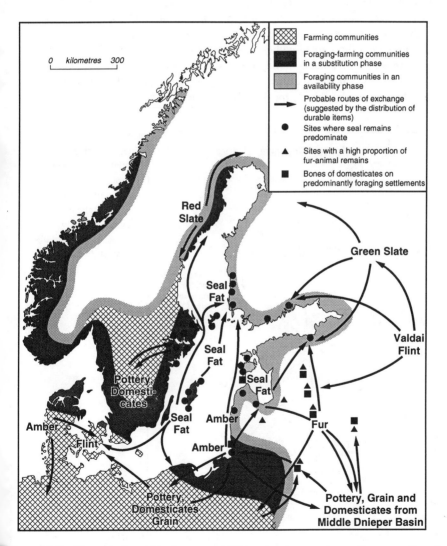

Figure 18.7   The agricultural frontier zone *c.* 2000 bc, showing putative trading networks and forager–farmer contacts in the eastern Baltic region between *c.* 2500 and 1500 bc.

term detriment of the forager economy
* hypergyny: the loss through marriage of forager women to farmers.

Hypergyny occurs where foragers are viewed by both parties as culturally and economically inferior to farmers. In such situations the emigration of forager women can amount to 15 per cent of the female population (Bailey & Annger 1989, Speth 1991), causing severe shortage of females among the hunter–gatherer males. Based on case studies in Africa, there seem to be two responses among forager men designed to increase their own standing with the women: an increase in commercial hunting by the men (Speth 1991), or the adoption of farming. Hypergyny, however, is an ideologically contingent practice, and something must have happened to render a farming community a more socio-economically attractive option than a hunting one. I suggest that the other long-term effects of the agricultural frontier, described above, were capable of disrupting the hunter–gatherer communities to the point where farming could offer greater social and economic benefits, and, initially, greater survivorship of children (Buikstra et al. 1986, Cohen 1989). In this way, hypergyny can be seen as a conditional but powerful vehicle for the demise of hunter–gatherer societies.

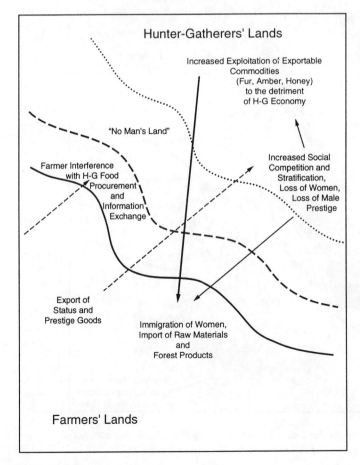

Figure 18.8 Competitive relations between foragers and farmers, which increase towards the end of the availability phase of the agricultural transition.

There are several indicators of conflict and competition within the agricultural frontier zone in northern Europe. These include marks of increased social competition, territoriality, and violence among the late mesolithic hunter–gatherers around the perimeter of the agricultural frontier on the North European plain (Keeley 1992) and in southern Scandinavia (Persson & Persson 1984, Bennike 1985, Meiklejohn & Zvelebil 1991, Price & Gebauer 1992); the presence of fortified farming villages on the farming side of the frontier; and, in some areas such as in Limburgh and Brabant, the existence of "no mans' land" (Keeley 1992). Similar apparently unoccupied areas of 20–40 km in width can be detected between the agricultural Bronze Age and forager inland neolithic sites during the first millennium bc in Finland, again suggesting antagonistic relations prior to the transformation of the hunter–gatherer communities there (Zvelebil 1981). Similarly, the presence of mesolithic armatures for arrows in neolithic assemblages in Poland, Germany and the Low Countries could be explained as a manifestation of conflict between foragers and farmers, and neolithic artefacts could be seen as loot rather than imports (Tomaszewski 1988, Gronenborn 1990, Keeley 1992). Even so, this evidence is somewhat ambiguous, in that some archaeological patterns can be a result of conflict as well as trade, and traces of violence on mesolithic skeletons may have been caused by anybody. On the whole, the evidence for exchange and co-operation is more extensive than that for conflict and competition.

The ambiguity of the evidence mirrors the theoretical argument where a case both for delay and for a rapid shift to farming can be made in a situation of contact between more sedentary foragers and farmers. In the historical situation of the western Baltic region, both the extended delay and then a rapid adoption of farming can be understood as a modified version of the forager–farmer interactions described earlier. The more complex hunter–gatherers of the coastal zone were better equipped demographically and technologically to interact with the farming communities on a more equal basis than the foragers of the interior. Here, the erosive effects of the competition may never have gained the upper hand. The early and extended phase of contact between forager and farmer communities in the fourth millennium bc may have established enduring kinship ties, and resulted in associated transferral of exchange from the intertribal to the tribal context, that is, from negative/unbalanced to generalized/balanced reciprocity. It would also have resulted in intermarriage rather than conflict and consequently in the blending of cultural traits and the development of a new archaeological culture.

The increase in conflict and competition towards the end of the Ertebølle would have reduced the benefits of maintaining the complex hunter–gatherer strategies and shifted the balance in favour of adopting farming. Because of their relative stability and population numbers, the coastal communities were able to acquire farming rapidly and to avoid the full destructive impact of the competition with farmers. The result was the transformation and evolution of hunter–gatherer social, ideological and economic strategies, rather than replacement – a process evident in continuities in material culture, economy, settlement location and burial practices (Rowley-Conwy & Zvelebil 1989, Madsen 1986, Solberg 1989, Price & Gebauer 1992, Jennbert 1985, Sherratt 1990, Bogucki 1988) between the Mesolithic and the first neolithic TRB (Trichterbeckerkultur) culture. In the western Baltic this process of transformation was accomplished fairly rapidly between *c.* 3200 and 3000 bc. Most authorities agree that we are dealing here with the acquisition of farming by local groups, with little or no immigration from the more established groups farther south (see Madsen 1986 for a review and Solberg 1989 for a contrary view). The genesis of the TRB culture in some areas of the north European Plain shows a similar blending of cultural attributes and continuity in settlement, and could be seen in a similar light (Bogucki 1988, Sherratt 1990, Midgley 1992).

In the eastern Baltic, agro-pastoral farming was adopted at a very slow rate over some two millennia (Zvelebil 1981, 1993, Dolukhanov 1979, Zvelebil & Dolukhanov 1991, Janik in press). Despite the presence of low numbers of domesticates on archaeological sites from *c.* 2500 bc, and despite a major change in material culture marked by the Corded Ware horizon *c.* 2500–1800 bc, the decisive shift to an agro-pastoral economy occurred between 1300 and 600 bc. This is attested to by the shift in the location of major settlements away from wetland and shoreline locations to areas with lighter soils suited to arable farming, by the rise in the presence of domesticates, and by the abandonment of symbolism associated with hunting and gathering in favour of agricultural symbols (Paaver 1965, Zvelebil 1981, 1985, 1992, 1993). In between, there was a society based principally on hunting and gathering for subsistence, yet making some occasional use of domesticates and possibly cultigens from about 2500 bc (Vuorela & Lempiainen 1988, Rimantiené 1992). The presence of domesticates in low numbers has been explained as a result of wide-ranging trading networks, elaborated within the context of the Corded Ware/Boat Axe culture (Dolukhanov 1979, Zvelebil 1993); their limited use, which continued until the end of the second millennium bc, fits with the notion of their ritual, rather than economic, significance (cf. Hayden 1990).

The transition to farming as a major economic activity (the substitution phase) during the Bronze Age occurred in conditions of strong cultural continuity and must have been accomplished by local groups. Although the details of this process are yet to be worked out, I suggest that the existence of trading networks may have upheld the viability of an essentially foraging economy and delayed the full adoption of farming. The increase in sealing in the area during the third and second millennia bc may have been particularly important, reflecting the commercial demand of the farming communities to the south and west of the agricultural frontier. In the eastern Baltic, then, the process of agricultural "transition" was arrested in the early stages and became a way of life, and as such remains suspended between our traditional notions of the Mesolithic and the Neolithic.

Conclusions

I have summarized an overall trend and ignored variation in both time and space. But we are dealing with a large area and it is the overall trend that is pertinent here. The major feature of this trend is the slow rate of the adoption of farming, and the variable timespan of the different phases in the process of adoption. In the eastern part of the Baltic region, this process gave rise to foraging–farming communities for which few parallels exist in the ethnographic record, and which followed their own historical trajectory of development.

Although many reasons have been advanced to explain the transition to farming in the circum-Baltic region (Price & Gebauer 1992) and in other areas of the world (Hayden 1990), less attention has been paid to the actual process of the transition. This is particularly true for areas such as temperate and northern Europe, which lie outside the centres of farming origins. Yet we need a better understanding of the process of the transition to farming in order to apprehend its causes.

Contacts between foragers and farmers, occurring within an agricultural frontier zone, must have had a direct effect on the nature and rate of the transition. Such contacts may have acted as a delaying mechanism in the process of the transition, as appears to have been the case in both the western and the eastern Baltic during the availability phase, or they may have acted to accelerate the adoption of farming, for example at the end of the Mesolithic in southern Scandinavia. In this way, the forager–farmer contacts, through which the transition to farming was mediated in many areas, acted as a mechanism regulating the rate of transition, and may be counted as one among the causes of the transition. Our next task is to identify more rigorously the specific content of the forager–farmer contacts and to link them to their specific archaeological signatures.

Acknowledgements

This paper was completed during my tenure as a visiting fellow at the Netherlands Institute for Advanced Study in the Humanities and Social Sciences (NIAS). I would like to thank NIAS for financial support and to staff at NIAS for providing secretarial assistance.

References

Alexander, J. 1978. Frontier studies and the earliest farmers in Europe. In *Social organisation and settlement*, D. Green, C. Haselgrove, M. Spriggs (eds), 13–29. Oxford: British Archaeological Reports, International Series 47.

Ammerman, A. J. 1989. On the neolithic transition in Europe: a comment on Zvelebil and Zvelebil (1988), *Antiquity* **63**, 162–5.

Ammerman, A. J. & L. L. Cavalli-Sforza 1984. *The neolithic transition and the genetics of population in Europe*. Princeton, NJ: Princeton University Press.

Andersen, S. H. 1975. Ringkloster. En jysk indlandsboplads med Ertebøllekultur. *Kuml* 1973–74, 10–108.

— 1987. Tybrind Vig: a submerged Ertebølle settlement in Denmark. In *European wetlands in prehistory*, J. M. Coles & A. J. Lawson (eds), 253–81. Oxford: Oxford University Press.

Aurenche, O. & J. Cauvin (eds) 1989. *Néolithisations, Proche et Moyen Orient, Méditeranée, orientale, Nord de l'Afrique, Europe méridionale, Chine, Amérique du Sud*. Oxford: British Archaeological Reports, International Series 516.

Barker, G. 1985. *Prehistoric farming in Europe*. Cambridge: Cambridge University Press.

Bailey, R. C. & J. R. R. Annger 1989. Net hunters vs archers: variation in women's subsistences strategies in the Ituri forest. *Human Ecology* **17**, 273–97.

Binford, L. R. 1965. Archaeological systematics and the study of culture process. *American Antiquity* **31**, 203–10.

Bennike, P. 1985. *Palaeopathology of Danish skeletons. A comparative study of demography, disease and injury.* Copenhagen: Akademisk Forlag.

Bogucki, P. I. 1987. The establishment of agrarian communities on the North European Plain. *Current Anthropology* **28**, 1–24.

— 1988. *Forest farmers and stockherders: early agriculture and its consequences in North-Central Europe.* Cambridge: Cambridge University Press.

Buikstra, J. E., L. W. Konigsberg, J. Bullington 1986. Fertility and the development of agriculture in the prehistoric Midwest. *American Antiquity* **51**, 528–46.

Case, H. 1969. Neolithic explanations. *Antiquity* **43**, 176–86.

Cavalli-Sforza, L. L. 1991. Genes, peoples and languages. *Scientific American* **265**(5), 72–8.

Clark, G. A. & M. Neeley 1987. Social differentiation in European mesolithic burial data. In *Mesolithic Northwest Europe, recent trends*, P. Rowley-Conwy, M. Zvelebil, H. P. Blankholm (eds), 121–30. Sheffield: University of Sheffield Press.

Clarke, D. 1968. *Analytical archaeology.* London: Methuen.

Cohen, M. N. 1989. *Health and the rise of civilization.* New Haven: Yale University Press.

Constandse-Westermann T. S. & R. R. Newell 1989. Limb laterisation and social stratification in western Mesolithic societies. In *People and culture in change*, I. Herskovitz (ed.), 405–34. Oxford: British Archaeological Reports, International Series 508.

Dennell, R. 1983. *European economic prehistory: a new approach.* London: Academic Press.

— 1985. The hunter–gatherer/agricultural frontier in prehistoric temperate Europe. In *The archaeology of frontiers and boundaries*, S. Green & S. M. Perlman (eds), 113–40. New York: Academic Press.

Dolukhanov, P. M. 1979. *Ecology and economy in Neolithic eastern Europe.* London: Duckworth.

— 1986. The late Mesolithic and the transition to food production in eastern Europe. In Zvelebil (1986: 109–20).

— 1993. Foraging and farming groups in north-eastern and north-western Europe: identity and interaction. In *Cultural transformations and interactions in eastern Europe*, J. Chapman & P. Dolukhanov (eds), 122–45. Aldershot: Avebury.

Edgren, T. 1970. Studier over den snörkeramiska kulturens i Finland. *Finska FornMinnesföreningens Tidskrift* **72**, 1–118.

Ehret, C. 1988. Language change and the material correlates of language and ethnic shift. *Antiquity* **62**, 564–74.

Fischer, A. 1982. Trade in Danubian shaft-hole axes and the introduction of neolithic economy in Denmark. *Journal of Danish Archaeology* **1**, 7–12.

Grayson, D. K. 1979. On the quantification of vertebrate archaeofaunas. In *Advances in archaeological method and theory* (vol. 2), M. Schiffer (ed.), 199–237. New York: Academic Press.

Green, S. & S. Perlman 1985. *The archaeology of frontiers and boundaries.* New York: Academic Press.

Gregg, S. A. 1988. *Foragers and farmers: population interaction and agricultural expansion in prehistoric Europe.* Chicago: University of Chicago Press.

Gronenborn, D. 1990. Eine Pfeilspitze vom altesband-keramisachen Fundplatz Friedberg-B Bruchenbrücken in der Wetterau. *Germania* **68**, 223–31.

Gronlund, E., H. Simola, P. Uimonen-Simola 1990. Early agriculture in eastern Finnish Lake District. *Norwegian Archaeological Review* **23**, 79–85.

Hastorf, C. & V. S. Popper (eds) 1988. *Current palaeoethnobotany.* Chicago: Chicago University Press.

Hamp, E. 1987. The pig in ancient northern Europe. In *Proto-Indo–European: the archaeology of a linguistic problem*, S. N. Skomal & E. C. Polome (eds), 185–90. Washington DC: Institute for the Study of Man.

Hayden, B. 1990. Nimrods, piscators, pluckers, and planters: the emergence of food production. *Journal of Anthropological Archaeology* **9**, 31–69.

Hedges, R. E. M., R. A. Housley, C. Bronk Ramsey, G. J. van Klinken 1995. Radiocarbon dates from the Oxford AMS system: *Arcaeometry* datelist 20. *Archaeometry* **37**, 417–30.

Hodder, I. (ed.) 1978. *The spatial organisation of culture.* London: Duckworth.

— 1982. *Symbols in action.* Cambridge: Cambridge University Press.

— 1990. *The domestication of Europe: structure and contingency in neolithic societies.* Oxford: Basil Blackwell.

Hunn, E. S. & N. M. Williams 1982. Introduction. In *Resource managers: North American and Australian hunter–gatherers*, N. M. Williams & E. S Hunn (eds), 1–16. Boulder: Westview Press.

Ingold, T. 1988. Notes on the foraging mode of production. In Ingold et al. (1988: 269–85).

Ingold, T., D. Riches, J. Woodburn (eds) 1988. *Hunters and gatherers: history, evolution and social change.* Oxford: Berg.

Janik, L. in press. The appearance of food producing societies in the southeastern Baltic region. In *Agricultural frontier and the transition to farming in the Baltic*, R. Dennell, L. Domańska, M. Zvelebil (eds). Sheffield: Sheffield Academic Press.

Jennbert, K. 1984. Den produktiva gåvan: tradition och innovation i Sydskandinavien för omkring 5300 år Sedan. [*Acta Archaeologica Lundensia*, Series in 4⁰, 16]. Lund: Gleerup.

— 1985. Neolithisation – a Scanian perspective. *Journal of Danish Archaeology* 4, 196–7.

Kabacinski, J. 1992. Dabki site 9 and its relation to the Stone Age cultures of the southern Baltic coastal zone. *Dorzecze* 1, 6–41.

Keeley, L. H. 1992. The introduction of agriculture to the western North European Plain. In *Transitions to agriculture in prehistory* [Monographs in World Archaeology 4], A. B. Gebauer & T. D. Price (eds), 81–97. Madison: Prehistory Press.

Kivikoski, E. 1967. *Finland.* London: Thames & Hudson.

Larsson, L. 1990. The Mesolithic of southern Scandinavia. *Journal of World Prehistory* 4, 257–309.

Leacock, E. & R. Lee 1982. *Politics and history in band societies.* Cambridge: Cambridge University Press.

Madsen, T. 1986. Where did all the hunters go? An assessment of an epoch-making episode in Danish prehistory. *Journal of Danish Archaeology* 5, 229–39.

Mallory, J. P. 1989. *In search of the Indo–Europeans.* London: Thames & Hudson.

Malmer, M. P. 1962. Jungneolithische studien. [*Acta Archaeologica Lundensia*, Series in 8⁰]. Lund: Gleerup.

Malinowski, B. 1950 (1922). *Argonauts of the western Pacific.* London: Routledge & Kegan Paul.

Meiklejohn, C. & M. Zvelebil 1991. Health status of European populations at the agricultural transition and the implications for the adoption of farming. In *Health in past societies: biocultural interpretations of human skeletal remains in archaeological contexts*, H. Bush & M. Zvelebil (eds), 129–45. Oxford: British Archaeological Reports, International Series 567.

Midgley, M. 1992. *TRB culture: the first farmers of the North European Plain.* Edinburgh: Edinburgh University Press.

Mithen, S. 1990. *Thoughtful foragers: a study of prehistoric decision making.* Cambridge: Cambridge University Press.

Moore, J. A. 1985. Forager–farmer interactions: information, social organisation and the frontier. In *The archaeology of frontiers and boundaries*, S. W. Green & S. Perlman (eds), 93–112. New York: Academic Press.

Neeley M. P. & G. A. Clark 1990. Measuring social complexity in the European Mesolithic. In *Contributions to the Mesolithic in Europe*, P. M. Vermeersch & P. van Peer (eds), 127–38. Leuven: Leuven University Press.

Neustupný, E. 1971. Whither archaeology? *Antiquity* 45, 34–7.

— 1982. Prehistoric migrations by infiltration. *Archeologickè Rozhledy* 34, 278–93.

— 1987. Comments on the establishment of agrarian communities on the North European Plain by P. Bogucki. *Current Anthropology* 28, 14–16.

Newell, R. 1984. On the mesolithic contribution to the social evolution of western European society. In *European social evolution: archaeological perspectives*, J. Biniliff (ed.), 69–82. Bradford: Bradford University Press.

Olsen, B. 1988. Interaction between hunter–gatherers and farmers: ethnographical and archaeological perspectives. *Archaeologia Polski* 33, 425–34.

O'Shea, J. & M. Zvelebil 1984. Oleneostrovskii Mogilnik: reconstructing social and economic organisation of prehistoric hunter–fishers in northern Russia. *Journal of Anthropological Archaeology* 3, 1–40.

Paaver, K. C. 1965. *Formirovaniye Teriofauny i Izmenchivost Mlekopytayushchikh Pribaltiki v Golt-sene*. Tartu: Akademiya Nauk Estonskoii SSR.

Perrson, O. & E. Persson 1984. *Anthropological report on the mesolithic graves from Skateholm, southern Sweden, excavation seasons 1980–1982*. Report Series 21, Institute of Archaeology, University of Lund.

Piggott, S. 1965. *Ancient Europe*. Edinburgh: Edinburgh University Press.

Price, T. D. 1985. Affluent foragers of mesolithic southern Scandinavia. In *Prehistoric hunter–gatherers: the emergence of cultural complexity*, T. D. Price & J. A. Brown (eds), 341–60. Orlando: Academic Press.

— 1987. The Mesolithic of western Europe. *Journal of World Prehistory* 2, 225–305.

Price, T. D. & A. B. Gebauer 1992. The final frontier: foragers to farmers in southern Scandinavia. In *Transitions to agriculture in prehistory* [Monographs in World Archaeology 4], A. B. Gebauer & T. D. Price (eds), 97–116. Madison: Prehistory Press.

Renfrew, C. 1987. *Archaeology and language: the puzzle of Indo–European origins*. London: Jonathan Cape.

Rimantiené, R. 1992. Neolithic hunter–gatherers at Šventoji in Lithuania. *Antiquity* 66, 367–76.

Rowley-Conwy, P. 1980. *Continuity and change in the prehistoric economies of Denmark, 3700–2300 bc*. PhD dissertation, Department of Archaeology, University of Cambridge.

— 1983. Sedentary hunters: the Ertebølle example. In *Hunter–gatherer economy in prehistory: a European perspective*, G. Bailey (ed.), 111–26. Cambridge: Cambridge University Press.

Rowley-Conwy, P. & M. Zvelebil 1989. Saving it for later: storage by prehistoric hunter–gatherers in Europe. In *Bad year economics*, P. Halstead & J. O'Shea (eds), 40–56. Cambridge: Cambridge University Press.

Sahlins, M. 1974. *Stone Age economics*. London: Tavistock.

Schiffer, M. 1976. *Behavioral archaeology*. New York: Academic Press.

Schrire, C. (ed.) 1984. *Past and present in hunter gatherer studies*. Orlando: Academic Press.

Schwabedissen, H. 1981. Ertebølle/Ellerbek – Mesolithikum oder Neolithikum? In *Mesolithikum in Europa*, B. Gramsch (ed.), 129–43. Berlin: VEB Deutscher Verlag der Wissenschaten.

Shennan, S. J. 1989. Introduction: archaeological approaches to cultural identity. In *Archaeological approaches to cultural identity*, S. J. Shennan (ed.), 1–32. London: Unwin Hyman.

Sherratt, A. 1982. Mobile resources: settlement and exchange in early agricultural Europe. In *Ranking, resource and exchange: aspects of the archaeology of early European society*, C. Renfrew & S. Shennan (eds), 13–26. Cambridge: Cambridge University Press.

— 1990. The genesis of megaliths: monumentality, ethnicity and social complexity in neolithic northwest Europe. *World Archaeology* 22, 148–67.

Solberg, B. 1989. The neolithic transition in southern Scandinavia: internal development or migration? *Oxford Journal of Archaeology* 8, 261–96.

Speth, J. 1991. Some unexplored aspects of mutualistic Plains–Pueblo food exchange. In *Farmers, hunters, and colonists: interaction between the Southwest and the southern Plains*, K. Spielmann (ed.), 18–35. Tucson: University of Arizona Press.

Spielmann, K. A. (ed.) 1991. *Farmers, hunters, and colonists: interaction between the Southwest and the southern Plains*. Tucson: University of Arizona Press.

Thomas, J. 1987. Relations of production and social change in the Neolithic of North-West Europe. *Man* 22, 405–30.

— 1988. Neolithic explanations revisited: the mesolithic–neolithic transition in Britain and south Scandinavia. *Proceedings of the Prehistoric Society* 54, 59–66.

— 1991. *Rethinking the Neolithic*. Cambridge: Cambridge University Press.

Timofeev, V. I. 1987. On the problem of the early Neolithic of the East Baltic area. *Acta Archaeologica*, 58, 207–12.

— 1990. On the links of the East Baltic Neolithic and the Funnel Beaker Culture. In *Die Trichterbeckerkultur*, D. Jankowska (ed.), 135–49. Institute of Prehistory, University of Poznan, Poznan.

Tomaszewski, A. J. 1988. Foragers, farmers and archaeologists. *Archaeologia Polski* 33, 434–40.

Vankina, L. V. 1970. *Torfyanikovaya Stoyanka Sarnate*. Riga: Zinatne.

Vencl, S. 1986. The role of hunting–gathering populations in the transition to farming: a Central-European perspective. In Zvelebil (1989: 43–51).

Vuorela, I. 1970. The indication of farming in pollen diagrams from southern Finland. *Acta Botanica Fennica* **87**, 1–40.

— 1972. Human influence on the vegetation of the Katinhanta bog, Vihiti, S. Finland. *Acta Botanica Fennica* **98**, 1–21.

— 1975. Pollen analyses as a means of tracing settlement history in SW Finland. *Acta Botanica Fennica* **104**, 1–48.

— 1986. Palynological and historical evidence of slash-and-burn cultivation in South Finland. In *Anthropogenic indicators in pollen diagrams*, K. E. Behre (ed.), 53–64. Rotterdam: Balkema.

— in press. Transition to farming in southern Finland. In *Agricultural frontier and the transition to farming in the Baltic*, R. Dennell, L. Domańska, M. Zvelebil (eds).Sheffield: Sheffield Academic Press.

Vuorela, I. & T. Lempiainen 1988. Archaeobotany of the oldest cereal grain find in Finland. *Annales Botanici Fennici* **25**, 33–45.

Welinder, S. 1989. Mesolithic forest clearance in Scandinavia. In *The Mesolithic in Europe*, C. Bonsall (ed.), 362–77. Edinburgh: John Donald.

Woodburn, J. 1982. Egalitarian societies. *Man* **17**, 431–51.

Woodburn, J. 1988. African hunter–gatherer social organization: is it best understood as a product of enscapulation? In *Hunters and gatherers, 1: history, evolution and social change*, T. Ingold, D. Riches, J. Woodburn (eds), 31–64. Oxford: Berg.

Zvelebil, M. 1981. *From forager to farmer in the Boreal zone: reconstructing economic patterns through catchment analysis in prehistoric Finland*. Oxford: British Archaeological Reports, International Series 115.

— 1985. Iron Age transformations in northern Russia and the northeast Baltic. In *Beyond domestication in prehistoric Europe: investigations in subsistence archaeology and social complexity*, G. Barker & C. Gamble (eds), 147–80. London: Academic Press.

— 1986a. Mesolithic prelude and neolithic revolution. In Zvelebil (1986c: 5–15).

— 1986b. Mesolithic societies and the transition to farming: problems of time, scale and organisation. In Zvelebil (1986c: 167–88).

— (ed.) 1986c. *Hunters in transition: mesolithic societies of temperate Eurasia and their transition to farming*. Cambridge: Cambridge University Press.

— 1989. On the transition to farming in Europe, or what was spreading with the Neolithic: a reply to Ammerman (1989). *Antiquity* **63**, 379–83.

— 1992. Les chasseurs pêcheurs de la Scandinavie préhistorique. *La Recherche* **246**, 982–90.

— 1993. Hunters or farmers? The Neolithic and Bronze Age societies of north-east Europe. In *Cultural transformation and interactions in Eastern Europe*, J. Chapman & P. Dolukhanov (eds), 146–62. Aldershot: Avebury.

— 1994. Plant use in the Mesolithic and its role in the transition to farming. *Proceedings of the Prehistoric Society* **60**, 35–74.

— 1995. Hunting, gathering or husbandry? Management of food resources by the late Mesolithic communities of temperate Europe. In *Before farming: hunter–gatherer society and subsistence*, D. Campana (ed.). MASCA Research Papers in Science and Archaeology, vol. 12, supplement. The University Museum of Archaeology and Anthropology, University of Pennsylvania, Philadelphia.

— 1996. What's in a name: the Mesolithic, the Neolithic and social change at the mesolithic–neolithic transition. In *Understanding the Neolithic of North-West Europe*, M. Edmonds & C. Richards (eds), 1–35. Glasgow: Cruithne Press.

Zvelebil, M. & P. Rowley-Conwy 1984. Transition to farming in northern Europe: a hunter–gatherer perspective. *Norwegian Archaeological Review* **17**, 104–28.

— 1986. Foragers and farmers in Atlantic Europe. In Zvelebil (1986c: 67–93).

Zvelebil, M. & K. V. Zvelebil 1988. Agricultural transition and Indo–European dispersals. *Antiquity* **62**, 574–83.

Zvelebil, M. & P. Dolukhanov 1991. Transition to farming in eastern and northern Europe. *Journal of World Prehistory* **5**, 233–78.

CHAPTER NINETEEN

The first farmers of southern Scandinavia

T. Douglas Price

Introduction

Agriculture arrived in prehistoric Europe in the form of plants and animals originally domesticated in Southwest Asia. Until the past ten years or so, this spread was
thought to reflect the arrival of foreign colonists bearing ceramic containers and
domesticated plants and animals and introducing to Europe permanent villages, pottery, new architecture, storage facilities, long-distance trade and elaborate burial rituals. Indigenous hunter–gatherers were thought to have been largely aceramic,
dependent on wild foods, residentially mobile, socially amorphous and eventually
overwhelmed. More recently, however, it appears that colonization may well have
been the exception, rather than the rule, in the spread of farming into Europe (cf. Halstead, Thomas and Zvelebil in Chs 16, 17 and 18 in this volume, Price 1987, 1991,
Runnels & van Andel 1988, Zvelebil & Rowley-Conwy 1984, 1986, Zvelebil & Zvelebil 1988). In this context, the question of why foragers shifted to farming is very
intriguing.

Information from northern Europe, because of both its abundance and its quality,
is particularly well suited to addressing questions regarding the transition to agriculture. This paper concentrates on Denmark and the rest of southern Scandinavia for
several reasons. The archaeology of the region is very rich. In spite of its relatively
small size and population, it has a long history of superb archaeological research. The
National Museum of Denmark has directed scientific excavations of prehistoric sites
for more than 150 years. Chronologies are highly detailed. Christian Thomsen first
defined the Stone Age in Copenhagen in 1819; there are now some 11 divisions of
the mesolithic period alone in Denmark. There are more studies, more dated sites, and
more archaeological information per square kilometre than anywhere else in the world.

Southern Scandinavia is also very well suited for the study of the transition to agriculture in the context of climate and other aspects of the environment. The environmental evidence from the area is exceptional. Danish natural historians have
examined myriad sources of evidence to provide a detailed picture of changes in sea
level, vegetation and climate over the past 10,000 years or so. This is also a region
with remarkable organic preservation. The combination of chalky soils and wetland

topography means that organic materials that seldom survive to the present elsewhere occasionally do so here. The lake, bog and offshore coastal deposits of Denmark and southern Sweden contain bone, wood, antler, even skin, hide and vegetable remains. It is possible to see a larger assortment of the material remains of the past in this region than it is elsewhere.

Prehistoric southern Scandinavia is essentially a laboratory for human prehistory. Not colonized by humans until the retreat of Pleistocene ice around 14,000 years ago, it was first a region of tundra and reindeer hunters. By 10,000 years ago the forest had returned to the warming landscape and the first postglacial foragers appeared, hunting and collecting a variety of species. By 6,000 years ago the ideas and materials of farming communities began to appear in the region, heralding the onset of the Neolithic. Evidence for farming appeared suddenly in this area around 3900 BC (calibrated radiocarbon years) with the arrival of domesticated plants and animals, a range of new ceramic containers, large tombs, bog offerings, prestige items and long-distance exchange.

The Linearbandkeramik farming culture spread thousands of kilometres across Central Europe in a shorter period of time than is resolvable by radiocarbon dating. Yet it took more than 500 years before domesticates were introduced into northern Europe from Linearbandkeramik farmers only a few hundred kilometres away in northern Germany and Poland. Certain ideas, or actual objects such as pottery, stone and antler axes and bone combs, were obtained in trade from the farmers to the south during this period, but agricultural foodstuffs were among the last items to be introduced in the late Mesolithic. The only reasonable explanation for this delay is the presence of successful fishing–hunting peoples who had little immediate use for domesticated plants and animals.

The focus of interest here, then, is on the nature and cause of the transition from hunting and gathering to farming adaptations in southern Scandinavia. The next two sections provide a brief introduction to the archaeology of mesolithic and neolithic Denmark, and a synthesis of current theoretical debates regarding the neolithic transition in the region. Current evidence from southern Scandinavia suggests that the primary correlates of the transition to agriculture were not climatic deterioration, resource decline, or population growth, but rather increasing status differentiation and trade. The information from this region is also applicable to broader questions concerning the general phenomenon of the origins and spread of agriculture. The implications of this study for understanding the more general phenomenon are summarized in the final section of this paper. If we cannot shed light on the question of agricultural transition with the evidence from southern Scandinavia, we may not be ready to resolve it anywhere.

A brief prehistory of southern Scandinavia, 6800–2800 BC

The time period of concern extends from approximately 6800 to 2800 BC, encompassing the later Mesolithic (*Kongemose* – KGM and *Ertebølle* – EBK) and the first half of the Neolithic (*Tragtbæger* – TRB) in the region (Fig. 19.1).

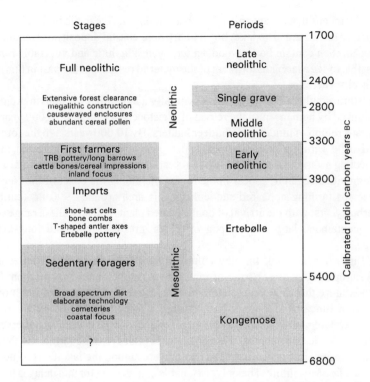

Figure 19.1 Chronology and periodization of the later Mesolithic and early Neolithic in southern Scandinavia.

The Kongemose is the middle Mesolithic, dating from 6800 BC to 5400 BC. This period witnesses the first evidence for extensive coastal adaptation, sedentary occupation, and shellfish consumption. The Ertebølle or late Mesolithic (5400–3900 BC) represents the culmination of several trends in the Mesolithic (Price 1987, 1991, Andersen 1993a). More artefact types and more complex facilities were made; previous forms become more functionally specific. Cemeteries are known from a number of later mesolithic sites such as Vedbæk (Albrethsen & Brinch Petersen 1976) in Denmark and Skateholm (Larsson 1984) in southern Sweden (Fig. 19.2); burials are generally simple inhumations with a limited range of utilitarian grave goods.

An intensification in food procurement can also be traced through the Danish Mesolithic. The variety of extraction sites including the construction of large fish weirs, and the remains of a wide range of marine fish and mammals, including seals, dolphins and whales, demonstrates the diversity of the subsistence base. The coastal focus is pronounced; inland sites are known almost exclusively from small, summer camps. Carbon isotope ratios in human bone point to the predominance of marine foods in the diet (Tauber 1981).

Significant regional variation in artefact types and styles is documented from the later part of the Ertebølle; differences between eastern and western Denmark, and among smaller areas within Zealand, have been reported (Andersen 1981, Vang

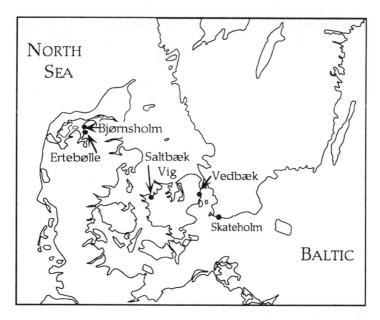

Figure 19.2 Southern Scandinavia and the location of sites mentioned in the text.

Petersen 1984). Some form of territoriality can be inferred from the limited, local distributions of certain artefact types (Vang Petersen 1984). Several instances of violent death in the cemeteries emphasize the possibility of conflict among territorial groups. Exchange in exotic materials is documented by the presence of a variety of foreign objects obtained from farmers to the south. In addition to pottery, bone combs, T-shaped antler axes, and shoe-last axes of amphibolite from a source in southeastern Europe, appear in an Ertebølle context in Denmark (Andersen 1973, Fischer 1982, Jennbert 1984).

Funnelbeaker (TRB) pottery is the hallmark of the early Neolithic, first appearing around 3900 BC. The earliest radiocarbon dates for the Neolithic come not from settlements but from long barrows with timber burial chambers, bog-site offerings and flint mines. There are relatively few initial neolithic settlements; the first TRB settlement dates are 100 years younger, often at sites in continuous use from the Ertebølle period. Residential sites are small with a thin cultural layer compared to the Ertebølle, suggesting that co-resident groups in the Neolithic were smaller and perhaps more mobile. Early neolithic sites exhibit a more inland location than mesolithic sites; they are often found at lakes or streams where fresh water was easy obtainable and conditions for grazing were favourable (Madsen & Jensen 1982, Nielsen 1985, Madsen 1991). The shift from a coastal focus is also indicated by carbon isotope ratios in neolithic skeletons, which indicate a greater dependence on terrestrial resources. Evidence for cereals and domesticated animals is found after 3900 BC (Andersen & Rasmussen 1993), but hunting, fishing, and gathering still played an important role during the first 600 years of the Neolithic (Skaarup 1973, Andersen 1993).

From the beginning of the middle Neolithic around 3300 BC, substantial residential sites began to reappear on the coast as well as at inland locations and the number of hunting sites decreased. Territorial demarcation among settlements appears to be fixed by 3300 BC, emphasized by the construction of one or more megalithic tombs in relation to settlements (Madsen 1991, Skaarup 1973, 1985). Marked forest clearance, together with more evidence for cereal growing and stock rearing, indicates an agricultural expansion (Andersen & Rasmussen 1993). Wheats comprise 96 per cent of the cereals at the beginning of the middle Neolithic, but barley accounts for 22 per cent of the cereal remains at the later Funnelbeaker sites (Jørgensen 1977). Cattle were the most important livestock and they became more common through the Funnelbeaker period, representing more than 80 per cent of the domestic animals at some later sites.

The introduction of farming was accompanied by technological innovations: thin-walled pottery and new pot shapes, large polished flint axes for forest clearing and timber-working (along with a related flint-mining industry), weapons such as ground-stone battle axes and mace heads, copper axes and flint daggers, personal ornaments made of amber and copper, grinding stones for processing cereals, and the ard – the first primitive type of plough.

Theories and evidence

The transition to agriculture is a subject of considerable debate in southern Scandinavia. Prior to the 1970s the primary topic of debate was whether the transition represented a colonization by TRB people or a transformation of the indigenous Ertebølle foragers into an agrarian society. Invading TRB people were thought by some to derive from either the western or the eastern part of Central Europe, or even from the Ukraine (e.g. Becker 1948, Lichardus 1976). Others argued that the TRB represented an independent Scandinavian development from the local Ertebølle (Troels-Smith 1953).

Most recent theories about why Ertebølle foragers opted for agriculture involve either stress resulting from changes in population or environment, or demands from increasing social differentiation. Competing explanations have been suggested, ranging from a combination of small-scale migration and indigenous adoption by late mesolithic groups (Larsson 1987), to climate change (Rowley-Conwy 1985, Larsson 1987), the gradual spread of ideas and products (Nielsen 1985), resource-poor inland groups seeking a productive source of food (Madsen 1986), or exchange cycles and competition for prestige (Fischer 1982, Jennbert 1984, 1985). The paragraphs below outline this debate in terms of four major issues: colonization versus adoption, population, resource availability and social demands. The question of colonization concerns *how* agriculture arrived in southern Scandinavia; the issues of population, resources, and social demands involve causality, or *why* foragers became farmers. In each section there is a discussion of the arguments involved and some of the evidence that pertains to them.

Colonization versus indigenous adoption

The question of how agriculture was introduced in southern Scandinavia is a complex one. There are three major hypotheses:

- that the early Neolithic was intrusive, brought by colonists (Becker 1948, 1955, Lichardus 1976)
- that the early Neolithic was an autochthonous development from the local late Mesolithic (Kossinna 1921, Troels-Smith 1953)
- that the early Neolithic developed from the local Mesolithic, under the influence of various Danubian cultures (Childe 1949, Chmielewski 1952, Schwabedissen 1967, 1981, Fischer 1982, Nielsen 1985, Madsen & Petersen 1984, Jennbert 1984, 1985, Larsson 1987).

The evidence for and against colonization has come largely from material culture. Arguments for colonization pointed to the introduction of a variety of new materials such as TRB pottery and new practices involving domestic plants and animals and monumental tombs. Today, however, most archaeologists believe that the TRB developed from the local Mesolithic under greater or lesser influence from various Danubian groups (Paludan-Müller 1978, Fischer 1982, Jennbert 1984, 1985, Madsen & Petersen 1984, Zvelebil & Rowley-Conwy 1984, 1986, Nielsen 1985, 1986, Rowley-Conwy 1985, Andersen 1993b). Continuity in flint and ceramic technology, and to some degree in burial ritual, suggests that an introduction of the TRB through colonization is unlikely. Nielsen (1985) has described the similarities and differences between the late Mesolithic and the early Neolithic in Zealand and southern Scania. Evidence from some 17 sites documents a continuity between the Ertebølle and the TRB. Flint technology appears to be derived from the Ertebølle; the pottery in the TRB tradition, and perhaps the technology of food preparation, is relatively new. However, only minor differences are noted between the Ertebølle and the utilitarian wares of the early TRB (Gebauer 1995, Nielsen 1987); the TRB funerary ceramics, on the other hand, do reflect innovation in shape and decoration.

Settlement evidence from Bjørnsholm (Andersen 1993b) and elsewhere documents continuity with the early Neolithic at places of Ertebølle residence. Bjørnsholm is a large "kitchen-midden" site in the central Limfjord area of northern Jutland, which dates from the late Mesolithic and early Neolithic (Fig. 19.2). The shell midden itself is more than 300m long and 10–50m wide and extends along the coast of the fjord, not far from the sea. The Ertebølle layers at Bjornsholm date from 5050–4050 BC and the early Neolithic there from 3960–3530 BC. New finds from the early Neolithic include a stone-axe blade, which imitates a central European copper axe, and a typical Danubian shaft-hole axe. TRB pottery is present in the stratigraphic sequence before a shift in subsistence from oysters to cockles is noted in the shell midden. Neolithic subsistence was generally similar to mesolithic subsistence, with the addition of wheats, barley, sheep, cattle, and pig. And, with the habitation, there is a striking example of an early neolithic monumental grave in the form of an earthen long barrow.

Comparison of the skeletal characteristics of mesolithic and neolithic populations indicates that the skeletal morphology of neolithic peoples continues trends observed in the Mesolithic (Meiklejohn & Zvelebil 1991). This is seen particularly in a decrease in tooth size and a reduction in stature. Given current archaeological and anthropological evidence, the consensus among Scandinavian archaeologists today is that the introduction of agriculture was largely the result of indigenous adoption.

Population

One of the major hypotheses concerning the transition to agriculture suggests that population growth resulted in too many people and too little food (e.g. Binford 1968, Cohen 1977). Agriculture provided increased yields of food per unit of land to feed growing numbers of people.

The question of population is best examined in southern Scandinavia in terms of the number and size of sites by time period. There appears to be an intensification in subsistence and settlement through the Mesolithic, with sedentary communities present at least by the Kongemose period (Fig. 19.1). However, the number of sites from the Mesolithic is never particularly large. No increase in the total number of settlements is seen in the earliest Neolithic; if anything, there may have been a decrease in the number of settlements from the late Mesolithic to the earliest Neolithic.

The systematic archaeological survey of the Saltbæk Vig area (Fig. 19.2) in northwestern Zealand (Price & Gebauer 1992) provides some information on the number and size of sites from the time of the transition. To date, the survey has examined approximately 18 km² of the research area and registered more than 350 sites (Fig. 19.3). The survey has revealed a variety of settlements (Tables 19.1, 19.2), primarily from the Mesolithic and Neolithic, including a number of important new sites. Settlement locations are concentrated on points of land and peninsulas on or very near the former coastlines (Fig. 19.3). Most mesolithic and neolithic sites are found on the southern shore of the inlet, concentrated towards its mouth. Mesolithic and neolithic

Table 19.1   Types of sites located in the Saltbaek Vig survey

Type of site	Stray find	Settlement	Lithic scatters	Barrow/dolmen	Total
Sites	108	126	118	4	356

Table 19.2   Chronology of sites located in the Saltbaek Vig survey.

Chron. period	Palaeolithic	Mesolithic	Mesolithic/Neolithic	Early Neolithic	Neolithic	Late Neolithic	Bronze Age	Mixed/Unknown	Total
Sites	1	68	40	6	214	11	5	11	356

sites generally tend to be in similar locations, suggesting a continuity of occupation. Neolithic sites tend to be richer in terms of artefact density and more diverse in settlement size, whereas some of the mesolithic sites surpass in size the larger neolithic sites. This pattern does not suggest any dramatic changes in population density, but

Figure 19.3   The distribution of mesolithic (upper) and neolithic (lower) sites in the Saltbaek Vig research area, northwest Zealand, Denmark. Contours are at intervals of 0, 2.5, 5, 15 , and 25 m above sea level. The 2.5 m contour is included because it represents the approximate level of the sea at the time of the transition to agriculture in southern Scandinavia. The water of the Saltbaek Vig, shown in grey, lies at −1.2 below sea level because this area has been dammed and drained to create more farmland. The Saltbaek Vig is approximately 7 km long and 2.5 km wide. North is to the top of the map.

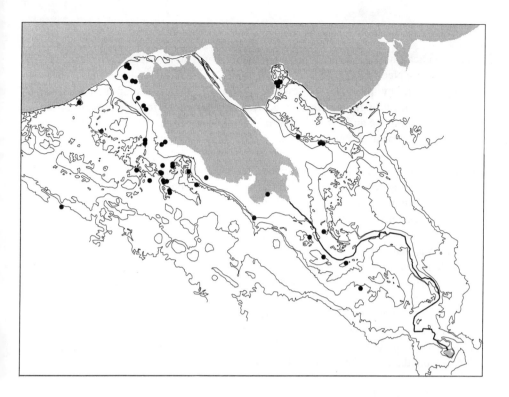

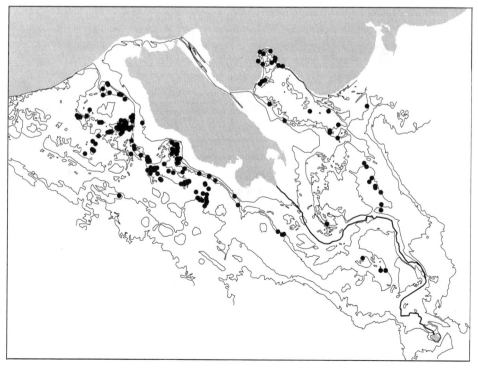

it may indicate a trend toward a larger population and a more varied economic organization in the Neolithic.

Similar survey information elsewhere indicates an intensification in subsistence and settlement through the Mesolithic, with sedentary communities present during the late Kongemose and Ertebølle periods. Settlements in the later Mesolithic were large, with linear occupation areas often more than 100m in length (e.g. Andersen 1993b).

There was a relatively dense population at the coast during the Ertebølle. In southern Scandinavia, changes in the landscape increased population density, even if population numbers were stable. Rising sea levels and the establishment of closed-canopy forest during the Mesolithic reduced the amount of land available for the population. Marine transgression was the hallmark of the early Holocene, while the vegetation was changing from more open birch and pine woodlands to more dense, closed-canopy deciduous forest with reduced biomass (Clutton-Brock & Noe-Nygaard 1990).

There is, however, no obvious evidence for population pressure preceding the transition to agriculture. Human skeletal remains from this period are robust with few pathologies (Bennike 1985, 1993). The first farmers settled in small scattered habitations combined with seasonal resource-extraction camps. Population size does appear to increase somewhat around 3300 BC, but there is no indication of increasing population immediately before or after the introduction of agriculture.

Resource availability

Binford (1968) and others have argued that agriculture was adopted either as a result of growing population or of declining food resources. Some imbalance between population levels and available resources in southern Scandinavia is implied in several papers (Andersen 1973, 1981, Paludan-Müller 1978, Rowley-Conwy 1983, 1984, 1985, Zvelebil & Rowley-Conwy 1984, Larsson 1987). Madsen (1986, 1991), for example, has argued that resource-poor inland groups sought a productive source of food to compete with their coastal neighbours. Larsson (1987) considers environmental changes and small-scale immigration of neolithic farmers to be the explanation for the introduction of neolithic elements and their rapid spread over all of southern Scandinavia. According to Larsson (ibid.), changes in the coastal environment, attributable to the retreat of the sea and a decline in temperature, diminished the role of marine resources and increased the exploitation of inland plants and animals. Rowley-Conwy (1985) argues that the transition was a result of changing climate at the end of the Atlantic climatic episode. Reduced salinity as a result of lower ocean temperature may have been responsible for a demise of the shellfish beds, an important supplement to the diet. This loss required new sources of food for the existing population, and farming was available nearby to supply that need. However, shellfish were exploited only in certain areas of southern Scandinavia and their local demise cannot explain the widespread appearance of cultigens and TRB pottery at 3900 BC.

For Denmark, possible environmental changes that might have affected the relationship between people and food include changes in climate, sea level, marine resources, usable land area, and vegetation. Colder air temperatures could have reduced or in other ways changed vegetation, and lowered the temperature and level of the sea. During the early Atlantic period, around 6000 BC, rising sea levels created the North Sea and turned the western part of the Baltic Sea into a salt-water ocean. These changes in sea level greatly reduced the land surface available to human populations in northwestern Europe. The shift from Atlantic to Sub-Boreal conditions occurred c. 3900 BC at the same time as the transition to agriculture. Oscillating transgressions and regressions continued throughout the Atlantic and Sub-Boreal periods, but these later changes in sea levels were less dramatic. The bays, inlets, and estuaries created by rising sea levels were among the richest resource zones for mesolithic groups.

The Sub-Boreal was slightly cooler and drier than the preceding Atlantic period. A decrease in the pollen of ivy indicates cooler winters when the fjords and inlets might be frozen. Even though winter temperatures may have been slightly lower, annual averages remained higher than today. Simulations of past climate (e.g. Kutzbach & Guetter 1986) also suggest that conditions in southern Scandinavia at 4000 BC would have been slightly warmer than at present, particularly in the summer. The presence in the Sub-Boreal of mistletoe and a species of tortoise, both found only to the south of Denmark today, suggests that environmental conditions after 3900 BC were still quite favourable. Thus, the environmental changes associated with the shift from the Atlantic to the Sub-Boreal were not major. The Littorina Sea continued to be rich in fish and sea mammals, and a considerable game population inhabited the forest. Climate did change frequently and dramatically throughout the early Holocene in northwestern Europe, but it is difficult to argue for one specific moment having had more impact on human populations than another. Given current evidence, it is not possible to argue for an ecological crisis at the time of the adoption of farming.

The physical anthropology of the inhabitants of the late Mesolithic and the early Neolithic also suggests that there was no significant change in resource availability (Meiklejohn & Zvelebil 1991). Bennike (1993), in fact, reports a slight decrease in stature of approximately 1 cm for both males and females from the Ertebølle to the early TRB. Such a decline does not suggest an improvement in food resources immediately following the transition to agriculture. It is difficult to argue that agriculture was adopted in order to obtain more food in the face of environmental degradation.

Social demands

Some scholars have suggested that the transition to agriculture was caused not by excess population or environmental constraints but by factors involving social structure and the emergence of inequality (e.g. Bender 1978, 1990, Hayden 1990, 1992). Hypotheses invoking social causes for the transition suggest that leaders or higher-status individuals may have directed their followers to adopt agriculture as a means for producing food surpluses and increasing exchange.

In southern Scandinavia, Fischer (1982) and Jennbert (1984, 1985) have argued for close connections between the farmers of north-central Europe and the foragers of Denmark, pointing to borrowed artefacts and ideas, including ceramics and certain stone and antler axes in the late Mesolithic. They suggest that these successful foragers did not require additional sources of food, and that the only obvious reason for farming was to generate surplus. Jennbert argues that certain leaders were probably responsible for encouraging the accumulation of wealth through cultivation and herding. Competition between higher-status individuals for prestige might then explain why successful foragers adopted farming.

It is clearly the case that changes in social, economic and religious spheres are more pronounced in the earliest Neolithic than are changes in subsistence. It is important here to recall the three categories of sites that have the earliest radiocarbon dates from the Neolithic: long barrows, bog sacrifices and flint mines. Evidence for social differentiation comes from large earthen long barrows, one of the earliest dated manifestations of the Neolithic. Early neolithic long barrows with wooden funeral structures were first recognized in Denmark in the early 1970s. Almost 40 non-megalithic barrows are known today, predominantly in Jutland in western Denmark. The barrows are low (1–2 m in height) and they vary in length from 50 to 150 m. Certain distinctive features are normally incorporated in their construction: rectangular or trapezoidal palisade enclosures surround the mound, the interior of the barrow is transversely partitioned by rows of stakes, and massive timber facades are usually placed at the eastern end of the mound, associated with deposits of pottery (Madsen 1979, Gebauer 1990, Kristensen 1991).

Earthen long barrows were often multi-stage monuments with one or more segments added sequentially to the western end. Even so, only one or a few graves have been found in each of the mounds. The appearance of the barrows at the onset of the Neolithic suggests changes in the social system and perhaps in territorial claims related to the creation of fields and pastures. There is no evidence of elite, mound-covered burials from the Mesolithic. Obviously, a limited segment of the population was entitled to such monumental burial. Communal participation in the construction and maintenance of, and additions to, these monuments must have been necessary and it suggests that the barrows represent more than places for the disposal of the dead. The earthen long barrows probably formed local ceremonial centres, some of which maintained their significance for several centuries. The later megalithic burial constructions were a continuation and aggrandizement of this tradition.

Bog sacrifices, which are found more commonly in eastern Denmark than elsewhere in southern Scandinavia, represent another manifestation of the earliest Neolithic. Such sacrifices consist of one or more cooking pots, animal bones or skulls, or human bodies. In the simplest form these offerings included only a pot, presumably filled with food. More elaborate examples include the construction of wooden platforms along the shoreline and sacrifices of humans, as well as of cattle, and the offering of various artefacts. Repeated sacrifices appear to have taken place at the same bog and there is a trend towards larger bog offerings over time during the early Neolithic (Nielsen 1983). Distinctive evidence of communal feasting, where humans made up part of the menu, is reflected in the heaps of smashed bones found at some sites (Becker 1948, Ebbesen 1975, Rech 1979, Skaarup 1985, Bennike & Ebbesen 1987).

Both earthen long barrows and bog sacrifices represent communal involvement and participation, and both types of site helped to define a ceremonial landscape. They both involved the consumption of labour, either through monumental construction and a range of funeral activities or through feasting and sacrifices of pots with food, cattle and occasionally people. Consumption of labour is also evident in the withdrawal of luxury items from circulation with the deposition of flint axes, amber beads, and copper items in votive hoards from the early Neolithic into the middle Neolithic. The expense of labour in the early Neolithic represents a considerable increase in surplus production invested in activities beyond basic subsistence.

The third category of sites that date from the earliest Neolithic is the flint mines. One of the most visible remains of the Neolithic are the tens of thousands of polished flint axes and fragments that dot the landscape of southern Scandinavia. Much of the tabular flint for the manufacture of these axes came from mines and quarries in the chalk belts that cross northern Denmark and southern Sweden (Becker 1973, 1980, 1993, Nielsen 1977, Vang Petersen 1993). Flint axes of Danish origin are known from the Neolithic in the Netherlands and Germany (Rech 1979). An extensive network of exchange promoted the trade of amber as well as flint and axes within southern Scandinavia. Far-reaching connections to south-central Europe are reflected in the import of copper ornaments and jewellery, axe blades, and the battle axe, a model for the Scandinavian axes (Randsborg 1979). Metallurgical analyses indicate that the copper artefacts have a very low arsenic content, which is characteristic of copper from southern Europe, and it may have come from sources in western Austria (Madsen & Petersen 1984). The materials traded in return are unknown. Organic products such as fur, feathers, lamp oil from seals, and honey, were probably included among the exports from Scandinavia.

The transition to agriculture in southern Scandinavia

Most models of agricultural transitions are still governed by assumptions about the pre-eminence of technology and subsistence. Archaeologists, still perhaps constrained by the Three Age Model, tend to regard the Mesolithic and Neolithic as separate entities and to assume that boundaries between them mark a threshold across which all aspects of social and economic life were transformed simultaneously (Bradley & Edmonds 1992: 18): wild became tame, flaked became polished, mobile became sedentary, foragers became farmers.

Rather than follow this traditional view for northern Europe, one can interpret the shift to agriculture as a four-part transition that took place over several millennia from foraging, to contact, to first farmers, and finally to a fully neolithic way of life (Fig. 19.1). From this perspective, there was no sudden change from foraging to farming, but rather a gradual incorporation of imported tools and weapons, prior to the adoption of domestic plants and animals, and the eventual dominance of these products in the diet. Rather than view the neolithic revolution in terms of a dichotomous shift from one way of life to another, it is more useful to consider individually the long-term social, economic and environmental changes that took place over several millennia in southern Scandinavia. Sedentary foragers in the late Mesolithic began to import items of neolithic manufacture from the south after 4600 BC. It is clear that contact with farmers preceded actual cultivation and herding by at least 500 years. The appearance of TRB pottery, domesticates and long barrows marks the beginning of the Neolithic around 3900 BC, but a fully neolithic economy is not in place until after 3300 BC. Agriculture only became the primary subsistence regime a millennium later, following a period of experimentation and major changes in technology, settlement and burial practices.

Several general conclusions regarding the transition to agriculture can be drawn on the basis of current evidence from southern Scandinavia.

- The spread of agriculture into northern Europe took place in the context of indigenous adoption. There is a distinct similarity between the late Mesolithic and the early Neolithic in most aspects of the technologies of stone and pottery, and in simple traditions of burial. In spite of certain innovations in the early Neolithic, such as new types of pottery and burial practice, the overall impression is one of continuity. There are no indications in the physical anthropology of the inhabitants that outside peoples are involved. It seems to be the case that the introduction of agriculture into southern Scandinavia took place largely through the indigenous adoption of foreign plants and animals, tools and practices, value and belief systems; the introduction of agriculture here is an inside job.
- The beginning of food production in southern Scandinavia was a long-term phenomenon, delayed by the success of resident hunter–gatherers in the area. There was no sudden shift from foraging to farming, but rather a very gradual transition involving the adoption of specific imported tools and weapons, and ideas, prior to the incorporation of domestic plants and animals. Contact with farmers preceded actual cultivation and herding by at least 500 years. Agriculture became the primary subsistence regime only a thousand years later, following a period of experimentation and changes in technology and settlement.
- It is very striking that the first evidence of the Neolithic, confirmed by radiocarbon dates and the presence of TRB pottery, comes from objects and activities that are more clearly associated with status differentiation, exchange and exotic materials, than with changes in subsistence and settlement. This emphasis suggests that the search for causality should focus on the realm of internal decisions in society, rather than external changes in climate, environment, or population. Human groups at the onset of the Neolithic participated in a larger sphere of trade than previously and accorded higher status to certain individuals. It seems reasonable to suggest that interaction through exchange networks among foragers and farmers fostered the rise of an elite component in late mesolithic societies and ushered in the surplus production and trade monopolies of the Neolithic.

Brunton (1975) may have provided some insight into this matter in his consideration of "Why do the Trobriands have chiefs?". The Trobriand Islanders have neither exceptional population density nor agricultural productivity. Brunton argues that it is participation in a closed system of kula exchange that limits the range of people who can effectively compete for leadership. Such a situation results in the emergence of a few "big men" who encourage the creation of surplus. Hayden (1990) has suggested specifically that it is the competitive and feasting aspects of big-man rivalry that are the driving force behind early food production. Certain parts of the Danish data fit such a model nicely, including the evidence for feasting at the bog sacrifices, the burials of single individuals in the first large tombs, the number of trade items in circulation, and perhaps even the adoption of domestic plants and animals.

Implications

In conclusion, the prehistoric spread of agriculture can be considered in a broader frame of reference. The information from southern Scandinavia and recent research in several other areas of the world (e.g. papers in Harris & Hillman 1989, Cowan & Watson 1992, Gebauer & Price 1992, Price & Gebauer 1995, and this volume) suggest that significant revision of current assumptions about the transition to agriculture is necessary. Several important, yet controversial, hypotheses emerge from a review of these studies (Gebauer & Price 1992: 8). New perspectives on the question of agricultural transitions should include the following tenets.

- Agriculture appeared first in areas with an abundance of resources, in lands of plenty rather than in marginal or poor environments. People already in an environment of risk seldom try new subsistence strategies that carry even greater risk (Wills 1992). New strategies are initiated in situations where the risk is affordable. This situation seems to have prevailed in such areas as the Levant, northern Europe, Japan, and the American Southwest. As one example, Bar-Yosef & Belfer-Cohen (1992) and others (e.g. Garrard et al. in Ch. 11 in this volume) point out that the earliest evidence for cultivation in Southwest Asia comes from the ecologically rich "Levantine Corridor".
- In prehistory, agriculture generally spread through the diffusion of ideas and products rather than people. The spread of agriculture across most of Southwest Asia and Europe appears to have been largely an inside job. With only a very few exceptions, the first farmers were the last hunters. No one has argued that the spread of agriculture through Southwest Asia was accomplished by colonists (Byrd 1992). Agriculture spread across Europe in largely the same fashion, through the movement of ideas and materials rather than individuals. There is no reason and no justification for suggesting that languages or genes spread with domesticated plants and animals.

Foragers became farmers. This pattern can be seen virtually on a global scale in the rapid spread of agriculture in the Levant itself, across much of Mesoamerica, the American Southwest, Japan and elsewhere. The exceptions to this pattern are often found in situations where new adaptations permit the occupation of previously uninhabited areas. Examples would include the Linearbandkeramik expansion into the dense forests of Central Europe or the movement of cattle pastoralists into the Eastern Sahara (Close & Wendorf 1992). Colonization should be understood as the exception rather than the rule in the spread of agriculture.

- Agriculture appeared initially among more sedentary and complex groups of hunter–gatherers. In southern Scandinavia and Southwest Asia, for example, sedentism clearly precedes the beginning of domestication. Elsewhere sedentary or semi-sedentary communities of foragers are the first to begin to experiment with the new cultigens and domesticated animals. Complex hunter–gatherers in Japan, northern Europe, and North and South America are the first foragers to shift to agriculture in those areas at the end of the Pleistocene.

Information from southern Scandinavia and elsewhere clearly suggests that new perspectives are needed if we are to understand the transition to agriculture. It seems evident now that agriculture began among *complex* hunter–gatherers. Farming spread quickly, along with many other items and ideas, among similar groups of foragers. Status differentiation and extensive trade in exotic materials appear to accompany this spread. I suggest that, to understand better the spread of agriculture in the prehistoric world, we need to look closely at the origins of status differentiation, social inequality and surplus production.

References

Albrethsen, S. E. & E. Brinch Petersen 1976. Excavation of a Mesolithic cemetery at Vedbæk, Denmark. *Acta Archaeologica* **47**, 1–28.

Andersen, S. H. 1973. Overgangen fra ældre til yngre stenalder i Sydskandinavien set fra en mesolitisk synsvinkel. In *Bonde – veidemann Bofast – ikke bofast i Nordisk forhistorie*, P. Simonsen & G. Stamsø Munch (eds), 26–44. Tromsø: Universitetsforlaget.

— 1981. *Danmarkshistorien. Jægerstenalderen.* København: Sesam.

— 1993a. Mesolithic coastal settlement. In *Digging into the past: 25 years of Danish archaeology*, S. Hvass & B. Storgaard (eds), 65–8. Aarhus: Universitetsforlag.

— 1993b. Bjørnsholm, a stratified køkkenmødding on the Central Limfjord, North Jutland. *Journal of Danish Archaeology* **10**, 59–96.

Andersen, S. T. & P. Rasmussen 1993. *Geobotaniske undersøgelse af kulturlandskabets historie.* Copenhagen: DGU & Miljøministeret.

Bar-Yosef, O. & A. Belfer-Cohen. 1992. From foraging to farming in the Mediterranean Levant. In Gebauer & Price (1992: 21–48).

Becker, C. J. 1948. Mosefundne lerkar fra Yngre Stenalder. Studier over yngre stenalder i Danmark. *Aarbøger for Nordisk Oldkyndighed og Historie* **1947**, 1–318.

— 1955. Stenalder bebyggelsen ved Store Valby i Vestsjælland. Problemer omkring tragtbægerkulturens ældste og yngste fase. *Aarbøger for Nordisk Oldkyndighed og Historie* **1954**, 127–97.

— 1973. Studien zu neolitischen Flintbeilen. *Acta Archaeologica* **44**, 125–86.

— 1980. Katalog der Feuerstein/Hortnstein/Bergwerke, Dänemark. In *5000 jahre feuersteinbergbau*, G. Weisgerber (ed.), 456–73. Bochum: Deutschen Bergbau-Museum.

— 1993. Flintminer og flintdistribution ved Limfjorden. *Kort- og råstofstudier omkring Limfjorden* [Limfjordsprojektet Rapport 6]. Aarhus: Moesgard.

Bender, B. 1978. From gatherer–hunter to farmer: a social perspective. *World Archaeology* **10**, 204–22.

— 1990. The dynamics of nonhierarchical societies. In *The evolution of political systems*, S. Upham (ed.), 247–63. Cambridge: Cambridge University Press.

Bennike, P. 1985. *Palaeopathology of Danish skeletons: a comparative study of demography, disease and injury.* Copenhagen: Akademisk Forlag.

— 1993. The people. In *Digging into the past: 25 years of Danish archaeology*, S. Hvass & B. Storgaard (eds), 34–9. Aarhus: Universitetsforlag.

Bennike, P. & K. Ebbesen 1987. The bog find from Sigersdal. Human sacrifice in the early Neolithic. *Journal of Danish Archaeology* **5**, 83–115.

Binford, L. R. 1968. Post-Pleistocene adaptations. In *New perspectives in archeology*, S. R. Binford & L. R. Binford (eds), 313–41. Chicago: Aldine.

Bradley, R. & M. Edmonds 1993. *Interpreting the axe trade.* Cambridge: Cambridge University Press.

Brunton, R. 1975. Why do the Trobriands have chiefs? *Man* **10**, 544–58.

Byrd, B. 1992. The dispersal of food production across the Levant. In Gebauer & Price (1992: 49–62).

Childe, V. G. 1949. The origin of Neolithic culture in northern Europe. *Antiquity* **23**, 129–35.

Chmielewski, W. 1952. Zagadnenie Grobowcow kujawskich w swietle ostatnich badan. *Biblioteka Muzeum Archeologicznego w Lodzi* **2**, 37–52.

Close, A. E. & F. Wendorf 1992. The beginnings of food production in the Eastern Sahara. In Gebauer & Price (1992: 63–72).

Clutton-Brock, J. & N. Noe-Nygaard 1990. New osteological and C-isotope evidence on Mesolithic dogs: companions of hunters and fishers at Star Carr, Seamer Carr and Kongemose. *Journal of Archaeological Science* **17**, 643–53.

Cowan, C. W. & P. J. Watson (eds) 1992. *The origins of agriculture: an international perspective.* Washington DC: Smithsonian Institution Press.

Cohen, M. N. 1977. *The food crisis in prehistory.* New Haven: Yale University Press.

Ebbesen, K. 1975. *Die jüngere Trichterbecherkultur auf den Dänischen Inseln* [Arkæologiske Studier II]. Copenhagen: National Museum.

Fischer, A. 1982. Trade in Danubian shaft-hole axes and the introduction of neolithic economy in Denmark. *Journal of Danish Archaeology* **1**, 7–12.

Gebauer, A. B. 1990. The Asnæs dolmen. A long dolmen with a wooden chamber. *Journal of Danish Archaeology* **9**, 1–37.

— 1995. Pottery production and the introduction of agriculture in southern Scandinavia. In *The emergence of pottery,* W. B. Barnett & J. Hoopes (eds), 99–112. Washington DC: Smithsonian Institution Press.

Gebauer, A. B. & T. D. Price (eds) 1992. *Transitions to agriculture in prehistory.* [Monographs in World Archaeology 4]. Madison: Prehistory Press.

Harris, D. R. & G. C. Hillman (eds) 1989. *Foraging and farming: the evolution of plant exploitation.* London: Unwin Hyman.

Hayden, B. 1990. Nimrods, piscators, pluckers, and planters: the emergence of food production. *Journal of Anthropological Archaeology* **9**, 31–69.

— 1992. Models of domestication. In Gebauer & Price (1992: 11–20).

Jennbert, K. 1984. *Den produktiva gåvan: tradition och innovation i Sydskandinavien för omkring 5300 år Sedan* [Acta Archaeologica Lundensia, Series in 4°, 16]. Lund: Gleerup.

— 1985. Neolithisation – a Scanian perspective. *Journal of Danish Archaeology* **4**, 196–7.

Jørgensen, G. 1977. Et kornfund fra Sarup. Bidrag til Belysning af Tragtbæ gerkulturens Agerbrug. *Kuml* **1976**, 47–64.

Kossinna G. 1921. Entwicklung und Verbreitung der steinzeitlichen Trichterbecher, Kragenflaschen und Kugelflaschen. *Mannus* **13**, 13–259.

Kristensen, I. K. 1991. Storgård iv: an early Neolithic long barrow near Fjelsø, North Jutland. *Journal of Danish Archaeology* **8**, 72–87.

Kutzbach, J. E. & P. J. Geutter 1986. The influence of changing orbital parameters and surface boundary conditions on climate simulations for the past 18,000 years. *Journal of Atmospheric Sciences* **43**, 1726–59.

Larsson, L. 1984. The Skateholm Project. A late Mesolithic settlement and cemetery complex at a southern Swedish bay. *Meddelanden från Lunds Universitets Historiska Museum* **1983–84**, 5–38.

Larsson, M. 1987. Neolithization in Scania – a Funnel Beaker perspective. *Journal of Danish Archaeology* **5**, 244–7.

Lichardus, J. 1976. *Rössen – Gatersleben – Baalberge. Ein Beitrag zur Chronologie des Mitteldeutschen Neolitikums und zur Entstehung der Trichterbecher-Kulturen.* Bonn: Habelt.

Madsen, T. 1979. Earthen long barrows and timber structures: aspects of the early Neolithic mortuary practice in Denmark. *Proceedings of the Prehistoric Society* **45**, 301–20.

— 1986. Where did all the hunters go? An assessment of an epoch-making episode in Danish prehistory. *Journal of Danish Archaeology* **5**, 229–39.

— 1991. The social structure of early Neolithic society in south Scandinavia. In *Die Kupferzeit als historische Epoche,* J. Lichardus (ed.), 489–96. Bonn: Saarbrücken Beiträge zuer Altertumskunde.

Madsen, T. & H. J. Jensen 1982. Settlement and land use in early Neolithic Denmark. *Analecta Praehistorica Leidensia* **15**, 63–86.

Madsen, T. & J. E. Petersen 1984. Tidligeolitiske anlæg ved Mosegården. Regionale og kronologiske forskelle i tidligneolitikum. *Kuml* **1982–83**, 61–120.

Meiklejohn, C. & M. Zvelebil 1991. Health status of European populations at the agricultural transition and the implications for the adoption of farming. In *Health in past societies: biocultural interpretations of human skeletal remains in archaeological contexts,* H. Bush & M. Zvelebil (eds), 129–45. Oxford: British Archaeological Reports, International Series 567.

Nielsen, E. K. 1983. *Tidligneolitiske keramikfund.* PhD dissertation, Institute of Archaeology, Copenhagen University.
— 1987. Ertebølle and Funnelbeaker pots as tools. On traces of production techniques and use. *Acta Archaeologica* **57**, 107–20.
Nielsen, P. O. 1977. Die Flintbeile der frühen Trichterbecherkultur in Dänemark. *Acta Archaeologica* **48**, 61–138.
— 1985. De første bønder. Nye fund fra den tidligste Tragtbægerkultur ved Sigersted. *Aarbøger for Nordisk Oldkyndighed og Historie* **1984**, 96–126.
— 1986. The beginning of the Neolithic – assimilation or complex change? *Journal of Danish Archaeology* **5**, 240–3.
Paludan-Müller, C. 1978. High Atlantic food gathering in northwest Zealand, ecological conditions and spatial representation. *New Directions in Scandinavian Archaeology* **1**, 120–57.
Price, T. D. 1987. The Mesolithic of western Europe. *Journal of World Prehistory* **1**, 225–332.
— 1991. The Mesolithic of northern Europe. *Annual Review of Anthropology* **20**, 211–33.
Price, T. D. & A. B. Gebauer 1992. The final frontier: foragers to farmers in southern Scandinavia. In Gebauer & Price (1992: 97–116).
— (eds) 1995. *Last hunters – first farmers: new perspectives on the prehistoric transition to agriculture.* Santa Fe, New Mexico: School of American Research Press.
Randsborg, K. 1979. Resource distribution and the function of copper in Early Neolithic Denmark. In *The origins of metallurgy in Atlantic Europe* [Proceedings of the Fifth Atlantic Colloquium], M. Ryan (ed.), 303–18. Dublin: Stationery Office.
Rech, M. 1979. *Studien zu Depotfunden der Trichterbecher- und Einzelgrabkultur des Nordens* [Offa-Bücher 39]. Neumünster: K. Wachholtz.
Rowley-Conwy, P. 1983. Sedentary hunters: the Ertebølle example. In *Hunter–gatherer economy,* G. Bailey (ed.), 111–26. Cambridge: Cambridge University Press.
— 1984. The laziness of the short-distance hunter: the origin of agriculture in western Denmark. *Journal of Anthropological Archaeology* **3**, 300–24.
— 1985. The origin of agriculture in Denmark: a review of some theories. *Journal of Danish Archaeology* **4**, 188–95.
Runnels, C. & T. H. van Andel 1988. Trade and the origins of agriculture in the eastern Mediterranean. *Journal of Mediterranean Archaeology* **1**, 83–109.
Schwabedissen, H. 1967. Ein horizontierter "Breitkeil" aus Satrup und die mannigfachen Kulturverbindungen des beginnenden Neolithikums im Norden und Nordwesten. *Palæohistoria* **12**, 409–68.
— 1981. Ertebölle/Ellerbeck – Mesolithikum oder Neolithikum? *Veröffentlichungen des Museum für Ur- und Frühgeschichte, Potsdam* **14/15**, 129–42.
Skaarup, J. 1973. *Hesselø-Sølager. Jagdstationen der südskandinavischer Trichterbecherkultur* [Arkæologiske Studier 1]. Copenhagen: Akademisk Forlag.
— 1985. *Yngre stenalder på øerne syd for Fyn.* Rudkøbing: Langelands Museum.
Tauber, H. 1981. δ^{13}C evidence for dietary habits of prehistoric man in Denmark. *Nature* **292**, 332–3.
Troels-Smith, J. 1953. Ertebøllekultur – bondekultur. Resultater af de sidste 10 aars undersøgelser i Aamosen. *Aarbøger for Nordisk Oldkyndighed og Historie* **1953**, 5–62.
Vang Petersen, P. 1984. Chronological and regional variation in the late Mesolithic of eastern Denmark. *Journal of Danish Archaeology* **3**, 7–18.
— 1993. *Flint fra Danmarks oldtid.* Copenhagen: Høst & Søn.
Wills, W. H. 1992. Foraging systems and plant cultivation during the emergence of agricultural economies in the prehistoric American Southwest. In Gebauer & Price (1992: 153–76).
Zvelebil, M. & P. Rowley-Conwy 1984. The transition to farming in northern Europe: a hunter–gatherer perspective. *Norwegian Archaeological Review* **17**, 104–28.
— 1986. Foragers and farmers in Atlantic Europe. In *Hunters in transition: mesolithic societies of temperate Eurasia and their transition to farming,* M. Zvelebil (ed.), 67–93. Cambridge: Cambridge University Press.
Zvelebil, M. & K. V. Zvelebil. 1988. Agricultural transition and Indo–European dispersals. *Antiquity* **62**, 574–83.

CHAPTER TWENTY

Arboriculture in Southwest Europe: *dehesas* as managed woodlands

Richard J. Harrison

Dehesa arboriculture as an agricultural system

Raising tree crops of native oaks and other nut-bearing trees is an ancient practice in Mediterranean Europe, once widespread, and now in decline. In discussions of agricultural systems, tree crops usually get short shrift, or are forgotten entirely, despite their importance throughout historical times and their continuance today as magnificent parkland landscapes that cover thousands of square kilometres in the western Mediterranean and northern Africa. These landscapes hold clues to ancient patterns of land use, and the modern systems provide detailed analogues, which take us beyond technical information and into a world of social relationships defined by the permanence of the tree crops. Enduring for millennia, they have left an indelible mark on rural cultures and diets.

Among the best studied are the systems of arboriculture in Spain and Portugal. They have been remarked upon by travellers from Roman times to the present day, and they share an important defining characteristic: all use autochthonous species of trees and shrubs, which, by a combination of grazing by domestic livestock and occasional pruning or firing, are brought into a condition of enhanced productivity. Although evergreen oaks are the most common species, ash, chestnuts and wild olive are also managed deliberately. One geographer has described them neatly: "These open oak groves or *dehesas* with their abundant sweet acorns and winter pasturage, represent an unstable forest formation maintained only by the continuing intervention of man, who has long exploited them for food, fodder, fuel and construction material" (Parsons 1962: 213).

Apparently little studied by prehistorians (except Lewthwaite 1982), *dehesas* nevertheless provide information of the greatest interest to archaeologists working on agricultural systems and their related social structures. Behind the term *dehesa* lie three different intertwined concepts of arboriculture (Montoya Oliver 1985).

- A type of land holding: *dehesa* is a name derived from *defesa* or *defensa*, describing a large enclosed area of land protected from the depredations of the sheep of the Castilian Mesta. These date only from the thirteenth century AD, and are most common in southwestern Spain.

- A production system based on pastoral exploitation of cork oak (*Quercus suber*) and holm oak (*Q. ilex*) forests by domestic animals, principally pigs, goats, sheep and cattle, with important secondary products such as charcoal, cork, tannin and timber. Specialized subtypes may include woodlands of sweet chestnut, wild olive, ash and other tree species.

- A description of a characteristic type of parkland, where oak trees cover between 10 and 30 per cent of the surface, and where grazing has created pastures with a specific composition. The term is used particularly for the landscapes of western Spain from Salamanca to Cádiz, and in southern Portugal, although place names show that *dehesas* formerly extended across Old Castile, to the foothills of the Spanish Pyrenees, the Iberian Mountains and into the Spanish Levant (Martín Bolaños 1943: 37–9, with excellent landscape photographs). Both the system and the landscape type may date back to the Neolithic.

Dehesas are distinctive plant communities managed by man, which have been artificially created and maintained over many years. It is best to imagine them as a form of arboriculture where animals are used to harvest the crops and convert them into dung, flesh and labour, as Smith (1977) explains. Fundamentally, they are a form of pastoral exploitation closely linked to a particular landscape and highly adapted to the natural environment (Martín Galindo 1966).

Formerly extensive and widespread in the Balkans and possibly in Turkey, *dehesas* survive now only in southern Portugal, southwestern Spain, the Balearics, the Maghreb, Corsica and northwestern Italy. Until recently, the origins of the *dehesa* production system were shrouded in obscurity, although they were thought to be linked to historically recent developments in southwestern Spain, particularly the Christian reconquest in the thirteenth century AD (Pérez Díaz et al. 1991). However, palynological investigations by Stevenson & Harrison (1992) have now shown that it is very likely that in southwestern Spain *dehesa* landscapes and production systems were being created by grazing from the early fourth millennium bc, and that they had reached a sophisticated environmental equilibrium by the first millennium bc. Analysis of the pollen records left in mires, and trapped in palaeosols beneath neolithic tumuli, does therefore now offer archaeologists the possibility of recognizing, and tracing the history of, these landscapes.

The *dehesa* system of production

However measured, it is clear that on the poor, shallow and often acid soils of the western Mediterranean, food outputs from *dehesa* management usually exceed those that can be got from growing cereals. Parsons gives reasonable estimates when he says: "An eighteen-month-old Iberian hog will more than double its weight in the three months of *montanera*, say from 60 kilograms to 140–150. Occasionally animals may be permitted to reach 170 kilograms or more. . ." (1962: 222). The pigs feed on the sweet acorns which the holm oaks, and to a lesser extent the cork oaks, produce at the rate of 600–700 kg per ha, although there are individual trees that exceed these figures many times, such as the wonderful holm oak described by Smith (1977: 157–8) at St Blas (Algarve, Portugal) which stood alone, attained a spread of 18 m, and cropped so heavily that it provided complete economic support for the widow who owned it. This one tree yielded 1200 litres of acorns in a mast year and 240 litres in other years, or an average of 720 litres per year. Many other trees are known to yield regularly 100–400 kg of acorns in mast years. Interestingly, when holm oaks grow together in stands over many hundreds of hectares, they fruit annually and do not have a pronounced masting cycle. A definite mast cycle occurs when the trees grow in continental climatic conditions where late frosts can damage the flowers; then a good crop of acorns is produced once every two or three years (Montoya Oliver 1989: 85). Exploiting the acorns demanded some skill: a herd would typically comprise 40–60 pigs in their second year, and the swineherd would ensure that they ate the acorns from trees growing on broken ground and steep slopes first. As the pigs fattened and lost their initial agility, they would consume the acorns from trees growing on flatter ground. Acorns would fall in showers when the humidity changed, and not all trees in a *dehesa* would release their mast at the same time; nor would the pigs find them equally palatable, preferring the sweeter varieties. Trees that cropped heavily, or had sweet fruits, were marked out and their nuts were used to propagate the variety. At a conservative conversion ratio of 10:1 a yield of 60–70 kg of pork per hectare could be expected every year from an average-sized holm oak *dehesa* (Parsons 1962: 222). However, lower yields of pork were obtained from cork oaks – only 7–20 kg per hectare according to Montoya Oliver (1988: 222) – because of the smaller acorn crops and their relative bitterness. Similar figures come from Portugal, where Smith (1977: 169) cites yields of 68 kg of pork per hectare of holm oak woodland as against 34 kg of pork from cork oaks, and he goes on to say that "Careful experiment in central Portugal has shown that 5.3 litres of acorns will make one pound of pork" (ibid.: 167) – a quite remarkable figure of absolute productivity. Although the holm oaks fruit from the age of 10 to 12 years, they do not reach their full masting potential for about 30 years and then often remain productive until the trees are 300 years old (Montoya Oliver 1989: 99).

Data on charcoal and browse production are also available. For example, Martín Galindo (1966) calculated that holm oak *dehesas* were expected to yield an average of 40 kg of charcoal per hectare per year. The annual weight of browse varies from 2500 to 1000 kg, depending on the quality of the *dehesa* and the density of animals allowed to graze in it (Montoya Oliver 1989: 100). Furthermore, these figures do not include the tannin from the holm oaks, the highly valued bark of the cork oaks, various succulent edible fungi, and the wild animals such as boar, deer, rabbits and doves, which habitually live in these woodlands and are hunted for food and sport.

Even higher yields have been obtained from sweet chestnuts in southern France and northern Italy. In 1938 1.6 million acres (648,000 ha), or 15 per cent of Italy's forests, were given over to this tree. Mature trees 70 years old, growing 12 to the hectare, yield 4000–5000 kg of nuts in a good year, and half that in an average year. These are outputs twice as high as any cereal crop that could be grown on the same land (Smith 1977: 133–4, quoting figures from Lavaille 1906).

Originally, the oaks in the Iberian *dehesas* were all wild; but the grafting of varieties of oak with superior acorn yield, greater sweetness, and early or late cropping or other beneficial characteristics has been practised widely in Portugal and Mallorca, reaching the point where most holm oaks on Mallorca, and many on estates in the Portuguese Algarve, are grafted varieties. The undergrowth has to be cleared away to permit the young trees to grow, and it is important to prune young trees at the ages of six to eight years to create the required low, branched shape. The parklands then flourish with little attention other than occasional pruning for forage and the removal of dead or infertile trees.

Most domestic animals, including fowls and geese, relish sweet acorns, and forage and prunings are available for many months of the year in winter, spring and even during the summer drought. The mast is enjoyed by cattle, horses and sheep, and there are many individual holm oaks with acorns suitable for human consumption; indeed, so sweet and free of tannin are some acorns that they can be eaten directly from the tree without any preparation. The root systems of the oaks also bring subsoil nutrients close to the surface, enriching the pasture in their immediate vicinity, and improving the soil structure. Montoya Oliver (1988: figs 73 and 64) shows cattle browsing dried cork-oak leaves in summer, and green prunings in spring, in the *dehesas* of Sehouls (Morocco). Rustic animal breeds are best adapted to the *dehesa* system, and their hardiness, mobility and the ease with which they are controlled by shepherds and swineherds compensates for their relatively low yields or slow maturation.

The *dehesa* system of production is well suited to the inclemencies of the Mediterranean climate, with its frequent droughts and soils prone to erosion when denuded of cover. Although yields vary considerably from year to year, they fail only when plagues of oak-moth caterpillars (*Tortrix viridiana*) or larger caterpillars (e.g. *Lymantria dispar* or *Malacosoma neustria*) strike. Other small insects (*Balaninus* sp.) may attack the flower and enter the acorns when they are forming, reducing their value as feed and seed, but an infestation can be controlled by letting pigs forage the acorns and larvae. There is also a fungus that attacks holm oaks (*Taphrina kruchii* or witch's broomstick), but otherwise the oaks in *dehesas* are quite resistant to defoliating parasites and diseases (Montoya Oliver 1989: 35–8). This means that production is stable and buffers risks of most kinds, even in lean years. Furthermore, it is a system where the labour inputs can be low and spread throughout the year. It is therefore well suited to pre-industrial societies with simple technology, land in surplus, and a labour scarcity – conditions that must have been common throughout much of later prehistory in the Mediterranean region.

From the pastoralists' point of view, a *dehesa* conferred far more benefits than cereal farming or irrigation agriculture. Among the additional advantages were the shelter *dehesas* provided for game, and their longevity. For example, parklands around the Laguna de las Madres and Acebrón (Huelva) are known to have persisted for more than a millennium (Stevenson & Harrison 1992). Since the late 1950s, political changes and attendant industrialization have provoked a demographic transformation of Spain, and the *dehesas*' products are now less in demand. But a recovery may happen as agronomists and foresters rediscover the value of *dehesas* as ecologically sustainable resources – a process that is being encouraged by the recent establishment of a research station at the Dehesa de Moncalvillo in the foothills of the Sierra de Guadarrama north of Madrid (Montoya Oliver et al. 1988).

For the prehistorian, *dehesas* are worth studying in detail as analogues for systems of production formerly widespread around the Mediterranean and possibly elsewhere in the Old World. Their former existence can sometimes be detected palynologically, and we have suitable models to understand how they functioned. It would be a great pity if the opportunity to study this unique system of production were now missed, because the arcane skills of *dehesa* management are disappearing fast.

References

Lavaille, J-B. 1906. *Le chataignier*. Paris: Vigot Frères.

Lewthwaite, J. 1982. Acorns for the ancestors: the prehistoric exploitation of woodland in the west Mediterranean. In *Archaeological aspects of woodland ecology*. S. Limbrey & M. Bell (eds), 217–30. Oxford: British Archaeological Reports, International Series 146.

Martin Bolaños, M. 1943. *Consideraciones sobre los encinares de España*. Instituto Forestal de Investagaciones y Experiencias [27], Madrid.

Martín Galindo, J. L. 1966. La dehesa extremeña como tipo de explotación agraria. *Estudios Geográficos* **599**, 431–44.

Montoya Oliver, J. M. 1985. Techniques traditionelles du contrôle du "matorral" dans la fôret méditerranéenne: la dehesa. *Fôret Méditerranéenne* **7**, 137–40.

— 1988. *Los alcornocales*, 2nd edn. Madrid: Ministerio de Agricultura.

— 1989. *Encinas y encinares*. Madrid: Mundi-Prensa.

Montoya Oliver, J. M., Mª. L. Mesón Garcia, J. Ruíz del Castillo 1988. *Una dehesa testigo. La Dehesa de Moncalvillo, San Agustin de Guadalix, Madrid* [ICONA Serie Técnica 5]. Madrid: Ministerio de Agricultura.

Parsons, J. J. 1962. The acorn-hog economy of the oak woodlands of southwestern Spain. *Geographical Review* **52**, 211–35.

Pérez Díaz, A., J. Fernández Nieva, M. A. Melón Jiménez, F. Sánchez Marroyo, J. Mª. Cruz Caballero, F. Espárrago Carande, A. Ristorí Peláez 1991. Dehesa. In *Gran enciclopedia extremeña* (tomo 4), K. Pellitero Aja (ed.), 34–49. Mérida: Ediciones Extremeñas.

Smith, J. R. 1977. *Tree crops: a permanent agriculture*, 4th edn. New York: Devin-Adair.

Stevenson, A. C. & R. J. Harrison, 1992. Ancient forests in Spain: a model for land-use and dry forest management in south-west Spain from 4000 BC to 1900 AD. *Proceedings of the Prehistoric Society* **58**, 227–47.

PART FOUR
Central Asia to the Pacific

CHAPTER TWENTY-ONE

The beginnings of agriculture in western Central Asia

David R. Harris & Chris Gosden

Since the Second World War, study of the origins and early development of agriculture on a world scale has been dominated by the concept of primary or "nuclear" centres where, it has been assumed, hunter–gatherers initiated crop cultivation and animal breeding and from where agriculture and pastoralism later spread to secondary or "non" centres (cf. Harris in Ch. 1 in this volume) . The fundamental question of how far this core–periphery model of agricultural origins fits the data now available for Eurasia as a whole is addressed, implicitly or explicitly, by many contributors to this volume. It has particular relevance to this contribution because Central Asia has not generally been regarded as a primary centre of early agriculture, despite the discovery in the western part of the region of much evidence of early neolithic food-producing communities. Our aim in this contribution is to summarize this evidence and to set it in a broader Southwest Asian context, rather than to present a detailed account of our recent investigations at the early neolithic type-site of Jeitun in southern Turkmenistan – which are published elsewhere (Masson 1992, Harris et al. 1993 and in press).

For present purposes, Central Asia can be regarded as the vast region of mountains and deserts that extends eastwards from the Caspian Sea to the Takla Makan Basin. Very little is known archaeologically about the beginnings of agriculture and settled life over most of the region, but in its western part a series of early neolithic sites has been identified in the relatively narrow zone between the Iranian Plateau and the Kara Kum Desert. These sites share many aspects of material culture and they collectively constitute the Jeitun Culture. They are the earliest well studied agro-pastoral settlements in the region, dating back to the sixth millennium bc, and they are distributed along the piedmont at the foot of the Kopet Dag range which forms the northern edge of the Iranian Plateau (Fig. 21.1).

This major physiographic boundary between mountainous upland and alluvial lowland is comparable in scale, and perhaps also in prehistoric significance, to the western and eastern margins of the Iranian Plateau, where, respectively, the Zagros Mountains and the hills of Baluchistan overlook the alluvial lowlands of the Tigris–Euphrates and Indus valleys. This comparison has also been made by Allchin & Allchin (1982: 99–100), who suggest that "we may . . . expect to find broadly parallel

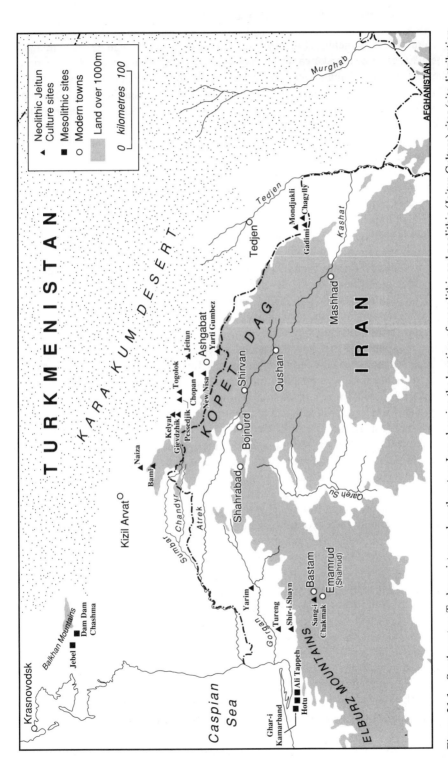

Figure 21.1 Southwestern Turkmenistan and northeastern Iran showing the location of mesolithic and neolithic (Jeitun Culture) sites (site distribution after Kohl 1984: 46–7 and Sarianidi 1992: 111).

. . . cultural developments taking place in . . . these three border regions of the Iranian plateau . . . creating a vast area which may be loosely defined as a cultural interaction sphere, with contacts maintained by land routes in the interior of the plateau" (ibid.: 100). Tosi (1973–4), too, has referred to the boundary between the Kopet Dag and the Kara Kum as "the northeastern frontier of the ancient Near East". Later in the paper we consider the evidence for early agricultural settlement in southern Turkmenistan in its broader Southwest Asian context, with particular reference to possible antecedents of the Jeitun Culture. Ideally, we should also compare the Turkmenian evidence with equivalent data on early agricultural settlement from farther east in Central Asia, but because archaeological information on the neolithic occupation of the region is so meagre we do not attempt to do so here.

It is also important to place the evidence for early agriculture in southern Turkmenistan in its biogeographical context, in terms of the distribution of the wild progenitors of the principal cultivated plants and domesticated animals associated with neolithic settlement in the region. The Russian botanist Vavilov, whose worldwide studies of centres of origin of cultivated plants had a profound effect on students of early agriculture (Harris 1990), included western Central Asia (and northern India) in his Southwest Asiatic Centre, which was one of the five centres he identified in his first major publication on the subject (Vavilov 1992a (1926): 126–7). He subsequently (1992b (1935): 337–42) added a separate Inner Asiatic Centre which encompassed northwestern India, Afghanistan, Tadjikistan, Kirgiziya and eastern Uzbekistan, but not the mountains of Turkmenistan, which remained part of his Southwest Asiatic Centre, now described as corresponding to Asia Minor in a wide sense (a division he later abandoned and returned to his original concept of a single, large Southwest Asiatic Centre; Vavilov 1992c (1940): 430–1; Dorofeyev & Filatenko 1992: xxii). These changes in the delineation of the western Asiatic centres reflect the fact that the less mountainous country that separates the eastern Kopet Dag from the western Hindu Kush is not a significant biogeographical boundary, and that the wild ancestors of some of the Southwest Asian cereals (e.g. barley, rye), pulses (e.g. lentil, grass pea) and fruits (e.g. grapevine, apple, pear, almond, walnut, pomegranate) are, or may be, native to western Central Asia as well as to Southwest Asia (Zohary & Hopf 1993). The importance of Vavilov's observations lies not in any minor differences between his western and central Asian centres but in the fact that the southern Turkmenian area of early agriculture is part of the extensive combined region from which most of the crops of neolithic Southwest Asian agriculture originated. Study of the distribution of the wild progenitors of the main domesticated animals associated with neolithic agriculture in Southwest Asia leads to a comparable conclusion; indeed, southern Turkmenistan occupies a central position within the area of overlap of the ranges of the progenitors of the four main domesticates: goat, sheep, aurochs and pig (Clutton-Brock 1981: 19), although the probable centres of sheep and goat domestication lie farther west in Southwest Asia (see below).

On archaeological and biogeographical grounds, therefore, western Central Asia, particularly southern Turkmenistan, can, and probably should, be regarded not as a marginal area distant from the main foci of early agriculture farther west but as an integral part of a Southwest Asian "cultural interaction sphere" in which agro-pastoral settlements became widely established from the Levant to the northern and eastern margins of the Iranian Plateau between the ninth and sixth millennia bc. It is within this regional framework that the specific evidence of early agricultural settlement in the piedmont zone of southern Turkmenistan should be viewed.

Early agricultural settlement in southern Turkmenistan

Professional archaeological investigations in the piedmont zone of southern Turkmenistan began with Pumpelly's partial excavation in 1904 of two conspicuous tells or *kurgans* at Anau on the piedmont southeast of Ashgabat (Pumpelly 1908). Further sporadic explorations took place during and after the First World War, for example the important tell site of Namazga-depe was discovered in 1916, but it was not until the Combined Archaeological Expedition to Southern Turkmenistan (IuTAKE) was established after the Second World War that systematic research on early prehistoric settlement in the region was initiated. From the late 1940s to the early 1960s a series of investigations – for example, Okladnikov's excavation of the mesolithic–neolithic site of Jebel Cave in the western Balkhan Mountains near the Caspian coast (Okladnikov 1956), Kuftin's excavations at Namazga-tepe (Kuftin 1956) and, most importantly, Masson's excavations at the small tell site of Jeitun at the edge of the Kara Kum Desert 25 km northwest of Ashgabat (Masson 1957, 1961, 1971; Masson & Sarianidi 1972: 33–46) – established a regional archaeological sequence and demonstrated the existence of agro-pastoral neolithic settlements (Kohl 1984: 45–55). Masson's comprehensive excavation of the upper levels at Jeitun revealed a settlement of rectangular one-roomed dwellings built of cylindrical clay blocks and containing large ovens. Walled yard areas and outhouses were found between and adjacent to many of the houses. No plant remains were recovered, but impressions of barley and wheat grains in the clay blocks, and the bones of domestic sheep and goat, indicated that the inhabitants grew cereal crops and herded livestock. No radiocarbon dates were obtained at Jeitun, but Masson proposed, on the grounds of close similarities between the artefact, especially the ceramic, assemblages at Jeitun with those from the upper layers at Jarmo and Tepe Guran in Iran, that the site had been occupied in the sixth millennium BC (Masson & Sarianidi 1972: 36, 171).

As archaeological survey and excavation continued in the piedmont zone through the 1950s and 1960s, more sites whose structural features and artefact assemblages resembled those at Jeitun were discovered, and three successive phases of the Jeitun Culture – differentiated by changes in pottery decoration – were distinguished. Radiocarbon dates were obtained from two of these sites: at Togolok west of Jeitun "Middle Jeitun" levels were dated to 5370 ±100 bc (Mellaart 1975: 212), and at Chagylly in the eastern piedmont "Late Jeitun" levels were dated to 5050 ±110 bc (Masson & Sarianidi 1972: 33). At Chagylly grains of two-row barley (reported as *Hordeum distichum*) and of wheats (reported as *Triticum vulgare* and *T. compactum*) were also identified (ibid.: 42). In all, some 13 sites (and 5 surface scatters) attributable to the Jeitun Culture were found in the piedmont zone (Fig. 21.1), and the radiocarbon dates for the Middle and Late Jeitun levels not only confirmed Masson's ascription of the

Jeitun Culture to the sixth millennium but also implied that the "Early Jeitun" phases, represented at Jeitun itself, probably dated back to *c*. 5500 bc. However, no radio-carbon dates were obtained for that phase, which is represented not only at Jeitun but also in the lower levels at the nearby sites of Chopan and Togolok. The middle phase is represented in the upper levels at the latter two sites and at Bami, Pessedjik and New Nisa, as well as in the lower levels at Mondjukli and Chagylly (where the late phase is also best represented). This spatial and temporal pattern of site distribution suggests that Jeitun Culture settlements were established earlier in the western than the eastern piedmont, although this inference must remain tentative because it is pos-sible that other early neolithic sites on the piedmont have been buried by subsequent colluvial, alluvial and aeolian deposits and have thus remained undetected. Indeed, this process is evident at the major Bronze Age sites of Altyn-depe and Namazga-depe, where soundings have revealed cultural deposits several metres below the present surface of the piedmont (Kohl 1981: x–xi).

The distribution of Jeitun Culture sites in the piedmont zone may also reflect dif-ferences in the geomorphology and hydrology of the zone itself. In its western section between Kizil Arvat and Ashgabat, which is known as Akhal Atak, short streams debouch on to the upper piedmont from narrow gorges cut through the steep mountain front of the Kopet Dag, traverse the coalesced alluvial fans that make up the piedmont, and flow into the sands of the Kara Kum where they dissipate through percolation and evaporation. The discharge of these streams is smaller and, because they are fed largely by groundwater, more stable than that of the longer rivers – the Tedjen and the Murghab – at the eastern end of the piedmont zone. The flow of the western streams is at a maximum from March to May, when it is augmented by rainfall and some snow-melt, and at a minimum from June to October (Dolukhanov 1981: 366). Precipitation throughout the piedmont zone is too low to sustain rainfed cereal cultivation: annual rainfall varies from 140 to 250mm and precipitation exceeds potential evapotranspi-ration only in January (data provided by the Institute for Desert Research, Ashgabat).

On the assumption that the seasonal moisture regime that prevailed in the Early Jeitun phase did not differ significantly from the present one and, even if, as Dolukhanov suggests (1981: 375), annual precipitation was greater then and spring floods more pronounced, the rainfed cultivation of cereals would have been impossi-ble. It must therefore be assumed that the crops of the earliest Jeitun cultivators depended on irrigation and/or groundwater through the growing season. These hydro-climatic conditions may help to explain why the earliest Jeitun settlements are located in the western section of the piedmont and also at or near the outer margins of the alluvial fans. There streamflow would have been slower than higher up on the pied-mont, spring floods would have been less destructive, and the sediment deposited by them finer and more fertile.

The site of Jeitun itself exemplifies these locational advantages. It lies at the margin of the alluvial fan of a piedmont stream – the Kara Su – which cuts through the south-ernmost dune ridge of the Kara Kum Desert. Today the Kara Su is fed from an arti-ficial lake created as part of a large-scale irrigation scheme, but it still maintains a channel through the dune ridge and flows into the desert past the small dune on which Jeitun itself is situated. In the immediate vicinity of the site there is a depression which today receives irrigation overflow and provides water for livestock and which in the past could have provided Jeitun cultivators with water for irrigation. It is also quite possible that the water table below the interdune flats around Jeitun, which would have been recharged by the spring floods of the Kara Su and by the infiltration of rainwater through the dunes, would have been high enough to permit small-scale cultivation of winter-sown cereals without irrigation, as we have previously suggested (Harris & Limbrey 1992; Harris et al. 1993: 327–8). Cultivation might also have been possible on the extensive clay formations or *takyrs* which are a conspicuous feature of the southern Kara Kum Desert. *Takyr* surfaces are sufficiently impermeable to retain standing water temporarily and farther north, in the desert, cereals are still sometimes grown on them. Furthermore, Lisitsina found evidence in a test pit beneath a *takyr* surface close to Jeitun of a buried soil consisting of a gleyed, humus-rich sandy loam (Dolukhanov 1981: 375).

More recently, in a review of the history of irrigation agriculture in southern Turkmenia, Lisitsina has gone further and stated that "in the soil horizons laid down near the Jeitun settlements [typical desert soils] are underlain by loams of varying thickness preserving obvious signs that they had been used in ancient agriculture and she described the distinguishing features of the "archaic agro-irrigated horizon" as "darker colour due to elevated humus content, considerably increased density, lumpy granular structure, presence of biogenic activity, and weak salinization" (Lisitsina 1981: 352). In her interpretation, Lisitsina assumes that cultivation at Early Jeitun sites was exclusively dependent on runoff on and from the piedmont. However, Kohl (1981: xii) cites evidence obtained from satellite imagery for an extensive zone of *takyrs* extending from the (subaerial) deltas of the Murghab and Tedjen rivers to the central piedmont some 50km west of Ashgabat, which he assumes to have been formed when those rivers extended farther northwest (as they did in historical times) than they do today; he further points out that the northeastern edge of this *takyr* zone corresponds almost precisely with the locations of Bronze Age settlements along the lower Murghab, and goes on to suggest that several of the Early Jeitun sites, including Jeitun itself, may have been situated not exclusively near streams that flowed across the piedmont but "on the edge of terminal swamps created by the Tedjen" (Kohl: ibid.). This possibility invites further field investigation,[1] and it may help to account for the apparent concentration of the Early Jeitun sites near the outer margins of the western piedmont. Perhaps, for the earliest Jeitun farmers, location near cultivable swamp margins or close to seasonally flooded clay surfaces where they could practice recessional (*décrue*) cultivation (cf. Harlan & Pasquereau 1969) was as important or more important than proximity to piedmont stream channels.

Thus, both the site-distributional evidence and inference from local geomorphological, hydrological and pedological conditions point to the western piedmont as the area of earliest known agricultural settlement in southern Turkmenistan. However, the possibility of earlier agricultural settlements having been established at higher elevations in the foothills of the Kopet Dag range and in intermontane valleys such as the Sumbar and the Atrek, where the rainfed cultivation of cereals and other crops would have been more feasible, should not be disregarded. As yet no such settlements have been found in Turkmenistan, but neolithic Jeitun-type horizons have been identified at a few sites in northeastern Iran (discussed below), and it is quite possible (in our view likely) that systematic archaeological survey in the uplands on both sides of the Iran/Turkmenistan frontier would reveal the existence there of agricultural settlements that were precursors of the Early Jeitun sites in the piedmont zone.

From the early fifth to the middle of the third millennia bc (the Aeneolithic and Early Bronze Age), following the earliest (Jeitun) phases of agro-pastoral settlement in the western piedmont, irrigation agriculture was developed farther east on the delta plain of the Tedjen River. Detailed investigations in the area of the Geoksyur Oasis in the eastern Tedjen delta have shown that here the irrigation system was elaborated and extended through the Aeneolithic period, from small ditches to a network of canals drawing water from the main delta channels and associated reservoirs (Dolukhanov 1981: 376–9; Lisitsina 1981: 353–5). Still later, in the second and early first millennia bc (Late Bronze Age and Early Iron Age), more complex irrigation systems were developed on the delta plains of the Murghab and Atrek rivers; cultivation on the piedmont was intensified around the major, now "proto-urban", settlements (Namazga-depe, Altyn-depe, Ulug-depe); and *kiariz* (= *kanat*, i.e. artificial galleries dug into water-bearing deposits), which have been dated to the first millennium bc at Ulug-tepe, began to be constructed (Dolukhanov 1981: 380–2; Lisitsina 1981: 355–6). Thus, in the three millennia following the (Jeitun) Neolithic, agricultural settlement expanded on the piedmont and also spread beyond it to the deltaic plains of the Tedjen, Murghab and Atrek rivers. However, according to Dolukhanov (1981: 383), by the first millennium bc most of the deltaic settlements had been abandoned as a result of increasing climatic aridity.

Investigations of early agro-pastoralism at Jeitun

Jeitun itself is the most thoroughly investigated site of the Jeitun Culture. It was first visited by archaeologists in 1952, when Kuftin and Marushchenko tried to date it by means of a small sounding, the result of which was inconclusive (Kohl 1984: 48). More systematic investigation was begun in 1955, and in 1959 and 1962–3 the second structural level of the site was almost completely excavated (the uppermost level having been badly eroded, principally by deflation). Masson and his colleagues suggested, on the basis of soundings, that five successive building levels were represented in the *c.* 3m of cultural deposits which had accumulated to form the small (0.7ha) tell (Fig. 21.2). Excavation was resumed at Jeitun in 1987, when Kurbansakhatov opened a 10×10m trench at the eastern end of the mound. This revealed house structures that were thought to represent the third level, and it was carried out in anticipation of a programme of collaborative work at the site by an international team of British, Russian and Turkmenian archaeologists, which was begun in 1989 (Masson 1992, Harris et al. 1993 and in press). The principal aim of the new investigations was to gain more detailed information about the ancient economy and environment of the site and to establish a radiocarbon chronology for its occupation. A particularly important objective was to obtain plant remains by systematic sampling and flotation and to date them directly by the accelerator mass spectrometric (AMS) radiocarbon technique. These investigations continued for six field seasons, from 1989 to 1994, and so far only preliminary results are available. They do, however, provide conclusive evidence that domesticated einkorn and emmer wheat (*Triticum monococcum* and *T. dicoccum*) and six-row barley (both naked-grain and hulled-grain varieties of *Hordeum sativum*) were being cultivated locally by 7000 bp (6000 cal BC) (Harris et al. 1993: 330–2 and in press). Masson's original assumption that domestic cereals were cultivated by the inhabitants of Jeitun during the sixth millennium BC was thus confirmed, and, indeed, agriculture at the site was shown to date back to the very beginning of that millennium.

The archaeobotanical investigations undertaken since 1989 at Jeitun have (so far) demonstrated the presence there of the remains of only two domesticated plants: wheat and barley. Einkorn wheat is much more abundant in the samples than either emmer wheat or barley, and a very small number of grains of a hexaploid-type wheat – probably bread wheat (*Triticum aestivum*) – have also been found. In addition to these cereals, the charred plant remains contain a range of weedy taxa, the most abundant of which are sea club-rush (*Scirpus maritimus*) and goat-face grass (*Aegilops squarrosa = A. tauschii*). The preponderance of club-rush implies that the cereal crops were grown on areas of high water table and high soil salinity, and goat-face grass can also grow on saline soils. Charles & Hillman (1992) infer that these two species grew as weeds among the cereals – a conclusion which independently reinforces the suggestion made in the previous section of this paper that the Jeitun cultivators may well have grown their cereal crops on the local interdune flats and/or the *takyr* surfaces characterized by high water tables. This suggestion does not of course exclude the possibility that fields were also irrigated. Surface water from streams and/or *takyrs* may have been directed on to fields along artificial channels – a possibility that is reinforced by our discovery in 1993 of a ditch-like feature exposed in the bank of a modern irrigation canal close to the site.[2]

Further information on how the cereals were cultivated was gained from Hillman's on-site examination of the plant temper that was used in building the walls and ovens at Jeitun. He found that the temper consisted of cereal straw, which strongly suggests that the crops were cultivated locally (Hillman 1981), and the lack of culm bases and basal ear nodes in the temper implies, respectively, that the cereals were harvested by sickle (see below) rather than by uprooting, and that the ears were reaped separately from the straw in a "double-harvest" system (Hillman 1984, 1985).

When the archaeobotanical data so far analyzed are viewed in relation to the 11 AMS radiocarbon dates we have obtained at Jeitun there is no indication of changes in plant use through time; more specifically, there is no evidence in the lower levels of greater use of wild plant foods and cereal cultivation appears to have been the main form of plant exploitation from the initial occupation of the site to its abandonment (Harris et al. in press).

The excavations at Jeitun, from the 1950s onwards, have yielded abundant corroborative evidence of cereal cultivation in the form of stone sickle blades and grindstones. Sickle blades alone are said to account for 37 per cent of all the tools found in the earlier excavations (Masson & Sarianidi 1972: 41). The blades – usually only two or three flakes – were inserted into straight wooden or bone handles to form harvesting knives. Korobkova (1981) has claimed, on the basis of her extensive experimental studies of harvesting and micro-wear on the blades, that the knives found at Jeitun could each be used for 20–25 hours before it was necessary to retouch the blades. She further concludes, in the absence of any traces of retouching on the blades, that the knives were seasonal implements repaired from one year's harvest to the next; and from this she calculates, by reference to the average area that can be harvested in an hour and the total number of knives (527) inferred to come from the second structural level, that an area of 21–33 ha would have been cultivated annually at Jeitun (ibid.: 343–5). This extended chain of inference involves several speculative assumptions (e.g. that all blades were recovered and used in a single year), but it is worth noting that the annual cultivated area estimated by this method corresponds quite closely to Masson's estimate of 20–22 ha based on calculations of the annual need for grain of the population of Jeitun, which he assumes to have been between 150 and 180 people (Masson 1971: 101–3). Grindstones, which were probably made on site from imported slabs of sandstone, also attest to the importance of cereal grains in the Jeitun domestic economy; but no stone tools resembling hoe blades or other tillage implements have been found – perhaps wooden digging sticks and/or hoes were used.

A third approach to estimating the cultivated area at Jeitun, in addition to Korobkova's and Masson's, has been proposed by Lisitsina (summarized in Kohl 1984: 53–4). Using comparative field data from her investigations of the later prehistoric economy of the Geoksyur Oasis, and assuming a population at Jeitun of only 120, she infers that c. 15 ha would have been cultivated annually, divided equally between spring-sown cereals on irrigated land and winter-sown cereals on dry (rainfed) land. All three of these speculative calculations rest on the assumptions that Jeitun was occupied year-round (i.e. that its population was fully sedentary) and that barley and wheat provided most of the food supply. However, neither assumption is necessarily justified, and that the latter is probably incorrect is suggested by the evidence for animal exploitation.

Animal remains in the form of bones, teeth and shell are well preserved and quite abundant at Jeitun. Shevchenko (1960) reported on an assemblage of 1,771 bones from Masson's earlier excavations of the upper structural levels and identified 10 species of mammal, including caprines (goats and sheep), which she regarded as wild, and domestic dogs. However, Masson (1971: 86) argued that most of the caprines were domesticated and that they supplied most of the meat in the diet. Kasparov (1992) has so far studied and reported on about half of the bone assemblage that was recovered (by hand and dry sieving) during the excavations carried out between 1989 and 1992 – 2,007 whole and fragmented bones from the third, and 123 from the fourth, structural level – and Legge (1992) has analyzed 79 caprine mandibles from the same assemblage. Altogether, 15 taxa have been identified: twelve mammals, one species of bird, one lizard and one tortoise. Fish vertebrae and other fish bones have been recovered by flotation since 1992, but they have not yet been studied.

The caprines are the most abundantly represented mammals in the assemblage that Kasparov has examined. He argues that, as well as domestic dogs, domestic goats and sheep *and* both the wild bezoar goat (*Capra aegagrus*) and the wild urial sheep (*Ovis vignei*) are represented. It is often difficult to distinguish between the bones of wild and domestic caprines, especially when, as here, the sample size is small, but it is probable that most of the goat and sheep bones at Jeitun derive from domesticated animals. However, Jeitun lies within the ranges of the wild bezoar and urial, and Kasparov's identification of both domestic and wild caprines at Jeitun, which is based largely on differences in their size,[3] is probably correct. According to his analysis of the minimum numbers of individuals represented in the whole assemblage that he has studied, domestic animals comprise 57 per cent (91 individuals) and wild animals 43 per cent (68) of the total (159).

The domestic animals in the assemblage consist almost entirely of sheep and goats.[4] Only four dogs are represented, and no bones of domestic or wild cattle, horses or onagers have been found at Jeitun – although the remains of both cattle and onagers have been found in Late Jeitun levels at Chagylly (Masson & Sarianidi 1972: 44; Kohl 1984: 53). Among the wild animals, the goitred gazelle (*Gazella subgutturosa*) is the most abundant (21 individuals), followed by wild goat and sheep (11 individuals in all), red fox (5), wild boar, tolai hare, steppe cat and tortoise (each 3). These small samples should not be taken to indicate the relative importance as prey of the wild animals hunted by the inhabitants of Jeitun, although it is likely that gazelles were the chief prey. They may well have been hunted seasonally close to the site because large herds used to migrate from the mountains and upper piedmont to winter in the Kara Kum before returning to the higher country in the spring (Valerii Kuznetsov: pers. comm. 1992) and they could readily have been intercepted as they moved into and out of the desert. Wild sheep and goats, on the other hand, did not migrate seasonally over long distances, and hunting them from Jeitun would probably have involved journeys to the foothills of the Kopet Dag of at least 40–50 km each way.

There is insufficient zooarchaeological data from Jeitun to assess with any accuracy the importance of hunting in the domestic economy, although the abundance of gazelle bones recovered both in Masson's earlier, and our recent, excavations, suggests that their meat contributed substantially to the diet. However, Masson has drawn attention to the surprising absence of arrow- or spear-heads in the lithic assemblage and has suggested that geometric microliths, which are present in large numbers, may have been mounted in wooden shafts to form some form of hunting missile; he also suggests that slings were used in hunting (Masson & Sarianidi 1972: 44).

The preponderance of sheep and goat bones in the assemblage recently analyzed by Kasparov (1992), most of which are from domesticated animals, implies that caprine pastoralism was important in the domestic economy. Although no structures suggestive of animal pens or stalls have been found at Jeitun, micromorphological analysis by Limbrey (1992) of deposits from one of the yard areas has demonstrated the presence of small humus-stained ovoid masses that she interprets as goat droppings, and pellets of goat/sheep dung have been found in most of the excavated samples processed by floatation. Possibly the animals were brought into the settlement at night to protect them from predators, after they had grazed and browsed locally during the day. Some seasonal transhumance may have been practised, alternating summer grazing in the foothills of the Kopet Dag with winter grazing of pastures in the desert closer to Jeitun, but this cannot be determined, particularly in the absence of known upland sites of the Jeitun period.

The question of whether the sheep and goats were managed primarily or exclusively for meat, or also for milk, has been considered by Legge (1992), who analyzed slaughter patterns by determining age at death from the caprine mandibles. He concluded that there was no strong seasonal pattern of slaughter because the teeth exhibit all stages of eruption and wear, and from this he inferred, following Payne's (1973) study of caprine mandibles as indicators of kill-off patterns, that the sheep and goats at Jeitun were exploited mainly for meat, although they may also have provided milk, as well as hair, wool and skins. He also argued that the lack of evidence for a seasonal pattern of slaughter implied that Jeitun was likely to have been occupied throughout the year.

Kasparov (1992) examined the distribution of bones in one house and its associated yard and outhouse and found that the sheep/goat bones in the house came from the meatiest parts of the carcasses, whereas almost all skeletal elements were present in the yard and outhouse deposits (which latter also contained fox, cat and wild boar), and many of those bones also showed evidence of gnawing by dogs – suggesting that carcasses (of sheep, goat and boar) were butchered and skins (of fox and cat) dressed in the yard and outhouse, and cooked meat eaten in the house. It is interesting, too, to speculate on the economic and social role of dogs at Jeitun. Masson (1971: 86) assumes that they were used in hunting, and Sarianidi (1992: 119) thinks that they may have assisted shepherds tending flocks of sheep and goats. That their role was not simply utilitarian is, however, suggested by the presence of small animal figurines made of clay, some of which are distinctly dog-like, and, more convincingly, by our discovery of the skeleton of a dog which had been interred, with a pottery vessel, in a wall of one of the houses at Jeitun. No human bones were associated with this dog burial – nor have any been found elsewhere in the excavations – but it brings to mind the evidence of dogs buried with their (presumed) owners at the neolithic site of Burzahorn in Kashmir (which is unparalleled in the Indian subcontinent) and, even farther afield, the neolithic dog burials of northern China and Manchuria (Allchin & Allchin 1982: 113, 116).

When the results of our investigations of the plant and animal remains recovered at Jeitun are added to what is known about the stone and bone artefacts, as a result especially of the analyses of microwear by Korobkova and her colleagues (1992), a clear picture emerges of an economy based on cereal cultivation, caprine pastoralism and hunting, but the relative dietary contribution of these three subsistence activities cannot be estimated with any confidence. It is even more difficult – in the absence as yet of direct evidence – to judge whether any crops other than wheat and barley were cultivated, or whether wild plants were exploited for food on a significant scale. We hope that, as analysis continues of the samples recovered between 1989 and 1994, we shall be able to add more detail to this picture of the economy and general way of life of the people who inhabited Jeitun at the beginning of the sixth millennium bc.

The regional context and possible antecedents of the early agricultural Jeitun Culture

The evidence for early agricultural settlement, at Jeitun itself and at other sites in the piedmont zone, shows that the Jeitun Culture represents a "developed" neolithic economy, in the sense that both cereal cultivation and caprine pastoralism were well established and the settlements were small (< 2 ha) farming villages, most (if not all) of which were probably occupied throughout the year. The sites with evidence of Early Jeitun occupation (Jeitun, Chopan, Gievdzhik, Pessedjik and Togolok) cluster near the outer margin of the western piedmont, whereas the sites situated on the eastern piedmont (Chagylly, Gadimi and Mondjukli) lack such evidence. This appears to indicate an eastward spread of agricultural settlement during the sixth millennium from Early to Late Jeitun times, although this assumption must remain tentative in the absence of well dated sequences from most of the known sites and because other early neolithic sites may have been buried by more recent alluviation. Nevertheless, the fact that *all* the known Early Jeitun sites are in the western piedmont strongly suggests that the antecedents of the Jeitun Culture should be sought to the west and south of the piedmont rather than to the east.

We can be confident that the cultivation of einkorn and emmer wheat did not begin independently on the western piedmont, by means of local plant domestication and without any external influence, because the areas of origin of these wheats, both of which were cultivated at Jeitun, lie farther west within the distribution areas of their wild progenitors, respectively *Triticum monococcum* subsp. *boeoticum* and *T. turgidum* subsp. *dicoccoides* (Zohary 1989: 359–62, and in Ch. 9 in this volume). Barley too was probably introduced from farther west as an already domesticated crop, but its local domestication cannot be excluded on phytogeographical grounds because its wild progenitor, *Hordeum vulgare* subsp. *spontaneum*, is known to occur in northern Iran and southern Turkmenistan,[5] and even as far east as the western Himalayas and Tibet (Zohary 1989: 359, citing Witcombe 1978 and Shao 1981). Goats, too, could have been domesticated locally, because Jeitun lies within the natural range of the wild bezoar. However, it is very unlikely that sheep were, because the urial is not regarded as a direct ancestor of domestic sheep, which are believed to derive from the Asiatic mouflon, *Ovis orientalis*, the natural range of which extends from Asia Minor eastwards as far as the Elburz Mountains, where it intergrades with the urial, but not into Turkmenia (Clutton-Brock 1981: 53–4; Uerpmann 1987: 126–30). Furthermore, the fact that the remains of domestic sheep and goats have been found at neolithic sites of the seventh and eighth millennia farther west in Iran, Syria, Turkey and the Levant (cf. Garrard et al., Legge and Hole in Chs 11, 13 and 14 in this volume), and that the smaller domestic forms are present at Jeitun in all the excavated levels, argues for their introduction into southern Turkmenia from the west as already domesticated animals.

It is difficult to try to trace the antecedents of the Jeitun Culture westwards and southwards towards the Caspian Sea and into Iran because the area is poorly surveyed archaeologically and few early neolithic or mesolithic sites have been excavated. There are, however, three sites in northeastern Iran from which ceramics closely resembling Jeitun pottery have been reported. Two of them – Tureng and Yarim – are situated on the plain traversed by the Gorgan River between the eastern Elburz Mountains and the southeastern coast of the Caspian (Fig. 21.1). The Jeitun-like ceramics were found in the basal levels of both sites, although at Tureng the resemblance was to Late Jeitun pottery (Crawford 1963, Deshayes 1967; Sarianidi 1992: 113).

The third site – Sang-i Chakmak (Sang-e Caxmaq) – is located on the Iranian Plateau on the eastern side of the Elburz Mountains near Bastam north of Emamrud (Shahrud) (Fig. 21.1). The site consists of several small tells on alluvial land, two of which were excavated by Masuda in 1971 and 1973 (Aurenche 1988: 83; Masuda 1974a, 1974b, 1976; Kohl 1984: 46; Sarianidi 1992: 114–5). The eastern mound was found to contain abundant pottery and other stone, bone and clay artefacts which closely resemble the material culture of the Jeitun sites as well as that represented in the lowest level at Yarim. The buildings were made of cylindrical clay blocks the same size and shape as those used at Jeitun, and the finds included clay figurines of animals and wooden sickle handles decorated with animal designs. There are no radiocarbon dates for the eastern mound, but it is thought to date to the Late Jeitun phase.

In contrast to the eastern mound at Sang-i Chakmak, the western one was almost devoid of pottery – only three ceramic sherds were found in the five levels excavated – but the rectangular plan and buildings of the settlement resemble those of the Jeitun Culture (Aurenche 1985: 236 and fig. 3). Two radiocarbon dates, of 5505 ±155 bc and 5540 ±130 bc, were obtained (apparently both from the third level), which, when calibrated, give values (at two standard deviations) of 6381 BC and 6373 BC (Possehl 1994: 92). The maximum time span (at two standard deviations) of the 11 AMS radiocarbon dates that we have obtained at the site of Jeitun is 6300–5700 cal BC, but only one of those dates (OxA–2914) produced (two) calibrations (just) over 6300 BC and both of them have very low probabilities (0.2 and 0.3 per cent) of representing the "true date" (Harris et al. in press). The dates from Jeitun essentially indicate an occupation there at c. 6000–5800 BC, so it does appear that the western mound at Sang-i Chakmak was occupied at least two or three centuries before Jeitun – probably earlier because only the third level has been dated. We conclude therefore that Sang-i Chakmak is both the westernmost and the earliest dated neolithic settlement at present attributable to the Jeitun Culture. There is another site – Shir-i Shayn – in the Gorgan Valley northwest of Sang-i Chakmak (Fig. 21.1) which has produced ceramics decorated with simple line and zigzag patterns reminiscent of Jeitun pottery, but it lacks excavated structures (Sarianidi 1992: 115), and, as far as we know, has not been dated. The almost complete absence of pottery in the western mound at Sang-i Chakmak has led Gupta (1979, II: 49–52) to suggest that the site may represent a transitional stage between the south Caspian Mesolithic – as revealed in the caves of Ghar-i Kamarband (Belt), Hotu and Ali Tappeh (Fig. 21.1) (Coon 1957: 141–204, McBurney 1968; Sarianidi 1992: 112–13) – and the Jeitun Neolithic. There are some suggestive similarities (for instance, in the stone-tool assemblages and the presence in both of small cones made of baked clay, but without more detailed investigation of the Sang-i Chakmak sites this intriguing hypothesis must remain untested.

In considering the possible origins of the "developed" Jeitun Neolithic we should also ask whether its antecedents might in part be found at the east Caspian mesolithic sites between Krasnovodsk and the Balkhan Mountains (Fig. 21.1). It was at the site of Jebel Cave that Oladnikov (1956) first established a mesolithic–neolithic strati-graphic sequence for southern Turkmenistan. Markov (1966) subsequently argued, on grounds of similarities in the lithic assemblages, that Level 4 at the cave of Dam Dam Chashma 2 was synchronous with the Early Jeitun phase. The east Caspian sites were occupied from approximately the tenth to the fifth millennium bc, and the bones of domestic goats and sheep, morphologically distinct from the wild forms, are present in levels dated to the sixth to early fifth millennia (Levels 4 at Jebel and at Dam Dam Chashma 2) (Aurenche 1988: 88; Kohl 1984: 41–2; Sarianidi 1992: 115–16). There is, however, no evidence of crop cultivation, and abundant bones of gazelle, onager and fish in the later levels suggest that hunting and fishing continued to be important activities during the neolithic occupation of the caves. It is possible, as Aurenche (1988: 83) has noted, that the caves were used seasonally by transhumant pastoralists (and/or by hunters) from the agricultural villages of the Jeitun Culture in the piedmont zone. Alternatively, it could be suggested that the presence of domestic goats and sheep in the later levels indicates that the occupants of the caves had adopted domestic livestock and were themselves practising caprine pastoralism. A third possibility is that the bones derive from domestic goats and sheep which had become feral and were being hunted.

In whatever way the presence in the caves of the remains of goats and sheep is interpreted, the east Caspian Mesolithic does not appear to be a credible progenitor of the neolithic Jeitun Culture as a whole – most conclusively because there is no evi-dence of cereal cultivation at any of the sites. However, renewed investigation of the caves, using flotation and other modern techniques for the recovery and analysis of plant remains, would be worthwhile and could throw more light on the interesting question of what interactions there may have been between the people occupying the caves and those inhabiting the agricultural villages in the piedmont zone during the sixth millennium.

The admittedly meagre archaeological evidence of early neolithic sites with Jeitun-like features in northeastern Iran, and the fact that domesticated einkorn and emmer wheat, and probably barley, as well as domesticated sheep and probably goats, derive from farther west, suggests that the development of an agro-pastoral economy in the piedmont zone of southern Turkmenistan resulted from the spread of most – perhaps all – of the elements of the neolithic agricultural economy that had been developed earlier in western Iran, the middle Euphrates Valley, Anatolia and the Levant.

On present evidence, we cannot determine whether this process was essentially one of primary ("demic") diffusion, whereby migrant agriculturalists colonized the piedmont zone from the southwest, or whether it occurred more by secondary diffu-sion involving the selective adoption of domesticates and agricultural techniques by resident mesolithic populations. The fact – which is strongly reinforced by the archae-obotanical evidence from our recent excavations at Jeitun referred to above – that the Jeitun Culture first appears in southern Turkmenistan as a "developed" neolithic econ-omy appears to favour the former interpretation.

It is probable that the agricultural economy (or elements of it) spread to the piedmont via the upland valleys of northeastern Iran and southern Turkmenistan rather than through the narrow south Caspian lowland, which would have been wetter and heavily forested. Today, the upland valleys of the Atrek River and its tributaries such as the Chandyr and the Sumbar lie within a zone of mediterranean type or "dry summer subtropical" climate which – ameliorated by the vast water body of the Caspian Sea – extends eastwards approximately to longitude 60°E near Mashhad (Trewartha 1960). These valleys have deep fertile soils and support woodlands and grasslands which contain many arboreal and herbaceous elements of the mediterranean flora. The woodlands, which are sometimes classified as "steppe forest", typically contain species of *Amygdalus, Juniperus, Pistacia, Punica* and *Pyrus*, and the grasslands, which are sometimes classified as "annual grass steppe", are frequently dominated by annuals such as *Aegilops squarrosa, A. triuncialis* and *A. cylindrica, Hordeum vulgare* subsp. *spontaneum* and *Lolium* spp. (Daniel Zohary: pers. comm. 1995). At the beginning of the Neolithic, when annual precipitation may have been higher than today (Dolukhanov 1981: 375) within an essentially mediterranean climate, this environment would have been well suited to the establishment of rainfed agriculture. We consider it likely that forms of rainfed agriculture were practised in the uplands before techniques of groundwater cultivation and irrigation were developed at Jeitun Culture sites in the drier piedmont zone, although such speculation must remain untested until evidence is found of early neolithic agricultural settlements in the Kopet Dag mountains and the upland valleys to the southwest.

Although there is a strong presumption that the Jeitun agricultural economy derived, in whole or in part, from northeastern Iran, we should not exclude the possibility that agro-pastoral settlements were established during the sixth millennium, or even earlier, in areas immediately to the south and east of the Kopet Dag piedmont. Five surface sites with scatters of stone tools, which resemble Early Jeitun lithic assemblages in the high proportion of geometric microliths that they contain, have been found in the upper Murghab Valley in southeastern Turkmenistan, but there is no evidence of Jeitun-like mudbrick settlements there (Kohl 1984: 211–12). Nor is there at the mesolithic and neolithic sites at Ak Kupruk in the piedmont zone of the Balkhab River in northern Afghanistan.

At two of the sites at Ak Kupruk – Ghar-i Mar and Ghar-i Asp – stone flakes interpreted as sickle blades, grindstones, and bones of reputedly domestic sheep and goats have been recovered from aceramic and ceramic neolithic levels, and a series of (partly stratigraphically inconsistent) radiocarbon dates obtained which reach back to c. 8500 bc and span over six millennia (Dupree 1972; Perkins 1972; Shaffer 1978: 73–81; Kohl 1984: 211–12, 232–3; Sarianidi 1992: 124–5). Dupree (1972: 263) suggested that these sites may have been occupied by specialized pastoral nomads, but doubts remain about both the validity of the dating and the identification of the earliest remains of sheep/goat as domestic. Until new investigations can be undertaken of these and other mesolithic–neolithic sites in northern Afghanistan, using modern techniques such as flotation and AMS radiocarbon dating, their importance must remain a matter of conjecture. However, although they may have been occupied by agro-pastoralists, they do not appear to be likely progenitors of the Jeitun Culture.

Farther east, in the mountain valleys of northeastern Afghanistan and southern Tadjikistan, sites of the Hissar Culture, which are thought to date from the sixth to the early second millennium bc, may have been occupied seasonally by pastoralists, or perhaps in some cases permanently by agro-pastoralists; but there is no evidence of mudbrick architecture at the Hissar sites, and no close parallels with the Jeitun Culture are evident (Kohl 1984: 212; Sarianidi 1992: 124).

Conclusion

At the beginning of this chapter we compared the piedmont zone of southern Turkmenistan, between the Kopet Dag range and the Kara Kum Desert, with the two other great physiographic boundaries of the Iranian Plateau – the hills of Baluchistan and the Zagros Mountains which overlook, respectively, the valleys of the Indus and of the Tigris–Euphrates. All three are major resource-rich ecotonal zones between upland and alluvial lowland, and in all three there is evidence of early neolithic agro-pastoral settlement. Along the western boundary of the Iranian Plateau, in the eastern "hilly flanks" of the so-called Fertile Crescent, this evidence dates back, at such sites as Jarmo, Ganj Dareh, Tepe Guran and Ali Kosh to the eighth and the first half of the seventh millennium bc. Along the southeastern boundary in western Pakistan the evidence is more meagre and initial agricultural settlement appears to be later than in the west. The site of Mehrgarh, situated on the physiographic boundary at the foot of the Bolan Pass at the northern end of the Kachi Plain, has yielded convincing evidence of early neolithic agro-pastoralism based on the cultivation of barley and wheat and the herding of domestic cattle, sheep and goats (Costantini 1984, Jarrige & Meadow 1980, Meadow 1984 and in Ch. 22 in this volume). The radiocarbon dating of this extensive multi-period site is problematic, but the earliest levels, which are aceramic and contain mudbrick structures (some of which may be granaries) with imprints of einkorn, emmer and free-threshing wheat and of hulled two-rowed and hulled and naked six-rowed barley, probably pre-date 6000 bc (Allchin & Allchin 1982: 105–6; Jarrige 1984, Meadow in this volume). The discovery, in the uppermost of these early levels, of turquoise beads possibly imported from Turkmenistan, and the presence in the lithic assemblage of hump-back trapezes very similar to those of the Jeitun Culture, hints strongly at the existence of an exchange network linking the two piedmont zones across the Iranian Plateau (Allchin & Allchin 1982: 106–7).

The site of Mehrgarh has provided the earliest evidence of agro-pastoral settlement in the South Asian subcontinent, and it demonstrates that a transition from primary dependence on hunting and gathering to agriculture had taken place at the southeastern margin of the Iranian Plateau by the beginning of the seventh millennium, just as it had along the northeastern margin in southern Turkmenistan. In addition to Mehrgarh, other early agricultural sites have been discovered in the southeastern marginal zone, from central Balochistan north to Kashmir, not all of which have been directly dated, but none has been shown to be as old as Mehrgarh and most are attributed to the fifth and fourth millennia (Allchin & Allchin 1982: 97–116; Khan et al. 1991; Sharif & Thapar 1992).

When the early agricultural Jeitun Culture of southern Turkmenistan is viewed in the wider context of neolithic Southwest and western Central Asia, it is not seen as an isolated epiphenomenon on the periphery of the "nuclear" centre of the Fertile

Crescent but as one of three piedmont zones around the Iranian Plateau in which neo-lithic agro-pastoral economies became established during the eighth and seventh mil-lennia bc. Our recent investigations at Jeitun, building on the work there of Masson and his colleagues, have provided new evidence of the process in one of those zones, but the course of "neolithicization" in the region as a whole is still not well under-stood. It is clear that the three piedmont zones did not develop in complete isolation from one another, but we still have much to learn about the relative importance of diffusion and autonomous development in the transition to agriculture in each of them.

Notes

1. From the air west of Ashgabat we have observed many *takyrs* in the southern Kara Kum just beyond the northern edge of the alluvial fans of the piedmont. We carried out a preliminary investigation of some of them near Jeitun in 1994, but unfortunately the samples were lost (in a stolen car) before they could be analyzed.
2. This interesting feature was first noticed and recorded by Susan Limbrey. It was then excavated by Keith Wilkinson and found to extend for *c.* 3 m towards the Jeitun mound. A charcoal sample from its base has been dated to 7140 ±220 bp (OxA–4916), which suggests that the "ditch" was in existence when Jeitun was occupied. A report on this discovery will be published elsewhere.
3. According to Juliet Clutton-Brock (pers. comm. 1995), it should be possible to distinguish between wild and domestic sheep and goats on the basis of size in assemblages dating to the sixth millennium bc.
4. One pig bone was found during the excavations in 1994, but no report on it is available.
5. In 1992 Gordon Hillman and one of us (DRH) observed apparently natural stands of wild barley growing profusely on volcanic soils in the Badkhys National Reserve close to the Afghanistan frontier in south-eastern Turkmenistan; and Daniel Zohary (pers. comm. 1995) informs us that he has observed "pock-ets" of wild barley in the intermontane valleys of northeastern Iran, e.g. near Shahrabad west of Bojnurd in a southern tributary valley of the Atrek River (Fig. 21.1). Although some or all of these isolated pop-ulations may consist of weedy forms that accompanied the spread of cereal cultivation from farther west, the possibility cannot be completely excluded that genuinely wild barley was present in north-eastern Iran and southern Turkmenistan when neolithic agricultural settlements were established there, and that it *could* have been domesticated locally.

Acknowledgements

We are deeply indebted to Professor V. M. Masson, Director of the Institute of the History of Material Cul-ture, St Petersburg, and to Dr K. Kurbansakhatov, the Head of IUTAKE in Ashgabat, for inviting us and our British colleagues to work at Jeitun from 1989 to 1994 and for providing logistical and administrative sup-port in Turkmenistan, assisted by Sergei Loginov. We are also indebted to – and greatly enjoyed working with – our many Russian archaeological colleagues who participated in the excavations at Jeitun, and we wish especially to thank Yuri Berezkin, Alexei Kasparov, Galina Korobkova, Nikolai Savvanidi, Tamara Sharovskaya and Natasha Solovyova. The Director and Deputy Director of the Desert Research Institute in Ashgabat, Dr A. G. Babaev and Dr N. S. Orlovsky, provided invaluable assistance with our off-site eco-logical surveys in the National Parks and Reserves of Badkhyz, Kara-Kala and Repetek, and Irina Annisi-mova, Katharine Judelson, Isabella Moskalyeva and Liya Orlovskaya acted, skilfully and patiently, as interpreters. Some 15 British colleagues have worked with us at Jeitun over the last six years (and are named in the acknowledgements in Harris et al. in press), and here we wish particularly to thank Michael Charles of Sheffield University, Susan Limbrey of Birmingham University and Gordon Hillman of the Institute of Archaeology, University College London. We gratefully acknowledge research grants received from the

British Academy, the British Institute for Persian Studies, the University of Oxford and the Gordon Childe Fund of the Institute of Archaeology, University College London (UCL). Financial and logistical assistance was also provided by the Institute of the History of Material Culture (St Petersburg), the South Turkmenian Multidisciplinary Archaeological Expedition (Ashgabat), Birmingham University, La Trobe University (Melbourne) and UCL. Figure 21.1 was kindly prepared by Tim Aspden at UCL. Professor Daniel Zohary of the Hebrew University, Jerusalem, made helpful comments on an earlier draft of this paper.

References

Allchin, B. (ed.) 1984. *South Asian Archaeology 1981*. Cambridge: Cambridge University Press.

Allchin, B. & R. Allchin 1982. *The rise of civilization in India and Pakistan*. Cambridge: Cambridge University Press.

Aurenche, O. 1985. La tradition architecturale à l'est de la Mésopotamie (Iran–Turkménistan) du 10e au 4e millénaires. In *L'archéologie de la Bactriane ancienne*, Actes du colloque franco–soviétique, Dushanbe, 27 octobre à 3 novembre 1982 (no eds), 235–40. Paris: Editions du CNRS.

— 1988. Remarques sur la néolithicisation de l'Asie centrale. In *L'Asie centrale et ses rapports avec les civilisations orientales, des origines à l'age du fer*, Actes du colloque franco–soviétique, Paris, 19–26 novembre 1985, 81–6. Paris: Mémoires de la Mission Archéologique Française en Asie Centrale, Tome 1, Diffusion de Boccard.

Charles, M. & G. C. Hillman 1992. Crop husbandry in a desert environment: evidence from the charred plant macro-remains. In Masson (1992: 83–94).

Coon, C. S. 1957. *Seven caves: archaeological explorations in the Middle East*. London: Jonathan Cape.

Costantini, L. 1984. The beginning of agriculture in the Kachi Plain: the evidence of Mehrgarh. In Allchin (1984: 29–33).

Clutton-Brock, J. 1981. *Domesticated animals from early times*. London: Heinemann & British Museum (Natural History).

Crawford, V. 1963. Beside the Kara Su. *Bulletin of the Metropolitan Museum of Art* 22, 263–73.

Deshayes, J. 1967. Céramiques peintes de Tureng Tepe. *Iran* 5, 123–31.

Dolukhanov, P. M. 1981. The ecological prerequisites for early farming in southern Turkmenia. In *The Bronze Age civilization of Central Asia*, P. L. Kohl (ed.) 359–85. New York: M. E. Sharpe.

Dorofeyev, V. F. & A. A. Filatenko 1992. Preface. In *N. I. Vavilov: origin and geography of cultivated plants*, V. F. Dorofeyev (ed.), xix–xxxi. Cambridge: Cambridge University Press.

Dupree, L. (ed.) 1972. *Prehistoric research in Afghanistan (1959–1966)*. Transactions of the American Philosophical Society 62, Part 4.

Gupta, S. P. 1979. *Archaeology of Soviet Central Asia and the Indian borderlands*, 2 vols. Delhi: B. R. Publishing Corporation.

Harlan, J. R. & J. Pasquereau 1969. *Décrue* agriculture in Mali. *Economic Botany* 23, 70–4.

Harris, D. R. 1990. Vavilov's concept of centres of origin of cultivated plants: its genesis and its influence on the study of agricultural origins. *Biological Journal of the Linnean Society* 39, 7–16.

Harris, D. R. & S. Limbrey 1992. The present-day environmental setting of Jeitun. In Masson (1992: 7–13).

Harris, D. R., V. M. Masson, Y. E. Berezkin, M. P. Charles, C. Gosden, G. C. Hillman, A. K. Kasparov, G. F. Korobkova, K. Kurbansakhatov, A. J. Legge, S. Limbrey 1993. Investigating early agriculture in Central Asia: new research at Jeitun, Turkmenistan. *Antiquity* 67, 324–38.

Harris, D. R., C. Gosden, M. P. Charles in press. Jeitun: recent excavations at an early neolithic site in southern Turkmenistan. *Proceedings of the Prehistoric Society* 62.

Hillman, G. C. 1981. Reconstructing crop husbandry practices from charred remains of crops. In *Farming in British prehistory*, R. Mercer (ed.), 123–62. Edinburgh: John Donald.

— 1984. Traditional husbandry and processing of archaic cereals in recent times: the operations, products and tools which might feature in Sumerian texts. Part I: the glume wheats. *Bulletin on Sumerian*

Agriculture 1, 114–52.

— 1985. Traditional husbandry and processing of archaic cereals in recent times: the operations, products and tools which might feature in Sumerian texts. Part II: the free-threshing cereals. *Bulletin on Sumerian Agriculture* 2, 1–31.

Jarrige, J-F. 1984. Chronology of the earlier periods of the Greater Indus as seen from Mehrgarh, Pakistan. In Allchin (1984: 21–8).

Jarrige, J-F. & R. H. Meadow 1980. The antecedents of civilization in the Indus Valley, *Scientific American* 243(2), 102–10.

Kasparov, A. K. 1992. Bone collection at the Jeitun settlement. In Masson (1992: 50–76).

Khan, F., J. R. Knox, K. D. Thomas 1991. *Explorations and excavations in Bannu District, North-West Frontier Province, Pakistan, 1985–1988* [British Museum Occasional Paper 80]. London: British Museum Press.

Kohl, P. L. (ed.) 1981. *The Bronze Age civilization of Central Asia: recent Soviet discoveries*. New York: M. E. Sharpe.

— 1984. *Central Asia: Palaeolithic beginnings to the Iron Age* [Synthèse 14]. Paris: Editions Recherche sur les Civilisations.

Korobkova, G. F. 1981. Ancient reaping tools and their productivity in the light of experimental trace wear analysis. In *The Bronze Age civilization of Central Asia: recent Soviet discoveries*, P. L. Kohl (ed.), 325–49. New York: M. E. Sharpe.

Korobkova, G. F., O. Lollekova, T. A. Sharovskaya 1992. Use-wear analysis of tools from the third level at Jeitun. In Masson (1992: 34–49).

Kuftin, B. A. 1956. Polevoi otchet: o rabote XIV otrade IuTAKE po izucheniiu kul'turi pervobitno-oshchinikh osedlozemledel'cheskikh poselenii epokhu medu i bronzi 1952 g. *Trudy IuTAKE* 7, 260–90.

Legge, A. J. 1992. The exploitation of sheep and goat at Jeitun. In Masson (1992: 77–83).

Limbrey, S. 1992. Micromorphological study of yard deposits. In Masson (1992: 94–6).

Lisitsina, G. N. 1981. The history of irrigation agriculture in southern Turkmenia. In *The Bronze Age civilization of Central Asia: recent Soviet discoveries*, P. L. Kohl (ed.), 350–8. New York: M. E. Sharpe.

Markov, G. E. 1966. Grot Dam Dam Cheshme 2 v vostochnom prikaspii. *Sovetskaya Arkheologiya* 2, 104–25.

Masson, V. M. 1957. Jeitun and Kara-tepe. *Sovetskaya Arkheologiya* 1, 143–60 [in Russian].

— 1961. The first farmers in Turkmenia. *Antiquity* 35, 203–13.

— 1971. *The Jeitun settlement: the emergence of a productive economy* [Materials and Research on the Archaeology of the USSR 180; in Russian]. Moscow: Nauka.

— (ed.) 1992. *New research at the Jeitun settlement: preliminary reports on the work of the Soviet–British Expedition.* Ashgabat: Academy of Sciences of Turkmenistan [in Russian].

Masson, V. M. & V. I. Sarianidi 1972. *Central Asia: Turkmenia before the Achaemenids.* London: Thames & Hudson.

Masuda, S. 1974a Tepe Sang-e Caxamaq. *Iran* 12, 222–3.

— 1974b Excavations at Tappeh Sang-e Caxamaq. *Proceedings of the IInd Annual Symposium on Archaeological Research in Iran*, 23–33. Tehran: Iranian Centre for Archaeological Research.

— 1976. Report of the archaeological investigations at Šahrud, 1975. *Proceedings of the IVth Annual Symposium on Archaeological Research in Iran*, 63–70. Tehran: Iranian Centre for Archaeological Research.

McBurney, C. B. M. 1968. The cave of Ali Tappeh and the Epi-Palaeolithic of northeastern Iran. *Proceedings of the Prehistoric Society* 34, 385–413.

Meadow, R. H. 1984. Notes on the faunal remains from Mehrgarh, with a focus on cattle (*Bos*). In Allchin (1984: 34–40).

Mellaart, J. 1975. *The Neolithic of the Near East.* London: Thames & Hudson.

Oladnikov, A. P. 1956. Peshchera Djebel – pamyatnik drevnei kul'turi prikaspiskikh Turkmenii. *Trudy IuTAKE* 7, 11–219.

Payne, S. 1973. Kill-off patterns in sheep and goats: the mandibles from Aşvan Kale. *Anatolian Studies* 23, 281–303.

Perkins, D., Jr 1972. The fauna of the Ap Kupruk caves: a brief note. In Dupree (1972: 73).

Possehl, G. L. 1994. *Radiometric dates for South Asian archaeology*. Philadelphia: University of Pennsylvania Museum (mimeograph).

Pumpelly, R. (ed.) 1908. *Explorations in Turkestan. Expedition of 1904. Prehistoric civilizations of Anau* [2 vols]. Washington DC: Carnegie Institution of Washington.

Sarianidi, V. 1992. Food-producing and other neolithic communities in Khorasan and Transoxania: eastern Iran, Soviet Central Asia and Afghanistan. In *History of civilizations of Central Asia* (vol. 1), A. H. Dani & V. M. Masson (eds), 109–26. Paris: UNESCO.

Shaffer, J. G. 1978. The later prehistoric periods. In *The archaeology of Afghanistan from earliest times to the Timurid period*, F. R. Allchin & N. Hammond (eds), 71–186. London: Academic Press.

Shao, Q. 1981. The evolution of cultivated barley. *Barley genetics* **4** [Proceedings of the 4th International Barley Genetics Symposium, Edinburgh], 22–5.

Sharif, M. & B. K. Thapar 1992. Food-producing communities in Pakistan and northern India. In *History of civilizations of Central Asia* (vol. 1), A. H. Dani & V. M. Masson (eds), 127–51. Paris: UNESCO.

Shevchenko, A. I. 1960. Towards a history of domestic animals in southern Turkmenistan. *Trudy IuTAKE* **10**, 464–77 [in Russian].

Tosi, M. 1973–4. The northeastern frontier of the ancient Near East. *Mesopotamia* **8–9**, 21–76.

Trewartha, G. T. 1960. Climates of the Earth (map). In *Goode's world atlas* (11th edn), E. B. Espenshade Jr (ed.), 8–9. Chicago: Rand McNally.

Uerpmann, H-P. 1987. *The ancient distribution of ungulate mammals in the Middle East* [Beihefte zum Tübinger Atlas des Vorderen Orients, Reihe A (Naturwissenschaften) 27]. Wiesbaden: Dr L. Reichert.

Vavilov, N. I. 1992a (1926). Centres of origin of cultivated plants. In *N. I. Vavilov: origin and geography of cultivated plants*, V. F. Dorofeyev (ed.), 22–143. Cambridge: Cambridge University Press.

— 1992b (1935). The phyto-geographical basis for plant breeding. In *N. I. Vavilov: origin and geography of cultivated plants*, V. F. Dorofeyev (ed.), 316–66. Cambridge: Cambridge University Press.

— 1992c (1940). The theory of the origin of cultivated plants after Darwin. In *N. I. Vavilov: origin and geography of cultivated plants*, V. F. Dorofeyev (ed.), 421–42. Cambridge: Cambridge University Press.

Witcombe, J. R. 1978. Two rowed and six rowed wild barley from the western Himalaya. *Euphytica* **24**, 431–4.

Zohary, D. 1989. Domestication of the Southwest Asian Neolithic crop assemblage of cereals, pulses, and flax: the evidence from the living plants. In *Foraging and farming: the evolution of plant exploitation*, D. R. Harris & G. C. Hillman (eds), 358–73. London: Unwin Hyman.

Zohary, D. & M. Hopf. 1993. *Domestication of plants in the Old World*, 2nd edn. Oxford: Oxford University Press.

CHAPTER TWENTY-TWO

The origins and spread of agriculture and pastoralism in northwestern South Asia

Richard H. Meadow

Introduction

In 1975 Sir Joseph Hutchinson summarized what was then known about the character of early South Asian plant and animal husbandry. The framework he created for his paper titled "India: local and introduced crops" (Hutchinson 1977) still stands, although the question of origins is somewhat less "obscure" than it was two decades ago. We now know that the development and spread of agriculture and pastoralism in South Asia are complex phenomena that have taken place over the course of more than 9,000 years. Within this period at least three major transformations occurred that can be related to the introduction and adoption of suites of major new crops and animals to the subcontinent. The first of these involved Southwest Asian forms, the second African and Asian species, and the third plants from the Americas. In addition to the imports, local forms of plants and animals came to be husbanded or continued to be gathered from the wild. Indeed, an important feature of South Asia is that it is one of those parts of the world where foragers and farmers lived side-by-side in many localities until quite recently.

The focus of attention in this paper is northwestern South Asia and the first two agricultural transformations, namely, those that took place between about 7500 and 5500 BC and between about 2500 and 1500 BC.[1] The period of the third transformation, from about AD 1500 onwards, is not discussed. We do not know precisely how long it took for specific crops and animals to become subsistence staples in any given region. The process may have been short in some cases, long in others, but when viewed at the scale of the whole subcontinent within a perspective of the past 11,000 years, the results of each transformation can be seen to have been nothing less than revolutionary.

Before reviewing the state of research and providing an overview of the evidence, however, it is important to follow Hutchinson's lead and emphasize that human subsistence activities are constrained by such environmental factors as timing, availability and amount of moisture, temperature range, day length, soils and topography. These affect the density, distribution and duration of vegetative growth, as well as the kinds of plants and animals that can be raised. For South Asia (Spate & Learmonth 1967, Schwartzberg 1992), the timings of floods and monsoon rains and the locations affected are of particular importance. In much of the region, the months of June through September are the wettest, with river flooding being a direct result of rainfall, although the large rivers of the north also carry snowmelt from the Himalaya. In the peninsula, on the heavy black-cotton soils, rains continue or occur later than farther north, and in the arid northwest winter and spring precipitation can be of great significance for vegetative growth. Another important factor is temperature, particularly the presence of colder weather during the winter months in the northwestern zone of alluvium. This has permitted the growth of such characteristically West Asian crops as wheat, barley, peas, lentils and flax during the cooler *rabi* period of November/December through April/May. In contrast, the Asian or African crops such as rice, and the millets that require warmth, are *kharif* crops grown in the period from May/June through October/November. The combination of warm temperatures and plentiful supplies of water is particularly important for rice cultivation, and areas with less available moisture can support the growing of millets in the same summer season. Of course, actual timings for planting and harvesting vary, depending upon the specific crop and upon local conditions that can differ significantly even within a single district.

State of research

In spite of the possibility of interesting studies on a range of questions concerning past agricultural and pastoral practices, and on relations between those and hunting and gathering, only limited bioarchaeological research was carried out in South Asia until recently, and what has been done is of uneven quality. An additional complication is that the dating of some of the key sites is unsure or debated.

Vishnu-Mittre (1989), Kajale (1991), Weber (1991, 1992) and Willcox (1992) have reviewed the archaeobotanical evidence up to the end of the 1980s, and Saraswat (1993) has carried the review into the 1990s. Vishnu-Mittre is particularly critical of the quality of the published record. He notes the need for the following: more care in the identification of remains, presentation of data, and interpretation of results; more and better comparative collections and illustrative texts; an up-to-date understanding of relevant taxonomy by all analysts; studying materials from "dependable archaeological provenance" and the precise dating of those contexts; and the systematic use of fine screening and flotation to ensure more complete and uniform recovery of remains. Taken at its most negative, Vishnu-Mittre's article can be seen as a general condemnation of much past work in archaeobotany in South Asia and leaves the non-specialist (including the author of this essay) at something of a loss about how much faith to put in the available literature. At the very least, it seems necessary to use general summaries such as those of Kajale (1974, 1991) with considerable circumspection.

The same criticisms and listing of needs can be made for the study of animal remains. The most comprehensive summary of such remains identified from South Asian sites to the end of the 1980s is that of B. P. Sahu, but "based primarily on the published faunal reports" (Sahu 1988: 17) it is largely uncritical of those materials. A more evaluative review is that of Rissman (1989), whereas the summaries of Thomas (1989, 1992) should also be mentioned. One helpful feature of many faunal reports from South Asia is the inclusion of photographs of selected bones and teeth. These assist the specialist (including this author) in determining whether identifications are correct or not. Unfortunately, in some cases they are not. The most common problems relate to distinguishing different forms of bovid (e.g. *Ovis/Capra* from *Gazella/Antilope*; *Bos/Bubalus* from *Boselaphus*; and each genus in a pair from the other), and even bovids from cervids. Such difficulties reflect the absence of suitable comparative collections, texts and expertise, and they lead to incorrect understandings of patterns of animal exploitation. What has proved to be a particularly unfortunate analytical practice has been to use bones identified from one site to help identify those from another. One suspects that similar methods may be employed in archaeobotanical studies as well, and although there is nothing inherently wrong with the practice when the material has been correctly identified in the first place, it does provide the means to perpetuate gross error into subsequent generations of analyses.

In spite of these disquieting realities, we continue to develop a picture of agricultural and pastoral adaptations in South Asia through the course of the Holocene. It is hardly more than a sketch, and an enormous quantity of high-quality work over an immense area is needed to complete the outlines and fill in the details.

A definitional and conceptual interlude

There are many definitions of the terms "agriculture" and "pastoralism," but more general ones are probably the best for our purposes. Thus, agriculture can be seen as the practice of growing crops, whereas pastoralism involves raising livestock. Anyone who sows or harvests domesticated plants is involved in agriculture, just as anyone who husbands grazing or browsing animals is a pastoralist. Under an even broader definition of agriculture, pastoralism can be included, but here it is useful to restrict the term to crop-growing. The development of agriculture and pastoralism involved the domestication of plants and animals, respectively. Domestication required a change in human attitudes and practices from those orientated towards gathering or hunting for immediate (or even deferred) consumption to those actively directed towards ensuring the reproduction of subsequent generations. The effect of the domestication process was to create behavioural, morphological and eventually genetic changes in the targeted plants and animals of a kind that made those forms greatly (if not always irreversibly) dependent upon humans for nourishment and especially for reproduction. On the cultural side, structural changes in the nature of socioeconomic relationships within and between human populations were facilitated by the ability of individuals or small groups to obtain and then maintain control over alienable subsistence resources that were very restricted in number and over the means for their production and reproduction. Thus, foundations for the development of increasing social differentiation and hierarchy were set. (For more detailed discussion and references see, for example, Harris 1989 and Meadow 1989a.)

Perennial questions in the archaeology of Eurasia are whether agricultural and pastoral origins were single or multi-centred phenomena and whether the spread of subsistence practices based on domestic taxa over vast areas reflects indigenous adoptions, colonizations, or both. The queries as posed here are stark and simplistic and some might argue meaningless. Yet they and their more elaborated cousins continue to generate much discussion and useful research. In the South Asian context (as noted above) agriculture and pastoralism involve both imported and indigenous taxa. How and whence were the imported taxa brought? Were local taxa domesticated as the result of experience with imported relatives or quite independently? Did intentional experimentation play a role? Were the adoption of agriculture and of pastoralism all-or-nothing affairs or can we define multidimensional continua of subsistence strategies with each consuming unit, however defined, falling at a different point? And a methodological question – are all consuming units equally visible in the archaeological record of the different periods, or do accident, intellectual history, archaeological practice, and taphonomic and site-formation processes affect the configuration of our understanding of pre- and protohistoric subsistence practices in South Asia? Although none of these questions is answered here satisfactorily, an attempt is made to indicate possible directions for future research.

The beginnings of agriculture in South Asia

What is probably the earliest evidence to date of agriculture and pastoralism in South Asia comes from the site of Mehrgarh situated on the North Kachi Plain at the foot of the Bolan Pass in the zone of transition between the Iranian Plateau and the Indus Basin (Fig. 22.1). Here on the easternmost margin of the Southwest Asian upland, a barley-dominated agricultural economy with some wheat has been defined, beginning in the earliest levels of the site (Costantini 1984). The evidence is in the form of impressions in mudbricks together with some charred remains of plant parts found within bricks that had been accidentally fired. Charcoal of any kind is rare in the aceramic-neolithic (Period IA) levels at Mehrgarh, and the eight samples that have been dated have provided results ranging from less than 4000 bc to greater than 8000 BC. Early ceramic-neolithic Period IB is rather more securely dated, to c. 5300–4700 BC (seven calibrated determinations), and therefore dates going back into the seventh millennium do not seem out of place for the 11 or more building levels of Period IA (Meadow 1993).

Dominating the plant assemblage of Mehrgarh Period I is naked six-row barley (*Hordeum vulgare* subsp. *vulgare* var. *nudum*) (more than 90 per cent of the seeds and imprints identified). Domestic hulled six-row barley (*H. vulgare* subsp. *vulgare*) and wild and domestic hulled two-row barley (*H. vulgare* subsp. *spontaneum* and *H. vulgare* subsp. *distichum*, respectively) are present in much smaller amounts (Costantini 1984, using the nomenclature of Zohary & Hopf 1988). The naked-barley grains even from the earliest levels are sphaerococcoid in form with "a short compact spike with shortened internodes and small rounded seeds. These characteristics, which in the aceramic Neolithic (Period I) can be ascribed to cultivated but perhaps

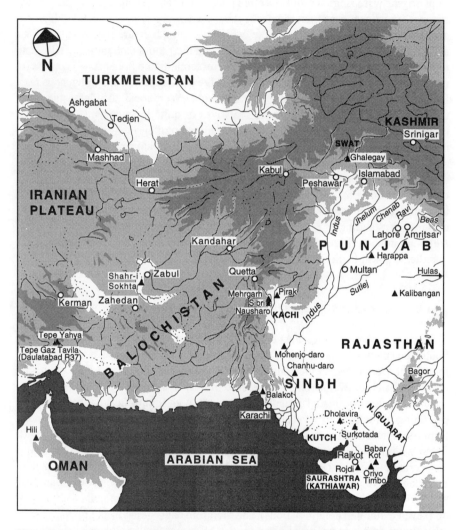

Figure 22.1 Northwestern South Asia, showing the location of the archaeological sites mentioned in the text.

not completely domesticated plants, are very marked in charred barley seeds of the subsequent Period II and III" (Costantini 1984: 29, 31). This domestic "shot" form, which Costantini calls *Hordeum sphaerococcum*, has been identified at sites of later periods in both Central and South Asia (Costantini 1990, Costantini & Costantini-Biasini 1985, 1986). As for wild barley, Zohary (1989: Fig. 22.2) shows that its distribution today, in "more isolated populations, usually of weedy forms," extends southeastwards to near Quetta at the head of the Bolan Pass. It seems possible, therefore, that the low proportion of truly wild forms in the Mehrgarh samples could be field weeds, and it may be significant that wild barley does not seem to have been identified from any deposits of a later period in South Asia.

Although there is a possibility that local wild barleys could have been brought under cultivation in the Mehrgarh area, this is much less likely for wheat. There has been no morphologically wild wheat identified in any South Asian macrobotanical assemblage. Present in very low proportions in the Mehrgarh IA samples are domestic einkorn (hulled: *Triticum monococcum*), domestic emmer (hulled: *T. turgidum* subsp. *dicoccum*), and a free-threshing form that Costantini (1984: 31) states "can be referred to as *Triticum durum*." By Period II (mid-fifth millennium), "the morphology of the seeds, although being within the range of variation of the tetraploid *Triticum durum*, shows characteristics of small-seeded forms. Not only does the morphology of the tetraploid wheat, which is probably dominant in Period II, seem to shift towards a sphaerococcoid form, but the hexaploid form dominant from Period V onwards also has a remarkable proportion of *Triticum sphaerococcum*" (Costantini 1984: 32). Indeed, by the Harappan period (third millennium), three forms of hexaploid wheat dominate in the region – what Costantini (1990) calls *Triticum aestivum*, *T. compactum* and *T. sphaerococcum* (or *T. aestivum* subsp. *vulgare*, *compactum* and *sphaerococcum* following Zohary & Hopf 1988). These wheats, and especially the last – shot wheat – have been identified at sites throughout South Asia from the Vale of Kashmir to the Deccan Plateau and east to the Ganga Valley in Bihar (Kajale 1991, Lone et al. 1993).

From their first cultivation in the region, barley and wheat continued to be the principal food grains of northwestern South Asia through the third millennium. Costantini (1990: 330) has made the point that the five forms of wheat and three forms of barley identified from the third millennium site of Nausharo – situated near Mehrgarh in the North Kachi Plain – indicate the existence of a large genetic pool that was being tapped within the context of a sophisticated agricultural system exploiting "all areas suitable for tilling." This fits well with our current understanding of prehistoric and early historic agricultural practices. These practices did not employ major irrigation works, but used for fields the margins of backswamps and oxbow lakes, together with periodically inundated areas where floodwater or runoff with its accompanying silts could be trapped using raised earthen or stone walls (*sailaba* agriculture). In addition, small canals and temporary diversion dams could be used to distribute water as needed from lakes, tanks (reservoirs), or even gently flowing channels. In the Indus Valley, major floods usually occur in the summer (July–September) when the monsoon rains add runoff to rivers just beginning to recede from having carried snowmelt from the northern mountains. Thus, a winter (*rabi*) cropping pattern for cereals decreases the possibility of fields being flooded by the rivers before harvest. In addition, as noted previously, winter rains in the northwestern part of the subcontinent provide essential supplemental moisture.

The prehistory of other crops that came to be part of the ancient South Asian *rabi* agricultural complex is even more poorly known than that of wheat and barley. Costantini (1990) has identified *Lens culinaris* (lentil) and *Linum usitatissimum* (flax/linseed) from mid- to late third millennium levels at Nausharo. Far to the southeast, in central Gujarat near Rajkot, Weber (1991: 23, 80–81) has noted the presence of a few charred seeds of *Lens esculenta* [=*L. culinaris*] (tentative identification) and *Linum* sp. from contemporary deposits at Rojdi. Cultivation of both lentils and linseed is known to be of considerable antiquity in Southwest Asia where they were probably domesticated (Zohary & Hopf 1988, Zohary 1989 and in Ch. 9 in this volume). They thus join wheat and probably barley as imported crops, although when they first arrived is not known. Also probably brought into South Asia were peas (*Pisum* sp.), which have been noted from Late Harappan/Early Historic deposits at Rojdi (Weber 1991) as well as from Harappan-period levels at Kalibangan (Vishnu-Mittre & Savithri 1982), Chanhu-daro (Mackay 1943: 250) and Harappa (Vats 1940: 467) (Fig. 22.1). The Chanhu-daro and Harappa identifications of *Pisum*, together with those of *Brassica* sp. and *Sesamum* sp., are now more than half a century old and are undocumented by photographs or detailed descriptions. They thus require modern substantiation, although all forms are well attested by the second millennium at other sites in South Asia, as is *Cicer arietinum* (chickpea), which Vishnu-Mittre & Savithri (1982) have reported from third millennium Kalibangan.

Important crops that are likely to have been native to South Asia include cotton (*Gossypium* sp.), gram bean (*Vigna* sp., previously sometimes classified as *Phaseolus* sp.), and dates (*Phoenix dactylifera*). Cotton was probably grown as a perennial, as it has been in parts of western South Asia even down to modern times (Hutchinson et al. 1947). Gram beans of different kinds can be planted and harvested throughout the year as a garden crop. Dates grow in areas where there are no killing frosts and are harvested in the summer. Another summer crop that is attested at least by the beginning of the third millennium are grapes (*Vitis* sp.). Costantini (1984: 32) notes that the pips identified at Mehrgarh (from Period V onwards) are clearly domestic and confirm "that grapes were introduced into the area following the development of cultivation techniques elsewhere."

Seeds ("stones") of dates have been identified from Period IB and II levels (ceramic neolithic) at Mehrgarh as well as from contemporary sixth millennium deposits at Tepe Gaz Tavila near Daulatabad south of Kerman in southeastern Iran (Costantini 1985). These are all single specimens, and although their contexts seem secure, they have not been directly dated to prove their antiquity. A much larger number of date stones has been identified from Nausharo, however, confirming the earlier evidence from Mohenjo-daro that, by the third millennium, dates were exploited in areas such as Sindh, southern Punjab and southern Balochistan, where they are commonly grown (Costantini 1990). Dates travel well, however, and thus it is not surprising to find their stones in sites situated in regions beyond where they are harvested.

Cotton presents a most interesting problem. It has long been supposed, because of specimens of cotton cloth preserved in the corrosion products of copper alloy and silver artefacts from Mohenjo-daro, that the fibres from a species of this plant were first exploited in the Indus Valley at least by the third millennium (Gulati & Turner 1928; Gulati in Mackay 1938: 591–4; Hutchinson et al. 1947). These findings stood in isolation until Costantini (1984) identified seeds of *Gossypium* sp. from Period IIB (later ceramic neolithic, *c.* 5000 BC) at Mehrgarh. He termed the find "perplexing" and has not elaborated on his identifications since that time. In 1994 Alison Betts et al. reported on cotton fibres adhering to textile impressions in lime plaster that were directly dated to between 4450 and 3000 BC from what may have been a pastoral camp in eastern Jordan. This now stands as the earliest evidence for cotton fibre, and its location far to the west of its previously presumed locus of first use reopens the whole question of the origin of cultivation of this important fibre and oil plant.

Hutchinson et al. (1947: 69–70) noted that although "cotton was first used in the Indus valley, the cytogenetic evidence appears to be conclusive that the wild relatives of the earliest cultivated species are to be found among the African and Arabian **Anomala**, and not among the African, Arabian and Indian **Stocksiana** . . . It appears, therefore, that the progenitors of the early cottons of the Indus valley must have been introduced from southern Arabia or north eastern Africa" [bold face as in original]. This observation has been repeated and amplified in subsequent publications (e.g. Phillips 1976, Zohary & Hopf 1988) and takes on particular significance when considered in light of the introduction to South Asia of some *kharif* cereal grains ("millets") from their African homeland. By the early 1970s, however, a dissenting view had arisen that now seems to dominate the thinking of many specialists (Santhanam & Hutchinson 1974). This view agrees that, although there are major chromosomal differences that are impediments to the interbreeding of African and Indian cottons, these probably did not occur after the domestication of the African form (*Gossypium herbaceum*). Instead "*Gossypium* geneticists now generally prefer to postulate ancient natural divergence in the wild and independent domestication of the two species and perhaps even multiple domestications of different wild forms of *G. arboreum* [Indian cotton]" (Sauer 1993: 100).

Cotton provides an example of the continuing debate over single and multiple origins for domesticated crops and animals. Stated simplistically, those who advocate single origins prefer to see one unbroken ramifying thread of antecedents to descendants from the time of the earliest domestication to today. Increasing variability would have occurred under conditions of intentional or unintentional human selection in the context of the exploitation of habitats that were increasingly diverse and marginal to the preferred habitat of the single circumscribed wild ancestral population. Plants and animals came to these habitats because people took them there. In contrast, those who advocate multiple origins would not necessarily deny the existence of a ramifying thread or the role of humans in transporting domestic forms, but would argue that there were originally many of these threads that intertwined to form a broad belt. Within the fabric of this belt, multiple domestications, introgressions, hybridizations, replacements of one form by another, and extinctions of forms have all occurred. In this second scenario there is room for independent invention and for the spread of ideas and techniques without necessitating transport of the plants and animals themselves. In most areas of the world within the presumed natural range of possible wild ancestors it is not yet possible to reach a conclusion on which if either is a more useful perspective, because we lack assemblages that directly reveal the transition from hunting–gathering to cropping–herding. This is certainly the case for South Asia, where even Mehrgarh does not extend back to pre-agricultural times.

The third millennium agricultural transformation

The debate about single or multiple origins for the earliest domesticated plants is paralleled by one on later agricultural developments. Did experimentation with cultivation of some local wild forms and the intentional gathering of others continue after agriculture was initially adopted? Or should the inclusion of new domesticated or cultivated forms in one area be attributed to imports of seed stocks from another? In the South Asian context, these are continuing topics of discussion, particularly in relation to rice and the so-called "millets". The best answer is probably that both processes occurred to a greater or lesser degree depending upon the particulars of the case involved.

At the moment it appears that in the Indus Valley itself, and in foothill areas to the west and north, there was a relatively rapid shift from a predominantly *rabi* (winter-cropping) regime to one that included a major *kharif* (summer) component. These summer-crop adoptions took place at the very end of the third and into the second millennium BC, and the major cultivars were *Oryza sativa* (rice), *Panicum miliaceum* (common/proso/broomcorn millet), *Panicum sumatrense* (= *P. miliare* – little millet), *Setaria italica* (foxtail millet), *Sorghum bicolor* (*jowar*, sorghum), *Pennisetum typhoides* (= *P. glaucum*, = *P. americanum* – *bajra*, bulrush/pearl millet), and *Eleusine coracana* (*ragi*, finger millet). Some of these cereal grasses have local wild relatives in parts of South Asia, others probably do not, and the situation for a third set is debated. By 1000 BC, the domesticated forms of all of them were widespread in the northwestern part of the subcontinent as well as in Gujarat and the Deccan (cf. Kajale 1991). What is particularly interesting is that the earliest evidence for most are in areas peripheral to the core area of the urban Harappan civilization (c. 2600–1900 BC), which was centred in the alluvial areas of the Greater Indus Valley (the modern provinces of Sindh and Punjab in Pakistan, the states of Punjab, Haryana, Rajasthan (northern), and Gujarat (northwestern) in India).

The question of early rice cultivation in South Asia is discussed by Glover & Higham in Chapter 23 in this volume. There is little need to add more to their presentation, except concerning the apparently early evidence for rice at Ghalegay in the Swat region of North West Frontier Province (Pakistan). To quote Lorenzo Costantini's postscript (1987: 162) to his report on the plant remains from several sites in that valley:

> Pottery samples from Ghalegay (Periods I–III), filed by the Italian Archaeological Mission of IsMEO, were examined by the present author in October 1987 at Saidu Sharif, Swat.
>
> During the research it was possible to identify grain impressions and silicized remains of *Oryza sativa* on potsherds of Period II and III. Such identifications confirm our above-mentioned expectations, namely the possible occurrence of rice long before Period IV.
>
> According to this evidence, the rice cultivation in the Swat Valley is now already proved [sic] in the second half of the third millennium bc.

The pottery of Period II has general affinities to "late Early Harappan" or "late Kot Dijian" wares that can date as early as 2600 BC, although it is possible that these ceramics may have continued to be made much later in the northern areas than they were farther south (Shaffer & Lichtenstein 1989, Shaffer 1992). Such a possibility would be in accord with the single date for Ghalegay II which falls between 2043 and 2275 BC (calibrated, lab. no. R–378a, 1 sigma: 3760 ±55 BP).

Another report of rice comes from Harappa. Plant-opal phytolith analysis of samples from sediments, ash and pottery has led a Japanese team to identify both *Oryza* and *Eleusine* in Late Harappan Period samples (dating *c.* 2000/1900–1500 BC). In their very carefully worded report, Fujiwara et al. (1992) also note the identification of rice phytoliths in three pottery and two baked brick fragments that probably date to the Mature Harappan Period, as well as finger millet in one pottery fragment possibly of the same date. They state that the samples were too small to "give conclusive results" but that the "possible presence of rice and *Ragi* in the Mature Period should not be ruled out" (Fujiwara et al. 1992: 136; see also Pearsall et al. 1995 for an encouraging report on the use of phytoliths to identify rice in the archaeological record). Current work on the macrobotanical remains from Harappa by Steven Weber promises to provide important new data on changes in cropping systems at the end of the third millennium.

The distribution and characteristics of wild-growing rices (the annual *O. nivara* and the perennial *O. rufipogon*) in South Asia are not well documented. This fact, together with the absence of charred grains from deposits securely dated to the second half of the third millennium and earlier makes it impossible to assert unequivocally that domesticated rice (*Oryza sativa*) was grown before the second millennium. The use of wild rice, however, is a distinct possibility. The masses of domesticated rice remains documented from early second millennium levels at Pirak in the North Kachi Plain (Costantini 1979, 1981) show that rice very quickly became a staple crop even in areas where it is rarely grown today and which are likely to be outside of the zone of its wild distribution. Whether wild rice grows or could have grown in Swat also needs to be clarified. One possibility is that rice was brought to Swat from East Asia through the vast mountain massifs to the north and east which, as Stacul (1994) has so elegantly stated, "did not act as barriers, but very often corresponded to centres around which life and common traditions converged." In this scenario, domestic rice would have moved from east to west, through the mountains that border South Asia to the north, and been introduced into the lowlands from the northwest.

Just as the mountains did not act as barriers, neither did the seas. In the United Arab Emirates and Sultanate of Oman, excavators have found ceramics that were made in northwestern South Asia during the second half of the third millennium (e.g. Cleuziou & Tosi 1989, Méry 1991, Potts 1993). These demonstrate direct interaction along the Arabian Sea coast and into the Gulf, such as has long been postulated on the basis of scattered finds and a few Mesopotamian textual references. This is particularly important for our understanding of the means whereby the African crops finger millet, sorghum and pearl millet could have been introduced into South Asia (cf. Harlan 1992). That Arabia could have acted as a bridge between Africa and South Asia is supported by Costantini's identification of imprints of *Sorghum bicolor* in mudbricks from the site of Hili on the Oman Peninsula dating to *c.* 2500–2400 BC (Cleuziou & Costantini 1980), although the analyst is circumspect about making an unequivocal attribution.

Charred remains of finger millet (*Eleusine coracana*) are the single most commonly preserved seeds from Period A at Rojdi in central Saurashtra (peninsular Gujarat), where they constitute about 62 per cent of the assemblage identified by Weber (1991). Rojdi A has been dated by radiocarbon to *c.* 2500–2300 BC and thus represents a particularly early introduction of what is thought to be a crop of African origin derived from *E. coracana* subsp. *africana* (Hilu & de Wet 1976, Hilu et al. 1979, Phillipson 1993). There are some, however, who still believe in a South Asian origin (e.g. Portères 1976, Dixit et al. 1987). Also identified in Rojdi A are *Panicum sumatrense* (= *P. miliare*), *Setaria* spp. and *Hordeum* sp. (*rabi*, barley), the last represented by only 10 seeds. Of interest is the fact that barley, of West Asian origin, is not found after Rojdi A, and sorghum – like finger millet presumably an import from Africa (de Wet et al. 1976) – is not found before Rojdi C at the beginning of the second millennium, whereas pearl millet (*Pennisetum typhoides*, another African import) is not found at all. The variable distributions and quantities of the different domestic forms, together with the wide variety of wild plants attested at Rojdi, underline the potential (and probably normal) complexity of the archaeobotanical record and its formation processes, as well as of plant-exploitation practices and the history of introductions and adoptions.

If one takes the published record at face value, there appears to be a sequence of introductions from Africa spanning about 1,000 years – first finger millet followed by sorghum and then pearl millet (Possehl 1986, Kajale 1988, 1991, Weber 1989, 1991; although see Reddy 1994 for a report of a single broken charred specimen of *Pennisetum* in late third to early second millennium deposits at Babar Kot) (Fig. 22.1). But to judge by the debates that flare occasionally, identifying and distinguishing millets are not always straightforward tasks (e.g. Hilu et al. 1979, Savithri & Vishnu-Mittre 1979), and this is also true for sorghum. The identification of sorghum by Costantini (1979) for Pirak Period I (*c.* 1600 BC) is based on only three grains that are merely referred to that genus ("cf. *Sorghum* spp."). In contrast, the material from Rojdi numbers 113 seeds. But whereas the genus determination for the Rojdi sorghum seems secure, a species identification of *S. bicolor* is termed only "most likely" (Weber 1991: 93). Weber (ibid.) also notes that, as the seeds come from later levels (Rojdi C and Early Historic), they need to be directly dated to prove their antiquity.

At Hulas in western Uttar Pradesh, Saraswat (1993) has identified five charred grains as *Sorghum bicolor* from "Late Harappan" levels, dated by ceramic finds to *c.* 1700–1000 BC. Other economic plants from Hulas include rice (wild and domestic), shot wheat, bread wheat, barley, oats, finger millet, cowpea and mung (*Vigna* spp.), lentil (*Lens*), grasspea (*Lathyrus*), chickpea (*Cicer*), field pea (*Pisum*), horsegram (*Dolichos*), cotton (one charred seed), ivy gourd (*Coccinia*), pipal-tree fruit (*Ficus*), anjan grass (*Cenchrus*), walnut (*Juglans*), almond (*Prunus*) and castor (*Ricinus*). This wide range of both *rabi* and *kharif* crops is typical of second millennium sites in western India (cf. Kajale 1988, 1991) which are, relatively speaking, much better known archaeobotanically than are sites of the preceding millennia. In the territory encompassed by Pakistan, however, except for Pirak (Jarrige et al. 1979) and the Swat sites

(Stacul 1987), the second millennium is unknown archaeobotanically and not much better known archaeologically.

Complementing the so-called "African millets" at late third and second millennium sites in northwestern South Asia are the "Asian millets" *Panicum miliaceum* (broomcorn or common millet) and *Setaria italica* (foxtail millet). They are thought to have been brought in from the west, although the timing and route of entry remain poorly understood. Although both have wild relatives in the subcontinent (Savithri & Vishnu-Mittre 1978), their domestic forms are known early in the Chinese Neolithic (Crawford 1992). Broomcorn millet is also well attested in the Neolithic of Europe (summarized by Zohary & Hopf 1988) and even in southeastern Iran at sixth millennium Tepe Gaz Tavila (Daulatabad R37) and in third millennium levels of Tepe Yahya (Costantini & Costantini Biasini 1985, Meadow 1986a). So far, however, it is not reported from sites of the Indus alluvium in the third millennium, although this may be attributable to unsystematic collecting protocols and dearth of analysis. Foxtail millet is also attested in Rojdi A, although there are not many seeds of it preserved until second millennium Rojdi C. Wild forms of *Setaria* have been identified throughout the Rojdi sequence, underlining once again the need to consider the roles that local wild forms of domestic species may have played.

One millet that is likely to have been brought into cultivation locally in South Asia is *Panicum sumatrense* (previously called *P. miliare*), the wild form of which occurs in northern India and southeastern Asia (Purseglove 1972: 201). This "little millet" is the second most commonly occurring seed after *Eleusine* in Rojdi A and it continues to occur throughout the Rojdi sequence. It is also one of the most commonly represented forms at the late third and early second millennium sites of Oriyo Timbo and Babar Kot, both located east of Rojdi in the Kathiawar Peninsula (Fig. 22.1). In her study of this material and of modern South Asian agricultural practices, Reddy (1994) notes that both common millet and little millet can be grown successfully under very poor conditions and also as opportunistic crops on newly formed flood deposits immediately after the monsoon rains. Because it lacks the compact heads or ears characteristic of sorghum and pearl millet which can be easily cut off the stalk individually, *Panicum* is traditionally harvested like wheat and barley, that is, in sheaves. This practice has significance for subsequent processing of the grain and may also help to account for its relatively early cultivation on the margins of an area where the agriculture was long dominated by the Southwest Asian cereals.

In 1986 Gregory Possehl proposed the following hypothesis:

> . . . within the areas of peninsular India shadowed by the monsoon, village farming communities developed when a set of cultivars adapted to a summer growing season was integrated into the subsistence regime. As long as wheat and barley were the only food grains available to the cultivator, sedentariness was at best a marginal option in these areas . . . Now, with plants adapted to the summer monsoon conditions, the relative balances within the subsistence regimes of peninsular India were altered, and settled agriculture took on new potential. (Possehl 1986: 249)

The plants involved comprise the millets, sorghum and rice. To grow the last effectively may require extensive investments in fields and canals. The opposite is true of the first two, which are among the least demanding of all dry-farmed warm-weather cereal crops. And, as noted, all three have wild relatives native to South Asia, any of which may have been exploited for millennia by hunter–gatherer populations. The plant-use practices of these peoples, however, are very poorly known, and this topic remains one of the most important on the research agenda for South Asia.

Furthermore, as Jarrige (1985) and Meadow (1989b) have pointed out, the cultivation of *kharif* crops may not only have opened up new areas for extensive farming on the periphery of the Indus Valley, but, on the alluvium itself, it may have made productive lands that were marginal to *rabi* crop agriculture. It is important to note, however, that the (admittedly poor) evidence to date permits the suggestion that not until the end of the Harappan Civilization were *kharif* cereals exploited in the Indus alluvial zone, even though they had been known for some 500 years in areas around its margin. This in turn leads to questions about the nature of Harappan society and agricultural practices, the control of productive resources, and ultimately the deurbanization of the Indus Valley at the beginning of the second millennium. Continuing analyses of archaeobotanical remains from Nausharo (by Lorenzo Costantini), Harappa (by Steven Weber) and contemporary sites in India (by M. D. Kajale, K. S. Saraswat and others) promise a fuller understanding of Harappan period agricultural practices in the near future.

Pastoralism

Pastoralism involves the breeding and raising of grazing or browsing animals. This may involve intensive or extensive management, and in South Asia today (and historically) it is carried out by people with a continuum of lifestyles from completely sedentary to completely mobile, even within the same community. In the context of northwestern South Asia, the principal pastoral animals today are domestic cattle (*Bos indicus* and some *Bos taurus*), water buffalo (*Bubalus bubalis*), sheep (*Ovis aries*), goat (*Capra hircus*), camel (*Camelus* spp.), horse (*Equus caballus*), donkey (*Equus asinus*), and equid hybrids (mules and hinnies). It is also possible to include pigs (*Sus scrofa*) as pastoral animals, although one might better describe their feeding behaviour as foraging or rooting than grazing or browsing. And although there are *Sus* remains in faunal records throughout the prehistoric and protohistoric periods, there is as yet no evidence for pigs having been domestic animals (Meadow 1989c).

Our knowledge of the earliest use of domestic animals in South Asia, like that for plants, is based on the excavations at Mehrgarh (Meadow 1981, 1984a, 1993). This site, situated on the North Kachi Plain at the foot of the mountainous western edge of the Indus alluvium, is at an ecotone on the margins of foothill, plain and riverine environments. The wild animal remains that dominate the earliest levels of "aceramic neolithic" Period IA reflect this situation with 12 forms of "big game" represented: wild sheep (*Ovis orientalis*) and goats (*Capra aegagrus*) from the hills, gazelle (*Gazella bennetti*) from the foothills and plains, wild asses (*Equus hemionus*) and blackbuck (*Antilope cervicapra*) from the drier plains, and nilgai (*Boselaphus tragocamelus*), large deer (*Cervus* (?) *duvauceli*), smaller deer (*Axis* (?) *axis*), boar (*Sus scrofa*), water buffalo (*Bubalus arnee*), wild cattle (*Bos primigenius* or *Bos namadicus*), and possibly elephant (*Elaphas maximus*) from better-watered areas.

The wild sheep, goat, cattle and buffalo all comprise potential ancestral stock for the domestic forms. To judge from the occurrence of five kids in each of two burials, however, goats are likely to have been domesticated already in the first levels of Period IA dating to the early seventh or late eighth millennium. The domestic status of at least some of the goats is confirmed by the presence of the remains of relatively small sub-adult or adult animals in contemporary trash deposits. A decrease in body size of the grown or nearly grown animal is one characteristic of early domestic bovids (cf. Uerpmann 1979 for sheep and goat, Grigson 1989 for cattle). Goats are also the single most common animal in the Period IA assemblages after gazelle.

Through the course of Period I at Mehrgarh, the remains of sheep and cattle came increasingly to dominate the faunal assemblages of the successive strata, while the animals represented grew smaller in body size. By the "ceramic neolithic", cattle bones in particular make up well over 50 per cent of the remains recovered from Period IIA deposits that date to the second half of the sixth millennium. This coincident pair of trends – increasing representation and decreasing body size – was found to occur in two widely separated deep soundings and it strongly supports an hypothesis of local domestication. In addition, both osteological and figurine evidence indicate that zebu (humped) cattle (*Bos indicus*) were present and likely to have been the dominant form (Meadow 1984a). These findings (first published in Meadow 1981) confirmed proposals by others with regard to the indigenous origin of South Asian zebu (reviewed in Grigson 1985). In the mid-1990s the indigenous domestication of cattle in eastern Iran or South Asia from local wild stock was corroborated by the work of geneticists, who through examination of mitochondrial DNA have suggested that the divergence of the maternal ancestral lines for zebu and taurine cattle took place perhaps three-quarters to one million years ago (Loftus et al. 1994).

The situation with sheep is not so straightforward. Cytogenetic studies suggest that modern domestic forms are all descended from a single ancestor related to the current Southwest Asian population of *Ovis orientalis* (reviewed in Uerpmann 1987). This would seem to preclude a separate origin for South Asian domestic forms, unless the latter were replaced more recently by imported breeds (Meadow 1989d). Gradual decrease in the size of sheep at Mehrgarh continued well into "chalcolithic" Period III (fifth millennium) and then stabilized with relatively small animals being the norm at least into the second millennium in that region (at the sites of Sibri and Nausharo situated near Mehrgarh: Fig. 22.1). At Harappa in (Pakistani) Punjab, however, very large domestic sheep occur in third millennium Harappan period deposits that are contemporary with those at Nausharo and Sibri (Meadow 1991). This upward shift in the body size parallels a more or less contemporary one in Mesopotamia where the selective breeding of sheep is documented historically (Meadow: unpublished data compiled from published sources).

Metrical data also suggest the existence of different domestic populations (or breeds) of cattle (*Bos*) in northwestern South Asia in the third millennium (Meadow 1991). This is hardly surprising as, by that time, cattle had become the dominant domestic form at settlement sites excavated throughout most of the region (Sahu 1988). Indeed, cattle are as much a hallmark of the protohistoric and historic faunal collections in South Asia as they are of those from much of Europe, sites in the intervening areas being dominated by the remains of sheep and goats.

Although wild cattle probably existed through much of the subcontinent, wild sheep and goats seem to have been confined to the extreme western part on the eastern lowland margin of the Iranian Plateau. Thus, finds of these small bovids on sites farther east and southeast are presumed to reflect movement of the pastoral economy. But the mechanisms and timing of such a movement remain poorly understood, and the possibility of multiple local domestications of cattle (*Bos*) has never really been considered. In part, of course, this is linked to the poorly developed nature of our understanding of the earliest village-farming communities in these areas. Also imperfectly understood, however, are the nature and degree of use of domesticates (both plant and animal) by the inhabitants of so-called "mesolithic" or "microlithic" communities, which in the Indian context can date anywhere in the Holocene.

A good example of the problem is provided by the important "mesolithic" site of Bagor in southeastern Rajasthan (Fig. 22.1). Shah (cited in *Indian archaeology 1967– 68: a review*: 42) initially examined the faunal remains and suggested that only wild animals were exploited, at least in Phase I (somewhere between 5000 and 2800 BC). Alur (cited in Misra 1973: 105–7) subsequently studied part of the collection and identified sheep and goat as the most commonly represented taxa and domestic cattle as being present. Finally, Thomas (1975) added water buffalo to the list and continued to insist that domestic sheep/goat were the most frequently occurring forms in all periods (I–III – "mesolithic" to early historic).

This identification of sheep and goat (and to a lesser extent cattle) at Bagor in particular, but also at other similar sites, has led to the suggestion that domestic animals were adopted quite early by non-agricultural peoples who thus became hunter–pastoralist–gatherers. The fact that Shah identified only wild taxa has never been fully discussed, perhaps because no complete (or even partial) report by her own hand ever appeared. The problem lies in the fact that gazelle, blackbuck, sheep and goat all have morphologically similar skeletons, and the teeth especially can be hard to differentiate in the absence of a comparative collection and without careful comparative osteological work of a kind that has been largely absent in the case of South Asian bovids. That there may be a problem is demonstrated by examination of photographs in the Inamgaon report (Thomas 1988) where many bones labelled as coming from sheep or goat seem more likely to be from blackbuck or gazelle. Currently, comparative collections are being assembled and osteological expertise is being developed in India. The concerned scholars are aware of the problems, and re-analysis of collections is taking place. The above observations are made only to alert the reader to the fact that we can expect re-evaluation of the situation on the subcontinent in the near future.

If there are difficulties in distinguishing the bones of small bovids, the situation is equally problematical for large bovids including cattle (*Bos*), water buffalo and nilgai. This has hampered our understanding of the domestication of the water buffalo in particular. Occasional remains of what are presumably the wild form have been identified from Mehrgarh Period IA deposits (Meadow 1981). In Period III at that site (*c.* 4800–

3300 BC), a complete horncore was uncovered; it is long and sweeping, but the domestic or wild status of its original owner cannot be determined because there are also long-horned domestic forms (Meadow 1989c and personal observation). By the Harappan period, however, domestic water buffalo appear to have been kept, at least to judge from a small and also tightly curled horncore from the site of Balakot near the coast northwest of Karachi, Pakistan (Meadow 1979a). Buffalo were also hunted, as is attested in the iconography of the Harappan period (unpublished data from current excavations at Harappa). Their remains have also been identified from several other pre- and proto-historic sites in northwestern South Asia (compiled in Sahu 1988), but their wild or domestic status is not clear. As with the small bovids, current comparative osteological work promises to provide a more solid foundation for future research.

In sum, by the end of the third millennium the herding of domestic water buffalo, goats, sheep, and especially cattle, characterized village agricultural and urban sites throughout northwestern South Asia. In addition, the identification of sherd scatters, located in zones marginal to agriculture, as the remains of temporary pastoral encampments has been proposed by several scholars (especially Mughal, e.g. 1991). None of these sites has been excavated, however, and, as noted, the possible keeping of animals by presumed hunter–gatherers remains an open question, as does the relationship such communities may have maintained with their settled neighbours, particularly in places such as Rajasthan and North Gujarat. What also remains to be studied in a comprehensive fashion is what products besides meat were supplied by domestic stock. The evidence of miniature terracotta bullock-cart frames (from all Harappan sites in Punjab and Sindh) and yokes (from Harappan period levels at Nausharo: J-F. Jarrige: pers. comm.) suggests that cattle were harnessed for draft. Whether they (and water buffalo) were also used for milk is not yet confirmed, nor is the presumed use of sheep for wool.

By the middle of the second millennium, two and possibly three new species had been introduced into the animal economies of South Asia. These are the camel (probably *Camelus bactrianus*), the donkey (*Equus asinus*) and the true horse (*Equus caballus*). None of them is traditionally used principally as a food animal, but all are commonly employed for transport and communications. Some of the earliest evidence for all three comes from the site of Pirak (Fig. 22.1) located in the North Kachi Plain some distance from Mehrgarh (Meadow 1979b, 1984b, 1986b, 1987). Whereas remains of both of the equids and of camel come only from Period III (early first millennium BC; almost no faunal remains are available from the earlier levels), figurines of two-humped camels, horses and riders are present from Period I, probably dating between 1800 and 1500 BC (Jarrige et al. 1979). Additional reasonably well dated evidence from northwestern South Asia includes depictions of horses painted on pottery from the Swat Valley (Stacul 1987: fig. 46). Less sure is a camel skeleton from Mohenjo-daro, which may possibly date to the end of the Harappan period (Meadow 1984b) and bones of both horse and camel from the old excavations at Mohenjo-daro and Harappa (Sewell 1931, Nath 1962) – the context of none of which is secure. There are no convincing depictions of either horse or camel in Harappan iconography, and the suggestion of Shaffer (1988) that the camel was an animal important for overland trade in the second half of the third millennium does not stand close scrutiny of the evidence available to date.

Several claims have been made for the presence of the domestic horse in South Asia before the beginning of the second millennium. These are reviewed in Sahu (1988: 159–60, 224), but most cannot be substantiated because of the absence of proper documentation. The latter is essential because of the presence in northwestern South Asia of the khur (*Equus hemionus*). Bones of a large khur will overlap in size with those of a small horse, and bones of a small khur will overlap in size with those of a donkey. One collection that has been documented and discussed extensively is that from Surkotada, a late third and early second millennium site in Kutch, Gujarat, India (Joshi 1990, Sharma 1974, 1990, 1993, Meadow 1987, Bökönyi in press, Meadow & Patel in press). Although the author of this paper does not find identifications of true horse at Surkotada to be convincing, the prolonged and sometimes highly technical debate shows that study of this material is not always straightforward, and we face with equids the same problems as we do with small bovids and bovines.

Like wheat and barley, horses, donkeys and camels came into South Asia from the northwest. But like sorghum, rice and some of the millets, they became widespread only by the second millennium, complementing the existing complex of domestic animals and helping to change the economic and social face of the subcontinent. Horses were useful for transport, communication, raiding and warfare, although keeping them has always required special skills under conditions of extreme heat and humidity. Historically most horses were kept by the elite, whereas the donkey was very much a work animal of the village, especially in the foothill and hill regions of the northwest, where it is likely to have been most common. Camels have traditionally been used for long-distance trade and for carrying the households of transhumants, roles that they probably took over from *Bos*. This latter supposition is difficult to document, but cattle are still used by some peoples in eastern Baluchistan to carry their worldly possessions (including poultry and very young kids and lambs) from lowlands to highlands and back again (Meadow: personal observation). The early camels were probably of the two-humped variety (Meadow 1984b), supplemented only in the later second and first millennia, if not later, by dromedaries (cf. Köhler-Rollefson in Ch. 15 in this volume), with which they were cross-bred to produce a particularly strong caravan animal. This remains a topic that needs to be more thoroughly investigated in the South Asian context.

Conclusion

Our understanding of the origins and spread of agriculture and pastoralism in northwestern South Asia has advanced somewhat since the 1975 summary of Hutchinson (1977). In particular, the sites of the North Kachi Plain (Mehrgarh, Nausharo, Sibri, Pirak) have provided a long sequence of plant and animal remains reaching back to nearly the beginnings of agriculture and pastoralism in the region. In addition, many sites from across the vast expanse of the subcontinent have been excavated or had material examined in an increasingly detailed and systematic fashion.

We now accept that neither mountains nor seas were ever barriers to communication or to the movement of materials and peoples. Interaction with the regions to the northwest, west and southwest was continuous, although of varying intensity, and it provided the means for the introduction of new plants, people and animals. But in many ways our knowledge of northwestern South Asia is better than it is for the eastern Iranian Plateau, with the result that it is difficult to investigate the nature of exchange, infiltration, migration or colonization. A related problem is that the first third of the Holocene is unknown archaeologically over vast areas of Southwest and South Asia, and thus peoples' interactions with local plants and animals are unknown during the key formative period.

In the South Asian context, "mesolithic" or "microlithic" sites are recognized in Rajasthan, North Gujarat, the Gangetic plain and south into peninsular India (Possehl & Rissman 1992). Although these form part of a long tradition beginning in the early Holocene, few have been extensively excavated, carefully dated or thoroughly studied. What little we know confirms an expected intimate acquaintance with local wild animal and plant resources. But how these resources may have been exploited and whether any were locally husbanded are questions that have yet to be investigated. One has the suspicion that in better-watered areas of the subcontinent there was little impetus initially to develop or adopt agriculture and pastoralism, that it took colonization to effect such changes, and that even then they were only unevenly adopted by indigenous populations, much as appears to have been the case in Africa.

At settlement sites in or on the margins of the Indus alluvium, where the remains of domesticates dominate the plant and animal assemblages, wild forms continue to be found. These may have derived from the settled peoples themselves or from others who lived on the margins and still hunted and gathered. For the latter we have no evidence. Few "mesolithic" or "microlithic" sites have been identified in these northwestern areas, even though we must assume that they were inhabited during the late Pleistocene and early Holocene. This is probably a problem of site visibility as well as a reflection of reconnaissance techniques.

We should expect the relationships between peoples to be dynamic and fluctuating. What we have currently for South Asia in general and for the northwestern portion in particular is a patchy archaeological framework with little depth of understanding of any single region, let alone for the entire area. The study of plant and animal remains continues to be rather haphazard and the results are only now beginning to be integrated into the broader archaeological picture. Questions of archaeological provenance and sample integrity, particularly critical in archaeobotanical studies, are also just beginning to be addressed, with the work of Weber (1991) and Reddy (1994) being important examples. These latter reflect a level of sophistication in analysis and interpretation that is new to South Asia and that, if continued, promises to transform our understanding of agricultural practices. The greatest need now for those who analyze plant and animal remains in the South Asian context is that they understand the implications of their work for the archaeology of the region. This demands that results of analyses are not just presented but are critically evaluated, interpreted and presented in such a way that archaeologists understand their worth and significance.

Note

1. All dates referred to in this paper are derived from calibrated radiocarbon date ranges and are therefore given as BC or BP. When a specific calibrated date is cited, the laboratory number is also given.

Acknowledgements

Thanks are due many colleagues who assisted in the preparation of this paper by their analyses and by support for my work. I wish particularly to acknowledge the contributions of L. Costantini, the late G. F. Dales, J-F. and C. Jarrige, M. D. Kajale, C. C. Lamberg-Karlovsky, J. M. Kenoyer, H. M-L. Miller, A. Patel, G. Possehl, P. Rissman, S. Reddy, J. Shaffer and S. Weber. For his invitation to the 1993 conference, for arranging a travel grant, for his editorial expertise, and for his encouragement, great patience and good humour, I own an enormous debt to David Harris. Special thanks also to Mary Moloney for implementing editorial changes and last-minute additions to the manuscript.

References

Betts, A., K. van der Borg, A. de Jong, C. McClintock, M. van Strydonck 1994. Early cotton in north Arabia. *Journal of Archaeological Science* **21**, 489–99.

Bökönyi, S. in press. Horse remains from Surkotada. *Harappan Studies* **2**.

Cleuziou, S. & L. Costantini 1980. Premiers éléments sur l'agriculture protohistorique de l'Arabie orientale. *Paléorient* **6**, 245–51.

Cleuziou, S. & M. Tosi 1989. The southeastern frontier of the ancient Near East. In *South Asian archaeology 1985*, K. Frifelt & P. Sørensen (eds), 15–47. London: Curzon Press.

Costantini, L. 1979. Plant remains at Pirak, Pakistan. In *Fouilles de Pirak* (vol. 1), J-F. Jarrige & M. Santoni (compilers), 326–33. Paris: Diffusion de Boccard.

— 1981. Palaeoethnobotany at Pirak: a contribution to the 2nd millennium bc. agriculture of the Sibi–Kacchi Plain, Pakistan. In *South Asian archaeology 1979*, H. Härtel (ed.), 271–7. Berlin: Dietrich Reimer.

— 1984. The beginning of agriculture in the Kachi Plain: the evidence of Mehrgarh. In *South Asian archaeology 1981*, B. Allchin (ed.), 29–33. Cambridge: Cambridge University Press.

— 1985. Considerazioni su alcuni reperti di palma da dattero e sul centro di origine e l'area di coltivazione della *Phoenix dactylifera* L. In *Orientalia Iosephi Tucci memoriae dicata* (vol. 1), G. Gnoli & L. Lanciotti (eds), 209–17. Rome: Istituto Italianio per il Medio ed Estremo Orientale.

— 1987. Vegetal remains. Appendix B in *Prehistoric and protohistoric Swat, Pakistan*, G. Stacul (compiler), 155–65. Rome: Istituto Italiano per il Medio ed Estremo Orientale.

— 1990. Harappan agriculture in Pakistan: the evidence of Nausharo. In *South Asian archaeology 1987*, M. Taddei (ed.), 321–32. Rome: Istituto Italiano per il Medio ed Estremo Orientale.

Costantini, L. & L. Costantini Biasini 1985. Agriculture in Baluchistan between the seventh and the 3rd millennium BC. *Newsletter of Baluchistan Studies* **2**, 16–30.

— 1986. Palaeoethnobotanical investigations in the Middle East and Arabian Peninsula, 1986. *East and West* **36**, 354–65.

Crawford, G. W. 1992. Prehistoric plant domestication in East Asia. In *The origins of agriculture: an international perspective*, C. W. Cowan & P. J. Watson (eds), 7–38. Washington DC: Smithsonian Institution Press.

de Wet, J. M. J., J. R. Harlan, E. G. Price 1986. Variability in *Sorghum bicolor*. In *Origins of African plant domestication*, J. R. Harlan, J. M. J. de Wet, A. B. L. Stemler (eds), 453–63. The Hague: Mouton.

Dixit, A. S., S. S. Dixit, Vishnu-Mittre 1987. The occurrence of *Eleusine africana* Kennedy O'Byrne in India and its significance in the origin of *Eleusine coracana*. *Proceedings of the Indian Academy of Sciences (Plant Sciences)* 97 (1), 1–10.

Fujiwara, H., M. R. Mughal, A. Sasaki, T. Matano 1992. Rice and ragi at Harappa: preliminary results by plant opal analysis. *Pakistan Archaeology* 27, 129–42.

Grigson, C. 1985. *Bos indicus* and *Bos namadicus* and the problem of autochthonous domestication in India. *Recent advances in Indo-Pacific prehistory*, V. N. Misra & P. Bellwood (eds), 425–8. New Delhi: Oxford and IBH.

— 1989. Size and sex: evidence for the domestication of cattle in the Near East. In *The beginnings of agriculture*, A. Milles, D. Williams, N. Gardner (eds), 77–109. Oxford: British Archaeological Reports, International Series 496.

Gulati, A. N. & A. J. Turner 1928. *A note on the early history of cotton* [Bulletin 17, Technological Series 12]. Bombay: Indian Central Cotton Committee.

Harlan, J. R. 1992. Indigenous African agriculture. In *The origins of agriculture: an international perspective*, C. W. Cowan & P. J. Watson (eds), 59–70. Washington DC: Smithsonian Institution Press.

Harris, D. R. 1989. An evolutionary continuum of people–plant interaction. In *Foraging and farming: the evolution of plant exploitation*, D. R. Harris & G. C. Hillman (eds), 11–26. London: Unwin Hyman.

Hilu, K. D. & J. M. J. de Wet 1976. Domestication of *Eleusine coracana*. *Economic Botany* 30, 199–208.

Hilu, K. D., J. M. J. de Wet, J. R. Harlan 1979. Archaeobotanical studies of *Eleusine coracana* ssp. *coracana* (Finger Millet). *American Journal of Botany* 66, 330–3.

Hutchinson, J. 1977. India: local and introduced crops. In *The early history of agriculture*, Sir J. Hutchinson, J. G. D. Clark, E. M. Jope, R. Riley (eds), 129–38. Oxford: Oxford University Press.

Hutchinson, J. B., R. A. Silow, S. G. Stephens 1947. *The evolution of Gossypium and the differentiation of the cultivated cottons*. London: Geoffrey Cumberlege and Oxford University Press.

Jarrige, J-F. 1985. Continuity and change in the North Kachi Plain (Baluchistan, Pakistan) at the beginning of the second millennium BC. In *South Asian archaeology 1983*, J. Schotsmans & M. Taddei (eds) 35–68. Naples: Istituto Universitario Orientale, Dipartimento di Studi Asiatici.

Jarrige, J-F., M. Santoni, J-F. Enault (compilers) 1979. *Fouilles de Pirak* [2 vols]. Paris: Diffusion de Boccard.

Joshi, J. P. (compiler) 1990. *Excavation at Surkotada 1971–72 and exploration in Kutch*. Memoir 87, Archaeological Survey of India, New Delhi.

Kajale, M. D. 1974. Ancient grains from India. *Bulletin of the Deccan College Research Institute* 34, 55–74.

— 1988. Plant economy. In *Excavations at Inamgaon I(ii)*, M. K. Dhavalikar, H. D. Sankalia, Z. A. Ansari (compilers), 727–821. Pune: Deccan College.

— 1991. Current status of Indian palaeoethnobotany: introduced and indigenous food plants with a discussion of the historical and evolutionary development of Indian agriculture and agricultural systems in general. In *New light on early farming*, J. Renfrew (ed.), 155–89. Edinburgh: Edinburgh University Press.

Loftus, R. T., D. E. MacHugh, D. G. Bradley, P. M. Sharp, P. Cunningham 1994. Evidence for two independent domestications of cattle. *Proceedings of the National Academy of Sciences USA* 91, 2757–61.

Lone, F. A., M. Khan, C. M. Buth 1993. *Palaeoethnobotany: plants and ancient man in Kashmir*. New Delhi: Oxford and IBH.

Mackay, E. J. H. 1938. *Further excavations at Mohenjo-daro*. Delhi: Government of India.

— 1943. *Chanhu-daro excavations 1935–36*. New Haven: American Oriental Society.

Meadow, R. H. 1979a. Prehistoric subsistence at Balakot: initial consideration of the faunal remains. In *South Asian archaeology 1977*, M. Taddei (ed.), 275–315. Naples: Istituto Universitario Orientale.

— 1979b. A preliminary note on the faunal remains from Pirak. In *Fouilles de Pirak* (vol. 1), J-F. Jarrige & M. Santoni (compilers), 334. Paris: Diffusion de Boccard.

— 1981. Early animal domestication in South Asia: a first report of the faunal remains from Mehrgarh, Pakistan. In *South Asian archaeology 1979*, H. Härtel (ed.), 143–80. Berlin: Dietrich Reimer.

— 1984a. Notes on the faunal remains from Mehrgarh, with a focus on cattle (*Bos*). In *South Asian archaeology 1981*, B. Allchin (ed.), 34–40. Cambridge: Cambridge University Press.

— 1984b. A camel skeleton from Mohenjo-daro. In *Frontiers of the Indus civilization*, B. B. Lal & S. P. Gupta (eds), 133–9. New Delhi: Books and Books.

— 1986a. The geographical and paleoenvironmental setting of Tepe Yahya. In *Excavations at Tepe Yahya, Iran 1967–1975: the early periods*, C. C. Lamberg-Karlovsky & T. W. Beale, 21–38. American School of Prehistoric Research Bulletin 38, Peabody Museum, Harvard University.

— 1986b. Faunal exploitation in the Greater Indus Valley: a review of recent work to 1980. In *Studies in the archaeology of India and Pakistan*, J. Jacobson (ed.), 43–64. New Delhi: Oxford and IBH.

— 1987. Faunal exploitation patterns in eastern Iran and Baluchistan: a review of recent investigations. In *Orientalia Iosephi Tucci memoriae dicata* (vol. 2), G. Gnoli (ed.), 881–916. Rome: Istituto Italiano per il Medio ed Estremo Orientale.

— 1989a. Osteological evidence for the process of animal domestication. In *The walking larder: patterns of domestication, pastoralism and predation*, J. Clutton-Brock (ed.), 80–90. London: Unwin Hyman.

— 1989b. Continuity and change in the agriculture of the Greater Indus Valley: the palaeoethnobotanical and zooarchaeological evidence. In *Old problems and new perspectives in the archaeology of South Asia*, J. M. Kenoyer (ed.), 61–74. Wisconsin Archaeological Reports 2, Department of Anthropology, University of Wisconsin-Madison.

— 1989c. A note on the distribution of faunal remains during the later periods at Mehrgarh (Baluchistan, Pakistan). In *South Asian archaeology 1985*, K. Frifelt & P. Sørensen (eds), 167–75. London: Curzon Press.

— 1989d. Prehistoric wild sheep and sheep domestication on the eastern margin of the Middle East. In *Early animal domestication and its cultural context*, P. J. Crabtree, D. Campana, K. Ryan (eds), 24–36. MASCA Research Papers in Science and Archaeology, vol. 6, supplement. The University Museum of Archaeology and Anthropology, University of Pennsylvania, Philadelphia.

— 1991. Faunal remains and urbanism at Harappa. In *Harappa excavations 1986–1990: a multidisciplinary approach to third millennium urbanism*, R. H. Meadow (ed.), 89–106. Madison, Wisconsin: Prehistory Press.

— 1993. Animal domestication in the Middle East: a revised view from the eastern margin. In *Harappan civilization* (2nd edn), G. L. Possehl (ed.), 295–320. New Delhi: Oxford and IBH.

Meadow, R. H. & A. Patel in press. A comment on "Horse remains from Surkotada" by Sándor Bökönyi. *Harappan Studies* 2.

Méry, S. 1991. Origine et production des récipients de terre cuite dans la péninsule d'Oman àl'Age du Bronze. *Paléorient* 17, 51–78.

Misra, V. N. 1973. Bagor: a late Mesolithic settlement in northwest India. *World Archaeology* 5, 92–110.

Mughal, M. R. 1991. The Harappan settlement systems and patterns in the Greater Indus Valley (circa 3500–1500 BC). *Pakistan Archaeology* 25, 1–72.

Nath, B. 1962. Remains of horse and Indian elephant from prehistoric site of Harappa. *Proceedings of the 1st All-India Congress of Zoology* 2, 1–14.

Pearsall, D. M., D. R. Piperno, E. H. Dinan, M. Umlauf, Z. Zhao, R. A. Benfer Jr 1995. Distinguishing rice (*Oryza sativa* Poaceae) from wild *Oryza* species through phytolith analysis: results of preliminary work. *Economic Botany* 49, 183–96.

Phillips, L. L. 1976. Cotton. In *Evolution of crop plants*, N. W. Simmonds (ed.), 196–200. Harlow: Longman.

Phillipson, D. W. 1993. *African archaeology*. Cambridge: Cambridge University Press.

Portères, R. 1976. African cereals: eleusine, fonio, black fonio, teff, *Brachiaria, paspalum, Pennisetum*, and African rice. In *Origins of African plant domestication*, J. R. Harlan, J. M. J. de Wet, A. B. L. Stemler (eds), 409–52. The Hague: Mouton.

Possehl, G. L. 1986. African millets in South Asian prehistory. In *Studies in the archaeology of India and Pakistan*, J. Jacobson (ed.), 237–56. New Delhi: Oxford and IBH.

Possehl, G. L. & P. C. Rissmann 1992. The chronology of prehistoric India from earliest times to the Iron Age. In *Chronologies in Old World archaeology*, R. W. Ehrich (ed.), 465–90 (vol. 1), 447–74 (vol. 2). Chicago: University of Chicago Press.

Potts, D. T. 1993 Rethinking some aspects of trade in the Arabian Gulf. *World Archaeology* **24**, 423–40.

Purseglove, J. W. 1972. *Tropical crops: monocotyledons* 1. London: Longman.

Reddy, S. N. 1994. *Plant usage and subsistence modelling: an ethnoarchaeolgoical approach to the Late Harappan of northwest India* [PhD dissertation, Department of Anthropology, University of Wisconsin-Madison]. Ann Arbor Michigan: University Microfilms.

Rissman, P. 1989. The status of research on animal domestication in India and its cultural context. In *Early animal domestication and its cultural context*, P. J. Crabtree, D. Campana, K. Ryan (eds), 14–23. MASCA Research Papers in Science and Archaeology, vol. 6, supplement. The University Museum of Archaeology and Anthropology, University of Pennsylvania, Philadelphia.

Sahu, B. P. 1988. *From hunters to breeders*. Delhi: Anamika Prakashan.

Santhanam, V. & J. B. Hutchinson 1974. Cotton. In *Evolutionary studies in world crops: diversity and change in the Indian subcontinent*, J. B. Hutchinson (ed.), 89–100. New York: Cambridge University Press.

Saraswat, K. S. 1993. Plant economy of Late Harappans at Hulas. *Purātattva* **23**, 1–12.

Savithri, R. & Vishnu-Mittre 1978. *Setaria* species in ancient plant economy of India. *The Palaeobotanist* **25**, 539–62.

— 1979. Further contributions on protohistoric ragi – *Eleusine coracana*. *The Palaeobotanist* **26**, 10–15.

Sauer, J. D. 1993. *Historical geography of crop plants: a select roster*. Boca Raton, Florida: CRC Press.

Schwartzberg, J. E. (ed.) 1992. *A historical atlas of South Asia*, 2nd edn. New York: Oxford University Press.

Sewell, R. B. S. 1931. Zoological remains. In *Mohenjo-daro and the Indus civilization*, J. Marshall (ed.), 649–73. London: A. Probsthain.

Shaffer, J. G. 1988. One hump or two: the impact of the camel on Harappan society. In *Orientalia Iosephi Tucci memoriae dicata* (vol. 3), G. Gnoli (ed.), 333–48. Rome: Istituto Italiano per il Medio ed Estremo Orientale.

— 1992. The Indus Valley, Baluchistan, and Helmand traditions: neolithic through Bronze Age. In *Chronologies in Old World archaeology*, R. W. Ehrich (ed.), 441–64 (vol. 1), 425–46 (vol. 2). Chicago: University of Chicago Press.

Shaffer, J. G. & D. Lichtenstein 1989. Ethnicity and change in the Indus Valley cultural tradition. In *Old problems and new perspectives in the archaeology of South Asia*, J. M. Kenoyer (ed.), 117–26. Wisconsin Archaeological Reports 2, Department of Anthropology, University of Wisconsin-Madison.

Sharma, A. K. 1974. Evidence of horse from the Harappan settlement at Surkotada. *Purātattva* **7**: 75–6.

— 1990. Animal bone remains. In Joshi (1990: 372–83).

— 1993. The Harappan horse was buried under the dunes of . . . *Purātattva* 23, 30–4.

Spate, O. H. K. & A. T. A. Learmonth 1967. *Indian and Pakistan: a general and regional geography*, 3rd edn. London: Methuen.

Stacul, G. (compiler) 1987. *Prehistoric and protohistoric Swat, Pakistan*. Rome: Istituto Italiano per il Medio ed Estremo Orientale.

— 1994. Pit structures from early Swat, Pakistan. Paper presented at the 23rd Annual Conference on South Asia, Madison, Wisconsin, 4–6 November 1994.

Thomas, P. K. 1975. Role of animals in the food economy of the Mesolithic culture of western and central India. In *Archaeozoological studies*, A. T. Clason (ed.), 322–8. Amsterdam: North Holland/Elsevier.

— 1988. Faunal assemblage. In *Excavations at Inamgaon 1(ii)*, M. K. Dhavalikar, H. D. Sankalia, Z. A. Ansari (compilers), 825–961. Pune: Deccan College.

— 1989. Utilization of domestic animals in pre- and protohistoric India. In *The walking larder: patterns of domestication, pastoralism, and predation*, J. Clutton-Brock (ed.), 108–12. London: Unwin Hyman.

Thomas, P. K. 1992. Faunal background of the Iron Age culture in Maharashtra. *Man and Environment* **17**(2), 75–9.

Uerpmann, H-P. 1979. *Probleme der Neolithisierung des Mittelmeerraums* [Beihefte zum Tübinger

Atlas des Vorderen Orients, Reihe B (Geisteswissenschaften) 28]. Wiesbaden: Dr L. Reichert.
— 1987. *The ancient distribution of ungulate mammals in the Middle East* [Beihefte zum Tübinger Atlas des Vorderen Orients, Reihe A (Naturwissenschaften) 27]. Wiesbaden: Dr L. Reichert.
Vats, M. S. 1940. *Excavations at Harappa.* Delhi: Manager of Publications, Government of India.
Vishnu-Mittre 1989. Forty years of archaeobotanical research in South Asia. *Man and Environment* **14**(1), 1–16.
Vishnu-Mittre & R. Savithri 1982. Food economy of the Harappans. In *Harappan civilization*, G. Possehl (ed.), 205–21. New Delhi: Oxford and IBH.
Weber, S. A. 1989. Millets in South Asia: Rojdi as a case study. In *South Asian archaeology 1987*, M. Taddei (ed.), 333–48. Rome: Istituto Italiano per il Medio ed Estremo Orientale.
— 1991. *Plants and Harappan subsistence.* New Delhi: Oxford and IBH.
— 1992. South Asian archaeobotanical variability. In *South Asian archaeology 1989*, C. Jarrige (ed.), 283–90. Madison, Wisconsin: Prehistory Press.
Willcox, G. 1992. Some differences between crops of Near Eastern origin and those from the tropics. In *South Asian archaeology 1989*, C. Jarrige (ed.), 291–300. Madison, Wisconsin: Prehistory Press.
Zohary, D. 1989. Domestication of the Southwest Asian Neolithic crop assemblage of cereals, pulses, and flax: the evidence from the living plants. In *Foraging and farming: the evolution of plant exploitation*, D. R. Harris & G. C. Hillman (eds), 358–73. London: Unwin Hyman.
Zohary, M. & M. Hopf 1988. *Domestication of plants in the Old World: the origin and spread of cultivated plants in West Asia, Europe, and the Nile Valley.* Oxford: Oxford University Press.

CHAPTER TWENTY-THREE

New evidence for early rice cultivation in South, Southeast and East Asia

Ian C. Glover & Charles F. W. Higham

Introduction

In terms of both the number of people depending on a staple cereal crop and the intensity of its production, Asian rice (*Oryza sativa* L.) is the most important of the world's food grains;[1] but there has been less research into its domestication(s), its distribution as a wild plant, and its early cultivation systems than there has for other major cereal crops such as wheat, barley and maize.[2]

At the risk of oversimplification it can be said that, in Asia, rice is typically grown in two contrasting situations (ecotypes): in lowland, normally permanent and intensively cultivated, flooded fields (Fig. 23.1, plate section) which are usually bunded to retain water for the growing season; and in upland swidden fields, which rely on rainfall (Fig. 23.2, plate section). In many areas, however, terraces extend the lowland ecotype high into the mountains (Fig. 23.3, plate section), and in the estuaries of the great river valleys varieties of "floating rice" (Fig. 23.4, plate section) can grow in water 6 m deep at up to 30 cm a day, keeping pace with seasonal floods (Stoskopf 1985: 337–8). These contrasting ecotypes are often referred to as lowland wet, and upland dry, rice cultivation.

De Candolle (1884) and Vavilov (1992 (1926)) established that domesticated rice originated from wild forms in two parts of the humid tropics: southern and eastern Asia (Fig. 23.5)[3] and western Africa, and that African rice (*Oryza glaberrima* Steud.) had a different and even less well known history of domestication. Modern writing on the origin, domestication and differentiation of Asian rice essentially starts with a paper given by Chang (1976a) at the Royal Society in London in 1975 in which he argued that it evolved from a wild annual progenitor, which he called *O. nivara*, somewhere – and perhaps in more than one place – within a broad belt roughly between 20° and 23°N stretching from the central Ganga Valley in India to the South China Sea (Fig. 23.6). He argued that the development of the three main regional races, *indica*, *japonica* (now often called *sinica*) and *javanica*,[4] took place as people extended the plant's natural climatic range north into temperate China and Japan, east

413

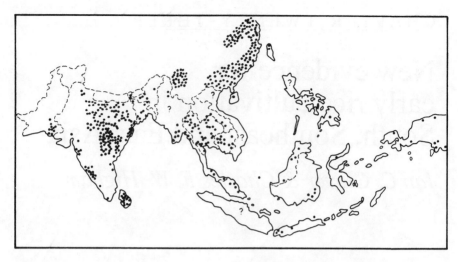

Figure 23.5   Known distribution of wild rices in Asia (redrawn from Harlan 1975: 215; and Ahn 1993).

into semi-arid western India and Pakistan, and south, through the equatorial belt, into Indonesia. Watabe (1984) presented a rather similar theory of origins (Fig. 23.7). Although there has been much disagreement among rice geneticists and botanists over the evolutionary history of rice and the relationships between the 22 species of *Oryza* and the more than 100,000 varieties of domesticated Asian rice recognized (Chang 1985), this broad picture still seems to hold, although Chang himself (1976a,b, 1983, 1987, 1988, 1989) and other writers (Chattarjee et al. 1978, Maloney 1990) have updated and modified the details. However, Oka (1988) presents a different scenario for rice domestication and puts less stress on the development of wild annual rices. Other writers (Yen 1982; Bray 1984: 477–510; Higham 1984, Glover 1985, Zhau & Wu 1988, Yan 1991, Bellwood et al. 1992, Thompson 1992a,b, Ahn 1993 and Maloney 1994) have added archaeological and archaeobotanical documentation.

The archaeology of rice in Asia

During the past three decades there have been many finds of rice at archaeological sites in Asia. Efforts have been made to wet- and dry-screen archaeological deposits for charred rice remains, to recover them from the clay matrix of pottery and bricks – because rice chaff is frequently used for pottery temper – and to categorize them according to whether they are wild or domesticated; and, if the latter, to determine the variety. To date, much more effort has gone into this type of research than into trying to understand early rice cultivation systems and their effect on social and cultural change,[5] or into palaeoecological research relating to rice, although this is now under way (Maloney 1991, Kealhofer & Piperno 1994). This situation is partly the result of less attention having been given, until recently, to archaeobotany in southern

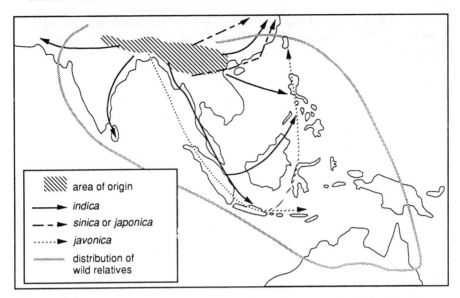

Figure 23.6   Postulated area of original domestication and early spread of Asian rice (redrawn from T. T. Chang 1976a).

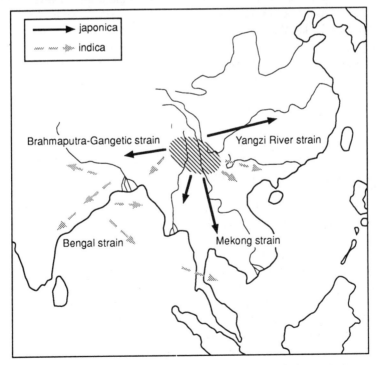

Figure 23.7   Postulated area of original domestication and early spread of Asian rice (redrawn from T. Watabe 1984).

and eastern Asia compared with Europe, the Americas and Southwest Asia, and partly it arises out of some particular and still unresolved archaeobotanical problems that we discuss briefly later in this chapter.

South Asia

The earliest claims for cultivated rice in the subcontinent of South Asia (Fig. 23.8) come from the "proto-neolithic" levels at Chopani–Mando on the River Belan on the margins of the Ganga floodplain in Uttar Pradesh, which the excavators date to the eighth–seventh millennia bc (Sharma et al. 1980). Vishnu-Mittre, who studied these remains, asserted that they were wild rice but without specifying the criteria on which this identification was based; and the evidence for dating this phase of the multi-period site is also far from clear (Ahn 1993: 73–4). At the nearby sites of Koldihwa and Mahagara neolithic settlements with hut circles, ground-stone axes and querns were excavated by Sharma and his teams (Sharma et al. 1980), and the coarse cord-impressed pottery contained many impressions of rice stalks, glumes and spikelets as well as charred grains which Chang and Vishnu-Mittre (in Sharma et al. 1980: 182) have identified as domesticated rice (*O. sativa*). Sharma has also claimed (ibid.: 135–6) – and this has appeared several times in print – that "neolithic" Koldihwa dates to the seventh millennium bc and Vishnu-Mittre (1976: 141) suggested that the rice remains found at the site were "the oldest recorded in the world". However, the evidence for this has not been substantiated[6] and both these sites are most unlikely to be older than the mid–late third millennium bc. Even so, they provide some of the earliest evidence for domesticated Asian rice within an agricultural system in South Asia.

Farther east in Uttar Pradesh a team from the Banares Hindu University excavated in the 1980s a neolithic mound at Khairadih on the Ghaghra river, and an organic-tempered sherd from Period 1 was dated to 2544 ±100 cal BC (CAMS 724). Bellwood et al. (1992: 164), who report this, note that the date was not definitely on rice-plant material, although other organic-tempered cord-impressed and black-and-red ware sherds in the layer clearly included charred rice; and more recently Kajale (1994) has reported finds of substantial quantities of charred rice at the multi-period site of Tara-dih, Gaya District in Bihar, which are ascribed to Period 1, described as neolithic and dated to 4000–3500 bp.

Some Indian archaeologists have tried to relate the cord-impressed pottery of these sites (which is unusual in the context of early Indian ceramic traditions) to the wide-spread cord-impressed pottery of Southeast and East Asia, but too few detailed descriptions of the Indian material have been published for any judgement to be reached; and cord-impressed pottery is so long-lasting and varied in eastern Asia that we doubt if any close and specific links could be made. However, it should be noted that quite a number of the late third to mid-second millennium bc finds of rice in eastern India come from areas where Austro–Asiatic languages such as Munda are, or were, spoken, and thus there is more than one possible, if unproven, link between early rice in India and Southeast Asia. We return to the relationship between the spread of early cultivation and the Austro–Asiatic and Austro–Tai language families at the end of this paper.

In a recent review of South Asian archaeobotanical finds Kajale (1991) lists over

60 sites at which rice grains or husks have been identified, and his data, together with additional records compiled by Ahn (1993), are summarized in Table 23.1. The location of most of the sites is shown in Figure 23.8. Some of these occurrences are identified as *O. sativa* or *sativa* type and others merely as *Oryza* spp., and they may include some wild rices. In constructing the table we have followed the periodization given by Kajale or the excavators, but when this is given as "neolithic" or "chalcolithic", or when more than one period is indicated, we have used other archaeological sources in order to determine which millennium the finds most probably belong to. Rather fewer sites than the 91 listed below in Table 23.1 are located on Figure 23.8 because some have more than one occupation phase and thus are counted more than once in the table.

Table 23.1   Archaeobotanical finds of rice in South Asian archaeological sites.

4th mill. bc	3rd mill. bc	2nd mill. bc	1st mill. bc	1st mill. AD	2nd mill. AD	Total
1	4	32	43	4	7	91

The single occurrence in the fourth millennium represents the finds from Koldihwa for which Kajale gives this date, but, as pointed out above, we doubt if the finds are quite so early. The four in the third millennium date to the end of the period and are mainly from Harappan sites such as Lothal and Rangpur, which may in fact be somewhat later. It is thus clear that only from the second millennium bc does rice become sufficiently common in many parts of South Asia for its cultivation to be regarded as certain.

The oldest known agricultural systems of the Indian subcontinent are clearly in the west, in present-day Pakistan, where they focused on wheat, barley, sheep, goats and cattle, and developed either as a result of demographic expansion eastwards of the food-producing communities of the Iranian Plateau, or from an independent but parallel trajectory towards domestication on its eastern margins. The most important early agricultural site here is Mehrgarh, which is discussed in Chapter 22 in this volume by Meadow.

By the fourth millennium bc, substantial agricultural settlements, including walled towns (e.g. Kot Diji, Rachman Dheri), had appeared on the plains of the Indus Valley and its northern tributaries, giving rise to the distinctive Harappan or Indus Valley civilization in the mid-third millennium bc. In the early and mature phases of the Harappan civilization wheat and barley were the dominant cereals, but from about 2000 bc rice appears to have been taken into cultivation as a summer crop, marking the beginning of the distinctive two-cropping (winter/*rabi*–summer/*kharif*) system of the subcontinent (cf. Meadow in Ch. 22 in this volume). Soon afterwards the range of rice cultivation expanded to sites such as Pirak (Costantini 1981) on the edges of the Indo–Iranian Plateau and to sites such as Aligrama, Loebanr and Semthan in the northern valleys of Swat and Kashmir (Costantini 1979, Buth et al. 1982).

Wet-rice cultivation was extended into the Himalayan foothills through extensive terracing and irrigation, and at Aligrama in Swat an Italian team (Tusa 1990) found spectacular evidence of an eleventh-century bc terraced and ploughed field on which rice was probably cultivated (Fig. 23.9, plate section). There then seems to have been

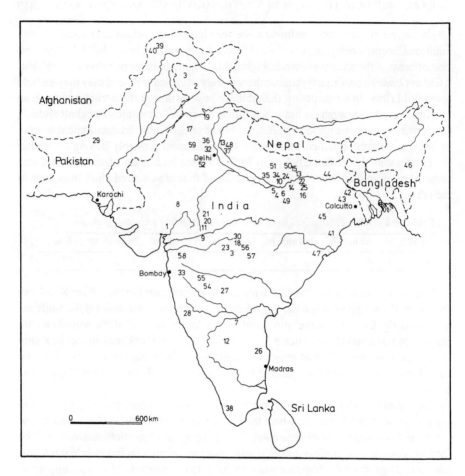

Figure 23.8 Distribution of prehistoric and protohistoric archaeological sites with preserved rice remains in South Asia; site locations from Kajale (1991: fig. 13.1) and Ahn (1993: appendix 1).

1 Lothal	13 Hastinapur	25 Rajgir	37 Hulas	49 Baraunha
2 Gufkral	14 Sonepur	26 Kunnatur	38 Adichanallur	50 Mahga
3 Semthan	15 Chirand	27 Ter	39 Aligrama	51 Sohgaura
4 Koldihwa	16 Taradih	28 Kolhapur	40 Loebanr III	52 Noh
5 Mahagara	17 Baidaypur	29 Pirak	41 Baidapur	53 Kakolia
6 Chopani Mando	18 Nevasa	30 Bhagi–Mohari	42 Mahisdal	54 Imangaon
7 Veerapuram	19 Rupar	31 Khairwada	43 Pandu Rajar Dhibi	55 Daimabad
8 Ahar	20 Ujjain	32 Lal Qila	44 Oriyup	56 Naikund
9 Navdatoli	21 Nagda	33 Walaki	45 Barudih	57 Paunar
10 Kausambi	22 Patilaputra	34 Narhan	46 Ambri	58 Bhokardan
11 Dangwada	23 Kaundinyapur	35 Sringverpur	47 Puri	59 Kokhrakot
12 Hallur	24 Rajghat	36 Daulatpur	48 Atranjikhera	

The following sites are also mentioned by Ahn (1993: app.1) as having preserved rice remains but we cannot identify the locations precisely enough to locate them on the map:

Kuchai (Bihar), Nandangarh (Bihar), Muzaffarpur (Bihar), Saharanpur (UP), Lahura-Dava (UP), Dadapur (UP), Manigara (UP), Kunjhun (Madhya Pradesh), Garh Kalika (Madhya Pradesh), Pauni (Maharashtra), Malappudi (Tamil Nadu), Gudavancher (Tamil Nadu), Kapa (Karnataka), Asanaghara (Sri Lanka), Ramba Vihara (Sri Lanka), Lekhania (UP), Bhag (Maharashtra).

a long delay before rice cultivation was carried farther west, across the Iranian Plateau and into Mesopotamia, Egypt and the Mediterranean Basin. We have not examined any archaeobotanical reports from this region, but our impression is that rice cultivation there did not significantly precede the expansion of Islam – implying an interval in the diffusion process of some 2,500 years. If true, this delay in the westwards spread of rice poses several interesting questions. [*Editor's comment*: This assumption appears to be essentially correct, but according to Watson (1983: 15–17) historical sources suggest that Asian rice was cultivated in parts of Persia, Mesopotamia and the Jordan Valley in pre-Islamic times.]

In summary, we can say that, towards the end of the third millennium bc, rice, including some domesticated varieties, appeared among the small-scale neolithic farming communities of the central and eastern parts of the Ganga Valley, perhaps brought by communities of farmers speaking proto-Munda languages expanding down the Brahmaputra Valley from a homeland in the region of Yunnan and northern Burma. By about 2000–1800 bc rice cultivation had spread into the socially and agriculturally more developed parts of the Indus Valley and adjacent regions where it was adopted as a summer (*kharif*) crop and probably contributed to the later expansion, and perhaps even the collapse, of the Harappan system, although its exact role in that system is still far from understood.

Mainland Southeast Asia and southern China

Study of the origins and spread of rice cultivation in Southeast Asia has been characterized more by speculation than rigorous analysis. Gorman (1977) speculated that rice was among the earliest plants to be domesticated in the region, but his own and others' archaeological evidence provides no support for this hypothesis. However, more recently the main components of a pattern, or at least a tenable model, have been identified. Mainland Southeast Asia, defined as the valleys of the Mekong, Chao Phraya, Red and Xijiang rivers and the intervening uplands (Fig. 23.10), has some coherence in terms of environmental variables and the pattern of human settlement in prehistory. Climatically the region, like India, is dominated by the monsoon, with alternate dry (November–April) and wet (May–September) seasons. Annual plants, including rice, flourish in the latter, and the regularly high temperatures, together with many lakes, rivers and a long coastline, provide abundant, naturally replenished food resources. The first historical records disclose the widespread presence of Austro–Asiatic languages with presumed deep prehistoric antecedents (Diffloth 1991). Cognates for rice and bronze are shared from Vietnamese in the east to the Munda languages of India in the west.

Speculation on early agriculture in this region began with the excavations of Spirit Cave and Non Nok Tha (Solheim 1972). The former, a small rockshelter perched on a hillslope, was in fact a temporary base for foragers. The latter has, at last, an internally consistent chronology based on AMS radiocarbon dating of rice chaff from pottery temper, and it belongs to the later second millennium bc.[7] Neither site has any relevance to the question of agricultural origins. The pattern of settlement before the first reliably identified rice had two foci. The first comprised upland rockshelters within a canopied forest habitat, a pattern that reveals long-term stability and little

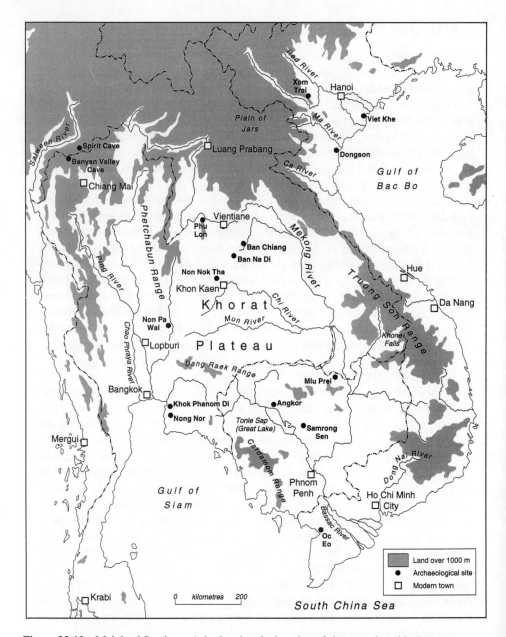

Figure 23.10 Mainland Southeast Asia showing the location of sites mentioned in the text.

cultural change by broad-spectrum foragers. These sites are often termed Hoabinhian after the type locality in northern Vietnam.

Rice remains have occasionally been found in Hoabinhian sites such as Banyan Valley Cave in northwestern Thailand (Yen 1977: 582–94, Reynolds 1992: 94), at Gua Cha in Kelantan State, Malaya (Bellwood 1985: 166), and at Xom Trai in Vietnam (Higham 1989: 43). The first two represent very late Hoabinhian survivals or post-Hoabinhian use of the sites, and the rice was almost certainly obtained via exchange with nearby lowland village farmers, but the finds at Xom Trai pose some problems.

Dao The Tuan (1983, 1984) reported finds of rice grains in 1982 at this 5m deep cave site at Xom Trai in Lac Son district of Ha Son Binh province, 150km southwest of Hanoi. In the lower levels (5–8) only a slender-grained rice was present, whereas both slender and round grains were present in the upper levels (4–1). Tuan presents measurements (1984: 144) for 30 grains of charred rice and implies that they were all from domesticated varieties, but he does not specify any criteria for this other than size and proportions. Viet (1989) lists 24 radiocarbon dates from the site, all from the top 2.5m. Whereas the top 0.7m is clearly disturbed, as Hoang (1984) had already pointed out, the 20 dates between 0.9 and 2.4m consistently fall in the period 17000–19000 bp. If rice was found in these levels (or lower) then it seems more likely that it would be *O. rufipogon* or *O. perennis*, rather than *O. sativa*, but whatever their status they constitute the earliest identified archaeological remains of rice in Asia.[8]

The second focus of settlement in mainland Southeast Asia was coastal and we know little about this adaptation before about 4000–5000 bc, because the rapid post-glacial rise in sea level and subsequent alluviation has covered relevant sites. When such settlements become archaeologically visible, and most are to be found on the raised beaches of northern Vietnam and Gwangdong, we encounter sedentary communities versed in pottery making and polishing stone adze heads. Vietnamese and Chinese colleagues refer to them as coastal neolithic, but this definition is based on material culture rather than on any archaeobotanical evidence for rice cultivation – or, indeed, on evidence of any other form of plant production, although dog, pig and cattle bones are regularly reported.

The investigation of such sites in central Thailand has been a main focus of the Bang Pakong Valley Research Programme (Higham & Bannanurag 1990, 1991, Higham & Thosarat 1993, 1994). Two sites, Khok Phanom Di and Nong Nor, formerly located close to the coast, have been excavated. Nong Nor, which was excavated in 1990–3, has two phases of occupation. The earlier phase, dated to *c.* 2450 bc, comprises a shell midden with abundant evidence for sea fishing and the hunting of marine mammals, pottery manufacture and the exchange of stone needed for polished adzes. But no evidence for rice has been found. There is then a gap in the occupation at Nong Nor, with re-occupation of the locality in the first millennium bc.

The other site, Khok Phanom Di (Higham & Bannannurag 1990, 1991, Higham & Thosarat 1993, 1994), which was excavated in 1985, was occupied from 2000–1500 bc. There, rice remains were abundant. They were found in the cultural deposits, as partially digested food in faeces in two of the burials (Figs 23.11; 23.12, plate section), as impressions on clay adhering to pottery vessels, and as a tempering agent in pottery vessels. Thompson (1992a) has identified the remains as cultivated rice on the basis of abcission scars and the lack of awns. Higham (1993) has also shown that the shell knives were probably used in rice harvesting.

Maloney (1991) has published several sediment cores from near Khok Phanom Di. They reveal episodes of burning, associated with increases in grass pollen and in the pollen of plants known today to colonize rice plots. These episodes date to about 6400 bp and 5560 bp. There are several possible explanations for them: early rice cultivation, clearance by foragers, or the result of natural conflagrations, of which there are many during the late dry season beyond the mangrove belt. These alternatives cannot be tested without further archaeological research. Rather, we must turn to the results of the excavations of the two sites and consider the possibility that rice cultivation was far later in Southeast Asia than in the Yangzi Valley.[9]

This proposition is now supported by the chronological framework available from neolithic or early bronze age sites found in the interior river valleys of Southeast Asia. In central Thailand, behind the coastal fringe, the earliest settlement known, at Non Pa Wai, has been dated to between 2400 and 2000 bc (Pigott 1992). In Northeast Thailand, there have been claims for fourth or even fifth millennium dates for two sites: Non Nok Tha (Bayard 1971) and Ban Chiang (Gorman & Charoenwongsa 1976). Both have revealed evidence for rice-chaff ceramic temper. But most of the recent AMS radiocarbon dates place the "Middle Period" occupation at Non Nok Tha in the late second millennium bc – clearly much later than claimed by Solheim and Bayard.[7] It is also argued here by Higham (and see Higham 1994a) that the early phase of settlement at Ban Chiang is much later than White (1990) has claimed. The application of stricter rules for the acceptability of radiocarbon dates to this site suggests to some archaeologists that the Ban Chiang sequence starts only in the late third millennium bc. These two sites, in fact, belong to a widely distributed series of settlements that share a black, incised pottery style. It is suggested that they represent a rapid expansion of agricultural groups that began, probably, about 2300–2000 bc.

The settlements in question are usually found along small tributary streams where the cultivation of rice could have been undertaken in naturally inundated areas. The village cemeteries document a social organization in which rank was obtained through achievement, signalled by the presence of grave goods such as marine shell, marble, slate, bronze and tin ornaments.

A major cultural dislocation occurred from about 500 bc, documented by the emergence of highly stratified chiefly societies and the growth of large centres each with dependent communities. These are found over most of the lowlands of Southeast Asia. The Dian culture of Yunnan in southwestern China is well known for its bronze models of agricultural ceremonies (Fig. 23.13, plate section) recovered from the princely graves of Shizhaishan (Ti & Wang 1983). From the Dongson Culture of the lower Red River, we encounter bronze ploughshares (Figs 23.14; 23.15, plate section), scenes on drums of rice husking (Fig. 23.16), and literary evidence for the preferential ownership of good agricultural land by members of the highest social echelon. In the arid zone of northeastern Thailand there are many moated settlements (Fig. 23.17, plate section) that probably have their origins in this period. Parry (1992) has identified reservoirs and canals from satellite photographs that suggest strongly that water control for agriculture was one of the uses to which such moats were put.

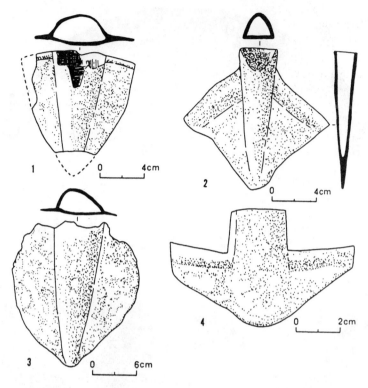

Figure 23.14   Bronze hoes (left) and ploughshares (right) from the first-millennium bc Dong-son Culture of North Vietnam (drawing from C. F. W. Higham).

Water control was, indeed, one of the reasons for the network of canals that cross the flat terrain of the lower Mekong as the river approaches its delta. These emphatically belong to the earlier centuries of the first millennium AD, and set a pattern that reached its apogee in the intricate system of water capture, storage and reticulation achieved at historic Angkor (Groslier 1979; van Liere 1980: fig. 4).

Our present understanding of the expansion of rice cultivation in Southeast Asia involves a late development within one of the richest habitats known, in terms of naturally replenished food resources. The adoption of rice cultivation, linked to the domestication of cattle and pigs, is seen here as a stimulus for a rapid expansion into the hitherto lightly populated interior river valleys by people who spoke early Austro–Asiatic languages. This expansion, which probably originated in the context of expanding rice agriculturalists from the Yangzi Basin, reached into Yunnan, down the Mekong, Red and Chao Phraya rivers and as far west as India. It was within these agricultural communities that we find the development of bronze working from about 1500 bc, and iron a millennium later. The widespread adoption of iron forging and the spread of imported glass and semi-precious stone jewellery were but two of the variables that underwrote the development of political centralization, and, with it, more intensive methods of rice cultivation.

Figure 23.16 Tympanum of first-millennium bc Dongson Culture bronze drum from Co Loa, North Vietnam, with (enlarged) scene of rice husking (from Pham 1990: 9).

Figure 23.18   Island Southeast Asia showing the location of sites mentioned in the text.

Island Southeast Asia

The environment and culture history of Island Southeast Asia (Fig. 23.18) contrasts in many respects with that of the mainland. Since the early Holocene this has
been an island realm with a higher ratio of coastline to landmass than anywhere except
Japan. Being mainly south of the Equator, the wet and dry seasons are reversed (rain
from November to March), there are few large river valleys or alluvial plains, and soil
regeneration is dependent in many areas on chains of very active volcanoes, which
are absent from the mainland. The equatorial belt (Sumatra, Malaya, Borneo/Kali-
mantan, Mindanao) was, at least from the early Holocene, largely covered by dense
rainforest which provided a meagre living for both hunter–collectors and primitive
cultivators, except along rivers, lakes and coasts.

Even the archaeological cultures of the late Pleistocene and early Holocene, which
are dominated by regionally varied flake-and-blade industries (Bellwood 1985: 193–

203) show a marked contrast with the Hoabinhian pebble-tool assemblages of the mainland. The evidence for a "classical" neolithic phase of settled village agriculture with pottery and ground stone tools, such as we find at Ban Kao and Khok Phanom Di in Thailand and in the Phung Nguyen Culture of northern Vietnam, is almost entirely lacking; indeed, most "neolithic" materials have been recovered from the upper levels of cave deposits.

Bellwood (1985: 204–45 and in Ch. 25 in this volume) has argued that a fully agricultural economy, including rice cultivation, was carried into the Indo–Malaysian archipelago, via Taiwan and the Philippines, by Austronesian-speaking peoples from after 3000 bc, from a starting point on the south coast of China. As Austronesian speakers expanded their settlements into Melanesia and the western Pacific, cereals, which probably included foxtail millet as well as rice, were gradually replaced by tubers and tree fruits. The western branch of Austronesian settlement, moving into Sulawesi, Borneo, Java and Sumatra, retained rice as a significant crop plant and this developed into the intensive terrace-field paddy systems of recent times, following the introduction of iron, domestic buffaloes and cattle in the early centuries of the Christian era.

Much of this reconstruction depends on the analysis of linguistic data and items of material culture such as pottery and polished stone tools. Remarkably little archaeobotanical evidence has been recovered, precisely identified and dated. Finds from caves in Timor and southern Sulawesi (Glover 1979, 1985) give some support to the model, although the dating of the substantial quantity of charred rice grains and chaff from Ulu Leang 1 cave in Sulawesi is still unresolved.[10]

From other locations in Island Southeast Asia, Snow et al. (1986) report a date of 3700 bp from the site of Andarayan in northern Luzon, Philippines, and from excavations at the cave site of Gua Sireh, inland of Kuching in Sarawak, East Malaysia, a charred rice grain extracted from a sherd in a layer overlying a preceramic occupation phase was dated by the AMS radiocarbon method to 2334 ±260 cal BC (CAMS 725), with conventional dates from above and below the sample supporting this age (Bellwood et al. 1992: 166–7). More reliably dated materials are urgently needed from Island Southeast Asia, but at present it appears that, once established, rice cultivation spread very rapidly throughout the region.

Central China

When one of us (Glover 1985) last summarized the evidence for the domestication and early cultivation of rice in Asia it was already apparent that by far the earliest and most abundant evidence for the cultivation of domesticated rice came from sites around Lake Taihu in the lower Yangzi Valley, and especially from the site of Hemudu (Homutu) a little farther southeast on the swampy coastal plains south of Hangzhou Bay (Fig. 23.19). The neolithic sequence in this area is summarized in Table 23.2.[11]

The Hemudu site is itself divided into two phases, and the material from Layers 3 and 4 of the earlier (5000–3900 bc) Hemudu phase is of greatest interest (Zhao & Wu 1988). Because of the waterlogged ground, much wood from pile dwellings and some agricultural tools were preserved, as well as abundant pottery, bone and stone tools, and, importantly, rice. Accumulations 10–50 cm thick of rice grains, husks, stalks and leaves were found in almost all the excavated areas. Yan (1982: 22) estimated that

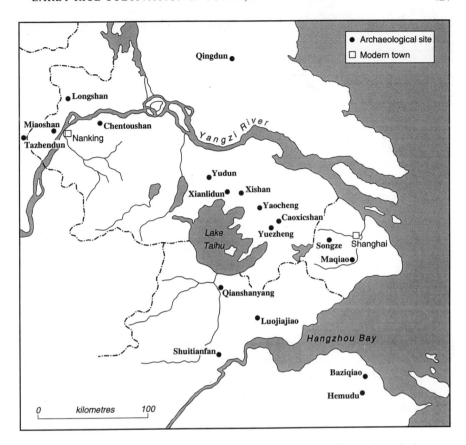

Figure 23.19 Lower Yangzi Valley, China, showing the location of Hemudu and other neolithic sites (redrawn from Ahn 1993: fig. 4.10).

the rice remains represent about 120 tonnes of harvested crop – almost certainly the largest archaeobotanical find made in an Asian archaeological site.

The rice remains from Hemudu have been examined by You (1976: 20–1) and Zhou (1981: 3–4) who both concluded that, on the grounds of their size and proportions (see Ahn 1993: 195–7 for details), this was domesticated rice and it comprised about 77 per cent *indica* and 22 per cent *japonica* varieties. Finding *indica* established so far north, so early, raises questions that cannot immediately be answered. Chang's (1976a) reconstruction of the sequence of the spread of domesticated varieties of *O. sativa* carried the implication that *indica* should be a later arrival in Central China, but this archaeological evidence suggests that this was not so. It seems to lend some support to the notion that there were two rather separate but contemporary domestications from *O. rufipogon*; the one leading to *japonica* in Central China, and the other to *indica* in southern China or northern Vietnam. Furthermore, Oka (1988) suggests regionally different links between perennial wild rices and domesticates. However, there is no convincing archaeological evidence to support this – except perhaps these anomalous rice remains from the Hoabinhian Xom Trai site referred to above.

Table 23.2 Lower Yangzi Valley: cultural sequence and evidence of agriculture (after Ahn 1993: fig. 4.10).

bc	Culture	Rice remains *indica:japonica* ratio	Other agricultural remains	Sites
5000	Majiabing (Hemudu phase)	7:3	water caltrop, bottle gourd dog, pig, water buffalo bone and wood spades	Hemudu, Luojiajiao
4500	Majiabing (Majiabing phase)	6:4	dog, pig, water buffalo stone spade	Caoxienshan, Songze, Baziqiao, Yudun
3500	Majiabing (Songze phase)		water buffalo, pig, dog stepped adze, shouldered axe, plough-share, harvesting knife	Quingdun, Xianlidun, Miaoshan (?)
3300	Liangzhu	most *japonica*	water buffalo, pig, dog, sheep peach, melon, silk? stepped adze, ploughshare, winged cultivation implement, harvesting knife, sickle	Qianshanyang, Maqiao, Shuitianfan, Yaocheng, Yuezheng, Longshan, Chentoushan
2400 –1000	Maqiao Hushu		stone ploughshare, sickle, knife, shouldered hoe	Xishan Xiatang

The designs on some potsherds from Hemudu are interpreted as representing ears of rice, and the agricultural tools include wooden-handled bone spade-like implements (Fig. 23.20) and possible reaping knives but no obvious plough shares, although it is argued that the water buffalo may have been domesticated there as well as pig and dog among the nearly 50 species of mainly wild animals.[12] Other identified plant remains at Hemudu include bottle gourd (*Lagenaria* sp.), water caltrop (*Trapa natans*), a date-like fruit (*Choerospondia axillaris*) and acorns (*Quercus* sp.).

Around Lake Taihu, between the Yangzi and Hangzhou deltas, rather similar remains have been found at the site of Luojiajiao (Fig. 23.19) which is dated to *c.* 4500 bc, and both *indica* and *japonica* rices (differentiated by grain length:width ratios) are abundant in many sites of the later phases of the Majiabang and Liangzhou cultures (Ahn 1993: 122–4). In the Songze phase of the Majiabang Culture (*c.* 3500–3300 bc), stone spades replace bone ones and triangular-shaped stone ploughshares appear, indicating that more intensive cultivation in fixed, probably bunded, fields had developed by this time.

In the central parts of the Yangzi Valley, around Lake Dong Ting, and south to the city of Changsha, a separate cluster of neolithic sites (Fig. 23.21) have been known for some time and grouped as the Daxi Culture of the fourth millennium bc. Rice remains are also regularly found in these sites and incorporated as charred grains and chaff in pottery. In 1988 an excavation was made at the site of Pengtoushan in Lixian County. The mound, 3–4 m above the rice fields, covered some 10,000 m² had four phases of occupation, and evidence for semi-underground houses, post-holes and fireplaces, and 19 burials, indicating a fairly stable settlement. Some 20 samples of charred rice extracted from the pottery (Fig. 23.22, plate section), and fired lumps of clay and soil charcoal, were dated in Beijing and at the Oxford AMS Radiocarbon Laboratory to between 5500 and 7000 bc (Pei 1989, Yan 1991; Hedges et al. 1992: 156).

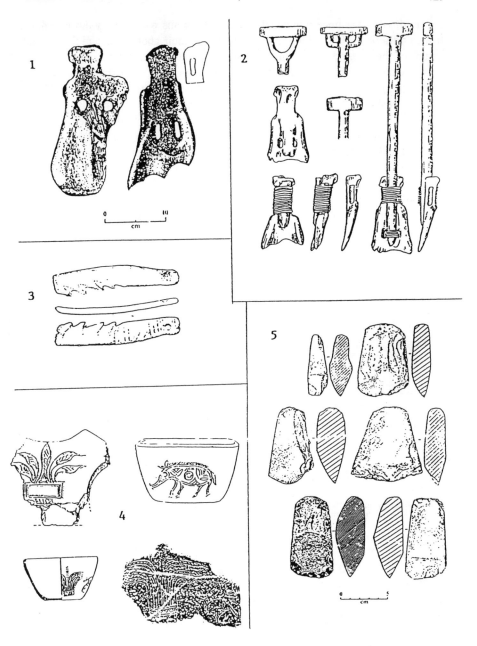

Figure 23.20   Artefacts from the site of Hemudu, lower Yangzi Valley, China.
1: spade-like digging implements made from ox and buffalo scapulae; 2: suggested reconstructions of "spades" using surviving wooden handles; 3: bone artefact interpreted as either a saw
or a (broken) harpoon; 4: pottery with incised designs interpreted as ears of rice (lower pair),
a pig, and a 5-leaved unknown plant; 5. stone axe/adze blades (from Ahn 1993: fig. 4.11).

Pei (ibid.:103) was uncertain whether the rice remains were clearly those of domesticated varieties,[13] but, taking into consideration their abundance and the sedentary
nature of the site, he argued that rice was cultivated. Yan (ibid.), who we believe
closely examined the material but did not excavate there, argued that the rice grains
were quite large and close in form to those of modern cultivars. However, Maloney
(1994) has shown some scepticism regarding these claims and certainly this material
should be closely examined by competent archaeobotanists, given their importance
as the earliest dated site in East Asia yielding abundant rice remains.[14]

   Despite the lack of clarity regarding the finds from Pengtoushan itself, rice remains
found in many sites on the swampy plains of the central and lower Yangzi and adjacent rivers is so widespread and abundant that we can be reasonably confident that
rice agriculture became well established in this region between the late sixth and the
third millennium bc, that is, some 3,500 years before, on the evidence presently available, it appeared in India or Southeast Asia.

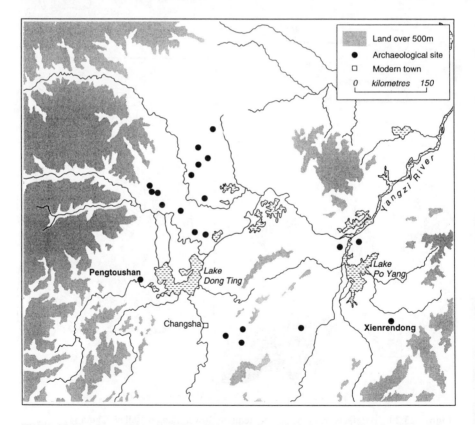

Figure 23.21   Central Yangzi Valley, China, showing the location of Lake Dong Ting, Pengtoushan and other early archaeological sites.

North China, Korea and Japan

As Crawford (1992a,b) and Ahn (1993) both provide recent and comprehensive summaries of the expansion of agricultural systems into Northeast Asia and the supporting archaeobotanical finds, and Imamura, elsewhere in this volume, discusses the introduction of rice into Japan, we refer readers to these accounts. In general the evidence suggests a northerly expansion of rice from the Yangzi Valley from about 3000 bc as it is taken into northern Chinese neolithic cultivation systems based primarily on millet. Rice-husk imprints have been found at Lijiacun and Hejiawan in Xixiang County, southern Shaanxi (Ahn 1993: 211). The Lijiacun Culture, a provincial variant of the proto-Yangshao cultures of the Huanghe (Yellow) River, is dated to the sixth millennium bc. However, the context of these finds is not clear, nor whether the rice is domesticated, locally cultivated, or imported from sites farther south. It is also possible that the climatic warming in the mid-Holocene permitted *Oryza rufipogon* to expand northwards from the Yangzi Valley.

Rice remains were long ago reported by Andersson from the eponymous Yangshao site which is now placed in the Miaodikou II phase of the Late Yangshao Culture dated to between 5000 and 4200 bp, and rice is first found in Korea at the site of Hunamni about 3000 bp. Crawford (1992a: 25) also reports occasional finds of short-grained *japonica* rices in Late and Final Jomon sites in Japan, such as Nabatake, Uenoharo and Kazahari, dated between 1000 and 400 bc, and from his own research on the Sakushu–Kotoni River in Hokkaido, which is the most northerly reported archaeological rice. While the context of individual grains must always be suspect, and their association with dated samples is seldom precisely specified, it is worth noting the direct AMS radiocarbon dating of a single rice grain from the Kazahari site in Aomori Prefecture, northern Honshu to 2540 ± 240 bp (TO–2022) (Crawford 1992b: 121). However, it is not until the Yayoi Period in the fourth century bc that rice is widely reported, from over 100 sites, and clearly becomes a staple crop in southwestern Japan, subsequently expanding into central and northeastern Japan (cf. Imamura in Ch. 24 in this volume).

By the Late Yayoi Period (c. AD 100–300), intensive rice agriculture based on transplanting seedlings from a nursery bed into small rectangular bunded fields seems to have been widespread, and Japanese archaeologists have carried out the most extensive and careful excavations of such field systems anywhere in the world. Barnes (1990) makes some mention of this, but one has to go to Japanese archaeological publications, such as Masaoka & Takaoka (1984), to get some idea of the scale of this impressive research.

Criteria for the identification of domesticated rice

As we mentioned earlier, there has been more discussion of, and rather more research into, the development of reliable criteria for the identification of domesticated rice than into the role of rice-cultivation systems in the development of ancient culture in Asia. The problems, and attempts to resolve them, are set out at length by Ahn (1993), by Thompson (1992a,b) and most recently by Maloney (1994), and only a brief summary of the important points need be given here.

The distinctions made between wild and domesticated rice are, as with most other cereals, based on the development of non-shattering spikelets, seed dormancy, and size of the grains (especially length:width:breadth ratios). To identify useful discriminating characters, archaeobotanists need abundant charred remains, and yet, as Thompson (1992b) has pointed out, rice is less often found charred than is wheat, barley or maize because it is seldom parched or deliberately heated before storage. Usually rice is bulk-stored in spikelet form and dehusked in individual households in small quantities on a daily basis. In China mudbrick and pisé building materials often preserve spikelets and husks (the huge quantity of material at Hemudu is quite exceptional), but the traditional raised wooden pile dwellings of Southeast Asia offer fewer chances for the preservation of ancient rice. However, rice husks (with some grains) were regularly used as an early pottery temper and this provides the main source of archaeobotanical samples. Although often distorted and fragmentary, rice remains embedded in pottery do permit direct dating of cultural material by the AMS radiocarbon method, and this is increasingly being done on samples from Thailand and China.

Japanese, e.g. Matsuo (1952) and Oka (1988), and Indian researchers such as Vishnu Mittre relied mainly on the size and proportions of the grains to distinguish domesticated from wild rice, and *indica* from *japonica* varieties, but, as Garton (1977) has shown, charring can significantly distort the proportions of rice grains, especially of the *japonica* type. Ahn (1993) has also shown that the use of Matsuo's (1952) scheme can lead to a high proportion of misclassifications for single grains or small samples.

In the 1970s T. T. Chang, following earlier Japanese work, introduced into archaeobotany the notion that the regularity of alignment and smoothness of the tubercles on rice glumes could be used to distinguish wild from domesticated rice, and his reports on archaeological rice from Non Nok Tha and Ban Chiang in Thailand and from Ulu Leang 2 cave in Indonesia relied on these features. But later independent studies by Ahn (1993), Thompson (1992b) and Kealhofer (pers. comm.) show that these "hair cell" patterns can vary dramatically from one end of the glume to the other. Chang's method did have the advantage that whole grains (which seldom survive in secure contexts) were not needed and abundant material was available embedded in bricks and pottery. This approach was developed further by Yen (1982) on material from Ban Chiang, an important neolithic to Bronze Age settlement in northeastern Thailand, and he came to the conclusion that the rice, although cultivated, was intermediate in character between wild and domesticated. As Ahn (1993) has pointed out, Chang has never published his criteria in sufficient detail for others to use his method, and in any case there is great variability in smoothness and regularity between different spikelets on the same plant and between different parts of the husks of the same grain of rice.

The chemical signature of rice, as determined by infrared spectroscopy, is clearly different from that of other Southeast Asian food plants (Hill & Evans 1989), but experiments to differentiate between strains of domesticated rice, and between its wild and weedy relatives, have not proved very successful (Ahn 1993). Thompson (1992a), however, has successfully identified domesticated rice at Khok Phanom Di in Thailand on the basis of the abcission scars on the rachilla, and the lack of awns, but these are features only rarely preserved on rice remains from archaeological sites. The study of rice phytoliths offers another approach that is showing promise, and discrimination between the *rufipogon, nivara* and *sativa* complexes and other species of *Oryza* is now possible (Kealhofer & Piperno 1994, Kealhofer 1994). But, as yet, a relatively easy and reliable method of identifying domesticated rice using small samples of the sort of material commonly found in archaeological sites in southern and eastern Asia has not been developed.

Early rice cultivation systems

The archaeological investigation of early cultivation systems for rice has barely begun, although Barnes (1990) has discussed the problems of recognizing and excavating rice paddy soils, and van Liere (1980) and Moore (1988) have pioneered the investigation of traditional water-management systems in Cambodia and Northeast Thailand. Indeed, van Liere (1985) has provided the outlines of a model for the development of rice cultivation practices. Today, and certainly in the popular perception, rice cultivation is dominated by intensive production methods of irrigation, terracing, ploughing, transplanting and staggered cropping in adjacent fixed, bunded or terraced fields. But these methods are very labour intensive and have become widespread only in the past 200 years, and sometimes much more recently (Hanks 1972).

In van Liere's scheme – and this is to some extent supported by recent archaeological finds – the earliest form of rice cultivation is likely to have been receding-flood agriculture around the many "reservoir" lakes and oxbows in the middle courses of the great river valleys of mainland Southeast Asia and South China. Seed would be broadcast as the floods receded, leaving the ground clean and moist. Only digging sticks and stone hoes would have been needed for cultivation, and ground-edge slate or flaked chert knives for harvesting. In the late second millennium bc in some regions bronze sickles came into use and bronze ploughshares are found (only in North Vietnam and South China) from the mid-first millennium bc.

A recent analysis of the associations and distribution of agricultural hoes and harvesting tools by Yokokura (1992) gives some support to this scenario from another perspective. Yokokura sees two phases of rice cultivation in Southeast Asia between the Neolithic and the Iron Age. In the first, cultivation was by stone and wooden hoes and digging sticks with little or minimum tillage of the soil, and individual ears of rice were harvested with small stone or shell hand-knives such as those found at Khok Phanom Di and the iron finger-sickles (*ani-ani*) of recent use in Indonesia. Bronze hoes (which we identify here as ploughshares) and bronze sickles were added to the tool kit in northern Vietnam in the last few centuries bc, and iron agricultural tools appear at about the same time in China, southern Vietnam and Thailand. However, the basic methods of cultivation and harvesting in Southeast Asia did not change and they differed from those of China, although Chinese Han-style iron hoes were adopted in northern and central Vietnam following the Han expansion there. Yokokura (ibid.) postulates that Indian methods of cultivation, with buffalo-drawn ploughs and harrows, were introduced in Southeast Asia only in the mid-first millennium AD.

Bunding to hold back the receding floodwaters was probably practised from the earliest stage of cultivation, and by the end of the first millennium bc large moated mounds with multiple banks and ditches were present throughout the Mun-Chi river basin in northeastern Thailand, and extended east across Cambodia into Vietnam. Similar large-scale water-management systems were present in Peninsular India and the dry zone of Sri Lanka at this time. Water diversion, storage and irrigation are all evidenced or probable, and certainly rice was being cultivated on a considerable scale, iron came into use, and buffaloes were probably used for ploughing, replacing the puddling of flooded fields by teams of cattle – a technique still practised in some of the eastern Indonesian islands. The first real field systems for rice cultivation recognizable in Southeast Asia (we cannot speak for India or China) are the square bunded fields of the early Khmer kingdoms, which can still be seen across much of Cambodia and northeast Thailand in areas previously uncultivated. According to van Liere (1980: 271) more than 50 million of these were built; their purpose was to trap rainfall rather than to be linked to a planned irrigation system; and rice was transplanted into them from nursery beds. But soon after AD 1000 the Khmers seem to have remodelled the smaller-scale water-catchment and irrigation systems of later prehistoric cultures and built long canals and huge reservoirs or barays. Whether they were built to intensify rice production, as Groslier (1979) once argued, or whether they were purely "theocratic hydraulics" to meet the year-round need for water in temple moats and ponds and to project on to the landscape an ideal cosmological scheme, as van Liere (1980) and Stott (1992) believe, is still unresolved. Recent surveys by the UNESCO Angkor "ZEMP" Project of the water-catchment systems around Angkor suggest a dual function for the most of the great barays and canals (Englehardt 1994).

Archaeolinguistics

Although it is beyond the main scope of this chapter, a highly significant recent development in linguistics deserves mention because it offers the possibility of a plausible and elegant synthesis of the cultural sequences in the Yangzi Valley, eastern India and Southeast Asia, and of the evidence for the origins and spread of rice agriculture (Higham 1994b). There are two major language families in question: Austro–Tai (AT) and Austro–Asiatic (AA). The former is distributed in southern China and Thailand, the latter is found from eastern India across Southeast Asia to Vietnam. Austronesian, according to Benedict and other linguists, is related to AT. In 1906, Schmidt suggested that AA and Austronesian were distantly related and he named the proto-language Austric (Schmidt 1906). There the matter has rested: the hypothesis has neither been rejected nor confirmed.

If the two language families are unrelated, and current attempts to correlate language distributions with the expansion of agriculturalists are justified (cf. Renfrew and Bellwood in Chs 5 and 25 in this volume), one could postulate two transitions to rice cultivation: one associated with Proto AT centred in the Yangzi catchment, the other associated with Proto AA in tropical Southeast Asia. However, Reid (1993) and

Figure 23.1 Lowland "wet" rice fields in Sulawesi, Indonesia. Taro (Colocasia esculenta), rice's "sister" crop, has been planted in a flooded field in the foreground (photograph I. C. Glover).

Figure 23.2 Harvesting "dry" rice in a mountain swidden field, central Timor (photograph I. C. Glover).

Figure 23.3 Rice terraces near Banue in the mountains of central Luzon, Philippines (photograph I. C. Glover).

Figure 23.4 "Floating" rice being harvested after floods have receded at Ban Krabuk, Kanchanaburi Province, Thailand ((photograph I. C. Glover).

Figure 23.9 Ploughed field of eleventh century bc, probably for rice and buried by alluvial deposits; at Aligrama Swat, Pakistan (photograph S. Tusa).

Figure 23.11   Rice-grain inclusions in a human coprolite from a second millennium bc burial at Khok Phanom Di, Thailand (micrograph G. B. Thompson).

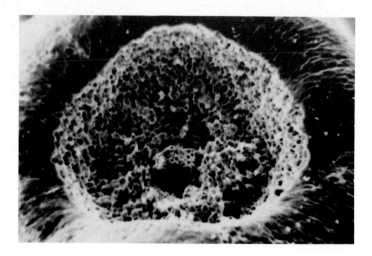

Figure 23.12   Scanning-electron micrograph of a rice grain from a human coprolite at Khok Phanom Di, Thailand, showing the surface and abscission scar of the grain (micrograph G. B. Thompson).

Figure 23.13 Cast tableau on the top of a second-century bc bronze drum from Shihzhaishan, Yunnan, China, showing an agricultural ceremony.

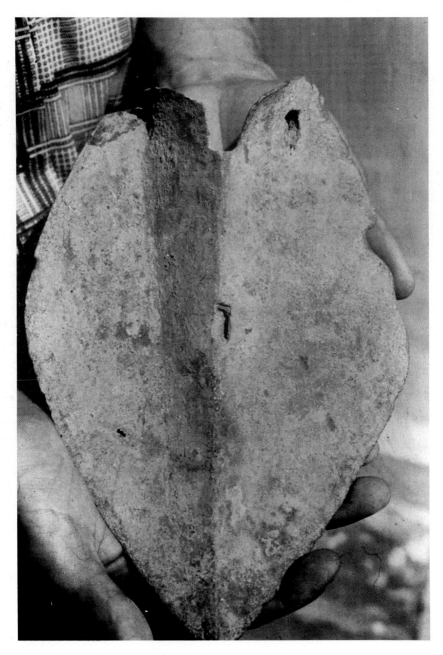

Figure 23.15 Bronze ploughshare from Co Loa, North Vietnam, from the first millennium bc Dongson Culture (photograph C. F. W. Higham).

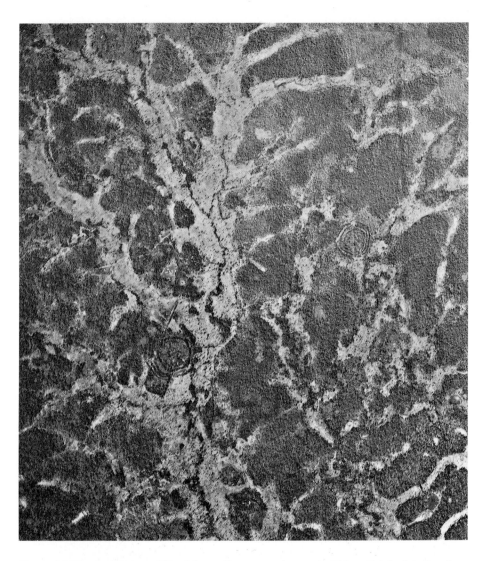

Figure 23.17 Aerial view of Ban Muong Tang moated mounds, Nakon Ratchasima Province, northeastern Thailand (from the Williams Hunt photographic collection, School of Oriental and African Studies, University of London).

Figure 23.22 Early neolithic pottery from Pengtoushan, China, showing rice-grain inclusions (photograph I. C. Glover).

Blust (1993) have recently identified evidence in shared morphemes that supports the Austric hypothesis, although lexical attrition has ruled out the survival of cognates. Blust (ibid.) has proposed that rice cultivation began in the Assam/Yunnan border area, from which agriculturalists expanded eastwards down the Yangzi (Proto AT) to reach Hemudu by 5000 bc, and westwards via the Brahmaputra into eastern India, bringing Proto-Munda languages. He also postulates southward expansion down the Mekong River (Proto Mon–Khmer) and down the Red River (Proto-Viet). The archaeological evidence for this intrusion suggests that it occurred during the third and second millennia bc, and is manifested archaeologically by similar dentate stamped pottery in sites from central Thailand to Yunnan, Cambodia and northern Vietnam.

Conclusion

Returning to the archaeological evidence, we can summarize the present position – which is of course sure to change as archaeological and palaeoecological research in Asia progresses – by suggesting that rice was first domesticated and came into regular cultivation, probably behind areas of seasonally receding floodwaters around lakes in the middle and lower reaches of the Yangzi River, at least 8,000 years ago. Soon afterwards the two major varieties of *indica* (*hsien*) and *japonica* (*keng*) rice were being grown in Central China, but the expansion of rice cultivation south from the Yangzi Basin into South and Southeast Asia seems, on the present patchy archaeological evidence, to have been rather slow. By 5,000 years ago it was being cultivated, probably as a "dry" or rain-fed crop on the southern margins of the millet belt of northern China, and only in the late third millennium bc can we recognize a rapid expansion of rice cultivation into mainland Southeast Asia and westwards across India and Pakistan. There its spread halted for some 2500 years before it was taken by Islamic cultures across Southwest Asia and the Mediterranean Basin. No doubt these fluctuations in the apparent rate of expansion related to the need to evolve appropriate strains of rice to meet new conditions of temperature, day length, seasonality and moisture variation as the crop encountered new environments.[15]

Notes

1. Chang (1985: 426) noted that rice provides some 20 per cent of the calories and 13 per cent of proteins for human consumption worldwide and is the major staple for over 2,000 million people. Over 100 million ha are under rice cultivation throughout the world, more than 90 per cent of which is in South and East Asia. Chang (1988) notes that brown rice has a higher calorific value than other cereals, and that average production from 1 ha of rice can support 5.63 persons in comparison to 3.67 for wheat and 5.63 for maize.
2. In preparing this paper we have drawn heavily on the publications of T. T. Chang, former Senior Rice Geneticist at the International Rice Research Institute, Los Banos, Philippines, who for over twenty years dominated research and writing in English on the origins, domestication and differentiation of Asian rice. In addition, we have relied heavily on the PhD dissertation of Dr Sung-Mo Ahn, of the National Museum, Chongju, Korea and formerly a research student at the Institute of Archaeology, Uni-

versity College London. Dr Ahn's knowledge of Japanese and Chinese, as well of Korean sources, has given us access to some of the many publications in those languages essential for a proper study of the history of rice and its cultivation. We gratefully acknowledge these sources as well as very helpful comments on a draft of the paper by Lisa Kealhofer.

3. De Candolle (1882: 385–7) saw China as the area of the earliest domestication of rice on the basis of its place in ritual, whereas Vavilov (1992 (1926: 29)) suggested eastern India on the basis of the presence of wild rice and the abundance of cultivated varieties, an approach also favoured by Chang (1976a,b).

4. Some authors, such as Oka (1988), accept just two cultivated races of *O. sativa: indica* (*hsien*) and *japonica* (*keng*), whereas Chang (1976a,b) adds *javanica* which Oka (ibid.) has shown to be so closely related to *japonica* that it could be considered only a subtropical variety of *japonica*. It is also argued that temperate long-grain rices, which tolerate cold and are fairly insensitive to variations in day length, are exclusively derived from *japonica* (Angladette 1974).

5. On the basis of historical sources (Ho 1956) showed that the introduction in the eleventh century AD of early-ripening rice varieties into southern China from Champa in central Vietnam led to a major population increase and, ultimately, to a shift in political and economic power from North to South China (see also Bray 1984: 477–510); and in Thailand Hanks (1972) documented the interrelationships between recent rice cultivation systems and demographic, political and technological change in lowland Thailand.

6. D. P. Agrawal, who dated samples from Koldihwa, made it clear that they came from a nearby geological deposit, not from the archaeological levels. He disassociated himself from G. R. Sharma's claims for a seventh millennium bc age for Koldihwa, and this view was confirmed to one of the present authors (ICG) by D. P. Sharma of the National Museum, New Delhi, who worked at the site and who, while a Master's student at the Institute of Archaeology in London, wrote a critical review of the dating of mesolithic and neolithic sites in the middle Ganga Valley.

7. [By ICG] The dating of Non Nok Tha has been disputed since the first dates were published. Bayard (1971: 26–31) suggested three possible chronologies on the basis of 26 radiocarbon and 4 thermoluminescence dates from 7 laboratories with a preferred "long" chronology starting about 3000 bc. This was challenged by Higham (1994) among others and more recently Bayard (pers. comm. to ICG) suggested that the first Early Period burials were no earlier than 2000 bc. In 1989, 11 charcoal samples of rice-tempered pottery from the Early and Middle Periods were dated at the Oxford AMS radiocarbon laboratory. However, only two of these came from secure contexts: OxA–2383: 3650±90 bp from EP 1, and OxA–2392: 3065±70 bp from MP 4. The other samples appear to have come from disturbed contexts and do nothing to resolve the problem of dating the site (Hedges et al. 1991: 292–3). [By CFWH] I differ from Glover in the interpretation of the AMS dates from Non Nok Tha. The submission form to the Oxford Laboratory stated that all samples were of secure provenance. The results, with three exceptions that are undoubtedly too late, indicate that the cemetery belongs within the period 1500–1000 bc.

8. In a conference paper given in early 1994 Hoang (1994) suggests that the rice at Xom Trai came only from the disturbed upper levels, but this is explicitly contradicted by the reports of Viet (1989), who was one of the excavators of the site and who dated the various charcoal samples.

9. On the basis of the pollen grains and the rice and weed phytoliths from the core KL2 taken from near the Khok Phanom Di site in 1985, Maloney (1994) says that "it is clear that rice cultivation began before the known occupation of the Khok Phanom Di site (*c.* 2000 bc) and probably as early as 7000 bp, if not indeed earlier, than the oldest certain evidence from China, that from Hemudu". However, he also says in the same conference paper that domesticated rice cannot unambiguously be identified from pollen, that rice–phytolith research is in its early stages, that "the best expectable outcome is that *O. glaberrima* (African rice) will prove to be separable from *O. sativa* . . . and that certainty of identification must rest with the discovery of plant macrofossil remains" (and there is as yet no certain evidence of such remains associated with human cultural remains in Thailand earlier than the early second millennium bc). Kealhofer (1994) has also presented phytolith evidence from mid-Holocene palaeosoils in the Lopburi region of central Thailand, which seems to indicate vegetational disturbance and perhaps even rice cultivation, but there are no archaeological materials associated with these soils.

10. The Toalian Culture cave site of Ulu Leang 1 in southern Sulawesi, Indonesia, yielded many charred rice grains, some isolated and possibly derived from recent disturbances, but a well sealed hearth, in

context J9, 7–8, contained over 50 complete or partial charred grains and many thousands of husk fragments that were identified as domesticated *O. sativa* by T. T. Chang. The stratigraphic position, and an overlying date of 4172 ±90 bp (HAR–1734), suggested to Glover (1979: 22–4) that this hearth dated from about 6000 bp, but another charcoal sample from near the hearth gave a much later date that suggests some unobserved disturbance in the area. Unfortunately, all the charred grains sent to Dr Chang were damaged or lost during investigation and none seems to have survived, so there is no possibility of dating them directly by the AMS radiocarbon method.

11. There is little agreement between Chinese archaeologists as to the division and grouping of these sites and phases. Some refer to the Majiabang Culture as the southern phase of the Qingliagang Culture and others separate the first, Hemudu phase, of the Majiabang Culture as a quite distinct culture. See Chang (1986: 208) for a more extended discussion in English of these relationships.

12. Because the water buffalo (*Bubalus bubalis*) is so important for ploughing rice fields when production is intensified through transplanting, archaeologists commonly take the appearance of the domesticated animal to mark this stage of rice cultivation.

13. Temper extracted from two sherds from Pengtoushan and dated at the Oxford AMS laboratory yielded uncalibrated dates of 7550 ±90 bp (OxA–2210) and 7040 ±140 bp (OxA–2214) (Hedges et al. 1992: 156)

14. Glover saw the pottery and other finds from Pengtoushan at the Hunan Province Institute of Archaeology in Changsha in 1991 and can confirm that charred rice grains (Fig. 23.22) and chaff are very common in the pottery and lumps of clay. However, a soil sample from the site, which he was told should contain some rice grains and which he brought to London for examination, was found to contain only some twigs and a few small potsherds.

15. The scenario for the domestication and expansion of rice assumes a relatively coherent single hearth of domestication which is suggested to us by the existing archaeological data. However, some botanists and palaeoecologists favour multiple centres of domestication within a very broad area such as that outlined by Chang (1976) and argue that the rice isozyme evidence supports this (Kealhofer: pers. comm, January 1994).

References

Ahn, S. M. 1993. *Origin and differentiation of domesticated rice in Asia – a review of archaeological and botanical evidence*. PhD dissertation, Institute of Archaeology, University College London.

Angladette, A. 1974. Rice in humid tropical Asia. In *Natural resources of humid tropical Asia* [Natural Resources Monograph XII], 415–38. Paris: UNESCO.

Barnes, G. L. 1990. Paddy soils now and then. *World Archaeology* 22, 1–18.

Bayard, D. T. 1971. *Non Nok Tha – the 1968 excavation*. University Monographs in Prehistoric Anthropology 4, University of Otago.

Bellwood, P., R. Gillespie, G. B. Thompson, J. S. Vogel, I. W. Ardika, Ipoi Datan 1992. New dates for prehistoric Asian rice. *Asian Perspectives* 31, 161–70.

Bellwood, P. 1985. *Prehistory of the Indo–Malaysian archipelago*. Sydney: Academic Press.

Blust, R. 1993. Beyond the Austronesian homeland: the Austric hypothesis and its implications for archaeology. Paper read at a meeting on Austronesian languages at the University Museum, University of Pennsylvania, Philadelphia, November 1993.

Bray, F. 1984. *Science and civilization in China*, vol. VI(2): *agriculture*, J. Needham (ed.). Cambridge: Cambridge University Press.

Buth, G. M., R. S. Bisht, G. S. Gaur 1982. Investigation of palaeoethnobotanical remains from Semthan, Kashmir. *Man and Environment* 6, 41–5.

Chang, K. C. 1986. *The archaeology of ancient China*, 4th edn. New Haven, Connecticut: Yale University Press.

Chang, T. T. 1976a. The rice cultures. *Philosophical Transactions of the Royal Society of London B* 275, 143–55.

— 1976b. The origin, evolution, cultivation, dissemination and diversification of Asian and African rices. *Euphytica* 25, 425–41.

— 1983. The origins and early cultures of the cereal grains and food legumes. In *The origins of Chinese civilization*, D. N. Keightley (ed.), 65–94. Berkeley: University of California Press.

— 1985. Crop history and genetic conservation: rice – case study. *Iowa State Journal of Research* **59**, 425–55.

— 1987. The impact of rice on human civilization and population expansion. *Interdisciplinary Science Review* **12**, 63–9.

— 1988. Ethnobotany of rice in Insular Southeast Asia. *Asian Perspectives* **26**, 69–76.

— 1989. Domestication and the spread of the cultivated rices. In *Foraging and farming: the evolution of plant exploitation*, D. R. Harris & G. C. Hillman (eds), 408–17. London: Unwin Hyman.

Chattarjee, P. G., R. Ranava, A. K. Ghosh 1978. On the origin of rice in India: some remarks. *Science and Culture* **44**, 145–8.

Costantini, L. 1979. Notes on the palaeobotany and protohistory of Swat. In *South Asian archaeology 1977*, M. Taddei (ed.), 73–8. Naples: Istituto Universitario Orientale.

— 1981. Palaeoethnobotany at Pirak. In *South Asian archaeology 1979*, H. Härtel (ed.), 271–7. Berlin: Reimer.

Crawford, G. W. 1992a. Prehistoric plant domestication in East Asia. In *The origins of agriculture: an international perspective*, C. W. Cowan & P. J. Watson (eds), 7–38. Washington: Smithsonian Institution Press.

— 1992b The transitions to agriculture in Japan. In *Transitions to agriculture in prehistory* [Monographs in World Archaeology 4], A. B. Gebauer & T. D. Price (eds), 117–32. Madison: Prehistory Press

de Candolle, A. 1882. *Origine des plantes cultivées*. Paris: Germer Baillière.

Diffloth, G. (1991). Linguistic prehistory from a Mon–Khmer perspective. Paper presented at the Conference on The High Bronze Age in Southeast Asia and China, Hua Hin, Thailand, January 1991.

Englehardt, R. 1994. New directions for archaeological research on the Angkor plain: use of remote sensing technology for research into ancient Khmer environmental engineering. Paper presented at the 15th Indo–Pacific Prehistory Association Congress, Chiangmai, Thailand, 5–12 January 1994.

Garton, D. 1977. *A study of the effects of charring on rice grains*. BA Report, Institute of Archaeology, University of London.

Glover, I. C. 1979. Prehistoric plant remains from Southeast Asia with special reference to rice. In *South Asian Archaeology 1977*, M. Taddei (ed.), 7–37. Naples: Istituto Universitario Orientale.

— 1985. Some problems relating to the domestication of rice in Asia. *Recent advances in Indo–Pacific prehistory*. V. N. Misra & P. Bellwood (eds), 265–74. New Delhi: Oxford University Press and IBH.

Gorman, C. F. 1977. *A priori* models and Thai prehistory: a reconsideration of the beginnings of agriculture in southeastern Asia. In *Origins of agriculture*, C. A. Reed (ed.), 321–55. The Hague: Mouton.

Gorman, C. F. & P. Charoenwongsa 1976. Ban Chiang: a mosaic of impressions from the first two years. *Expedition* **18**, 14–26.

Groslier, B-P. 1979. La cité hydraulique angkorienne. Exploitations ou surexploitations du sol? *Bulletin de l'Ecole française d'Extrême Orient* **66**, 161–202.

Hanks, L. M. 1972. *Rice and man*. Chicago: Aldine–Atherton.

Harlan, J. R. 1975. *Crops and man*. Madison, Wisconsin: American Society of Agronomy Crop Science Society of America.

Hedges, R. E. M., R. A. Housley, C. R. Bronk, G. J. van Klinken 1991. Radiocarbon dates from the Oxford AMS system: *Archaeometry* datelist 14. *Archaeometry* **33**, 279–96.

— 1992. Radiocarbon dates from the Oxford AMS system: *Archaeometry* datelist 14. *Archaeometry* **34**, 141–59.

Higham, C. F. W. 1984. Prehistoric rice cultivation in Southeast Asia. *Scientific American* **250**, 100–7.

— 1989. *The archaeology of mainland Southeast Asia – from 10,000 BC to the fall of Angkor*. Cambridge: Cambridge University Press.

— 1994a. Chronometric hygiene and the Bronze Age of Southeast Asia. Paper presented at the 15th Indo–Pacific Prehistory Association Congress, Chiangmai, Thailand, 5–12 January 1994.

— 1994b. Archaeology and linguistics in Southeast Asia: implications of the Austric hypothesis. Paper presented at the 15th Indo–Pacific Prehistory Association Congress, Chiangmai, Thailand,

5–12 January 1994.

Higham, C. F. W. & R. Banannurag (eds) 1990. *The excavation of Khok Phanom Di – a prehistoric site in central Thailand*, vol. 1. London: Society of Antiquaries.

— 1991. *The excavation of Khok Phanom Di – a prehistoric site in central Thailand*, vol. 2. London: Society of Antiquaries.

Higham, C. F. W. & R. Thosarat (eds) 1993. *The excavation of Khok Phanom Di – a prehistoric site in central Thailand*, vol. 3. London: Society of Antiquaries.

— 1994. *Khok Phanom Di: adaptation to the world's richest habitat.* Fort Worth, Texas: Harcourt Brace Jovanovich.

Higham, T. F. G. 1993. The shell knives. In Higham & Thosarat (1993: 177–212).

Hill, H. E. & J. Evans 1989. Crops of the Pacific: new evidence from the chemical analysis of organic residues in pottery. In *Foraging and farming; the evolution of plant exploitation*, D. R. Harris & G. C. Hillman (eds), 418–25. London: Unwin Hyman.

Ho, P. T. 1956. Early-ripening rice in Chinese history. *Economic History Review* 9, 200–18.

Hoang, Xuan Chinh 1984. The Hoabinhian culture and the birth of botanical domestication in Viet Nam. In *Southeast Asian Archaeology at the XV Pacific Science Congress*, D. T. Bayard (ed.), 169–72. Dunedin: University of Otago Monographs in Prehistoric Anthropology 16.

— 1994. The development stages of early agriculture in Vietnam. Paper presented at the 15th Indo–Pacific Prehistory Association Congress, Chiangmai, Thailand, 5–12 January 1994.

Kajale, M. D. 1991. Current status of Indian palaeoethnobotany: introduced and indigenous plants with a discussion of the historical and evolutionary development of Indian agriculture and agricultural systems in general. In *New light on early farming – recent developments in palaeoethnobotany*, J. Renfrew (ed.), 155–89. Edinburgh: Edinburgh University Press.

— 1994. Domestication of rice (*Oryza sativa* Linn.) in parts of eastern India and its relevance to the theory of expansion of rice cultivation from China. Paper presented at the 15th Indo–Pacific Prehistory Association Congress, Chiangmai, Thailand, 5–12 January 1994.

Kealhofer, L. 1994. Holocene palaeoenvironments in central Thailand: the phytolith evidence from the Lopburi region. Paper presented at the 15th Indo–Pacific Prehistory Association Congress, Chiangmai, Thailand, 5–12 January 1994.

Kealhofer, L. & D. R. Piperno 1994. Early agriculture in southeast Asia: phytolith evidence from the Bang Pakong valley, Thailand. *Antiquity* 68, 564–72.

Maloney, B. K. 1990. Grass pollen and the origins of rice agriculture in North Sumatra. *Modern Quaternary Research in Southeast Asia* 11, 135–61.

— 1991. Palaeoenvironments of Khok Phanom Di: the pollen, pteridophyte spore and macroscopic charcoal record. In *The excavation of Khok Phanom Di – a prehistoric site in central Thailand* (vol. 2), C. F. W. Higham & R. Banannurag (eds), 7–134. London: Society of Antiquaries.

— 1994. The origins of rice cultivation: recent advances. Paper presented at the 4th International Conference on Thai Studies, London, July 1994.

Masaoka, M. & T. Takaoka 1984. *Excavation of Hykkengawa Haraojima Site II.* Okayama: Educational Board of Okayama Prefecture.

Matsuo, T. T. 1952. Genetic and ecological studies on cultivated rice. *Bulletin of the National Institute of Agricultural Science, Japan* D3, 1–111.

Moore, E. 1988. *Moated sites in early North East Thailand.* Oxford: British Archaeological Reports, International Series 400.

Oka, H-I. 1988. *Origin of cultivated rice.* Amsterdam: Elsevier.

Parry, J. T. 1992. The investigative role of Landsat-TM in the examination of pre- and proto-historic water management sites in northeast Thailand. *Geocarto International* 4, 5–24.

Pei, A. 1989. Rice remains in Pengtoushan culture in Hunan and rice growing in prehistoric China. *Nongye Kaogu* 1989 (2), 102–8.

Pham, Huy Thong (ed.) 1990. *Dong Son drums of Viet Nam*: Ha Noi: Vietnam Social Science Publishing House.

Pigott, V. 1992. The archaeology of copper production at prehistoric Non Pa Wai and Nil Kham Haeng in central Thailand. Paper presented at the 4th International Conference of the European Association of Southeast Asian Archaeologists, Rome, September 1992.

Reid, L. A. 1993. Morphological evidence for Austric. Paper presented at the Conference on Asia-Mainland/Austronesian Connections, University of Hawaii, May 1993.

Reynolds, T. E.g. 1992. Excavations at Banyan Valley Cave, northern Thailand: a report on the 1972 season. *Asian Perspectives* **31**, 77–98.

Schmidt, P. W. 1906. *Die Mon-Khmer Völker: ein Binderglied zwischen Völkern Zentralasiens und Austronesiens*. Braunschweig: Friedrich Vieweg.

Sharma, G. R., V. D. Misra, D. Mandal, B. B. Misra, J. N. Pal 1980. *Beginnings of agriculture: epi-palaeolithic to neolithic: excavations at Chopani–Mando, Mahadaha and Mahagara*. Allahabad: Abinash Prakashan.

Solheim, W. G. 1972. An earlier agricultural revolution. *Scientific American* **206**(4), 34–41.

Snow, B. E., R. Shutler, D. E. Nelson, J. S. Vogel, J. R. Southon 1986. Evidence for early rice cultivation in the Philippines. *Philippine Quarterly of Culture and Society* **14**, 3–11.

Stoskopf, N. C. 1985. *Cereal grain crops*. Reston, Virginia: Prentice-Hall.

Stott, P. 1992. Angkor: the shifting paradigm. In *The gift of water*, J. Rigg (ed.), 47–58. London: School of Oriental and African Studies.

Thompson, G. B. 1992a. *Archaeobotanical investigations at Khok Phanom Di, central Thailand*. PhD dissertation, Department of Prehistory, Research School of Pacific Studies, Australian National University.

— 1992b. Archaeobotanical indicators of rice domestication – a critical evaluation of diagnostic criteria. Paper presented at the 4th International Conference of the European Association of Southeast Asian Archaeologists, Rome, September 1992.

Ti Huang & Wang Dadao (eds) 1983. *The Chinese bronzes of Yunnan*. London: Sidgwick & Jackson (in co-operation with the Cultural Relics Publishing House, Beijing).

Tuan, Dao The 1983. Chaff found at Xom Trai Cave – the evolution of rice plants in Vietnam. *Khao Co Hoc* 1983 (3), 1–6 [in Vietnamese].

— 1984. Remarks on samples of rice unearthed at Xom Trai Cave. *Khao Co Hoc* 1984 (1–2), 142–8 [in Vietnamese].

Tusa, S. 1990. Ancient ploughing in northern Pakistan. In *South Asian Archaeology 1987*. M. Taddei (ed.), 349–76. Rome: Istituto per il Medio ed Estremo Oriente.

van Liere, W. 1980. Traditional water management in the lower Mekong Basin. *World Archaeology* **11**, 265–80.

— 1985. Early agriculture and intensification in mainland Southeast Asia. In *Prehistoric intensive agriculture in the tropics*, I. S. Farrington (ed.), 829–34. Oxford: British Archaeological Reports, International Series 232 ii.

Vavilov, N. I. 1992 (1926). *Studies on the origin of cultivated plants* [Papers on Applied Botany and Plant Breeding, Institut Botanique Appliqué et d'Amélioration des Plantes (Leningrad) 16, 139–248 [in Russian]]. English version: Centres of origin of cultivated plants. In *N. I. Vavilov: origin and geography of cultivated plants*, V. R. Dorofeyev (ed.), 22–143. Cambridge: Cambridge University Press.

Viet, Nguyen Van 1989. *Die Radiocarbon-Chronologie für die Ur- und Frühgeschichte in Nord Vietnam*. DPhil. thesis, Akademie der Wissenschaften, Berlin (DDR).

Vishnu-Mittre 1976. Comment on Hutchinson, J. India: local and introduced crops. *Philosophical Transactions of the Royal Society of London B* **275**, 141.

Watabe, T. 1984. Origin and dispersal of rice in Asia. *East Asian Cultural Studies* **24**, 33–9.

Watson, A. M. 1983. *Agricultural innovation in the early Islamic world*. Cambridge: Cambridge University Press.

White, J. 1990. The Ban Chiang chronology revised. In *Southeast Asian Archaeology 1986*, I. C. & E. A. Glover (eds), 121–9. Oxford: British Archaeological Reports, International Series 561.

Yan Wenming 1982. The origin of rice agriculture in China. *Nongye Kaogu* **1982**(1), 19–54.

— 1991. China's earliest rice agriculture remains. In *Indo–Pacific prehistory 1990* (vol. 1), P. S. Bellwood (ed.), 118–26. Canberra & Jakarta: IPPA and Asosiasi Prehistorisi Indonesia. *Bulletin of the Indo–Pacific Prehistory Association* II.

Yen, D. E. 1977. Hoabinhain horticulture? The evidence and the questions from northwest Thailand.

In *Sunda and Sahul: prehistoric studies in Southeast Asia, Melanesia and Australia*, J. Allen, J. Golson, R. Jones (eds), 567–99. London: Academic Press.

— 1982. Ban Chiang pottery and rice. *Expedition* **24**, 51–64.

Yokokura, M. 1992. Early agriculture in Southeast Asia [in Japanese with an English summary]. *Southeast Asian Studies* **30**, 272–314.

You, X-L. 1976. A few observations on rice grains and bone "Si" unearthed from the 4th layer of the Hemudu site. *Wenwu* 1976 (8), 20–3 [in Chinese].

Zhao, Songqiao & Wei-Tang Wu 1988. Early neolithic Hemudu culture along the Hangzhou estuary and the origin of domestic paddy rice in China. *Asian Perspectives* **27**, 29–34.

Zhou, J. 1981. Report of the examination of ancient rice from the middle and lower Yangzi. *Yunnan Nongye Xuexi* 1981 (1), 1–6 [in Chinese].

CHAPTER TWENTY-FOUR

Jomon and Yayoi: the transition to agriculture in Japanese prehistory

Keiji Imamura

The purpose of this chapter is to present a general overview of two distinctive aspects of Japanese prehistory: the development of complex, non-agricultural subsistence strategies during the transitional period from the Pleistocene to the Holocene, and the subsequent adoption and spread of full-scale agriculture after a long stable period of development based on gathering, fishing and hunting. Because the intention here is to present a synopsis of these aspects of Japanese cultural evolution and to elucidate the essential points, many sites and associated phenomena are described only briefly, without full explanation of their individual characteristics and contexts. Also, because of limitations of space, and to ensure clarity and simplicity of presentation, discussion of differing interpretations is necessarily restricted.[1]

The unique sequence of prehistoric cultures in Japan

Prehistoric development in Japan did not follow a "Three Age" pattern that can be periodized as a sequence of cultures from the Neolithic to the Bronze Age and the Iron Age. Whereas pottery and stable sedentary settlements are usually regarded elsewhere in Eurasia as typical of neolithic farming communities, in Japan these phenomena are associated with hunting–gathering communities. Full-scale agriculture, and bronze and iron tools, were introduced into Japan at the same time. There was in this sense neither a distinct neolithic period of agriculture without bronze, nor a Bronze Age without iron. In addition, edge-ground stone tools, which are commonly regarded as diagnostic of the Neolithic, are found in large quantities from 30,000 years ago, thus necessitating a redefinition of the Palaeolithic in Japanese prehistory.

The sequence of prehistoric economies in Japan can be summarized as follows:
(a) an archaic economy of mobile hunting and gathering with ground-stone tools
(b) a hunting–gathering economy with pottery and sedentary settlements
(c) an agricultural economy with bronze and iron.
This sequence is reflected in the periodization of Japanese prehistoric cultures into

the Preceramic or Palaeolithic (corresponding to (a) above), the Jomon period (b), and the Yayoi period (c). The term Jomon derives from the Japanese word for the cord marking that was commonly applied to the surface of pottery of that period, and Yayoi is the name of the site from which the first specimen of the "Yayoi" type of pottery was discovered. The change from (a) to (b) took place earlier than 12,000 years ago, whereas the change from (b) to (c) took place around 2400 to 2500 years ago in northern Kyushu (the region of Japan closest to the Asian continent) and around 2100 to 2200 years ago at the northern tip of Honshu Island (Fig. 24.1). The so-called Epi-Jomon hunting–gathering culture, however, continued in the northernmost island of Hokkaido, where the climate was too cool for rice cultivation.

Figure 24.1   Japan showing the location of sites mentioned in the text.

The Jomon period is divided into six phases: Incipient, Initial, Early, Middle, Late and Final; and the Yayoi is divided into four: Initial, Early, Middle and Late. The Initial phase of the Yayoi is seen only in southwestern Japan because the final phase of the Jomon culture lasted in northeastern Japan until the time of the Early Yayoi. The Yayoi is followed, from the end of the third century AD, by the Kofun period (d), which is characterized by a uniform type of mounded tomb called *kofun*. The dispersal of this standardized type of tomb, made for the ruling class, is interpreted as indicative of the political unification of Japan.

The origins of agriculture in China

Recognition of the very early origins of agriculture in China has been one of the most important recent discoveries in world archaeology, and it has accentuated the contrast between the long tradition of agriculture in China and the persistence of hunting–gathering communities, with pottery, in Japan. An extended discussion of the origins of Asian agriculture is not required here, particularly because Glover & Higham present in Chapter 23 in this volume detailed information on early rice cultivation in the middle and lower reaches of the Yangzi Valley. Therefore, only a cursory outline of early Chinese agriculture is provided by way of comparisons with the situation in Japan. In China, early evidence of foxtail millet dates back to 7000 bp at several sites, including Cishan and Peiligang, in the Huanghe (Yellow) River Valley (Shao 1982), and evidence of rice dates back to about 8000 bp at Pengtoushan and other sites in the middle reaches of the Yangzi Valley (Ren 1982, S. Nakamura 1991).

There is much research to be done, including archaeobotanical investigation and explication of the processes of domestication, before the origins of Chinese agriculture can be fully understood. However, judging from the kinds of tools used for farming and the processing of cereals, such as the stone sickles and querns of the northern area, and the large settlements and functionally diversified pottery forms of both the northern and southern areas, the cereal remains are believed to be the product of cultivation beyond the level of gathering seeds from wild plants. Indeed, it is now apparent that agriculture in East Asia began in two areas, the cool dry Huanghe River Valley and the warm humid Yangzi Valley, and that in each it developed around, and was dependent on, different cereals adapted to their respective climates: foxtail millet in the former and rice in the latter (Matsumura 1991). The early dates, together with the kinds of cereals cultivated, militate against the long-held view that agriculture spread to China from Southwest Asia and suggest that it originated independently in East Asia.

The oldest known pottery in China is from Xiangrendong in Jiangxi Province, and from Zengpiyan in Guanxi Province, which, after allowing for the effect of inert carbon dissolved in waters in the limestone has been dated to between 8000 and 9000 bp (C_{14} Lab. 1982). More recently some pottery fragments were discovered from a layer dated to 10000 bp at Nanzhuangtou in Hebei Province (Baoding 1992). The simple forms of the pottery, as well as the site locations (with the exception of Nanzhuangtou) in caves with abundant remains of collected shellfish and hunted animals, make it difficult to postulate any form of agriculture at those sites. In summary, although the precise origins of Chinese pottery as well as agriculture cannot be completely ascertained at present because of insufficient evidence, it appears that pottery originated before agriculture and that the establishment of agriculture and the elaboration of pottery then progressed rapidly during the early Holocene.

Developments in Japan during the final Pleistocene and early Holocene

Almost contemporaneous with the beginnings of agriculture in China, different developments took place in Japan. The first innovation was pottery. According to radiocarbon dates from the Fukui Cave (Kamaki & Serizawa 1967) in Nagasaki Prefecture, the Kamikuroiwa rockshelter in Ehime Prefecture (Esaka et al. 1967) and other sites, pottery began to appear from around 12000 bp in hunting–gathering communities in Japan. Objections have been raised against this date based on the assumption that the oldest pottery, as well as the oldest ground-stone tools, in the world could not come from the remote Japanese islands, off the Asian mainland. Thus, it was argued that the radiocarbon dating that placed Japanese prehistory outside the general trajectory of cultural developments elsewhere in the world must be fundamentally flawed (Yamanouchi & Sato 1962). However, those who rejected the radiocarbon dates had suggested the same basic sequence of cultures that the ages of the radiocarbon dates indicated. The most important point is that radiocarbon dates for evidence in Japan of worldwide natural phenomena, such as rising postglacial temperatures and sea levels, show no discrepancy from dates obtained on similar samples in other parts of the world. Thus, to argue that the radiocarbon dates for Japanese prehistory are wrong is to suggest that only those samples taken from human settlements are incorrect – to the extent of being double to triple their true ages.

The date of the earliest Japanese pottery that originally generated this controversy goes back even further. Recently, the Mikoshiba-Chojakubo and related stone-tool assemblages, which had been placed at the end of the preceramic (palaeolithic) period, were found associated with very small quantities of pottery at several sites (Research Party Ushirono 1976, Miyake et al. 1979, Suzuki & Shiraishi 1980). Although there are no radiocarbon dates from these sites with pottery, they are almost certainly older than the linear appliqué-type pottery, which is dated to between 12,000 and 12,500 bp in the Incipient Jomon. Therefore, the emergence of pottery in Japan may date back to around 13000 bp.

However, the extent to which pottery was used at that time was very limited. Only a few among the dozens of sites known of that period have pottery fragments, and when they occur they do so in very small quantities. Thus, although the technique of pottery manufacture was known, it was only used on rare occasions. It seems that the nomadic life of the time, which was largely dependent on hunting, neither required the use of pottery nor was suited to the transport of fragile pots.

From about 12000 bp there is evidence that the use of pottery became quite common, but it is not until after 9000 bp, when plant foods become dominant among subsistence resources and many stable settlements appear, that there is evidence of the mass use of pottery. So a close correspondence is recognized between pottery, plant foods and sedentary life. This marks the establishment of the basic Jomon economic system.

Establishment of the Jomon economic system and stable settlements

The phase from the emergence of pottery until the appearance of the Yoriitomon series of pottery types is called the Incipient Jomon and is distinguished from the next phase, the Initial Jomon. Modes of life changed greatly between the two phases. The changes included greater dependence on plant foods and marine resources and in increase in the scale of settlements, all of which imply a stable life.

The main features of the Incipient Jomon are as follows: small-scale settlements with few if any dwellings (those that did exist lacked firm structures), a high frequency of habitation sites in caves and rockshelters, large quantities of stone tools compared with pottery, and a high percentage of hunting tools such as spearheads or tanged points (Fig. 24.2; Nakamura 1960) with a correspondingly low percentage of plant-food processing tools such as grinding stones, hammer stones or pitted stones. There is no evidence of sea fishing, but it is difficult to judge whether it was practised during the Incipient Jomon or whether all traces of sea-fishing settlements were submerged following the postglacial rise of sea level of 40–50 m.

Only in southernmost Japan, in southern Kyushu, does a different picture emerge, during the time of the linear appliqué pottery in the Incipient Jomon. Despite thick layers of volcanic ash overlying cultural deposits of the Incipient Jomon and obstructing the discovery of sites, and despite the comparatively slow progress of archaeological surveys, many sites of the Incipient Jomon have been discovered in Kyushu. Indeed, a much denser distribution of sites from this phase is assumed for southern Kyushu than for the Tokyo region, where intensive surveys have been carried out.

One of the sites in southern Kyushu that has been investigated is the Sojiyama site of the linear appliqué stage in Kagoshima Prefecture (Amamiya et al. 1992). Two pit dwellings (semi-subterranean houses) with quite substantial structures and characteristic fire-pits with ventilation shafts were found there. Among the artefacts, there was much pottery, 12 arrowheads (which are rarely found in contemporary sites in other areas), five grinding and hammer stones, two pitted stones and four grinding slabs. This assemblage of artefacts is very different from those characteristic of normal Incipient Jomon sites in other areas. On the whole it is similar to those of later Jomon sites, and suggests that plants foods were important in southern Kyushu at that time. One other piece of evidence, which supports the postulated importance of plant foods, is a storage pit for acorns which was unearthened at Higashi–Kurotsuchida in Kagoshima Prefecture (Kawaguchi 1982).

All this evidence suggests the spread from the south of a stable lifestyle which was based on plant foods and which accompanied rising temperatures and the florescence of the temperate forest (Miyoshi & Yano 1986). The acorns from Higashi–Kurotsuchida were those of deciduous oaks. Although the cold climate had passed and it was becoming warmer, deciduous forests, which are characteristic of northeastern Japan,

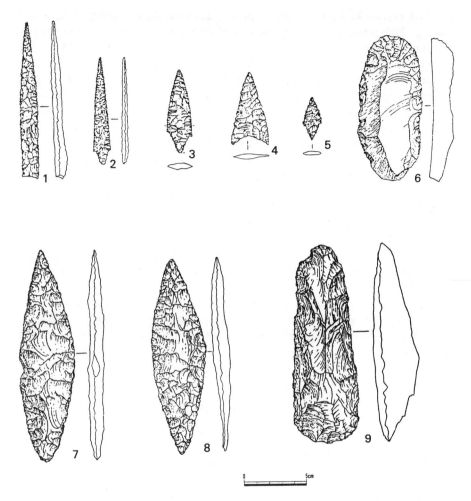

Figure 24.2 Typical stone tools of the Incipient Jomon from Kosegasawa, Niigata Prefecture (from Nakamura 1960): 1 = slender point; 2, 3 = tanged point; 4, 5 = arrowheads; 6 = end scraper; 7, 8 = spearheads; 9 = unifacially edged axe (adze).

initially extended farther south to include southwestern Japan where today evergreen forests are found. Whereas the acorns of evergreen oaks only require leaching to make them edible, the acorns of deciduous oaks require special processing to remove their higher content of tannic acid. This is done either by boiling them for several hours or by neutralizing them with a solution of wood ash. The storage of deciduous-oak acorns at Higashi-Kurotsuchida suggests that such techniques were already known, and the increasing abundance of pottery in these sites suggests that pottery was closely involved with the processing of plant foods (Watanabe 1987).

This economic change, the first appearance of which is associated with a warmer climate and extensive terrace-deposits of volcanic ash in southern Kyushu, next becomes evident in the Kanto region around Tokyo at the beginning of the Initial Jomon, which is marked by the appearance of the Yoriitomon series of pottery types. Yoriitomon pottery first appears in central Japan, in Honshu, around 9000 bp. The term Yoriitomon refers to a characteristic cord-mark which was applied by the rolling and impressing of cord-wrapped dowels. During this phase the number of sites increased rapidly. Some of them have many pit dwellings; for example, at the Musashidai sites, Tokyo City, 19 pit dwellings were distributed in an arc in the excavated area (Hayakawa & Kawachi 1987). If this arc represents one section of a circle, which is the basic arrangement of dwellings in large settlements during the Jomon, then it is clear that this settlement layout must have been established by this time.

The number of pit dwellings unearthed at all sites associated with Yoriitomon pottery in the Kanto region exceeds 200 – a large number compared to the total of 10, including doubtful cases, reported from all Incipient Jomon sites throughout Japan. However, not only was there an increase in the number and size of settlements, but significant changes also took place in subsistence patterns.

An interesting example of Initial Jomon settlement is a site at the Tokyo Astronomical Observatory (Fig. 24.1; Imamura et al. 1983). There, three pit dwellings were found in a small area during the rescue excavation of a planned construction site, but there are undoubtedly more unexcavated pit dwellings because the excavation area covered only one section of the settlement. Of particular interest was pit dwelling 3 – a rectangular structure measuring up to 8.2×8.4m, which is larger than most other Jomon dwellings. The post-holes, which only measured 10–20cm in diameter, were

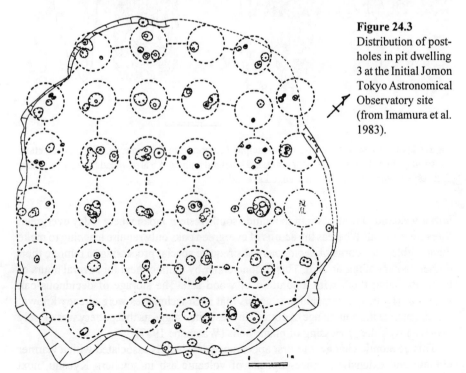

Figure 24.3
Distribution of post-holes in pit dwelling 3 at the Initial Jomon Tokyo Astronomical Observatory site (from Imamura et al. 1983).

clustered in groups of three to five holes, and these groups were arranged in such a way as to mark out three concentric squares (Fig.24.3). This clustering of post-holes cannot be explained by the successive building of new dwellings at the same spot, nor by the building of extensions. It is interpreted as evidence of a long period of occupation during which old posts were replaced by new ones placed nearby or alongside the old ones to reinforce them. This example clearly demonstrates long-term occupation and suggests a stable life-style. What was the economic base that supported this stable life? Neither animal bones nor plant remains were preserved in the acidic soil, and a few arrowheads are the only indication of hunting gear. However, there are 538 grinding or pitted stones, 64 grinding slabs, and 185 stamp-shaped stone tools, most of which were presumably used for processing plants foods (Fig. 24.4). This clearly shows how important plant foods were at this site.

Another major change apparent in the Initial Jomon is the earliest evidence of sea fishing. The Natsushima shell midden supplied good evidence of this (Sugihara & Serizawa 1957). It is located in a small bay at Yokosuka, Kanagawa Prefecture, in central Honshu (Fig. 24.1). The major species of mollusc were oyster (*Crassostrea*

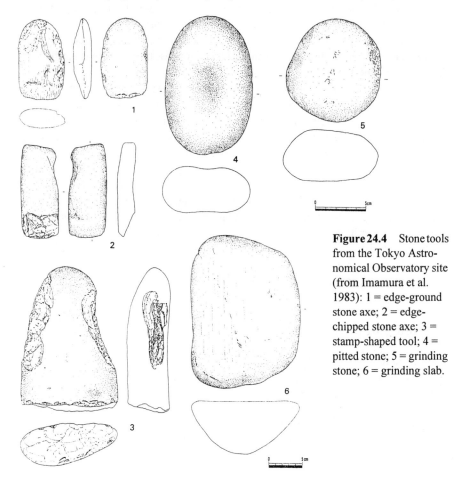

Figure 24.4 Stone tools from the Tokyo Astronomical Observatory site (from Imamura et al. 1983): 1 = edge-ground stone axe; 2 = edge-chipped stone axe; 3 = stamp-shaped tool; 4 = pitted stone; 5 = grinding stone; 6 = grinding slab.

gigas) and cockle (*Tegillarca granosa*), and 15 species of fish were identified. Three fish-hooks made of antler provide evidence for fishing by hook and line. As well as the evidence for fishing in bays, there is also evidence for open-sea fishing, for instance, at the Shimotakabora site on the western coast of Oshima Island south of the Tokyo region (Fig. 24.1; Research Party Shimotakabora 1985). This site is dated to 8500 bp by the Hirasaka type of palin pottery, which immediately followed the Yoriitomon series. The variety of fish, including tuna, moray, rock bream, opal eye, scad mackerel, chub mackerel and parrot fish, as well as marine turtle and dolphin, presents clear evidence of active fishing on the open sea.

Adaptive strategies other than agriculture

Most of the basic economic features of the Jomon were in place by the middle of the Initial Jomon. These included the processing of plant foods, marine fishing both in bays and on the open sea, hunting with bows and dogs, the common use of pottery and of pit dwellings, and the circular arrangement of houses in large settlements. Some of these traits are first recognized in the Incipient Jomon of southern Kyushu, and pottery is adopted in Hokkaido later than in other areas of Japan. The correspondence between these traits and the northward spread of a warmer climate is hardly surprising or accidental.

Moreover, the correspondence in dates between the establishment of the Jomon economy and the emergence of agriculture in China is not accidental. It can be understood as reflecting two different adaptive strategies pursued in response to changing vegetational environments under conditions of increasing temperature and humidity during the postglacial epoch (Yasuda 1982). In Japan, adaptation was mainly towards the exploitation of plant-food resources provided by the temperate forests, which flourished under conditions of increased, mainly summer, precipitation.

If economic changes outside the early centres of agriculture are also seen as adaptations to a changing environment, it is inappropriate to regard hunting–gathering economies as primitive. It is suggested in the next section that the Jomon economy was an extremely successful adaptive strategy that incorporated many phenomena similar to features associated with neolithic communities, such as stable sedentary settlement and developments in material and spiritual culture.

Stability of the Jomon economy

The Jomon lasted without any fundamental changes to its economic base for about 10,000 years, until 2,400 years ago when it was replaced in the Yayoi period by an economic system based on wet-rice cultivation. This long timespan should be seen as a reflection of very successful adaptation to the natural environment of Japan rather than the result of lack of innovation. Judging from the number and scale of settlements, it reached a peak of prosperity in the Middle Jomon (5000–4000 bp) in northeastern Japan.

The remains of acorns, walnuts, and sweet and horse chestnuts provide evidence of the use of tree nuts. Tubers are also thought to have been exploited, although there is as yet no direct proof of this because the inference is based on the assumed digging function of so-called chipped-stone axes. In addition to such plant foods, there were also abundant fishing resources in many bays and inland waters. Fish-hooks, harpoons, fish-spears and nets were used, and fish-weirs were constructed in small streams. Hunting was also actively pursued, with deer and wild boars, which lived in the forests, as the most important game. Jomon people capitalized on these varied resources in many ways, one of the most ingenious and multi-faceted subsistence techniques being the pit-trap and accessory devices employed in hunting (Imamura et al. 1983).

The existence of hundreds of large settlements must be cited first as evidence of the stability brought about by a favourable environment and its efficient utilization. In the Kowashimizu site (Fig. 24.1) in Chiba Prefecture, 260 pit dwellings arranged in a circle with more than 1000 pits in the central space were excavated. Many of the pits were flask-shaped in cross-section and are thought to have been used for storage. There are also shallow pits thought to be burial pits at the centre of the settlement (Research Party Kowashimizu 1976). At the Nishida site (Fig. 24.1) in Iwate Prefecture, a settlement was discovered with a clearly recognizable concentric layout: burial pits in the centre surrounded by buildings evidenced only by post-holes, followed by an outer ring of pit dwellings, with storage pits located at the periphery (Fig. 24.5; Sasaki et al. 1980, Nagamine 1981).

The stability of settlements also facilitated the development of crafts and fine art, including lacquer ware and elaborately decorated pottery (Fig. 24.6), as well as cult objects such as ceramic female figurines and stone rods, some of which are in the form of phalluses. Further evidence for the stability of Jomon settlement and subsistence is provided by items of food shaped like biscuits, which were found at the Ondashi site (Fig. 24.1) in Yamagata Prefecture. Analysis of the fatty acids and sterols they contained revealed the following ingredients: chestnut and walnut flour, animal meat and blood, wild bird's eggs, salt, and natural yeast (Nakano 1989). In addition to these surprising ingredients, beautiful patterns were applied on the surface of these "biscuits" (Fig. 24.7).

Presence of cultivated plants during the Jomon period

Although Jomon culture basically depended on gathering, fishing and hunting, a few plants were cultivated, for example, green grams (*Vigna radiata* L.), perilla (*Perilla frutescens* Britt. var. *japonica* Hara. and/or *Perilla frutescens* Britt. var. *crispa* (Thunb.) Benth.), and the bottle gourd (*Lagenaria siceraria* var. *gourda*) were cultivated by 5500 bp (Kasahara 1981, Umemoto & Moriwaki 1983). However, these plants cannot be considered to have been staple foods. Perilla is used for seasoning foods in Japan, and gourds were raised until recently to use the woody fruits as containers. Also, the possibility that chestnut trees (Chino 1983) and tubers such as the Japanese indigenous yam were protected and cared for is suggested by indirect evi-

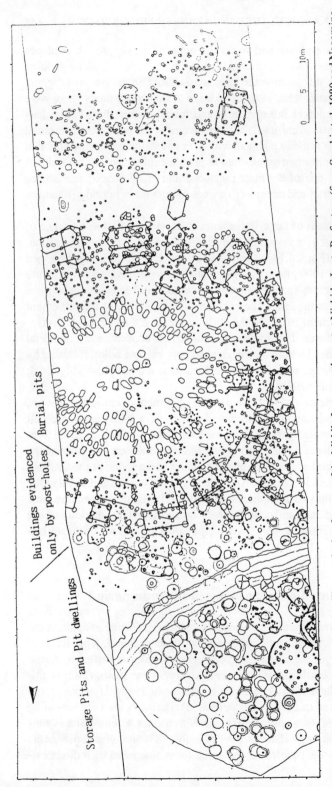

Figure 24.5 Distribution of pit dwellings and other features of the Middle Jomon settlement at Nishida, Iwate Prefecture (from Sasaki et al. 1980 and Nagamine 1981).

Storage Pits and Pit dwellings

Buildings evidenced
only by post-holes / Burial pits

0 5 10m

Figure 24.6   Richly decorated Middle Jomon pottery from Sori, Nagano Prefecture.

Figure 24.7   Biscuit-like food from the Early Jomon Ondashi site, Yamagata Prefecture (from Nakano 1989).

dence. Some archaeologists and archaeobotanists have even argued, on the basis of pollen analysis from several sites, that buckwheat (*Fagopyrum esculentum* Moench) was cultivated (Yasuda 1984).

By 3,000 years ago, rice and barley appear to have been added to the list of cultivated plants (Research Committee Uenohara 1971), although remains of these crops are very sparse. But although it must be admitted that the cultivation of cereals had begun in southwestern Japan by the Late Final phases of the Jomon, to take this as evidence for the existence of agricultural communities would lead to a basic misunderstanding of the essential character of the Jomon culture. In spite of their knowledge of plant cultivation, Jomon people did not proceed from the partial and sporadic use of cereals to full-scale agriculture. Indeed, the introduction of cereals in the Late Final Jomon did not replicate the prosperity of the Middle Jomon, and it is difficult to recognize any effect on society which might have been brought about by the cultivation of such plants. This stands in stark contrast to the Yayoi period, which is characterized by an abundance of cereal remains, a rapid and continuing increase in the number and scale of settlements, and major social changes brought about by intensive plant cultivation.

The beginning of agriculture

In Japan, agriculture began suddenly about 2,400 years ago, with the appearance of highly developed wet-rice fields and stone tools in the tradition of the East Asian mainland. It was also accompanied by iron and bronze tools, although evidence of these is very rare. The technology of the early rice fields can best be demonstrated by describing the detailed investigations undertaken at the Initial Yayoi site of Itatsuke in northern Kyushu (Figs 24.1, 24.8; Yamazaki 1979).

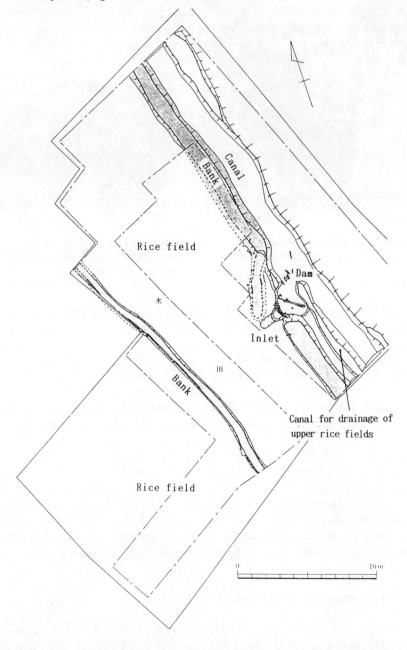

Figure 24.8   Plan of rice fields and canals at the Initial Yayoi site of Itatsuke, Fukuoka Prefecture (from Yamazaki 1979).

The Itatsuke site is located at the centre of the Fukuoka Plain, and consists of a settlement on a high terrace with rice fields on a low terrace. The settlement was encircled by an oval moat measuring 110 by 80m, within which many storage pits, pit burials and jar burials were excavated. The rice fields had been formed on a low terrace between the high terrace and alluvial lowlands. Water was supplied by a canal which was traced along the edge of the high terrace over the rice field. Dams had been built in the canal in order to collect water, and outlets beside the dams allowed water to flow into the rice fields. There were also drainage canals below the rice fields designed to recycle drained water to the main canal. Rice fields were segmented and enclosed by banks 50cm wide and 10cm high. Although the full extent of the field system is not known because of the limited area of excavation, an area of 80 by 400m is inferred on the basis of the local topography. A crucial point to note is that these rice fields were not developed in natural swampy land but rather on a low terrace above the swampy lowland, and so they had to be supplied with water by canal. Thus, water in the rice fields was artificially managed and the fields could be alternately drained and dried, or flooded, as needed. Such rice fields are not only more easily controlled but also more productive than swampy fields, which are submerged under water for most or all of the year.

A set of more primitive paddy fields has been unearthed at Nabatake southwest of Itatsuke (Fig. 24.1). They are slightly earlier in date and are located at the bottom of a small valley where artificial irrigation was not necessary (Nakajima & Tajima 1982). This evidence should not be interpreted as a progression from the Nabatake type to the Itatsuke type, but rather that varied methods were used in accordance with local conditions. The transplanting method of rice cultivation is also known to have been practised, at least by the Late Yayoi phase, as is demonstrated by the evidence of traces of seedlings on excavated rice fields at Hyakkengawa-Haraojima in Okayama Prefecture (Figs 24.1, 24.9; Masaoka et al. 1980, 1984).

Although as yet no evidence of prehistoric rice fields has been found on the East Asian continent, we can neither assume that rice field technology did not progress during 5000 years of experience there, nor that it developed with extraordinary speed immediately after being introduced to the Japanese islands. Wet-rice cultivation in Japan, which had begun in the Initial Yayoi with such advanced technologies, spread as far as the northern tip of Honshu Island during the following 200–300 years. Excavation of rice fields at Sunazawa in Aomori Prefecture, the oldest known rice fields on the northern tip of Honshu, provide evidence for this swift spread (Fig. 24.1; Murakoshi 1983).

On grounds of geographical proximity and archaeological evidence, we can be certain that wet-rice cultivation was introduced to Japan from the Korean Peninsula. However, the change from gathering, fishing and hunting to an agricultural economy, namely from the Jomon to the Yayoi, cannot be explained simply by population replacement. The evidence from pottery argues against such a hypothesis. It is known that in each region of Japan the final type of local Jomon pottery was modified into the first type of local Yayoi pottery, and only the Ongagawa type of early Yayoi pottery, which originated in northern Kyushu and spread in southwestern Japan, shows influence in manufacturing techniques from Korean pottery (Yane 1984). This sug-

Figure 24.9   Traces of the root holes of rice seedlings on the surface of an excavated field at the Late Yayoi site of Hyakkengawa-Haraojima, Okayama Prefecture (from Masaoka et al. 1980, 1984).

gests that, if any immigrants came from the Korean Peninsula, there was not any wholesale displacement of indigenous pottery makers. It is more likely to have been a situation in which the knowledge and technology of wet-rice cultivation, introduced by some immigrants, was quickly appropriated by local populations.

However, this question must also be considered in relation to anthropological studies of prehistoric populations, and a recent view put forward by K. Hanihara emphasizes the large contribution of continental Asian genes to the formation of the modern Japanese population (Hanihara 1987). He assumes migration on a very large scale from the Yayoi period to the early historical period, not only for the spread of the genes but also for the increase in population during those periods. A discussion of the discrepancy between this view and the view based on archaeological evidence would require a separate publication in order to do it justice. Here I simply want to question the assumption that the population in Japan could not have experienced exceptionally high rates of growth in protohistoric and early historic times – which could have become possible when advanced means of food production well suited to the Japanese natural environment were adopted. Indeed, an exceptional increase in population had previously occurred during the Middle phase of the Jomon period. Thus, the expansion of the continental Asian genes could have been caused not only by migration but also by high rates of population growth in groups with advanced food-production technologies.

Why did agriculture begin relatively late in Japan?

The geographical situation of Japan as an offshore archipelago did not isolate it completely from continental Asian cultures during the Jomon period. Indeed, there is considerable indirect evidence of prehistoric navigation between Kyushu and Korea, as well as Hokkaido and northeastern Russia, in the form of the exchange of pottery and obsidian. However, such exchanges did little to change the fundamental economy and culture of the Jomon.

The relatively late beginning of agriculture in Japan can be explained very simply by the fact that it also began late in southern Korea, and there was thus no chance for agriculture to be introduced early from there. A more fundamental question is why it took so long for agriculture to spread to the northeastern margin of the Asian mainland, which is not very far from the areas of origin of agriculture in China. This cannot be explained by a general assumption that cultures diffuse slowly. Indeed, some cultural elements, such as the unique microblade industry of the Late Palaeolithic, spread rapidly throughout northeastern Asia including the Japanese islands; and, as we have seen, wet-rice agriculture spread some 1200 km from northern Kyushu to the northern tip of Honshu in 300 years – a direct distance similar to that between northern Kyushu and the earliest area of agriculture in northern China. As previously noted, a few cultivated plants had already been adopted during the Jomon. Their exact areas of origin are more difficult to determine than that of cultivated rice, but they are usually thought to have been introduced from the Asian mainland. Their introduction, however, did not lead to the adoption of agriculture.

The major gateway to the Asian mainland was northern Kyushu, which is closest to the Korean Peninsula. Although there are three inferred possible routes by which domesticated rice could have reached Japan (Fig. 24.10), the northern route via the Korean Peninsula is the only one supported by a wealth of archaeological evidence (Takakura 1991). Rice had to spread north from its likely area of origin in central China before it reached Japan through the Korean Peninsula. It is possible that this process took a long time because varieties of rice had to evolve which were adapted to the cool and fairly arid environment of northern China where, also, other kinds of agriculture had previously developed. This may partly explain the time-lag for the beginning of rice cultivation in southern Korea and Japan.

Japanese climate and the adoption of agriculture

It is important to remember, however, that the first full-scale agriculture in Japan was wet-rice cultivation and not dry-field agriculture, although the latter had previ-

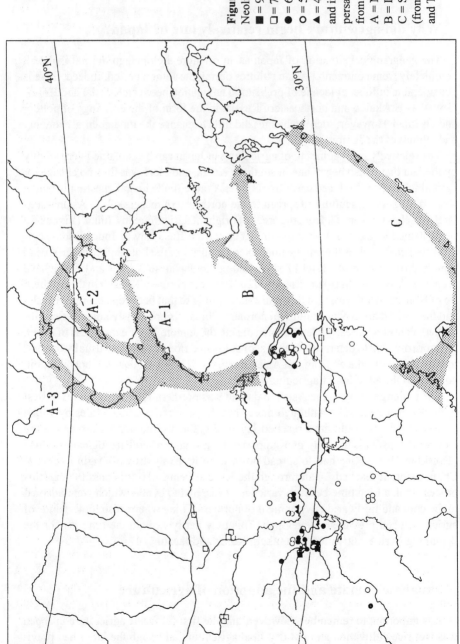

Figure 24.10
Neolithic rice remains:
■ = 9000–7000 bp
□ = 7000–6000 bp
● = 6000–5000 bp
○ = 5000–4000 bp
▲ = 4000–3000 bp
and inferred routes of dispersal of rice cultivation from China to Japan:
A = Northern Route
B = Direct Route
C = Southern Route
(from Matsumura 1991 and Takakura 1991).

ously spread throughout northern China and was in much closer geographical proximity to Japan than the wet-rice agricultural area of central and southern China. The question then is why wet-rice agriculture, which was only introduced later, was adopted, whereas dry-field agriculture, which could have been introduced much earlier, was not. A possible explanation of this apparent anomaly is as follows.

The warm and humid climate of southwestern Japan is more favourable for wet-rice cultivation than for millet cultivation on dry fields. However, because dry-field agriculture is not impossible there, this answer alone cannot suffice. Another point that must be considered is the high productivity and stability of the system of wet-rice agriculture in which the water supplies nutrients and suppresses weed growth as well as providing almost endless annual harvests. Excavated wet-rice fields and agricultural tools indicate that Japanese rice agriculture began with already highly developed technologies.

The stability and development of the Jomon culture depended on the abundant resources of the temperate rainforest as well as those of the rivers and seas. Jomon people exploited these resources in varied ways, largely in seasonally scheduled subsistence patterns. Only a more advantageous subsistence pattern could have changed their mode of life. Thus, dry-field agriculture, which was not well adapted to the Japanese climate and forested environment, could not surpass the affluence of the Jomon subsistence economy based on gathering, fishing and hunting.

Some further explanation should be added as to why the Japanese environment is said to be unfavourable to dry-field agriculture. Japan's temperate climate and high precipitation, especially in the summer, promotes the sustained growth of vegetation but does not necessarily promote the growth of crops. Under Japanese climatic conditions, cereals readily succumb to the vigorous growth of weeds and other herbaceous plants. The herbaceous plants in turn give way to shrubs and trees, which monopolize and screen-out the sunlight (Yano 1988). Grasses cannot become the dominant natural vegetation, and it is even more difficult for crops introduced from overseas. However, the removal of plant competitors by humans give crops the opportunity to respond to the favourable climatic conditions and become dominant. The technique of raising rice seedlings on preparatory plots, and then transplanting them onto fields which had previously been ploughed to suppress weed growth, is a most effective way of giving rice a competitive advantage over other plants. This process requires much human care and co-operation. The produce will be naught if clearance and weeding is not done, but the area that one person can weed is limited. Thus, the precondition for the adoption of agriculture is sufficient productivity to counterbalance the amount of labour which must be invested and which might otherwise be directed towards other subsistence activities.

The critical level of productivity was accomplished for the first time by wet-rice cultivation, which was the mainstay of Yayoi agriculture even though dry-field cultivation was also practised. It was no accident that the first system of agriculture to be adopted was highly productive because, under Japanese climatic conditions, it was only advantageous to adopt a highly productive system. The key point was not the presence or absence of cultivation but rather the techniques that could convert invested labour into a high-yield agricultural product.

The capacity of the Jomon people to adopt agriculture

It is necessary to ask whether the Jomon people had the capacity to adopt such an advanced system of agriculture. It is clear that the introduction of wet-rice cultivation techniques depended on immigrants from the Korean Peninsula. As has been suggested, however, and as the change from Jomon to Yayoi pottery suggests, there were no massive population replacements. Therefore, it is clear that the local populations must have had the capacity to appropriate and implement this system of agriculture. Jomon people had already adopted a sedentary life, which is the basic condition for agriculture. They also practised annual scheduling of food production and storage, as seen in the storage of nuts in large underground pits. Moreover, the habits of hard work required to carry out wet-rice cultivation were already well developed among the Late Jomon people who routinely practised such painstaking processes of food preparation as the making of horse chestnuts edible (Kanahako 1989). Their manual skills had also been developed in the manufacture of sophisticated tools for hunting and fishing.

Cultural diffusion is not principally a question of transport and transmission. It is more a question of whether the object or technique in question is sufficiently attractive to warrant adoption and whether it can be effectively used once it is appropriated.

Societal changes following the introduction of agriculture

Once accepted, wet-rice cultivation set off a chain reaction of increased production, increased population, the development of new rice fields and then again increased production. Before long, disputes arose, possibly over cultivable land and access to water. By about 100 BC, some three centuries after the beginning of wet-rice agriculture, there is for the first time evidence of frequent warfare, in the form of defensive settlements encircled by moats (Haraguchi et al. 1990), defensive settlements on hilltops (Morioka 1986), the mass production of large arrowheads (Sahara et al. 1964) that differ from those used for hunting, and even the skeletons of war victims in which arrowheads or the broken tips of stone and bronze weapons are lodged (Hashiguchi 1986).

The emergence of distinct social classes is also evident at this time. Burials with special goods such as bronze weapons, bronze mirrors and glass ornaments were located separately from normal burials without grave goods; and, soon after these developments, further social differentiation can be observed in the form of only one or two completely isolated burials with exceptionally rich grave goods (Shimada & Umehara 1930, Yanagida 1985), which appear to have been the tombs of chiefs who ruled comparatively small areas.

There is also evidence that a few chiefs began to conduct diplomatic exchanges with the Han Dynasty of China, probably with the aim of gaining advantageous positions over neighbouring chiefs. A Chinese chronicle of the Late Han Dynasty records that the king of the Na in Japan sent messengers to the capital city of Luoyang in AD 57 and that the Emperor Guang-wu bestowed on him a golden seal. The seal itself has been discovered at a site in northern Kyushu. Seals that Chinese emperors gave to their vassals and to foreign kings were strict status markers, differentiated by material, colour of tassle, and the last character of the inscription. Such seals symbolized a pyramid-shaped hierarchy with the emperor's seal on the top, corresponding to the ideal order of Chinese society (Kurihara 1961). Bestowal of such a seal by the Chinese emperor indicated the positioning of Japan into their own world. The seal itself symbolizes the entry of Japan into international relations.

Local Japanese chiefs, or kings, soon began to make mounded tombs each in their own style, which were, by the late third century AD, standardized into a uniform style called *kofun*. One of the oldest *kofuns*, known as Hashihaka (Fig. 24.1), was built in the Nara Basin where the earliest recorded capital of Japan was located in the sixth century AD. It is 278 m long and represents a tremendous increase in scale over any previous mounded tombs. The standardization of *kofun* tombs is believed to have been brought about by the coalition of powerful clans (Kondo 1983) and to reflect the process of political unification. Thus, it took only seven to eight centuries from the beginning of wet-rice agriculture for a unified political system to be formed. A century later, in AD 391, the unified state (or coalition) despatched military expeditions into Korea and waged war against the kingdom of Koguryo, as is recorded on a monumental epitaph of that north Korean kingdom.

Conclusion

From this overview of Japanese prehistory, several points arise that have general relevance to the study of other hunting–gathering communities and the processes by which they may have been transformed into agriculturalists. Six such points are summarized here by way of conclusion.

- There were other successful adaptive subsistence strategies than agriculture well suited to the changing postglacial environment.
- Hunting–gathering communities may develop sufficiently to exhibit many cultural features similar to those seen in neolithic communities.
- Such development can have the effect of delaying the acceptance of agriculture and can also influence the selection of a form of agriculture that is acceptable.
- Once agriculture is adopted, sedentism, annual scheduling and skills previously acquired by hunting–gathering communities can contribute to the smooth and swift transition to an agricultural economy.
- Hunting–gathering communities that develop stable, sedentary life, handicrafts and religious cults do not evolve stratified social systems or political structures.
- Once advanced agricultural technology is acquired, however, such social innovations can become established in a very short time.

Note

1. It is hoped that such shortcomings will be corrected with the forthcoming publication in English of an introduction to Japanese prehistory by the author (to be published by UCL Press and the University of Hawaii Press).

Acknowledgements

I wish to thank Professor David Harris and Dr Ian Glover for their encouragement to contribute to this volume and for their invaluable comments on drafts of this chapter. I would also like to thank Mr Mark Johnson who kindly took the trouble to correct my writing in English.

References

All of these references are translated from the original Japanese, except for Hanihara (1987) and Miyoshi & Yano (1986).

Amamiya, M. et al. 1992. *The Sojiyama site*. Kagoshima City Report Series of Excavation of Buried Cultural Properties 12.

Baoding Prefectural Administration of the Preservation of Ancient Monuments, Xushui Country Administration of the Preservation of Ancient Monuments, Archaeology Department of Beijing University, and History Department of Hebei University 1992. Trial digging at the Nanzhuangtou site in Xushui Counrtry, Hebei Province. *Archaeology* **11**, 961–70, 986.

C14 Laboratory, Department of Archaeology, Course of History, Beijing University and C14 Laboratory, Institute of Archaeology, Chinese School of Social Sciences 1982. Question of reliability of dates on carbon-14 samples from limestone areas such as Zengpiyan. *Acta Archaeologica Sinica* **2**, 243–50.

Chino, H. 1983. Chestnuts and the vegetational environment of the Jomon settlements. *Bulletin of Tokyo Metropolitan Center for Buried Cultural Properties* **2**, 25–41.

Esaka, T., K. Okamoto, S. Nishida 1967. The Kamikuroiwa rock shelter, Ehime Prefecture. In *Cave sites of Japan*, Committee for Cave Researches, The Japanese Archaeological Society (ed.), 224–36. Tokyo: Heibonsya.

Hanihara, K. 1987. Estimation of the number of the early migrants to Japan: a simulative study. *Journal of the Anthropological Society of Nippon* **95**(3), 391–403.

Haraguchi, S. et al. (eds) 1990. Moated sites and the origin of nations. *Archaeology Quarterly* **31** [special issue].

Hashiguchi, T. 1986. War victims. In *The world of the Yayoi people,* vol. 9 of *Researches of Yayoi culture,* 104–13. Tokyo: Yuuzankaku Press.

Hayakawa, I. & K. Kawachi 1987. Settlement remains of the Early Jomon Period: the third research of the Musashidai site, Huchu City. *Archaeological Journal* **284**, 23–6.

Imamura, K. et al. 1983. *A site in Tokyo Astronomical Observatory*. Tokyo: Research Party of a Site in Tokyo Astronomical Observatory.

Kamaki, Y. & C. Serizawa 1967. The Hukui Cave, Nagasaki Prefecture. In *Cave sites of Japan*. Committee for Cave Researches, The Japanese Archaeological Society (ed.), 256–65. Tokyo: Heibonsya.

Kanahako, H. 1989. *Akayama*. Report of Kawaguchi City Research Party of Archaeological Sites 12.

Kasahara, Y. 1981. Plant seeds and detected perilla frutescens from the Torihama shell midden. In *The Torihama shell midden: preliminary report on the research in 1980*. Hukui: Educational Board of Hukui Prefecture.

Kawaguchi, S. 1982. A storage pit of the Incipient Jomon Period: Higashi–Kurotsuchida site, Kagoshima Prefecture. *Archaeology Quarterly* **1**, 63.

Kondo, Y. 1983. *The age of key-hole shaped mounded tombs*. Tokyo: Iwanami Press.

Kurihara, T. 1961. Research on seals of Qin-Han dynasties recorded in documents. In *Studies of the Qin-Han history*. Tokyo: Yoshikawa Kobunkan Press.

Masaoka, M. & T. Takabatake et al. 1980, 1984. *The site of Haraojima, Hyakkengawa*, vols. 1 & 2. Okayama Prefecture: Research Report Series of Buried Cultural Properties 39 & 56.

Matsumara, M. 1991. Cereal remains of Asian Neolithic; distributions by the period. *Archaeology Quarterly* **37**, 33–5.

Miyake, T. et al. 1979. *Excavation report on the Odai–Yamamoto I site.* Research Report Series of Aomori Prefectural Museum 5.

Miyoshi, N. & N. Yano 1986. Late Pleistocene and Holocene vegetational history of the Ohnuma moor in the Chugoku Mountains, western Japan. *Review of Palaeobotany and Palynology* **46**, 355–76.

Morioka, H. 1986. Hill-top settlements. In *Yayoi settlements,* vol. 7 of Researches in Yayoi culture, 55–72. Tokyo: Yuzankaku Press.

Murakoshi, K. 1983. The most northern wet rice fields of the Yayoi period. *Geography* **28**(10).

Nagamine, K. 1981. The Middle Jomon phase as a major division. In *Great compilation of the Jomon pottery* **2**, 130–37. Tokyo: Kodansha.

Nakajima, N. & R. Tajima 1982. *The Nabatake site.* Karatsu City: Research Report Series of Buried Cultural Properties 5.

Nakamura, K. 1960. *Kosegasawa.* Nagaoka: Nagaoka City Museum of Science.

Nakamura, S. 1991. Early neolithic culture of the middle reaches of Changjiang. *Bulletin of Japan Society for Chinese Archaeology* **1**, 20–40.

Nakano, M. 1989. Reconstruction of ancient times with surviving fatty acid. In *What fruits has new methodology brought about to archaeology?* Organizing Committee for the Third Public Seminars, "Universities and science" (ed.), 114–31. Tokyo: Kubapuro.

Ren, S. N. 1982. Early Neolithic Culture of the Taihu Plain and Hangzhou Bay Area. In *Archaeological discoveries and researches of the new China.* Institute of Archaeology, Chinese School of Social Sciences (ed.), 143–57. Beijing: Wenwu Press.

Research Committee of the Uenohara Site 1971. *Report on researches of the Uenohara site.*

Research Party of the Kowashimizu Shellmidden 1976. *The shellmidden of Kowashimizu.* Matsudo City Report Series on Buried Cultural Properties 7.

Research Party of the Shimotakabora Site 1985. *The Shimotakabora site, Oshima Town, Tokyo.* Oshima: Educational Board of Oshima Town.

Research Party of the Ushirono site 1976. *The Ushirono site.* Katsuta City: Educational Board of Katsuta City.

Sahara, M. et al. 1964. *Shiude.* Kyoto: Shinyosya.

Sasaki, M. et al. 1980. *Report on excavations of buried cultural properties carried out in relation to the New Tohoku Main Railway,* 7 (The Nishida site). Morioka: Educational Board of Iwate Prefecture.

Shao, W. P. 1982. Remains of Mesolithic and Early Neolithic. In *Archaeological discoveries and researches of the new China,* Institute of Archaeology, Chinese School of Social Sciences (ed.), 33–41. Beijing: Wenwu Press.

Shimada, S. & S. Umehara 1930. *Research of a prehistoric site at Suku, Chikuzen.* Archaeological Research Report Series, Department of Archaeology, Kyoto Imperial University 11.

Sugihara, S. & Serizawa, C. 1957. *Shell mounds of the earliest Jomon culture at Natsushima, Kanagawa Prefecture, Japan.* Report on the Research by the Faculty of Literature, Meiji University, Archaeology 2.

Suzuki, J. & H. Shiraishi, 1980. *The Terao site.* Kanagawa Prefecture: Research Report Series of Buried Cultural Propertie 6.

Takakura, H. 1991. The route of rice arrival. *Archaeology Quarterly* **37**, 40–45.

Umemoto, K. & T. Morikawi 1983. Identification of seeds of leguminous plants: green gram (*Phaseolus radiatus L.*) from the Torihama shellmidden. In *The Torihama shellmidden: preliminary report on the researches in 1981 and 1982.* Hukui: Educational Board of Hukui Prefecture.

Watanabe, M. 1987. Acorns as food in Japan and Korea and the origin of Jomon pottery. *Bulletin of Faculty of Letters, Nagoya University,* History 33.

Yamanouchi, S. & T. Sato 1982. The age of the Jomon pottery. *Scientific Yomiuri* **12**(13), 18–26, 84–8.

Yamazaki, S. 1979. *Preliminary report on a research at Itatsuke.* Fukuka City: Research Report Series of Buried Cultural Properties 49.

Yanagida, Y. 1985. *The Mikumo site: Minamishouji location.* Fukuoka Prefecture: Research Report Series of Buried Cultural Properties 69.

Yane, Y. 1984. From Jomon pottery to Yayoi pottery. In *From Jomon to Yayoi,* Katada (ed.), 49–70. Nara: Tezukayama Institute of Archaeology.

Yano, N. (ed.) 1988. *Vegetation of Japan*. Tokyo: Tokai University Press.

Yasuda, Y. 1982. Climatic changes. In *Researches of Jomon culture* 1, 163–200. Tokyo: Yuzankaku Press.

— 1984. Cultural changes in the Japan Sea circumference area. *Bulletin of National Museum of Ethnology* 9, 761–98.

CHAPTER TWENTY-FIVE

The origins and spread of agriculture in the Indo–Pacific region: gradualism and diffusion or revolution and colonization?

Peter Bellwood

Since I began my oceanic research in the late 1960s I have been intrigued by the many ways through which the study of language can illuminate prehistory. More recently I have become even more intrigued by the possibility that links exist between major language-family distributions and the origins and spreads of agriculture. I have approached this question from the vantage point of Oceania and the eastern part of Asia, and thus overlap in the Indian subcontinent with Colin Renfrew's similar interpretations for agricultural language dispersals in the western Old World (Renfrew 1987, 1989, 1992a, 1992b).

My current views on worldwide linguistic prehistory and agricultural origins have already been published or are in press (Bellwood 1991, 1993a, 1996 in press). In 1992, while on leave in Berkeley, I began research on the topic for the first time with respect to the origins of agriculture in the Americas. I now feel that certain underlying observations are of immense significance. They illustrate clearly the limits of the archaeological record alone for charting the genesis of the major ethnolinguistic groupings that inhabit the world today. Regional archaeological records are obviously an essential part of the multidisciplinary mix, but to understand the genesis of ethnolinguistically defined populations, as opposed simply to geographically defined and archaeologically defined ones, it is necessary to take a worldwide comparative perspective employing the disciplines of linguistics, biological anthropology, historically focused cultural anthropology and, of course, archaeology.

Comparison reveals patterning on a worldwide scale within the data of the major disciplines, especially in the form of foci and clines of diversity and homogeneity. These foci and clines are of great importance and they remain invisible to researchers trapped within disciplinary or regional boundaries. Here, scale is essential: a pan-continental pattern of archaeological data will be quite different in its implications from a record based on one site or region, just as language change on a continental or family scale can be attributable to a different overall process from language change in a single community. This chapter is devoted to the macro scale, but the micro scale is still essential from a theoretical viewpoint because one must know the range of ways by which, for instance, groups of people can change their languages in real-life situations, change their physical characteristics through intermarriage, react demographically to opportunities for colonization, or react in the case of hunter–gatherers to the availability of agricultural products and technology. Comparative patterns within these fields of behaviour can be of inestimable value for interpreting the past.

If applying a comparative perspective to language, culture and biology, one might ask if it is possible to combine the results in some way to increase understanding of prehistory without succumbing to circularity of reasoning. I believe that patterns can be compared without resort to circularity, because each discipline produces an independent dataset not founded on prior knowledge derived from one of the other disciplines. For instance, linguists do not use archaeological data in determining the patterns of shared linguistic innovations that produce the orders of subgroup differentiation within a language family. Archaeologists do not use linguistic information to date their cultures. Furthermore, an emphasis on comparison of overall patterning is often more productive than an exclusive focus on one-to-one linkages such as those between individual proto-languages and archaeological cultures. Such linkages can often be made with high degrees of certainty (e.g. the Proto-Oceanic/Lapita correlation in the western Pacific), but they can also be very elusive, especially in continental situations.

There is also the contentious question of whether similar models for the explanation of situations of shared ancestry versus diffusion/borrowing can be applied to the records of biological, cultural and linguistic variation. I will avoid any firm commitment on this question by simply pointing out a fairly obvious fact: biological descent is Darwinian rather than Lamarckian, whereas cultural and linguistic descent are at least partially Lamarckian in that acquired characteristics can be and usually are transmitted through time from one human generation to another. In biological inheritance, parental genes disaggregate with each generational transmission and recombine in relatively random ways to produce an approximately 50:50 contribution by each parent to an offspring. Cultures and languages obviously do not disaggregate and recombine in this way; their element combinations are much more strongly related to each other through time than are the individual genes and alleles in biological gene pools. Yet, despite this level of coherence in transgenerational transmission, cultures and languages can also be changed drastically and rapidly through Lamarckian forms of trait acquisition by choice and intent.

That biology and language/culture sometimes do not relate closely to each other often leads archaeologists and linguists to shy away from multidisciplinary comparison. For instance, not all the Austronesian-speaking peoples of Southeast Asia and Oceania reflect a single common biological background (except at a basic *sapiens* level). Conversely, some neighbouring groups in lowland New Guinea appear closely related biologically and culturally, yet may speak totally unrelated Papuan and Austronesian languages (e.g. Welsch et al. 1992). The real world contains many examples of this type, yet in my opinion such observations reflect no more than the expected when a multidisciplinary understanding of the prehistory of the region concerned is brought to bear on the situation.

The significance of language families for prehistory

One of the central points of this chapter is that the processes through which individuals or small groups have changed their languages or cultures on a local group-to-group scale are not necessarily the appropriate processes to explain the existences of very widespread language families such as Indo–European, Austronesian or Uto–Aztecan. Processes that are often claimed by archaeologists to explain such major language-family distributions, probably because they see them at work in societies in the ethnographic record, include language shift or borrowing through bilingualism, the existence and spread of lingua francas to facilitate trade and communication, and that very intriguing sociolinguistic phenomenon called "élite dominance" (Renfrew 1989). All of these processes can lead, and have led many times, to shifts from indigenous languages and dialects to external target languages. But we must ask if they alone can produce shifts from vernaculars to a target language through total populations (not just élites) across regions of major language-family size (e.g. Ireland to Bangladesh (Indo–European), Madagascar to Easter Island (Austronesian), Mexico City to Idaho (Uto–Aztecan)), and eventually produce entities that linguists can identify with confidence as genetically structured language families.

In my view, these processes explain nothing at the language-family scale, because they are, by their very natures, of restricted geographical extent and tied to specific areas of intensive cultural interaction. Not even the historical spreads of Arabic, Spanish or English can be explained by such processes alone, even though, in these cases, mass communication, literacy, state authority and charismatic religion undoubtedly have given them a massive advantage in ways unthinkable for the languages of pre-state societies of prehistory. Without trying to bring in the voluminous data from historical records that illustrate the point, I will state here what I increasingly believe to be the only explanation for the major language families of the world, both hunter-gatherer and agriculturalist, that is, that they record processes of colonization by growing populations expanding outwards from homeland regions. In the cases of some extremely large agriculturalist language families, such as Indo–European and Austronesian, these colonizations occurred on a massive and sometimes a chronologically rapid scale, undoubtedly incorporating existing peoples but also leading to major reconstructions of the world patterns of humanity that existed at the end of the Pleistocene. Given our understanding of the range of rates at which linguistic change can occur, it is apparent that many of these colonizations spread almost to their eventual limits between the beginning of the Holocene and the period of the development of states and written records in the various regions of the world, mostly between 9,000 and 3,000 years ago.[1] They are thus predominantly neolithic or formative in their cultural associations and there are good grounds for seeking strong (but not total) associations between the spreads of language families, people and agriculture in prehistory.

Five years ago such a statement might have caused an uproar. Colonization has not been a popular concept with archaeologists recently, although it is clear that ideas are now changing in some areas (e.g. Anthony 1990). In order to defend my opinions on the significance of colonization I bring in at this point some linguistic and ethnographic ammunition:

- A language family, as a set of genetically related languages, cannot be a product of convergence but must have a source region and a history of expansion: "The fact that a set of languages can be shown to be genetically related entails that there was a real proto-language, spoken by a particular group of people, in a particular region, at a particular time period" (Kaufman 1990: 21).
- Expansion on the scale of a major language family cannot be by language shift alone: "The only plausible explanation of the currency of [Indo–European] languages so similar over so large an area at the beginning of historical periods is that they derive from dialects of a fairly homogeneous prehistoric language which had been disseminated by migrations out of a smaller region" (Friedrich 1966); and "'entire' spoken languages do not and cannot diffuse through space save in the mouths of (some of) their speakers" (Diebold 1987: 27).

These two "rules" suggest that families such as Indo–European and Uto–Aztecan cannot be explained by postulating that unmoving indigenous peoples, whatever their cultural backgrounds, adopted an in-moving target language (or a group of related dialects) across anything more than a few localized cultural boundaries. Such massive chain- or mesh-like language shift through a region of existing linguistic diversity would lead to sufficient interference in the target language concerned that no genetic family could possibly be the eventual result on anything like a continental scale. The same observation applies to culture; relatively homogeneous and extensive neolithic/ formative entities such as the Lapita in the Pacific, the Linearbandkeramik and the Early Formative in Mesoamerica could not be "borrowed in" by culturally differentiated hunter–gatherers and still remain coherent and homogeneous as they spread.

The ethnographic record also records that, while some hunter–gatherers have adopted agriculture in the recent past, most have not converted willingly or very successfully (Smith 1972, and see Peterson 1976 for an illuminating Australian example). The essence here concerns the remote past; were the hunter–gatherers of the Mesolithic and Archaic in the Old and New Worlds any different from the ethnographic Aborigines of Australia or the tribes of California in this regard? I see no reason why they should have been, although I am aware that some archaeologists argue for eager agricultural adoption by ancient hunters. Of course adoption occurred, but in my view it did so more via assimilation and outsider pressure (especially in agriculturally marginal environments) than via free choice in unpressured social situations. Again the ethnography here is voluminous and fascinating (see Headland 1986 for an excellent case study on the Philippine Agta).

Reasoning from the above points, I find that there is a coherence of worldwide patterning in the archaeological and linguistic records, which indicates that language families and agriculture have not simply diffused through innumerable communities of resident and unmoving hunter–gatherers across the world, without large-scale population movement. If we ignore the linguistic isolates and focus purely on the large and widespread families, then it is apparent that:

- relatively large numbers of these families intersect geographically in regions of early agricultural development;[2] and
- in cases where language-family homelands and histories can be reconstructed in terms of shared innovation patterning in space and time (cf. the "shape of the

tree", below), homelands tend again to correlate with such regions of early (primary) agriculture.

Thus, we have the apparent equations, many in the western Old World noted already by Renfrew (1992b), listed in Table 25.1 and shown in Figures 25.1 and 25.2. There is insufficient space here to justify all these in detail, but the equations indicate to me that the language families concerned were spread from the early regions of agriculture, presumably (as the most economical hypothesis) with the agricultural economy itself in the mouths and hands of actual speakers. The most likely time for such spread would be at the regional beginnings of agriculture, when a steep demographic gradient between indigenous hunter–gatherers and incoming agriculturalists would have existed. Whole language-family spreads are harder to justify after relatively dense agricultural populations have already developed throughout a large region, as pointed out by Renfrew (1987) for Indo–European and by Bellwood (1985, 1991) for Austronesian. Pacific prehistory in fact gives very strong backing for this viewpoint because documented language replacements (e.g. in the Polynesian Outliers) have only taken place on very small islands or pockets of coastline, never over the whole extents of large islands.

I should add the proviso that this linkage of agricultural and major language family dispersal is a statement of strong tendency rather than absolute correlation. Clearly, some later but still pre-Columbian spreads of language have occurred in historical times, although generally under sociopolitical circumstances that seem inapplicable to the cultural conditions of the Neolithic/Formative, which obtained at the recon-

Table 25.1   Regions of early agricultural development and the language families which appear to have expanded from them with agricultural colonists.

Region of early agriculture	Associated language families
Sub-Saharan Africa	Niger–Congo
Southwest Asia	Sumerian Elamo–Dravidian Indo–European Turkic Afro–Asiatic (?) (certainly Semitic)
China	Sino–Tibetan Austroasiatic Austronesian Tai Hmong–Mien
New Guinea	Many Papuan families
Mexico	Otomanguean Uto–Aztecan Mayan Mixe–Zoque
Andes/Upper Amazon	Chibchan/Paezan Quechua/Aymara Arawakan Panoan

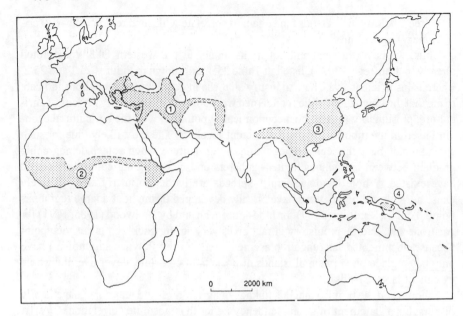

Figure 25.1 Regions of independent agricultural development in the Old World.

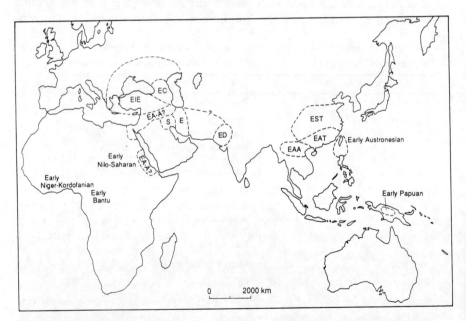

Figure 25.2 Postulated homeland regions for Old World language families which are believed to have undergone expansion with agricultural colonists. EA–A, Early Afro–Asiatic; EIE, Early Indo–European; S, Sumerian; E, Elamite; ED, Early Dravidian; EST, Early Sino–Tibetan; EAT, Early Austro–Tai (Tai and Austronesian, after Benedict); EAA, Early Austroasiatic.

structed time depths of origin of the major families themselves. Adoptions by indigenous hunter–gatherers of agricultural plants introduced from external sources, together with aspects of agricultural economy, probably occurred also in some areas, as many archaeologists have claimed.[3] Hunter–gatherers have certainly adopted agriculture under situations of contact with agriculturalists, but we might ask how often, how successfully, and with what overall significance for world prehistory such adoptions have taken place.

Rates of spread

There is another generalized point that merits discussion. I am here arguing that language families and agricultural technologies have spread mainly through colonization. But how rapid, how intensive, and how assimilatory with respect to existing hunter–gatherers in the regions affected were these colonizations? Certain underlying regional differences here are obvious. Western Asia produced, uniquely, a very important set of domestic animals that gave its agricultural system an unchallengeable advantage in terms of productive capacity. The Americas suffered somewhat in this respect, with no major domesticated animals and only one major cereal (maize). China fell somewhere in the middle with pigs, chickens and, in the south, perhaps domesticated water buffalo as well. Additionally, agriculture in western Asia and Europe spread along the environmentally less stressful latitudinal route (Diamond 1991: 222), whereas in the Americas it spread north and south in the more difficult longitudinal direction, with consequent and sometimes abrupt transitions to conditions of hostile climate and unsuitable day length.

Archaeological data can indicate the rates of spread of early agricultural societies – some fast, such as Lapita and Linearbandkeramik (Danubian), some presumably too slow to be even visible as colonizations in the archaeological record because they changed faster than they spread. Examples of the latter seem to occur where environmental or latitudinal barriers intervene, thus allowing a much greater contribution of prior hunter–gatherer societies to the eventual cultural expression (e.g. the relatively late spread of agriculture to regions such as northern Europe (cf. Chs 17, 18 and 19 in this volume, by Thomas, Zvelebil and Price), much of the USA and southern Canada). In such marginal circumstances this spread can sometimes be associated with a return by some former cultivators to a predominantly hunting and gathering existence, as in southern New Zealand, interior Borneo and (I suspect) in regions such as the Great Basin and parts of northern Europe.[4]

Rates of agricultural spread are therefore important (cf. Cavalli-Sforza in Ch. 4 in this volume). In this regard there is another observation of close relationships between patterns in the archaeological and linguistic records. Put simply, the relative rapidity or slowness of spread of a proto-language can be read from the shape of a language family "tree", just as the tempo of a cultural expansion can be read from the extent and degree of cultural homogeneity visible in the archaeological record.

For instance, it can be seen in Figure 25.3 that the tree of Oceanic Austronesian subgroup relationships, excluding the Western Oceanic and Central Pacific subgroups

(Ross 1989), becomes in effect a "rake" in much of Melanesia with no branching structure and no time gradient of differentiation. This is evidently because this region was settled, from the Bismarcks to western Polynesia, very rapidly. Many archaeologists and linguists equate this settlement with the dispersal of the Lapita cultural complex between 1600 and 1200 bc (Pawley & Green 1984, Kirch 1988, Spriggs 1991, Pawley & Ross 1993). A better-differentiated tree with a succession of subgroup separations exists in the case of Polynesia, settled over a much longer period of 2000 years from Tonga/Samoa (c. 1200 bc) to New Zealand (c. AD 1000) (Bellwood 1987, Irwin 1992, and see Ross 1991 for Melanesian minor subgroup examples). Linguistic differentiation requires centuries of time for the creation of sufficient unique innovations to define subgroups (Polynesian has many such innovations), and in cases of rapid colonization the time factor lacks a sufficient geographical gradient for nested subgrouping to occur.

In fast-moving cases of colonization or language spread, language differentiation will be of an equal order over the whole geographical range, giving rise to the rake-like patterns that seem to characterize the lower nodes of the so-called family trees of language families such as Indo–European, Uto–Aztecan, and perhaps Pama–Nyungan (much of central and southern Australia). Family trees with a more branching pattern in the lower nodes, and thus a relatively longer chronology of expansion, could be represented by examples such as Iroquoian and Dravidian. If, as I believe, language-family trees are real, and not just epiphenomena of cladistic reasoning, then tree shape, or absence thereof, may be a factor of great historical significance. It may correlate with the speed and extent of proto-language dispersal.

Some archaeological cultures can also reveal very wide spatial spreads with little regional differentiation (the presumed equivalent of the linguistic "rakes"). Others tend to be highly localized and to belong to patterns of high regional diversity (equivalent perhaps to the "trees"). Equivalently rake-like archaeological cultures (with their possible linguistic equivalents in parentheses) include Lapita in the western

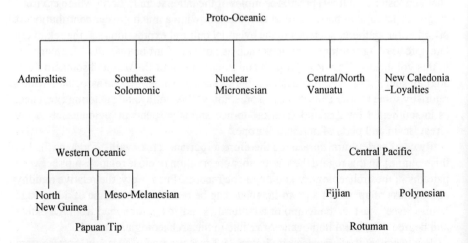

Figure 25.3 A partial subgrouping of Oceanic languages (after Pawley & Ross 1993: fig. 2).

Pacific (Proto-Oceanic), Linierbandkeramik in Europe (early Indo–European), the Mesoamerican and Andean Early Formatives (uncertain, but probably covering early Otomanguean, Mayan, Chibchan and Quechumaran families),[5] early neolithic cultures in China (early Sino–Tibetan, Tai–Kadai, Austronesian, Austroasiatic; see further discussion below), earliest Iron Age cultures in sub-Saharan Africa (early Bantu), and the Pre-Pottery Neolithic B (PPNB) of the Levant (early Semitic). It will be noted that all of these archaeological entities are close in time to the origins or introductions of agriculture in the regions concerned, and in all cases they are succeeded in time by increasing degrees of regionality and cultural differentiation. Not even the Aztecs or the Incas could, by conquest, recreate the degree of cultural homogeneity we see across the Americas in the Early Formative (Ford 1969), or even in the Middle Formative Olmec and Chavin phases.

In my view these archaeological equivalents of linguistic "rakes" in many cases do not indicate diffusion, but full colonization by demographically expanding agricultural populations moving rapidly into new territories occupied by hunter–gatherers. Such populations spoke related languages (as with the spreads of English and Spanish in the recent past) and created archaeological landscapes that many archaeologists with anti-colonization ideologies tend to shy from interpreting. This is partly because the recent ethnographic past shows us few such landscapes; most tribal peoples, apart from a few expansive rainforest groups such as the Iban and Kayan of Borneo, have been in geographical retreat since Europeans located them.

A model for mid-latitude agricultural origins derived from Southwest Asia

I now wish to turn to the main theme of this chapter – early agriculture in the Indo–Pacific region, including examination of the Chinese and New Guinea foci of early agriculture in terms of how they compare with our understanding of other regions of similar significance, especially Southwest Asia. In order to do this, given my commitment to broad-scale comparison, I first briefly develop a model based on Southwest Asia, the only region in the world with a detailed archaeological record of a primary transition to agriculture (Mesoamerica and the Andes fall far behind in this regard).

My observations of the trajectories of environmental change and cultural change in Southwest Asia in the period 18000 to 7000 bp are grouped under six subheadings, which focus on data of major comparative significance. The same six subheadings are then used later for discussion of China and New Guinea.

Environmental parameters   Very rapid climatic amelioration in the terminal Pleistocene after 14000 bp replaced a regime of low temperature, low and relatively non-seasonal rainfall and persistent cloud cover with a regime of warmer temperature, high and strongly winter-focused rainfall and higher insolation (Byrne 1987, Maley 1987, COHMAP 1988, Broecker & Denton 1990, Blumler & Byrne 1991, McCorriston & Hole 1991, Wright 1993, cf. Hillman and Hole in Chs 10 and 14 in this volume).

The change was quite abrupt and led rapidly to an establishment of modern climatic and vegetational conditions by 11000 bp, the latter including predominantly annual as opposed to perennial cereals and legumes.

The immediate cultural background to agriculture   Hunters and gatherers exploited the newly expanding plant resources and over a period of several millennia (Kebaran–Natufian) developed a degree of "complex sedentary foraging" (Henry 1989) with food (presumably including grain) storage, and settlement sizes up to a maximum of 0.5 ha (Bar-Yosef & Belfer-Cohen 1991: 191).

Some process or combination of processes (one of the most hotly debated questions in modern archaeology), eventually prompted some late Natufian/early PPNA groups to shift to a conscious regime of cereal and legume planting, rather than collecting, by about 10500 bp. Likely processes, perhaps working in combination, include forms of environmental stress on food supplies – for instance, the Younger Dryas model preferred by Henry (1989), Bar-Yosef & Belfer-Cohen (1991, 1992) and Moore & Hillman (1992), but disputed by Wright (1993) – and "social production" as dressed in varied guises by Bender (1978) and Hayden (1990, 1992). A contributory cause might also have been a preference among Natufians to harvest wild grain slightly unripe in order to maximize the quantities harvested by forestalling the problem of shattering (Unger-Hamilton 1989, Bar-Yosef & Belfer-Cohen 1991). This habit could have reduced the densities of wild stands over time and thereby could have promoted the planting of small quantities of specially harvested and stored grain each autumn, thus starting the process of domestication (Limbrey 1990).

Each of these processes probably had some part to play in the shift to plant cultivation and domestication in Southwest Asia, although I believe that the unprecedented environmental changes (at least for the previous 130,000 years) in the terminal Pleistocene were the most essential of the processes listed for the shift to take place where and when it did. Neither environmental stress on food supplies nor social production alone seem to be sufficient causes. For instance, the archaeological and ethnographic records contain many examples of hunter–gatherer societies that practised competitive exchange (especially in California and the North American Northwest Coast), and in the early Holocene societies in many parts of the Northern Hemisphere, apart from those considered in this chapter, probably experienced the Younger Dryas climatic regression (Zhou 1991: 5). Yet none of these appears to have made a primary shift to agriculture. The missing element is probably the existence of suitable plants and animals that would respond to domestication. Many of these had circumscribed regions of origin, not only in geographical terms, but also in terms of the actual transitions from wild to domesticated, as suggested for Southwest Asia by Zohary's observation (1989, and in Ch. 9 in this volume) that the major cereals and legumes were probably each domesticated only once, not multiple times.

The edge-of-the-range factor   It is relevant to draw attention here to the theory that plant domestication will be most likely to occur at the edge of the geographical range of the vegetation type, or ecosystem, concerned, because here resource stresses of a non-catastrophic type likely to induce a sowing/planting habit in human populations will be most frequent. The oldest sites with domesticated plant remains in Southwest Asia, such as Tell Aswad, Netiv Hagdud and Jericho, were located where localized lake or spring resources were available in climatically dry regions outside the higher rainfall belts of expansive cereal and forest growth (van Zeist 1988). Such areas were probably marginal for the bulk of the population in the Levant in the late Natufian. If groups accustomed to harvesting wild cereals had attempted to settle in such locations, for instance during a phase of climatic dryness such as the Younger Dryas, they could have found it advantageous to begin planting, as pointed out many years ago by Binford (1968). As stated by Flannery (1969: 80): "pressures for domestication may not be as strong in the heart of the wild cereal habitat as elsewhere."

Tempo   The shift from "complex" hunting and gathering to cereal sowing, with consequent selection of domesticated characteristics (whether unconscious or intentional on the part of the human groups concerned), was potentially a very rapid event in Southwest Asia (Hillman & Davies 1990, Bar-Yosef 1991). Domesticated cereals and legumes are well in evidence by the PPNA (Hopf 1983, Miller 1991), *c.* 10300 bp, although hunting and gathering clearly continued while there were still resources available to be hunted and gathered. In the latter respect it is of great relevance that the beginnings of Southwest Asian animal domestication seem to reflect a reaction to the local extirpation of wild meat sources (Legge & Rowly-Conwy 1987, Helmer 1988).

Technological background to domestication   The selection of domesticated characteristics in Southwest Asian cereals and legumes has been suggested by various researchers to be a partial result of harvesting habits. In particular, many Natufian and PPNA populations used flint sickles, thus selecting for tough-rachised seed heads during harvest – a process that would undoubtedly have led to very rapid selection for domesticated characteristics once actual planting had begun (Wilke et al. 1972, Unger-Hamilton 1989, Hillman & Davies 1990).

Consequences   The consequences of the shift to cultivation in Southwest Asia, following *c.* 10500 bp, were of course immense. But for the purposes of this chapter I wish to focus on the PPNA and PPNB. The former, characterized by sites much greater in size than Natufian settlements (Bar-Yosef & Belfer-Cohen 1991: 190–1) and culminating in the 2.5–3 ha walled settlement of Jericho, represents a relatively homogeneous cultural expression that spread through the Levant, possibly into northern Iraq (the sites of Nemrik and Qermez Dere; Bar-Yosef 1989), and, as a more distant, time-delayed possible outlier, to Cyprus (Khirokitia?). The PPNA appears not to have spread farther into the Zagros or Anatolia.

The PPNB was more expansive (Cauvin 1988, Zarins 1990; Miller 1991: 141; Byrd 1992) and has long seemed to me to be the origin of the agglutinative cell-like form of architecture found at many eighth to seventh millennium bc sites, some up to 12 ha in size, as far apart as Çatal Hüyük, Çayonu, Bouqras, Abu Hureyra, Basta, Ganj Dareh layer D and even perhaps Mehrgarh. Not all of these sites are classifiable directly as PPNB in archaeological terms, but one might ask here if the PPNB could also have represented some degree of population colonization outwards from the Levant, either carrying on from the PPNA or overlaying it. If colonization was involved, we might ask who, in an ethnolinguistic sense, was doing the colonizing? My hunch here, following Renfrew (1992a, 1992b), would be to give the linguistic concept of a Proto-Nostratic founder language some very careful consideration, perhaps placing it within the late Natufian, and relating the Levantine PPNB perhaps to a phase of early Semitic (Afro–Asiatic) expansion (Zarins 1989, 1990).

But because the main subject of this chapter is neither Southwest Asia nor Nostratic, and because tying something as elusive as Proto-Nostratic to any particular archaeological time and place is unlikely to be an easy task, I will not follow this line of thought further here. The role of Southwest Asia in this chapter is purely a comparative one and a source of structure for the discussion that follows. I now turn to examine how the Southwest Asian "model" with its six subheadings presented above can help to illuminate the faintly known outlines of early agricultural development in China and New Guinea.

The Indo–Pacific regions of early agriculture

The two regions of the eastern Old World where archaeology indicates that developments of agriculture were probably primary and independent – China and the New Guinea highlands – were remarkably different. The New Guinea highlands lacked cereals and native domesticated animals and had a predominantly non-seasonal climate in the regions of earliest agricultural activity. Production and population increase were probably more limited than in eastern Asia, hence the propensity of New Guinea prehistory to indicate gradual *in situ* intensification of agricultural systems rather than outflow of population and economy to adjacent areas. Eastern Asian early agriculturalists had access to greater productive capacity with the monsoon-climate cereals, rice and the two millets, *Setaria italica* and *Panicum miliaceum*, together with domestic animals. They were more orientated to rivers and coasts than early New Guinea agriculturalists, who were located in the high-altitude interior of the island. The eastern Asian early agriculturalists also took opportunities to colonize by land in southerly (Austroasiatic, Tai) and southwesterly (Munda of northeast India) directions, and by sea in southerly and easterly directions (Austronesian).

Reference should be made at this point to an important observation concerning China and Southeast Asia generally. Since the famous publication on agricultural origins by Sauer (1952), many archaeologists have accepted that some form of vegetative horticulture, involving the cultivation of fruits and tubers, is extremely ancient in Southeast Asia, where it preceded the rice-based agricultural systems that dominate the region today. The plant remains from Hoabinhian contexts excavated by Gorman (1970) in Spirit Cave in northern Thailand seemed to support this view, although Gorman himself eventually felt that rice was one of the earliest plants to be domesticated (Gorman 1977). Without repeating published work at length, I can only state that this early pre-cereal horizon today seems to be a mirage as far as China and Southeast Asia are concerned (see Yen 1977 for Spirit Cave; and for general accounts covering Southeast Asia see Bellwood 1985, 1992, Higham 1989, Glover & Higham in Ch. 23

in this volume). However, it certainly does reflect reality in New Guinea and western Oceania, where cereals were absent throughout prehistory.

China

Unlike Southwest Asia, the beginnings of agriculture in China are associated with cultures already at a high level of technological development and settlement size. All have pottery of a skilled level of manufacture – there are no signs of incipient experiment as seen among the "white wares" and occasional items of fired clay in the western Asian Pre-Pottery Neolithic. Semi-sedentary complex forager villages like those of the Natufian are not yet recorded; even the oldest Neolithic sites in central China were used for storing or processing huge quantities of domesticated grain. Store-pits at Cishan, c. 6000 BC,[6] could have held 100 tonnes of millet; Hemudu, a site of at least 4ha at 5000 BC (Zhao & Wu 1988), produced waterlogged rice remains equivalent to 120 tonnes of fresh grain (Yan 1993). The impression one receives is that early Holocene foragers with microlithic tool kits could have been transformed very quickly into pottery-using agriculturalists, and many publications comment on the apparent absence of any transition (Chang 1986: 87; Pearson & Underhill 1987, An 1988). The oldest Chinese neolithic sites also have domestic animals – certainly pig, dog and chicken, and possibly also water buffalo in the Yangzi Valley rice zone at Pengtoushan and Hemudu (Han 1988, Yan 1993). The Chinese Neolithic differs greatly from that of Southwest Asia in this regard, where animal domestication generally follows plant domestication, in some regions by as much as two millennia (Helmer 1988).

The impression I derive, especially after seeing the material culture from many Chinese neolithic sites displayed in Chinese museums, is that the beginnings of agriculture in China only first become visible at a stage more culturally evolved than in western Asia, Mesoamerica or the Andes. Why should this be? Alas, I cannot answer this question with ease. Perhaps there is a preceramic "Natufian" in China, so far unrecognized in the archaeological record. If so, then the beginnings of agriculture in China could go back even further in time than those in Southwest Asia. On the other hand, perhaps the transition to agriculture and ceramic life in central China really was so fast that it is archaeologically invisible.

Whatever the answer, the transition was under-way by at least 6000 BC in both the Huanghe (Yellow) and middle–lower Yangzi basins, involving foxtail[7] and broomcorn millet in the former and rice in the latter. I thus regard early East Asian agriculture as focused in the Huanghe–Yangzi region and not the tropical south of China, which remained the preserve of Hoabinhian hunter–gatherers before their replacement or assimilation by agriculturalists.

Our present, admittedly faint, knowledge of the structure of early agriculture in central China can now be reviewed using the same six subheadings already applied to Southwest Asia.

Environmental parameters   As in Southwest Asia, the climatic amelioration at the end of the Pleistocene in eastern Asia involved a rise of temperature, approaching present levels by 13000 bp, and also the development of a much stronger summer monsoon (Walker 1986, Broecker et al. 1988, COHMAP 1988). As with the wheats and barleys, the ancestors of the cultivated millets and rice probably spread from refugia after the glacial maximum (Whyte 1983). For rice, an annual habit would have become emphasized because of the increased seasonality of rainfall, particularly in the northern cold-winter regions along the Yangzi (Oka 1988, Chang 1989, and see below). It is precisely here that the oldest evidence for domesticated rices, similar to both the modern *indica* and *japonica* types (Li 1985), has been found. Indeed, climatic conditions between 8000 and 2000 BC were slightly warmer and wetter than now and would have been very favourable for summer rice crops in the swamps and lakes of the Yangzi valley (Han 1988, Sun & Chen 1992). As in Southwest Asia, there is some evidence that the overall climatic amelioration was temporarily reversed by a Younger Dryas interval between 9000 and 8200 BC (Zhou 1991: 5; EATQN 1992: 82), but whether this would have had any impact on the shift to cultivation, as currently claimed by some scholars for Southwest Asia, remains uncertain. Any temporary shortening of the summer growing season on the northern edge of wild-rice distribution could, however, have been quite significant for populations targeting it as a food source.

The immediate cultural background to agriculture   Unfortunately, there is little to say on this topic. We have "a critical gap of about 1,000–1,500 years" (Chang 1986: 87) spanned by no sites at all, except for some rather dubious and probably disturbed cave assemblages from the south (ibid.: 95–106), which I find unconvincing because they are not backed up by well dated stratified open sites older than 5000 BC. However, it seems a reasonable hypothesis that terminal Pleistocene gatherers would have begun to exploit stands of annual broomcorn and foxtail millet, and/or rice, as part of their subsistence rounds, once these wild cereals became widespread. I have not been able to search for new references on the millets (apart from Chang 1983, Fogg 1983 and Whyte 1983) and so the following discussion is focused on rice, *Oryza sativa*, derived from the wild *Oryza rufipogon* with both annual and perennial habits according to Oka (1988), but via an intermediate wild annual form, *Oryza nivara*, according to Chang (1976).

As in Southwest Asia, the shifts to cultivation of both rice and the millets appear to have been rapid in China, although exactly which factors stimulated them (or was there just one shift to agriculture?) remains unknown. The morphological and genetic changes in rice – reduced shattering, greater synchronicity of germination and ripening, increased panicle (rather than grain) size, reduced awns and glumes, tendency to evolve self-pollination – were probably stimulated by the same kinds of harvesting and management activities that led to the comparable changes in wheat and barley in Southwest Asia (Oka 1988, Chang 1989, Thompson 1992). Such activities include the use of a sickle/reaping knife, selection of non-shattering stock for planting, and winter storage of seed leading to reduced selection pressures for tough protective glumes. According to Oka (1988: 101), some of these changes could have taken place rapidly, as in Southwest Asia (cf. Hillman & Davies 1990 for einkorn wheat). The rice of Hemudu (dated to *c.* 5000 BC) is described by Yan (1993: 121) as being already "of a fairly advanced form" and according to Li (1985) it was already differentiated into *indica* and *japonica* types. However, early rice sites seem to show few signs of the parching and roasting of husked grain or the heavy grinding equipment characteristic of Southwest Asia; presumably the earliest cultivated rices did not require this kind of treatment.

The edge-of-the-range factor   According to T. T. Chang (1983: 73):

The true domestication process [of rice] undoubtedly first took place in China because the cooler weather and shorter crop season there exerted great selection pressure on the early cultivars and made them more dependent on human care for perpetuation than were their tropical counterparts.

According to Oka (1988: 131–2), wild rice today grows only as far north as Fujian, but grew as far north as the Yangzi until the Song dynasty. In the warmer climatic conditions of the early Holocene we might expect wild rice to have grown well north into the region between the Huanghe and Yangzi rivers. It certainly appears to have been first domesticated in the swampy regions lining the middle and lower courses of the Yangzi River (Glover 1985, Yan 1991, 1993, Bellwood et al. 1992), and thus towards the edge of its natural range in a region where winter storage and synchronized annual planting would have been encouraged. As Yan (1993: 121–2) states:

. . . many grain crops [including rice] were no doubt first cultivated in temperate regions, where the four seasons are clearly distinct and the ripening period for such grain crops is relatively short . . . As soon as the inhabitants discovered [the value of wild rice] as a foodstuff and its capacity to sustain long periods of storage, they would naturally have made every effort to cultivate it and to expand production. This is one major factor which helps explain why the agricultural technology for rice cultivation in the Chiangjiang [Yangzi] River area was more advanced than in the south . . .

It is worth commenting here that plant cultivation not only seems to have begun on the edges of the ranges of the wild progenitors in both China and Southwest Asia, but there also seems to have been a focus on wetlands in both regions (as, perhaps not surprisingly, in New Guinea: see below and Gorecki 1986, Bayliss-Smith & Golson 1992, Bayliss-Smith in Ch. 26 in this volume). Planting perhaps began around the edges of seasonally inundated patches of soil, especially at times when water levels were falling rapidly after a summer-monsoon flood peak. A dry Younger Dryas climatic phase, if indeed one occurred in China, would probably have produced an adequate level of stimulus for cultivation to begin by reducing available moisture and promoting an increasing focus on low-lying wet areas.

In this regard it is apparent, and obviously important, that rice began its cultivated life as a wet-field crop rather than a dryland swiddened crop. Dryland swiddening in China and Southeast Asia may be regarded as a secondary development undertaken when good swampy or riverine terrain was already fully occupied. Modern ethnographic situations suggest that simple forms of swamp cultivation need be no more labour-demanding than swidden, and they can be a lot more productive (e.g. Padoch 1985 for East Kalimantan).

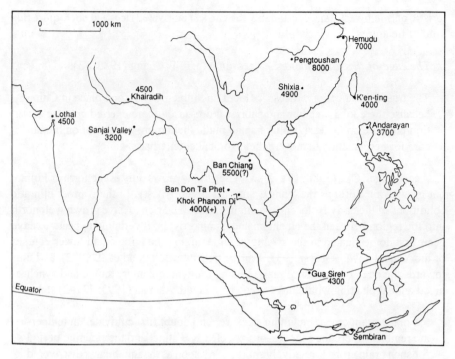

Figure 25.4   A sample of radiocarbon ages (cal BP, approximated) for the early presence of rice, presumed cultivated (from Bellwood et al. 1992: fig. 1).

Tempo   Evidence that the development of domesticated rice was quick has been presented above and similar data for the millets may be expected. However, the spread of rice out of its homeland in the Yangzi Valley seems to have taken place more slowly than the spread of wheat and barley cultivation out of Southwest Asia into Europe and Pakistan (Bellwood et al. 1992: Fig. 25.1, reproduced here as Fig. 25.4). This surely reflects in part the latitudinal factor. The spread of early rice cultivation in eastern Asia took place mainly across latitudes (i.e. north–south) rather than along latitudes (i.e. east–west). Because the wild rices, and presumably the early cultivated ones, were sensitive to day-length variations (Oka & Chang 1960), they probably would not have flowered successfully if moved too quickly across latitudes. The equatorial latitudes across which rice eventually travelled to reach much of Indonesia were also zones of low rice productivity owing to low sunlight (especially in the crucial 45 days before harvest), high night temperatures, lack of seasonality and perhumid rainfall conditions (Chang 1968). Thus, rice first appeared in central Thailand and Borneo some 3,000 years after its first domestication in central China (Bellwood et al. 1992). In the other direction, the ultimate transfer of rice to Japan in the second/first millennia BC required either an 800 km sea crossing from the Chinese mainland to Kyushu, or a land route going beyond 40°N and then back south through Korea (cf. Imamura in Ch. 24 in this volume). The fact that it does not appear in Japan until the Late Jomon / Early Yayoi period is thus not surprising.

The technological background to domestication in China   As in Southwest Asia, the oldest neolithic sites in the Huanghe basin have reaping knives or sickles of stone, shell and even pottery (Chang 1986: 93). However, among the earliest rice-growing societies in the south, such knives are absent, appearing only in the Majiabang phase (post-Hemudu 4) in the lower Yangzi and later than the oldest pottery assemblages in the P'eng-hu Islands and Taiwan (Tsang 1992a,b). Today, metal finger knives, which allow individual harvesting of panicles without prior weeding and also selection of ripe panicles as they mature, are widely used in Southeast Asia (Miles 1979). In function, therefore, these modern reaping knives and their prehistoric forebears are probably similar to the flint sickles of Natufian-PPNA Southwest Asia, although I am not aware of any studies of edge residues like those carried out on Southwest Asian stone knives by Unger-Hamilton (1989).

The absence of stone reaping knives in earliest neolithic southern China may be illusory – perhaps bamboo was used, or shell, as at Peiligang or at Khok Phanom Di in central Thailand (Thompson 1992). However, if their absence in the south is real, we may have to allow for some diffusion of technology from the millet zone into the rice zone after the beginnings of agriculture.

Consequences   The consequences of the shift to agriculture in China were massive indeed, if we examine both archaeological and linguistic sources of evidence (the biological evidence relating to a dispersal of Mongoloid populations through Southeast Asia and Oceania is also of major importance, albeit outside the range of this chapter: see Bellwood 1996, Hill & Serjeantson 1989, Pietrusewsky 1992).

Starting with the archaeology, I refer to Chang's interesting discussion of the growth of the "Chinese Interaction Sphere" (1986: ch. 5). In that discussion he accepts the putatively "early" dates for pottery from some southern Chinese caves, although, as stated above, I am suspicious of these because they have no support from sedentary village sites and I favour omitting them from further consideration. If they are omitted, then we have three phases, following Chang:

- Seventh millennium BC – a cluster of related sites in the Huanghe basin (Peiligang, Cishan: Shih 1993), plus the newly discovered Pengtoushan rice-growing complex in the middle Yangzi (Yan 1993, Glover & Higham in Ch. 23 in this volume). From published data it is not clear to me whether we have here one primary development of agriculture with two minor subfoci, or two independent developments.
- *c.* 5000 BC – the Yangshao, Dawenkou, Hemudu and Majiabang cultures, plus assemblages distributed down the southern coast of China to Fujian and Guangdong (Chang 1992, Tsang 1992a,b, and see Meacham 1984–5a for some possible dates of this order for assemblages of painted pottery from Hong Kong and Macau). Chang seems to think that these assemblages are still "distinctive and individual" (1986: 237), but I believe, having seen much of the material in Chinese museums, that the assemblages from coastal regions south of the Yangzi, including Taiwan, are all fairly closely related in terms of ceramic detail (e.g. red slip, cord marking, perforated pedestals, general shape repertoire, etc.) as well as in a very broad range of non-ceramic material culture from stone adzes

to the widespread presence of rice. The situation appears to be similar to that of the earlier phase, with slightly separate but overlapping style zones in the Huanghe basin and the regions south of the Yangzi.

- *c.* 4000 BC onwards – Chang now recognizes a high degree of regional integration, but still with northern (Huanghe river) and southern ("Lungshanoid") divisions. He believes this occurred because of a "process of linkage" and that "regional cultures reached out to touch each other physically, interacted culturally, and show tangible and growing evidence of sustained and significant interaction" (ibid.: 237). This suggests that he believes that a homogeneous cultural entity (his "Chinese or proto-Chinese sphere of interaction": (ibid. 1986: 242)) developed by convergence from relatively unlike ancestral cultural forms. Although I must respect Chang's views on this, we do at this point tend to part interpretive company. My view is that the interaction sphere was there from the beginning of the Neolithic; it did not develop by convergence after 4000 BC, but simply continued to track relationships between people and cultures who shared one, possibly two, foci of common origin at the beginnings of expansive millet and rice agriculture.

At this point we are on the verge of a vast archaeological odyssey through time and space. I can only state that for many years I have held strongly the view that a dispersal, via human colonization, of neolithic material culture and agricultural systems took place from the general region of China south of the Yangzi through the entirety of Southeast Asia, eastern India, and Oceania beyond the region of independent early agriculture in New Guinea and western Melanesia (Bellwood 1984–5, 1985, 1991, 1992, Tsang 1992a,b, Spriggs 1989, and, for a contrary view, see Meacham 1984–5b). I do not wish to go over all this ground again, but will note that there are no dates, either archaeological or palynological, for arguable agricultural activities anywhere in Southeast Asia older than about 3000 BC (see Flenley 1988 and Stuijts 1993 on the palynology). The same applies to the Indian subcontinent outside the Harappan sphere of influence in the northwest (Liversage 1991, Bellwood & Barnes 1993).

This brings up the question of who was doing the colonizing, and with this I return to the archaeological and linguistic discussion foreshadowed at the beginning of this chapter. In brief, the general area of East Asia between the Huanghe river, Yunnan and northern Vietnam can be stated on firm linguistic grounds to been the homeland of the Tai-Kadai (TK), Miao-Yao (MY, also known as Hmong-Mien) and the vast Austronesian (AN) language families, and on slightly less firm grounds to be the homeland of the Austroasiatic (AA) and Sino–Tibetan (ST) families (Bellwood 1994). As already noted, areas of primary agricultural origin, including China, Southwest Asia, Africa between the Sahara and the Equator, Mesoamerica with the northern Andes, and New Guinea support absolutely high densities of language family and primary subgroup geographical intersections. They also correlate geographically with deep phylogenetic splits within language family trees. In short, they are regions of high phylogenetic diversity within and between language families, and as such must be given recognition as regions of common origin of major language families (Figs 25.1, 25.2). In general, populations have remained stable within, or have flowed outwards from, these regions. Only rarely have they flowed inwards on any major scale; had they done so, the phylogenetic linguistic diversity so visible now would have been reduced or erased.

Within East and Southeast Asia, the location of Proto-Austronesian (PAN) in Taiwan has long been accepted by a majority of linguists (Blust 1984–5, 1992, Sirk 1987, Starosta 1992, Zorc 1994, Pawley & Ross 1995, Tryon 1995, despite arguments to the contrary by Dyen 1992, and Wolff 1992). A southern Chinese origin also applies to TK (Benedict 1975, Chamberlain 1990). An early propinquity of ancestral TK and AN is supported by the phylogenetic claims inherent in Benedict's Austro–Tai hypothesis (Benedict 1975), or, should these prove incorrect, by an allied claim by Thurgood (1993) for early borrowing between the two phyla. For AA an origin in China is now masked by the expansion of Chinese, but traces of early AA place names as far north as the Yangzi (Norman & Mei 1976), together with claims for an AA–AN genetic relationship (the Austric hypothesis, recently supported by Diffloth 1993), suggest that the AA languages spread from a homeland adjacent to those of AN and TK (surviving Mon–Khmer subgroup data suggest a homeland no farther south than the middle Mekong: ibid.). For ST, homeland estimates by linguists tend to fall in the western part of the range (e.g. Matisoff 1991 favours a source in the upper basins of the Huanghe, Yangzi and Mekong rivers), but in my view this could reflect the loss of early ST diversity in China proper due to the expansion of Chinese within the past 2,500 years. A source for ST close to the presumed Chinese archaeological homeland, squarely in the Huanghe River early agricultural zone, would make excellent sense and would help to explain why, during the Conference on Asian Mainland/Austronesian Connections recently held in 1993 in Honolulu, so many varied links, some genetic, some due to ancient borrowing, were claimed between all the language families of eastern Asia (Bellwood 1994).

Archaeologically, the expansions of AA and AN speakers through mainland and island Southeast Asia respectively can be followed, in so far as the archaeological record is able to illuminate such processes, in terms already indicated by me in several publications (Bellwood 1984–5, 1991, 1992). Within Indonesia, the earliest ANs probably found AA agriculturalists already in occupation in Sumatra, to judge from language substratum indications in Acehnese (including placenames: Diffloth pers. comm.), in western Borneo (Aslian substratum: Adelaar 1995), and possibly in Sumbawa (non-AN features noted by Blust 1987). Palynological indications of forest clearance, putatively for agriculture, from c. 3000 BC onwards in Sumatra and Java (Flenley 1988, Stuijts 1993), commence at a date too early for AN (Western Malayo–Polynesian) linguistic colonization of this region (Blust 1984–5) and thus may relate to older AA agricultural activity spread by colonists from the c. third millennium BC agricultural societies of the Malay Peninsula (Bellwood 1993). ANs have thus replaced AAs in several places in western Indonesia and have also replaced AA (Aslian) populations on the Malay Peninsula, just as the Tai and ST (Tibeto–Burman, including Pyu, Burmese, Karen) languages overall have probably replaced earlier AA languages in much of mainland Southeast Asia. I make this point because I do not wish to give the impression that I believe all agricultural colonizations replaced previous hunter–gatherers – there have certainly been agriculturalist-over-agriculturalist replacements many times in prehistory, but mostly within the recent millennia of state formation and never on a total language-family scale.

As well as these observations about ancient linguistic geography and inter-phylum relationships, we also have the evidence of proto-language vocabularies, a mine of information for archaeologists, as can be realized by scanning the huge number of reconstructions for all aspects of life for Proto-AN, spoken probably in Taiwan some time in the fourth millennium BC (Blust 1984–5, Sirk 1987, Pawley & Ross 1993, Zorc 1994). Reconstructions of this type for other language families leave no doubt that the proto-languages of all those mentioned above contained terms for domesticated plants and cultivation, especially of rice, well before the dispersal of populations from the common East Asian homeland region (e.g. Zide & Zide 1976 for Munda, Benedict 1975 for TK, Chamberlain 1990 for Tai).

Within Oceania, the colonizations of Austronesian-speaking agricultural populations can be tracked by both archaeology and linguistics. The AN Oceanic languages spread quickly eastwards out of the "Lapita Homeland" region of the Bismarck Archipelago at about 1600 BC (Pawley & Ross 1993, 1995), carried by speakers with an agricultural economy, here minus rice, which was evidently dropped from cultivation in the difficult climatic zone along the Equator in eastern Indonesia (Bellwood 1980). Western Oceanic prehistory has almost as long and complex a trajectory as that of Southeast Asia, far beyond recapitulation here (see Bellwood 1989, Irwin 1992). But I do wish to stress one very important archaeological and linguistic point. The Lapita agricultural repertoire, as reported by archaeologists such as Kirch (1989) and Gosden (1990), together with the reconstructed Proto-Oceanic agricultural terms (Pawley & Green 1984), indicate that the first AN settlers of Oceania carried a range of crops very similar, except for the loss of rice, to those of their contemporaries and close cousins in Indonesia. However, some of these crops, including sugar cane, taro, canarium nuts and some kinds of bananas (Australimusa section), are believed by Yen (1990, 1993) also to have been domesticated independently from local progenitors in New Guinea. Indeed, since the 1970s it has been assumed that New Guinea was an independent centre for the development of tuber and fruit agriculture (e.g. Bellwood 1978: 238; Yen 1980) and that it must have played some role, perhaps an important one, in the dispersal of agriculture through the Pacific. Let us now examine this assumption.

New Guinea: a different trajectory?

Among the large islands that lie between Asia and Australia, New Guinea is unique in having a continuous highland spine almost 2,000 km long, as opposed to the smaller discontinuous areas of highland characteristic of other large islands such as Borneo and Java. The New Guinea highlands, with their large valleys and dense populations, mostly lying between 1,300 m and 2,300 m above sea level (ground frosts start at c. 2,600 m), contain evidence for a locally generated transition to agriculture in a context of dramatic terminal Pleistocene/early Holocene environmental change. I will here examine New Guinea with respect to the six subheadings already considered for Southwest and East Asia, with the proviso that the archaeological and linguistic records from the island are very sparse. There are no simple answers, and New Guinea certainly does not fit well with any scenario derived from either of the other two regions.

Environmental parameters   By 10500 bp the climate in the highlands had ameliorated to present conditions and the tree line had risen almost 2,000 m in a remarkably short period, perhaps only one millennium, to its present altitude at *c.* 4,000 m (Swadling & Hope 1992, Haberle 1994). Reversing the trend characteristic of Southwest Asia and China, the climate at this equatorial latitude seems to have become less rather than more seasonal with the retreat of the ice (Morley & Flenley 1987). Relatively non-seasonal climates developed in the regions of the Irian Jaya and Papua New Guinea highlands where palynological and archaeological data suggest agriculture first developed, some time in the range 10,000 to 7,000 bp (Hope 1983, Haberle et al. 1991). Traditional New Guinea agricultural systems are focused on tubers and tree products which are less seasonal than the annual cereal and legume crops of Southwest Asia and China.

Given the above, it may be supposed that the stresses that might have given rise to agriculture in the New Guinea highlands should perhaps be looked for as much in the altitudinal rise of postglacial environments as in the shifts of rainfall seasonality and temperature (Mountain 1991a). I return to this point below.

The immediate cultural and technological backgrounds to agriculture   In New Guinea, unlike Southwest Asia or China, technology seems to have changed very little before, with or after the advent of agriculture. We see no rapid spreads of new art styles, pottery (never manufactured in the main highlands), or house forms. Neither are there any recognizable harvesting tools in the oldest agricultural contexts. Except for the appearance of ground-stone axes and the digging of ditches (presumably with wooden digging sticks), the archaeological face of early agriculture shows no real change from the prior hunter–gatherer assemblages of the Late Pleistocene.

The edge-of-the-range factor   Most of the New Guinea sites, and all of the "hard" evidence for early agriculture, occur between 1,300 m and 2,000 m in the highlands and were thus located well within the forest belt in the early Holocene. At Kuk in the Waghi Valley (1,550 m altitude) the main crops in Phases 1 and 2 (9000 and 6000 bp) are considered, in the absence of actual macrofossils or pollen, to have been taro, Australimusa bananas, yams and sugar cane (Golson & Gardner 1990, Bayliss-Smith & Golson 1992, Daniels & Daniels 1993). Today, yams grow up to about 1,700–2,000 m, bananas to about 2,000 m and taro to about 2,700 m (Bayliss-Smith 1988 and in Ch. 26 in this volume). Presumably in the last glacial these crops would not have grown at all in the broad fertile highland valleys above 1,300 m, and would have been restricted to lowland areas and to the steeply sloping terrain that surrounds the highlands in most directions. As postglacial temperatures rose, people might have moved with the rising upper limits of these plants into the highlands, then as now a region on the "edge of the range".

Any early Holocene stress factor, such as a long episode of locally unprecedented drought or frost (Brookfield 1989), could then have encouraged a switch to swamp-edge planting in favourable locations. Once swamp-edge planting was begun, probably in combination with some swiddening on adjacent terrain (Bayliss-Smith 1988), it is not hard to see communities being propelled towards increasing investment in new forms of production such as grassland tillage and tree-fallowing, as described for Kuk by Golson & Gardner (1990).

Could New Guinea agriculture have developed first in the lowlands and then spread into the highlands? I doubt it, as does Gorecki (1986). The altitudinal locations of early sites in New Guinea have been plotted by Haberle (1994), and the virtual absence of sites of all periods between 500 m and 1,300 m is very striking. Coastal sites are also few, and yield no evidence of early agriculture. Swadling's finds of plant remains at Dongan in the Sepik basin dated to c. 5500–6000 bp (candlenut, canarium, coconut, pandanus, possibly sago: Swadling et al. 1991) are of great interest here, but most are of nut-yielding species which could have been exploited from wild rather than planted trees. In the New Guinea lowlands there is no hard evidence for actual plant cultivation, as opposed to collection, prior to the arrival of Austronesian-speaking populations within the past 3,500 years (perhaps much less in the case of the New Guinea coasts). The lowlands also witnessed far less environmental change than the highlands, and the latter in this regard fit well with "edge-of-the-range" theory as applied to Southwest Asia and China.

Tempo   Perhaps as a result of the absence of any visible cultural change with the advent of agriculture in New Guinea, some archaeologists have suggested that agriculture developed gradually in the highlands from early settlement times, c. 30000 bp according to current highland dates (listed in Mountain 1991b), rather than rapidly in the early Holocene. This slow development is seen as a result of gradually developing forest and plant-management activities (Groube 1989, Swadling & Hope 1992: 27–8).

This suggestion has some validity in that certain pollen diagrams show instances of sporadic high charcoal counts going back as far as 30,000 years ago (Haberle 1994). However, my own view is that this gradualist stance is more an epiphenomenon of ideology than a product of hard data. The pollen diagrams that show signs of actual forest clearance – as opposed to sporadic high charcoal levels which could result from "firestick farming" (high charcoal peaks also occur in pollen diagrams in hunter–gatherer Australia) – all place it in the Holocene (Flenley 988, Golson 1991, Haberle et al. 1991) and accord well with the first archaeological dates for swamp drainage from Kuk at 9000 bp (Golson 1977, 1991, Golson & Gardner 1990, Bayliss-Smith & Golson 1992).

These data also integrate well with evidence of increased slopewash and sediment deposition in the New Guinea highlands after 9000 bp (Gillieson et al. 1987), and with increasing rates of artefact deposition in several highland sites after about the same time (Mountain 1991b). The ground-stone axe/adzes, perhaps essential tools for large-scale forest clearance, do not make a convincing appearance in the archaeological record in the highlands much before 6000–7000 bp.

Consequences   The New Guinea highlands, with their high diversity of language families and their evidence for early agriculture close to the Pleistocene/Holocene boundary, conform to the expectations derived from Southwest Asia and China. In terms of cultural consequences they may conform less well, although language distributions in the highlands do indicate some degree of agricultural dispersal according to Foley (1992: 147). However, the archaeological and linguistic records do not indicate any major colonizations from the highlands out into lowland New Guinea or the islands of Melanesia, and the total absence of any agricultural spread into Australia is very striking, despite the fact that it was probably still joined to New Guinea by dry land when the agricultural developments began (Barham & Harris 1983: 543–8; Harris 1995). In this regard the New Guinea situation lacks the explosiveness characteristic of other regions. Perhaps this situation reflects lack of domestic animals and cereals, as well as the isolation of the highlands by inhospitable terrain. Within the highlands also there seems to be a localization rather than a universality of early agricultural activity according to present information – some regions, such as the far western and eastern highlands of Papua New Guinea, have yet to produce evidence that they were also involved in such transitions to agriculture as are seen at Kuk (Feil 1987), or Kalela Swamp in the Baliem Valley of Irian Jaya (Haberle et al. 1991). However, this situation may reflect the constraints of a frustratingly sparse archaeological record as opposed to a firm reality.

Although there is currently a tendency among western Pacific archaeologists to suggest that the early Austronesian economy, which was spread by colonization across the Pacific after 3000 bp (c. 1600 cal BC), owed much to borrowing of crops and items of material culture from prior populations in the Bismarck Archipelago (e.g. Green 1991, Enright & Gosden 1992), actual evidence for this view remains weak. There is as yet no convincing evidence for agriculture (as opposed to a degree of tree-crop harvesting, not necessarily of "domesticated" or even planted species) in the pre-Lapita lowlands of western Melanesia (Spriggs 1993 and in Ch. 27 in this volume). Furthermore, an important point usually overlooked by archaeologists is that the initial Austronesian language dispersal into Oceania, which reached eastern Melanesia, Polynesia and Nuclear Micronesia, carried no identifiable traces of intensive borrowing from Papuan sources (as demonstrated in some detail by Ross 1989 and by Pawley & Ross 1993, 1995). Austronesian languages which do carry strong evidence of Papuan influence belong to the Western Oceanic subgroup of Ross (1989) (Fig. 25.3), and in all cases they appear to be the result of relatively recent (within the past 2,000 years) language spreads subsequent to Lapita times.

Of course, one could adopt a contrary view that pre-Austronesian agricultural sites do exist in the New Guinea lowlands but have been long buried out of archaeological reach by the millions of tonnes of sediment released by 9,000 years of agriculture in the New Guinea highlands. For instance, Swadling & Hope (1992: 21) state that the rate of soil erosion in the upper Ok Tedi Valley in the Western Highlands of Papua New Guinea is about 60 times the world average. A similar process may, I suspect, account for the similar lack of lowland neolithic sites in large alluviated Indonesian islands such as Java and Sumatra. But for New Guinea this question will not be resolved easily. The relative lack of Austronesian colonization of the lowlands of New Guinea could reflect an environmental hazard such as malaria (Groube 1993), or it could reflect the existence of a prior and dense Papuan-speaking agricultural, or at least tree-crop managing, population. At present we simply do not know.

Some comparisons

Southwest Asia and China are regions where agriculture began very early in the Holocene, probably because of a terminal Pleistocene environmental trigger, such as the Younger Dryas return to glacial conditions. In both regions, agriculture was associated with domesticated meat animals and in both the cultural results give the impression of being explosive and highly expansive. People, agricultural systems and languages colonized across very large regions, replacing or assimilating former hunter–gatherer populations. New Guinea seems to fit the Southwest Asian/Chinese model in terms of terminal Pleistocene/early Holocene timing and the edge-of-the-range factor, but not in terms of tempo or cultural and demographic consequences.

In the other regions of early agriculture the general picture is clearly different again, certainly in respect of timing although perhaps less so in respect of cultural consequences. I will leave Africa out of consideration because, despite the impressive range of Bantu colonization after 1000 BC (Ehret & Posnansky 1982, Vansina 1984), it is by no means certain that the origins of agriculture in the summer-rain belt of sub-Saharan Africa were entirely independent of developments farther north. They could have been triggered by a spread of pastoralism from Southwest Asia and the Nile Valley during the early to middle Holocene Saharan pluvial period (Harlan 1992). The same applies to India, which I also do not regard as a primary region of agricultural development (for reasons discussed in more detail in Bellwood et al. 1992, and Bellwood & Barnes 1993). Rice was probably introduced into the Indian subcontinent by Munda (Austroasiatic) speakers moving in from Southeast Asia after 2500 BC, and the spread of agriculture through the Deccan was evidently stimulated by the introduction of African millets into Gujarat and Maharashtra, during the late Harappan period, some time in the third millennium BC (Possehl 1986, Weber 1991, Meadow in Ch. 22 in this volume).

This leaves the Americas, an area where modern scholars seem willing to accept two, perhaps three, independent developments of agriculture (Eastern Woodlands of North America, Mesoamerica, northern Andes in South America). Yet a careful searching of the literature for these regions will indicate that strong, viable claims for the domestication of major food plants (ignoring condiment or container species such as peppers and gourds) are nowhere older than 3000 BC, and indeed in most regions post-date 2000 BC (for some current statements see Flannery & Marcus 1983, Sharer & Grove 1989, de Tapia 1992, Pearsall 1992, Pozorski & Pozorski 1992, Smith 1992). Claims for older cultigens in cave deposits or based on phytolith data from pollen cores are quite common in the literature and suggest some degree of human–plant coevolution, to use Rindos' (1984) term, going back into the earliest Holocene period. But given the conflicting views on the dates and domesticated status of these remains (e.g. Mangelsdorf 1986, Benz & Iltis 1990, and the American papers in Harris & Hillman 1989), together with Flannery's early hypothesis of a maize "take-off" after 2000 BC (Flannery 1973), perhaps we should beware of reading more than a minor degree of forager–plant coevolution into the record prior to the third millennium BC. There is a danger that the search for "early agriculture" by archaeologists becomes automatically self-fulfilling.

Nevertheless, the data from Mesoamerica and the northern Andes still give the same hints, as in Southwest Asia and China, of explosive cultural change and expansion following the establishment of sedentary agricultural villages, despite the fact that these developments are delayed in the Americas by about 4,000 years. Here a terminal Pleistocene timing does not seem to fit. A similar delay applies to the Eastern Woodlands, although here the links between early seed agriculture and cultural changes are far more difficult to discern.

In a sense, therefore, Mesoamerica and the Andes give the impression of being quite different from New Guinea in terms of timing (mid-Holocene versus terminal Pleistocene/early Holocene), tempo (rapid versus gradual) and consequences (geographical expansiveness versus stability), and of opposing Southwest Asia and China in terms of timing. However, to make these broad comparisons is obviously to lift the lid of a huge Pandora's box of interesting questions.

Are there any regularities in early agriculture?

The above discussion will suggest that I disagree with two recently published statements:

Agriculture generally spreads through the diffusion of ideas and products rather than people . . . Colonization must now be seen as the exception rather than the rule in the spread of agriculture.   (Gebauer & Price 1992: 8)

[The development of agriculture involved] rather a long and painfully slow process of plant and animal manipulation.   (Mellaart 1989: 4)

I see only limited evidence that systematic agriculture, as opposed to "coevolutionary" tinkering with the habitats of wild plants by hunter–gatherers, either developed slowly or diffused to hunter–gatherers anywhere in the world, although I am aware that such diffusion is likely to have occurred in certain environments on the fringes of agricultural viability (e.g. northern Europe, Southeast Asian rainforests, southern Californian semi-desert). Any large-scale hunter–gatherer adoption of agriculture, so large in scale that it could have served as the main process whereby agriculture spread from its homeland regions, seems to me to be entirely negated by the structures of the linguistic and early neolithic/formative records of human affairs.

Indigenous agricultural developments from hunter–gatherer backgrounds were also quite rare events in world prehistory, dependent on specific concatenations of place, time and the existences of domesticable plants and animals. Not just any plants and animals would do; the archaeological and botanical/osteological records indicate quite clearly that a few species have had phenomenal significances for human food production.

With these opinions in mind, I would like finally to offer a draft "model" of the shape and impact of an "ideal" agricultural revolution, against which data awaiting recovery from the several relevant parts of the world can be compared. The model will clearly fit some Old World cases well because it is of course derived from them. Other cases, as we should expect, will not fit so well.

First, I suggest that genuinely primary Old World agricultural revolutions, those that pulled themselves up by their own boot-straps out of the Palaeolithic/Mesolithic, were related to the massive environmental changes that occurred at the end of the Pleistocene (cf. Wright 1993). The American revolutions, for reasons that will no doubt be very interesting if we ever discover them, seem not to fit in this regard.

Secondly, agriculture spread from the primary regions mainly by population colonization, rather than by diffusion alone. The linguistic evidence for this I believe to be particularly strong, and was never really considered before in any meaningful way by the archaeological community until the publication of Colin Renfrew's 1987 book. The rates and intensities of spread seem to relate to the precise natures of the economies concerned, with greater "explosiveness" related to cereals and domestic animals, as opposed to tubers and continued hunting – a point previously made by Harris (1972) on ecological grounds. As we might expect, Southwest Asia, China and Bantu Africa seem to rate highest on the scale, the Americas in the middle, with New Guinea showing very few signs of agricultural spread. The Eastern Woodlands of North America remain to me quite enigmatic on this point.

Thirdly, there should be a short period of time in each region of genuine agricultural origin during which "complex foraging" behaviour shifted into systematic agriculture, rapidly and with revolutionary changes in social organization and population density. All regions apart from New Guinea seem to fit this aspect of the model fairly well. A rapid shift in lifestyle from foraging to agriculture accords with the general view, which I hold, that the fundamental developments in human prehistory have all been of rather a revolutionary (or punctuational) nature. I am unable to visualize agriculture as a gradual and unconscious shift out of foraging – were it more than marginally so we would have to rethink entirely the nature of neolithic/formative archaeological patterning and the concomitant but independent linguistic patterning across the globe.

Finally, the rate of agricultural expansion should be visible in the extents and degrees of homogeneity of the archaeological cultures involved, and also in the shapes of the phylogenetic trees of the language families which, through language palaeogeography and proto-language reconstruction, can putatively be associated with the various regions of agricultural revolution.

At the beginning of this chapter, I emphasized the importance of co-operation between archaeology and linguistics in understanding the remote human past, especially that pertaining to the origins of agriculture. I conclude by returning to this topic because a careful understanding of it can indicate to us what to look for in future research. Back in 1978, as a result of discussions with the linguist Andrew Pawley, I made the following statement based on my understanding of the linguistic situation in New Guinea:

It is my own belief that some kind of cultivation may have commenced independently in New Guinea before Austronesians arrived, on the grounds that the latter, who probably were cultivators, were not successful colonisers of New

Guinea because quite dense populations of Papuan speakers with their own methods of plant cultivation had probably developed there before them. (Bellwood 1978: 238)

In other words, the surviving presence of a high diversity of Papuan languages in New Guinea, within a vast swathe of more closely related Austronesian languages extending more than half way around the world, suggested to me at that time that New Guinea had something special going for it. Today, 20 years since the above was written, it seems more and more likely that this prognosis was true, and that regions which lack such linguistic diversity, such as much of Indonesia, were not foci of the origins of agriculture.

In stating this, however, it is not my intention to impose a linguistic straightjacket on archaeological interpretation. Nor is it my intention to isolate an archaeological model that will fit every situation of agricultural origins. The essence is to understand the archaeological and linguistic records as independent clues to the past patterning of human affairs on a macro scale. No source of data relevant to this scale should be dismissed as being incomprehensible or of no relevance if we wish to understand the human past.

Notes

1. It should not be forgotten that I am here discussing whole language families. Of course, many individual languages such as Thai, Arabic, Chinese, English and Spanish have spread widely in historical times, but most language families had already reached close to their geographical limits before history began.
2. Some hunter–gatherer regions also have high linguistic diversity, especially northern Australia and the western coast of North America. The meaning of this is that populations, over time, have tended to flow outwards from these areas (which are mostly productive and densely populated) rather than inwards, exactly as with agricultural homelands.
3. Such adoptions probably occurred, for instance, around the Atlantic fringes of Europe, among those Dravidian speakers in the northwestern part of the Indian subcontinent who received African millets in the third millennium BC (Possehl 1986), and among Yuman speakers in the American Southwest. But, for reasons given in this chapter, I am unable to accept this kind of transmission as the worldwide norm.
4. I do not wish to give the impression that I believe hunter–gatherers outside the primary agricultural zones have never adopted agriculture. Many doubtless have, just as many agriculturalists have often gone the other way and "adopted" hunting and gathering. Archaeological evidence in the Pacific indicates that initial agricultural colonists frequently resorted to economies based heavily on hunting and gathering in pristine environments. These were normally only temporary reactions to plentiful supplies and were later succeeded by a switch back to agriculture. On a longer-term basis it is clear that some one-time agriculturalists have actually shifted on a long-term basis to hunting and gathering in marginal environments, such as equatorial rainforests and semi-arid zones (discussed in Bellwood 1990, 1991, in press). But the shift the other way, from hunting and gathering to systematic and temporally successful agriculture, would have been far more difficult (Hunn & Williams 1982, Bellwood 1990). This is not because hunter–gatherers necessarily lack any will to cultivate, but more because any inmoving group of agriculturalists that serves as the source of crops, animals and knowledge for the existing foragers will probably not tolerate competition on the best agricultural lands (cf. Headland 1986).
5. Note that Proto-Mayan, Proto-Otomanguean, and two Amazonian proto languages (Proto-Arawakan and Proto-Panoan) seem to share a single term for maize (Matteson 1972: 52; "corn" *iSi-ki/?im), which is presumably a result of very early borrowing. If correct, this could be very significant for understanding the dispersal of agriculture in the Americas.

6. In this chapter radiocarbon dates given as BC are derived from calibrated date ranges whereas those given as bc and bp are from uncalibrated date ranges.
7. I am intrigued that foxtail millet was also grown in the Southeast European Neolithic c. 3000 BC (Rimantiené 1992). Where did it originate? [As I suggest in Ch. 29 in this volume, foxtail millet may have been domesticated independently in East Asia and elsewhere in Eurasia: Ed.]

References

Adelaar, K. A. 1995. Borneo as a cross-roads for comparative Austronesian linguistics. In Bellwood et al. (1995: 75–95).

An Zhimin 1988. Archaeological research on Neolithic China. *Current Anthropology* **29**, 753–9.

Anthony, D. W. 1990. Migration in archaeology: the baby and the bathwater. *American Anthropologist* **92**, 895–914.

Barham, A. J. & D. R. Harris 1983. Prehistory and palaeoecology of Torres Strait. In *Quaternary coastlines and marine archaeology*, P. M. Masters & N. C. Flemming (eds), 529–57. London: Academic Press.

Bar-Yosef, O. 1989. The PPNA in the Levant – an overview. *Paléorient* **15**, 57–63.

— 1991. The early Neolithic of the Levant: recent advances. *The Review of Archaeology* **12**(2), 1–18.

Bar-Yosef, O. & A. Belfer-Cohen. 1991. From sedentary hunter–gatherers to territorial farmers in the Levant. In *Between bands and states*, S. A. Gregg (ed.), 181–202. Occasional Paper 9, Center for Archaeological Investigations, Southern Illinois University.

— 1992. From foraging to farming in the Mediterranean Levant. In Gebauer & Price (1992: 21–48).

Bayliss-Smith, T. P. 1988. Prehistoric agriculture in the New Guinea Highlands: problems in defining the altitutidinal limits to growth. In *Conceptual issues in environmental archaeology*, J. Bintliff, D. Davidson, E. G. Grant (eds), 153–60. Edinburgh: Edinburgh University Press.

Bayliss-Smith, T. P. & J. Golson 1992. Wetland agriculture in New Guinea highlands prehistory. In *The wetland revolution in prehistory*, B. Coles (ed.), 15–27. Exeter: The Prehistoric Society and the Wetland Archaeology Research Project.

Bellwood, P. S. 1978. *Man's conquest of the Pacific*. Auckland: Collins.

— 1980. Plants, climate and people: the early horticultural prehistory of Austronesia. In *Indonesia: the making of a culture*, J. J. Fox (ed.), 57–73. Canberra: Research School of Pacific Studies, Australian National University.

— 1984–5. A hypothesis for Austronesian origins. *Asian Perspectives* **26**, 107–17.

— 1985. *Prehistory of the Indo–Malaysian archipelago*. Sydney: Academic Press.

— 1987. *The Polynesians*, revised edn. London: Thames & Hudson.

— 1989. The colonization of the Pacific: some current hypotheses. In *The colonization of the Pacific*, A. V. S. Hill & S. W. Serjeantson (eds), 1–59. Oxford: Oxford University Press.

— 1990. Foraging towards farming: a decisive transition or a millennial blur? *The Review of Archaeology* **11**(2), 14–24.

— 1991. The Austronesian dispersal and the origin of languages. *Scientific American* **265**(1), 88–93.

— 1992. Southeast Asia before history. In *The Cambridge history of Southeast Asia*, N. Tarling (ed.), 55–136. Cambridge: Cambridge University Press.

— 1993. Cultural and biological differentiation in peninsular Malaysia: the last 10,000 years. *Asian Perspectives* **32**, 37–60.

— 1994. An archaeologist's view of language macrofamily relationships. *Oceanic Linguistics* **33**, 391–406.

— in press. Prehistoric cultural explanations for the existence of widespread language families. In *Understanding ancient Australia: perspectives from archaeology and linguistics*, P. McConvell & N. Evans (eds). Melbourne: Oxford University Press.

— 1996. Early agriculture and the dispersal of the southern Mongoloids. In *Prehistoric dispersal of Mongoloids*, T. Akazawa & E. Szathmary (eds), 287–302. Oxford: Oxford University Press.

Bellwood, P. S. (ed.) 1991. *Indo–Pacific prehistory 1990* (vol. 2). *Bulletin of the Indo–Pacific Prehis-*

Haberle, S. 1994. Anthropogenic indicators in pollen diagrams: problems and prospects for late Quaternary palynology in New Guinea. In *Tropical archaeobotany: applications and new developments*, J. G. Hather (ed.), 172–201. London: Routledge.

Haberle, S. G., G. S. Hope, Y. DeFretes 1991. Environmental change in the Baliem Valley, montane Irian Jaya, Republic of Indonesia. *Journal of Biogeography* **18**, 25–40.

Han Defen 1988. The fauna from the Neolithic site of Hemudu, Zhejiang. In *The palaeoenvironment of east Asia from the mid-Tertiary* (vol. II), P. Whyte (ed.), 868–72. Hong Kong Centre of Asian Studies, University of Hong Kong.

Harlan, J. 1992. Indigenous African agriculture. In Cowan & Watson (1992: 59–70).

Harris, D. R. 1972. The origins of agriculture in the tropics. *American Scientist* **60**, 180–93.

— 1995. Early agriculture in New Guinea and the Torres Strait divide. In *Transitions: Pleistocene to Holocene in Australia and Papua New Guinea*, J. Allen & J. F. O'Connell (eds), 848–54. *Antiquity* **69** [Special Number].

Harris, D. R. & G. C. Hillman (eds) 1989. *Foraging and farming: the evolution of plant exploitation*. London: Unwin Hyman.

Hayden, B. 1990. Nimrods, pescators, pluckers and planters: the emergence of food production. *Journal of Anthropological Archaeology* **9**, 31–69.

— 1992. Models of domestication. In Gebauer & Price (1992: 11–19).

Headland, T. 1986. *Why foragers do not become farmers*. Ann Arbor: University Microfilms International.

Helmer, D. 1988. Les animaux de Cafer et des sites précéramiques de sud-est de la Turquie. *Anatolica* **15**, 37–48.

Henry, D. O. 1989. *From foraging to agriculture: the Levant at the end of the Ice Age*. Philadelphia: University of Pennsylvania Press.

Higham, C. F. W. 1989. *The archaeology of mainland Southeast Asia – from 10,000 BC to the fall of Angkor*. Cambridge: Cambridge University Press.

Hill, A. V. S. & S. W. Serjeantson (eds) 1989. *The colonization of the Pacific*. Oxford: Oxford University Press.

Hillman, G. C. & M. S. Davies. 1990. Measured domestication rates in wild wheat and barley. *Journal of World Prehistory* **4**, 157–222.

Hope, G. S. 1983. Palaeoecology. *Journal of Human Evolution* **12**, 37–42.

Hopf, M. 1983. Jericho plant remains. In *Excavations at Jericho* (vol. 5), K. M. Kenyon & T. A. Holland (eds), 576–621. London: British School of Archaeology in Jerusalem.

Hunn, E. S. & N. M. Williams 1982. Introduction. In *Resource managers: North American and Australian hunter–gatherers*, N. M. Williams & E. S. Hunn (eds), 1–16. Boulder: Westview Press.

Irwin, G. J. 1992. *The prehistoric exploration and colonization of the Pacific*. Cambridge: Cambridge University Press.

Kaufman, T. 1990. Language history in South America. In *Amazonian linguistics*, D. L. Payne (ed.), 13–73. Austin: University of Texas Press.

Keightley, D. N. (ed.) 1983. *The origins of Chinese civilization*. Berkeley: University of California Press.

Kirch, P. V. 1988. The Talepakemalai Lapita site and Oceanic prehistory. *National Geographic Research* **4**, 328–42.

— 1989. Second millennium BC arboriculture in Melanesia. *Economic Botany* **43**, 225–40.

Legge, A. J. & P. A. Rowley-Conwy 1987. Gazelle killing in Stone Age Syria. *Scientific American* **257**(2), 88–97.

Li Kunsheng 1985. The origin of Asiatic rice cultivation. *Bulletin of the Ancient Orient Museum* **7**, 93–112.

Limbrey, S. 1990. Edaphic opportunism? *World Archaeology* **22**, 45–52.

Liversage, D. 1991. South Asian radiocarbon datings: calibration and computer graphics. *Bulletin of the Indo–Pacific Prehistory Association* **10**, 198–205.

Maley, J. 1987. Fragmentation of the African rainforest and extension of montane biotopes during the Late Quaternary. *East Asian Tertiary/Quaternary Newsletter* **7**, 73–5.

Mangelsdorf, P. 1986. The origin of corn. *Scientific American* **255**, 72–8.

Matisoff, J. 1991. Sino–Tibetan linguistics: present state and future prospects. *Annual Review of Anthropology* **20**, 469–504.

Matteson, E. 1972. Toward Proto Amerindian. In *Comparative studies in Amerindian languages*, E. Matteson (ed.), 21–89. The Hague: Mouton.

McCorriston, J. & F. Hole 1991. The ecology of seasonal stress and the origins of agriculture in the Near East. *American Anthropologist* **93**, 46–69.

Meacham, W. 1984–5a. C14 dating of pottery. *Journal of the Hong Kong Archaeological Society* **11**, 108–11.

— 1984–5b. On the improbability of Austronesian origins in southern China. *Asian Perspectives* **26**, 89–106.

Mellaart, J. 1989. *Çatal Hüyük and Anatolian kilims*. Volume 2 of *The goddess from Anatolia* [4 vols], J. Mellaart, U. Hirsch, B. Balpiner. Milan: Eskenazi.

Miles, D. 1979. The finger knife and Ockham's razor. *American Ethnologist* **6**, 223–43.

Miller N. 1991. The Near East. In *Progress in Old World palaeoethnobotany*, W. van Zeist (ed.), 133–60. Rotterdam: Balkema.

Moore, A. & G. C. Hillman 1992. The Pleistocene to Holocene transition and human economy in Southwest Asia: the impact of the Younger Dryas. *American Antiquity* **57**, 482–94.

Morley, R. J. & J. R. Flenley 1987. Late Cainozoic vegetational and environmental changes in the Malay Archipelago. In *Biogeographical evolution of the Malay Archipelago*, T. C. Whitmore (ed.), 50–9. Oxford: Oxford University Press.

Mountain, M. J. 1991a. Landscape use and environmental management of tropical rainforest by pre-agricultural hunter–gatherers in northern Sahulland. In Bellwood (1991: 54–68).

— 1991b. Bulmer Phase I. In *Man and a half: essays in honour of Ralph Bulmer*, A. Pawley (ed.), 510–20. Memoir 48, The Polynesian Society, Auckland.

Norman, J. & Tsu-lin Mei 1976. The Austroasiatics in ancient south China: some lexical evidence. *Monumenta Serica* **32**, 274–301.

Oka, H-I. 1988. *Origin of cultivated rice*. Amsterdam: Elsevier.

Oka, H. I. & T. T. Chang 1960. Survey of variations in photoperiodic response in wild *Oryza* species. *Botanical Bulletin* **1**, 1–14. Taipei: Institute of Botany, Academia Sinica.

Padoch, C. 1985. Labor efficiency and intensity of land use in rice production. *Human Ecology* **13**, 271–89.

Pawley, A. K. & R. C. Green 1984. The Proto-Oceanic language community. *Journal of Pacific History* **19**, 123–46.

Pawley, A. K. & M. Ross 1993. Austronesian historical linguistics and culture history. *Annual Review of Anthropology* **22**, 425–59.

— 1995. The prehistory of the Oceanic languages: a current view. In Bellwood et al. (1995: 39–74).

Pearsall, D. M. 1992. The origins of plant cultivation in South America. In Cowan & Watson (1992: 173–205).

Pearson, R. & A. Underhill 1987. The Chinese neolithic: recent trends in research. *American Anthropologist* **89**, 807–21.

Peterson, N. 1976. Ethno-archaeology in the Australian Iron Age. In *Problems in economic and social archaeology*, G. de G. Sieveking, I. H. Longworth, K. E. Wilson (eds), 265–75. London: Duckworth.

Pietrusewsky, M. 1992. Taiwan Aboriginals, Asians and Pacific Islanders: a multivariate investigation of skulls. Paper presented at the International Symposium on Austronesian Studies relating to Taiwan, Academia Sinica, Taipei, December 1992.

Possehl, G. 1986. African millets in South Asian prehistory. In *Studies in the archaeology of India and Pakistan*, J. Jacobson (ed.), 237–56. New Delhi: Oxford & IBH.

Pozorski, S. & T. Pozorski 1992. Early civilization in the Casma Valley. *Antiquity* **66**, 845–70.

Renfrew, C. 1987. *Archaeology and language: the puzzle of Indo–European origins*. London: Jonathan Cape.

— 1989. Models of change in language and archaeology. *Transactions of the Philological Society* **87**, 103–55.

— 1992a. Archaeology, genetics and linguistic diversity. *Man* **27**, 445–78.

— 1992b. World languages and human dispersals: a minimalist view. In *Transition to modernity*, J. A. Hall & I. C. Jarvie (eds), 11–68. Cambridge: Cambridge University Press.

Rimantiené, R. 1992. Neolithic hunter–gatherers at Šventoji in Lithuania. *Antiquity* **66**, 367–76.

Rindos, D. 1984. *The origins of agriculture: an evolutionary perspective*. London: Academic Press.

Ross, M. D. 1989. Early Oceanic linguistic prehistory. *Journal of Pacific History* **24**, 135–49.

— 1991. How conservative are sedentary languages? In *Current trends in Pacific linguistics*, B. Blust (ed.), 433–51. Canberra: Research School of Pacific Studies, Australian National University.

Sauer, C. O. 1952. *Agricultural origins and dispersals*. New York: American Geographical Society.

Sharer, R. J. & D. C. Grove (eds) 1989. *Regional perspectives on the Olmec*. Cambridge: Cambridge University Press.

Shih, Xing-bang 1993. Neolithic cultural systems in China. In *Pacific Northeast Asia in prehistory*, C. M. Aikens & Song Nai Rhee (eds), 133–7. Pullman: Washington State University Press.

Sirk, U. 1987. On the geographical location of early Austronesian. In *A world of language*, D. C. Laycock & W. Winter (eds), 623–30. Canberra: Research School of Pacific Studies, Australian National University.

Smith, P. 1972. *The consequences of food production*. Reading, Mass: Addison–Wesley.

Smith, B. D. 1992. *Rivers of change: essays on early agriculture in eastern North America*. Washington: Smithsonian Institution Press.

Spriggs, M. 1989. The dating of the Island Southeast Asian Neolithic: an attempt at chronometric hygiene and linguistic correlation. *Antiquity* **63**, 587–613.

— 1991. What happens to Lapita in Melanesia? In *Poterie Lapita et peuplement: actes du colloque Lapita, Nouméa, Nouvelle Calédonie, janvier 1992*, J. C. Galipaud (ed.), 219–30. Nouméa: ORSTOM.

— 1993. Island Melanesia: the last 10,000 years. In Spriggs et al. (1993: 187–205).

Spriggs, M., D. E. Yen, W. Ambrose, R. Jones, A. Thorne, A. Andrews (eds) 1993. *A community of culture: the people and prehistory of the Pacific*. Occasional Papers in Prehistory 21, Department of Prehistory, Research School of Pacific Studies, Australian National University.

Starosta, S. 1992. A grammatical subgrouping of Formosan languages. Paper presented at the International Symposium on Austronesian Studies relating to Taiwan, Academia Sinica, Taipei, December 1992.

Stuijts, I. M. 1993. *Late Pleistocene and Holocene vegetation of West Java, Indonesia*. Rotterdam: Balkema.

Sun, X. J. & Y. S. Chen 1992. Palynological records of the last 11,000 years in China. *East Asian Tertiary/Quaternary Newsletter* **14**, 92–4.

Swadling, P., N. Araho, B. Ivuyo 1991. Settlements associated with the inland Sepik–Ramu Sea. In Bellwood (1991: 92–112).

Swadling, P. & G. Hope 1992. Environmental change in New Guinea since human settlement. In *The naive lands*, J. Dodson (ed.), 13–42. Melbourne: Longman Cheshire.

Thompson, G. B. 1992. *Archaeobotanical investigations at Khok Phanom Di, central Thailand*. PhD dissertation, Department of Prehistory, Research School of Pacific Studies, Australian National University.

Thurgood, G. 1993. Tai-Kadai and Austronesian: the nature of the historical relationship. Paper presented at Conference on Asia Mainland/Austronesian Connections, University of Hawaii, May 1993.

Tryon, D. 1995. Proto-Austronesian and the major Austronesian subgroups. In Bellwood et al. (1995: 17–38).

Tsang, Cheng-hwa 1992a. *Archaeology of the P'eng-hu Islands*. Taipei: Institute of History and Philology, Academia Sinica.

— 1992b. New archaeological data from both sides of the Taiwan Strait. Paper presented at the International Symposium on Austronesian Studies relating to Taiwan, Academia Sinica, Taipei, December 1992.

Unger-Hamilton, R. 1989. The Epi-Palaeolithic southern Levant and the origins of cultivation. *Current Anthropology* **30**, 88–103.

Vansina, J. 1984. Western Bantu expansion. *Journal of African History* **25**, 129–45.

van Zeist, W. 1988. Some aspects of early neolithic plant husbandry in the Near East. *Anatolica* **15**,

49–67.

Walker, D. 1986. Late Pleistocene–early Holocene vegetational and climatic changes in Yunnan Province, Southwest China. *Journal of Biogeography* **13**, 477–86.

Weber, S. A. 1991. *Plants and Harappan subsistence*. New Delhi: Oxford & IBH.

Welsch, R. L., J. Terrell, J. A. Nadolski 1992. Language and culture on the north coast of New Guinea. *American Anthropologist* **94**, 568–600.

Whyte, R. O. 1983. The evolution of the Chinese environment. In Keightley (1983: 1–20).

Wilke, P. J., R. Bettinger, T. F. King, J. F. O'Connell 1972. Harvest selection and domestication in seed plants. *Antiquity* **46**, 203–9.

Wolff, J. 1992. The position of the Austronesian languages of Taiwan within the Austronesian group. Paper presented at the International Symposium on Austronesian Studies relating to Taiwan, Academia Sinica, Taipei, December 1992.

Wright, H. E. 1993. Environmental determinism in Near Eastern prehistory. *Current Anthropology* **34**, 458–69.

Yan, Wenming 1991. China's earliest rice agriculture remains. *Bulletin of the Indo–Pacific Prehistory Association* **10**, 118–26.

— 1993. Origins of agriculture and animal husbandry in China. In *Pacific Northeast Asia in prehistory*, C. M. Aikens & Song Nai Rhee (eds), 113–23. Pullman: Washington State University Press.

Yen, D. E. 1977. Hoabinhian horticulture? The evidence and the questions from northwest Thailand. In *Sunda and Sahul: prehistoric studies in Southeast Asia, Melanesia and Australia*, J. Allen, J. Golson, R. Jones (eds), 567–99. London: Academic Press.

— 1980. The Southeast Asian foundations of Oceanic agriculture: a reassessment. *Journal de la Société des Océanistes* **66–7**, 140–6.

— 1990. Environment, agriculture and the colonisation of the Pacific. In *Pacific production systems: approaches to economic prehistory*, D. E. Yen & J. M. J. Mummery (eds), 258–77. Occasional Papers in Prehistory 18, Department of Prehistory, Research School of Pacific Studies, Australian National University.

— 1993. Pacific subsistence systems and aspects of cultural evolution. In Spriggs et al. (1993: 88–96).

Zarins, P. 1989. Jebel Bishri and the Amorite homeland: the PPNB phase. In *To the Euphrates and beyond*, O. M. C. Haex (ed.), 29–52. Rotterdam: Balkema.

Zarins, J. 1990. Early pastoral nomadism and the settlement of Lower Mesopotamia. *Bulletin of the American Society for Oriental Research* **280**, 31–65.

Zhao, S-Q. & W-T. Wu 1988. Early Neolithic Hemudu culture. *Asian Perspectives* **27**, 29–34. Zhou, Li-ping 1991. Report on the 13th INQUA Congress. *East Asian Tertiary/Quaternary Newsletter* **13**, 2–6.

Zide, A. & N. Zide 1976. Proto-Munda cultural vocabulary: evidence for early agriculture. In *Austroasiatic studies* (vol. II), P. N. Jenner, L. C. Thompson, S. Starosta (eds), 1295–334. Honolulu: University of Hawaii Press.

Zohary, D. 1989. Domestication of the Southwest Asian Neolithic crop assemblage of cereals, pulses, and flax: the evidence form the living plants. In Harris & Hillman (1989: 358–73).

Zorc, R. D. 1994. Austronesian culture history through reconstructed vocabulary. In *Austronesian terminologies: continuity and change*, A. K. Pawley & M. Ross (eds), 541–94. Canberra: Australian National University.

CHAPTER TWENTY-SIX

People–plant interactions in the New Guinea highlands: agricultural hearthland or horticultural backwater?

Tim Bayliss-Smith

Research into the prehistory of the New Guinea highlands[1] began in 1959, less than 30 years after highlands prehistory had come to an end in the 1930s. When Susan Bulmer carried out surveys of archaeological sites in 1959–60, existing models of world prehistory relegated New Guinea to the status of a neolithic backwater. For example, the region received no mention from Gordon Childe in his book *Man makes himself* (1936), and in Carl Sauer's survey of *Agricultural origins and dispersals* (1952) New Guinea was seen as a passive and late recipient of domesticated plants and animals that diffused to it from a Southeast Asian hearthland.

The excavations of Bulmer and others in Papua New Guinea in the 1960s were accompanied by productive work in many related fields, including ethnoarchaeology, palynology and geomorphology, so that by the mid-1970s it became possible for general models of New Guinea's culture history to be constructed (Fig. 26.1). In 1975 Susan Bulmer herself published the first comprehensive review of the New Guinea evidence. She concluded that the antiquity of agriculture was not in doubt: what she termed "intensive agriculture" seemed to be well established by about 5,000 years ago, and she felt that "it must be only a matter of time before earlier direct evidence of food plants is discovered". However, it was also clear that it was not possible from the evidence available to assess the relative importance of hunting and gathering compared to domestic animals and agriculture. Moreover, the relationships in prehistory between economic patterns in Southeast Asia and Indonesia and those in New Guinea were "by no means clear" (Bulmer 1975: 67–8).

Despite another two decades of research effort in New Guinea, all of the areas of doubt that Bulmer highlighted still remain. When did agriculture begin? How significant was it, compared to hunting and foraging? How much of what has been interpreted as agriculture is indigenous, and how much the result of interaction with the outside world? And at what point is it justifiable to describe New Guinea cultivation as constituting "intensive agriculture"? The evidence that is claimed to demonstrate early agriculture in the New Guinea highlands remains, to a frustrating degree, indirect. We now know a great deal more than we did in 1975 about regional changes in forest cover. We have estimates of soil erosion rates, and maps showing traces of swamp drainage. There is archaeological evidence for the prehistoric stone axes that in modern times were associated with swidden cultivation, and for wooden spades and digging sticks that could have been used for ditching and soil tillage. But to what extent is this evidence for fully agricultural societies?

Although most scholars have regarded the recent research findings as strengthening the case for early agriculture, there is also a growing need for reassessment, for three main reasons:

- From palynological studies in Australia we have accumulating evidence for a substantial impact by Aboriginal hunter–gatherers upon tropical and montane rainforests (Kershaw 1986, Kershaw et al. 1991, Hopkins et al. 1993). Should we interpret the early evidence for deforestation in the highlands in New Guinea as unambiguous evidence for agricultural clearance?
- Some of the archaeological evidence cited as demonstrating the antiquity of pig husbandry and hence of agriculture itself must now be challenged. Following a programme of radiocarbon accelerator dates on pig teeth, using samples collected from apparently early stratigraphic contexts in the highlands, the dates for pig all turn out to be recent, that is, within the past 500 years (Hedges et al. 1995: 428).
- There is now increasing scepticism about a rapid and early transition to agriculture in the Papuan lowlands, including the Torres Strait Islands (Harris 1995), and in Island Melanesia (Spriggs 1993 and in Ch. 27 in this volume). Twenty years ago implicit notions of a "revolutionary" arrival of the Neolithic still lingered, but today we expect there to be many intermediate stages involving the production of wild plant foods and their cultivation, before domestication and agriculture become fully established (Rindos 1980, Harris 1989).

It is therefore time to look again at claims that have been made about New Guinea's agricultural prehistory. Exactly what form of plant–people interaction is being envisaged? And how far can these claims be substantiated from all the evidence now available? In this chapter I first briefly consider five versions of highlands prehistory that were proposed in the years 1975–86. Following Daryl Feil (1987) and Les Groube (1989), I then explore the possibility that each ecological zone within the highlands needs to be considered separately, as a means to reconcile the contradictions that are implied by the earlier models. Finally, I return to the global model of plant exploitation proposed by David Harris (1989). The model is based on intensification from foraging to agriculture via intermediate stages, with "energy thresholds" that need to be overcome in between each stage. Can such thresholds be identified for the highlands, and if so were these thresholds overcome as a result of technologies developed within New Guinea, or because of technologies introduced from the outside? Each region in the highlands may well have its own unique agricultural prehistory, if in some regions the available technologies were able to overcome local ecological constraints, and so push intensification beyond an energy threshold, whereas elsewhere, in more constrained regions, people were obliged to maintain a more stable relationship with their plant and animal resources.

Use of plants in the New Guinea Highlands

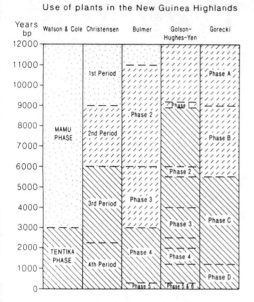

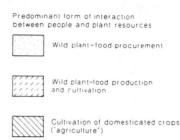

Figure 26.1   Five models of the agricultural prehistory of the New Guinea Highlands.

Highlands agricultural prehistory: five models

New Guinea can be divided into agro-ecological zones that approximately correspond to the altitudes shown in Table 26.1. The mountains above 2,700m (zone E)

Table 26.1   Agro-ecological zones in New Guinea.

A. 0–600m	Lowlands zone
B. 600–1,200m	Highlands Fringe or Intermediate zone
C. 1,200–1,800m	Highlands zone
D. 1,800–2,700m	High Altitude zone
E. Above 2,700m	Upper Montane and Alpine zones

are too high for significant agricultural activity, because of the persistently cool and damp conditions that prevail. These altitudes support an upper montane forest and cloud forest above which there is a transition to tropical alpine grassland, little used even today except for occasional visits to hunt and to forage (Smith 1985). The transition between the Fringe (B) and the Highlands zone (C) corresponds approximately to the transition from hill forest to lower montane forest, although the forests are degraded to grassland in areas of heavy human impact, especially in the drier Eastern Highlands. This boundary (at approximately 1,200–1,400m) also marks the normal upper limit of malaria. In Figure 26.2 the extent of zones C, D and E, as defined by the lower limit of the lower montane forest, is shown for Papua New Guinea. Rainfall seasonality subdivides zone C into wet and dry areas. The dry Eastern Highlands are

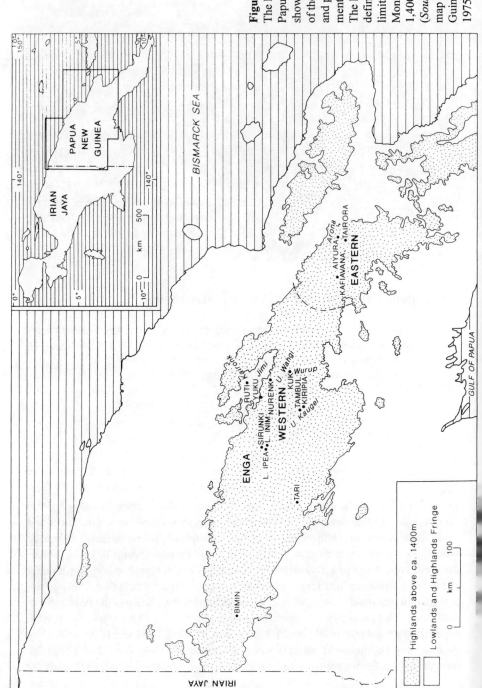

Figure 26.2
The highlands in Papua New Guinea, showing the location of the archaeological and pollen-core sites mentioned in the text. The highland area is defined by the lower limit of the Lower Montane Forest, at 1,400m altitude. (*Source*: Vegetation map of Papua New Guinea (Paijmans 1975)).

also shown in Figure 26.2, together with the location of the main archaeological and pollen-core sites.

Modern agricultural populations are most densely concentrated in the drier and warmer valleys of the Highlands zone (C) at 1,500–1,700m altitude, and most pre-historic sites are also found in the same region. However, the origins of agriculture in the Highlands zone should probably be sought at lower altitudes. Golson (1991a), citing R. M. Bourke's unpublished data on the altitudinal range of 160 food species, points out that the upper altitudinal limit of some of the important lowlands tree crops occurs within the Fringe Highlands zone. Most of the important non-tree crops (including the yam species *Dioscorea esculenta* and *D. alata* and bananas, *Musa* spp.) also originate at lower altitude, and do not thrive above 1,750–1,900m. The only important exception is taro (*Colocasia esculenta*), which matures slowly above 2,000m but can actually be found in cultivation almost as high as the recently introduced sweet potato (*Ipomoea batatas*), around 2,700m. The Fringe zone will therefore be an important area in which to trace the origins and spread of Lowlands agriculture, and the High Altitude zone can provide information about when taro cultivation became widespread in the highlands generally. The discussion in this chapter mainly focuses on the Highlands zone proper (1,200–1,800m), but the term "highlands" is also used more loosely to refer to all three ecological zones in the altitudinal range 600–2,700m.

Bulmer's post-Pleistocene proto-agriculturalists

The study of the archaeology of the wider "highlands" (i.e. the entire area above 600m) began in 1959–60 with the surveys of Susan Bulmer, who, together with Ralph Bulmer, proposed a four-phase model of prehistory that initially lacked a firm chronology from radiocarbon dates (Bulmer & Bulmer 1964). However, by 1974, 34 radiocarbon dates were available covering 11 highlands sites, all from Papua New Guinea (then as now almost no data were available for West New Guinea, Irian Jaya). Based on her synthesis of all the work up to 1974, Bulmer (1975, 1977) felt that the four-phase model could be sustained with a few modifications.

Phase 1 in the Pleistocene was interpreted as a sparse population foraging and hunting in the montane forests and grasslands, between 26,000 and 11,000 years ago. There was little evidence for plant foraging, but Bulmer suggested that the nuts and fruits of *Pandanus* spp. probably provided an important food resource. Around 11000 bp, at a time of climate changes, there were innovations in stone technology, and there is evidence for trade in marine shell, in a period she termed Phase 2 (11000 to 6000 bp). Bulmer thought that the economy would still have depended upon generalized hunting in the montane forests and pandanus collecting, but in addition "it is conceivable that some groups were cultivating plants in forest clearings, for they at least possessed an implement [the lenticular axe/adze] capable of clearing substantial amounts of forest" (Bulmer 1975: 62). There was insufficient evidence to say whether the shift towards cultivation was a highlands development or reflected the advent of agriculture in the lowlands.

By Phase 3 (6000 to 3000 bp) "there can be little doubt that cultivation was widespread in montane New Guinea" (ibid.: 63). The pollen evidence for deforestation in several sites in the Highlands zone was interpreted as the result of a substantial clearing of land for cultivation, using the polished axe-adzes for felling trees, and the hafted tanged implements for tilling, ditching or digging for roots (Bulmer 1977). Exotic finds suggested there was long-distance trade in stone tools and marine shell, which in turn implied that any introduced Southeast Asian cultigens would have been transferred easily from the coast to the highlands. At the Fringe rockshelter site of Yuku (1,280 m altitude) fragments of sugar cane were found in a crevice associated (on the basis of similarity in stone artefacts) with a layer dated from bone collagen to 4570 ± 220 bp (Bulmer 1975: 48–9). If this relates to *Saccharum officinarum*, then it provides the first direct evidence for the cultivation of domesticated plants and it suggests some sort of link to eastern Indonesia (Halmahera/Sulawesi), which is the area identified as the likely hearth for sugar cane domestication (Daniels & Daniels 1993). The apparent presence of early pig in many sites also suggested to Bulmer the presence of "agriculture", because most of the pigs would need to be reared (even today feral pigs are not common above about 1,500 m altitude), and because pigs must have arrived in New Guinea through human agency and as already domesticated animals. However, despite these hints of agricultural activity, all rockshelter sites were still dominated by evidence of hunting and pandanus collecting, and there was almost no information about settlements.

About 3000 bp, with the beginning of Phase 4, a series of changes in both lowland and highland sites were interpreted as side-effects of the expansion into Melanesia of Austronesian-speaking trading people and a new technology of tools and crops. Bulmer linked this to the evidence then becoming available from swamps in the Upper Wahgi valley of systematic drainage for cultivation, with the use of digging sticks dated to 2300 bp. She suggested more sedentary settlement, the abandonment of rockshelters because hunting was no longer feasible in their vicinity, and a transition to full agriculture. These patterns all intensified with the adoption of the sweet potato in Phase 5, beginning 400 years ago.

Watson & Cole: no pre-Austronesian horticulture in the Eastern Highlands?

The surveys and excavations of Virginia Watson & David Cole (1977) were not published in time to be included in Bulmer's (1975, 1977) reviews. Their work related to an area of 3,400 km² in the Auyana–Tairora region in the seasonally dry and deforested Eastern Highlands. It was unusual in its systematic coverage of a quite extensive area, and because of its focus on the location and excavation of settlement sites. There were surface collections from 68 sites, and excavations at a further 8 open settlement sites. Nothing of this kind has been achieved in the highlands before or since and, although the archaeological data were limited in range, the findings deserve careful consideration. For the predominant Nanoway tradition to which most sites belonged, two phases were identified. The first (Mamu Phase) was dated to the Pleistocene at 18000 bp, and the phase continued without obvious break until 3,000 years ago. As well as houses, there was a material culture based on flaked stone tools, with stone mortar and bowl fragments appearing only in the final millennium, after 4000 bp. The assumed economy was wild game hunting and plant foraging. The Tentika Phase that follows (3000 bp to present) has a different assemblage of flaked stone tools, polished axe-adzes, pottery, pigs, circular houses and an assumed economy based on horticulture. The last 400 years of this phase is considered to be a period of "Ipomoean Revolution", because of the dramatic improvement in the productivity of agriculture made possible in the Eastern Highlands with the introduction of the sweet potato (Sorenson & Kenmore 1974, Golson 1982b).

Although the assumption of an abrupt transition from hunting and collecting to horticulture 3,000 years ago can be criticized, the Eastern Highlands evidence is valuable in demonstrating how limited and how late is convincing evidence for plant cultivation. It is an impression not refuted by the rockshelter at Kafiavana (White 1972), about 40 km distant from the sites surveyed by Watson & Cole, but in the same ecological zone. If we discount stray pig finds from early horizons at Kafiavana that are now shown to be recent (Hedges et al. 1995: 428), the evidence almost all relates to wild fauna. Kafiavana seems largely to have been a place to which various animals – mammals hunted in forests and grassland, birds, reptiles and fish – were brought, eaten, and their bones discarded, between about 11000 and 4500 bp. Although Peter White was aware of the claims for early agriculture elsewhere in the highlands, he could find no evidence to support these claims in rockshelter sites like Kafiavana:

> The adoption of horticulture presumably allowed a general increase in population density, with increasing pressure on the forests leading to the formation of grasslands in environmentally less favourable areas. In the Eastern Highlands the faunal evidence suggests that this process had not greatly advanced by about 900 BP [bp].   (White 1972: 148)

The apparent abandonment of Kafiavana around 4500 bp could be taken as an indirect signal of a more sedentary, horticultural settlement pattern, but equally it could reflect some other factor such as the reduction of hunting possibilities in the vicinity. From the evidence of stone and bone artefacts, there is nothing in the rockshelter evidence from the Eastern Highlands to contradict Watson & Cole's (1977) conclusion that horticulture emerged from a predominantly foraging–hunting economy well within the period of Austronesian influence on the coast. Isolation cannot be invoked, since Kafiavana shows evidence of a prestige economy based on trade with the coast. From about 9000 bp onwards, marine shells appear from time to time, presumably playing the same social role, as an exotic item of decoration, as they did at the time of European contact.

Christensen: upslope effects of valley agriculture

A third model is based on the excavations of Ole Christensen (1975) at four rockshelters in the Wurup valley, which is a tributary of the upper Wahgi valley in the Central Highlands of Papua New Guinea, at an altitude of about 1,680 m. Christensen's material was never fully analyzed, because of his untimely death. However, his preliminary analysis deserves to stand as a general model of highlands prehistory not only because it is based on a review of all the archaeological and palynological evidence then available, but also because his interpretation is guided by valuable ethnographic observations of forest management and rockshelter use. Christensen's own archaeological data include more than just faunal and lithic evidence from one site. His sites cover an altitudinal gradient that shows the changing importance of hunting and the changing use of pandanus. His four rockshelters span the altitudinal range 1,770–2,450 m, and so provide very useful clues to the use of forests adjacent to and beyond the upper limits of plant cultivation in the Highlands zone.

These 4 rockshelters were carefully chosen from 76 that were recorded in the Wurup valley, and if we accept the logic of Christensen's ethnographic model, they provide us with a measure of the intensity of horticulture. He suggests that in the early phase of horticultural activity the cultivation of plants would have had very little effect on the natural vegetation, and would be below the level of archaeological and palynological visibility, because it was focused on naturally open areas, some of them seasonally flooded, situated along water courses or near swamps:

> If one proposes a model of little interference with the landscape during an early agricultural period, one might expect more interference with the initiation of more widespread, complex agricultural practices. . . . Around 2400 BP [bp] . . . palynological data and a comparison with the ethnographic model suggest that agricultural activities may have expanded upslope as well as into the swamps, and that Kamapuk [a rockshelter at 2,050 m] and Manim [a rockshelter at 1,770 m] have become a focus for regrowth forest hunting activities and women's garden site activities, and that Etpiti [2,200 m] and Tugeri [2,450 m] have now come to be within the distance that overnighting is considered to be worthwhile. (Christensen 1975: 33–4)

The first period in his tentative scheme is attributed to Pleistocene hunters and gatherers, but their occupation of the Wurup valley was too fleeting for any reliable record to survive even in the low-altitude rockshelter sites. In the second period, between about 9000 and 6000 bp, the types of stone tool that were found, plus the overwhelming predominance of fragments of pandanus drupes, suggested an economy based on the seasonal occupation of the valley for forest foraging, and focused on the production of nuts from managed pandanus groves. Varieties of *Pandanus julianettii* are planted today in the Wurup valley, in forest groves that are cleared and weeded, but D. Donaghue (cited in Golson 1991a) has identified the early Manim fragments as *P. anaresensis*, a type now neither common nor much eaten in the highlands. The apparent evidence from Christensen's sites for domestication of *Pandanus*, which Golson (in Christensen 1975: 24) originally described as "a change over time from thick-walled, allegedly wild, to thin-walled, allegedly cultivated, varieties", is in fact a switch from wild *anaresensis* to *julianettii*, which is the species that was ultimately domesticated. Its earliest date in Manim is after 2500 bp (Golson 1991a).

Only in the third period, starting about 6000 bp, does Christensen record "sweeping changes" in the Manim rockshelter, and these he linked to pollen evidence of forest clearance for horticulture and archaeological traces of cultivation in the Wahgi swamps. The fauna from Kamakuk (2,050 m) was later shown by K. Aplin to indicate a degraded montane forest, when the site first comes into use as a hunting camp at 4300 bp (Golson & Gardner 1990). A continuing upslope agricultural expansion can be detected in the fourth period, starting around 2400 bp, with further pressures on the forests inferred from the growing scarcity of game animals at lower levels and from the first evidence of occupation for hunting of the rockshelters above 2,200m. Thus, Christensen's model is in agreement with Bulmer's in detecting important changes towards agriculture at 6000 bp, but it places more emphasis on the vulnerability to over-hunting of local game resources and on the use of indigenous plants as the basis for agricultural intensification before about 2400 bp, rather than change depending upon the arrival of the presumed domesticates of Southeast Asian origin (yams, taro and pigs).

Golson's Kuk sequence: wetland agriculture 9,000 years ago?

The best known model of highlands agricultural prehistory is based on the archaeological excavations of Jack Golson (1977b), supported by the geomorphology of Philip Hughes (Golson & Hughes 1980, Hughes et al. 1991), the palynology of Jocelyn Powell (1982), and the ethnobotany of Douglas Yen (1982, 1990, 1991). Golson has modified and extended details of his original model in its various subsequent versions, but in essence it remains unaltered:

> The hierarchy of propositions that Golson [1977b] developed in his attempt to correlate the sociopolitical characteristics of upper Wahgi society with the region's agricultural history . . . has not proved uniformly robust. The broader claims . . . concerning the antiquity of various aspects of agricultural technology and the feedback relationship between their agricultural contexts and effects, have been strengthened by subsequent research and analysis . . . The evidence from Arona [Eastern Highlands] and the Baliem valley [Irian Jaya] suggests . . . that the model is applicable to the highlands as a whole. (Golson & Gardner 1990: 411–12)

The model is based on six phases of wetland drainage identified in the Kuk swamp during the period from 9000 bp to the present day. Kuk is at 1,550m in the upper Wahgi valley, and events there are seen by Golson as symptoms of wider events in the agricultural prehistory of the highlands. Wetland cultivation is regarded as representing only the intensive end of a whole spectrum of activities. As well as production from wetland cultivation, resources in the Wahgi valley would also have included hunting and the collection and production of wild plants (especially *Pandanus* spp.), but in Golson's view the most important component of all post-glacial economies was dryland cultivation.

Unfortunately, little can be said about dryland agriculture, because it is almost invisible archaeologically and because it cannot be traced in the local pollen record where there is a hiatus in organic sedimentation until the second half of the Holocene. Discussion of Golson's model is also hindered by an absence of published detail on all of the phases of drainage except Phase 4 (around 2000 until 1200 bp), which has been investigated in two parts of Kuk swamp but without full publication yet of radiocarbon dates (Bayliss-Smith & Golson 1992a,b, Bayliss-Smith 1994).

In earlier publications Golson used the term "agriculture" to describe the entire period from 9000 bp onwards, and he has followed Yen's (1982) argument that "the timing of the agricultural beginnings at Kuk also recommends that we look downhill for their origins" (Golson 1982a: 299). Apart from taro, the crops that are proposed as likely cultigens in the early gardens at Kuk are today all within 600 m of their ceiling of productive growth. The pollen record indicates that climates similar to those of the present day first became established in montane areas around 9500 bp. Because the beginnings of agriculture follow so closely after this date, it is argued that agriculture came into the highlands from lower altitudes as soon as rising temperatures and diminished cloudiness made it ecologically feasible. Kuk Phase 1 (*c.* 9000 bp) therefore becomes "an archaeological record of environmental manipulation that is part of the domestication process, with the adaptation of plants already domesticated in other environments as the stimulus" (Yen 1990: 263).

The difficulty in evaluating this claim is an absence of published detail about the archaeological features themselves; the lack of any means for a firm identification of the plants involved; and severe doubts about the presence of pig in New Guinea at this time, an animal whose supposed presence at Kuk and whose close association with agricultural disturbance initially lent support to the claims for 9,000 year-old agriculture. These claims have themselves been modified in the 20 years since Golson's (1977a) paper was written. A comparison of the changing interpretations of Phase 1 (Table 26.2) shows a number of trends.

The Kuk evidence was initially seen as reflecting the early arrival the Southeast Asian domesticates (*alata* and *esculenta* yams, taro, Eumusa section bananas, pigs), but this interpretation was later abandoned. In the 1980s Kuk came to be seen as a centre for the early cultivation of the indigenous plants, such as *Pandanus* fruit and nut species, Australimusa section bananas, sugar cane and various green vegetables. It must have been these plants that were the most important components of Pleistocene mid-montane strategies for hunting and gathering (Mountain 1991), and it is at Kuk in Phase 1 that we see the first evidence for their deliberate cultivation. More recently the focus has shifted back to taro and native yam species. This followed from the realization that these species are not necessarily Southeast Asian introductions. Instead, taro is now seen as probably a wild plant of the New Guinea lowlands (*Colocasia esculenta* var. *aquatilis*) that was independently domesticated there (Yen 1990, Matthews 1991). There is, however, an alternative view, that although these wild taro plants were at one time gathered in New Guinea, as they were in Australia, they "may have had no role in agriculture" (Matthews & Terauchi 1994: 257).

Interpretations of the grey clay that covers the enigmatic wetland features of 9000 bp have been more consistent (Table 26.2). Since 1977 the clay has been seen as evidence for dryland cultivation. It was deposited in Kuk swamp between 9000 and 6000 bp and is interpreted as the product of accelerated erosion in the catchment of Kuk swamp, following forest clearance (more recently, "forest disturbance") for swidden cultivation. Golson's present view is that this shifting cultivation was for "crops like taro under a forest fallow regime" (Golson in press).

Phases 2 and 3 (?6000 to 5500 bp, and ?4000 to 2500 bp) are further periods during which there were "horticultural" episodes in the wetland, with the organization of drainage remaining relatively simple:

Table 26.2 Interpretations of 9,000 year-old agriculture at Kuk.

Source	WETLAND Evidence cited	Tentative interpretation	DRYLAND Evidence cited	Tentative interpretation	Possible basis for food production
1.	Shallow basins	Pig wallows	Grey clay	Bush clearance for shifting agriculture	SE Asian cultigens (e.g. *alata* and *esculenta* yams, taro, Eumusa bananas), pigs
2.	(a) Shallow basins, gutters, hollows, pits and stakeholes (b) Map of artificial channel 2m wide and 1m deep, close to and contemporary with (a)	Early gardening Wetland drainage	Grey clay	Bush clearance for gardening	Indigenous NG plants (e.g. Australimusa bananas as staple; greens like *Oenanthe javanica*); pigs (?)
3.	(a) Artificial channel (b) Hollows, basins and "stake holes" (c) Pigs	Drainage Early agriculture Domestication	Grey clay	Beginning and continuation of bush clearance for swidden agriculture	Both indigenous NG plants (*Pandanus*, Australimusa bananas, sugar cane (?), *Saccharum edule*, *Setaria palmifolia*, greens, minor yams) and some plants of SE Asian origin
4.	Artificial channel associated with features (basins, pits, stakeholes)	Agricultural activities on land surfaces near the channel	Grey clay	Forest clearance	Unknown: indigenous and/or SE Asian crops and pigs
5.	(a) Single major disposal channel (b) Gardening features	Drainage Simultaneous planting of different crops	Accelerated deposition	Beginning of forest disturbance	Early cultivation of indigenous plants that were the useful parts of a hunting–gathering flora
6.	(a) Channel (b) Basins, pits and stakeholes	Drainage Agricultural activities	Grey clay	Forest clearance for agriculture	Unknown. The NG domesticates are Australimusa, sugar cane, *Setaria palmifolia*, greens *Rungia klossii* and *Abelmoschus manihot*, nut and fruit forms of *Pandanus*
7.	Features associated with channel	Experimental planting surfaces	Grey clay	Continued dryland gardening	Unknown. Could have included bananas and sugar cane, probably yams and possibly taro, but probably not *Pandanus antaresensis*
8.	(a) Channel and associated features	Possible evidence for an early phase of wetland management	(Grey clay)	Sustained disturbance accompanied by fire, for agriculture	Indigenous NG plants, possibly including taro-yam complex
9.	Structurally diversified features to provide for crops of different requirements	Unintensive horticulture	(Grey clay)	Dryland cultivation	Main focus was on dryland cultivation of crops like taro under a forest fallow regime

Sources (in order of writing): 1. Golson (1977a). 2. Golson (1977b). 3. Golson & Hughes (1980). 4. Golson (1981). 5. Yen (1982); Golson (1982a). 6. Golson (1985). 7. Golson (1991a). 8. Golson (1991b); Yen (1991). 9. Golson in press.

. . . [The] structural features [of Phases 1–3] are not linear and uniform but consist in part of small basins and interconnecting runnels which can admit and circulate water, as well as dispose of its excess . . . These earlier systems are thought to represent mixed gardening with the intercropping of different plant species and allowance for their varying soil and moisture requirements (Golson 1990:145)

Phases 4–6 which follow, beginning about 2000 bp, are more straightforward, because they have direct analogues in the relatively intensive monocultures based on taro and sweet potatoes, which are found at the present day. The major break in the dryland sphere comes around 2500 bp with the deposition of soil aggregates in Kuk swamp, interpreted as the beginning of large-scale soil tillage in the grassland soils that by then dominated the landscapes of the upper Wahgi valley.

Golson has recently reiterated his view that the changes signalled in the Kuk sequence are general trends across the New Guinea highlands as a whole (Golson 1989, Golson & Gardner 1990, Golson in press). He cites pollen evidence from the Baliem valley in Irian Jaya that shows forest disturbance before 7000 bp (Haberle et al. 1991), and traces of agricultural activities and forest disturbance at Ruti in the Fringe Highlands (Gillieson et al. 1985), at Arona in the Eastern Highlands (Sullivan et al. 1987), and at Tambul in the High Altitude zone (Golson: pers. comm.). In this model not all highlands environments became equally and simultaneously "agricultural", but there was sufficient integration between all areas to ensure that societies everywhere experienced the same gradual intensification towards agricultural production that the Kuk sequence records.

Gorecki: 9,000 years of sedentarized swamplanders and shifting drylanders

One of the archaeologists working at Kuk swamp in the 1970s was Pawel Gorecki (1979, 1986), and his interpretation of the Kuk sequence deserves separate treatment because it is based on his own first-hand knowledge of the archaeological data from the Wahgi valley, as well as benefiting from his insights from later ethnoarchaeological work in the Fringe Highlands. Gorecki also conducted excavations in a lowland swamp site in the Ruti flats near the confluence of the Lai and Jimi rivers (Gillieson et al. 1985, 1987). There are three ways in which his model differs from Golson's.

First, he disagrees that swamp abandonment at the Kuk site after Golson's Phases 1 and 2 can be taken as a signal of regional processes. Only small areas have been excavated at Kuk and at three other locations in the Waghi valley. Gorecki believes that an uninterrupted (but locally episodic) use of wetlands after 9000 bp is more logical than invoking periods of abandonment. What Kuk shows us are occasional glimpses of the continuing process of domestication of New Guinea cultigens and the evolution of wetland gardening techniques. In his view, dryland agriculture changed much less, and it may have still been based on swidden technology until 400 years ago.

Secondly, Gorecki interprets the changes between 5500 and 4000 bp in social rather than in technological or demographic terms. This period falls within his first full agricultural phase (Phase C), in between Golson's wetland Phases 2 and 3, and within Bulmer's poorly dated Phase 3. It also corresponds to the last millennium of the Mamu Phase in the Eastern Highlands when fragments of stone mortars and bowls begin to appear among hunting debris. At Kuk the field systems switch from Golson's assumed polyculture at the end of his Phase 2 (5500 bp) to a rather more organized system of drainage (but still, to Golson, an assumed crop polyculture) in Phase 3 at 4000 bp. Gorecki disagrees that the new drainage system was polycultural, and he suggests that a new social organization can be inferred:

The [Kuk] evidence from around 4000 BP [bp] is different from anything found before in terms of the organisation of the major channels . . . It appears that the whole gardening activity was now planned, and the organisation and management was now communal rather than individual as during Phases A and B. The overall pattern has a geometric aspect, with major channels regularly spaced and receiving tributaries at right angles . . . The crop . . . could well have been taro, used both as food and as pig fodder. This change probably resulted in the creation of mixed gardens distinct from those where the staple was grown, a segregation still noted today (Gorecki 1986: 163).

More and more sophisticated use of wetlands by these increasingly well organized, sedentized groups provided them with privileged access to wealth. Gorecki agrees with Modjeska (1982) that the wetlands were "hotspots" of productivity and the centres for ritual exchange networks between centre and periphery. Hunting, gathering and, increasingly, dryland swiddens sustained groups at lower population density in the periphery, and these groups also acted as middlemen in the trade networks that drew into the highlands coastal shells, and furs and plumes from the Fringe Highlands.

His third point of disagreement concerns the role of the sweet potato. Golson accounts for the end Kuk Phase 4 (1200 bp) by suggesting that dryland cultivation was boosted at that time by the adoption of agroforestry practices involving a managed bush fallow using the nitrogen-fixing tree *Casuarina*. Gorecki accounts for this change by suggesting that instead 1200 bp saw the first of three waves of sweet potato introduction. The first sweet potato from Polynesia improved the productivity of dryland swiddens in the main valleys and led to a disintensification of wetland land use. The second wave of introduced sweet potato via the East Indies initiated the generally recognized Ipomoean Revolution of 400 bp. Finally, after 1933 the Australian and Dutch colonial presence in the highlands resulted in a third wave of improved varieties, which had transformed yields in all ecological zones by the 1950s.

The regional geography of agricultural origins

Feil's "regional division of labour"

Since Harold Brookfield's (1964) perceptive paper on "The ecology of highland settlement", few archaeologists can have been unaware of the radically different opportunities and constraints within different highlands environments. Brookfield examined the regional incidence of drought, frost and cloud cover and explored their implications for present-day agriculture, and he also pointed to the fear of sickness and death, which limits migration of highlanders to altitudes below 1,200m where epidemics of malaria can be transmitted. He concluded that optimal conditions for settlement based on sweet potato cultivation are quite rare today, although conditions that verge on the marginal are rather widespread. As a result, good land is always in short supply, and access to it provides the key to social organization, exchange relationships and warfare.

An awareness of the ecological limits imposed by altitude was a particular feature of Golson's agricultural history at Kuk, as is shown by the title of his major paper, "No room at the top" (Golson 1977b). As already discussed, there has also been a growing recognition of the scarcity of wetland sites for agricultural intensification such as Kuk, and their increasing value in a dryland landscape progressively degraded by swidden cultivation and the spread of grasslands. Modjeska (1982), Golson (1982b), Bayliss-Smith (1985a) and Gorecki (1986) all recognized that the Kuk findings implied the establishment of centre–periphery relationships. Such places as the upper Waghi wetlands must have been rather special agricultural centres set within a broad periphery of regions that were higher in altitude, lower and more seasonal in rainfall, or which had precipitous or malarial terrain. Nevertheless, Daryl Feil (1987) was the first to translate these insights into an explicitly regional model:

> Prior to the arrival of the sweet potato there were quite distinct forms of the division of labour in the highlands . . . In the Eastern Highlands a mixed economy was practised: hunting and collecting with intermittent, supplemental agriculture . . . There were few pigs and populations were highly dispersed, small, non-sedentary and unstable residentially, and the level of their interaction was infrequent and unregularised . . . In the Western Highlands, at Kuk for instance, the situation was vastly different . . . Men had long abandoned hunting (or had been forced to do so by diminishing forests) . . . We find a dominant, purely agricultural economy linked to the domesticated pig. (Feil 1987: 35)

Details of this model may need to be challenged: the antiquity of the pig, for example, and the chronology of the sweet potato's arrival are still uncertain. The pollen record in the Eastern Highlands and its relationship to agriculture needs to be clarified. The position of other environments that might be close analogues to the Western Highlands, such as the Tari Basin in Papua New Guinea and the Baliem Valley in Irian Jaya, also need to be considered. Nevertheless, Feil's insistence on different pre- sweet potato societies in east and west, because of insoluble agricultural problems of seasonal drought or occasional frost away from the agricultural centres such as the Wahgi, is useful because it accounts successfully for the apparent contradictions in existing models (Fig. 26.1). Alongside Groube's (1989) model for lowland agricultural origins through the process of rainforest management, Feil's highlands model can provide a new and more regionally focused research agenda for future investigations.

No room at the top revisited

The High Altitude zone above 1,800 m is a key area for resolving some of the many contradictions in New Guinea prehistory. The vegetation history of this region is relatively well known, helped by the many suitable sites in mires and lakes for the analysis of pollen and sediments. There are many fewer archaeological sites, but this may reflect the limited use of this zone until the new agricultural possibilities that were provided by new domesticated species. Settlement and deforestation today extends up to 2,700 m and is based on an intensive monoculture of sweet potatoes assisted by mounding techniques designed to reduce soil waterlogging, concentrate compost and minimize frost damage (Brookfield & Allen 1989). The evidence from pollen diagrams and lake cores shows unmistakably that the scale of forest clearance and soil disturbance we see today began in this zone only some 300 years ago. Moreover, all pollen diagrams above 1,900 m show no rise in *Casuarina* pollen until the past 260–300 years, whereas in sites below this altitude a rise in pollen between 1200–1400 bp can often be detected as well as the recent peak (Haberle 1994). The High Altitude evidence thus supports very strongly the "classic" model of an Ipomoean Revolution following the recent introduction of the sweet potato (Bayliss-Smith 1985a, 1988).

Circa AD 1650 marked the beginnings of a large-scale agricultural colonization of the High Altitude zone, but there is evidence for a more limited use of some areas much earlier in prehistory. Just as the recent date for intensive impacts provides conclusive evidence for the arrival of modern sweet potatoes in the highlands, so we can gauge the progress of domestication or adoption of previous crops from the timing of their impacts in the High Altitude zone. The upper limits for the cultivation of crops today (Table 26.3) show that, whereas a range of green vegetables and pandanus nut

Table 26.3   Normal upper altitudinal limit of cultigens in New Guinea Highlands.

Crop	Central Highlands, PNG normal limits	Enga Province, PNG usual maximum (extreme)
Starch staples		
Sago	1,200 m	1,150 (1,290 m)
Breadfruit	1,200 m	1,150 m (1,240 m)
Yams		
Dioscorea esculenta	1,500 m	n.s.
D. pentaphylia	1,550 m	n.s.
D. bulbifera	1,750 m	n.s.
D. alata	1,900 m	1,900 m (1,920 m)
Bananas (Eumusa section)	2,100 m	2,200 m (2,350 m)
Pueraria lobata	2,300 m	n.s.
Taro	2,700 m	2,400 m (2,620 m)
Sweet potato	2,750 m	2,700 m (2,850 m)
Green vegetables		
Sugar cane	2,600 m	2,600 m (2,730 m)
Oenanthe javanica	2,700 m	2,700 m (3,000 m)
Setaria palmifolia	2,700 m	2,700 m
Rungia klossii	2,750 m	1,950 m (2,510 m)
Rorippa (*Nasturtium*) *schlecteri*	n.s.	2,700 m (2,850 m)
Pandanus nuts		
Marita (*Pandanus conoideus*)	n.s.	1,750 m (1,780 m)
Karuka (*P. julianettii*)	2,550 m	2,500 m (2,730 m)
P. antaresensis	2,350 m	n.s.
P. brosimos/P. iwem	3,100 m	n.s.

n.s.: altitude not stated

Sources: Central Highlands: Bayliss-Smith (1985a: 286), based on fieldwork observations in Upper Kaugel valley and data of R. M. Bourke (pers. comm. 1980); *P. antaresensis* and *P. brosimos/P. iwen*: R. M. Bourke, cited by Golson (1991a: 88); Enga Province: Bourke & Lea (1982: 89–90).

species will grow above 2,000 m, the only starch staple of any significance at all is taro.

From an extensive review of the performance of crops in this zone, Bayliss-Smith (1985a) concluded that no permanent agricultural settlement would have been feasible in valleys or on plateaux above 2,000 m unless and until taro was available as an agricultural staple. It could have been grown as a swidden crop with a forest fallow, as occurs today in the Bimin valley near Telefomin (Bayliss-Smith 1985b). Alternatively, taro could have been produced in a more intensive way using the Kuk technology of wetland drainage. However, experimental data from taro grown in drained wetlands at Kiripia in the upper Kaugel valley (2,200 m) showed that such a technology generates poor yields despite high labour inputs. Wetland drainage would not have been viable as a subsistence strategy, and so must have been reserved for the small-scale cultivation of high-status but ecologically marginal crops such as vegetables, sugar cane and bananas. The main subsistence base would have been provided by taro swiddening, pandanus collecting and hunting. This economy could have supported small communities of sedentary settlers maintaining exchange relationships with people at lower altitudes, or it could have been an activity of seasonal migrants primarily concerned with hunting and the pandanus nut harvest (ibid.).

All this ethnobotanical and experimental information provides a basis for the interpretation of the archaeological, sedimentological and pollen evidence from areas in the High Altitude zone. It is important to include here the negative evidence of non-impact on soils and vegetation, as well as the fairly sparse data that does suggest some sort of agricultural presence. A summary of the data and their sources is shown in Figure 26.3.

Small-scale anthropogenic disturbance to the montane forest can be inferred from an increase in secondary taxa in pollen diagrams and from an increased influx of sediment and carbonized particles into lakes and mires. These symptoms of probable agriculture are neither simultaneous nor universal in the High Altitude zone. Lake Inim (2,550 m), for example, was undisturbed until 1600 bp, whereas at Nurenk, in an area at 1,950 m which today is being overtaken by the expanding frontier of sweet potato cultivation, there is no evidence of forest disturbance until the past 300 years. Neither of the high rockshelters in the Wurup valley, Tugeri (2,450 m) and Etpiti (2,200 m), shows any sign of use by hunting parties, let alone nearby cultivation, until after 2,500 years ago. However, Sirunki Swamp and Lake Ipea at 2,400–2,500 m show minor disturbance followed by partial regeneration between about 4300 bp and 3000 bp, although no forest clearance that was irreversible or sustained until the past 300 years. A wooden spade from Tambul (2,280 m) in the upper Kaugel valley is identical to implements used at Kuk for digging agricultural ditches, and has been dated to 3930 ±80 bp (Golson: pers. comm.). This spade has been taken as direct evidence for High Altitude zone cultivation, and it has a parallel in the artefact assemblage in Kamapuk rockshelter (2,050 m) at around the same time, which Christensen (1975) interpreted as showing agricultural activities in the vicinity. These data would suggest the possibility of a taro-based swidden economy becoming established in some localities at altitudes above 2,000 m at about the time of Golson's Phase 3 at Kuk. This is the same time as Gorecki's Phase C of communal and well organized agriculture centred, he suggests, around an integrated wetland taro monoculture/dryland swidden system.

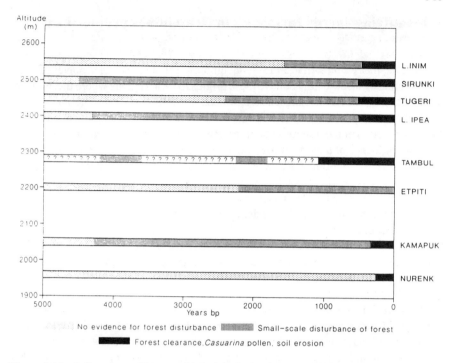

Figure 26.3   Inferred use of forests at high-altitude sites between 1,900 m and 2,600 m altitude. (*Sources:* Lake Inim, Lake Ipea: Walker & Flenley 1979, Oldfield et al. 1985; Sirunki swamp: Flenley 1988; Tambul: Golson pers. comm., Bayliss-Smith 1985a; Tugeri, Etpiti and Kamapuk (Wurup valley): Christensen 1975; Nurenk: Hope et al. 1988).

The existence of this inferred small-scale cultivation at high altitude (in particular the Tambul spade) is the strongest evidence yet available that domesticated taro did not exist in the highlands in anything like its present form until after 4500 bp. If taro was in cultivation at Kuk 9,000 years ago, as Golson has at times suggested, then it is very hard to explain why it was not being cultivated in otherwise suitable high-altitude sites until 5,000 years later. Indeed, if the early post-glacial millennia were slightly warmer than the subsequent period, then the absence of a taro-based agricultural colonization of these altitudes (where pandanus nuts are seasonal and other resources are notably sparse) is even harder to explain. The conclusion seems inescapable that the New Guinea wild taro (*Colocasia esculenta* var. *aquatilis*) described by Matthews (1991) was either not domesticated, or it was not cultivated until after 5000 bp, or it was a very inferior cultigen in the High Altitude zone. This zone remained an impossible area for agricultural settlement until Southeast Asian taro was introduced, and it remained difficult right up to the era of the modern sweet potato.

Identifying energy thresholds in New Guinea people–plant interactions

It is clear that we remain in almost total ignorance about the origins of New Guinea agriculture, because we now believe these origins to lie in regions where the evidence is unexplored and in the Pleistocene era, which is too remote for ethnographic analogy to be reliable. Equally, much uncertainty remains about the subsequent evolution of agriculture. Neither the ignorance nor the uncertainty will be resolved simply by more information being obtained from a wider range of sites, unless better ways can be devised to generate information about the plant species that were being managed or cultivated, and about the true status of the pig. However, it is now possible to produce a descriptive model that gives a regional picture of changing subsistence over the past 9,000 years (Fig. 26.4), but the model is highly speculative and it provides little in the way of explanation.

We can be fairly sure that the past 9,000 years have seen a shift in the New Guinea highlands from a primary dependence on wild plant foods to a primary dependence on cultivated crops. Following Harris (1989), we might hope to be able to identify "energy thresholds" that mark important steps along this road, marking points of substantial change in the output:input ratio obtainable from systems of plant management. In the New Guinea case it is difficult to be convinced that any very significant changes in energy ratio have resulted from new tools or new techniques. That part of the tool kit which is archaeologically visible – stone tools and ditching for water control – has changed little in 9,000 years (Golson & Steensberg 1985). There is reason to believe, however, that the plants being managed have undergone dramatic changes, both

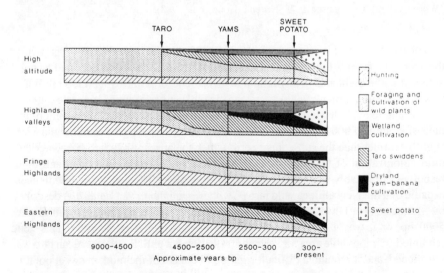

Figure 26.4 A regional model of agricultural prehistory in the New Guinea highlands: the changing importance of different resources, and the predicted impact of Colocasian, Dioscorean and Ipomoean "Revolutions".

because of a gradual, indigenous process of domestication and because of more dramatic jumps in productivity resulting from crop introductions from the outside world.

Of the cultivated crops, we can be sure that the modern South American sweet potato came in 300 years ago, even if earlier, inferior varieties may have arrived from Polynesia somewhat before this date (Hather 1992: 75–6). Of the other staple crops, *alata* and *esculenta* yams and Eumusa section bananas arrived in the Highlands zone, possibly together but possibly at very different times, from Southeast Asia via the lowlands. Taro also came from the lowlands, but its ultimate origin, whether exotic (Southeast Asian) or indigenous, is in doubt. In the absence of these starchy staples, highlands agriculture would have been very depleted in productivity and nutritional balance, and in the Eastern Highlands and at high altitude in particular it is hard to imagine an agricultural economy becoming established at all.

The evidence upon which to base a chronology of innovations in land use in the highlands is ridiculously flimsy, and likely to require revision as soon as hard botanical evidence becomes available. The negative evidence from the High Altitude zone is crucial in implying the absence of domesticated taro before about 4500 bp, and following its arrival a kind of Colocasian Revolution can therefore be hypothesized across the highlands as a whole. Even at high altitude, some sparse agricultural settlement became feasible, based on this new crop. In the main valleys taro made possible high-yielding cultivation from wetland systems, and these became more and more organized during Golson's Phases 3 and 4 at Kuk. If Bulmer's (1975) 4500 bp date for sugar cane in the Fringe Highlands is confirmed, then this crop too might have been implicated in the same energy threshold, being cultivated alongside taro in fertile wetland sites. In dryland sites, but not in the drought-prone Eastern Highlands, taro made possible a large increase in the labour productivity of swidden agriculture, but this expansion of swiddening caused deforestation and a crisis that could be resolved only by innovations in agricultural technology.

A second "energy threshold" seems to be identifiable around 2500 bp. This represents a period after Austronesian languages had arrived on the coast, and after Lapita culture had begun its inexorable expansion, together with its "transported landscape" of agriculture based on the complex of taro–yams–bananas–pig along with Melanesian tree and vegetable crops. As a faint echo of these coastal developments, we can hypothesize in the Highlands zone the development of a new, more intensive form of dryland agriculture using introduced *alata* and *esculenta* yams and Eumusa bananas. These new crops made possible a more productive use of the grasslands that, after two millennia of taro swiddening, had replaced forest over wide areas. These changes in turn led to increases in population density and a greater intensity of exchange networks, something noted in almost all archaeological sites. To grow yams properly requires soil tillage, and this change has been noted in the stratigraphy at Kuk at *c.* 2500 bp with the deposition of soil aggregates derived from a more intensive use of soils in the catchment. Brookfield (1989: 308) has even suggested that "an apparent retrogression of high-altitude interference around 2500 bp may correlate with the development of tillage at lower and middle altitudes to reclaim for cultivation grasslands earlier created by shifting cultivation". The evidence of agricultural activities in the Kaironk valley of the Fringe Highlands (Bulmer 1977), and from the lowland margin of same zone (Gillieson et al. 1985), also points to an external impulse towards intensification. *Casuarina* agroforestry practices beginning at 1200 bp may be a further development of yams–banana based agriculture, or may possibly signal the arrival of an inferior Polynesian sweet potato. However, none of these innovations affected land use in the High Altitude zone, which remained low in its intensity and impact, and continued to be centred on taro swiddens, pandanus and hunting.

The third introduced crop was the sweet potato, which resulted in a revolutionary change in some previously marginal environments: the degraded grasslands, especially in the Eastern Highlands, and the areas at high altitude. As with previous introductions, the opportunity to move through the new energy threshold did not result in highlanders completely abandoning their pre-existing activities, but resulted instead in a shift in emphasis within their systems of production. Despite Colocasian, Dioscorean and Ipomoean Revolutions, in all four highlands environments some trace still remains of all the previous forms of people–plant interaction. Unlike hunting practices, which over the past 10,000 years must have changed considerably because of deforestation, over-exploitation and the extinction of various megafauna (Mountain 1991), with plant cultivation and even with the management of wild plants we can expect much more continuity. Most of the wild plant species, the indigenous cultigens and the earlier introduced crops are still utilized today, even if their nutritional role is much diminished.

It is unlikely that this attempt at an integrated model of highlands agricultural history will long survive the onslaught of new data. It is presented not as an explanation for change, but as a framework specifying the intermediate steps that must have happened in between plant collecting and farming. To construct the regional and chronological framework that specifies fully when and where these changes took place will demand much more work. Once we can agree on these various steps, described in this chapter as *outputs* from the people–plant relationship, then we can begin to consider some more difficult but perhaps more rewarding questions of the necessary *inputs* at each stage, in terms of the organization of work, social and political relationships, exchange, and the transmission of knowledge.

Conclusion: explaining diffusion, environmental constraints and the social landscape

This chapter has concentrated on the tangible symptoms of prehistoric agriculture: ditches and tools, crops, impacts on vegetation and rates of soil erosion. We have seen that for the New Guinea highlands, even to establish the basic facts about these phenomena is not at all a straightforward task. We have found that when the facts that are available are put into regional and chronological frameworks, then to make sense of the patterns we have had to invoke diffusionist explanations. At different times in the past the people of the New Guinea highlands have adopted new cultigens that have spread into the region from outside, and these seem to have provided highlanders with dramatic improvements to agricultural productivity. The impact of these innovations (taro, yams, sweet potatoes) has varied in different environments, implying again an adaptation by highlanders to an external factor, namely the ecological constraints imposed by soils, by altitude and by location.

This chapter has shown that an appreciation of the variable geography of the New Guinea highlands helps us to construct more meaningful facts about the region's agricultural past. Alongside indigenous domestication we see in the highlands evidence of a willingness to innovate, a process stimulated by adoption of the new crops coming in from the outside. These new resources represent a series of "energy thresholds" that mark important steps in an increasing intensity of control over the social landscape. But to recognize that sometimes new crops are adopted, and that seasonality and altitude do impose constraints on crop productivity, is not to explain agricultural history as merely the outcome of diffusion and environmental determinism.

What I am proposing in this chapter is a better framework in which to understand the changing agricultural landscape, rather than a new explanatory model. The analysis has emphasized the importance of the diffusion of cultigens and the role of environmental constraints as controls over the process of long-term, regional change. In themselves, these factors cannot explain change, or lack of change. The rich ethnographic record for this region at the close of its neolithic prehistory shows that the landscapes of the highlands are cultural artefacts, constructed by people who are using hunting, gathering, swiddening and intensive cultivation to pursue social goals. The enhancement of prestige through what Brookfield (1972) termed "social production" is what shapes a large part of "intensive agriculture", and ritualized exchange between individuals provides a better explanation for "trade" than models that stress only the economic geography of resource scarcity (Gosden 1986, Ballard 1994). In some parts of the highlands the subordinate position of women is emphasized, and agriculture is characterized by a strong sexual division of labour (Donaldson 1982). We should be considering these cultural landscapes in terms of a gendered division of social space in which men and women pursue rather different social goals, in ways that are sometimes complementary and sometimes antagonistic.

In other words, the evidence from the recent past supports very strongly the idea that the agricultural landscapes of Melanesia are social products, "spaces carved out by patterns of action, which then help to channel future action" (Gosden 1994: 81). However, the processes by which such landscapes are generated are mutual ones, reflecting the interplay between nature and culture. The environmental spaces that are available for human action do not determine the responses of those who occupy these spaces, and the reverse is also true. Space is not just a raw material to be shaped by the social process, and landscapes are not merely symbolic constructs. Chris Gosden's notion of mutuality in the construction of the social landscape is the way in which we should seek to explain agricultural landscapes of the past.

V. Gordon Childe (1957) came to much the same conclusion after a lifetime spent studying the prehistory of Europe. That continent offered much space for the societies that adopted the new domesticated plants and animals that were spreading in from western Asia, and its environment offered a diversity of habitats for the subsequent divergent development of different Bronze Age cultures. But Childe emphasized that neither diffusion nor environment determined the course of events during "the dawn of European civilisation". Change cannot be explained "by some mystic property of

European blood or soil, nor yet by reference to mere material habitat, but rather in sociological and historical terms" (Childe 1957: 396).

In the New Guinea highlands, too, we need to construct a social history of agricultural origins and dispersals. There is still much painstaking work to be done to map the spread of plants and animals into new environmental niches. This work inevitably requires some emphasis on diffusion and environmental diversity, and this carries with it the danger that we see highlanders as being involved in no more than an iterative, but essentially passive, process of ecological adaptation. This is not at all the model that I wish to propose. Instead – and once the facts are better revealed – I believe we must return again to New Guinea ethnography, hungry for the insights that it can provide. It is ethnography that can show us how highlanders have adapted agriculture to the cultural landscape as they find it, in order to shape that world further through social action.

Acknowledgements

For helpful discussion during the preparation of this chapter, I am much indebted to the participants in the first meeting of the Pacific–Australia Archaeology Group at the Institute of Archaeology, University College London, in March 1994. In particular Chris Gosden, Les Groube and David Harris provided valuable suggestions. Jack Golson was, as always, prompt and generous in his reply to queries and in sending me unpublished material. Michael Young helped at short notice to prepare the map and the diagrams.

Note

1. In this chapter "highlands" denotes the general montane zone of New Guinea (without specified altitudinal limits), whereas initial capital letters are used to denote the five altitudinally defined zones A–E (see text).

References

Ballard, C. 1994. The centre cannot hold. Trade networks and sacred geography in the Papua New Guinea Highlands. *Archaeology in Oceania* **29**, 130–48.

Bayliss-Smith, T. P. 1985a. Pre-Ipomoean agriculture in the New Guinea Highlands above 2000 metres: some experimental data on taro cultivation. In *Prehistoric intensive agriculture in the tropics*, I. S. Farrington (ed.), 285–320. Oxford: British Archaeological Reports, International Series 232 i.

— 1985b. Subsistence agriculture and nutrition in the Bimin Valley, Oksapmin sub-district, Papua New Guinea. *Singapore Journal of Tropical Geography* **6**, 101–15.

— 1988. Prehistoric agriculture in the New Guinea Highlands; problems in defining the altitudinal limits to growth. In *Conceptual issues in environmental archaeology*, J. Bintliff, D. Davidson, E. G. Grant (eds), 153–60. Edinburgh: Edinburgh University Press.

— 1994. Melanesian interaction at the regional scale: spatial relationships in a fluid landscape. In *Migration and transformations: regional perspectives on New Guinea*, A. J. Strathern & G. Stürzenhofecker (eds), 295–311. Pittsburgh: University of Pittsburgh Press.

Bayliss-Smith, T. P. & J. Golson 1992a. A Colocasian Revolution in the New Guinea Highlands? Insights from Phase 4 at Kuk. *Archaeology in Oceania* **17**, 1–21.

— 1992b. Wetland agriculture in New Guinea highlands prehistory. In *The wetland revolution in prehistory*, B. Coles (ed.), 15–27. Exeter: The Prehistoric Society and the Wetland Archaeology Research Project.

Bourke, R. M. & D. A. M. Lea 1982. Subsistence horticulture. In *Enga: foundations for development*, B. Carrad, D. A. M. Lea, K. Talyaga (eds), 76–92. Armidale, NSW: Department of Geography, University of New England.

Brookfield, H. C. 1964. The ecology of highlands settlement: some suggestions. *American Anthropologist* **66**(4: Part 2), 20–38 [Special Publication].

— 1972. Intensification and disintensification in Pacific agriculture: a theoretical approach. *Pacific Viewpoint* **13**, 30–48.

— 1989. Frost and drought through time and space, Part III: what were conditions like when the high valleys were first settled? *Mountain Research and Development* **9**, 306–21.

Brookfield, H. C. & B. Allen 1989. High-altitude occupation and environment. *Mountain Research and Development* **9**, 201–9.

Bulmer, S. 1975. Settlement and economy in prehistoric Papua New Guinea: a review of the archaeological evidence. *Journal de la Société des Océanistes* **31**, 7–75.

— 1977. Between the mountain and the plain: prehistoric settlement and environment in the Kaironk valley. In *The Melanesian environment*, J. H. Winslow (ed.), 61–73. Canberra: Australian National University Press.

Bulmer, S. & R. N. H. Bulmer 1964. The prehistory of the Australian New Guinea Highlands. *American Anthropologist* **66**(4: Pt 2), 39–76 [Special Publication].

Childe, V. G. 1936. *Man makes himself*. London: Watts.

— 1957. *The dawn of European civilization*, 6th edn. London: Routledge & Kegan Paul.

Christensen, O. 1975. Hunters and horticulturalists: a preliminary report of the 1972–4 excavations in the Manim valley, Papua New Guinea. *Mankind* **10**, 24–36.

Daniels, J. & C. Daniels 1993. Sugarcane in prehistory. *Archaeology in Oceania* **28**, 1–7.

Donaldson, M. 1982. Contradiction, mediation and hegemony in pre capitalist New Guinea: warfare, production and sexual antagonism in the Eastern Highlands. In *Melanesia: beyond diversity* (vol. 2), J. May & H. Nelson (eds), 435–60. Canberra: Research School of Pacific Studies, Australian National University.

Feil, D. K. 1987. *The evolution of Highland Papua New Guinea societies*. Cambridge: Cambridge University Press.

Flenley, J. R. 1988. Palynological evidence for land use changes in South-East Asia. *Journal of Biogeography* **15**, 185–97.

Gillieson, D., P. Gorecki, G. Hope 1985. Prehistoric agricultural systems in a lowland swamp, Papua New Guinea. *Archaeology in Oceania* **20**, 32–7.

Gillieson, D., P. Gorecki, J. Head, G. Hope 1987. Soil erosion and agricultural history in the Central Highlands of Papua New Guinea. In *International Geomorphology 1986*, Part II, V. Gardiner (ed.), 507–22. Chichester, England: John Wiley.

Golson, J. 1977a. The making of the New Guinea Highlands. In *The Melanesian environment*, J. H. Winslow (ed.), 45–60. Canberra: Australian National University Press.

— 1977b. No room at the top: agricultural intensification in the New Guinea Highlands. In *Sunda and Sahul: prehistoric studies in Southeast Asia, Melanesia and Australia*, J. Allen, J. Golson, R. Jones (eds), 601–38. London: Academic Press.

— 1981. New Guinea agricultural history: a case study. In *A time to plant and a time to uproot: a history of agriculture in Papua New Guinea*, D. Denoon & C. Snowden (eds), 484–91. Port Moresby: Institute of Papua New Guinea Studies.

— 1982a. Kuk and the history of agriculture in the New Guinea Highlands. In *Melanesia: beyond diversity* (vol. 2), R. J. May & H. Nelson (eds), 297–307. Canberra: Research School of Pacific Studies, Australian National University.

— 1982b. The Ipomoean Revolution revisited: society and the sweet potato in the upper Wahgi valley. In *Inequality in New Guinea Highlands societies*, A. Strathern (ed.), 109–36. Cambridge: Cambridge University Press.

— 1985. Agricultural origins in Southeast Asia: a view from the East. In *Recent advances in Indo–Pacific prehistory*, V. N. Misra & P. Bellwood (eds), 307–14. New Delhi, Bombay and Calcutta: Oxford and IBH.

— 1989. The origins and development of New Guinea agriculture. In *Foraging and farming: the evolution of plant exploitation*, D. R. Harris & G. C. Hillman (eds), 678–87. London: Unwin Hyman.

— 1990. Kuk and the development of agriculture in New Guinea: retrospection and introspection. In *Pacific production systems: approaches to economic prehistory*, D. E. Yen & J. M.J. Mummery (eds), 139–47. Occasional Papers in Prehistory 18, Department of Prehistory, Research School of Pacific Studies, Australian National University, Canberra.

— 1991a. The New Guinea Highlands on the eve of agriculture. In *Indo–Pacific prehistory 1990* (vol. 2), P. Bellwood (ed.), 82–91. Canberra and Jakarta: IPPA and Asosiasi Prehistorisi Indonesia. *Bulletin of the Indo–Pacific Prehistory Association* 11.

— 1991b. Bulmer Phase II: early agriculture in the New Guinea Highlands. In *Man and a half: essays in Pacific anthropology and ethnobiology in honour of Ralph Bulmer*, A. Pawley (ed.), 484–91. Polynesian Society Memoir 48, The Polynesian Society, Auckland.

— in press. From horticulture to agriculture in the New Guinea Highlands: a case study of people and their environments. In *Historical ecology of the Pacific Islands: prehistoric environmental and landscape change*, P. V. Kirch & T. L. Hunt (eds). New Haven, Connecticut: Yale University Press.

Golson, J. & D. S. Gardner 1990. Agriculture and sociopolitical organisation in New Guinea Highlands prehistory. *Annual Review of Anthropology* 19, 395–417.

Golson, J. & P. J. Hughes 1980. The appearance of plant and animal domestication in New Guinea. *Journal de la Société des Océanistes* 36, 294–303.

Golson, J. & A. Steensberg 1985. The tools of agricultural intensification in the New Guinea Highlands. In *Prehistoric intensive agriculture in the tropics*, I. S. Farrington (ed.), 347–84. Oxford: British Archaeological Reports, International Series 232 i.

Gorecki, P. P. 1979. Population growth and abandonment of swamplands: a New Guinea Highlands example. *Journal de la Société des Océanistes* 35, 97–107.

— 1986. Human occupation and agricultural development in the Papua New Guinea Highlands. *Mountain Research and Development* 6, 159–66.

Gosden, C. 1986. The interpretation of Mailu prehistory: the tyranny of distance. *Archaeology in Oceania* 21, 180–6.

— 1994. *Social being and time*. Oxford: Blackwell.

Groube, L. M. 1989. The taming of the rain forests: a model for Late Pleistocene forest exploitation in New Guinea. In *Foraging and farming: the evolution of plant exploitation*, D. R. Harris & G. C. Hillman (eds), 292–304. London: Unwin Hyman.

Haberle, S. 1994. Anthropogenic indicators in pollen diagrams: problems and prospects for late Quaternary palynology in New Guinea. In *Tropical archaeobotany: applications and new developments*, J. G. Hather (ed.), 172–201. London: Routledge.

Haberle, S. G., G. S. Hope, Y. DeFretes 1991. Environmental change in the Baliem Valley, montane Irian Jaya, Republic of Indonesia. *Journal of Biogeography* 18, 25–40.

Harris, D. R. 1989. An evolutionary continuum of people–plant interaction. In *Foraging and farming: the evolution of plant exploitation*, D. R. Harris & G. C. Hillman (eds), 11–26. London: Unwin Hyman.

— 1995. Early agriculture in New Guinea and the Torres Strait divide. In *Transitions: Pleistocene to Holocene in Australia and Papua New Guinea*, 848–54. *Antiquity* 69 [Special Number].

Hather, J. G. 1992. The archaeobotany of subsistence in the Pacific. *World Archaeology* 24, 70–81.

Hedges, R. E. M., R. A. Housley, C. Bronk Ramsey, G. J. van Klinken 1995. Radiocarbon dates from the Oxford AMS system: *Archaeometry* datelist 20. *Archaeometry* 37, 417–30.

Hope, G. S., D. Gillieson, J. Head 1988. A comparison of sedimentation and environmental change in New Guinea shallow lakes. *Journal of Biogeography* 15, 603–18.

Hopkins, M. S., J. Ash, A. W. Graham, J. Head, R. K. Hewett 1993. Charcoal evidence of the spatial extent of the Eucalyptus woodland expansions and rainforest contractions in North Queensland during the late Pleistocene. *Journal of Biogeography* 20, 357–72.

Hughes, P. J., M. E. Sullivan, D. Yok 1991. Human-induced erosion in a Highlands catchment in Papua New Guinea: the prehistoric and contemporary records. *Zeitschift für Geomorphologie* suppl. band 83, 227–39.

Kershaw, A. P. 1986. Climatic change and aboriginal burning in North East Australia during the last two glacial/interglacial cycles. *Nature* 322, 47–9.

Kershaw, A. P., D. M. D'Costa, J. R. C. McEwen Mason, B. E. Wagstaff 1991. Palynological evidence for Quaternary vegetation and environments of mainland South East Asia. *Quaternary Science*

Reviews 10, 391–404.

Matthews, P. 1991. A possible tropical wildtype taro: *Colocasia esculenta* var. *aquatilis*. In *Indo–Pacific prehistory 1990* (vol. 2), P. Bellwood (ed.), 69–81. Canberra and Jakarta: IPPA and Asosiasi Prehistorisi Indonesia. *Bulletin of the Indo–Pacific Prehistory Association* 11.

Matthews, P. & R. Terauchi 1994. The genetics of agriculture: DNA variation in taro and yam. In *Tropical archaeobotany: applications and new developments*, J. G. Hather (ed.), 251–62. London: Routledge.

Modjeska, C. N. 1982. Production and inequality: perspectives from central New Guinea. In *Inequality in New Guinea highlands societies*, A. Strathern (ed.), 50–108. Cambridge: Cambridge University Press.

Mountain, M-J. 1991. Landscape use and environmental management of tropical rainforest by pre-agricultural hunter–gatherers in northern Sahulland. In *Indo–Pacific prehistory 1990* (vol. 2), P. Bellwood (ed.), 54–68. Canberra and Jakarta: IPPA and Asosiasi Prehistorisi Indonesia. *Bulletin of the Indo–Pacific Prehistory Association* 11.

Oldfield, F., A. T. Worsley, P. G. Appleby 1985. Evidence from lake sediments for recent erosion rates in the highlands of Papua New Guinea. In *Environmental change and tropical geomorphology*, I. Douglas & T. Spencer (eds), 185–96. London: Allen & Unwin.

Paijmans, K. 1975. *Vegetation map of Papua New Guinea*. In *Explanatory notes to the vegetation map of Papua New Guinea*. Land Research Series 35, Commonwealth Scientific and Industrial Research Organization, Melbourne.

Powell, J. M. 1982. Plant resources and palaeobotanical evidence for plant use in the Papua New Guinea Highlands. *Archaeology in Oceania* 17, 28–37.

Rindos, D. 1980. Symbiosis, instability and the origins and spread of agriculture; a new model. *Current Anthropology* 21, 751–72.

Sauer, C. O. 1952. *Agricultural origins and dispersals*. New York: American Geographical Society.

Smith, J. M. B. 1985. Vegetation patterns in response to environmental stress and disturbance in the Papua New Guinea highlands. *Mountain Research and Development* 5, 329–38.

Sorenson, E. R. & P. E. Kenmore 1974. Proto-agricultural movement in the Eastern Highlands of New Guinea. *Current Anthropology* 15, 67–74.

Spriggs, M. J. T. 1993. Island Melanesia: the last 10,000 years. In *A community of culture: the people and prehistory of the Pacific*, M. Spriggs, D. E. Yen, W. Ambrose, R. Jones, A. Thorne, A. Andrews (eds), 187–205. Occasional Papers in Prehistory 21, Department of Prehistory, Research School of Pacific Studies, Australian National University.

Sullivan, M. E., P. J. Hughes, J. Golson 1987. Prehistoric garden terraces in the Eastern Highlands of Papua New Guinea. *Tools and Tillage* 5, 199–213, 260.

Walker, D. & J. Flenley. 1979. Late Quaternary vegetational history of the Enga Province of upland Papua New Guinea. *Philosophical Transactions of the Royal Society of London B* 286, 265–344.

Watson, V. D. & J. D. Cole 1977. *Prehistory of the Eastern Highlands of New Guinea*. Seattle: University of Washington Press.

White, J. P. 1972. *Ol Tumbuna: archaeological excavations in the Eastern Central Highlands*, Papua New Guinea. Terra Australis 2, Department of Prehistory, Research School of Pacific Studies, Australian National University.

Yen, D. E. 1982. The history of cultivated plants. In *Melanesia: beyond diversity* (vol. 1), R. J. May & H. Nelson (eds), 281–96. Canberra: Research School of Pacific Studies, Australian National University.

— 1990. Environment, agriculture and the colonisation of the Pacific. In *Pacific production systems: approaches to economic prehistory*, D. E. Yen & J. M. J. Mummery (eds), 258–77. Occasional Papers in Prehistory 18, Department of Prehistory, Research School of Pacific Studies, Australian National University.

— 1991. Domestication: the lessons from New Guinea. In *Man and a half: essays in Pacific anthropology and ethnobiology in honour of Ralph Bulmer*, A. Pawley (ed.), 558–69. Memoir 48, The Polynesian Society, Auckland.

CHAPTER TWENTY-SEVEN

Early agriculture and what went before in Island Melanesia: continuity or intrusion?

Matthew Spriggs

Island Melanesia consists of the archipelagos to the east and southeast of the island of New Guinea: the Bismarcks (New Britain, New Ireland and Manus), the Solomons, Vanuatu and New Caledonia. I have recently discussed the distinctiveness of Island Melanesia in relation to New Guinea to the west and Fiji–West Polynesia to the east (Spriggs 1993). On present evidence the Bismarcks and the main Solomons chain were occupied by people by about 35000–30000 bp, but the eastern outer islands of the Solomons (the Reef–Santa Cruz group), Vanuatu and New Caledonia do not appear to have been reached before about 3200 BP during the expansion of the Lapita cultural complex. The boundary between the main Solomons and the eastern outer islands is a major biogeographical divide, separating what Green (1991a) has called Near and Remote Oceania. This boundary may have represented an absolute barrier to pre-agricultural settlement (Spriggs1989a).

My purpose in this chapter is to introduce a comparative perspective on early agriculture from Island Melanesia and the wider Pacific. The Pacific evidence of relevance to the Eurasian region can be summarized in three points. All of them are likely to be contentious. First, the process of domestication of plants may have begun very early in Island Melanesia, perhaps by 28000 bp. But, in the larger historical picture of the development of agriculture in the region, this had little significance. Secondly, cultivation of plants began very early there and can be attested before 13000 bp. Again, this didn't matter. Thirdly, when full-scale agriculture appeared at about 3500 BP, it was an intrusive phenomenon that led to a complex "frontier" situation. And it did matter. Nothing in the previous archaeological sequences of the region suggests any inevitable tendency in the direction of agriculture.

Terms of engagement

Before looking at the Island Melanesian evidence we need to consider frameworks for interpreting what we might find. Simple distinctions between hunter–gatherers and agriculturalists have broken down since the early 1980s and a more sophisticated appreciation of terminology is necessary to the discussion that follows. None of the rather abstract schemes of classification of the supposed evolutionary continuum from foraging to agriculture is really adequate to our purpose. The most useful is that of David Harris (1989), whose scheme runs from wild plant-food procurement or foraging, through wild plant-food production with minimal tillage, cultivation with systematic tillage, to agriculture or farming. He sees each of these stages as involving major energy thresholds, but this is not necessary to the model. In fact I will argue that there is only one important threshold in his scheme, that between cultivation and agriculture. Foraging to wild plant-food production is certainly a continuum. The former may include burning of vegetation to open up forest and encourage useful plants, and protective tending or nurturing of plants by weeding around them. This is already beyond the most simplistic definitions of what a hunting and gathering lifestyle involves. Wild plant-food production may involve replacement planting of the tops of wild tubers or vines, transplanting of useful species such as nut trees, reducing competition by selective weeding or clearing, and even simple forms of irrigation and drainage. It is Harris's next two stages that require some reconsideration. He places domestication as the important threshold between cultivation and agriculture. Cultivation includes systematic soil tillage and land clearance for gardens. Agriculture involves cultivation of domesticated crops and the creation of agro-ecosystems.

Harris (1989: 19) sees crop domestication as the key criterion here, but in relation to Pacific cultigens thought to have been derived from wild forms in the area, Yen (1985: 323) has questioned whether they are in fact wholly domesticated today:

> Firstly, in many cases the wild species still exist, taxonomically classifiable with cultivated forms, and economically with identical uses. Secondly, the genetic fixation that ensures, if not agricultural stability, then at least consistency in classification, has not been achieved . . . The application of such criteria in the categorisation of "degrees of domestication", however, may prove an inconsistent and unsatisfactory exercise.

So, for the Pacific at least, it no longer seems relevant whether we can detect that a particular cultivated plant shows morphological evidence of domestication and when that domestication first occurred. It is more important to identify when dependence upon agriculture began, defined here in terms of the creation of agro-ecosystems that limit subsistence choice because of environmental transformation or labour demands. This threshold has greater implications for changes in human behaviour and organization than whether cultivated plants are domesticated or whether indeed some form of cultivation of crops is being carried out.

In the following discussion, I treat cultivation (including within it the possibility of domesticated plants) as not significantly different than wild plant-food production, merely part of a continuum with no clear energy threshold between the two. In this I seek to downplay the importance of morphological domestication as a significant threshold in the continuum of plant-exploitative activities in the Pacific (and of course by extension, elsewhere). Systematic tillage and land clearance on a small scale do not appear sufficiently different from practices already included under wild plant-food production to warrant the threshold status that Harris has given them. So we are left with a foraging baseline, a continuum from wild plant-food production to culti-vation, and then a major threshold between this and agriculture.

This threshold represents the break between what Guddemi (1992) calls a "hunter–horticultural subsistence style" and sedentary agriculture. He argues that this style should not be seen as a transition state between true foraging and agriculture but as a distinct economic and social pattern that shares many features with societies more usually described as foragers or hunter–gatherers rather than with sedentary horticul-turalists.

The situation at initial settlement

The nature of the economic system of the initial colonizers of Island Melanesia, 30,000 or more years ago, has recently become of wider than regional interest because of the hypothesis that it is impossible for foraging or hunting–gathering groups to live in tropical rainforests without neighbouring farming groups with whom they can trade forest products in return for staple foods (Headland 1987, Bailey et al. 1989). This is because such foods, particularly carbohydrates, may be so poor, variable and dis-persed in undisturbed tropical rainforests that they cannot support viable populations of hunters and gatherers. A major problem with the original definition of "undis-turbed" by Bailey et al. is that it is unlikely that such an environment ever existed in Melanesian rainforests (or perhaps anywhere). They excluded rivers, swamps and lakes, as well as proximity to the coast or to any non full-canopy rainforest type of vegetation. This led one commentator to wonder how one can have an undrained rain-forest (Brosius 1991: 134)! Also, as others have noted (Bahuchet et al. 1991: 219; Blumler & Byrne 1991: 24; Stearman 1991: 246–7), ecologists are becoming increas-ingly aware that disturbance is so pervasive in natural environments that most plant species are maladapted to completely undisturbed conditions.

Despite their clearly overstated criteria for a "real" rainforest, Bailey et al. do make the point that tropical rainforests are not the Gardens of Eden they are sometimes por-trayed as. However, their view of possible early inhabitants of these forests presents far too passive a picture. Changes in vegetation attendant on the opening of the canopy through natural tree-fall or along rivers and other natural clearings would have been apparent to early settlers. Cutting, ring-barking or burning of vegetation would extend such habitats where various edible species might be expected to grow.

In the depauperate forests of Island Melanesia, transplanting of useful plants spe-cies from more productive habitats may have been necessary from initial occupation of areas beyond the coastal fringe. Thus, there may never have been true foragers in the Island Melanesian rainforests, a condition of regular exploitation being a form of wild plant-food production from the beginning. Bailey et al. therefore may be right in one sense. Perhaps foragers could not have lived in these forests, but people did not have to wait for the advent of agricultural colonists to open up the canopy through clearance for gardens. Wild plant-food production and cultivation may have been developed early on as a set of strategies to make occupation of the forests possible, starting with initial settlement in Island Melanesia (cf. Groube 1989 for mainland New Guinea). Potential staples would have included the root vegetable taro *(Colocasia esculenta)*, whose natural range may have included the Solomon Islands as well as New Guinea and Southeast Asia. Domesticated forms may have derived from wild types that produced very little starch, and it has been suggested that other properties such as the edibility of shoots and leaves and medicinal uses may have led to initial interest in the plant, with later selection for starch content (Matthews 1991). The analysis of residues on stone flake tools from Kilu cave on Buka in the northern Solomons raised the possibility that this process of domestication was under way by 28000 bp and that starch-rich tubers were already available by that time (Loy et al. 1992). The natural distribution of taro in swamps and along streams could have suggested artificial irrigation to recreate the natural habitat, and ditched beds in swamps could have developed from efforts at extending plantings or reducing competition from other swamp vegetation.

Additional naturally occurring root vegetables that may have suggested themselves for cultivation include other aroids such as species of *Alocasia* and *Cyrtosperma* (cf. Hather in Ch. 28 in this volume). A range of cultivation techniques could have been applied to them: vegetation clearance by fire, tillage of the soil, and selection of non-spiny (*Cyrtosperma*) or less acrid (*Alocasia*) varieties for replanting.

Sago palms (*Metroxylon*) occur as several different species in the archipelagos of Island Melanesia, suggesting a wide natural distribution and local domestication (Yen 1985). Rhoads (1982) documents the range of management practices involved in sago exploitation, from the cutting of natural stands through to the planting and tending of palm suckers by canopy clearance and/or the creation of artificial swamps. Sago can thus be transplanted from its natural habitat of alluvial, freshwater swamps to areas it would not naturally colonize. It may have formed an alternative or complementary staple to taro in lowland parts of the region (cf. Townsend 1990). Indeed, this possibility for a pre-agricultural subsistence base in relation to New Guinea, Borneo and some other islands in Southeast Asia is entertained by Bailey & Headland (1991: 276) in an attempt to reformulate their model in the light of critical comment.

The above plants are given as examples of possible staples that might have been encountered by the first colonists. All would have been familiar to them from their previous homes to the west, as would have been many other forest plants. However, the animals encountered coming out of Asia would not have been familiar, being mainly marsupial instead of placental mammals. Faunal diversity too would have decreased as the colonists moved from Southeast Asia to New Guinea. A further major reduction in mammal species with the move from New Guinea to the Bismarcks may have been a significant limitation to early settlement of the island interiors.

Settling in: 20000 bp to 3500 BP

The major subsistence changes that occurred during this period were the apparently deliberate introduction from New Guinea of wild animal species. Examples are the phalanger (*Phalanger orientalis*) into the New Ireland forests from 20000 bp onwards and the bandicoot (*Echymipera kalubu*) into Manus before 13000 bp. There is also evidence for the transplantation of New Guinea nut trees such as *Canarium* to New Ireland and Buka by the beginning of the Holocene, and much earlier (well before 13000 bp) in Manus. Making a conscious move to recreate the richer environment of the New Guinea forests, or at least to compensate for the poverty of the ones they arrived in, the early island Melanesians overcame the natural limits on productivity of the forest environment and took an active part in shaping it. The addition of the animal component of the transported economy necessitates an adjustment to Harris's (1989) terminology. Instead of wild plant-food production, we should talk of wild-food production.

Although foraging to wild-food production as a sequence demonstrates a continuum rather than a sharp break, it is clear that the system from 20000 bp represents the latter kind of economy. The economy of the first settlers may also have gone beyond simple foraging by necessity, but the evidence is much clearer for this later period. It may be that the economy at least from 20000 bp represents what Harris calls cultivation, what Guddemi (1992) calls hunter–horticulturalism, and perhaps what Zvelebil (1986) calls complex hunting and gathering. I do not see the kind of changes that occur in the Holocene as foreshadowing further change to a fully agricultural life-style. The gulf between cultivation and agriculture seems to me to represent a major transition for which the sequences of change prior to about 3500 BP give no hint.

Other researchers have interpreted the evidence differently, seeing the firm evidence for agriculture after 3500 BP associated with the Lapita culture as representing an almost inevitable unfolding from what came before. This interpretation is based on three main assumptions:

- The evidence for a system of swamp drainage in the New Guinea highlands at 9000 bp which is interpreted as evidence for agriculture; a lowland derivation for this is assumed and therefore it is thought likely that such a system also existed in the Bismarcks (Allen 1993: 145).
- Suggestions from the pollen evidence at the site of Balof 2 on New Ireland of short-term local clearance in the early Holocene (Allen et al. 1989: 558).
- The progressive abandonment in the early to mid-Holocene of all the rockshelters in Island Melanesia for which we have evidence of Pleistocene occupation. The inference is that there was a settlement shift at the time related to a more sedentary, agriculturally based village existence.

The first question is whether the evidence in the New Guinea highlands for drainage is itself firm support for an agricultural existence. Such practices may be part of a wild-food production economy within Harris's schema. Here the scale of the landscape transformation is important and this is by no means clear for either the 9000 bp or the 6000 bp systems at the Kuk Swamp (Golson 1991 and cf. Bayliss-Smith in Ch. 26 in this volume). The assumption of an earlier origin in the lowlands too is based on the natural distribution of the plants presumed to have been grown at Kuk. As there are no plant remains identifiable at the site in this early period, that too begs a few questions. Even if in one area of Melanesia, and one with very distinctive climatic conditions, there was a fully agricultural economy at this early time, there is no evidence that it was widespread in the tropical parts of the region or that it inevitably had to have reached the Bismarcks by 3500 BP. The pollen evidence from Balof 2 in New Ireland, suggestive of short-term local clearance, can certainly be accommodated at least as well within a wild-food production or cultivation model as one of full-scale agriculture.

I have discussed the issue of rockshelter abandonment in some detail elsewhere (Spriggs 1993: 189). A link between this phenomenon and the development of agriculture is unpersuasive in the light of comparable periods of abandonment of these sites at times during the Pleistocene. In addition, if Holocene abandonment is related to the adoption of agriculture, one also has to ask what change led to reoccupation of these same rockshelters at various times between 3,500 and 1,600 years ago? Other rockshelter sites appear to come into use in the period after 6000 bp, but there are no signs from them of the movement towards Lapita agriculture that we seek. It is all more of the same until the Lapita culture, and then the archaeological signatures change dramatically.

If there is no convincing evidence of full-scale agriculture in the early Holocene, is there any evidence for a "Mesolithic Prelude" in Clark's (1980) phrase? The evidence is equivocal, but some degree of economic intensification is likely to have occurred during this period (cf. Spriggs 1993: 189–90). The basic pattern, however, is one of subsistence continuity from 20000 bp through to about 3500 BP. Even with an improved subsistence base the population may have been bumping up against the limits set by malaria (Groube 1993). Without a much more sedentary life-style than in the previous era, the population constraints that appear to be imposed by the disease could not be broken. On Groube's arguments, an agricultural economy seems almost a prerequisite to overcoming the brake to population that malaria may have imposed.

The Lapita culture: continuity or intrusion?

The Lapita culture represents a major change in archaeological visibility in Island Melanesia: large village sites, distinctive pottery, a range of preserved plant materials, and a greater range of other artefact types than hitherto. Its geographical spread over a vast area from the Bismarcks (and very ephemerally on New Guinea) to Tonga and Samoa in West Polynesia represents the first human settlement across the Remote Oceania barrier at the southern end of the main Solomons chain. The rapidity of that spread over a period of only some 500 years is also notable. Argument rages over the degree to which Lapita is an intrusive Southeast Asian neolithic culture or an indigenous development in the Bismarck Archipelago, which then spread rapidly to the east. The details of the argument cannot detain us here; they are summarized in a partisan manner in several of my recent papers (Spriggs 1989b, 1990, 1993, 1996, cf. Bellwood 1984 and in Ch. 25 in this volume, Green 1991b, 1992), and in a no less partisan way on the other side (Allen & White 1989, Gosden 1992, Gosden & Specht 1991, Specht et al. 1991, White et al. 1988).

A key assumption of the indigenist view of Lapita as having originated in the Bismarck Archipelago has to be that there were distinct trends in pre-Lapita times towards the development of the kind of agriculture that was clearly practised by the Lapita communities living in large sedentary villages in the Bismarcks, and which was almost certainly a prerequisite for permanent settlement in Remote Oceania, including Vanuatu and New Caledonia. There seems to be no hint in the pre-Lapita period of the changes that were to occur after 3500 BP. It is true that there had been economic changes since 20000 bp, with a more intensive form of hunter–horticulturalism probably in existence by the end of the period. But it is not at all obvious that this was leading somehow inevitably along an evolutionary path towards Lapita agriculture.

Examination of what agriculture looks like archaeologically on Pacific islands where we have no pre-Lapita occupation can give clues as to what the archaeological traces are that one should expect. First, if we look at the Lapita settlement pattern in Remote Oceania, we see quite large villages and rapid population growth from initial permanent settlement. Eastern Fiji and Tongatapu provide examples (Best 1984, Spennemann 1989). Secondly, we note that domestic animals (pig, dog, chicken) were present. A third signature of early agriculture on these islands is a pioneering pattern of initial settlement followed by serious erosion in the local landscape, abandonment of an area for, sometimes, many hundreds of years, and a later more conservation-orientated re-use with continuing occupation. This appears to reflect large-scale clearance for agriculture leading to significant environmental degradation. The response to this was to move to another area where presumably the process was repeated. In a more fully occupied environment such a land-use pattern was unsustainable, and so conservation practices such as terracing had to be developed to allow continued settlement (Spriggs in pres).

Major impacts on vegetation, and direct evidence of increased rates or erosion, are witnessed in the pollen records of various Pacific islands soon after initial evidence of agricultural groups, either Lapita or Lapita-derived. Within Island Melanesia the pollen record of a coastal swamp on Aneityum at the southern end of Vanuatu shows dramatic changes from forest to more open vegetation around 3000 BP, accompanied by high carbonized-particle counts resulting from burning. Clay sediments, which washed into the swamp at the same time, give direct evidence of the increased erosion rates one would expect to accompany such changes (Hope & Spriggs 1982). This is precisely the timeframe when initial settlement might be expected on Aneityum.

Another common pattern soon after settlement on the islands of Remote Oceania, in Polynesia as well as Island Melanesia, is the rapid extinction of many endemic species of birds and reptiles (Steadman 1989). This is linked to direct predation by humans in some cases, but more clearly to habitat alteration by forest clearance for agriculture, or competition with introduced species such as rats, dogs and chickens. Fossil evidence from New Caledonia and occurrences of bird bones only in earlier settlement sites there suggest that about 40 per cent of bird species became extinct not long after human occupation of the island. In addition, a primitive crocodile, a horned turtle and a large lizard also became extinct (Balouet & Olson 1989). Extinctions are also documented from Erromango in Vanuatu (Spriggs & Wickler 1989) and from Tikopia and Anuta in the eastern Solomons (Steadman et al. 1990).

Moving back across the boundary of Near Oceania, we do not see these kinds of impacts at earlier dates than Lapita, despite a much longer human history. In the main Solomons, the north Guadalcanal pollen sequences begin at about 3800–3500 BP. Burning of vegetation by humans was a feature of the environment from at least this time, but the earliest major impact of human activity on the vegetation through forest clearance occurred only some 2,200 years ago (Haberle 1993). This later impact is seen too in the layers of sediment washed into several of the cave occupation sites, the result of increased erosion rates in local catchments (Roe 1993). The Guadalcanal evidence contrasts interestingly in its timing with that from several sites in the Bismarcks, suggesting that the agricultural frontier reached Guadalcanal several hundred years later. It is also relevant that no Lapita sites have yet been located on the island, despite the presence of archaeological deposits spanning that period. These deposits suggest continuity from previous hunter–horticultural phases and have produced no bones of domestic animals.

The Balof 2 pollen evidence from New Ireland has already been alluded to. It suggests a fundamental subsistence change from about 3,000 years ago when a probable regrowth of secondary forest becomes a significant feature of the pollen record, previously dominated by rainforest species, although with some suggestion of localized and short-term clearance (Allen et al. 1989: 558). A similar pattern is evident on Manus, where a pollen core from Lahakai near the south coast attests to early Holocene burning at the site, but with a major episode of forest clearance beginning around 3000 BP (Southern n.d. & pers. comm.).

Several Lapita sites in New Britain show direct evidence of erosion associated with, or occurring immediately prior to, the first evidence of Lapita occupation around 3400 BP. These are interpreted as evidence for large-scale vegetation clearance for gardens. Three Lapita sites in the Arawe Islands off the south coast of New Britain produced deposits of clays washed in from higher ground. At one of these the clay overlay Lapita pottery, and a sample two-thirds of the way down the deposit gave an age of 2690 BP. Similar clay deposition was noted at the Lapita site of Apugi, near Kandrian to the east of the Arawes, and also at the earliest of the Watom Island Lapita sites, where it overlay the beach deposit at the base of the sequence (Gosden et al. 1989). Such major impacts on the landscape by human groups were unprecedented in the region and suggest not only new patterns of subsistence but also a radically different attitude to the environment and the place of humans in it.

It is known that bird and other animal extinctions occurred in Near Oceania, but they are not yet fully reported. Several species that were present in pre-Lapita times have not been found in any post-Lapita contexts: the endemic rats *Solomys spriggsarum* and *Melomys spechti* and some birds on Buka (Flannery & Wickler 1990), and several bird species including rails at New Ireland sites such as Panakiwuk (Marshall & Allen 1991).

If Lapita does represent in its initial stages the movement into the area of pottery-using agriculturalists from Island Southeast Asia, these groups must initially have been small, gaining numbers over time by natural increase and recruitment from neighbouring groups. Agriculture would have spread out from Lapita centres to non-Lapita groups across a "frontier" by varying processes and at varying rates. The spread of agriculture and the relations between Lapita and non-Lapita populations are important topics in Island Melanesian archaeology, but the deficiencies of our evidence are glaringly obvious. The comparative European material has been of some use in understanding agricultural spread and the nature of relations across agricultural "frontiers" (Spriggs 1993: 194, citing Zvelebil 1986).

In summary, Lapita represents the first convincing evidence for agriculture in the region, as is indicated by:
- macrofossils of a range of domesticated plants (Gosden et al. 1989, Kirch 1989)
- evidence for accelerated erosion and deposition consistent with gardening on hillslopes
- the extension of settlement to areas where a non-agricultural subsistence base would be unlikely or impossible, i.e. Remote Oceania (Polynesia in particular)
- the very size and nature of Lapita settlements as large sedentary villages
- the first appearance of the three animal domesticates found in the Pacific (all of Southeast Asian origin): pig, dog and chicken, and therefore the beginnings of Pacific animal husbandry.[1]

The origins of the Lapita crops

Many Island Southeast Asian neolithic cultures were rice-using and yet rice was not transferred across to New Guinea or Island Melanesia (cf. Bellwood and Glover & Higham in Chs 23 and 25 in this volume). The question then arises of the origins of the Oceanic agricultural complex, based on tubers, spread by the Lapita culture to previously unoccupied parts of the Pacific. Traditionally the crops were seen as of Asian or Southeast Asian origin (Yen 1973) but more recently Yen (1990, 1991, 1992) has challenged this derivation, suggesting many as New Guinea domesticates and pointing to the evidence for early agriculture in the New Guinea highlands as support for an independent centre of plant domestication in Melanesia.

How can it be that so many of the plants cited by Yen as Melanesian domesticates are also suggested on linguistic grounds as being present in the pre-Lapita period in Island Southeast Asia (Pawley & Green 1984: 130)? Several possibilities can be considered. The first is mistaken interpretation of the botanical and/or genetic distributional data. The argument would run that the plants in question were really Southeast Asian domesticates that were later carried to and diversified in Melanesia. Alternatively, it might be argued that they were plants generally distributed in Southeast Asia and Melanesia which were domesticated more than once in different areas. A third possibility is an early domestication in New Guinea and subsequent (but pre-Austronesian) spread westwards into Southeast Asia. The integration of these plants into an intrusive neolithic culture could therefore have occurred in Southeast Asia rather than in Melanesia, or of course it could have occurred more than once in both areas.

Archaeologists who have stressed the local, indigenist model for the development of Lapita seem to have read Yen's treatment of these issues too literally. Both the likely pre-Lapita Southeast Asian occurrence of many of the key putative New Guinea domesticates, and the poorly developed state of research on these crops, undermine simplistic statements about their supposed introduction from local sources into the Lapita sites in the Bismarcks. Further genetic and distributional studies of wild and cultivated varieties will be informative, as will greater application of current techniques of recovery and analysis of tropical archaeological plant remains (Hather 1994). Even assuming that it can ultimately be shown that many of the plants involved were domesticated in New Guinea, the timing and geography of their integration into the cultural complex, which is currently best represented in the Bismarcks as Lapita, is an entirely open question.

Conclusion

The contrast has been drawn here between systems of cultivation or hunter–horticulturalism, which in Island Melanesia go back to the Pleistocene, and agriculture which appears in the guise of an intrusive culture of Southeast Asian origin at about 3500 BP. The archaeological signatures of these two life-styles are quite distinctive and there is no evidence in the region that the earlier forms were developing in any inexorable way towards agriculture. The migration into Island Melanesia of populations with a different subsistence base, and a very different relation with and attitude to the environment, created an entirely new situation for autochthonous groups. Competition for land with migrant groups, assimilation, adoption of all or part of the agricultural package on offer, expansion of groups able or willing to take up an agricultural life-style at the expense of demographically weaker groups, and a variety of other responses can be expected to have been generated by the events. The current state of archaeological research, in many areas still in an exploratory state, has meant that modelling such responses has barely begun. Our knowledge of the agricultural frontiers in the region over space and time is thus non-existent.

There are some comparative lessons, or points for consideration, raised by the Island Melanesian case. Domestication, at least in its early stages, may not be as significant for the origins of agriculture as is often assumed. The starch-residue evidence from Kilu suggests that the process was already underway in Island Melanesia some 28,000 years ago. Movement of plant and animal species between islands was also well underway by the end of the Pleistocene. But none of this led to the development of agriculture in the region. The extent to which the region is agricultural today is itself variable, with hunter–horticultural groups still common well into this century in the interiors of several of the larger islands.

The agricultural system as it exists today is not directly a legacy of the Pleistocene cultivators. In many of its crops, certainly in its domesticated animals (pig, dog, chicken), and also in its attitude to and use of the environment, it is a result of the expansion of Island Southeast Asian agricultural populations into a previously non-agricultural region and subsequent processes of development, assimilation and adjustment. Although there may well have been centres of plant domestication in the wider Melanesian area, I am dubious as to whether there was a centre of agricultural origins either there or anywhere in the adjacent insular parts of Southeast Asia. The ultimate origins of the agricultural system of these areas must be sought, as Bellwood (1985 and in Ch. 25 in this volume) has argued, on the Asian mainland.

The message of this chapter is that neither evidence of domestication nor of cultivation is enough when talking about the origins of agriculture. Subsistence systems incorporating both could well have been widespread (in appropriate environmental contexts) in the late Pleistocene and early Holocene in many parts of the world, and had no necessary trajectory in the direction of agriculture in any particular case. The question of the origins of agriculture requires quite different types of evidence, and those relating to cultivation and domestication are not necessarily of relevance in generating an answer.

Note

1. Current data from AMS radiocarbon dates on pig teeth from New Guinea suggest that earlier claims for pig there at 10000 bp and more confidently at 6000 bp need to be revised (Hedges et al. 1995: 428). It is on present evidence quite possible that the pig was not introduced to New Guinea until the post-Lapita time period. The term for pig is in fact an Austronesian loan word in many New Guinea non-Austronesian languages. That said, perhaps it would not be surprising if pig were a pre-Lapita import from Southeast Asia. We know from islands to west and east of New Guinea that wild animals were being intentionally moved around in the late Pleistocene and early Holocene. However, the contexts in which pig remains occur in some Lapita sites strongly suggest that fully domesticated varieties must have been involved. A two-stage introduction of pigs is possible: wild pigs in the early to mid-Holocene to New Guinea, and domestic varieties at the time of Lapita to New Guinea and Island Melanesia.

References

Allen, J. 1993. Notions of the Pleistocene in Greater Australia. In Spriggs et al. (1993: 139–51).

Allen, J., C. Gosden, J. P. White 1989. Human Pleistocene adaptations in the tropical Island Pacific: recent evidence from New Ireland, a Greater Australian outlier. *Antiquity* 63, 548–61.

Allen, J. & J. P. White 1989. The Lapita homeland: some new data and an interpretation. *Journal of the Polynesian Society* 98, 129–46.

Bahuchet, S., D. McKey, I. de Garine 1991. Wild yams revisited: is independence from agriculture possible for rain forest hunter–gatherers? *Human Ecology* 19, 213–43.

Bailey, R. C. & T. N. Headland 1991. The tropical rain forest: is it a productive environment for human foragers? *Human Ecology* 19, 261–85.

Bailey, R. C., G. Head, M. Jenike, B. Owen, R. Rechtman 1989. Hunting and gathering in tropical rain forests: is it possible? *American Anthropologist* 91, 59–82.

Balouet, J. C. & S. L. Olson 1989. *Fossil birds from Late Quaternary deposits in New Caledonia* [Smithsonian Contributions to Zoology 469]. Washington DC: Smithsonian Institution Press.

Bellwood, P. S. 1984. The great Pacific migration. In *Yearbook of science and the future for 1984*, 80–93. Chicago: Encyclopaedia Britannica.

— 1985. *Prehistory of the Indo–Malaysian archipelago*. Sydney: Academic Press.

— (ed.) 1991. *Indo–Pacific prehistory 1990* (vol. 2). Canberra and Jakarta: IPPA and Asosiasi Prehistorisi Indonesia. *Bulletin of the Indo–Pacific Prehistory Association* 11.

Best, S. 1984. *Lakeba: the prehistory of a Fijian island* [PhD dissertation, Department of Anthropology, University of Auckland]. Ann Arbor: University Microfilms.

Blumler, M. A. & R. Byrne 1991. The ecological genetics of domestication and the origins of agriculture. *Current Anthropology* **32**, 23–35, 44–54.

Brosius, P. 1991. Foraging in tropical rain forests: the case of the Penan of Sarawak. *Human Ecology* **19**, 123–50.

Clark, J. G. D. 1980. *Mesolithic prelude*. Edinburgh: Edinburgh University Press.

Flannery, T. F. & S. Wickler 1990. Quaternary murids (Rodentia: Muridae) from Buka Island, Papua New Guinea, with descriptions of two new species. *Australian Mammalogy* **13**, 127–39.

Golson, J. 1991. Bulmer Phase II: early agriculture in the New Guinea Highlands. In Pawley (1991: 484–91).

Gosden, C. 1992. Production systems and the colonization of the western Pacific. *World Archaeology* **24**, 55–69.

Gosden, C., J. Allen, W. Ambrose, D. Anson, J. Golson, R. Green, P. Kirch, I. Lilley, J. Specht, M. Spriggs 1989. Lapita sites of the Bismarck Archipelago. *Antiquity* **63**, 561–86.

Gosden, C. & J. Specht 1991. Diversity, continuity and change in the Bismarck Archipelago, Papua New Guinea. In Bellwood (1991: 276–80).

Green, R. C. 1991a. Near and Remote Oceania: disestablishing "Melanesia" in culture history. In Pawley (1991: 491–502).

— 1991b. The Lapita Cultural Complex: current evidence and proposed models. In Bellwood (1991: 295–305).

— 1992. Definitions of the Lapita Cultural Complex and its non-ceramic component. In *Poterie Lapita et peuplement: actes du colloque Lapita, Nouméa, Nouvelle Calédonie, janvier 1992*, J. C. Galipaud (ed.), 7–20. Nouméa: ORSTOM.

Groube, L. M. 1989. The taming of the rain forests: a model for Late Pleistocene forest exploitation in New Guinea. In *Foraging and farming: the evolution of plant exploitation*, D. R. Harris & G. C. Hillman (eds), 292–317. London: Unwin Hyman.

— 1993. Contradictions and malaria in Melanesian and Australian prehistory. In Spriggs et al. (1993: 164–86).

Guddemi, P. 1992. When horticulturalists are like hunter–gatherers: the Sawiyano of Papua New Guinea. *Ethnology* **31**, 303–14.

Haberle, S. 1993. Environmental history of the northern plains of Guadalcanal, Solomon Islands. In *Prehistory without pots: prehistoric settlement and economy of North-West Guadalcanal, Solomon Islands*, D. Roe, Appendix 1, 1–25. PhD dissertation, Department of Prehistory, Research School of Pacific Studies, Australian National University.

Harris, D. R. 1989. An evolutionary continuum of people–plant interaction. In *Foraging and farming: the evolution of plant exploitation*, D. R. Harris & G. C. Hillman (eds), 11–26. London: Unwin Hyman.

Hather, J. G. (ed.) 1994. *Tropical archaeobotany: applications and new developments*. London: Routledge.

Headland, T. N. 1987. The wild yam question: how well could independent hunter–gatherers live in a tropical rain forest ecosystem? *Human Ecology* **15**, 463–91.

Hedges, R. E. M., R. A. Housley, C. R. Bronk Ramsey, G. J. van Klinken 1995. Radiocarbon dates from the Oxford AMS system: *Archaeometry* datelist 20. *Archaeometry* **37**, 417–30.

Hope, G. & M. Spriggs 1982. A preliminary pollen sequence from Aneityum Island, southern Vanuatu. *Indo–Pacific Prehistory Association Bulletin* **3**, 88–94.

Kirch, P. V. 1989. Second millennium BC arboriculture in Melanesia: archaeological evidence from the Mussau Islands. *Economic Botany* **43**, 225–40.

Loy, T. H., M. Spriggs, S. Wickler 1992. Direct evidence for human use of plants 28,000 years ago: starch residues on stone artefacts from the northern Solomon Islands. *Antiquity* **66**, 898–912.

Marshall, B. & J. Allen 1991. Excavations at Panakiwuk Cave, New Ireland. In *Report of the Lapita Homeland Project*, J. Allen & C. Gosden (eds), 59–91. Occasional Papers in Prehistory 20, Department of Prehistory, Research School of Pacific Studies, Australian National University.

Matthews, P. 1991. A possible tropical wildtype taro: *Colocasia esculenta* var. *aquatilis*. In Bellwood (1991: 69–81).

Pawley, A. (ed.) 1991. *Man and a half: essays in Pacific anthropology and ethnobiology in honour of Ralph Bulmer*. Memoir 48, The Polynesian Society, Auckland

Pawley, A. & R. C. Green 1984. The Proto-Oceanic language community. *Journal of Pacific History* **19**, 123–46.

Rhoads, J. W. 1982. Sagopalm management in Melanesia: an alternative perspective. *Archaeology in Oceania* **17**, 20–7.

Roe, D. 1993. *Prehistory without pots: prehistoric settlement and economy of North-West Guadalcanal, Solomon Islands.* PhD dissertation, Department of Prehistory, Research School of Pacific Studies, Australian National University.

Southern, W. n.d. *The vegetation of Lahakai Swamp, Manus Island, Papua New Guinea: a preliminary report.* Typescript.

Specht, J., R. Fullagar, R. Torrence 1991. What was the significance of Lapita pottery at Talasea? In Bellwood (1991: 281–94).

Spennemann, D. H. R. 1989. *'Ata ' Tonga mo 'ata 'o Tonga: early and late prehistory of the Tongan Islands.* PhD dissertation, Department of Prehistory, Research School of Pacific Studies, Australian National University.

Spriggs, M. 1989a. The Solomon Islands as bridge and barrier in the settlement of the Pacific. Paper presented at the Circum-Pacific Prehistory Conference, Seattle, August 1989.

— 1989b. The dating of the Island Southeast Asian Neolithic: an attempt at chronometric hygiene and linguistic correlation. *Antiquity* **63**, 587–613.

— 1990. Dating Lapita: another view. In *Lapita design, form and composition: Proceedings of the Lapita Design Workshop, Canberra, Australia, December 1988*, M. Spriggs (ed.), 6–27. Occasional Papers in Prehistory 19, Department of Prehistory, Research School of Pacific Studies, Australian National University.

— 1993. Island Melanesia: the last 10,000 years. In Spriggs et al. (1993: 187–205).

— 1996. What is southeast Asian about Lapita? In *Prehistoric dispersals of mongoloids*, T. Akazawa & E. J. E. Szathmary (eds), 322–46. Oxford: Oxford University Press.

— in press. Landscape catastrophe and landscape enhancement: are either or both true in the Pacific? In *Historical ecology of the Pacific Islands: prehistoric environmental and landscape change*, P. V. Kirch & T. L. Hunt (eds). New Haven, Connecticut: Yale University Press.

Spriggs, M. & S. Wickler 1989. Archaeological research on Erromango: recent data on southern Melanesian prehistory. *Indo–Pacific Prehistory Association Bulletin* **9**, 68–91.

Spriggs, M., D. E. Yen, W. Ambrose, R. Jones, A. Thorne, A. Andrews (eds), 1993. *A community of culture: the people and prehistory of the Pacific*, . Occasional Papers in Prehistory 21, Department of Prehistory, Research School of Pacific Studies, Australian National University.

Steadman, D. W. 1989. Extinction of birds in eastern Polynesia: a review of the record, and comparisons with other Pacific Island groups. *Journal of Archaeological Science* **16**, 177–205.

Steadman, D. W., D. S. Pahlavan, P. V. Kirch 1990. Extinction, biogeography and human exploitation of birds on Tikopia and Anuta, Polynesian outliers in the Solomon Islands. *Occasional Papers of the Bishop Museum* **30**, 118–53.

Stearman, A. M. 1991. Making a living in the tropical forest: Yuqui foragers in the Bolivian Amazon. *Human Ecology* **19**, 245–60.

Townsend, P. K. 1990. On the possibility/impossibility of tropical forest hunting and gathering. *American Anthropologist* **92**, 745–7.

White, J. P., J. Allen, J. Specht 1988. Peopling the Pacific: the Lapita homeland project. *Australian Natural History* **22**, 410–16.

Yen, D. E. 1973. The origins of Oceanic agriculture. *Archaeology and Physical Anthropology in Oceania* **8**, 68–85.

— 1985. Wild plants and domestication in Pacific Islands. In *Recent advances in Indo–Pacific prehistory*, V. N. Misra & P. S. Bellwood (eds), 315–26. Delhi: Oxford University Press and IBH.

— 1990. Environment, agriculture and the colonisation of the Pacific. In *Pacific production systems: approaches to economic prehistory*, D. E. Yen & J. M. J. Mummery (eds), 258–77. Occasional Papers in Prehistory 18, Department of Prehistory, Research School of Pacific Studies, Australian National University.

— 1991. Domestication: the lessons from New Guinea. In Pawley (1991: 558–69).

— 1992. Polynesian cultigens and cultivars: the questions of origin. In *Islands, plants, and Polyne-*

sians: an introduction to Pacific ethnobotany, P. A. Cox & S. A. Banack (eds), 67–95. Portland: Dioscorides Press.

Zvelebil, M. 1986. Mesolithic societies and the transition to farming: problems of time, scale and organisation. In *Hunters in transition: mesolithic societies of temperate Eurasia and their transition to farming*, M. Zvelebil (ed.), 167–88. Cambridge: Cambridge University Press.

CHAPTER TWENTY-EIGHT

The origins of tropical vegeculture: Zingiberaceae, Araceae and Dioscoreaceae in Southeast Asia

Jon G. Hather

Introduction: the seasonal environment

Traditional agriculture in Oceania is a complex amalgamation of arboriculture and vegeculture. The latter – cultivation largely of the corms and tubers of members of the Araceae and Dioscoreaceae plant families, and to a lesser extent the Zingiberaceae – is ethnographically well documented, and although little direct archaeological evidence has so far been recovered (see Hather 1992 for a review), is assumed to be an ancient system of plant-food production and to have originated somewhere to the west of eastern Melanesia. Although relatively few in number, the crops of the Araceae and Dioscoreaceae support considerable geographical and temporal variation in agricultural practice, both in terms of the importance of individual taxa and in methods of cultivation. These crops are often cited as being of great importance in understanding the origins of agriculture in the tropics (Harris 1972, 1981), and many questions about them can be asked of plant assemblages from archaeological sites in Southeast Asia.

The question of the origin of vegeculture as a method of agrarian subsistence has received much attention but relatively little debate. Sauer (1952: 24–5) made an important link between the seasonal environment and vegetative reproduction, although he barely defined the ecological implications. Harris (1969) explored in detail the ecological/environmental aspect of the link between seasonality and the origins of vegeculture. Drawing on the fact that many tuberous plants store starch and, because of this, are able to survive short periods of both lower temperature and rainfall, he made the assumption that the wild ancestors of tuberous crop plants must have lived in climatically seasonal environments. He further inferred that the first attempts at their cultivation must have taken place in such environments. Hawkes (1969: 23) writing at the same time echoed this view, stating that "Tropical root crops must have originated . . . in areas with a well marked wet and dry season, since the plant stores up in its underground organs sufficient food reserves to tide it over the dry period". Much more recently Hole (1992: 374–5) reiterated the idea in discussing the origins of vegeculture, remarking that such plants "need an annual dry interval of more than 2 months for successful propagation".

The topic of this chapter is a re-examination of the link between seasonal environments and the origins of vegeculture, with particular reference to the origins of agriculture in the Indo–Pacific. The nature of tuberous plants and their life-forms is explored and a model suggested in the light of evidence linking the origins of vegeculture of some of the world's most important root and tuber crops with a non-seasonal, continuously warm and humid tropical environment.

The tuberous habit

Corms, rhizomes, roots, and other storage organs – often conveniently, although rather misleadingly, termed "roots and tubers" – are represented in most natural ecosystems around the world by only a limited number of morphological structures. Such structures have been variously classified in terms of many different criteria (Hather 1994). An important dichotomy in many such classifications is made by differentiating between structures derived from stem and from root tissue, a distinction that is important in terms of developmental anatomy, ecology, reproductive potential and life-cycle. The plant life-form central to the theme of this chapter is represented by morphological structures falling under the categories rhizome, corm and tuber. By definition, rhizomes and corms are formed from stem tissues, as is also the case for the particular tubers discussed in this chapter. In terms of their developmental anatomy, ecology, reproductive potential and life-cycle this distinction is fundamental to an understanding of their morphological adaptation to the restrictions of their anatomy in their environment. Two considerations are critical to this theme: vascular potential and bud meristem potential.

Vascular potential

All vascular plants (i.e. all plants with the exception of the Algae and the majority of Bryophytes) transport water, containing dissolved minerals, carbohydrates and sugars, throughout their tissues in specialized cells. These cells and their associated tissues account for all wood and much plant fibre used by people. In herbaceous plants, these conducting tissues are located in what are known as vascular bundles, composed of xylem and phloem. Xylem is a lignified tissue conducting water, and phloem a non-lignified tissue conducting carbohydrates and sugars in solution. Plants that have the potential to become woody contain a third tissue, the infrafascicular cambium, a meristematic tissue that, together with the interfascicular cambium, is responsible for secondary growth: the creation of more vascular tissues linking up the vascular bundles in annular rings of woody growth (Fig. 28.1). In the Angiosperms this occurs only in the class Dicotyledonae. The Angiosperm plant families Araceae, Zingiberaceae and Dioscoreaceae, important in tropical agriculture, are in the class Monocotyledoneae, almost all members of which lack the meristematic tissues of infrafascicular and interfascicular cambium and so lack the potential to become woody.

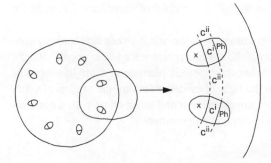

Figure 28.1 Vascular potential in many dicotyledons. x = xylem; ph = phloem; c^i = interfasicular cambium; c^{ii} = infrafasicular cambium.

Secondary, woody growth is the commonest strategy by which plants attain longevity in many environments, including the non-seasonal humid tropics. Longevity is achieved by a continuous supply of buds to produce shoots on which to support ephemeral leaves, and woodiness is of course the dominant life-form in all forests, whether tropical or temperate. It is, however, not the only strategy by which plants may be long-lived: those that cannot undergo secondary growth attain longevity by other methods: the pseudo-woody growth of many monocotyledons, best exemplified by the Arecaceae (the Palm family), and vegetative propagation, exemplified by the Zingiberaceae, Araceae and the Dioscoreaceae. It is this second strategy that is the focus of interest in this chapter.

Bud meristem potential

One of the most outstanding features of vascular plant evolution from the earliest palaeontological evidence to the present is the phenomenon of branching. The ability of a plant to place its photosynthetic organs, usually leaves, in positions that meet its requirements exactly results largely from the division of meristematic cells which give rise to buds that will develop into shoots and later branches. This is achieved with an accuracy that meets a level of mathematical precision rarely found in other organisms (Thompson 1942: 912). Branching may be described in terms of phylotaxy, which characterizes the positions of buds, or in terms of monopodial and sympodial growth which characterizes the potential of buds.

In monopodial growth a high degree of apical dominance is maintained, the bud at the top of the leading shoot growing at the expense of lateral shoots. Where lateral shoots arise, these become dominant over buds along their length (Fig. 28.2a). The degree of apical dominance is hormonally controlled, so that the degree of branching is dependent on a chemical balance within the meristematic tissues. However, it is not uncommon for the leading shoot at germination to maintain dominance throughout the plant's life. Such growth is exhibited by many Gymnosperms.

In sympodial growth, apical dominance of the leading shoot is lost after a period of growth, in temperate zones often after a single growing season, and a lateral bud close to the apical bud assumes dominance. This bud in turn gives way to one of its own lateral buds. The growth between each apical bud and the lateral position from which it arose is called the sympodial unit. Monocotyledons, including the Zingiber-

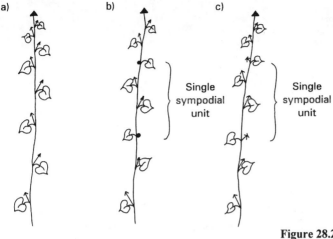

Figure 28.2 Bud meristem potential: (a) monopodial; (b) sympodial determinate; (c) sympodial indeterminate.

aceae, Araceae and Dioscoreaceae, almost universally have sympodial growth of which there are two types:

- determinate, where the apical bud that loses dominance to a lateral bud dies, becomes unspecialized tissue (parenchyma) or becomes a tendril or other organ (Fig. 28.2b);
- indeterminate, where the bud continues subordinate growth or may become dormant and resume continued indeterminate sympodial growth later, either as an entity separate from the parent plant or as a subordinate branch (Fig. 28.2c).

Tropical cultivars

The life-forms exemplified by three tropical plant families, members of which have been taken into cultivation, characterize how plants may attain longevity by vegetative propagation rather than by secondary growth, and how the phenomenon of sympodial branching is central to this pattern of growth.

Zingiberaceae

The Zingiberaceae are a family of rhizomatous plants that include the cultivated taxa *Alpinia* (galangal), *Curcuma* (turmeric), *Zingiber* (ginger) and many others. The Zingiberaceous plants are used in Southeast Asia as minor starchy staples (especially *Curcuma* spp.; Cronquist 1981: 1180), but they are more important in cultivation as spices. As such they are perhaps less likely to have been important as staples in the early stages of agrarian subsistence, although they may have been among the earliest plants to be cultivated. Rhizomatous plants are typified by having a perennial axis in a horizontal position, and ephemeral axes, leaves and infloresences in the vertical

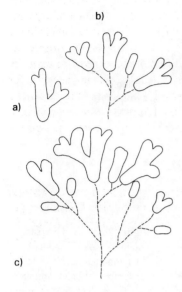

Figure 28.3 Diagrammatic representation of growth in *Zingiber*: (a) a young plant begins to branch; (b) the initial stages of growth decay; and (c) numerous ramets grow away from the region of original growth.

position. Thus, growth is parallel to the ground and not perpendicular. Plants that have a main vertical axis and put out horizontal axes terminating in vegetatively produced young plants which, once established, break ties (vascular and otherwise) with the parent plant are termed stoloniferous (see Hather 1994 for a discussion of this terminology).

The indeterminate sympodial growth of the Zingiberaceous rhizome ensures that along its length dormant buds are positioned which have the potential to become sympodial branches (Fig. 28.3a). In the course of time the end of the rhizome opposite the leading shoot, the distal end, begins to die. As it does so, the dormant buds grow, and as the rotting of the distal end proceeds along the length of the rhizome these lateral sympodial units become detached (Fig. 28.3b). The leading shoot, the proximal end, keeps up in growth with the death of the distal end and continues to produce dormant sympodial buds. Eventually the plant will have formed of separate sympodial units, known as ramets, which describe an arc at their leading edge (Fig. 28.3c). Ramets of the same plant are of the same genetic make-up and, although they may be many metres apart, they still genetically constitute a single plant. Such plants have been calculated to be many hundreds of years old and have potential immortality (Bell 1974, 1986, Bell & Tomlinson 1980).

Araceae

The Araceae are a family of plants that includes one of the most important carbohydrate-rich staple crops in the tropics, *Colocasia esculenta*, taro. It also contains several crops locally important in Southeast Asia, such as *Alocasia macrorrhiza*, *Cyrtosperma chammisonis* and species of *Amorphophallus*. *Xanthosoma sagittifolia*, an Araceous crop of tropical American origin, is important in parts of the Americas. The life-form of the majority of Araceae, and of all those that have been taken into cultivation as staples, is that of the corm. A corm is functionally similar to a rhizome, with a vertical orientation. Sympodial units form around the circumference of a parent corm and, when the parent corm dies and rots, they exist as independent ramets of the same plant. Some members of the Araceae, for example *Colocasia* and *Cyrtosperma*, have a propensity for secondary sympodial units or cormells to grow to maturity alongside the primary sympodial unit or corm (Figs 28.4a,b). This may continue for several "generations" so that a large clump of corms will form. In time this dies at the centre so that a ring of plants remains (Fig. 28.4c). By contrast, in *Amorphophallus*, a parent plant is replaced by one or sometimes two corms, so that at any one time the plant has only one or two sympodial units (Fig. 28.5).

Dioscoreaceae

The Dioscoreaceae are a family of only five genera, of which the genus *Dioscorea*, the yams, is the largest with around 600 species, mainly in the tropics. *Dioscorea* species are important cultivated crops throughout the tropics: *D. trifida* in the Americas, *D. rotundata* and *D. cayenensis* in the humid tropics of Africa, and *D. alata*, *D. esculenta*, *D. nummularia* and *D. pentaphylla* in Southeast Asia. Many others are of local importance, including *D. bulbifera* which has a pan-tropical distribution. The life-form of most *Dioscorea* species is that of a vine growing from a large fleshy tuber formed from either the epicotyledonary or young hypocotyledonary growth. This is very different from the rhizomatous growth of the Zingiberaceae and from the cormous growth of the Araceae.

Figure 28.4   Diagrammatic representation of growth in *Colocasia*: (a) a corm begins to reproduce vegetatively; (b) more corms are produced; and (c) the oldest corms at the centre of the colony wither and die, separating the colony into two ramets.

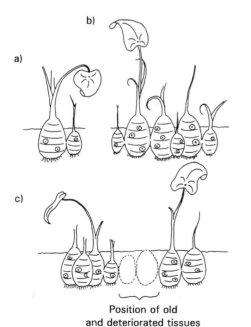

Figure 28.5   Diagrammatic representation of growth in *Amorphophallus*: the youngest corm lies above the withered corm of the previous year which itself lies above the decayed corm of the year before that.

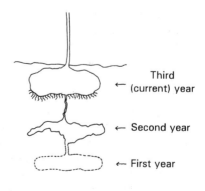

Position of old
and deteriorated tissues

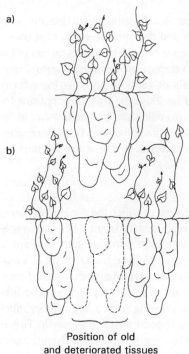

a)

b)

Position of old
and deteriorated tissues

Figure 28.6   Diagrammatic representation of growth in *Dioscorea alata*: (a) a single mature plant grows to form a massive colony; and (b) where the oldest tubers at the centre of the colony wither and die, separating the colony into two ramets.

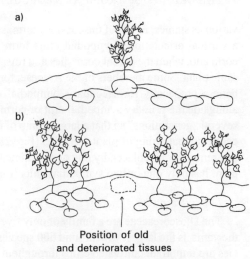

a)

b)

Position of old
and deteriorated tissues

Figure 28.7   Diagrammatic representation of growth in *Dioscorea esculenta*: (a) an original tuber vegetatively reproduces second-generation tubers; and (b) the original tuber decays and the now separated second- generation tubers vegetatively reproduce third-generation tubers.

The tuber of *Dioscorea* acts as a reservoir of dormant buds, either along the top of a flattened surface or along the vertical length of the tuber – the basal nodal region (Degras 1993: 10). Both the sympodial branching form and adventitious growth play a part in the formation of new buds, and tubers tend to be static and individually long-lived. However, fragmentation by the death and rotting of the central part of a large tuber will produce ramets that are functionally independent although genetically identical (Figs 28.6a,b). Similarly, individual tubers that form at the end of stolons will also achieve independence on the deterioration of the stoloniferous contact (Figs 28.7a,b).

Agricultural origins in non-seasonal tropical environments

Wild tubers

Holttum (1955) and Holdsworth (1961) both remark on the fact that the massively tuberous or rhizomatous life-form of certain Monocotyledonous families, including the ones under discussion here, adapted to longevity, originated in the continuously hot and humid forests in tropical regions of the world. Such a life-form comprises a strategy formed by plants that lack fasicular cambia and therefore the potential to become woody. Rhizomes, corms and tubers provide a platform for the growth of adventitious roots, which have the advantages of greater support and increased water uptake over simple primary root structure. Both these features allow the support of a much increased leaf area, necessary for any large plant with continuous growth in a tropical rainforest. The dormant apical buds of the indeterminate sympodial system grow and either replace the parent plant laterally (*Zingiber officinale*, *Curcuma domestica*, *Alpinia galanga*, *Colocasia esculenta*, *Alocasia macrorrhiza*, *Dioscorea* spp.) or vertically (*Amorphophallus* spp.), allowing a continuous supply of buds which can grow into shoots that can support an ephemeral photosynthetic leaf area. Without the ability to produce a continuous supply of leaves, the plants would soon die.

The life-form of these plants relies heavily on successful vegetative propagation, an asexual method of reproduction. This must not be confused with other forms of asexual reproduction – apomixis, aneuspory, diplospory, parthenogenesis, and so on. In their wild state the Zingiberaceae, Dioscoreaceae and Araceae flower and set seed successfully. However, this is a character that has been affected by their cultivation and incorporation into agrarian systems, as is discussed below.

This form of growth, where a plant may exist as individual spatially separated ramets, each genetically identical and able to function as an independent plant, has, perhaps, elements of a Dawkinsian theory of genetic survival (Dawkins 1978, 1982). There are many examples of this growth form, especially from the plant families described here, in the humid tropics, and while there is certainly an aspect of this growth form that relates to a storing up of reserves, continuous green growth is exhibited, and there is no period of perennation (Dafni et al. 1981).

Previous models of the origins of vegeculture do not account for the fact that the plants concerned can and do grow naturally and propagate in the non-seasonal tropics. The model presented here views the rhizomes, corms and tubers of these taxa not as perennating organs of seasonal environments but as the main perennial body of plants in non-seasonal humid tropical environments. In other words, in temperate and arid environments where seasonality exists, we naturally view the truly perennating organs of corm, rhizome and tuber in the same way as the trunk, branches and twigs of deciduous trees. As organs of perennation they are functionally similar: corms, rhizomes and tubers perennate in temperate and arid regions because that is what is demanded of them in seasonal environments. In the non-seasonal humid tropics the organs of corm, rhizome and tuber have no more a perennating function than the trunk, branches and twigs of the non-deciduous trees in that environment. However, this is not to make a firm statement on seasonal versus non-seasonal distribution. It is rather to make the point that the incorporation of these plants into agrarian systems cannot be seen to be *restricted* to the seasonal tropics by virtue of their morphology.

Corner (1964) termed the life-form expressed by massively cormous, tuberous or rhizomatous organs "pachycaully" (i.e. thick-stemmed, referring to the primary body of the plant). He views this state, exhibited by the earlier monocotyledonous plants, to have evolved in and be associated with the tropics. Leptocaully (i.e. narrow-stemmed) is an advanced and derived character, exhibited by temperate taxa and more recently evolved tropical families. The majority of the members of the Araceae and Dioscoreaceae originated in the humid tropics and display pachycaully to some extent. Members of the Alocasia genus are extreme in this respect. The tropical Zingiberaceae, Araceae and Dioscoreaceae differ in the ways in which they have adapted to the low-light conditions of the humid forests in which they have evolved. The Araceae display large, often fleshy, leaves, a character also thought to be primitive. The Dioscoreaceae have developed vines by which they can climb up narrow shafts of light and position their leaves to the maximum advantage for capturing light. The Zingiberaceae have long strap-like leaves, typical of many Monocotyledons and associated with life on the forest floor.

Non-seasonal perennation

There is however a direct and important relationship between the non-perennating corms and tubers of monocotyledons growing in non-seasonal tropical humid environments and the perennating structures typical of more northerly and southerly latitudes During the evolution of the monocotyledons, their natural spread to seasonal tropical and eventually to temperate climates involved two possibly conflicting processes:

- a reduction in the "primitive" pachycaul life-form leading to the "advanced" leptocaul life-form, i.e. a reduction in the massive "tropical" geophytic life-form;
- selection for the reduced geophytic organ as an organ of perennation, resulting in the many monocotyledons with perennating rhizomes, corms and tubers that occur in temperate latitudes in such families as the Liliaceae, Amaryllidaceae and Iridaceae as well as the Araceae.

This, seen by many as a neotenous evolutionary advance by the selection of the juvenile pachycaul form, certainly accounts for the generally small size of temperate corms and tubers. It also enables the model for the origins of vegeculture in the tropics, developed here, to be extended to explain the relative lack of root and tuber staples in Old World temperate regions (for a more detailed discussion see Hather 1994).

Initial propagation and cultivation

The life-form of members of the Araceae, Dioscoreaceae and Zingiberaceae is the key to their present importance as starch-rich staples. An overriding feature of that life-form is the dormant sympodial bud, which can grow at a time when the parent plant needs to expand in order to maintain its life by the production of a new photosynthetic leaf area. The removal of these buds, with enough tissue to support their short-term growth before they can produce leaves of their own, is the basis of vegeculture. This process almost certainly began with the removal of fragments of tissue, coincidentally containing buds, from wild plants, and observation of their independent growth when discarded. From there, it is but a short step to deliberate propagation and cultivation.

An interesting result of the cultivation of these crops is that is has led to a reduced incidence of both flowering and the setting of viable seed (different and independent functions, although of course the latter is dependent on the former). Whether the plants' ability to reproduce sexually has been diminished by cultivation, or whether it is just the opportunity to do so that has been reduced, due to harvesting before flowering, is difficult to determine. Whichever is the case, the reduced incidence of flowering has unfortunately led to these plants being relatively invisible in the pollen record (Haberle 1994), a problem that has plagued research into the early exploitation and spread of them as crops.

The origins of vegeculture in the tropics

The model proposed here is that the rhizomes of the Zingiberaceae, the corms of the Araceae and the tubers of the Dioscoreaceae, and also incidentally the vegetative structures of the Taccaceae, Cannaceae, Marantaceae and analogous structures in the Musaceae, evolved as an adaptive strategy for longevity in humid tropical forests rather than as a strategy adapted to seasonally dry conditions in the more arid tropics. The earliest cultivation of these taxa probably took place in the regions of distribution of their wild ancestors, as Harris pointed out (1969), but it is suggested here that this would have been in the humid, rather than in the seasonally dry, tropics. However, this model does not imply that many of the dicotyledonous root and tuber staples also originated in the non-seasonal humid tropics, rather than in more climatically seasonal environments. The tubers of *Solanum tuberosum* (Solanaceae) and *Ipomoea batatas* (Convolvulaceae) and the root of *Manihot esculenta* (Euphorbiaceae), for example, may indeed have originated in seasonally dry or cold environments, their respective tuberous organs having a perennating function.

In relating this model to the origin of vegeculture in Southeast Asia, and in terms of the broad location or locations of the areas in which these plants were first cultivated, two points must be recognized. First, that the distribution of non-seasonal rainforests today may not be the same as that at the time of the earliest cultivation of this resource. Second, that tectonic changes and the changing pattern of sea-level and rainforest distribution may have left isolated populations of plants suited to the humid tropics but also capable of living in more seasonal environments. The evidence discussed here indicates that the rhizomes, corms and tubers of some present-day crop plants evolved in the humid tropics and that their natural distribution is within the humid tropics. However, the possibility of their having been taken into cultivation in more seasonal climates cannot be ruled out. The natural wild distribution of the Zingiberaceae and Araceae is within the humid tropics, and members of these families that live in seasonal environments are few, and, in terms of the general characters of the family, are thought to be unusual (Cronquist 1981, Grayum 1990, Heywood 1978). The Dioscoreaceae are also mainly found in the humid tropics although the family includes species living in seasonal environments both within and beyond the tropics (Coursey 1967). However, the tuberous life-forms of *Dioscorea* species on the Australian continent are likely to be residual of a less seasonal past environment, as must be the life-form of *Tamus communis* (Dioscoreaceae) in Europe. As it happens, neither of these taxa were brought into cultivation in their respective continents.

The cultivation of cormous, tuberous and rhizomatous crops represents a relatively simple progression from their being gathered for food from wild populations, and from the exploitation of these plants as a wild resource. The wild progenitors of the crops that have become central to Southeast Asian vegeculture are native to tropical non-seasonal forests in Southeast Asia and this agrarian strategy almost certainly began independently in many, possibly isolated, pockets of human activity within this region. This mirrors the likely pattern of agricultural origins in Southwest Asia as proposed by Moore & Hillman (1992). Evidence for tropical origins are, however, likely to be, at best, scanty. Domestication, in the sense of genetic selection of plants in ways that are more suitable to human needs – higher yield, easier cultivation, detoxification, and so on – may occur after many generations of selection in an agrarian environment, although for some cereals it has been shown experimentally to happen within relatively few generations (Hillman & Davies 1990). It is the morphological, anatomical, chemical or genetic differences between domesticates and their wild progenitors that allow archaeologists to differentiate between them. It might be possible to determine the time of domestication of a crop (or at least a time shortly thereafter), but by definition this must be after the point at which cultivation began.

In his evolutionary model of plant exploitation – "an evolutionary continuum of people–plant interaction" – Harris (1989) defines agriculture as succeeding cultivation only after the domestication of the crops involved. However, he acknowledges that house-garden horticulture may incorporate plants that are "adventitious wild and weedy taxa rather than domesticates" (Harris 1989: 19–20) and he excludes small-scale horticulture from his definition of agriculture that involves "larger-scale field cultivation".

Many crops in Southeast Asian agricultural systems are grown in multi-cropping and mixed cropping systems, not necessarily in house-gardens but also in larger swidden plots. Taro is cultivated alongside such other crops as the different species of yam, other Aroids, and, more recently, crops introduced from the American tropics and Europe. In traditional systems one or two yam taxa, taro or in some instances another Aroid, dominate and other crops, grown alongside them, are fewer in number. These minor crops, for example *Dioscorea hispida*, *Colocasia gigantea*, *Lasia spinosa* and *Schismatoglottis calyptrata*, differ markedly from the staples – *Colocasia esculenta*, *Dioscorea alata*, *D. esculenta* – in that they are not domesticated, that is, there is no genetic difference between the plants cultivated in gardens for food and wild plants within the area of natural distribution.

A solution to the problem such a traditional agricultural system poses for Harris's definition of agriculture, is to suggest that "domestication" is a statement about the genetic status of a plant and as such should be removed from a model that aims to define the point at which agriculture can be said to have originated (cf. Harris's 1996 modification of his 1989 model, and Table 1.1a in this volume). Domestication is not something that can be defined as a single event; it is a process that begins with minor changes and continues as long as the crop is under selective pressure. By removing domestication from the model, we are left with a process of change that begins with wild-plant procurement and ends with sophisticated agriculture. The beginning of cultivation is the point where part of a plant (a seed or vegetative part) is planted, managed and harvested. Agriculture can be said to begin when this process becomes a strategy that people have come to rely on for subsistence. Domestication, defined as genetic change, can begin to take place at any point along the continuum and will continue as long as the particular plant continues to be under selective pressure.

As in Southeast Asia, so in many other regions of the world, some systems of agriculture have evolved and proved long lasting, whereas others may have been abandoned in favour of other subsistence strategies. The nature of plants in humid, non-seasonal tropical forests, the nature of such environments, and the interactions between them and past human populations differ considerably from those extra-tropical regions, such as Southwest Asia, on which most models of the origins of agriculture have been based. This examination of the origins of vegeculture, with particular reference to Southeast Asia, has not only permitted a reformulation of models for the origins of tropical agriculture, but can also, by broadening their basis, contribute towards a re-examination of more general models of the origins of agriculture.

References

Bell, A. D. 1974. Rhizome organization in relation to vegetative spread in *Medeola virginiana*. *Journal of the Arnold Arboretum* **55**, 458–68.
— 1986. The simulation of branching patterns in modular organisms. *Philosophical Transactions of the Royal Society B* **313**, 143–59.
Bell, A. D. & P. B. Tomlinson 1980. Adaptive architecture in rhizomatous plants. *Botanical Journal of the Linnean Society* **80**, 125–60.
Corner, E. J. H. 1964. *The life of plants*. Chicago: University of Chicago Press.
Coursey, D. G. 1967. *Yams*. London: Longman.
Cronquist, A. 1981. *An integrated system of classification of flowering plants*. New York: Columbia University Press.
Dafni, A., D. Cohen, I. Noy-Meir 1981. Life-cycle variation in geophytes. *Annals of the Missouri Botanical Garden* **68**, 652–60.
Dawkins, R. 1978. *The selfish gene*. Oxford: Oxford University Press.
— 1982. *The extended phenotype*. Oxford: Oxford University Press.
Degras, L. 1993. *The yam: a tropical root crop*. London: Macmillan.
Grayum, M. H. 1990. Evolution and phylogeny in the Araceae. *Annals of the Missouri Botanical Garden* **77**, 628–97.
Haberle, S. 1994. Anthropogenic indicators in pollen diagrams. In *Tropical archaeobotany: applications and new developments*, J. G. Hather (ed.), 172–201. London: Routledge.
Harris, D. R. 1969. Agricultural systems, ecosystems and the origins of agriculture. In *The domestication and exploitation of plants and animals*, P. J. Ucko & G. W. Dimbleby (eds), 3–16. London: Duckworth.
— 1972. The origins of agriculture in the tropics. *American Scientist* **60**, 180–93.
— 1981. The prehistory of human subsistence: a speculative outline. In *Food, nutrition and evolution*, D. M. Walker & N. Kretchmer (eds), 15–35. New York: Masson.
— 1989. An evolutionary continuum of people–plant interaction. In *Foraging and farming: the evolution of plant exploitation*, D. R. Harris & G. C. Hillman (eds), 11–26. London: Unwin Hyman.
— 1996. Domesticatory relationships of people, plants and animals. In *Redefining nature: ecology, culture and domestication*, R. Ellen & K. Fukui (eds), 437–63. Oxford: Berg.
Hather, J. G. 1992. The archaeobotany of subsistence in the Pacific. *World Archaeology* **24**, 70–81.
— 1994. A morphological classification of roots and tubers and its bearing on the origins of agriculture in southwest Asia and Europe. *Journal of Archaeological Science* **21**, 719–24.
Hawkes, J. G. 1969. The ecological background of plant domestication. In *The domestication and exploitation of plants and animals*, P. J. Ucko & G. W. Dimbleby (eds), 17–30. London: Duckworth.
Heywood, V. 1978. *Flowering plants of the world*. Oxford: Oxford University Press.
Hillman, G. C. & M. S. Davies 1990. Measured domestication rates in wild wheats and barley under primitive cultivation and their archaeological implications. *Journal of World Prehistory* **4**, 157–222.
Holdsworth, M. 1961. The flowering of rain flowers. *Journal of the West African Science Association* **7**, 28–36.

Hole, F. 1992. Origins of agriculture. In *The Cambridge encyclopedia of human evolution*, S. Jones, R. Martin, D. Pilbeam (eds), 373–9. Cambridge: Cambridge University Press.

Holttum, R. E. 1955. Growth-habits of Monocotyledons – variations on a theme. *Phytomorphology* **5**, 399–413.

Moore, A. M. T. & G. C. Hillman 1992. The Pleistocene to Holocene transition and human economy in Southwest Asia: the impact of the Younger Dryas. *American Antiquity* **57**, 482–94.

Sauer, C. O. 1952. *Agricultural origins and dispersals*. New York: American Geographical Society.

Thompson, D. W. 1942. *Growth and form*, 2nd edn, vol. 2. Cambridge: Cambridge University Press.

PART FIVE
Conclusion

CHAPTER TWENTY-NINE

The origins and spread of agriculture and pastoralism in Eurasia: an overview

David R. Harris

Introduction

The essential aims of this book are, as I suggested in the Introduction, to gain greater understanding of how, where and when agriculture originated and spread, both by focusing upon the single large landmass of Eurasia and by introducing into the discussion distinctive, and in part novel, multidisciplinary perspectives. I have already commented in the Introduction on some of the general concepts that recur throughout the book and influence the ways in which we interpret the evidence: the terminology we use to define interactions between people, plants and animals; the concept of centres of origin; and the role of diffusion. My aim in this concluding chapter is not to return to these important concepts but to turn to the substantive evidence and attempt a partial – although highly provisional – interpretation of the beginnings of agriculture and pastoralism in Eurasia as a whole. This is an imposing task, but one that is worth attempting to gain an overview as much of what we do not know as of what we more securely understand.

Such an attempt is also timely because the subject has moved on from the 1960s and 1970s, when the generation of high-level "explanatory" models had such a stimulating effect on it, and is now benefiting from the more regionally and chronologically focused interpretation of existing and new evidence. Many contributors to this volume stress, in their interpretations of the evidence, the importance of particular conjunctions of circumstances in particular places at particular times. This does not represent a return to narrowly conceived particularism, nor does it imply any rejection of a comparative perspective, but it does signify an important shift of emphasis away from attempts to "explain" the origins of agriculture in terms of *general* processual models (which often lacked testable "middle-range" propositions) to a greater concern with what Sherratt (in Ch. 8 in this volume) refers to as "the chapter of accidents that forms the background to the processes we want to explain" – in a phrase, historical *contingency*.

It is fascinating, but not unexpected, that at the same time a parallel conceptual shift has been taking place in ecology towards what Blumler (in Ch. 3 in this volume) describes as "a non-equilibrium view of nature" – a shift that he thinks "reflects the accumulation of a huge mass of empirical ecological data" (as well as being "in part a logical extension of previous paradigm shifts in the physical sciences"). The study of early agriculture is likewise faced with an abundance of new data, and, as has already been suggested, the time is ripe to attempt continental-scale, comparative interpretations of the evidence we have. In what follows, which I do not claim is anything more than a preliminary "historical" sketch, the evidence is reviewed regionally and chronologically. However, it must be emphasized that the temporal framework is not rigorously defined, partly because of the problems involved in interpreting radiocarbon dates, a minority of which have been calibrated (and not all by the same method) and many of which suffer from contextual uncertainties.

Before embarking on the review, there is one other important matter to clarify. This relates to the distinctions, drawn in the Introduction, between agriculture and cultivation and between the raising of livestock and the hunting, taming or herding/management of essentially wild animals. I assume, and indeed have long argued, that "hunter–gatherers" around the world have for many millennia routinely manipulated plant and animal populations in diverse ways to optimize their use of them (e.g. Harris 1984, 1989: 16–20; see also many papers in Harris & Hillman 1989). The manipulation of plants has included activities that amount to small-scale "cultivation", such as local clearance of vegetation and the planting, sowing, drainage and irrigation of mainly wild plants; and the manipulation of animals has included the keeping of pet mammals and birds and the "protective herding" and "free-range management" of wild ungulates. Rindos (1984: 152–66) labels such "co-evolutionary" activities "incidental" and "specialized" domestication and distinguishes them from "agricultural domestication". This distinction is very similar to mine between small-scale cultivation and larger-scale cultivation and agriculture (see Table 1.1) in that both regard the scale and environmental impact of human actions as important criteria in the definition of agriculture. This point is also stressed by Spriggs (in Ch. 27 in this volume) in his discussion of my earlier model of people–plant interaction (Harris 1989), where he argues that whether a plant is domesticated or not is less significant in defining agriculture than the "creation of agroecosystems, which limit subsistence choice because of environmental transformation or labour demands". Hather also suggests (in Ch. 28 in this volume) that "domestication" should be removed from definitions of agriculture. Although each of us places different emphases on particular points, there is a general consensus here that "agriculture" (and by extension livestock raising) differs in spatial scale, in labour demands/energy input, and in environmental impact from the procurement and small-scale production/protection of (mainly) wild plants and animals. It is necessary to emphasize this important distinction here because, in what follows, discussion focuses on "agriculture" in that sense, not on evidence for the manipulation of plant and animal resources by "hunter–gatherers". And, to anticipate, a general conclusion that can be drawn from this review is that agriculture, so defined, originated independently only very rarely – possibly only twice – in the history of Eurasia.

The Levantine region

The earliest well attested evidence we have at present for agriculture and pastoralism anywhere in Eurasia comes from the western half of the so-called "Fertile Crescent" in Southwest Asia: more specifically, from sites in the "Levantine Corridor" of woodland, moist steppe and rift-valley oases and in the middle Euphrates Valley. Here the remains of domesticated cereals (barley, einkorn and emmer wheat) and pulses (pea, chickpea, lentil) and flax have been dated at such sites as Jericho, Tell Aswad and Tell Abu Hureyra, to the eighth millennium bc. By the seventh millennium these "founder crops" of neolithic Southwest Asian agriculture (with the addition of bitter vetch) occur at other sites in the Levant ('Ain Ghazal, Beidha, Ramad, Yiftah'el), in the Euphrates Valley (Bouqras), in the foothills of the Zagros Mountains (Jarmo, Ali Kosh) and in Anatolia (Çayönü, Çan Hassan, Haçilar) (cf. Fig. 9.1). More uncertainty attaches to the earliest evidence for domesticated caprines – goat and sheep being the earliest ungulates to be domesticated (cf. Garrard et al., Legge and Hole in Chs 11, 13 and 14 in this volume). Few if any sites in Southwest Asia provide firm evidence of domestic caprines before 7000 bc. Legge argues (in this volume) for the presence of domestic goats and sheep at Tell Abu Hureyra as early as 7400 bc, and for the possible presence of domestic goats at Jericho in the eighth millennium. He also notes the absence of sheep from the Levantine sites, and suggests that "their origin as domesticates lay to the north or east" whence they were introduced to the Damascus region by about 6600 bc. This latter point accords well with Hole's view (in this volume) that caprine domestication is likely to have begun in the lower mountain valleys of the Zagros–Taurus region, between about 600 m and 1,300 m altitude, "a thousand years or so later than cereal agriculture began in the Levant", either in association with, or relatively independently of, the beginnings of cereal agriculture in the region. Garrard et al. (in this volume) review the evidence for domestic goats and sheep in the Levant and conclude that it is very limited and uncertain before 6500 bc, but that it increases dramatically, at such sites as Basta in southern Jordan, in the Damascus region, and at Tell Abu Hureyra on the Euphrates in the next few centuries.

The earliest evidence for domestic cereals, pulses and caprines in Southwest Asia appears to sustain the following summary interpretation:

- that seed-crop agriculture based on cereals and pulses began to be practised in the Levant and the middle Euphrates Valley soon after the beginning of the eighth millennium, during the Pre-Pottery Neolithic A (PPNA: *c.* 8300–7600 bc)
- that agriculture spread during the late eighth and early seventh millennia (Early and Middle PPNB: *c.* 7600–6500 bc) northwards and eastwards into the uplands of Anatolia and the Zagros, where pastoralism based on the raising of goats and sheep also developed during this period
- that domestic caprines only became part (or at least an important part) of systems of agro-pastoral production in the Levant after 6500 bc, during the Late PPNB.

It is not my intention in this chapter to try to explain *why* the developments that the evidence suggests took place. However, two factors that are often regarded as "explanatory", and which several of the contributors to the Southwest Asian section of this book stress, deserve mention. The first is the role of sedentism as a precursor to agriculture; and the second is the proposition that environmental, essentially climatic, change was an important factor in bringing about the transition to agriculture. The idea that sedentary life preceded and made possible the beginning of agriculture is not new – indeed it was proposed as long ago as 1952 by Carl Sauer – but it has seldom been demonstrated archaeologically. However, there is now a considerable body of evidence in support of the view that some resource-rich locations in the Levant were occupied year-round during the terminal Pleistocene (more specifically in the Natufian and Khiamian periods: *c.* 10500–8300 bc) by "sedentary foragers" who developed more intensive techniques of plant exploitation, including storage and possibly small-scale cultivation, than their "hunter–gatherer" predecessors and who lived year-round in settlements of up to half a hectare in area (Henry 1989, Bar-Yosef & Belfer-Cohen 1991). This does not in itself explain *why* the transition to agriculture occurred, but it does lead to what many of us regard as a necessary condition for it to take place, and it further implies that the sedentary populations would be likely to increase, with resultant intensified exploitation of local plant and animal resources (Harris 1990: 19–28).

Intensified resource exploitation focusing on particularly "responsive" or "domesticable" plants and animals, and leading to the development of agriculture and pastoralism, may also have been induced by the impact of climatic and other environmental (including sea-level) changes on the food supplies of the Natufian "sedentary foragers". In particular, the cold dry interval that occurred between *c.* 9500 and *c.* 8600 bc in the eastern Mediterranean, and which corresponds to the period of the Younger Dryas in Europe, is likely to have reduced the wild plant-food resources available to Late Natufian populations in the Levant and to have increased their dependence on the small-scale cultivation of large-seeded grasses and herbaceous legumes – the progenitors of the domesticated cereals and pulses that first appear in the succeeding PPNA. Several contributors to this volume (Bellwood, Blumler, Garrard et al., Hillman, Hole) see late Pleistocene to early Holocene climatic change, particularly the period equivalent to the Younger Dryas, as an important stress factor that helped bring about the transition from foraging to cereal and pulse agriculture in the Levant. This hypothesis is supported by other authors, for example Bar-Yosef & Belfer-Cohen (1992), who further suggest that the rapid return to wet conditions after the "Younger Dryas" in the eastern Mediterranean "ensured the existence of many small lakes and ponds and provided for the success of many PPNA sites along the Levantine Corridor" (ibid.: 39).

Turning next to the question of the spread of agriculture within western Southwest Asia, it has first to be said that the hypothesis that cereal and pulse agriculture originated in the southern Levant earlier than elsewhere and then spread north up the Levantine Corridor, as McCorriston & Hole (1991) and Bar-Yosef & Belfer-Cohen (1992) argue, or whether it originated contemporaneously over a larger area encompassing the northern Levant and southeastern Anatolia, cannot at present be conclusively demonstrated. Blumler points out (in this volume) that wild einkorn does not grow south of the Bekaa Valley today because the rainy season there is too short, and he concludes that either it was domesticated somewhere to the north or the rainy season was longer (in the south) when agriculture began. Hillman infers from his detailed re-examination of the palynological data (in Ch. 10 in this volume) that the climatic changes that followed the Glacial Maximum, including the "Younger Dryas", occurred almost synchronously in the southern Levant *and* farther north, and he also points out that at least some cereal domestication occurred independently in the north, for instance, of annual rye, which is present in domestic form at Tell Abu Hureyra some 500 years earlier than the earliest domesticated cereals and pulses in the southern Levant. Furthermore, finds of domestic einkorn and emmer wheat, dated to the second half of the eighth millennium, have recently been reported from the southeastern Anatolian sites of Cafer Höyük and Çayönü (de Moulins 1993, van Zeist & de Roller 1994, Willcox 1995). It can therefore be argued that the presently available archaeobotanical data point to a quite widespread process of cereal domestication in western Southwest Asia during the eighth millennium. This is not necessarily inconsistent with the spread of cereal/pulse agriculture northwards from the southern Levant, but it does indicate, as Zohary says (in Ch. 9 in this volume) that, as yet, we know "very little about the way the Southwest Asian neolithic crop 'package' was assembled". It remains an open question whether different crops were taken into cultivation together in the same place, or whether different crops were domesticated (perhaps each only once) in different places.

Improved knowledge of the time and place of "domestication events" in neolithic Southwest Asia depends on the acquisition of more precisely identified plant and animal remains, but there is sufficient evidence to demonstrate that agro-pastoral production became widely established by the end of the Late PPNB (*c.* 6000 bc). Byrd (1992) has recently reviewed much of this evidence for the Levant and he concludes that agricultural villages with domestic goats and sheep, as well as cereals and pulses, were established throughout the more fertile areas by then. He further hypothesizes that the sedentary economy spread by colonization and through contact and exchange with local hunter–gatherers, and speculates that the shift from round to rectangular architecture that occurred at many sites during the Pre-Pottery Neolithic may indicate that process (Byrd 1992: 52–3). Bellwood too (in Ch. 25 in this volume) associates the origin of what he calls "the agglutinative cell-like form of architecture" with the PPNB and suggests that the latter may represent "some degree of population colonization outward from the Levant". In their contribution (to this volume) Garrard et al. show that crop cultivation and livestock herding did not become established until the terminal PPNB in the drier "Marginal Zone" east and south of the Levantine Corridor, where caprine pastoralism may have served a valuable function as a buffer against risks of crop failure. There is no direct evidence to suggest at present that agro-pastoralism developed in the Negev and Sinai during the PPNB, but the fact that most of the Southwest Asian founder crops, and domestic sheep and goats, had reached the Nile Valley by 5000 bc (Goring-Morris 1993) implies that pastoralism and probably some cultivation was being practised in the Negev and Sinai in the sixth millennium.

It is now apparent that some 2,000 years elapsed between the appearance of the first domesticates and the establishment of an agro-pastoral economy and settlement pattern through most of western Southwest Asia, but we cannot ascertain, on the basis of presently available evidence, how far this process depended on colonization by farmers and how far on the adoption of agriculture and pastoralism by hunter–gatherers. However, it can be argued on more general grounds that the sedentary agricultural populations of neolithic Southwest Asia would have tended to expand both numerically and territorially because shifts from mobile to settled life tend to bring about population growth, particularly by reducing the average birth interval (Lee 1972, 1980; Harris 1977: 411–14; and cf. Groube's discussion in Ch. 7 in this volume of the relationship between sedentism, disease and population growth). Increasing dietary dependence on seed-crop agriculture (and livestock raising) would also have provided more assured supplies of cereal-based weaning foods such as gruel and porridge (Molleson 1994: 64) – as well as milk, once the domestic caprines began to be milked – that would have shortened the period of human lactation, led to earlier conception and thus accentuated the tendency for the average birth interval to be reduced. Infant mortality may also have been lowered by easier access to weaning foods, although this effect may have been countered by increased incidence of diseases in the sedentary settlements.

It can further be argued that populations practising systems of seed-crop agriculture that incorporate cereals and pulses and thus yield a well balanced dietary combination of vegetable proteins, lipids and carbohydrate, which provides most of the essential nutrients, have an inherent tendency to expand spatially. If domestic livestock are also incorporated into the system of production as providers of meat and (at some stage in the process) milk, the dietary "package" becomes even more self-sufficient and the capacity for expansion is enhanced. This contrasts, as I suggested long ago (Harris 1972, 1973), with "vegecultural" systems focused on the cultivation of root crops that provide mainly carbohydrate. In these systems, which developed particularly in the tropics, most of the necessary protein and fat is usually obtained by fishing and/or hunting and therefore the cultivators remain "tied" to habitats where these wild resources are available; they tend not to expand territorially but to remain localized – a point to which I return in the later discussion of Southeast Asia and Melanesia. These considerations highlight the unique dietary effectiveness of the Southwest Asian early neolithic "package" of cereals, pulses, goats and sheep, which was not matched in any other "centre" of agriculture in the world (Harris 1981). They also give strong support to the view that the establishment of seed-crop agriculture and caprine pastoralism within and beyond western Southwest Asia during and after the PPNB probably owed more to the spread of farming populations by migration and colonization than to the adoption of agro-pastoralism by local hunter–gatherers.

Other contributors to this volume, notably Bellwood and Renfrew, also postulate outward dispersal of agricultural populations from the Levant during the Neolithic. In suggesting that the distribution of PPNB sites may signify this process, Bellwood goes as far as to speculate, following Renfrew (1992), that the Levant may have been the homeland, in the late Natufian, of a "Proto-Nostratic founder language", and that the PPNB may perhaps reflect "a phase of early Semitic (Afro–Asiatic) expansion" – a view that accords closely with Renfrew's hypothesis (1991 and Ch. 5 in this volume) that the Afro–Asiatic language family originated in the Levantine region.

Anatolia and southeastern Europe

From this cursory review of the origins and early spread of agro-pastoralism in the Levantine region, we can now follow the trail northwestwards across Anatolia and into Europe. Relatively little is known about the nature and chronology of earliest agricultural settlement in the vast area of Anatolia as a whole, but, where early neolithic sites have been investigated in any detail (e.g. at Süberde, Can Hasan III, Erbaba and Çatal Hüyük (east) in south-central Turkey), bioarchaeological evidence for agriculture, in the form of the remains of crops and domestic animals, dates no earlier than the late seventh millennium (c. 6200 bc at Süberde and Can Hasan III, c. 5600 bc at Erbaba and Çatal Hüyük east).

It is of particular interest that these early agricultural sites in Anatolia tend to be – as Roberts (1991) has clearly shown – located on or close to hydromorphic soils, which retain moisture and allow crops to be grown for more of the year under a "Mediterranean" climatic regime of warm, wet winters and hot, dry summers than on drier free-draining soils. Roberts's detailed survey of early neolithic sites in the Beyşehir-Suğla and Konya Basins demonstrated that they were all located on alluvial deposits, typically at the margins of fans and seasonal lakes, suggesting that these locations were selectively settled by agriculturalists because of the water-retentive characteristics of their soils. In a seminal paper published a decade earlier, Sherratt (1980) had drawn attention, in a more comprehensive way, to the consistency with which early agricultural sites were located, in Southwest Asia and Europe, on alluvial soils with high groundwater and/or were close to surface-water sources such as springs, seepage areas, seasonal stream channels, floodplains, levees, low terraces and the margins of existing or former lakes. He also inferred that the earliest systems of cultivation were small-scale and locally intensive: "horticultural" rather than "agricultural" (Sherratt 1980: 313–16). Halstead (in Ch. 16 in this volume) arrives at a similar conclusion – although from different premises – when he suggests that in neolithic Greece "farming may have more closely resembled recent intensive horticulture than agriculture". In a recent paper on the beginnings of agriculture in Greece, van Andel & Runnels (1995) present a strong case for the earliest farmers having preferentially settled on higher surfaces, especially inactive levees, within floodplains, rather than in upland areas where the soils would have had low water-holding capacity; and they also refer to the observations of Dennell & Webley (1975) on Bulgaria, Barker (1975) on southern Yugoslavia, and Kosse (1979) on the Hungarian Plain, all of which show a consistent correlation between the distribution of early neolithic sites and floodplains and river and lake margins.

The implication of these studies of early neolithic site distribution in Anatolia and southeastern Europe is that seed-crop agriculture began there as a small-scale activity that focused on hydromorphic soils and developed "patchily" in the landscape. In the paper already cited, van Andel & Runnels make the further point that the areas selected for agricultural settlement in Greece and the southern Balkans appear not to have been occupied by indigenous mesolithic populations (unlike areas farther west and north in Europe, where this was not the case), and they regard this as evidence in favour of the demic-diffusion hypothesis for the beginnings of agriculture in the region. They go on to modify Ammerman & Cavalli-Sforza's (1984) demographic "wave-of-advance" model by stressing the relative sparsity and discontinuous distribution of floodplains and other "target" areas for agricultural settlement. This, they suggest, helps to account both for the relatively rapid spread of agriculture westwards that the radiocarbon chronology indicates and for the apparently paradoxical absence of palynological and other evidence for agricultural "impact" on the landscapes of the Balkans until *c*. 4000 bc (Willis & Bennett 1994). In other words, they replace the Ammerman & Cavalli-Sforza assumption of more or less continuous migration caused by continuing population growth immediately behind the advancing front of agricultural settlement, with a model of migration occurring in discrete steps, the intervals between the steps being "dictated by geography and by the population growth in each of a slowly rising number of parent areas" (van Andel & Runnels 1995: 497). In Greece, one such – perhaps the main – parent area was the Thessalian floodplain. Here, judging by the gradual increase in the number and average size of sites that occurred in the Larisa Basin during the early and middle Neolithic (a period of over 1,500 years) population growth remained low until the late Neolithic when the number of sites increased relatively rapidly in and beyond the floodplain – a process that may have led to the agricultural colonization of the southern Balkans north of Thessaly (van Andel & Runnels: ibid.).

The western Mediterranean

This model of relatively slow, step-by-step expansion of (initially small-scale) seed-crop agriculture, in neolithic southeastern Europe – driven mainly by population increase by incoming neolithic farmers but not excluding the possibility of some adoption of domesticates by indigenous mesolithic groups, as Halstead suggests (in this volume) might have occurred at Franchthi Cave in the early Neolithic – appears to fit the available archaeological, geomorphological and palynological evidence quite well. It may also help us to interpret the spread of agriculture farther west and north around the northern Mediterranean and into Central and Northwest Europe. In a recent review of models for the transition to agriculture in Mediterranean Europe, Donahue (1992) emphasized the piecemeal character of the spread of domesticates and of the "fully neolithic economy" in the region. For example, he accepts (ibid.: 76–7) the case, made by Geddes (1985) and others, for domestic sheep having reached France during the sixth millennium before the "full" neolithic economy became established there in the fifth millennium (but see Zilhão 1993: 43–5, 48–9 for a critical discussion of the stratigraphy of the caves in which the sheep remains were found, which casts severe doubt on their presence there – and in southern Spain at the site of Cova Fosca – during the Mesolithic).

In southern Italy and along the Dalmatian coast of the Adriatic, the earliest evidence for neolithic agricultural settlement dates to the first half of the sixth millennium (Whitehouse 1987, Chapman & Muller 1990), which accords well, in terms of the chronology of the Neolithic, with the region's intermediate position between eastern Greece and southern Spain, and according to Donahue (ibid.) domestic sheep (and ceramics) also appear there well before the advent of the full neolithic economy. However, in a recent discussion of the evidence for the spread of agro-pastoral economies across Mediterranean Europe, which contains a detailed review of much of the Portuguese and some of the Spanish evidence, Zilhão (1993) rejects suggestions that the transition to agriculture began there with the piecemeal introduction of pottery and of some domesticates, particularly sheep, and their adoption as prestige items acquired through long-distance exchange networks by still-mobile mesolithic communities (as proposed by Lewthwaite in 1986), with the establishment of sedentary agricultural villages occurring as much as a millennium later. Zilhão concludes that in the Iberian Peninsula and southern France the earliest Neolithic does not pre-date *c.* 4800 bc and that its beginning is signalled by the appearance of "classic" Cardial pottery, which "is associated right from the beginning with a full agro-pastoral system (ibid.: 28), a conclusion largely endorsed by Rowley-Conwy (1995: 346–8) in a recent review of the western European evidence. Zilhão also demonstrates that in central Portugal the earliest neolithic settlements occur in areas, or "enclaves", between nuclei of late mesolithic settlement in the valleys of the Tejo, Sado and Mira rivers; and he interprets this pattern as suggesting "initial settlement by small Neolithic seafaring groups in areas that were not exploited (or were only marginally exploited) by local hunter–gatherers, followed by a more or less delayed assimilation of the latter into the new economic system" (ibid.: 50). His suggestion that the initial neolithic settlers were "small seafaring groups" may seem surprising, but is not unreasonable in the light of Cherry's (1990) and Broodbank & Strasser's (1991) demonstrations of the antiquity of colonization and seafaring in the Mediterranean. And the tendency for early neolithic settlements to be concentrated in enclaves, where mesolithic settlement was sparse or non-existent, parallels the pattern in eastern Greece described by van Andel & Runnels (1995). Indeed, it may be a more general characteristic of early neolithic settlement elsewhere in Europe.

Central, northern and northwestern Europe

If the appearance of neolithic agro-pastoral economies in southern France, southeastern Spain and central Portugal was broadly contemporaneous and occurred between *c.* 4800 and *c.* 4400 bc, as Zilhão concludes, he may be right to suggest that the spread of "cardial cultures" in the western Mediterranean broadly resembles the Linearbandkeramic (LBK) expansion across Central and into Northwest Europe, which occurred in the sixth and fifth millennia. From this comparison he develops a two-phase model for the neolithization of central and western Europe (ibid.: 51–2), which is summarized in a map reproduced as Figure 5.3 in Renfrew's contribution to this volume. The first phase begins about 4800–4400 bc and is characterized by the spread of agro-pastoral settlers out of the Balkans and southern Italy northwest along the (upper) Danube and west via the Mediterranean; it is followed by a period of stabilization during which well defined but permeable boundaries exist between neolithic and mesolithic populations; and after *c.* 4000–3500 bc the second phase ensues during which "the Mesolithic groups living beyond the agricultural frontier . . . in the

Atlantic fringe of Europe – the coasts of northern Portugal, Cantabrian Spain, western France, Belgium, the Netherlands and Great Britain – are finally assimilated" (ibid.: 52). Zilhão's model is not inconsistent with evidence for the transition to agriculture in temperate Europe north of the Alpine mountain chain (the Carpathians, Alps and Pyrenees); and it also accords well with Renfrew's hypothesis (1991 and in this volume) that proto-Indo–European originated in central Anatolia and spread westwards into and through Europe as part of the neolithic "farming dispersal".

There is general (but not universal) agreement that the LBK represents colonization by immigrant farming groups who introduced to Central Europe the Southwest Asian "founder" crops and domestic animals (goats, sheep, probably cattle and possibly pigs – cf. Uerpmann in Ch. 12 in this volume for comments on the possibility of there having been several centres of cattle domestication in Southwest Asia and on the lack of information on pig domestication), and who spread eastwards and westwards across the North European Plain from Poland and the Ukraine to northern France. But the question of how they interacted with the indigenous hunter–fisher–gatherers of temperate Europe is more contentious. Keeley (1992), discussing the introduction of agriculture to the western North European Plain, maintains that the LBK farmers "completely and permanently replaced the indigenous RMS [Rhine–Meuse–Schelde] Mesolithic culture" and "avoided or even fought . . . the RMS groups living beyond the area of LBK settlement", some of whom, however, "did adopt elements of a neolithic way of life, specifically ceramics and stock-rearing" (ibid.: 92).

On the other hand, Thomas, Zvelebil and Price (in Chs 17, 18 and 19 in this volume) all emphasize the reciprocal nature and variability of neolithic/mesolithic interactions around the western and northern margins of the "core" area of LBK settlement on the loess soils of Central Europe. Thus, Thomas criticizes the concept of the Neolithic as a unified, intrusive phenomenon; stressing that "the introduction of food plants and of domestic animals, the use of pottery and of ground and polished stone tools, the emergence of sedentary villages, the first construction of earth and stone monuments and the development of new funerary practices might each have had a separate temporality" and "in some regions [of prehistoric Europe], all of the elements appeared at roughly the same time, whereas in others there were major time lags, or particular changes failed to manifest themselves altogether". He accepts that the LBK represents a "rapid colonization of a large area by a distinct population" practising "a relatively uniform subsistence strategy (cattle herding with small-scale cultivation)" and maintaining "a uniform material culture (timber-framed longhouses, band-decorated pottery and stone adzes)"; but he also argues for a reformulation of the Neolithic by the late mesolithic communities living on the North European Plain, beyond the loess zone of the LBK, who selectively appropriated elements of material culture, including crops and domestic animals from the agriculturalists by a process he felicitously describes as "judicious adoption of aspects of what the Neolithic had on offer".

This interpretation differs subtly but not in essence from those of Price and Zvelebil, who, in their analyses (in this volume) of farmer–forager interaction in southern Scandinavia and the circum-Baltic region, focus on the gradual and complex processes that gave rise first to distinctive foraging–farming communities and eventually to the more comprehensive adoption of agriculture around the northern fringe of the

North European Plain. By focusing on the nature of the transition itself, their contributions illuminate what is likely to have been a complex and variable phenomenon around the maritime margins of northern and western Europe, from northern Spain to the Baltic, where regional differences in the spatial and temporal pattern of the transition are beginning to become apparent – differences that Dennell (1992) has recently examined comprehensively from an archaeobotanical perspective.

The processes by which agriculture and pastoralism became established in prehistoric Europe as a whole are thus now seen as much more complex than was previously thought when the "demic-diffusion" model of colonization by neolithic farmers from Southwest Asia tended to be uncritically accepted. What is replacing that model is a more subtle interpretation more finely tuned to ecological, regional and cultural variation across the continent and over the 4,000 and more years that separate the earliest evidence of crops and domestic animals in Greece from that in southern Scandinavia and the British Isles (e.g. in northeastern Scotland, where domestic wheat, barley and flax have been directly dated to *c.* 2800 bc: Fairweather & Ralston 1993). The transition appears to have been initiated by small-scale colonization of well watered cultivable areas, in Greece and farther west in the Mediterranean, which were not intensively exploited by hunter–gatherers. No profound ecological adjustment was involved in this initial spread of the Southwest Asian founder crops to these areas of "Mediterranean" climate. Population densities in the "enclaves" of settled agriculturalists increased, if only gradually, and came to exceed those of the more mobile indigenous hunter–gatherer groups, and further agricultural colonization of new areas eventually took place. The most extensive (LBK) expansion was from Greece through the Balkans and into Central Europe, where settlement focused on the valley systems and loess soils. The spread of agriculture into temperate Europe north of the Alps involved a major ecological transition, from the Mediterranean lands, where summer drought was the main limitation on crop growth, to the North European Plain, where winter cold was the main limiting factor. The transition also required adjustment to the pronounced seasonal differences in day length between the two regions. It now became more difficult to maintain livestock through the winter without supplementary feeding – a problem that was partly solved by the elaboration of such techniques as hay-making and stall-feeding. A long period of coping with the new climatic conditions – and generally more acid soils – ensued before the integrated system of mixed grain–livestock farming evolved, which was to prove both ecologically sustainable and nutritionally highly effective, and during this period relatively stable but socially dynamic "frontier zones" existed between the mainly farming and mainly foraging populations. In due course, however, almost all the remaining forager groups adopted agriculture and pastoralism, and, by the middle of the third millennium, agro-pastoralism had become the dominant system of food production throughout prehistoric Europe from the Mediterranean to northern Britain, Ireland and southern Scandinavia.

Central and South Asia

Agriculture and pastoralism did not only spread into Europe from western Southwest Asia. The founder crops and domestic caprines were also dispersed eastwards across the Iranian Plateau to both Central and South Asia. Cereal agriculture based on wheat and barley, and pastoralism based on the raising of goats and sheep, were established in western Central Asia, in the relatively well watered piedmont zone along the northeastern margin of the Iranian Plateau in southern Turkmenistan, by the sixth millennium bc. Harris & Gosden discuss (in Ch. 21 in this volume) the possible antecedents of this local neolithic economy – the Jeitun Culture – which is character-ized by rectangular mudbrick architecture comparable to the early neolithic architec-ture of the Levant and Anatolia. We conclude that domestic einkorn and emmer wheat, and probably barley, sheep and goats, were introduced into southern Turkmenistan from farther west, probably via the Atrek and other upland valleys in northeastern Iran. We cannot, on present evidence, determine definitely whether this was the result mainly or entirely of colonization by migrant agriculturalists, or whether resident mes-olithic populations adopted the domesticates and agrarian techniques, but the fact that, when the Jeitun Culture appears, it does so as a "developed" neolithic economy strongly supports the former interpretation. Less is known about the beginnings of agriculture farther east in Central Asia. Some sites in northern Afghanistan and south-ern Tadjikistan, for example those of the Hissar Culture, may have been occupied sea-sonally by pastoralists, or possibly permanently by agro-pastoralists, as early as the sixth millennium, but they do not resemble the Jeitun sites in their material culture, and the evidence for agro-pastoralism is not secure (Kohl 1984: 212; Sarianidi 1992: 124).

In South Asia the site of Mehrgarh in western Pakistan has provided the earliest evidence of agro-pastoral settlement, dating to about the beginning of the seventh mil-lennium. The evidence takes the form mainly of impressions in mudbrick of domestic barley and wheat, and the bones of domestic goats, sheep and cattle (Meadow in Ch. 22 in this volume). In assessing whether these early domesticates are more likely to have been introduced or domesticated locally, Meadow concludes that wheat and goats, and probably barley and sheep, were introduced from Southwest Asia, whereas cattle – both *Bos taurus* and *Bos indicus* (zebu or humped cattle), which comprise well over 50 per cent of the faunal assemblage by the second half of the sixth millennium – may well have been domesticated locally, perhaps more than once, in eastern Iran and/or South Asia. Other early agricultural sites have been discovered along the south-eastern margin of the Iranian Plateau from central Balochistan to Kashmir, most of which are attributed to the fifth and fourth millennia and none of which has been shown to be as old as Mehrgarh (Allchin & Allchin 1982: 97–116; Meadow in this volume).

On the basis of these findings, it appears that agro-pastoralism had become estab-lished in the lowlands adjacent to the southeastern edge of the Iranian Plateau by *c.* 6000 bc and that it was dependent from the start on some at least of the Southwest Asian domesticates. It is therefore probable that it began here, as it did along the north-ern edge of the Iranian Plateau in southern Turkmenistan, as a result of diffusion from western Southwest Asia, even though some local domestication, at least of cattle, sub-sequently took place. This conclusion can be seen as lending support to Renfrew's tentative hypotheses (in this volume) concerning the origins of the proto-Dravidian and proto-Altaic languages, which propose that the former spread across southern Iran from the southern Zagros region to South Asia in association with agriculture, and that the latter originated in Turkmenia and gave rise, in association with pastoral nomadism, to the Early Altaic languages of Central Asia.

In his contribution to this volume, Meadow outlines the main changes that took place in the agricultural systems of northwestern South Asia after the earliest known agro-pastoral economy was established at Mehrgarh. He discusses the – at present rather meagre – archaeobotanical evidence for the presence of other crops of Southwest Asian, South Asian and African origin, and suggests that in the Indus Valley region a major shift took place late in the third millennium from a predominantly winter cropping (*rabi*) agricultural regime to one that also included a significant component of summer crops (*kharif*). The latter included Asian and African millets and, notably, Asian rice, which raises the much-debated question of the origin of rice as a "founder crop" of early Asian agriculture.

In their thorough review (in Ch. 23 in this volume) of the currently available archaeological evidence for the earliest cultivation and spread of domestic rice in South, Southeast and East Asia, Glover & Higham pay careful attention to the uncertainties that often relate to the identification and dating of rice remains. Although claims have been advanced for the cultivation of domestic rice in northern India, in the region of the Ganga Valley, as early as the seventh millennium bc, the chronology of the sites from which rice has been reported (Chopani–Mando, Koldihwa and Mahagara) is problematic, and in the case of Chopani–Mando the rice is reported by the archaeobotanist concerned to be wild. If these putative early finds are disregarded, it appears that rice did not become a component of South Asian agriculture until the late third millennium, when it was evidently cultivated in parts of the eastern and central Ganga Valley; and by about 2000 bc it was adopted in the area of the Indus Valley (Harappan) Civilization, probably as a component of the *kharif* system of summer cropping.

There have also been claims for very early rice cultivation in mainland Southeast Asia, particularly in Thailand, but after critically assessing the evidence Glover & Higham conclude that rice is likely to have entered Southeast Asian agriculture only in the late third millennium, probably as a result of the expansion of agricultural groups down the Mekong, Red and Chao Phraya rivers from the Yangzi Basin in central China, a process that may also have led to the introduction of domestic rice into northeastern India, perhaps via the Brahmaputra Valley from Yunnan. They speculatively associate these expansions with the southward spread of languages of the Austro–Asiatic family from Yunnan – a hypothesis that also receives support (in this volume) from Bellwood, and, more tentatively, from Renfrew.

East Asia

The relatively late appearance of domestic rice in South and Southeast Asia, probably introduced initially by migrant farmers from the north, implies that it has greater antiquity as a crop in China. Many recent discoveries of domesticated rice in archaeological contexts in the central and lower Yangzi Valley – most spectacularly at the site of Hemudu where large accumulations of rice remains have been found in almost all the excavated areas, associated with agricultural tools and dated to between 3900 and 5000 bc – have demonstrated conclusively that rice agriculture was well established by the fifth millennium and possibly earlier (see Glover & Higham's chapter in this volume for discussion of the uncertainties surrounding the identification and dating of the rice remains at the putatively sixth millennium site of Pengtoushan). From what appears on present evidence to be the earliest region of rice cultivation, in the Yangzi Valley, the crop evidently spread north from about 3000 bc and was incorporated into pre-existing systems of seed-crop agriculture in the Huanghe Valley and other parts of northern China, which were at that time based primarily on the "temperate millets" *Panicum miliaceum* (broomcorn millet), *Setaria italica* (foxtail millet) and *Echinochloa utilis* (barnyard millet). The earliest rice known archaeologically in Korea dates to *c.* 1200 bc at the site of Hunamni (Choe 1982: 520), and there are reports of occasional finds of rice in Late and Final Jomon sites in Japan (Crawford 1992: 25) dated to between 1000 and 400 bc. But, as Imamura demonstrates (in Ch. 24 in this volume), rice did not become a staple crop – raised by wet-padi methods – in southwestern Japan until the fourth century bc, whence its cultivation spread within 300 years to the whole Japanese archipelago except the northernmost island of Hokkaido.

Although there is now a coherent body of evidence for the origin and spread of rice agriculture in East Asia, we still largely lack dependable evidence for the prehistoric exploitation of other crops that were cultivated in northern China in early historical times. These include – in addition to the "temperate" millets, all three of which were probably domesticated in East Asia (although foxtail millet may have been independently domesticated elsewhere in Eurasia: Rao et al. 1987: 111) – soybean (*Glycine max*), Chinese cabbage (*Brassica campestris*) and a wide range of tree fruits and other cultigens (Crawford 1992). Botanical considerations suggest that most of these crops were domesticated in East Asia, but without adequate archaeobotanical data we can at present only infer that a wide variety of herbaceous and tree crops were cultivated in northern (and probably central and southern) China before rice agriculture became widely established.

This indirect evidence for early (pre-rice) agriculture in northern China raises the interesting question of the prehistoric presence there of domestic barley and wheat. Both crops have a long history of cultivation in East Asia. *Hordeum vulgare* subsp. *spontaneum*, the wild progenitor of domestic barley, has been reported from Tibet and Szechwan (Chang 1983: 78; Shao 1981), so its domestication in China independently of its origin as a domesticate farther west in Southwest/Central Asia cannot be completely excluded, but no archaeological finds of it have been reported from China. The earliest proven occurrence of it in East Asia comes from Korea at *c.* 1200 bc, which implies that it was grown in northern China at least by the time of the Shang Dynasty: *c.* 1700–1100 BC (Crawford 1992: 22). There is no botanical case for wheat having been domesticated in East Asia; nor is there any unequivocal archaeological evidence of its early presence in China (ibid.: 25). In the absence of firm evidence, all we can conclude is that both crops probably reached northern China from Southwest/Central Asia by the middle of the second millennium bc.

Despite the sparsity of accurately identified and dated plant and animal remains from Chinese archaeological sites, there is incontrovertible archaeological evidence for the establishment in northern China, at least by the mid-seventh millennium bc, of substantial villages, with pottery and storage pits, supported by a mixed economy of hunting, fishing, gathering, the cultivation of millets and a few other crops, and the raising of domestic pigs, dogs and probably chickens (Chang 1986: 87–95; Crawford 1992: 13–14). This evidence, and that of early rice cultivation in the Yangzi Valley, strongly suggests that agriculture began in East Asia independently of influences from Southwest Asia, although certain crops of Southwest/Central Asian origin, notably barley and wheat, and probably hemp (*Cannabis sativa*), which is thought to be of Central Asian origin (Purseglove 1968: 41), were introduced during the prehistoric period.

Southeast Asia, New Guinea and the southwestern Pacific

We can now turn our attention to the last part of Eurasia to be considered in this overview: Southeast Asia including New Guinea and the southwestern Pacific. It has already been suggested that rice is unlikely to have become a staple crop of mainland Southeast Asian agriculture until after about 3000 bc. There is very little direct archae-obotanical evidence of early plant use in the region, but it has long been regarded as the homeland of many cultivated plants, particularly root-and-tuber and tree crops (Li 1970; Harris 1981: table VII). Recent investigations of "coastal neolithic" sites in Vietnam and Thailand dated to the third millennium have yielded evidence of sedentary pottery-making communities with dogs, pigs and cattle but without evidence of plant exploitation. This negative evidence may be a function of the difficulty of retrieving and identifying the remains of the crops, such as yams and taro, which may have been staple foods before the advent of rice agriculture (as they have been historically in much of Southeast Asia), but it is also possible that the occupants of these coastal neolithic sites obtained most of their carbohydrate from wild plants and most of their protein and fats from fish, marine mammals, pigs and cattle (the bones of which are commonly recovered at these sites: Glover & Higham in this volume). Whatever the role of root "crops" may have been in the region before the arrival of rice, we have no evidence at present for the earlier widespread existence of specialized "vegecultural" systems focused on such crops. Small-scale mixed "horticultural" production of root and tree crops, and "wild" plants, in "gardens" within and near the settlements, combined with hunting, fishing, gathering and the raising of some domestic animals, is a more plausible model for the earliest system of cultivation practised in Southeast Asia (as elsewhere in the seasonally dry and humid tropics; Harris 1973: 398–401; and cf. Hather's innovative examination of the origins of tropical vegeculture in this volume).

The same generalization can be applied to the early Holocene populations of Island Southeast Asia – although there evidence of sedentary settlements with pottery is almost entirely lacking – but there is some evidence for the early development of specialized systems of root-crop production based principally on taro and yams (and latterly sweet potato). At present this phenomenon has been demonstrated archaeologically only in the intermontane valleys of highland New Guinea, and we do not know whether similar systems evolved early in the lowlands. There is also very little firm evidence on which to construct a chronology for the spread of rice through Island Southeast Asia. Isolated finds of rice have been made in the Philippines, in Sarawak and in Sulawesi, the first two of which date respectively to *c.* 1700 and *c.* 2300 bc (Glover & Higham and Bellwood (Fig. 25.4) in this volume). Bellwood argues (1991 and in this volume) that rice agriculture was introduced into the Indo–Malaysian archipelago from southern China, via Taiwan and the Philippines, by Austronesian speaking peoples after 3000 bc, a process that he believes partly overlaid somewhat earlier agricultural settlement in Sumatra, western Borneo and possibly Java and Sumbawa by speakers of Austro–Asiatic languages who had spread from the Malay Peninsula. He further proposes that the Austronesian expansion, which continued eastwards through Island Southeast Asia and spread out of the "Lapita Homeland" region of the Bismarck Archipelago into the southwestern Pacific about 1500 bc, continued the process of agricultural colonization, but that rice dropped out of the crop repertoire in the equatorial zone in eastern Indonesia. This hypothesis carries conviction, but it is complicated by the presence, in the path of the Austronesian agricultural expansion, of the very large island of New Guinea, which Golson (1977, 1991, in press), Yen (1991, 1995) and others have shown to have a distinctive agricultural history of its own.

Thanks to the archaeological, geomorphological, palynological, ethnobotanical and ethnographic fieldwork that has been carried out in the highlands of Papua New Guinea since the 1960s, a general picture of the evolution of human subsistence and environmental change there is beginning to emerge. In particular, a long sequence of cultivation and local environmental change has been revealed by the work of Golson and his colleagues at the site of Kuk Swamp in the western highlands, and much has been learned about late Pleistocene and Holocene vegetation changes in the highlands from the palaeoenvironmental investigations of Flenley, Haberle, Hope, Hughes and others (see references in Ch. 26). In Chapter 26, Bayliss-Smith reviews much of this research in relation to the long-debated question of whether (highland) New Guinea was an early and independent "centre" of agriculture. He emphasizes that the data available are still insufficient to answer that fundamental question, but he does offer a descriptive regional model (summed up in Fig. 26.4) of changing subsistence in the highlands over the past 9,000 years, and concludes that this evolutionary process has involved both "indigenous" plant domestication and "crop introductions from the outside world". The latter include the arrival in the highlands, perhaps 4,500 years ago, of taro (*Colocasia esculenta*) from the lowlands, it having been domesticated there or in Southeast Asia; the introduction, perhaps 2,500 years ago, of the greater and lesser yams (*Dioscorea alata* and *D. esculenta*), and bananas of the Eumusa section, as domesticates from Southeast Asia; and the introduction of the sweet potato (*Ipomoea batatas*), of South American origin, 300 years ago or possibly slightly earlier.

An important inference that can be drawn from Golson's sustained archaeological investigations at the Kuk Swamp (see, for example, Golson 1977, 1989, 1991, in press) is that only very small-scale production of a few (wild and possibly domesticated) plants can be inferred at the beginning of the sequence at *c.* 9000 bp, although by *c.* 6000 bp there is evidence of larger-scale cultivation of the swamp with, probably, taro as the principal crop. In a recent discussion of early agriculture in New Guinea, I have postulated an evolutionary sequence of subsistence there suggesting that:

- late Pleistocene populations in Melanesia as a whole selectively exploited a range of wild plants – particularly tree and root-and-tuber "crops" – in a system of "wild plant-food production" that foreshadowed the later development of "house-garden horticulture"
- between *c.* 10,000 and *c.* 6000 bp both small-scale wetland and shifting (swidden) cultivation were initiated
- between *c.* 6000 and *c.* 3500 bp larger-scale wetland cultivation was developed, accompanied by continued swidden cultivation and house-garden horticulture
- after *c.* 3500 bp further intensification of production took place in the highlands, but did not cause agricultural expansion into the lowlands (Harris 1995).

This last point can be seen as a particular example of what – as has already been suggested in this chapter – is a fundamental contrast between agricultural systems based mainly on seed crops, which have an inherent tendency to expand into new areas, and those based mainly on root-and-tuber and tree crops, which tend to remain localized. We would therefore not expect the agricultural systems evolved in (perhaps only parts of) the New Guinea highlands to have expanded widely or rapidly, if at all – that is, local intensification rather than spatial expansion of production could be predicted – which outcome is precisely what Golson proposed in 1977 in his "no room at the top" model.

In trying to model the evolution of subsistence in New Guinea, we need also to address the controversial question of when pigs were first introduced, probably as domestic animals, from Southeast Asia. Their presence in the highlands as long as 6,000 or even 10,000 years ago has been suggested, but recent AMS radiocarbon dates on six pig teeth from two archaeological sites (Nombe and Kafiavana) in the highlands have shown them all to be less than 500 years old (Hedges et al. 1995: 428). Finds of pig remains thought to be of early to mid-Holocene age have also been reported from lowland sites north of the highlands (Gorecki et al. 1991: 121; Swadling et al. 1991: 106–7) and at Matenbek on New Ireland (Gosden 1995: 813, where direct dating by the AMS method was unsuccessful). One – in my view strong – possibility is that pigs reached New Guinea, perhaps with some of the Southeast Asian plant domesticates such as the greater and lesser yams, as a direct or indirect result of the Austronesian expansion, the main route of which lay north of New Guinea via the Bismarck Archipelago and the Solomon Islands out into the Pacific. This supposition gains support from the fact that, according to Spriggs (in this volume), the term for pig is an Austronesian loan word in many non-Austronesian languages of New Guinea. Further general support for the view that New Guinea was essentially "by-passed" by the initial Austronesian expansion into the Pacific comes from Bellwood's statement (in this volume, following Pawley & Ross 1993) that the Austronesian languages involved in this dispersal show no signs of intensive borrowing from Papuan sources; and he also suggests that the apparent lack of Austronesian colonization of the New Guinea lowlands might reflect an environmental hazard such as malaria (Groube 1993). Despite all that has been learned since the 1960s about early human subsistence in New Guinea, many basic questions remain unanswered. The role in plant domestication of New Guinea itself is enigmatic, and there are many uncertainties about the chronology and routes of dispersal of the Southeast Asian crops and domestic animals that were introduced into the Pacific. There is a strong case for suggesting, as Spriggs does (1993 and in this volume), that the Lapita Culture of Island Melanesia – the first manifestations of which in the Bismarck Archipelago at *c.* 3500 bp are associated with village sites and distinctive pottery – signals the arrival on the threshold of the Pacific of intrusive "neolithic" agriculturalists from Southeast Asia. Their subsequent rapid spread in 500 years through the Solomon Islands and out into the uninhabited Pacific as far as New Caledonia, Fiji, Tonga and Samoa, carrying with them the staple crops and domestic animals (pig, dog, chicken) of Pacific agriculture, is one of the most dramatic episodes known of agricultural colonization – comparable, at a great geographical and chronological remove, to the less rapid but as extensive spread of the LBK farmers through neolithic Europe.

Conclusion

Vast gaps remain in our knowledge of early agriculture and pastoralism in Eurasia, but this provisional synthesis of much of what we do know suggests – to me at least – that we are observing a more unified phenomenon than is often supposed. What does *not* emerge from the evidence we have is a picture of multiple independent foci of agricultural beginnings at diverse times and places. On the contrary, the evidence best fits a model of very few – possibly only two – independent "centres" in which pristine transitions to agriculture, in the sense of dependence on the systematic cultivation of (mainly) domesticated crop plants, took place.

The most parsimonious interpretation of the available evidence suggests, first, that seed-crop agriculture based on cereals and pulses developed in western Southwest Asia during the eighth millennium bc, associated in the seventh millennium with the raising of domesticated goats and sheep, and, secondly, that seed-crop agriculture based on millets and rice, with domestic pigs and chicken, developed in East Asia, probably first in the basins of the Huanghe and Yangzi rivers, by, or possibly before, the mid-seventh millennium bc (whether separately in these two parts of China or as part of a single developmental process there we do not at present know).

This interpretation leads to a second general conclusion: that diffusion was the dominant process by which agriculture and pastoralism became established throughout the rest of Eurasia. How far this was the result of colonization by agricultural populations (demic diffusion) and how far it depended on the adoption of crops, domestic animals and agricultural techniques by hunter–gatherers remains a controversial question, but, in my view, the evidence suggests that expanding populations of seed-crop cultivators, associated in some areas with pastoralism, were mainly responsible for the spread of agriculture.

Thirdly, I conclude that the expanding agricultural and pastoral populations largely replaced or assimilated the pre-existing hunter–gatherers (where they existed), except in ecologically marginal zones where agriculture was difficult or impossible, such as the northern latitudes of Europe and Asia and the most humid tropical areas of Southeast and South Asia. However, where agricultural settlers approached these marginal zones and encountered partly sedentary groups of hunter–gatherers, as they did in places along the northern and western fringes of the North European Plain, relatively stable "frontiers" were established at which sustained social and economic interaction took place between the "intrusive" agriculturalists and the "indigenous" hunter–gatherers. We do not know whether comparable patterns of interaction developed in the humid tropical forests of South and Southeast Asia, but I suspect that the resident hunter–gatherer populations there would have been too small and too widely dispersed to "resist" the incoming agriculturalists, although in some areas they may well have evolved reciprocal economic and social relationships with larger agricultural populations of the kind known ethnographically in, for example, the Philippines (Peterson & Peterson 1977, Griffin 1989).

Although I have deliberately excluded from this essay discussion of the "why" question, and have therefore not reviewed alternative explanatory models for the origins of agriculture, I do wish to emphasize the weight of evidence in favour of there having been a link between the beginnings of agriculture in western Southwest Asia, and very possibly also in East Asia, and the drastic and widespread climatic and vegetational changes that occurred at and soon after the transition from the terminal Pleistocene to the early Holocene. This point is part of the more general "philosophical" conclusion, alluded to at the beginning of this chapter, that very particular, and therefore rare if not unique, conjunctions of circumstances brought about the initial "pristine" shift(s) from dependence on hunting and gathering to dependence on agriculture. This transition appears to have occurred at most only two or three times in the whole of Eurasia, but it gave rise to a new way of life that eventually spread from its Asian heartlands to the Atlantic coasts of Europe and to the islands of Japan and the Pacific – with truly revolutionary consequences for humanity.

References

Allchin, B. & R. Allchin 1982. *The rise of civilization in India and Pakistan*. Cambridge: Cambridge University Press.

Ammerman, A. J. & L. L. Cavalli-Sforza 1984. *The neolithic transition and the genetics of population in Europe*. Princeton: Princeton University Press.

Barker, G. 1975. Early Neolithic land use in Yugoslavia. *Proceedings of the Prehistoric Society* **41**, 85–104.

Bar-Yosef, O. & A. Belfer-Cohen 1991. From sedentary hunter–gatherers to territorial farmers in the Levant. In *Between bands and states*, S. A. Gregg (ed.), 181–202. Occasional Paper 9, Center for Archaeological Investigations, Southern Illinois University.

— 1992. From foraging to farming in the Mediterranean Levant. In Gebauer & Price (1992: 21–48).

Bellwood, P. S. 1991. The Austronesian dispersal and the origin of languages. *Scientific American* **265**(1), 88–93.

Broodbank, C. & T. S. Strasser 1991. Migrant farmers and the Neolithic colonization of Crete. *Antiquity* **65**, 233–45.

Byrd, B. F. 1992. The dispersal of food production across the Levant. In Gebauer & Price (1992: 49–61).

Chang, K. C. 1986. *The archaeology of ancient China*, 4th edn. New Haven: Yale University Press.

Chang, T. T. 1983. The origins and early cultures of the cereal grains and food legumes. In *The origins of Chinese civilization*, D. N. Keightley (ed.), 65–94. Berkeley: University of California Press.

Chapman, J. & J. Muller 1990. Early farmers in the Mediterranean Basin: the Dalmatian evidence. *Antiquity* **64**, 127–34.

Cherry, J. F. 1990. The first colonization of the Mediterranean islands: a review of recent research. *Journal of Mediterranean Archaeology* **3**, 145–221.

Choe, C-P. 1982. The diffusion route and chronology of Korean plant domestication. *Journal of Asian Studies* **41**, 519–29.

Crawford, G. W. 1992a. Prehistoric plant domestication in East Asia. In *The origins of agriculture: an international perspective*, C. W. Cowan & P. J. Watson (eds), 7–38. Washington: Smithsonian Institution Press.

de Moulins, D. 1993. Les restes de plantes carbonisées de Cafer Höyük. *Cahiers de l'Euphrate* **7**, 191–234.

Dennell, R. W. 1992. The origins of crop agriculture in Europe. In *The origins of agriculture: an international perspective*, C. W. Cowan & P. J. Watson (eds), 71–100. Washington DC: Smithsonian Institution Press.

Dennell, R. W. & D. Webley 1975. Prehistoric settlement and land use in southern Bulgaria. In *Palaeoeconomy*, E. S. Higgs (ed.), 97–110. Cambridge: Cambridge University Press.

Donahue, R. E. 1992. Desperately seeking Ceres: a critical examination of current models for the transition to agriculture in Mediterranean Europe. In Gebauer & Price (1992: 73–80).

Fairweather, A. D. & I. B. M. Ralston 1993. The Neolithic timber hall at Balbridie, Grampian Region, Scotland: the building, the date, the plant macrofossils. *Antiquity* **67**, 313–23.

Gebauer, A. B. & T. D. Price (eds) 1992. *Transitions to agriculture in prehistory* [Monographs in World Archaeology 4]. Madison: Prehistory Press.

Geddes, D. S. 1985. Mesolithic domestic sheep in West Mediterranean Europe. *Journal of Archaeological Science* **12**, 25–48.

Golson, J. 1977. No room at the top: agricultural intensification in the New Guinea Highlands. In *Sunda and Sahul: prehistoric studies in Southeast Asia, Melanesia and Australia*, J. Allen, J. Golson, R. Jones (eds), 601–38. London: Academic Press.

— 1989. The origins and development of New Guinea agriculture. In Harris & Hillman (1989: 678–87.

— 1991b. Bulmer Phase II: early agriculture in the New Guinea Highlands. In *Man and a half: essays in Pacific anthropology and ethnobiology in honour of Ralph Bulmer*, A. Pawley (ed.), 484–91. Polynesian Society Memoir 48, The Polynesian Society, Auckland.

— in press. From horticulture to agriculture in the New Guinea Highlands: a case study of people and their environments. In *Historical ecology of the Pacific Islands: prehistoric environmental and landscape change*, P. V. Kirch & T. L. Hunt (eds). New Haven, Connecticut: Yale University Press.

Gorecki, P., M. Mabin, J. Campbell 1991. Archaeology and geomorphology of the Vanimo Coast, Papua New Guinea: preliminary results. *Archaeology in Oceania* **26**, 119–22.

Goring-Morris N. 1993. From foraging to herding in the Negev and Sinai: the Early to Late Neolithic transition. *Paléorient* **19**, 65–90.

Gosden, C. 1995. Arboriculture and agriculture in coastal Papua New Guinea. In *Transitions: Pleistocene to Holocene in Australia and Papua New Guinea*, J. Allen & J. F. O'Connell (eds), 807–17. *Antiquity* **69** [Special Number].

Griffin, P. B. 1989. Hunting, farming, and sedentism in a rain forest foraging society. In *Farmers as hunters: the implications of sedentism*, S. Kent (ed.), 60–70. Cambridge: Cambridge University Press.

Groube, L. 1993. Contradictions and malaria in Melanesian and Australian prehistory. In *A community of culture: the people and prehistory of the Pacific*, M. Spriggs, D. E. Yen, W. Ambrose, R. Jones, A. Thorne, A. Andrews (eds), 164–86. Occasional Papers in Prehistory 21, Department of Prehistory, Research School of Pacific Studies, Australian National University.

Harris, D. R. 1972. The origins of agriculture in the tropics. *American Scientist* **60**, 180–93.

— 1973. The prehistory of tropical agriculture: an ethnoecological model. In *The explanation of culture change: models in prehistory*, C. Renfrew (ed.), 391–417. London: Duckworth.

— 1977. Settling down: an evolutionary model for the transformation of mobile bands into sedentary communities. In *The evolution of social systems*, J. Friedman & M. J. Rowlands (eds), 401–17. London: Duckworth.

— 1981. The prehistory of human subsistence: a speculative outline. In *Food, evolution and nutrition: food as an environmental factor in the genesis of human variability*, D. N. Walcher & N. Kretchmer (eds), 15–35. New York: Masson.

— 1984. Ethnohistorical evidence for the exploitation of wild grasses and forbs: its scope and archaeological implications. In *Plants and ancient man: studies in palaeoethnobotany*, W. van Zeist & W. A. Casparie (eds), 63–9. Rotterdam: Balkema.

— 1989. An evolutionary continuum of people–plant interaction. In Harris & Hillman (1989: 11–26).

— 1990. *Settling down and breaking ground: rethinking the Neolithic Revolution*. Twaalfde Kroon-Voordracht. Amsterdam: Stichting Nederlands Museum voor Anthropologie en Praehistorie.

— 1995. Early agriculture in New Guinea and the Torres Strait divide. In *Transitions: Pleistocene to Holocene in Australia and Papua New Guinea*, J. Allen & J. F. O'Connell (eds), 848–54. *Antiquity* 69 [Special Number].

Harris, D. R. & G. C. Hillman (eds) 1989. *Foraging and farming: the evolution of plant exploitation*. London: Unwin Hyman.

Hedges, R. E. M., R. A. Housley, C. Bronk Ramsey, G. J. van Klinken 1995. Radiocarbon dates from the Oxford AMS system: *Archaeometry* datelist 20. *Archaeometry* **37**, 417–30.

Henry, D. O. 1989. *From foraging to agriculture: the Levant at the end of the Ice Age*. Philadelphia: University of Pennsylvania Press.

Keeley, L. H. 1992. The introduction of agriculture to the western North European Plain. In Gebauer & Price (1992: 81–95).

Kohl, P. L. 1984. *Central Asia: palaeolithic beginnings to the Iron Age* [Synthèse 14]. Paris: Editions Recherche sur les Civilisations.

Kosse, K. 1979. *Settlement ecology of the Early and Middle Neolithic Körös and Linear Pottery Cultures in Hungary*. Oxford: British Archaeological Reports, International Series 64.

Lee, R. B. 1972. Population growth and the beginnings of sedentary life among the !Kung bushmen. In *Population growth: anthropological implications*, B. Spooner (ed.), 329–42. Cambridge, Massachusetts: MIT Press.

— 1980. Lactation, ovulation, infanticide and women's work: a study of hunter–gatherer population regulation. In *Biosocial mechanisms of population regulation*, M. N. Cohen, R. Malpass, H. Klein (eds), 321–48. New Haven, Connecticut: Yale University Press.

Lewthwaite, J. 1986. The transition to food production: a Mediterranean perspective. In *Hunters in transition: mesolithic societies of temperate Eurasia and their transition to farming*, M. Zvelebil (ed.), 53–66. Cambridge: Cambridge University Press.

Li, H. 1970. The origin of cultivated plants in Southeast Asia. *Economic Botany* **24**, 3–19.

McCorriston, J. & F. Hole 1991. The ecology of seasonal stress and the origins of agriculture in the Near East. *American Anthropologist* **93**, 46–69.

Molleson, T. 1994. The eloquent bones of Abu Hureyra. *Scientific American* **270**(8), 59–65.

Pawley, A. K. & M. Ross 1993. Austronesian historical linguistics and culture history. *Annual Review of Anthropology* **22**, 425–59.

Peterson, J. T. & W. Peterson 1977. Implications of contemporary and prehistoric exchange systems. In *Sunda and Sahul: prehistoric studies in Southeast Asia, Melanesia and Australia*, J. Allen, J. Golson, R. Jones (eds), 533–64. London: Academic Press.

Purseglove, J. W. 1968. *Tropical crops: dicotyledons 1*. London: Longman.

Rao, K. E. P., J. M. J. de Wet, D. E. Brink, M. H. Mengesha 1987. Infraspecific variation and systematics of cultivated *Setaria italica*, foxtail millet (Poaceae). *Economic Botany* **41**, 108–16.

Renfrew, C. 1991. Before Babel: speculations on the origins of linguistic diversity. *Cambridge Archaeological Journal* **1**, 3–23.

— 1992. Archaeology, genetics and linguistic diversity. *Man* **27**, 445–78.

Rindos, D. 1984. *The origins of agriculture: an evolutionary perspective*. London: Academic Press.

Roberts, N. 1991. Late Quaternary geomorphological change and the origins of agriculture in south central Turkey. *Geoarchaeology* **6**, 1–26.

Rowley-Conwy, P. 1995. Making first farmers younger: the west European evidence. *Current Anthropology* **36**, 346–53.

Sarianidi, V. 1992. Food-producing and other neolithic communities in Khorasan and Transoxania: eastern Iran, Soviet Central Asia and Afghanistan. In *History of civilizations of Central Asia* (vol. 1), A. H. Dani & V. M. Masson (eds), 109–26. Paris: UNESCO.

Sauer, C. O. 1952. *Agricultural origins and dispersals*. New York: American Geographical Society.

Shao, Q. 1981. The evolution of cultivated barley. *Barley genetics* **4** [Proceedings of the 4th International Barley Genetics Symposium, Edinburgh], 22–5.

Sherratt, A. 1980. Water, soil and seasonality in early cereal cultivation. *World Archaeology* **11**, 313–30.

Spriggs, M. 1993. Island Melanesia: the last 10,000 years. In *A community of culture: the people and prehistory of the Pacific*, M. Spriggs, D. E. Yen, W. Ambrose, R. Jones, A. Thorne, A. Andrews (eds), 187–205. Occasional Papers in Prehistory 21, Department of Prehistory, Research School of Pacific Studies, Australian National University.

Swadling, P., N. Araho, B. Ivuyo 1991. Settlements associated with the inland Sepik–Ramu Sea. In *Indo–Pacific prehistory 1990* (vol. 2), P. S. Bellwood (ed.), 92–112 Canberra and Jakarta: IPPA and Asosiasi Prehistorisi Indonesia. *Bulletin of the Indo–Pacific Prehistory Association* **11**.

van Andel, T. H. & C. N. Runnels 1995. The earliest farmers in Europe. *Antiquity* **69**, 481–500.

van Zeist, W. & J. G. de Roller. The plant husbandry of Aceramic Cayönü, SR Turkey. *Palaeohistoria* **33/34**, 65–96.

Whitehouse, R. 1987. The first farmers in the Adriatic and their position in the Neolithic of the Mediterranean. In *Premières communautés paysannes en Mediterranée occidentale*, J. Guilaine, J. Courtin, J-L. Roudil, J-L. Vernet (eds), 357–66. Paris: CNRS.

Willcox, G. 1995. Wild and domestic cereal exploitation: new evidence from Early Neolithic sites in the northern Levant and south-eastern Anatolia. *Arx World Journal of Prehistoric and Ancient Studies* **1**, 9–16.

Willis, K. J. & K. D. Bennett 1994. The Neolithic transition – fact or fiction? Palaeoecological evidence from the Balkans. *The Holocene* **4**, 326–30.

Yen, D. E. 1991. Domestication: the lessons from New Guinea. In *Man and a half: essays in Pacific anthropology and ethnobiology in honour of Ralph Bulmer*, A. Pawley (ed.), 558–69. Memoir 48, The Polynesian Society, Auckland.

— 1995. The development of Sahul agriculture with Australia as bystander. In *Transitions: Pleistocene to Holocene in Australia and Papua New Guinea*, 831–47. *Antiquity* **69** [Special Number].

Zilhão, J. 1993. The spread of agro-pastoral economies across Mediterranean Europe: a view from the far west. *Journal of Mediterranean Archaeology* **6**, 5–63.

H. sativum 51, 79, 148, **213**, 214, 377, 554, 563
H. sphaerococcum "shot" 394
H. vulgare, subsp. *vulgare* six-row 393
Harappan civilization 393, 394, 400, 417
barley, wild (*Hordeum* spp.) 42–3, 183, 189, 191
  genetics of 147, 154, 155–6
  H. murinum (wall barley) 177, 180, 182
  H. vulgare 143, **144**
    subsp. *spontaneum* 148, 161, 188, **213**, 214, 296, 381, 384, 393, 565
    subsp. *vulgare* (*nudum*) naked six-row 303, 377, 393
barrows, long 317, 349, 351, 356
Basque language 57, 65, 72, 87
Basque people, anomaly of 54, *61–3*, 64, 65, 86
Basta (Jordan) 218, 475
  caprines at 209, *246*, *247*, 255, *255*, 259, 554
Beaker culture *see* Trichterbeckerkultur (TRB)
bean
  domesticated 51
  Vicia faba (broad/faba) 144
  Vigna spp. 396, 400, 451
Beidha (Jordan) 21, 554
  caprines 208, *246*, 254, *255*, 259
Beisamoun (Israel) 209, 218, 253
Bekaa Valley 41, 555
Belgium 316, 560
bezoar *see* goat, wild
birds 188, **212**, 530–1
Bismarck archipelago (Melanesia) 472, 484, 487, 528, 567, 568, 569
  Lapita Culture and 529–30
  see also New Ireland
bitter vetch (*Vicia ervilia*) 143, **144**, 155, **213**, 303, 554
Bjørnsholm (Denmark), "kitchen midden" 351
blackbuck (*Antilope cervicapra*) 402, 404
boar (*Sus scrofa*) *see* pig, wild
Boat Axe Culture 331, 335, 340
bog deposits 317, 349, 356–7, 358
Bolling Allerød Interstadial 168, 171, 173, 264, 268, 270–1
Borneo 471, 473, 483, 567
Borneo/Kalimantan 425–6, 480
"bottlenecks", and origins of agriculture 133, 135, *135*, *136*
boundaries *see* agricultural frontier
Bouqras (Syria) 210, 270, 475, 554
Boyacá (Colombia) 19–20
Brahmaputra Valley 78, 419, 435, 564
Brassica spp. 396, 565

bricks (mud/clay)
  grain impressions 373, 398–400, 563
  plant temper 377
British Isles 82, 231, 317, 318, 560, 562
bronze 37, 419, 442
  artefacts 422–3, *423*, *424*, 433
broomrapes, food plants 178
buckthorn (*Rhamnus palaestina*) 183, 187
buckwheat (*Fagopyrum esculentum*) 453
buffalo, domesticated 51, 404–5, 426
buffalo, water
  (*Bubalus arnee*) 403
  (*Bubalus bubalis*) 402, 471, 477
bulbs, edible 182
burials 421
  dog 283, 332–3, 380
  grave goods 332, 460
  inhumations 318, 348
  Japan 451, 455, 461
  megalithic tombs 350
  Northwest Europe 318, 351
  single individuals 358, 460
  see also barrows; cemetery evidence
Burma 78, 419
burning to enhance yields 161, 177, 179, 182, 191, 276–7, 422, 525, 531
Burqu (Jordan) 211, **212**, 218

Cafer Höyük (Turkey) 241, 243, *244*, 246, 258, 556
California 33, 41
caltrop, water (*Trapa natans*) 428
Cambodia 423, 433, 434
camel, domesticated 54, 282, 284, 402, 406
  Bactrian 55, 288, 405, 406
  dromedary 55–6, 286, 287–8
    dispersal process 282, 291
    in India 284–5, 288–90
    pastoralism 285–7
    products 285, 286, 290–1
camel, wild **212**
Çan Hasan (Turkey) 241, 554, 558
cannabis 39, 566
caprines
  domestication of 263, 264, 276–8, 297, 554
  mixed herds 218, 219, 220–1
  pastoralism at Jeitun 379–80, 383
  sites in eastern Jordan **212**, 215, 220, 556
  see also animal bones; goat; ibex; sheep
carbonization *see* charcoal; charred plant remains
Caspian mesolithic cultures 382–3
Caspian Sea 148
caste system 56, 58, 284–5, 289–90, 291
Casuarina sp., tree crop 511, 513, 518

cat, steppe 379
Çatal Hüyük (Turkey) 1, 475, 558
cattle, domesticated 138, 263, 364, 403–4
   Bos indicus zebu (humped) 402, 403, 563
   Bos taurus 402, 563
   Europe 313, 314, 350, 561
   in Greece 297, 298, 302
   origins of 51, 52, 67, 236, 403, 561
   South Asia 283, 379, 402, 563
   Southeast Asia 421, 426, 566
   traded 334
   uses of 54, 405, 406
cattle, wild *see* aurochs
Caucasian languages 57, 72, 74, 75, **76**
Caucasus region 60, *62*, 85–6, 152
caves and rockshelters
   Greece 296–8, *299*–301, *303*, 559
   Island Melanesia 528, 529
   Japan 445, 446
   New Guinea 504, 506–7
   Southeast Asia 419–20, 421, 426, 432, 476
   Southwest Asia 267–8, 373, 382–3
Çayönü (Turkey) 475, 554, 556
   caprine bones 209, 238, 241, 244–7, *245*,
   246–7, 248, 258
cemetery evidence 348, 422
   demographic 108–9, 110, 121, 122, 124
   of social status 316, 332–3, 422
   see also burials
Cenozoic era, climatic history of 132, 136
Central America 51, 75, 473, 488, 489
Central Asia 233, 370, 372–3, 563
   nomadic expansion from 55, 76, 81–2
   see also Jeitun Culture; Kurgan Culture;
   Turkmenistan
Central Europe
   cultural groups *315*
   spread of agriculture 559, 561
   spread of Indo–European languages 82, 561
centres of origin (of cultivated plants) 1, 5–7,
   51–2, 134, 372, 532, 552, 569
   and language families source regions 468–9,
   469, **470**
cereal agriculture 76, 81, 318, 330
   extensive 301–2, 305
   harvesting evidence 233, 377–8, 401, 474,
   475
      rice 422, *424*, 478
   intensive 303, 304–5
   see also domestication
cereals
   DNA analysis of ancient 97–9
   founder crops 142, 143, 144–5, **144**, 554
   see also barley; einkorn wheat; emmer wheat;
   pulses; wheat

cereals, wild 33–4, 39, 42–3, 183
   early cultivation of 193–4, 266, 555
   in oak-park zone 30–1, 162–3, 191
Cerny Culture 314, 317, 319, 320
Chagylly (Turkmenistan) 373, 374, 379, 381
Chao Phraya river 419, 423, 564
chaos theory 25, 29
charcoal 393
   clay and soil 428
   wood 168, 171, 269, 364, 365, 486
charred plant remains 98, 168, 171
   Britain 318, 319
   Mehrgarh 393–4, 395–6
   rice 416, 426, 428, 432
Chenopodiaceae
   annual (*Chenolea arabica*) 183, 214
   perennial 176, 179, 183
chick pea (*Cicer* spp.) 150–1, *151*, **213**
   (*C. arietinum* subsp. *reticulatum*) 143, **144**,
   155, 396, 400, 554
chicken, domestic 236, 471, 477, 530, 533, 566
China 55, 83, 380, 413, 460–1, 482, 490, 564
   Central **39**, 40–1
      rice cultivation in 426–30, *427*, **428**, *430*
   languages 66, 473, 482–4
   millets in 401, 565
   North 66–7, 431
      centre of origin 5, 6, **39**, 40–1, 51
   origins of agriculture 66, 444–5, 471, 477–
   84, 565–6, 569
   pottery 426, 444–5, 477, 481–2, 566
   settlements 428, 432, 477, 566
   South 51, 434
   tools 426, 428, **428**, *429*, 444
   see also Hemudu
Chopan (Turkmenistan) 374, 381
Chopani Mando (India) 416, 564
Christ's thorn (*Paliurus spina-Christi*) 183,
   187
Cishan (China) 444, 477
climatic change 28, 40, 51–2, 94, 136, 161,
   277, 555, 562
   amelioration 103–4, 123, 213, 264, 273,
   473–4, 478
   Atlantic/Suboreal period 331, 354–5
   desertification 105, 133, 135
   and disease 111–12, 123–4
   effect of temperature 42–3, 181, 275, 391,
   562
   increasing aridity 28, 105, 124, 168, 171
   increasing variability 28, 161, 182–3, 187,
   192, 195
   plate tectonics and 131–2
   Pleistocene/Holocene transition 28, 40, 187,
   229, 555, 570

seasonal drought 33, 39–41, **39**, 42–3, 538–9, 545–6, 562
seasonal insolation 43, 182
seasonal rainfall 478, 485, 501
Southeast/eastern Asia 477–8
Southwest Asia 159, *160*, 161, 174–5, 267
see also Bolling Allerød Interstadial; environmental changes; Glacial Maximum; Ice Age; pollen analysis; Younger Dryas
"climax" state of vegetation **28**, 31–2, 33
coastal sites 560
north European 317, 339, 348, 349, 350
Southeast Asia 421, 486, 566
coconut, New Guinea 486
coevolution 35–6, 93–4, 488, 553
collection (gathering) **4**, 12–13, 17, 20, 474, 525
see also food; hunter–gatherers; production
Colombia, peasant farmers' view of land 19–20
colonization 57, 407, 455–7, 460, 476, 563
during Pleistocene 103, 105, 106, **106**
as exceptional 346, 350–1, 359, 489
initial 54, 57, 70, **76**, 82, 526–7
and spread of agriculture 298, 393, 482, 490, 532, 556–7, 562, 569
and spread of languages 70, **76**, 467–8, 471, 473, 483–4
see also demic diffusion; Lapita Culture; Linearbandkeramik; rate of advance
complex sedentary foraging 474, 526, 555, 570
adoption of neolithic elements 316–17, 318–20, 560–1
Baltic/southern Scandinavia 331–3, 339, 347, 357–8, 359–60, 562
Island Melanesia 526, 528, 530, 533
Japan 442–3, 450, 451, 453, 457, 459
copper, artefacts 350, 357
Corded Ware (Boat Axe) Culture 331, 335, 340
cork, from *dehesa* oak groves 364, 365
corms, structure and growth 539, 542–3, *543*
Corsica, *dehesa* oak groves 364
cotton (*Gossypium* spp.) 396–7
Crete 296, 298, 300, 303
crucifers (mustard) 180, 182, 183
cultivation
defined 21–3, 193, 525, 533, 548, 569
of plant foods **4**, 134, 135, 161, 276, 397, 527, 546–7, 568
small-scale **4**, 548, 553, 555, 558, 562
see also domestication; horticulture
cultural attitudes 392
to animals 282–4, 286, 290–1
cultural constraints, on reproduction 104–5, 108–9
cultural diffusion 7, 52, 359, 457, 460

culture
as behaviour 227
hybridity 316, 319
non-linear interaction with nature 26, 36, 482, 519
Cyprus 475

dairying 210, 219, 221, 303, 557
camel milk 285, 286, 290
caprine 380
Dam Dam Chashma cave (Turkmenistan) 383
Damascus region 207
caprines in 209, 252–3, 554
see also Aswad
Danebury hillfort (England) 98–9
Danube river 82, 560
Danubian Culture 314, 351
see also Linearbandkeramik
dates
Choerospondia axillaris (type) 428
Phoenix dactylifera 396
Dawenkou Culture, China 481
Daxi Culture, Yangzi Valley 428
deer 243, 402, 451
fallow (*Dama mesopotamica*) 234, 235
red (*Cervus elaphus*) 234, 235, 244, 270, 296
roe (*Capreolus capreolus*) 234, 235
dehesa oak grove 363–4
production system 364–7
demic diffusion 52–4, **77**, 95–6, 324, 333, 359, 383, 417, 558, 562, 569
genetic evidence and 53–4, **87**, 96–7
and spread of language 7, 473
see also colonization; diffusion; indigenous adoption
Denmark 231, 314, 335, 346–7, 348, 354–5, 356
see also Saltbaek Vig; Scandinavia, southern
desert steppe *164*, 165, *165*, 178, 179
desertification 105, 133, 135
Dhuweila (Jordan) **212**, **213**, 214, 217–18, 220
Dian Culture, Yunnan (China) 422
diet 557
diffusion
cultural 7, 52, 359, 457, 460
of farming technology 52, 310–11
role of 7–8, 489, 552, 569
theory of 25–6, 36–7
see also demic diffusion; independent invention; language
dinosaurs, extinction of 131
Dioscoreaceae 538, 539, 540, 543, 545–6, 547
sympodial growth 541, 543–4, *544*
see also yam

disease, infectious 73, 117, 334
    density-dependent disease (DDD) 110, 112–
        14, 115, 116, 119, 557
    epidemic interval 113–15, 116
    high-mortality epidemic 110, 113
        measles 110, 115
    low-mortality endemic 111
    macroparasitic 112
    mutability of microbes 111–12
    and population stagnation 113–20, 123–5
    progression of 114–15, 116–17
    rare high mortality 112
    vector-borne 112–13, 122, 123, 124
        see also malaria
    zoonotic (plague) 111, 112–13
disease, non-infectious 108, 109
diversity
    cultural 310, 313, 330–3, 348, 561
    language 73, 74–6, **76**, 77–85, 482–3, 491
    and niche concept 229
    of plant species 149–53
DNA
    ancient 88, 96–9
    chloroplast 148, 155–6
    mitochondrial 85, 88, 403
    nuclear 85, 99
    plastid 99
    polymorphism of founder crops 147–8
Dobe !Kung hunter–gatherers 117, 118, 121,
    122
dog
    burials 283, 332–3, 380
    domestic
        China 477, 566
        at Jeitun 378, 379, 380
        north Vietnam 421
        Remote Oceania 530, 532, 533
    domestication of 229–31, *230*, 263, 282–3
Dogon people, Mali 19
domestication
    centres of 51–2, 208–10, 258–9, 264
    and change in human attitudes 21–2, 23, 392
    and development of agriculture 71, 525,
        533, 553
    events 6–7, **38**, 142, 532, 556
    process of 194, 273–8, 312, 474, 478, 548,
        553
    as selective breeding 20–1, 232, 548
    theories of 14, 26, 93–4, 209–10, 393, 474–
        5
    timing of 264–7, 277–8
    see also domestication, of animals; domesti-
        cation, of plants
domestication, of animals 6, 21, 22, 263
    dog (wolf) 229–31, *230*, 263, 282–3

    herbivores 231–6
    local 298–9, 563
    multiple events 397, 404
    niche concept 230, 235–6
    recognition criteria 239–40, 242
    single event 232, 259, 273, 397, 553
    suitability of species 235, 274, 474, 489
    taming 231, 233, 234–5, 276, 282–3, 553
    see also animals, domesticated; camel; dog;
        goat; sheep
domestication, of plants 194
    characteristics of 207, 546–7
    genetics of 96–9, 145–8, 153–4, 525, 547
    local 81, 299
    multiple events 6, 96, 154, 155–6
    single event 6, 96, 142, 148, 149–51, 154,
        155–6, 474, 553
    suitability of species 149–53, 474, 489
    wild species unchanged 21, 525, 548
    see also cereals; plant foods; plants,
        cultivated
Dong Ting, Lake (Yangzi Valley) 428, 430,
    430
Dongson Culture, bronze artefacts 422, *423*,
    424
donkey (*Equus asinus*), domesticated 84, 236,
    402, 405, 406
Dravidian languages 56–7, 66, 72, 81, 472, 563

ecology
    of *dehesa* oak groves 365–6
    and farming dispersal 77, 331, 562
    and misconceptions about nature 27–34, **28**
    non-equilibrium view of nature 25, 28–30,
        526, 553
    and social context 26–7
    of wild cereals 42–3
ecosystems, concept of 27, 28, 36, 95
ecotones (transitional habitat zones) 5, 134
    North Kachi Plain 385, 395, 402, 406
    park woodland and woodland steppe 176,
        187
    plant domestication at 474–5, 479
Egypt 51, 136, 419
einkorn wheat, cultivated/domesticated
    (*Triticum monococcum* subsp. *monococcum*)
    153, 154, 155, 395, 556
    in Greece 297, 303
    at Jeitun 377, 381, 563
    Levant 207, **213**, 214, 215, 220, 554
einkorn wheat, wild (*Triticum monococcum*)
    41, 42, 143, **144**, 187–9, 215
    eastern Jordan **213**, 214, 215, 220
    present distribution of 162–3, *162*, 207, 215,
        555

subsp. *boeoticum* 153, 161–2, 188, **213**, 214, 381
subsp. *urartu* 153, 161–2, 188
Elamite language (Elamo–Dravidian) 57, **76**, *80*, 81, 88
elephant (*Elaphus maximus*) 403
emmer wheat, cultivated/domesticated 159, 207, 220, 554, 556
   Triticum dicoccum 99, 214, 395
      in Greece 296, 297, 299, 303
      at Jeitun 377, 563
emmer wheat, wild
   Triticum timopheevii 151–2, *152*
   Triticum turgidum 42–3, 189, 191, 381
      founder cereal crop 143, **144**
      genetics of 147, 154, 155
      and sibling species 151–3, *152*
energy thresholds model 500, 516–18, 519
energy yields from wild plant-foods 180–3
environmental changes 354–5, 547
   at Pleistocene/Holocene transition 7, 93–4, 105, 134–5, 490, 555
   at Younger Dryas 207–8, 555
   see also climatic change; sea levels
epidemics *see* disease
equids 217, 220, 402
   see also donkey; horse; onager/ass
Ertebølle mesolithic culture 314, 316, 347, 348–9, 354
   adoption of farming 339, 350–1
   variations within 332–3, 348–9
es-Sultan (Jericho) 238, 252, 253, 259
Eskimo–Aleut languages 73, **76**, 84
Ethiopia 52, 80
ethnography
   in New Guinea 505–6, 519
   and rate of advance 52–3, 312
   see also hunter gatherers
Etpiti rockshelter (New Guinea) 506, 514
Euphrates–Tigris region 57, 180, 204, 270, 554
Europe 55, 76, 104, 137, 401, 562
   spread of agriculture to 51, 52, 53–4, 95, 312, 471, 559
   spread of Indo–European languages to 82, 86–8, **87**
   see also Central Europe; Mediterranean; Northwest Europe
evolutionary theory
   gradualism in 34, 37–8, 39
   Lamarckian 466
   and non-equilibrium view of nature 25, 94
   as progressive **28**, 34
   see also coevolution
exchange 385, 421, 457
   among hunter–gatherers 331, 474, 519, 526

between farmers and foragers 324, 328, 333, 334–5, 349, 358, 556
   prestige 314, 320, 335, 560
   see also trade
exotic goods, status and 314, 356, 358, 360
extinctions 97, 276
   species 94, 131, 530–1

farmers 15–16
   conflict/competition with foragers 337–40, *338*, 349
   interaction with hunter–gatherers 313, 326, 333–7, *335–8*, 339–41, 355, 357–8
      intermarriage 53, 59, 324, 333, 339
   relations with pastoral nomads 56, 58–9, 60
   see also hunter–gatherers
farming dispersal
   genetic evidence 85–9, *87*
   and languages 70, 74, 75, 76–85, **76**, **77**, *79*, *80*, *83*, 560
   see also indigenous adoption of farming; three-stage model; wave of advance model
fecundity 77, 101, 104, 120, 193
   and fertility 120–3
Fertile Crescent 136, 165, 196
   early cereals in 41, 193–4
   plant foods of 178–81
   see also Iraq; Jordan; Levant; Syria
Fertile Crescent, northern
   climatic changes in 159, *160*, 161
   steppe vegetation 176–81, *190*
   wild einkorn 187–9
   woodland 183, 186–7, *190*, 195
fig (*Ficus carica*) 213
figurines
   animals 288, 380, 382
   bronze 422
   clay 271, 380, 382
   draft cattle 302, 403, 405
   human 305, 306, 451
Fiji (Polynesia) 530, 569
Finland 329–30, 331
fire
   as natural disturbance 30, 32, 33–4
   see also burning
fish and fishing **4**, 378, 421, 566
   fish weirs 348, 451
   Japan 446, 449–50, 451
   marine foods 331, 348, 421, 566
   see also molluscs; shells
flax (linseed) (*Linum* spp.) 396
   L. usitatissimum 143, **144**, 155, 395, 554
flint mines 317, 349, 350, 357
food
   collection (foraging) 12–13, 20, 525

processing 120, 444, 449, 460
storage 192, 304–5, 474, 477
see also production
food resource management (FRM) 264, 276
 Baltic region 331, 354–5
 in Greece 303, 304
food resources
 local abundance 359, 423, 555
 need to increase 124, 234, 474–5, 555
 new 105, 107
 see also animals, game; plant foods
foragers and foraging *see* food, collection;
 hunter–gatherers; plant foods
forest clearance 350, 483
 Island Melanesia 525–6, 528, 530, 531
 New Guinea 500, 503–4, 506, 508, 510,
  512–13
forest management 538
 New Guinea 508, 511, *515*, 518
forest steppe, late Pleistocene *164*, 165, *165*,
 384
fox 218, 234, 379
France 65, 316, 317, 318, 365
 farming dispersal to 82–3, 559–60
 pottery 316, 560
Franchthi cave (Greece) 296–8, 299–301, 559
frog, as food 234
frontier *see* agricultural frontier
fruits 318, 476
 tree 271, 277, 426, 484, 485, 565
 see also nuts
fur (animal), traded 334–5, 511

galangal (*Alpinia* spp.) 541, 545
Ganga Valley 413, 419, 564
Ganj Dareh (Iran) 271, 277, 385, 475
 goat bone analysis 241, 242, *244*, *246*, 249–
  51, *249–51*, *255*, 258
 goat management at 208, 240, 273, 276
 sheep bones 241, *247*, 251–2
gathering *see* collection; hunter–gatherers
gazelle 188, 210, 234, 235, 256, 270, 277, 379
 bone finds 208, 209, 242, 255, 257, 404
 in Levant **212**, 215, 217–18, 220, 271
 at Mehrgarh 402, 403
gene frequencies
 and chronology 64–5
 principal components (PC) analysis 53, 56,
  60–1, *61–3*, 86–7, *87*
genetic gradients
 in demic diffusion 53, 59, 324, 330
 in pastoral nomadic expansions 57–60
genetic isolation, and domestication 230, 232
genetic selection, and animal size 240
genetic transformation, co-evolutionary 93–4

genetics, *see also* DNA
genetics, of crops 26, 27, 37, 42, 155–6
 chromosome polymorphism 146–7, *146*
 DNA polymorphism 147, 148
 genetic polymorphism 145–6
 isozyme polymorphism 147, 148
 mutations and domestication traits 153–4,
  478
 protein polymorphism 147–8
genetics, human 456
 and languages 71, 85–9, 466
 molecular 71, 85–9
Geoksyur Oasis (Turkmenistan) 376, 378
Ghab (Syria), pollen cores 166, 168–9, *170*,
 171, 173–5
Ghalegay (Pakistan) 398–9
Ghoraifé (Syria), caprines 210, 252–3
Gilgal, Jordan Valley 207, 265
ginger (*Zingiber officinale*) 541, *542*, 545
Gird Chai (Zagros mountains), settlement site
 271
Glacial Maximum 166, 169
 effect on wild plant-foods 161, 173, 182–3,
  192, 556
glaciations, and population dispersal 133
glass, Southeast Asia 423
goat, domesticated (*Capra* sp.) 76, 248, 364,
 554, 561
 C. hircus 296, 298, 302, 303–4, 402
 at Ganj Dareh 208, 240, 241, 242, 249–51,
  258
 at Gritille 248, 258
 at Jeitun 373, 378–9, 381
 in Levant 252, 253, 258–9, 554
 origins of 51, 79, 81
goat, wild (*Capra aegagrus*)
 bone measurements 240, 241–3, *244–6*
 distribution 208, 217, 232, 372, 381
 domestication of 234, 235, 258–9, 381
 habitat 208, 210, 238, 256, 274, 275–6
 horn cores 248, 253, 254
 in Iran 248–9
 at Jeitun 378–9, 381
 marked sexual dimorphism 242, 249–50,
  257
 at Mehrgarh 402, 403
 at pre-neolithic sites 238
 Turkish sites 243–8
 see also animal bones; sheep
gourd 39
 bottle (*Lagenaria* sp.) 428, 451
 ivy (*Coccinia* sp.) 400
grasses
 annual 182, 188, 195, 384
  Aegilops squarrosa (goat-face grass) 148,

377, 384
perennial
Poa spp. (meadow grass) 176, 177
Stipa and *Stipagrostis* spp. (feather) 177,
178, 179–80, 182, 183
rye (*Lolium* spp.) 384
see also cereals
Greece *297*
adoption of domesticates 296, 298–9, 305,
559, 562
colonization from 57, *61–3*, 64–5, 82, 559
intensive horticulture in 302–3, 305–6, 558–
9
islands, settlements 298, 301, 303
pottery 297, 306
settlements 298, 299, 300, 303, 304–6, 559
see also Crete; Tenaghi Phillipon
greenstone, traded 219
Gritille (Turkey), caprines at 210, 248, 258
Gua Cha (Malaya), rice remains 421
Guilá Naquitz (Mexico), climate simulation
project 28
Gujarat province (India) 284, 395–6
Gwangdong province (China) 421

Haçilar (Turkey) 1, 554
hackberry 183
Hagener people, Papua New Guinea 18–19, 21
Hallan Çemi (Turkey) 171, 182, 271, 272, 273,
274, 278
Hambledon Hill (England) 319
Han Culture, China 433
Harappa (Pakistan) 396, 402, 403, 405
Harappan civilization 56, 288, 417, 482
crops 395, 396, 398, 402, 488
rice cultivation 398, 417, 419, 564
hare (*Lepus* spp.) **212**, 217, 218, 379
Hatoula (Israel) 209, 253
hawthorn 183, 187, 188, 195
Hayonim (Israel) 171, 174
hearths 272, 428
hemp (*Cannabis sativa*) 39, 566
Hemudu Culture, China 481
Hemudu (Yangzi Valley, China) 78, 426, 477
artefacts 426, *429*, 564
rice cultivation 426–8, *427*, **428**, 435, 478,
564–5
herding 4, 405, 553
herd following 231–2
herd management 208, 210, 252, 276, 380,
553, 562
herd population structure 239, 257–8
mixed sheep and goats 210, 218, 219, 220–1
mobile system of 218–19
selective culling 218, 240, 250, 257, 380

and summer transhumance 271, 277, 379
Hili (Oman) 399–400
Hissar Culture (Afghanistan/Tadjikistan) 384–
5, 563
Hoabinhian Culture 419, 421, 426, 476, 477
Hokkaido island (Japan) 443, 450, 457, 565
Holocene period
early, climate 40, 41
see also Pleistocene/Holocene transition
homicide, mortality from 109
honey, traded 334
Hong Kong, pottery assemblages 481
Honshu island (Japan) 443, 448, 455
hornbeam (*Carpinus* sp.), Greece 304
horse, domesticated (*Equus caballus*) 54–5, 76,
82–3, 138, 236
military use of 55, 83, 84
South Asia 56, 402, 405–6
uses of 83–4, 405–6
horticulture 3, **4**, 548
Greece 302–3, 305–6, 558–9
tropical forest 17–18, 505, 506, 566, 568
houses
courtyard enclosures 305, 306, 373
pit dwellings 448, *448*, 451
rectangular 304, 305, 373, 556, 563
round 214, 271, 505, 556
timber-framed long 313, 318, 561
see also bricks; caves and rockshelters
Huanghe (Yellow) River Valley, China 41,
444, 477, 481, 565, 569
Hula (Israel), pollen analysis from 166, *167*,
168, 169, 173, 175, 181
Hulas (India) 400
Hunamni (Korea) 431, 565
Hungarian Plain 95, 558
hunter–gatherers 13, 14, 53, **77**, 84, 383, 402,
526
acculturation to agriculture 59, 71, 317–18,
461, 489, 556, 557, 569
and adoption of domesticates 310, 312–13,
317, 471, 559
and advance of agriculture 53–4, 58–9, 71,
219, 312, 468–9, 569–70
birth intervals among 121–2, 124
conflict/competition with farmers 337–40,
338, 349, 570
interaction with farmers 313, 326, 333–7,
335–8, 339–41, 355, 556, 570
intermarriage with farmers 53, 59, 324, 333,
339
patterns of mobility 124–5, 274, 316–17,
320
pseudo-agricultural activity by 36, 276, 405
surviving 81, 117, 118, 121, 533

and wild plant-food yields 192–5, 474
  see also complex sedentary foraging; farmers
hunting **4**, 17, 231
  methods 217–18, 379, 450, 451
  and over-exploitation 105, 106–7, 210, 256–7
  seasonal 242, 256, 331
hunting farming groups, mixed 328–9, 561
hygiene, and disease 120
hypergyny 324, 338, 339

Iberian peninsula 54, 65, 82
  see also Portugal; Spain
ibex
  (*Capra ibex*) 208
  (*Capra nubia*) 253, 254
Ice Age
  effect on early man 105, 132–3
  see also Bolling Allerød Interstadial; Glacial
    Maximum; Younger Dryas
independent invention 7, 8, 36–7, 397, 553
India
  agriculture 488
  animals 283, 284–5, 288–90
  languages 57, 81, 434
  pastoral expansion to 55, 56
  pottery 416
India, North
  horse in 83, 84
  rice 416, 417, 564
indigenous adoption of farming 456, 471, 489,
  561, 569
  Greece 296, 298–9, 305
  New Guinea 518–19
  Northwest Europe 82, 83, 312, 324, 340,
    350–60
  selective 7, 317, 318, 357–8, 383
  South Asia 393, 407
  see also three-stage model
Indo–European languages 72, 74, **76**, *80*, 88,
  472
  Indo–Iranian branch 55, 66, **76**, 81
  origins 54, 65–6, 87–8, 561
  spread of 55, 82, 84, 332, 473
Indo–Malaysian archipelago 567
Indo–Pacific languages 73, 75, **76**
Indo–Pacific region 476–7, 484
  see also China; New Guinea; South Asia
Indonesia 413, 480, 483, 504
Indus Valley 287, 395, 402
  kharif summer crops 398, 402, 419, 564
  see also Harappan civilization; Mohenjo-
    Daro
infrared spectroscopy, for rice identification
  432

intentional experimentation, in domestication
  393
Iran 55, 57, 84, 209, 241, 248–9, 401, 563
  northeastern **371**, 376, 381–2, 384, 385
  see also Ganj Dareh; Zeribar
Iranian Plateau 370, 372–3, 385–6, 404, 407
  agricultural expansion from 417, 563
  spread of rice cultivation across 419
  see also Kopet Dag mountains
Iraq 209, 241, 248–52, 270, 475
  see also Nemrik; Qermez Dere
Ireland 82–3, 317
Irian Jaya *see* New Guinea
iron 423, 426, 442
Islam, and spread of rice cultivation 419, 435
Island Melanesia *see* Melanesia (Island)
Israel 147, 233
  see also 'Ain Mallaha; Hula; Netiv Hagdud;
    Yiftah'el
Italy 82, 364, 365, 559
Itatsuke (Japan) 454–5, *454*

Japan 72, 442–4, *443*, 460–1
  Jomon Culture 442, 445–53, *447*, 457
  pottery 442, 445–6, 447, 448, 450, 451, *453*,
    455–6
  settlements 445, 446, 448–9, *448*, *449*, 450,
    451, *452*, 460
  spread of rice to 413, 431, 455, 457, *458*,
    459, 480, 565
  spread of rice within 455, 565
  tools 442, 446, *447*, 449, *449*, 451, 453
  Yayoi Culture 431, 443, 450, 453–7
Jarmo (Iraq) 385, 554
Java 426, 483, 487, 567
Jebel Cave (Turkmenistan) 373, 383
Jeitun Culture 370, *371*, 374, 381–5, 563
Jeitun (Turkmenistan) 82, 373, 376–7
  domestic animals 378–80
  domestic crops 377, 378
  pottery 373, 381–2
  tools 377–8
  water supplies 374–5
Jericho 1, 135, 214, 218, 475
  animals 208, 209
  cereals 207, 265, 475, 554
  see also es-Sultan
Jilat (Jordan) **212**, 213
  caprine bones at 215, 218, 255–6
  cereal and legumes at **213**, 214–15, 220
Jomon Culture (Japan) 431, 443, 450, 460
  Incipient 445, 446, 448, 450
  Initial 446, 448
  Late Final 453, 565
  Middle 450–1, 453

stability of 450–1, 457
Jordan
  caprines in 209, 233, 241
  see also 'Ain Ghazal; Azraq; Beidha; Jilat
Jordan, eastern 204, *205, 206*, 211, **212**, 213–14, *216*
  caprine herding in 215–19, 556
  crops **213**, 397
Jordan Valley 168, 175, 194, 263
  see also Natufian Culture
juniper (*Juniperus* sp.) 384

Kafiavana rockshelter (New Guinea) 505, 568
Kamapuk rockshelter (New Guinea) 506, 514
Kara Kum Desert 370, 372, 374
  takyr clay formations 375
Kara Su river, Kopet Dag mountains 374–5
Karamik Bataklığı (Turkey) 169, 174
Karim Shahir (Iran) 271, 273
Kashmir 563
Kebaran sites, Levant 268
Khallat Anaza (Jordan) **212**, 215, 217
Kharaneh (Jordan) 211, **212**, 215
Khiamian Culture, Levant 555
Khmer Culture 434
Khok Phanom Di (Thailand) 421, 426, 432, 433, 481
khur, South Asia *see* onager/ass
Kilu Cave (Buka, Solomons) 526, 533
Knossos (Crete) 296, 298, 303
Koldihwa (India) 416, 417, 564
Kongemose Culture (Scandinavia) 347–8, 352, 354
Kopet Dag mountains 370, 372, 374, 375–6, 384
Korea 72, 431, 455–6, 457, 460, 461, 565
Kosegasawa (Japan) *447*
Kujavia, long mounds 317, 318
Kuk (New Guinea) 485, 486, 487, **509**, 514
  swamp 507–11, 528–9, 567–8
Kurgan Culture (Central Asia) 82
  expansion periods 55, 56, *61–3*, 64
  genetic gradients and 60–1
  and spread of Indo–European languages 55, 66, 87–8
Kyushu region (Japan) 443, 446, 447–8, 457

labour
  factor in productivity 327, 459
  organization of 326, 512, 519
  and surplus production 304–5, 327, 356–7
language
  distribution processes 7, 74–6, 472
    climate-related colonization 70, **76**
    élite dominance 70, 73, 74–5, **76**, 78, 85, 467
    farming dispersal 70, 74, 75, 76–85, **76**, **77**, *79*, *80*, *83*, 560
    initial colonization 70, 74, **76**, 78, 82, 84
    by population expansion 54, 55, 56–7, 65–7, 467–9
  genetic unit density ratio (GUDR) 73, 74, 75, 81
  isolates 72, 73
  rate of spread 471–2, 490
  replacements 75, 469
  vocabularies 484
  see also African languages; Afro–Asiatic; Austric languages; Dravidian; Indo–European; linguistics; literature; Sumerian; writing
language families
  classification of 72–4
  significance of 467–71
  source regions 468–9, **469**, **470**, 482–4
  "trees" and phylogenetic diversity in 471–3, **472**, 482–3
Lapita Culture (Pacific) 487, 517, 524, 528, 569
  crops 529, 530–1, 532–3
  domestic animals 530, 532
  origins 529–32
  rapid colonization by 468, 471, 472–3, 484, 529, 567, 569
  settlements 529, 530, 532
Lebanon 241
legumes *see* pulses
Lengyel Culture 314, 316, 317, 318, 320
lentil (*Lens culinaris* syn. *L. esculenta*)
  distribution of 207, 299, 395, 396
  founder crop 143, **144**, 554
  genetics 146–7, *146*, 154, 155
  subsp. *orientalis* **144**, 146–7, *146*, 150, *150*
lentil, wild (*Lens* sp.)
  distribution of 150, *150*, **213**
  Greece 296, 297–8, 299, 303
Levant 219, 287, 473
  caprine bone analysis in 252–6, 258–9
  climatic changes 159, 174–5, 213–14
  domestication of animals 208–10, 220, 258–9
  grassland expansion from 188–9
  landbridge 133, 135, *136*
  origins of agriculture in 263, 554, 555
  plant domestication in 207–8, 271, 359
  woodland and expansion 165–6, *167*, 168–75, 195
  see also Israel; Jordan; Syria
Lijiacun Culture, China 431
linear model of development 27, **28**, 31–3, 39

Linearbandkeramik (LBK) people 95, 320, 324
    expansion of 313, 314, 316, 319, 347, 359,
        468, 471, 562
    and mesolithic populations 560, 561
linguistic cognates 332, 419, 484, 532, 568
linguistics
    and language distribution 71–2, **76**, 465–6
    residual zones 73–4, 75
    spread zones 73, 74, 81
    see also language; language families
linseed *see* flax
literature 55, 287
    Indian 56, 83, 84
Lungshan Culture 482
Luojiajiao (lower Yangzi, China) 428, **428**

Magyars, in Hungary 55, 57
Mahagara (India) 416, 564
maize, cultivated/domesticated 26, 51, 75, 148,
    153, 471, 488
Majiabing Culture, Yangzi Valley 428, **428**,
    481
malaria
    as limit to expansion 487, 501, 511, 529,
        568
    Plasmodium vivax 112, 122, 123, 124
Malatya (Turkey) 165, 183, 186, *190*
Malay Peninsula 425–6, 483
Mali, Dogon people 19
malnutrition 105, 107, 108
Manim rockshelter (New Guinea) 506
manioc (*Manihot esculenta*) 17, 547
Marginal Zone *see* Jordan, eastern
marine foods 331, 348, 421, 566
    see also fish and fishing; seal
maritime trading 136–7, 299, 560
Mediterranean region 57, 94, 124, 136
    spread of agriculture to 52, 419, 559
Mehrgarh (Pakistan) 385, 393, 406, 475
    animals at 402–3, 404–5, 563
    plants at 81, 385, 393–7, 417, 563
Mekong river 78, 419, 423, 435, 564
Melanesia (Island) 78, 524
    animals in 530–1, 532
    domestication of plants 524, 532, 533–4
    language spread 472, 487, 532
    transition to agriculture 500, 524, 568
    see also Lapita Culture; New Guinea
mesolithic cultures *see* complex sedentary
    foraging; hunter–gatherers
Mesopotamia 124, *265, 266*, 419
Mexico 5, 6, 26, **38, 39**, 148
Miao Yao (Hmong–Mien) languages 78, 482
micropredation *see* disease, infectious
Midianites, and dispersal of camel 282, 287

migration 55, 73, 105, 559
    and "bottlenecks" 134–5, *135, 136*
    and epidemic disease 118–19
    and genetic gradients 59–60
    partial 57, 557
    small-scale (local) 60, 350
    see also colonization, initial
Milankovich fluctuations (of solar radiation)
    31, 132, 182
millets
    cultivation of 5, 19, 52, 435, 565
    Echinochloa utilis barnyard 565
    Eleusine coracana finger (*ragi*) 398, 399,
        400, 564
    Panicum miliaceum common/broomcorn
        398, 400, 401, 476, 477, 478
    Panicum sumatrense little 398, 400, 401,
        564
    Pennisetum typhoides pearl 398, 400
    Setaria italica foxtail
        Huanghe Valley **39**, 41, 444, 477, 478,
            565
        South Asia 398, 400, 401, 476
    in Southeast Asia 426
    spread from Africa 399, 400, 488
    see also sorghum
Mirabad, Lake, pollen cores 176, 181, 183,
    188, 269, *269*
M'lefaat (Iraq) 171, 182, 209, 271
mobility
    of early farmers 52, 320
    of hunter–gatherers 124–5, 274, 316–17,
        320
Mohenjo Daro (Indus Valley) 288, 396, 405
molluscs 272, 300, 351, 354, 449–50
    see also shells
Mon–Khmer languages 78, 435, 483
Mondjukli (Turkmenistan) 374, 381
Mongolian language subfamilies 67, 72, 82
monuments, Northwest Europe 311, 319
mortality
    causes of 107–13, 117–18, 119, 122
    reduced 77, 557
mosquito, anophelene 112, 123
mouflon *see* sheep, wild
mountain zones, New Guinea 485, 501, **501**,
    503, 511
Munda languages 78, 79, 81, 416, 419, 435,
    476, 488
Mureybet (Syria) 171, 217, 270
    sheep bones 241, *251*, 253
Murghab river, Kopet Dag mountains 374, 375,
    376, 384

Na–Dene languages (America) 57, 73, **76**, 84,

88
Nahel Oren (Israel) 208, 253
Namazga-depe (Turkmenistan) 373, 374, 376
Nanoway Culture (New Guinea) 504–5, 510–11
Natufian Culture 175, 208, 268, 474, 475, 555
  and language 476, 557
  wild caprines 252
nature
  ecological misconceptions about 27–34, **28**
  human conservation of 14
  human interaction with 20–4, 519–20, 526–7, 553
  human transformation of 12–16, 553
  indigenous peoples' knowledge and view of 17–20
  misconceptions about in evolutionary theory 34–9
  non-equilibrium view of 25–6, 29–30, *29*, 33
Nausharo (Pakistan) 395, 402, 403, 406
Nea Nikomedeia (Greece) 296, 303
Near East *see* Southwest Asia
Negev 208, 209, 213, 214
  cereals and caprines in 219, 221, 556
Nemrik (Iraq) 271, 273, 278, 475
neolithic cultures *see* Pre-Pottery Neolithic
Netherlands 82, 316, 560
Netiv Hagdud (Israel) 207, 253, 265, 475
New Caledonia (Melanesia) 530, 569
New Guinea
  agro-ecological zones 501–3, **501, 502,** 504–7, 512–13
  Austronesian influence in 504, 505, 517, 567, 568
  domestication events 532–3
  dryland agriculture 507, 508, **509,** 510, 517
  Hagener people (Mount Hagen) 18–19, 21
  highlands agricultural prehistory models 501–11, *501,* 566
  languages 73, 75, 466, 486–7, 490–1
  non-expansive agriculture 77, 84, 476, 484–8, 490, 499–500
  pigs 18, 21, 534
    introduced 500, 504, 505, 507, 508, 512, 516, 568
  role of sweet potato 511, 512, 513, 514
  settlements 504–5
  soil erosion 486, 487, 500
  tools 485, 486, 500, 503–4, 505, 514
  wetland agriculture 507–10, **509,** 528–9, 567–8
New Ireland (Bismarcks) 528, 529, 531
New Zealand 471, 472
Newgrange, (Ireland) 82–3

niche concept
  and animal domestication 229–31, *230,* 235–6
  and spread of agriculture 264, 270, 272
  and symbiosis 227–9
Nile Valley 124, 219, 221, 556
nilgai (*Boselaphus tragocamelus*) 402, 404–5
Nilo–Saharan languages 67, 73, **76,** 84
Nishida (Japan) 451, *452*
nomadic pastoralism 54–7, 58–60, 67, 81–2, 384–5
Non Nok Tha (Thailand) 419, 422, 432
North America 73, 88
  Eastern Woodlands **39,** 41, 488, 489, 490
North European plain, forager farmer contacts in *336,* 561
North Kachi Plain (Pakistan) 385, 395, 402, 406
Northwest Europe
  indigenous adoption of farming 82, 312–13
  late-mesolithic cultures 53–4, 313–16, *315,* 316, 320
Nostratic language macro-family (hypothetical) *80,* 476, 557
nuclear regions **77,** 139
  concept 5, 370
  population densities in 133–4
  species diversity in 5–6, 149–51
nuts 451, 486
  acorns 168, 364–5, 366, 428, 446, 451
  canarium 484, 486, 528
  hazelnuts 318, 331–2
  horse chestnuts 451, 460
  pandanus 486, 503, 506, 507, 508, 513–14
  water chestnuts 331–2
  see also almond

oak (*Quercus*) 183, 446–7
  dehesa groves 363–7
  in Zagros mountains 30–1, 272, 275
  at Zeribar (Iran) 176, *184–5,* 186
oak-park zone 30–1, 161, 191, 195, 269
  cereals in 42, 152, *152*
oak Rosaceae park-woodlands 162–3, 180, 186, 195
oases, Levant 204, 475, 554
oasis hypothesis, for domestication 194, 229
oat, wild (*Avena* sp.) 42–3, 296, 299
obsidian 278, 299, 457
Oceania
  Near and Remote 524
  see also Melanesia; Polynesia
Ohalo (Israel), early food plants at 168, 214
olive (*Olea* sp.) 269, 302, 363, 364
onager/ass (*Equus hemionus/asinus*) 188, 242,

256, 270, 271, 277, 379, 403
  domestication of 234, 235
  in eastern Jordan **212**, 215, 217
Ondashi (Japan), "biscuit" 451, *453*
ornaments 334, 350, 357, 385, 423
Otomanguean languages 75, 84, 473

Pacific *see* Indo–Pacific; Lapita Culture;
  Melanesia (Island); Polynesia
Pakistan
  animals 83, 288
  Dravidian languages in 57, 81
  early agriculture in 81, 417, 480
  pastoral expansion to 55, 56
  see also Harappan civilization; Mehrgarh
Palegawra Cave (Iraq) 241, 267–8, 269
palms (Arecaceae) 540
Pama–Nyungan languages (Australia) 73, 84,
  472
pandanus (*Pandanus* spp.) 486, 503, 506, 507,
  508, 513–14
Papua New Guinea *see* New Guinea
Paralia (Franchthi, Greece) 298, 300
pastoralism
  camel 285–7
  definition 392, 402
  development of 138, 554, 563
  transhumance 55, 271–2, 273–4, 277, 302,
    314, 379, 383
  see also goat; herding; nomadic pastoralism;
    sheep
pea, grass (*Lathyrus sativus*) 144, 303, 400
pea (*Pisum sativum*) 207, 303, 396, 400
  founder crop 143, **144**, 554
  genetic mutation in 154, 155
  subsp. *elatius* 149, *149*
  subsp. *humile* 147, 148, 149, *149*
pea, wild (*Pisum fulvum*) 149–50, *149*
pear (*Pyrus* sp.) 183, 187, 384
Peiligang (China) 444, 481
Pengtoushan (China) 428, 430, *430*, 444, 477,
  565
perilla (*Perilla frutescens*), Japan 451
Peru, centre of origin 6, **39**, 40
Pessedjik (Turkmenistan) 374, 381
Pevkakia (Greece) 302, 305
phalanger (*Phalanger orientalis*) 528
Philippines 425, 567, 570
Phung Nguyen Culture, north Vietnam 426
pig
  linguistic cognates 332, 568
  as livestock, South Asia 402, 421, 566
  New Guinea 18, 21, 500, 504, 505, 507,
    508, 512, 516, 568
  see also pig, wild

pig, domesticated 51, 236, 263, 561
  China 471, 477, 566
  and *dehesa* oak groves 364–5
  in Greece 296, 297, 298, 302
  Island Melanesia 533
  in mesolithic Europe 314, 316, 561
  Remote Oceania 530, 532
pig, wild (*Sus scrofa*) 234, 235, 243, 244
  distribution 372
  in Greece 296
  Japan 451
  at Jeitun 379
  mesolithic northern Europe 331–2
  sites in eastern Jordan **212**
pine, joint- (*Ephedra* spp.) 180, 188
Pirak (Pakistan) 399, 400, 405, 406, 417
pistachio *see* terebinth
pits 319
  storage 318, 446–7, 477, 566
plant foods, wild 161, 168, 173, 178, 181, 271,
  407, 503
  continued use of 318, 320
  grain of wild grasses 179–80
  production of **4**, 525, 527, 528
  seeds 179, 180
  yields from 180–1, 182–3, 189, 191–2, 195
  see also corms; rhizomes; root crops; tubers
plants
  Angiosperms
    Dicotyledonae 539, *540*
    Monocotyledoneae 539–41, 544, 546
  bud meristem potential 539, 540–4, *541*,
    545, 546–7
  community concept of **28**, 30–1
  indicator species 94
  medicinal and narcotic 318
  species diversity 5, 149–53
  storage organs 134, 183, 538–9, 545
  succession theory 31–3, *32*
  see also plant foods; plants, cultivated; pollen
    analysis; weeds
plants, cultivated
  centres of origin 1, 5–7, 51–2, 134, 372,
    532, 552, 569
  see also cereals
plate tectonics 130–1
  and genesis of agriculture 133–7, 547
  and genesis of *Homo* 131–3
Pleistocene epoch, climatic changes in 132–3
Pleistocene/Holocene transition
  climatic changes 28, 40, 187, 229, 555
  environmental changes at 7, 93–4, 105,
    134–5, 490, 555
plough 301, 302, 350
  China 422, *423*, 433

Poland 314, 316, 334, 335, 347, 561
pollen analysis 355, 422, 453, 488, 528, 530, 531
  and climatic change 159, *160*, 181, 267, 268–9
  core sites 169, 171, *172*, 213, *265*, *266*
  from Ghab 166, 168–9, *170*, 171, 173–5
  from Hula 166, *167*, 168, 169, 173, 175
  and genetic transformation 94–5, 99
  of grasses 187–8
  New Guinea 485, 486, 507, 510, 512–13
  oak grove 364
pollination systems 145, 150, 183
Polynesia
  colonization of 78, 472, 530–1, 532
  languages 72, 74, 487
pomegranate (*Punica* sp.) 384
poppy (*Papaver* spp.) 180, 182, 183
population density 58, 133, 331, 491, 562
  and disease 110, 112–14, 115, 116, 119, 557
population expansion 55, 557
  and genetic gradients 57–8, 60
  and spread of languages 65–7, 85–6, 468–9
  see also colonization, initial; migration
population increase 93, 456–7, 529, 555, 557
  and birth-spacing interval 121–2, 124, 557
  exponential growth **101**, 102, 103, 106–7, 114–15
  logistic growth 102, 103, 104, 106, *106*
  restraints upon 104–7, 529
  to early Holocene 51, 101–6, **101**, *102*
population pressure
  and agricultural origins 40, 51, 310–11, 312
  and "bottlenecks" 133, 134–6, *136*
  "carrying capacity" model 104, 105, 107, *108*, 116
  concept of 103–4, 139, 352, 354
  and disease 124–5
population stagnation
  and epidemic disease 115–17
  late Pleistocene 105, 106, 107
Portugal 363–7, 560
potato, sweet *see* sweet potato
pottery
  band-decorated 313, 561
  black incised 422
  black-and-red ware 416
  Cardial Ware 312, 316, 560
  cord-impressed 416
  decorated 306, 451, *453*
  dentate stamped 435
  depictions of horses 405
  grain impressions in 314
    rice 398–9, 416, 421
  late-mesolithic point-butted 314

  linear appliqué 445, 446
  neolithic Scandinavian 350
  traded 334, 335, 457
  western Mediterranean 560
pottery temper, rice chaff 414, 419, 421, 422, 428, 432
Pre-Pottery Neolithic A (PPNA)
  caprine bones 238, 252, 253, 258
  cereal domestication 220, 393–4, 554, 555
  lacking in eastern Jordan 213, 215
  no animal husbandry 233, 402–3
  western Asian 477
Pre-Pottery Neolithic B (PPNB) 266
  cultivated crops 143–4, 220, 394–5, 396
  domestication of animals 208–9, 233, 241, 252–3, 258–9, 556
  fauna changes 217–18, 403–4
  settlement types 214, 556, 557
production
  as manufacturing 16, 20
  surplus generation 305, 355–6, 357, 358, 360
production (of food)
  critical level 459
  distinct from collection 12–13
  human intervention 14, 15–16, 18, 19–20, 519–20, 525, 526, 553
  intensified 77, 568
pulses 34, 39, 302, 555
  seed yields from 182, 183
  species diversity 149–50
  see also bean; chick pea; lentil; pea
punctuated equilibrium model of evolution 34, 37
Pygmies 53, 58

Qermez Dere (Iraq) 271, 272, 273, 274, 278, 475
  food plants at 171, 182, 272

Raikas, (Hindu caste) 284–5, 289–90
rainforest 425, 526, 545–7
Rajasthan (India) 284, 287, 288–90
Ramad (Syria) 218, 554
  caprines 210, 253, 259
rate of advance theory 52–3, 471–3, 490
Rebaris (Hindu caste) 284, 285, 289, 290
Red River (Song Koi) 78, 419, 423, 435, 564
reindeer 4, 138, 330
religion, and attitude to animals 283, 285, 291–2
Rhine Meuse Schelde Culture 316, 561
rhizomes, structure of 539, 541–2, *542*
rice, cultivation of 402, 433–4, 476, 480, 532
  lowland wet 413, 417, 459, 479

Japan 450, 453–7, *454, 456, 458*, 565
transplanted 455, *456*
upland dry (swiddened) 413, 457, 459, 479
rice, domesticated (*Oryza* spp.)
    identification criteria 399, 431–3, 478, 564,
        565
    O. indica 413–14, 427, 428, 435, 478
    O. japonica (sinica) 413–14, 427, 428, 435,
        478
    O. javanica 413–14
    O. sativa 398–9, 400, 417, **417**, 478
    origins and spread of 51, *415*, 417, *418*, 419,
        476, **480**, 564–5, 567
    and spread of language 78, 81, 419, 434–5,
        484
rice, wild, aquatic (*Zizania*) 40–1
rice, wild (*Oryza* spp.)
    distribution 400, 413–14, *414*, 427, 479
    O. glaberrima (African) 413
    O. nivara (annual) 399, 478
    O. perennis 421
    O. rufipogon (perennial) 399, 421, 426, 431,
        478
Ringkloster (Denmark) 335
rockshelters *see* caves
rodents
    rat, Melanesia 530, 531
    at Warwasi 269
Rojdi (Pakistan) 396, 400, 401
Roman Empire, fall of 60, 64
root crops 178, 181, 539, 547, 566, 568
    New Guinea 527, 542, 543, 545, 546
    see also tubers
Rosaceae 183
    in oak Rosaceae park-woodlands 162
Rössen Culture 314, 316, 317, 320
Rowanduz (Turkey) 166, 183, 186, 188
rye, cultivated (*Secale cereale* subsp. *cereale*)
    144, 161
rye, wild 42, *43*
    annual (*Secale cereale* subsp. *vavilovii*) 161,
        162, 188, 189, 556

sago palms (*Metroxylon* spp.) 486, 527
Sahara 52, 54, 56, 67
"Saharan pump" process 133
Sahel, agricultural origins in **39**, 52
Sahuland (New Guinea Australia) 103, 104
sainfoins (*Onobrychis* spp.) 178, 180
Saltbaek Vig (Denmark) 352, **352**, *353*
Samoa 472, 569
Sarawak 567
Scandinavia, southern
    archaeology of 346–7
    arrival of agriculture in 52, 82, 347, 350–1,

562
    climatic changes 354, 355
    farmer–forager contacts in *336*, 561
    indigenous adoption of farming 83, 312,
        340, 350–60
    prehistoric chronology of 347–50, *348, 349*
    spruce woodland 95
    TRB culture in 317, 349–50, 351
    see also Baltic region
Scotland 562
Scythian peoples, migration 55, 64
sea levels
    fluctuations in 133, 555
    rising 105, 135, 354–5, 421
seal
    fat (oil) 334, 335
    as food 331, 348
seals (artefacts), Chinese 460–1
sedentism
    and domestication of animals 233–4, 274,
        359
    effect on health 110, 124–5
    of proto-neolithic hunter–gatherers 192–3,
        331, 333, 352, 354, 474, 555
    and territoriality 264
    see also complex sedentary foraging;
        settlements
seeds
    of crop progenitors **39**, 40, 183, 189, 207
    dispersal mechanisms 35–6, 154, 188, 207
    DNA analysis of 98–9
    inhibition of germination (wild) 154–5, 207
Semitic languages 72, 74, 473, 557
settlements
    abandoned 218, 278
    concentric 448, 450, 451, *452*
    earliest 264, 271–3
    fortified 339, 460
    longhouse, primary neolithic 318, 320
    moated 422, 455, 460
    mudbrick and pisé 432
    nucleation of 313
    permanent 266, 272, 273, 317, 381, 555
    raised wooden pile 426, 432
    seasonal 214, 273–4
    semi-underground 214, 272, 273, 428, 446
    walled yards 305, 373
    see also caves and rockshelters; houses
Shanidar (Iraq) *172*, 209, 269, 271
sheep, domesticated 51, 76, 79, 554
    and *dehesa* oak groves 364
    in Europe 316, 559–60, 561
    at Jeitun 373, 378–9
    Ovis aries 296, 298, 302, 402
sheep, wild 274, 275

bone measurement analysis 241, *246–7*, 251–2, *251*
distribution 232–3, 242, 275–6, 372, 381
Ovis orientalis (Asiatic mouflon) 209, 233, 238, 381
  domestication of 231–3, *231*, 234–6, 259
  Mehrgarh 402, 403
Ovis vignei (urial), at Jeitun 378–9, 381
  at Turkish sites 244, 245, 246–8
  see also goat
shells
  in pollen core 166, 169
  as tools 422, 433, 481
  traded (decorative) 503, 504, 505
Siberia, expansion from 60, *61–3*, 64, 65
Sibri (Pakistan) 403, 406
Sinai 208, 213, 214
  cereals and caprines in 219, 221, 556
  see also Ujrat el-Mehed; Wadi Tbeik
Sino–Tibetan languages 57, 72, **76**
  source region 482, 483
  spread of 66–7, 473
  Tibeto–Burman 483
Skateholm (Sweden) 332–3, 348
skeletal morphology, mesolithic/neolithic 351, 354, 355
snail
  Bulinus spp., bilharzia vector 112
  as food 234
social organization 77, 304–6, 317, 519–20
  and domestication 18–19, 312, 392, 474
  use of ceremonial 316, 319, 356
social status
  and exotic goods 314, 356, 360
  and plant foods 318–19, 326–7
  and surplus production 358
social stratification 58, 392, 460–1
  as cause of transition to agriculture 355–7
  of complex hunter–gatherers 331, 332–3, 347
  effect on animal husbandry 283, 284–5
  and reproductive patterns 118–19
  Southeast Asia 422, 460–1
  see also caste system
soil erosion
  Greek mainland 303–4
  Indonesia 487
  New Guinea 486, 487, 500
  Remote Oceania 530, 531
solar radiation, changes in 31, 132, 182
Solomon Islands 524, 527, 568, 569
sorghum
  cultivation of **39**, 52, 401–2
  Sorghum bicolor 398, 399–400
Sori (Japan), pottery *453*

South America 36, **39**, 51, 75
South Asia 391–2, *394*, 407
  agricultural transformations in 390, 398–402
  climate (monsoon) 391, 401, 419, 477
  kharif summer crop period 391, 398, 402, 417, 564
  pastoralism in 402–6
  rabi winter crop period 391, 395–6, 417, 564
  rice remains in 416–19, **417**, *418*
  spread of agriculture to 51, 396, 407, 563
  see also India; Mehrgarh; Pakistan
Southeast Asia
  Austro–Asiatic languages 434, 482, 483
  centre of expansion from 78, 81, 569
  centre of origin of cultivars 5, 6, **39**, 51, 76, 534, 566
  domestic animals *see* chicken; dog; pig
  and origins of Lapita Culture 529, 531–2
  see also China
Southeast Asia, island 566
  rice cultivation in 425–7, *425*, 567
Southeast Asia, mainland 419, *420*
  rice cultivation 410–23, 564
  see also China; Melanesia
Southwest Asia
  centre of origin of cultivars 5, **39**, 40, 41, 51
  crop domestication events **38**, 556, 569
  earliest settlements 264, 475
  languages 57, 79
  role as nuclear region 136–7, *137*, 144, 204, 475, 554, 569
  spread of agriculture from 52, 53, *61–3*, 79, 391, 488, 490, 557, 562–3
  wild cereals in 30–1, 33–4, 42, *43*
  see also Anatolia; climatic change; Fertile Crescent; Levant
soybean (*Glycine max*), China 565
Spain 40, 53–4, 363–7, 559–60
Spirit Cave (Thailand), rockshelter 419, 476
squash, domesticated 51
steppe 95, 163, *164*, 165, *165*, 195
  Artemisia Chenopodiaceae 176–8, 179, 275
  energy yields from food plants 180, 181–3
  fauna of 213
  Jordanian plateau (basalt) 210, 211
  late Pleistocene 165, *190*
  piedmont 275
  see also desert steppe; forest steppe; woodland steppe
steppes, Eurasian 54–5, 74, 95
Store Åmose (Denmark) 314
storksbill (*Erodium hirtum*) 178, 180
Stumble (England) 318
succession model of plant species 31–3, *32*

Sudan **39**, 80
sugar cane   484, 485, 504, 508, 517
Sulawesi (Indonesia)   426, 567
Sumatra   425, 426, 483, 487, 567
Sumbar valley, Kopet Dag mountains   375, 384
swamps, New Guinea   487, 507–11, 514, 528–9, 567–8
   drainage   500, 504, 527, 528
Swat region (Pakistan)   398–9, 400, 405
Sweden *see* Baltic; Scandinavia
sweet potato
   Ipomoea batatas
      New Guinea   18, 503, 504, 567
      Southeast Asia   547, 566
   role of   511, 512, 513, 514
swidden (shifting) cultivation   548
   New Guinea   500, 508, 510, 514, 517, 568
   rice   413, 457, 459, 479
Swifterbant late mesolithic culture   316
Syria   188, 209, 211, 241, 270
   see also Abu Hureyra; Aswad; Bouqras;
      Ghab; Ramad

Tadjikistan, Hissar Culture sites   384–5, 563
Taforalt (Egypt)   124
Tai Kadai languages   473, 476, 482–3
Taiwan   78, 481, 483
Tambul (New Guinea)   510, 514
taming of wild animals   4, 232, 233–5, 533
   see also domestication
taro (*Colocasia* spp.)   484, 527
   C. esculenta
      New Guinea   503, 508, 515
      Southeast Asia   542–3, *543*, 545, 566
   C. gigantea (wild)   548
   cultivation of   18, 485, 507, 508, 511, 514, 568
   introduced in New Guinea   515, 517, 567
Taurus mountains   165, 166
technological innovation
   New Guinea   503, 516
   in pottery   350, 351
   and spread of farming   52, 57, **77**, 331, 333, 334–5, 475, 481
Tedjen river, Kopet Dag mountains   374, 375, 376
Tell Abu Hureyra *see* Abu Hureyra and, *see also*
   Aswad; es-Sultan; Mureybet; Ramad
Tenaghi Phillipon (Greece)   169, 174
teosinte, wild (maize)   **39**, 148
Tepe Asiab (Iran)   271, 277
   caprine bones   238, 241, 248–9, *249*, 252, 258
Tepe Gaz Tavila (Iran)   396, 401
terebinth (*Pistacia*)   213, 384

expansion of   183, 186–7, 188, 269, 272
   at Zeribar (Iran)   176, *184–5*, 186
terebinth almond woodland steppe   163, 180, 186–7, 191, 195
territoriality
   among complex hunter–gatherers   264, 331, 349
   between farmers and foragers   339, 350
   of caprines   274, 275
Tethys Sea (former)   130, 132, 136
Thailand   422, 426, 434
   rice cultivation in   421–2, 432, 433, 434, 480, 564
Thessaly (Greece)   298, 299, 300, 559
three-stage model of availability   82, 318, 324–6, *325*, *329*, 357
   availability stage   324–5, 327, 328, 333, *335*, *337*
   consolidation stage   324, 325
   substitution stage   324, 325, 333–4, 340
      extended   318, 326, 328–30
   see also indigenous adoption of farming
Tibetan peoples, genetic origins   66–7
tillage, for cultivation   525–6
Togolok (Turkmenistan)   373, 374, 381
Tokyo Astronomical Observatory settlement
   (Japan)   448–9, *448*, *449*
Tonga   472, 569
tools
   adzes (stone)   313, 314, *429*, 561
   axes   503–4, 505
      antler   334
      copper   350, 351
      polished flint   350
      stone   334, 351, 416, 451, 500
   bronze   453
   digging sticks/hoes   378, *423*, 433, 500, 504
   fishing   450, 451
   flake and blades   384, 425, 504, 527
   grinding   264, 271, 378, 478–9
      querns   416, 444
   harvesting   233, 478
      iron finger sickles   433
      knives   422, 433, 481
      sickle (blades)   298, 377–8, 433, 444, 481
   iron   433, 453
   spades
      bone   428, **428**
      stone   428, **428**
      wooden   500, 514
   traded   334
   see also plough; weapons
Torres Straits Islands   500
tortoise (*Testudo*)   **212**, 215, 355, 378, 379
toxins, in food plants   179

trade 219, 399
    Baltic and Scandinavia 334–5, *337*, 340,
        347, 349, 357, 358
    maritime 136–7
    New Guinea 503, 504, 511
    see also exchange
tragacanth, spiny cushion- (*Astragalus* sp.) 178
transhumance *see* pastoralism
transport
    and agricultural expansion 54, 57, 84
    camel caravans 284, 286
    ox-carts 284, 405
tree crops 566
    New Guinea 503, 511, 513, 518, 568
Trichterbeckerkultur (TRB) (Beaker culture)
    316, 317–18, 319, 320, 339–40
    in southern Scandinavia 317, 349–50, 351
Trobriand Islanders 24, 334, 358
truffle, as food plant 178
tubers 451, 476
    Melanesia 426, 532, 538, 568
    New Guinea 484, 485
    structure and growth 539–41, *540, 541,*
        543–4, 544
    wild 544–6, 547
Tugeri rockshelter (New Guinea) 506, 514
Tungus language subfamilies 67, 72, 82
Turkey 166, 174, 364, 558, 588
    caprines 209, 241, 243–8
    plant species 147, 150, *150*, 207, 215
    see also Asikli Höyük; Cafer Höyük; Çatal
        Hüyük; Çayönü; Gritille; Haçilar; Hallan
        Çemi; Karamik Batakligi; Taurus moun-
        tains
Turkic language subfamilies 67, 72, 82
Turkmenistan 55, 82, 188, 370–3, *371*, 564
    camel in 286, 287, 291
    early agricultural settlement in 373–6, 383,
        563
    see also Jeitun

Ukraine 82, 83, 561
Ulu Leang cave (Sulawesi) 426, 432
Umbelliferae, in pollen cores 181
Uralic languages 60, *61–3*, 64, 65, 72, **76**
Urmia, Lake, pollen cores 181, 182
Uto–Aztecan languages 75, 84, 472
Uwaynid (Jordan) **212**, 215

Van, Lake, pollen profiles 180, 268, *269*
Vanuatu (Melanesia) 530, 531
vegeculture, origins of 538–9, 545–9
vegetables, green
    Brassica sp. 396, 565
    New Guinea 508, 513

Southeast Asia 566
Vietnam 421, 433, 566
    languages 78, 434
    rice cultivation 421, 427, 433–4
villages *see* settlements
vines (*Vitis* sp.) 302, 396
Volga Don region *see* Kurgan Culture

Wadi Jilat *see* Jilat
Wadi Judayid (Jordan) 209, 238, 252
Wadi Tbeik (Sinai) 217, 219
Wahgi Valley (New Guinea) 505, 506–7, 510,
    512
warfare
    between farmers and foragers 339, 349
    in Japan 460, 461
    mortality from 108, 109
    use of camel 287–8, 289–90
    use of horse 55, 83, 84
Warwasi (Iran) 252, 269
water supplies 475, 558
    canals 395, 422, 455
    floodplains 272, 391, 395, 558–9
        walled fields 395, 434
    irrigation 215, 527
        Jeitun area 374–5, 376, 377, 384
    management systems
        New Guinea 510, 511, 516
        for rice cultivation 413, 422–3, 433–4,
            455
    springs 193, 194, 211, 213
"wave of advance" model
    of farming dispersal 77, 80, 82, 94, 310–11,
        311, 324
    for Greece 306, 559
weapons 350, 357, 379, 460
    see also tools
weeds 33–4, 39
    crop 189, 303, 318, 377, 395
    suppression of 459, 525
wetlands 169, 180, 272, 375
    New Guinea 507–10, **509**, 510–12, 568
    rice cultivation 413, 417, 479
        Japan 450, 453–7, *454, 456, 458*, 459
    see also swamps; water supplies
wheat (*Triticum* spp.) 97–9, 350, 565
    cultivated/domesticated 51, 79, 395, 396,
        402, 417
    T. aestivum hexaploid bread 148, 303, 377,
        395, 563
    T. compactum 373, 395
    T. durum, Greece 303, 395
    T. spelta spelt 98–9
    T. sphaerococcum "shot" 395
    T. vulgare 373

tetraploid *see* emmer wheat
wheat, wild   189, 395
   see also einkorn wheat; emmer wheat
wolf, domestication of   229–31, *230*, *231*
women
   fecundity and fertility   101, 104, 120–3
   as gardeners   17, 506
   status of   332, 519
   see also hypergyny
woodland steppe
   distribution   *164*, 165, *165*
   spread of   166, 180, 183, 186–7, *190*, 195
   terebinth almond   163, 186–7, 188, 191, 195
   see also forest steppe; steppe
woodlands
   dating expansion of   166–75, *190*, 264, 268–
   9
   expansion of   95, 275, 277, 278
   Levantine   161, *167*, 554
   oak Rosaceae park-   162–3, 180, 186, 195
   refuges   165, 166, 183, 188–9, 195, 264,
   269, *269*
   xeric zone, distribution models of   163–6,
   164–5, 183
   see also forest steppe; oak-park zone;
   woodland steppe
wormwood (*Artemisia* spp.)   182
   seeds as food   179, 183
   steppe type   176–8, 179, 275
writing   37, 55, 57
   see also literature
Wurup Valley (New Guinea)   505–6, 514

Xom Trai (Vietnam), rice remains   421, 427

yam
   cultivation of   18, 451, 485, 507, 566

Dioscorea alata and *D. esculenta*   503, 508,
   517, 543–4, *544*, 567
Dioscorea hispida (wild)   548
Yangshao Culture   431, 481
Yangzi Valley
   central region   428, 430, *430*, 431, 435
   farming dispersal from   78, 79, 423, 564, 569
   and language distribution   434–5
   rice cultivation   444, 477, 481, 564, 565, 566
      lower Yangzi   426–8, *427*, **428**, *429*, 435
Yayoi Period (Japan)   431, 443, 450
Yiftah'el (Israel)   207, 208, 218, 554
Younger Dryas period
   climate models   41, 264, 267
   effect on wild plant foods   161, 181–2, 189,
      192, 195, 555, 556
   impact on southern Levant   41, 174, 207–8,
      213
   and settlement patterns   270–1
   in Southeast Asia   478, 479
   and woodland expansion   168, 169, 171,
      173–5, 186, 188, *190*, 277
Yunnan region (China)   422, 482, 564
   spread of rice from   419, 423, 435, 564

Zagros mountains   217, *265*, 273–8, 475, 563
   pollen record from   30–1, 165, *172*
   settlements in   267–73, 278, 554
Zarzian Culture (Zagros mountains)   *172*, 267–
   71
Zawi Chemi (Iraq)   *172*, 209, 269, 271, 273
Zeribar, Lake (Iran)
   pollen core site   169, 173–4, 176, 177, 181–
      2, 188–9, *266*, 268–9, *269*
      and woodland expansion   183, *184–5*,
         186–7, 188
Zingiberaceae   538, 539, 540–2, *542*, 546